The Anthropology of Development a

 University of the
West of England

BRISTOL

**FRENCHAY CAMPUS
(BOLLAND) LIBRARY**

Please ensure that this book is returned by the end of
the loan period for which it is issued.

UWE, BRISTOL   F366A.02.06
Printing & Stationery Services

Telephone Renewals: 0117 32 82092 (24 hours)
Library Web Address: www.uwe.ac.uk/library

Blackwell Anthologies in Social and Cultural Anthropology
Series Editor: Parker Shipton, Boston University

Series Advisory Editorial Board:
Fredrik Barth, University of Oslo and Boston University
Stephen Gudeman, University of Minnesota
Jane Guyer, Northwestern University
Caroline Humphrey, University of Cambridge
Tim Ingold, University of Aberdeen
Emily Martin, Princeton University
John Middleton, Yale Emeritus
Sally Falk Moore, Harvard Emerita
Marshall Sahlins, University of Chicago Emeritus
Joan Vincent, Columbia University and Barnard College Emerita

Drawing from some of the most significant scholarly work of the nineteenth and twentieth centuries, the *Blackwell Anthologies in Social and Cultural Anthropology* series offers a comprehensive and unique perspective on the ever-changing field of anthropology. It represents both a collection of classic readers and an exciting challenge to the norms that have shaped this discipline over the past century.

Each edited volume is devoted to a traditional subdiscipline of the field such as the anthropology of religion, linguistic anthropology, or medical anthropology; and provides a foundation in the canonical readings of the selected area. Aware that such subdisciplinary definitions are still widely recognized and useful – but increasingly problematic – these volumes are crafted to include a rare and invaluable perspective on social and cultural anthropology at the onset of the twenty-first century. Each text provides a selection of classic readings together with contemporary works that underscore the artificiality of subdisciplinary definitions and point students, researchers, and general readers in the new directions in which anthropology is moving.

1 *Linguistic Anthropology: A Reader*
   Edited by Alessandro Duranti
2 *A Reader in the Anthropology of Religion*
   Edited by Michael Lambek
3 *The Anthropology of Politics: A Reader in Ethnography, Theory, and Critique*
   Edited by Joan Vincent
4 *Kinship and Family: An Anthropological Reader*
   Edited by Robert Parkin and Linda Stone
5 *Law and Anthropology: A Reader*
   Edited by Sally Falk Moore
6 *The Anthropology of Development and Globalization: From Classical Political Economy to Contemporary Neoliberalism*
   Edited by Marc Edelman and Angelique Haugerud

The Anthropology of Development and Globalization

From Classical Political Economy to Contemporary Neoliberalism

Edited by

Marc Edelman and
Angelique Haugerud

Blackwell
Publishing

Editorial material and organization © 2005 by Blackwell Publishing Ltd

BLACKWELL PUBLISHING
350 Main Street, Malden, MA 02148-5020, USA
9600 Garsington Road, Oxford OX4 2DQ, UK
550 Swanston Street, Carlton, Victoria 3053, Australia

First published 2005 by Blackwell Publishing Ltd

5   2006

Library of Congress Cataloging-in-Publication Data

The anthropology of development and globalization : from classical political economy to
contemporary neoliberalism / edited by Marc Edelman and Angelique Haugerud.
    p. cm. — (Blackwell anthologies in social and cultural anthropology ; 5)
    Includes bibliographical references and index.
    ISBN 0-631-22879-9 (hardback : alk. paper) — ISBN 0-631-22880-2 (pbk. : alk. paper)
    1. Political anthropology.   2. Economic anthropology.   3. Economic development.
4. Rural development.   5. Globalization.   6. Hybridity (Social sciences)   I. Edelman, Marc.
        II. Haugerud, Angelique.   III. Series.

GN492.A5925 2004
306.2—dc22
2004012937

ISBN-13: 978-0-631-22879-0 (hardback : alk. paper) — ISBN-13: 978-0-631-22880-6 (pbk. : alk. paper)

A catalogue record for this title is available from the British Library.

Set in 9/11 pt Sabon
by Kolam Information Services Pvt. Ltd, Pondicherry, India
Printed and bound in India
by Replika Press Pvt. Ltd

The publisher's policy is to use permanent paper from mills that operate a sustainable forestry
policy, and which has been manufactured from pulp processed using acid-free and elementary
chlorine-free practices. Furthermore, the publisher ensures that the text paper and cover board used
have met acceptable environmental accreditation standards.

For further information on
Blackwell Publishing, visit our website:
www.blackwellpublishing.com

Contents

Acknowledgments

Our understanding of development and globalization owes much to conversations with interlocutors in Africa, Latin America, North America, and Europe – academics, students, farmers, activists, government officials, politicians, and NGO personnel. Portions of the Introduction draw on the editors' co-authored chapter, "Development" in *A Companion to the Anthropology of Politics*, edited by David Nugent and Joan Vincent (Blackwell, 2004). We are particularly indebted for helpful criticisms and suggestions generously provided by Laura Ahearn, Sara Berry, Michael Chibnik, George DeMartino, James Ferguson, Lesley Gill, Ilene Grabel, Maia Green, Ed Hartman, Frederick Klaits, Nicholas Jackson, Jackie Klopp, Micaela di Leonardo, Peter D. Little, Dillon Mahoney, Sarasij Majumder, Noelle Mole, Donna L. Perry, Louisa Schein, Parker Shipton, K. Sivaramakrishnan, Wendy Weisman, and the 2002–03 seminar participants in Rutgers University's Center for the Critical Analysis of Contemporary Culture. We appreciate as well the discerning comments offered by anonymous referees of the original prospectus and proposed contents list. Sara Berry, Michael Chibnik and K. Sivaramakrishnan kindly read a nearly final version of the entire introduction and we thank them for commenting so helpfully and so promptly at that crucial stage. It has been a delight to work with Jane Huber, our editor at Blackwell, and Parker Shipton, the series editor. Their fine editorial judgment and intellectual acumen have made this a better book. Its shortcomings are, of course, attributable to the volume editors alone.

It would not have been possible to include the range and number of works reprinted here without abridging them. In many cases, we have had to cut not only the main text but also some footnotes and references. The editors thank the authors for their understanding on this point. Full bibliographic citations of the original works are provided below.

The editors and publishers wish to thank the following for permission to use copyright material:

1 Smith, Adam, 1976 [1776] Of the Accumulation of Capital, or of Productive and Unproductive Labour. *In* An Inquiry into the Nature and Causes of The Wealth of Nations, Book II, pp. 256–257, 358, 359, 360, 363–364, 368, 369, 370 [excerpts]. Chicago: University of Chicago Press.

2 Marx, Karl, and Friedrich Engels, Manifesto of the Communist Party. Internet edition: www.marxists.org/archive/marx/works/1848/communist-manifesto/Copyleft:Marx/Engels Internet Archive (marxists.org) 1987, 2000. Permission is granted to copy and/or distribute this document under the terms of the GNU Free Documentation License. See www.marxists.org/admin/legal/fdl.htm.

3 Weber, Max, 1950 The Evolution of the Capitalistic Spirit. *In* General Economic History: 352–8, 364–9 [excerpts]. Glencoe, IL: Free Press.

4 Polanyi, Karl, 1957 [1944] The Self Regulating Market and the Fictitious Commodities: Labor, Land, and Money. *In* The Great Transformation: The Political and Economic Origins of Our Time: 68–76. Boston: Beacon Press. Reprinted by permission of Kari Polanyi Levitt.

5 Leys, Colin, 1996 The Rise and Fall of Development Theory. *In* The Rise and Fall of Development Theory, chapter 1: 3–44 [excerpts]. Indiana University Press and James Currey. Reprinted by permission of James Currey Publishers, London and Indiana University Press, Bloomington.

6 Cooper, Frederick, and Randall Packard, 1997 Introduction. *In* International Development and the Social Sciences: Essays on the History and Politics of Knowledge, Frederick Cooper and Randall Packard, editors: 1–41 [excerpts]. Berkeley: University of California Press. Reprinted by permission of the authors and University of California Press.

7 Ferguson, James, 1997 Anthropology and Its Evil Twin: "Development" in the Constitution of a Discipline. *In* International Development and the Social Sciences: Essays on the History and Politics of Knowledge, Frederick Cooper and Randall Packard, editors: 150–175 [excerpts]. Berkeley: University of California Press. Reprinted by permission of University of California Press.

8 Friedman, Jonathan, 2003 Globalization, Dis-integration, Re-organization:The Transformations of Violence. *In* Globalization, the State and Violence, Jonathan Friedman, editor: 1–14, 16–19, 20, 21, 22, 31–33 [excerpts]. Lanham, MD: AltaMira Press. Reprinted by permission of AltaMira Press, a division of the Rowman & Littlefield Publishing Group.

9 Graeber, David, 2001 The Globalization Movement: Some Points of Clarification. *In* Items and Issues 2(3–4): 12–14. New York: Social Science Research Council. Reprinted by permission of the author and Social Science Research Council.

10 Sassen, Saskia, 2002 Globalization After September 11. *In* Chronicle of Higher Education January 18, 2002: B11–14 [excerpts]. Reprinted by permission of Saskia Sassen.

11 Comaroff, Jean, and John L. Comaroff, 2001 Millennial Capitalism: First Thoughts on a Second Coming. *In* Millennial Capitalism and the Culture of Neoliberalism, Jean Comaroff and John L. Comaroff, editors: 1–13, 14–15, 19–23, 46–48, 50–56 [excerpts]. Durham, NC: Duke University Press. Copyright, 2001, Duke University Press. All rights reserved. Used by permission of the publisher.

12 Geertz, Clifford, 1984 Culture and Social Change: The Indonesian Case. *In* Man 19(4): 511–532 [excerpts]. Reprinted by permission of the author and Blackwell Publishing Ltd.

13 Little, Peter D., and Catherine S. Dolan, 2000 What It Means to be Restructured: Nontraditional Commodities and Structural Adjustment in Sub-Saharan Africa. *In* Commodities and Globalization: Anthropological Perspectives, Angelique Haugerud, M. Priscilla Stone, and Peter D. Little, editors: 59–78 [excerpts]. Boulder, CO, New York, Oxford: Rowman and Littlefield Publishers. Reprinted by permission of the authors and Rowman & Littlefield Publishing Group.

14 Schein, Louisa, 2002 Market Mentalities, Iron Satellite Dishes, and Contested Cultural Developmentalism. *In* Provincial China 7(1): 57–67, 70–2 [excerpts]. Reprinted by permission of Taylor & Francis Ltd. www.tandf.co.uk/journals.

15 Miller, Daniel, 1998 Conclusion: A Theory of Virtualism. *In* Virtualism: A New Political Economy, James G. Carrier and Daniel Miller, editors: 188–196, 199–204, 214–215 [excerpts]. Oxford and New York: Berg. Reprinted with permission from Berg Publishers. All rights reserved.

16 Crewe, Emma and Elizabeth Harrison, 1998 An Intellectual Heritage of Development. *In* Whose Development? An Ethnography of Aid: 43–46 [excerpt]. London and New York: Zed Books. Reprinted by permission of Zed Books.

17 Chant, Sylvia, and Matthew C. Gutman, 2002 "Men-streaming" Gender? Questions for Gender and Development Policy in the Twenty-first Century. *In* Progress in Development Studies 2 (4): 269–282 [excerpts]. Reprinted by permission of Arnold Publishers, a member of the Hodder Headline Group.

18 Collins, Jane L., 2002 Deterritorialization and Workplace Culture. American Ethnologist 29(1): 151–167, 167–171 [excerpts]. Reprinted by permission of the author and American Anthropological Association.

19 Riles, Annelise, 2001 Network! *In* The Network Inside Out: 172–174, 178–182, 183–184, 217–220, 222–227, 229, 231–233 [excerpts]. Ann Arbor, MI: University of Michigan Press. Reprinted by permission of University of Michigan Press.

20 Peluso, Nancy Lee, 1995 Whose Woods Are These? Counter-Mapping Forest Territories in Kalimantan, Indonesia. Antipode 27(4): 383–406 [excerpts]. Reprinted by permission of Blackwell Publishing Ltd.

21 Fairhead, James, and Melissa Leach, 1997 Webs of Power and the Construction of Environmental Policy Problems: Forest Loss in Guinea. In Discourses of Development: Anthropological Perspectives, R. D. Grillo and R. L. Stirrat, editors: 35–8, 40–55, 55–57 [excerpts]. Oxford and New York: Berg. Reprinted with permission from Berg Publishers. All rights reserved.

22 Cunningham, Hilary, 1998 Colonial Encounters in Postcolonial Contexts: Patenting Indigenous DNA and the Human Genome Diversity Project. Critique of Anthropology 18(2): 206–218, 228–33 [excerpts]. Reprinted by permission of the author and Sage Publications Ltd.

23 Fox, Jonathan, 2003 Advocacy Research and the World Bank: Propositions for Discussion. Development in Practice 13(5): 519–527 [excerpts]. Reprinted by permission of Taylor & Francis Ltd. www.tandf.co.uk/journals

24 Roe, Emery M., 1991 Development Narratives, Or Making the Best of Blueprint Development. World Development 19(4): 287–300 [excerpts]. Reprinted by permission of Elsevier Limited.

25 Harper, Richard, 2000 The Social Organization of the IMF's Mission Work: An Examination of International Auditing. In Audit Cultures: Anthropological Studies in Accountability, Ethics and the Academy, Marilyn Strathern, editor: 21–23, 25–36, 37, 38–48, 50–53 [excerpts]. London: Routledge. Reprinted by permission of Thomson Publishing Services on behalf of Routledge.

26 Arturo Escobar, 1992 Imagining a Post-Development Era. Social Text 31: 20–56. [excerpts]. Copyright, 1992, Social Text. All rights reserved. Used by permission of Duke University Press.

27 Gardner, Katy, and David Lewis, 1996 Beyond Development?. In Anthropology, Development and the Post-Modern Challenge: 153–168, 173, 175–183 [excerpts]. London: Pluto Press. Reprinted by permission of Pluto Press.

28 Isichei, Elizabeth, 2002 Village Intellectuals and the Challenge of Poverty, In Voices of the Poor in Africa: 169–187. Rochester, NY: University of Rochester Press. Reprinted by permission of Elizabeth Isichei.

29 Franke, Richard W. and Barbara H. Chasin, 1994 Kerala's Achievements. In Kerala: Radical Reform as Development in an Indian State, 2nd edition. Oakland, CA: Institute for Food and Development Policy: 10–21, 106–7, 118, 125, 126, 128, 131, 132, 133 [excerpts]. Reprinted by permission of the authors and Food First/Institute for Food and Development Policy.

30 Verdery, Katherine, 1996 What Was Socialism and Why Did It Fall? Abridged from What Was Socialism and What Comes Next? Princeton, NJ: Princeton University Press: 19–38. © 1996 Princeton University Press. Reprinted by permission of the author and Princeton University Press.

31 Gledhill, John, 2001 Disappearing the Poor? A Critique of the New Wisdoms of Social Democracy in an Age of Globalization. Urban Anthropology and Studies of Cultural Systems and World Economic Development 30(2): 124–9, 133–7, 138–9, 141–5, 147–9, 151–2, 154–6 [excerpts]. Reprinted by permission of the author.

Every effort has been made to trace copyright holders and to obtain their permission for the use of copyright material. The authors and publishers will gladly receive any information enabling them to rectify any error or omission in subsequent editions.

Introduction:
The Anthropology of Development and Globalization

Marc Edelman and Angelique Haugerud[1]

I Introduction

Development is a matter of life and death. It is both an urgent global challenge and a vibrant theoretical field. Even when anthropologists do not take development as their subject, they often surreptitiously slip assumptions about it into their ethnographies. But named or un-named, development questions lie at the discipline's theoretical and ethnographic core. An anthropologist with an eye on interdisciplinary development studies (which are usually dominated by political science and economics) might lament this wider field's neglect or oversimplification of culture. Yet a scholar contemplating anthropology itself may be struck (as the editors are) by a torrent of works on modernity, development, and globalization in which culture is on proud display while historical political economy and economic and financial globalization are largely absent. Rather than encourage continued separation of these analytical tracks, we need new intellectual hybrids: adventurous combinations of culture, economy, discourse, power, institutions, and history. We must imagine other paths as well: new modes of economic organization, moral aesthetics, and forms of social creativity. In the 21st century, the anthropology of development and globalization demands nothing less.

What is development?

"Development" is an unstable term.[2] Is it an ideal, an imagined future towards which institutions and individuals strive? Or is it a destructive myth, an insidious, failed chapter in the history of Western modernity (Escobar 1995)? Conventionally "development" may connote improvements in well-being, living standards, and opportunities. It may also refer to historical processes of commodification, industrialization, modernization, or globalization. It can be a legitimizing strategy for states, and its ambiguity lends itself to discourses of citizen entitlement as well as state control (Cooper and Packard 1997). A vision of development as improved well-being, especially in former colonies, has gradually replaced the unidimensional economistic measures that neoclassical economists favor, such as GDP growth or economic rates of return to particular projects.[3] Influenced by scholars such as Amartya Sen, the United Nations Development Program created a Human Development Index that combines indicators of health, life expectancy, literacy, formal education, political participation, and access to resources (UNDP 2001:14). During roughly the same period, a growing coterie of scholars and grassroots activists, some of them influenced by Michel Foucault's understandings of power, has rejected outright the desirability of "development," which they see as a destructive and self-serving discourse propagated by bureaucrats and aid professionals that permanently entraps the poor in a vicious circle of passivity and misery.[4]

Some scholars and activists in the latter category imagine a "post-development" era in which community and "indigenous" knowledge become a reservoir of creative alternatives to development (e.g., Esteva 1988; Escobar 1995; Rahnema 1997; Sachs 1992). The alternatives-to-development or "alternative development" position entails "the abandonment of the whole epistemological and political field of postwar development" (Escobar 1991:675), as discussed below. Others focus on development alternatives (alternatives _in_ rather than _to_ development) and favor reforms within the existing development apparatus (see Crewe and Harrison 1998; Little and Painter 1995; Nolan 2002). Some scholars in both camps celebrate the "local" and the "indigenous" – an inclination that figures in larger pendulum shifts during the past fifty to sixty years, notably in the differing views of community and "traditional" culture, with these alternately romanticized or demonized in development thought. Nearly all analysts agree that most development projects fail.[5] Nonetheless, a faith in progress (an assumed capacity to improve the conditions of existence)[6] continues amongst some supporters of all three positions – "development," development alternatives, and post-development alike.

What types of faith in progress motivate development theories and practices? The underlying historical teleologies include a presumed shift from kinship to contract, agriculture to industry, personalized to rational or bureaucratic rule, subsistence to capital accumulation and mass consumption, tradition to modernity, and poverty to wealth. As we explore writers such as Adam Smith, Max Weber, Immanuel Wallerstein, and others, we note explanatory shortcomings of views of human history in which the end or the process itself is made to fit a pre-existing design. Much debate about development in the 20th and 21st centuries, for example, explores whether all or most societies follow the same trajectory toward greater accumulation and well-being or, alternatively, whether wealth in some places or among certain social groups is causally related to poverty in other places or among other groups. Similarly, the notion of a single development trajectory implies that history, rather than reflecting the outcome of struggles between contending social groups – including at times very localized struggles – is simply a _deus ex machina_, in which culture and political processes play no role.

Whether analysts focus on "development" as discourse, as policy or project blueprint, as historical process, or as self-propelled evolutionary process, the concept has become increasingly contentious, and it has attracted attention from an astonishing array of scholars. Mostly gone are musty oppositions between "applied" and "mainstream" or "academic" anthropology. The topic of development is no less theory-worthy or theory-laden than any other in anthropology. The related term "applied anthropology" was coined well over a century ago, and "[d]ebates over practical anthropology and development anthropology have pervaded the history of the profession" (Vincent 1990:431; see also Firth 1981; Malinowski 1929, 1930; Rappaport 1993).[7] More fundamentally, however, the discipline itself was historically constituted as the "science of 'less developed' peoples," and although the social evolutionist underpinnings of this conception have eroded during the 20th century,[8] it remains relevant to anthropology's place in the academic division of labor (Ferguson, this volume). Anthropological discomfort with development, Ferguson argues, does not signal the discipline's critical distance from it but rather its uncomfortable intimacy with development.

The boundary between the "anthropology of development" and other modes of anthropology – like most boundaries – is permeable and at times nearly indiscernible. How such boundaries are made and unmade – and debated or ignored – is more revealing than any attempt to pin down a category definition. In the case of anthropology and development, then, our task is to explore the diverse ways anthropologists have intervened in and been influenced by debates about development.

Why globalization?

As this volume's title implies, development debates fuse with those on globalization – especially globalization as "free-market" or neoliberal economic policies, which became dominant during the 1980s and 1990s (see below). Globalization has at least two other common meanings: the increased integration of various places into the world economy, and the effects of vastly improved transportation and communication systems on multidir-ectional cultural flows. These three meanings are inter-related but far from identical. Many anthropologists emphasize globalization as cultural flows, leaving as shadowy or invisible the economic and political processes and institutions that both shape and are shaped by those flows. As globalization began to replace development as a fashionable buzzword, both terms remained profoundly ambiguous and prone to being hyped, maligned, or acclaimed. Development – in spite of those social scientists who wish for its disappearance – remains the "foundation concept" (Lewellen's term) of a powerful array of international organizations (such as the World Bank, UN agencies, Inter-American Development Bank, nongovernmental organizations) as well as most governments of poor nations.[9] But questions about what kind of development and for whom energize new forms of trans-border activism in pursuit of democratic alternatives to economic neoliberalism (see Graeber's chapter in this volume). Thus in the early 21st century, the idea that there is not just one type of globalization (economic neoliberalism) sparked lively discussion not only among radical economists and activists, but also among mainstream economists and policy-makers. In that sense, debates about globalization and development so compellingly engage one another that no analysis of one can afford to ignore the other.

Outline of the volume

This volume includes work by writers who would not define themselves as development anthropologists or anthropologists of development – an editorial decision that signals the interdisciplinarity of development thought since the 18th century, as well as a rich cross-fertilization of anthropological subfields. Works included here thus invite the reader to rethink the history and potential of this key disciplinary specialty. These selections illus-trate the vibrancy and centrality of development and globalization questions to a wide swath of the discipline.

Our anthology begins with classical roots of contemporary anthropological debates about development. Key theorists from the Enlightenment to the 20th century have shaped later development scholarship in powerful ways. Identifications of noteworthy authors from the past are almost unavoidably "presentist" (see Stocking 1968) and the category of "classics" is obviously problematic. But ideologically motivated, "presentist" appropri-ations and simplifications of ideas rooted in other ages and places are often interesting commentaries on and reflections of contemporary struggles over development doctrine and policies. Thus the introduction to Part I discusses several "classic" readings whose selection is in some sense "presentist," but which reflects as well a "historicist" argument – that is, an emphasis on particular theoretical works in relation to their own time and social context (Stocking 1968). The texts of Adam Smith, Karl Marx and Friedrich Engels, Max Weber, and Karl Polanyi are worth revisiting, partly so that we can move beyond the association of canonical thinkers with their "one big idea", and understand better the ideologically motivated representations of their thought that infuse contemporary development debates.

Part II offers three overviews of 20th-century development thought, all of which reflect the interdisciplinary sensibilities of development studies scholarship as well as the complex interplay of political economy, history and culture that shapes development processes themselves. In addition to Ferguson's essay on the place of development in anthropology, we include two chapters by non-anthropologists in this section (Cooper and Packard; Leys) because these scholars raise profoundly important issues that merit more anthropological attention (see below and the editors' introduction to Part II). In particular, the contentious history of development debates (e.g., modernization, dependency and world systems theories) and related institutional and policy changes is sometimes lost from view in anthropologists' fascination with cultural flows and fragmentation or local project outcomes.

Part III addresses the crucial 20th-century move from development to globalization – that is, the shift from the Bretton Woods system of development centered on nation-states to the rise of economic neoliberalism or contemporary globalization. Neoliberalism of course is not monolithic, but has varying forms and consequences nationally and locally. Its overall focus and its stunning silences are helpfully summed up by Farmer (2003:5):

> Neoliberalism generally refers to the ideology that advocates the dominance of a competition-driven market model. Within this doctrine, individuals in a society are viewed, if viewed at all, as autonomous, rational producers and consumers whose decisions are motivated primarily by economic or material concerns. But this ideology has little to say about the social and economic inequalities that distort real economies. As a physician who has worked for much of my adult life among the poor of Haiti and the United States, I know that the laws of supply and demand will rarely serve the interests of my patients.

The early1970s breakdown of the Bretton Woods system of fixed exchange rates and national controls of capital flows marked a major watershed in the globalization of trade, finance and investment (P. M. Garber 1993; Helleiner 1994; see also chapter by Friedman below). After several decades of post-World War II expansion, based – in most capitalist countries – on Keynesianism or other varieties of state intervention in the economy, a period of recession, "stagflation," and growing fiscal deficits provided an opening in politics and policy making for free-market radicals whose ideas previously had attracted little serious attention and were widely considered eccentric if not extremist. The subsequent, post-1980 period of market openings and public-sector retrenchment, frequently glossed as "globalization," saw immense disruptions, rising social tensions, and lively resistance to neoliberal policies and institutions (such as the globalization protestors who are the focus of Graeber's chapter in this volume).

Parts IV, V, and VI illustrate how contemporary anthropology has absorbed the momentous changes of the era of economic neoliberalism. These chapters include analyses of consumption, markets, gender, work, networks, the environment, and biotechnology – a range of topics that by no means exhausts anthropology's rich contributions to understanding development. The connections among these topics, however, are sometimes lost from view as intellectual specialization grows. Crafting a new political economy, we argue, is one way to reconnect the fragments and to recuperate an understanding of why they may best be examined in relation to each other, in broader analytical frameworks, rather than as distinct phenomena or even exotic curiosities (see Friedman's and Leys' chapters below).

Part VII considers two powerful supra-national economic governance institutions: the International Monetary Fund (IMF) and the World Bank. It offers an ethnographer's inside look at the International Monetary Fund (Harper's chapter), and explores ethical and other challenges facing anthropologists who work for the World Bank and other development institutions (Fox's chapter). In addition, Part VII addresses the forceful role that certain stock narratives or "blueprints" play in development projects and national policies (Roe's chapter). It further asks how anthropologists and other development practitioners might best respond to the frequent shortcomings of "blueprint"-oriented attempts at directed social change.

Part VIII looks at the recent history and future prospects of capitalism, why socialism collapsed, and proposed alternatives, from the utopian project of "post-development" to the radical popular mobilization and grassroots democratic participation that have given the Indian state of Kerala some of the developing world's best indicators of physical and social well-being. Part VIII concludes with a critical examination of the "normalization" of inequality and of recent proposals for a pragmatic, market-oriented "Third Way" version of social democracy, positioned between unfettered capitalism and bureaucratic state socialism (Gledhill's chapter).

This introductory essay outlines historical benchmarks in development theory and practice, and major 20th- and 21st-century theoretical debates about development and globalization. Classical precursors are discussed in detail elsewhere (in the editors' introduction to Part I). This essay first addresses the clash of radical and mainstream paradigms such as 20th-century theories of imperialism, modernization, and dependency; and the rise in the 1980s of economic neoliberalism. It then explores how anthropology absorbed the seismic changes of the new free-market regime, partly by culturalizing and de-historicizing globalization, and by downplaying its political, economic, and legal dimensions. A central aim of this volume is to make these historical and political-economic dimensions visible again, and to illustrate how integral they are to the cultural themes emphasized by many anthropologists of development, globalization, cultural hybridity and post-modernity. With that aim in mind, we review briefly anthropological connections between development and the following topics: NGOs, civil society, gender, population, culture, consumption, environment, and city and countryside. Next we examine the work of anthropologists in development agencies, issues that distinguish development anthropology from the anthropology of development,[10] and reasons why that boundary has blurred. Finally, we consider the post-development position: the choice between development alternatives and alternatives *to* development. In a world where nearly one-half of the population subsists on two dollars a day or less, the search for alternatives to the exhausted paradigms of the past and the harsh realities of the present is more timely than ever.

II Trends, Theories, Debates

Development: Three historical phases

Any periodization of economic or intellectual history is useful primarily as a heuristic tool. Thus we sketch here three historical phases simply to signal some benchmarks in thinking about development.[11] In addressing both historical trends and theories – broad global changes and paradigm shifts – we emphasize the latter, with brief suggestions about how historical trends and theories influence one another.

Notions of development can be traced back at least to the late-18th-century rise of industrial capitalism, which "for the first time allowed productive forces to make a spectacular advance," thus permitting people to imagine dramatic material progress (Larraín 1989:1). Development in late-18th- and 19th-century Europe "was meant to construct order out of the social disorders of rapid urban migration, poverty and unemployment" (Cowen and Shenton 1996:5). Our first phase of development thought thus includes attempts to understand the rise of capitalism in the 15th and 16th centuries, and the startling changes associated with the emergence of industrial capitalism in the late 18th century. These transformations helped to inspire the teleologies noted earlier, together with conceptions of a "universal history," including Enlightenment, Hegelian, Marxian, and other notions of progress. Indeed, development was seen by some (such as Comte) in the late 19th century as reducing the "disordered faults of progress" (Cowen and Shenton 1996:7), though for many in that era "the idea of development provided a way of narrating world history, but not necessarily a rationale for acting upon that history" (Cooper and Packard 1997:7).

The 18th- and 19th-century intellectual traditions of the first phase of development thought were seldom acknowledged in most of the second period,[12] which saw the emergence of a much narrower development theory in the 1950s to deal with "how the economies of the colonies of Britain, France, Portugal and other European powers, colonies comprising some 28% of the world's population, might be transformed and made more productive as decolonisation approached" (Leys 1996:5). Both the terms "development" and "underdevelopment" were invented well before World War II (though their visibility waxed and waned and their precise meanings changed), and neither was originally seen as "part of a new imperial project for the colonial and post-colonial 'Third World'" (Cowen and Shenton 1996:7, 366).

A key precursor to this second period was the 1944 establishment of the Bretton Woods financial institutions (International Monetary Fund and World Bank), together with a system of fixed currency exchange rates, limitations on capital movements across national boundaries, and the institutionalizing of national economic planning to promote growth. The idea of development here was strongly influenced by John Maynard Keynes, the chief British delegate to the Bretton Woods Conference and an advocate of public spending as an engine of growth and source of employment. This approach to development underlined the centrality of state sovereignty, as national governments – initially in war-ravaged Europe and soon after in Asia, Africa, and Latin America – pledged to improve the material circumstances of their citizens. The supranational finance and governance institutions (World Bank, IMF, UN) were to assist nation-states in the development quest. While after 1980 the IMF and World Bank became forceful proponents of trade and financial liberalization, before then their stance was distinctly unliberal, at least as regards finance and the role of the public sector (Helleiner 1994:164–165). This pre-1980 position took for granted and indeed encouraged extensive state intervention in the economy, whether this meant controlling exchange rates, subsidizing investment and consumption, or building infrastructural mega-projects such as hydroelectric and irrigation schemes, highways or modern port facilities.

Development took on new visibility as an effort to reduce world poverty after the 1944 Bretton Woods Conference and the end of World War II, and especially after Harry Truman's 1949 inaugural address, which proposed using US scientific and technological expertise to stimulate growth and raise living standards in "underdeveloped areas."[13] Policy theorists and planners rethought unequal relationships between rich and poor nations, and the development dream "colonized reality" (Escobar 1995:5).[14] Or as Hart (1992:215) put it, "The protagonists of the cold war designated the poor remainder of humanity 'the Third World' and gave the name 'development' to their economic predicament." A new generation of technocrats increasingly viewed poverty alleviation not as an outcome of "self-regulating processes of economic growth or social change" but of concerted action by both rich and poor nations working in cooperation with new international aid agencies and financial institutions (Cooper and Packard 1997:1). In a later path-breaking study, anthropologist James Ferguson (1990) portrayed these development institutions as an "anti-politics machine" that could only cast development problems in apolitical, ahistorical, techno-managerial terms – disguising the profound political questions at stake in common interventions in agricultural, health or education programs.

A third development phase begins in the 1970s with the breakdown of the Bretton Woods controls on capital movements (and a consequent weakening of states' capacities to promote national development), the 1971 termination of currency exchange rates fixed to a gold value through the US dollar, and – in the late 1970s and 1980s – a series of policy changes that were known (outside the United States) as economic neoliberalism. (Inside the United States, the new economic status quo was so taken for granted – so naturalized by institutions of power – that it was seldom labelled or debated at all [Korten 2001:78]).[15] What the rest of the world terms "neoliberalism" or "liberalism" – that is, doctrines or policies that accord the market rather than the state the main role in resolving economic and other problems – is typically considered "conservative" in the United States. Or put another way, in the United States neoliberalism is a blend of neoclassical economics and political conservatism.

In the 1970s, the World Bank, under Robert McNamara's leadership, shifted its focus from economic growth per se to poverty and equity issues. At the same time the US Agency for International Development began to emphasize poverty, basic human needs, and the equitable distribution of the gains from economic growth. However, skyrocketing petroleum prices, rising interest rates, and slowing economic growth forced many poorer countries, particularly in Latin America, to assume greater debt burdens. The 1980s debt crisis[16] was accompanied by diverging economic growth rates among Third World states and the emergence of the newly industrialized countries (NICs) – most notably the "Asian tigers" of Taiwan, South Korea, Singapore, and Hong Kong – as success stories. Rapid growth among the NICs (sometimes termed "NIEs" or "newly industrializing economies") was originally attributed to free-market policies, and occasionally to "Confucian culture," but later was recognized as the outcome of state subsidies and protectionism, radical agrarian reforms that contributed to building prosperous rural middle classes, and US concessions motivated by geo-political concerns (Castells 2000:256–299). The NICs received few loans from international financial institutions and only modest amounts of foreign aid.

During the 1980s and 1990s, the World Bank and International Monetary Fund promoted in poorer nations a key set of reforms known as structural adjustment. In contrast to these institutions' stance during their first three decades of existence, these programs sought to reduce the state role in the economy, and called for reductions in state expenditures on social services such as education and health care, introduction of user fees for such services, trade liberalization, currency devaluation, selling off of state-owned enterprises, and financial and labor market deregulation. The rationale for such policies is set forth particularly clearly in the highly visible 1981 World Bank publication known as the "Berg report" on African development (World Bank 1981).

By the mid-1990s, however, the World Bank was modifying these structural adjustment policies. Continuing debt problems prompted the Bank to develop social investment programs targeted at poor sectors hit hard by adjustment policies, as well as conditioned debt relief programs for a subset of nations it termed "heavily indebted poor countries" (HIPC), most of which were in Africa. The latter shift reflected in part the beginning of a breakdown of the "Washington Consensus" (see below), the neoliberal orthodoxy that had held sway in the international financial institutions and in many developing-country governments. The 1996 Heavily Indebted Poor Countries initiative taken by the G-7 countries in the face of heavy pressure from the Jubilee 2000 debt-forgiveness movement, the 1997 Asian financial crisis, and growing evidence of the shortcomings of orthodox neoliberalism all contributed to this unravelling. The intellectual hegemony of the

"Washington Consensus" crumbled in the mid- to late-1990s as several of its prominent architects – including a former World Bank vice-president – launched scathing criticisms of the impact of structural adjustment policies on the economies and living standards of the poorer countries (Stiglitz 2002; Sachs 1999; Soros 2002).

In just three decades, the official aims of world development efforts had been dramatically lowered – from the 1960s notion, associated with W. W. Rostow (see below), of catching up to the consumption levels of industrialized countries, to the more modest early 1970s aim of redistribution with growth, then the late-1970s program designed to meet the basic needs of the poor (with no expectation of equity with wealthier nations), and finally by the 1980s, fiscal austerity under structural adjustment programs that often sacrificed the basic needs of the poor (Leys 1996:26). By the late 1980s, Leys (1996:26, 24) argues, the recently expanded powers of global capital markets over national economies, together with other world economic changes, signalled that "'development theory' was in deep trouble"; indeed, "the only development policy that was officially approved was not to have one – to leave it to the market to allocate resources, not the state."[17] The latter position of free-market universalism, once held only by a dissenting minority, had become predominant in much of the world by the late 1980s.[18]

When fractures appeared in this dominant "free-market" approach, some mainstream economists distanced themselves from its more extreme versions. Thus John Williamson, who invented the term "Washington Consensus" in 1989, later attempted to refine the paradigm, subtly separating the original set of policies addressed by Washington-based institutions such as the World Bank and IMF on the one hand, and neoliberal or market fundamentalist policies on the other (Williamson 2002). Williamson (2002:252) distinguishes the so-called Washington Consensus policies from state minimalism or "an extreme and dogmatic commitment to the belief that markets can handle everything."[19] He rejects the idea that the latter approach is effective for reducing poverty (especially for the poorest countries), and he notes that by the early 21st century, the World Bank endorsed a "wider array of antipoverty instruments than was able to command a consensus in 1989" (Williamson 2002:259).[20]

Innovative economists such as Ilene Grabel and Ha-Joon Chang (2004), on the other hand, argue that it is misleading to think that the architects of the Washington Consensus have moved to a post-neoliberal position. Instead, Grabel and Chang suggest, mainstream economists such as Williamson attempt to save the Washington Consensus by modifying a few key policy prescriptions (for example, recognizing that liberalization of capital flows can lead to financial crisis). Grabel and Chang's book *Reclaiming Development* refutes myths about neoliberal development such as the claim that it promotes economic growth, that it accounts for the historical success of today's wealthy nations, that the latter nations converge on a single economic model, and that the Anglo-American policy model is universally applicable but the successful East Asian model cannot be replicated. In contrast to the revisionist architects of the Washington Consensus, Grabel and Chang (2004) aim to be part of a dialogue about real post-neoliberalism, and thus offer a range of alternatives to such policies (see also DeMartino 2000 and ILO 2004).

How have the world's poor fared during the past several decades of official development efforts? Positive indicators include an increase in world GNP from $1.3 trillion in 1960 to nearly $30 trillion by the late 1990s, and during the same period a 50 percent increase in the rate of school enrolment, a rise of 17 years in life expectancy in poor countries, and a 50 percent drop in child mortality worldwide (Nolan 2002:223). Nonetheless, at the end of the 20th century, over 840 million people were undernourished, and nearly 1.3 billion lived on the equivalent of less than one dollar per day (FAO 2003:6; UNDP 1999:22, 28). A half-century after the emergence of the narrow version of economic development theory that was to lift decolonizing nations out of poverty, and four decades after colonial rule ended in much of the Caribbean, Africa, and the Pacific, "developing" nations accounted for some four-fifths of the world's population (Leys 1996:5). Between 1950 and 1990, as the world's population doubled, so too did the number of people living in poverty (Nolan 2002:223).

Global economic inequality increased dramatically between 1960 and 1990: in 1960, the wealthiest 20 percent of the world's population received 30 times the income of the poorest 20 percent; in 1997, the richest 20 percent received 74 times as much (UNDP 1999:36). By the late 20th century, the world's 200 wealthiest individuals had assets equal to more than the combined income of 41 percent of the world's population; the assets of the three richest people were more than the combined GNP of all least developed countries (UNDP 1999:38). Debt levels as a percentage of export earnings in poor nations doubled between 1970 and 1986, and by 1986 more money flowed to the West in debt repayments than went to the Third World in loans and investments (Nolan 2002:54). In the late 1990s, Tanzania, for example, was spending one-third of its national budget on debt repayment – four times what it spent on primary education (Nolan 2002:56). Nicaragua's 1991 foreign debt was more than five times its GDP and its annual debt service more than twice its export earnings. Fully 43 percent of the foreign aid it received went for payments on the debt (Robinson 1997:34-35). Numerous other "developing" countries found themselves in a similar economic straightjacket. By the late 1980s, such trends led to pronouncements that the development process had been reversed (Portes and Kincaid 1989:489), and survival rather than development had become the "economic imperative of the day" (Hart 1992:219).

The British news weekly the *Economist* offers a counter-narrative to this picture of growing global poverty and worsening economic inequality.[21] That publication highlights several difficulties in assessing economic inequality trends: how to measure what people in poor nations actually consume (i.e., living standards),[22] how to value consumption in a way that allows meaningful comparisons across countries and over time, and how to define an appropriate basis of comparison (this is what economists often call adjusting per capita GDP for "purchasing power parity" or PPP). The *Economist* (2004:70) cites statistical studies based on national-accounts data, which it says show declining poverty in the 1980s and 1990s. By contrast, the more widely cited estimates (used by the UN and World Bank, for example) are based on direct surveys of households and show little or no decline in poverty in recent decades. Economists find combining the national-accounts and house-hold-survey data to be technically challenging, and hope eventually to produce more accurate figures.

Yet any statistics lend themselves to alternative manipulations and interpretations. For example, both the time period under analysis and the figure taken as the poverty baseline make a big difference, as World Bank functionary Martin Ravallion notes in his reply in a subsequent issue of the *Economist*. In the late 1980s and early 1990s, for instance, conditions worsened for the world's poor. But if a two-decade window and the frugal $1-a-day standard are used, the World Bank estimates that "the world poverty rate fell from 33% in 1981 (about 1.5 billion people) to 18% in 2001 (1.1 billion)." On the other hand, when judged by the $2-a-day standard, the Bank estimates that the number of people living in poverty *increased* from 2.4 billion to 2.7 billion between 1981 and 2001. And of course those who managed to move beyond the $1-a-day standard remain poor "even by the standards of middle-income developing countries" (Ravallion 2004:65). Furthermore, all of these figures show sharp regional differences in poverty trends. Although the number of people living on less than $1 a day in Asia has fallen during the last two decades, the number in that category in Africa has roughly doubled. During the early 1980s, "one in ten of the world's poorest lived in Africa"; two decades later the figure was about one in three

(Ravallion 2004:65). Few would deny the challenges of collecting reliable global economic data, and it is clear that statistics can be manipulated to support a variety of positions. Yet visible poverty is widespread and solutions – not just better statistics – are urgently needed.

Official foreign cooperation (termed "aid" in the United States) declined worldwide during the 1990s, dropping from about $60 billion in the early 1990s to about $55 billion in 1999 (Nolan 2002:225). The US contribution to these amounts fell sharply – from over 60 percent of the total in the mid-1950s to 17 percent by 1998 (Nolan 2002:228). In 1947, at the start of the post-World War II Marshall Plan, US foreign aid as a percentage of GDP was nearly 3 percent, while by the late 1990s it was a mere 0.1 percent – the lowest of any major industrialized nation (Soros 2002:17).[23] Among bilateral aid donors, only Japan has substantially increased its development aid during the past two decades. While official aid flows have diminished, private direct investment in developing countries has increased, rising to more than three times the dollar amount of official aid by 1997 (Nolan 2002:231). Such private investment is very unevenly distributed, with much of it going to Asia and most African countries receiving little.

Whatever the practical ambitions of the last fifty years of development theory, poverty remains widespread and remedies are still elusive. In the late 20th century, this stark reality contributed to widespread disillusionment with those agents (such as the World Bank, International Monetary Fund, bilateral aid agencies, and national governments) to which the responsibility for development was entrusted (Cowen and Shenton 1996:4). Yet none of the alternative trustees, such as NGOs, communities, or grassroots social movements, have proven to be effective substitute agents for humanizing markets, alleviating poverty, or ensuring equity and social justice. But before we consider this dilemma, let us review some 20th-century development debates.

From imperialism to dependency and the world-system

This section outlines the convergence of early-20th-century theories of imperialism with the radical analyses of dependency and underdevelopment that became influential in anthropology in the 1970s. It also examines how these radical understandings of dependency engaged mainstream paradigms, especially "modernization" approaches, and how dependency in turn became a target for the critiques of orthodox Marxist and historically minded anthropological theorists.

Max Weber's concern with "traditionalism" as an impediment to development, first articulated at the dawn of the 20th century (see Part I), combined an Enlightenment notion of progress with a modern understanding of the history of capitalism. Apart from briefly discussing speculation in the seventeenth to early nineteenth centuries (Weber 1950), Weber accorded little attention to capitalist crises, an issue that had engaged Marx and that animated development debates in the first half of the 20th century. The frequent booms and busts in European and North American economies, as well as the sudden imperial expansion of the major European states after 1870 and of the United States following the 1898 Spanish-American War, led to closer scholarly scrutiny of a system that increasingly appeared to contain both extraordinary dynamism and immense destructive powers.

The approach that had the most impact in the capitalist West, particularly during the 1930s depression in the United States, was John Maynard Keynes's "pump-priming" economic policy, which sought to temper the business cycle through government measures to stimulate demand and increase employment (see Heilbroner 1972:261-272). But while demand-side policies might alleviate the worst effects of a major slump, they did little to explain imperialism or uneven development.

In the late 19th century, "imperialism" referred specifically to the colonialism of the great maritime powers – to the extension of political sovereignty *overseas*, first by Portugal and Spain, then by Britain, France and other European countries, and finally by the United States and Japan (B. J. Cohen 1973:10). In 1902, an English liberal and advocate of free trade, John A. Hobson, noting that the term was "on everybody's lips," published a work that virtually single-handedly reshaped in economic terms popular and academic understandings of imperialism (Hobson 1965:xvii). Arguing that the "taproot of Imperialism" was the persistent tendency to produce more goods than could be sold at a profit and to accumulate more capital than could be profitably invested, he suggested that "manufacturers, merchants, and financiers . . . are tempted more and more to use their Governments in order to secure for their particular use some distant undeveloped country by annexation and protection" (Hobson 1965:80-81). While Hobson influenced radical socialist opponents of capitalism, notably V. I. Lenin and Rosa Luxemburg (Lenin 1965; Luxemburg 1972), he nonetheless believed that increasing workers' purchasing power and taxing excess capital could obviate the "need to fight for foreign markets or foreign areas of investment" (Hobson 1965:86). Often ignored by those who accepted Lenin's characterization of Hobson as a social reformer and pacifist (Lenin 1965:11) are the unabashedly social Darwinist dimensions of his work, such as the assertion that "civilized Governments" ought to "undertake the political and economic control of lower races" if this were done to "secure the safety and progress of the civilization of the world and not the special interest of the interfering nation" (Hobson 1965:232).

The various Marxist theories shared the view that imperialism grew out of capitalist crises, even though they differed on the importance of underdeveloped regions as sources of cheap or strategic raw materials, markets for manufactured goods, outlets for excess capital, and places where super-profits could be derived from super-exploitation of poorly paid workers (Barratt Brown 1972; Bleaney 1976; B. J. Cohen 1973). In Latin America, and particularly in Peru, as Cristóbal Kay (1991) has argued, heated polemics during the 1920s and 1930s between heterodox Marxist revolutionaries, such as José Carlos Mariátegui, and anti-imperialist reformist populists, such as Víctor Raúl Haya de la Torre, set the stage for debates in the 1960s between proponents of radical and "structuralist" versions of dependency theory. Both strands of theory – in the 1920s and in the 1960s – viewed underdevelopment and development as products of a single, worldwide process of accumulation that continually reproduced both outcomes. Perhaps the central innovation of these theorists, many of them grouped around the independent US socialist magazine *Monthly Review*, derived from the observation that – contrary to the predictions of Hobson and Lenin – capital flows from underdeveloped to developed areas generally exceeded developed-country exports of surplus capital. As Paul Baran and Paul Sweezy concluded,

> foreign investment, far from being an outlet for domestically generated surplus, is a most efficient device for transferring surplus generated abroad to the investing country. Under these circumstances, it is of course obvious that foreign investment aggravates rather than helps to solve the surplus absorption problem (Baran and Sweezy 1966:107–108).

This inversion of the classical theories of imperialism, which had seen developed countries' need to export excess capital as one of the principal dynamics or "laws" impelling imperial expansion, became the germ of the circulationist or market-based approaches to dependency, underdevelopment, and the world-system that strongly influenced anthropology and sociology in the 1960s and 1970s, particularly in Latin America.[24] But while the intellectual genealogy of dependency theory can be traced back to a radical lineage associated with *Monthly Review* (which published an influential Spanish-language edition), it also originated in the work of individuals and institutions that were in the mainstream of economic policy-making in Latin America.

Founded in 1948, and directed after 1950 by Argentine economist Raúl Prebisch, the United Nations Economic Commission on Latin America (ECLA) initiated an "intellectual revolution" in Latin America that had a profound impact on development policy in the hemisphere and beyond, as well as on a generation of social scientists (Bulmer-Thomas 1994:234; Sikkink 1988). ECLA doctrine held that Latin American countries which relied on primary product exports were negatively affected by the long-term decline in terms of trade; in other words, over time a larger quantity of exports (say, bags of coffee or tons of bauxite) was required to purchase the same volume of imports (for example, jeeps or machine tools). This process occurred primarily because of the monopoly and monopsony powers in what Prebisch called the "center" of the world economy that facilitated the extraction through international trade of surplus from the "periphery."[25] Export-led development thus entailed chronic foreign exchange shortages and vulnerabilities to market fluctuations – many Latin American countries in the mid-20th century earned half or more of their export earnings from one or a handful of commodities. ECLA, under Prebisch's direction, promoted a "structuralist" approach to economics and an inward-looking, rather than export-oriented, development model based on import substitution industrialization (ISI) and dynamizing domestic markets.[26]

In addition to Prebisch, several influential Latin American social scientists were associated with ECLA during the 1960s and early 1970s, including economist Celso Furtado and sociologist Fernando Henrique Cardoso. Cardoso co-authored with Enzo Faletto one of the most widely read treatises on dependency and development (Cardoso and Faletto 1969). In 1994 Cardoso would be elected president of Brazil on a neoliberal platform. Cardoso and Faletto's "historical structuralist" study of dependency noted that the larger Latin American countries had begun to industrialize during the 1930s, when developed-country demand for their traditional primary-product exports contracted. This incipient industrialization brought to the fore a new national, urban-industrial bourgeoisie that formed a "developmentalist alliance" with the expanding working class. This alliance wrested power from traditional oligarchies and established populist political experiments and a development style that relied increasingly on foreign rather than national, capital. Populist class pacts were typically fragile, however, and their rupture often led to authoritarian political outcomes, a conclusion Cardoso and Faletto based on the Brazilian experience after 1964, but which would soon be confirmed with the military coups in Chile, Uruguay and Argentina in the 1970s (Cardoso and Faletto 1969:160).

A second influential strain of dependency analysis arose among radical theorists enthused by the 1959 Cuban revolution. The best known of these writers in the English-speaking world was the prolific and peripatetic German-American economist Andre Gunder Frank, although he was but one figure in a large, transdisciplinary intellectual-political nexus that spanned Latin America. Frank (and others in this group) sought to demolish the "dual society" thesis, which was rooted in Weberian and Parsonian sociology and in the works of anthropologist Robert Redfield (1953) and economist W. A. Lewis (1955). The "dual society" argument held that Latin America (and by extension other poor regions) included a dynamic capitalist sector and a stagnant "traditional" or "feudal" one, which could only be modernized through assimilation or incorporation into the "advanced" sector. Instead of "dualism," Frank, Mexican anthropologist Rodolfo Stavenhagen (1969), and others proposed a model of "internal colonialism" that saw urban zones as beneficiaries of surpluses extracted from rural areas. This pattern mirrored the "metropolis-satellite" (or what Prebisch had termed "center-periphery") relations that linked developed and underdeveloped regions as outcomes of a single historical process and which Frank defined as "capitalist" since the 16th century (Frank 1969:9).

The claim that development and underdevelopment were the results of the same "capitalist" historical process had implications for development policy and for those seeking radical political change. Marxists – and particularly the pro-Soviet Communist Parties – had long argued that Latin American societies were significantly "feudal." This characterization was based primarily on the widespread existence in the countryside of coerced, non-waged labor relations and vast, extensively exploited properties owned by seemingly traditional elites whose aspirations and sumptuary practices (such as elaborate displays of wealth in dwellings, luxury goods consumption and political influence buying) were said to resemble those of medieval European nobles. Progress, according to this analysis, based on Stalin's (1940) simplification of Marx, could only occur if "feudalism" were overthrown and replaced by capitalism, as had occurred in Europe; the Left and working class ought, therefore, to align with the "progressive bourgeoisie" to break the back of the traditional landed oligarchy. If, however, as Frank maintained, Latin America had always been "capitalist," it followed that there was not really a "progressive bourgeoisie" opposed to a "feudal" oligarchy; the upper class was, in his view, thoroughly "capitalist," with a strong interest in preserving the existing social order. In the absence of a "progressive bourgeoisie" the political task for radicals was to topple the entire capitalist class through revolutionary struggle (Frank 1969:371-72). Structuralist Marxist critics dodged these pressing issues of strategy, but nonetheless castigated Frank for "conceptual imprecision" and for failing to distinguish the "capitalist mode of production," characterized in classical Marxism by wage-labor relations, from the "capitalist system" of market-based commodity exchange, in which wage labor might be present or absent (Laclau 1971:24).

Although Frank was trained in the orthodox neoclassical economics department at the University of Chicago, he had early sympathies for Keynesianism and the heterodox, visionary economics of Kenneth Boulding. Even at Chicago, as he later reported in an intellectual autobiography, he "spent more and more . . . time studying and associating with the anthropologists," largely because they – like him – assumed "that the determinant factors in economic development were really *social*" (Frank 1991:17, original emphasis). As early as 1959, he participated with Margaret Mead in a session at the American Anthropological Association meetings and, in the early 1960s, Darcy Ribeiro invited him to teach anthropology at the new University of Brasilia (a position followed by a prolonged sojourn in Chile, Mexico, and Germany). In 1968, he issued a passionate call for "liberation anthropology" in *Current Anthropology* and, in another paper, lambasted both "formalist" and "substantivist" economic anthropologists[27] for ignoring the effects of colonialism and imperialism on underdevelopment (Frank 1969:137-45; 1991:38-39). Later he wrote appreciatively of Kathleen Gough, Rodolfo Stavenhagen, Eric Wolf, and June Nash, as well as of Clifford Geertz, whose *Agricultural Involution* (1966) he considered an incisive refutation of the "dualism" thesis (Frank 1991).

While Frank remarked that dependency theory "succumbed to the [1973] coup in Chile,"[28] the approach took on a second life in 1974 with the appearance of US sociologist Immanuel Wallerstein's *The Modern World-System*, the first volume of a planned multivolume work on the history of the world economy (Frank 1991:36; Wallerstein 1974). Wallerstein drew inspiration from Fernand Braudel's 1972 magnum opus on the 16th-century Mediterranean, European debates about the transition from feudalism to capitalism (see Hilton 1976), and an extraordinarily wide and insightful reading of the history of world regions and of development-related theory, ranging from Eric Wolf and Barrington Moore to Pierre Chaunu and R. H. Tawney. Wallerstein sought to explain the emergence in "the long sixteenth century" of a single world economy, larger than any empire, and its functional division into what he called – in an unacknowledged reworking and expansion of Prebisch's categories – "core," "semiperipheral" and "peripheral" regions, characterized respectively by the prevalence of wage labor, tenant farming and sharecropping, and coerced labor.

Many of the arguments of world-system theory are, as Alejandro Portes and Douglas Kincaid point out (1989:482), "at least implicit in dependency theory, and many analysts do not regard them as distinct approaches. . . . Nevertheless, in one essential point the world-system approach . . . goes beyond dependency: the concept of national development is subsumed into that of a higher level social system, the capitalist world economy" (Portes and Kincaid 1989:482).[29] In addition, dependency theorists tended to view the hierarchy of nations as fairly stable, while world-system theorists posited national movements up or down the hierarchy without fundamentally changing the functioning of the system as a whole.

Despite its erudite commentary on a vast literature of secondary sources, Wallerstein's work, like that of the dependency group, was not fundamentally historical in the sense of understanding uneven development, labor arrangements, stratification patterns, or political systems as outcomes of struggles between contending social groups located in concrete social formations. Some critics took him to task for not distinguishing sufficiently between relations of production and relations of exchange and for according the latter explanatory priority in accounting for the shape of the world-system (Brenner 1977). Others, notably Mintz (1977), maintained that even the history of the world-system had to be understood from the bottom up, not just as an expanding sphere of exchange but as an outcome of diverse local initiatives and local responses, themselves the outcomes of social struggles that sought varying relationships with international and other markets.

This critique of world-system theory contributed, particularly in the works of Wolf (1982) and Mintz (1985), to solidifying the position of historically-oriented political economy within US anthropology. In Europe, Latin America, and South Asia, debates between and among Marxists and world-system theorists produced vigorous, heterodox development-studies traditions and had more influence on mainstream development theory than the critique of world-system theory did in the United States. Marxist and world-system theory debates affected agrarian studies (Roseberry 1995) and, eventually, those strains of post-colonial studies that sought to root changing identities in historical processes of nation-state formation and transitions to new kinds of global spaces and governmentality (Gupta 1998). Thus by the 1970s, a new critical anthropology emerged as the discipline was profoundly reshaped by outside influences, especially dependency theory, world-system theory, and neo-Marxist critiques of both modernization theory (see below) and traditional functionalist anthropology. "[H]istory, political economy, and colonialism began to gain new legitimacy as bona-fide anthropological topics" that were central to disciplinary theory (Ferguson 1997:162), rather than consigned to the "applied" slot. In that sense "development" – or rather "underdevelopment" – had become a hot topic in the discipline's mainstream. Now the notion of development itself was critiqued, particularly its presumed equation with moral and economic progress, and its understanding of the world as a set of individual societies moving independently through history (Ferguson 1997:163; Wolf 1982).

In a parallel change, the 1970s move beyond narrowly economistic indicators of development helped to create new employment opportunities for anthropologists in development agencies, and contributed to the emergence of a new subfield of development anthropology (Hobart 1993; Hoben 1982; Escobar 1991; Little and Painter 1995; Ferguson 1997; Nolan 2002). Many of these development anthropologists straddled (sometimes uneasily) the worlds of academe and development agencies, and brought the discipline's new critical perspectives on development to the very institutions and organizations charged with implementing the policies that they critiqued (see below and Part VII introduction).

From modernization to neoliberalism, development to globalization

The modernization paradigm that the dependency theorists attacked had antecedents in Weber and attracted followers in sociology, particularly Talcott Parsons (1937), Edward Shils (1957), and Bert Hoselitz (1952); in psychology, where David McClelland (1961) designed a "need for achievement" or "NAch" scale that purportedly measured an essential attitudinal component of development; and in the work of anthropologists such as Manning Nash (1966) and Robert Redfield (1941), whose "folk society" category – juxtaposed to "urban society" or "civilization" – was in effect an early articulation of the dualism or dual society thesis. Parsons claimed that his concern with moral codes (or "pattern variables") as the key factors structuring social action derived from Weber's principle that modernization involved a transition from particularistic, collectivity-oriented practices and beliefs to universalistic and self-oriented ones.

The Chicago-based journal *Economic Development and Cultural Change*, launched in 1952, became a significant venue for the work of anthropologists and sociologists interested in development issues, most of whom backed some version of the modernization paradigm.[30] In its first issue, Hoselitz lamented "the obstinacy with which people hold to traditional values, even in the face of a rapidly changing technology and economic organization" (1952:9). However, he also indicated that "value systems" would adjust when economic conditions improved and lambasted the "naive . . . opinion that economic development will result essentially in a repetition of the American experience," as well as the "dangerous [and] . . . false" doctrine that development was necessarily tied to a particular form of government or ideology (1952:19).

Much of Clifford Geertz's early work directly engaged the central questions of modernization theory and a Weberian preoccupation with the relation between religion and development.[31] In a series of works, the first of which appeared in *Economic Development and Cultural Change*, he compared a Javanese and a Balinese town, dominated respectively by Islamic and Hindu elites, with a view to explaining contrasting patterns of economic activity and attitudes toward accumulation (Geertz 1956, 1962, 1963). The traders in the Javanese bazaar were, according to Geertz, heirs to an early-20th-century reform movement in Islam that created "a genuinely bourgeois ethic," akin to the Protestant ethic that Weber saw as propelling the rise of European capitalism (1963:49). The largely agrarian Hindu aristocrats in Bali, on the other hand, eschewed the individualism of the Javanese bazaar merchants in favor of employing non-economic, cross-class ties to mobilize labor and intra-class ties to amass capital in large, firm-like enterprises. In the opening sentence of *Peddlers and Princes* (1963), Geertz hailed the notion of "take-off" elaborated in economist Walt Whitman Rostow's recently published *The Stages of Economic Growth* (1960) and proposed that Indonesia was in "a pre-takeoff period" (although he also criticized the assumption of Indonesian social homogeneity that national planners typically articulated when discussing the impending "take-off") (Geertz 1963:1-3, 153–155).

As Geertz's invocation of Rostow indicates, *The Stages of Economic Growth* became a basic reference point for all subsequent discussions of the modernization paradigm. Rostow saw his work, subtitled "A Non-Communist Manifesto," as "an alternative to Karl Marx's theory of human history" (rather as Weber and Parsons earlier had viewed their own) and to Soviet hubris about the superiority of socialism (Rostow 1960:2, 134).

Rostow played major foreign policy roles in the Kennedy and Johnson administrations, including service as one of the main architects of US policy in Vietnam (his brother, named for US socialist leader Eugene Victor Debs, held important foreign policy posts in the Johnson and Reagan administrations).

Rostow is most frequently cited for his claim that all countries eventually pass through the same stages:

(1) "traditional society," characterized by "pre-Newtonian" technology, little or no social mobility, a fatalistic ethos, and strong family- or kin-based ties that limit investment and circumscribe economically rational decision making;
(2) a pre-take-off period in which consolidated nation-states emerge and traditional institutions and values begin to break down and coexist alongside ideas of progress and new types of enterprises;
(3) "take-off," when traditional impediments to economic growth are overcome, agriculture modernizes, industry expands, and investment rates rise;
(4) "the drive to maturity," marked by technological innovation and enlargement and specialization of the industrial base; and
(5) "the age of high mass-consumption," a period of widespread affluence, growing urbanization, service-sector expansion, and ubiquitous consumer durables, such as automobiles and refrigerators.

Modernization theory – and Rostow in particular – was much criticized for emphasizing economistic measures of progress, such as GNP growth, as well as for a "culturalist" preoccupation with "traditional" values and institutions and a corresponding neglect of structures of exploitation, and for assuming that all societies traveled the same historical trajectory, albeit at different paces. While such objections are largely valid, critics rarely acknowledge that one of the main criteria of development for most modernization theorists was not so much economic growth per se, but rather increasing structural complexity in the economy (a notion with clear origins in Durkheimian sociology). Moreover, from the vantage point of the early 21st century, several other dimensions of Rostow's work – and of the modernization paradigm in general – stand out as the antithesis of the neoliberal version of free-market fundamentalism. First, Rostow stressed the central role of the state in economic development, as a provider of the "social overhead capital" (ports, railways, roads, and so on) necessary for growth and, especially in the stage of "mass consumption," as a guarantor of social welfare and security. Second, he not only considered the state a central agent of development, but saw the nation as the geographical and political space in which progress along the five-stage trajectory would be made or arrested. This focus on individual countries – which some in recent years have condemned as an obsolete "methodological nationalism" (Beck 2003) – was entirely consonant with how the world economy was then organized and with the World Bank and the International Monetary Fund's vision of the development of *national* economies, each with its particular resource endowments and forms of *national* protectionism (Helleiner 1994). Finally, Rostow considered that one feature of the "drive to maturity" stage would be the production at home of goods formerly acquired abroad, an affirmation consistent with those of protectionist advocates of import substitution industrialization, such as his "structuralist" critics in ECLA.

It should hardly be surprising that modernization theory, derided by its critics as a legitimating ideology for capitalism, had a statist dimension. From the end of World War II until the collapse of the Bretton Woods system of capital controls and fixed exchange rates in the early 1970s, the intimate links between state and market were part of the prevailing common sense of the economics profession and policy-makers. Economic historian Karl Polanyi's work on reciprocity, redistribution, and exchange, which became the charter for the "substantivist" school of economic anthropology in the 1960s (see Polanyi 1958; Neale and Mayhew 1983), reflected the consensus of mid-1940s intellectuals when he declared that the "self-regulating market" was a 19th-century "utopian experiment" that had failed and that

> economic history reveals that the emergence of national markets was in no way the result of the gradual and spontaneous emancipation of the economic sphere from governmental control. On the contrary, the market has been the outcome of a conscious and often violent intervention on the part of government which imposed the market organization on society for non-economic ends (Polanyi 1957:250).

In the post-World War II era in most wealthy nations (and in many "semiperipheral" countries as well), this view underlay the rise of welfare state institutions. In western Europe, in particular, where the welfare state derived from social democratic pacts between labor and capital, development theory was more open to influences from Marxism and more heterodox than in the United States, where modernization theory had originated in a cold war confrontation with Soviet-style socialism. The 1944 Bretton Woods Agreement that established the International Monetary Fund created a liberalized trade regime but, influenced by Keynes and his disciples, was distinctly nonliberal in the financial arena, endorsing the use of national controls on capital movements. By the early 1970s, a combination of market pressures (expanding demand for international financial services, "stagflation," OPEC states' accumulation of petrodollars), technological changes (telecommunications and computer revolutions), and calculated actions by key state actors (deregulation of US financial markets) contributed to scuttling the Bretton Woods system of fixed exchange rates and controls on capital and to encouraging speculative financial movements that complicated any national defense of the Keynesian welfare state (Helleiner 1994; P. M.Garber 1993).

The demise of the Bretton Woods controls was, according to Philip McMichael, the "beginning of the end of the [national as opposed to global] development project:" national sovereignty diminished with the loss of government currency controls; under the new form of globalization "money became increasingly stateless," offshore money markets expanded, and debt management was globalized (2000:115, 113–114). Neoliberal economists such as Friedrich von Hayek, whose *Road to Serfdom* appeared in 1944 (the same year as Polanyi's *Great Transformation*), had been widely viewed as outlandish extremist zealots.[32] But in the recession, stagflation and fiscal crises of 1974, their ideas began to gain support, part of an epochal shift that helped lay the ideological and policy groundwork for the neoliberal globalization era. The elections on neoliberal platforms of Margaret Thatcher in Britain in 1979 and Ronald Reagan in the United States in 1980 initiated the political ascendance of a new free-market regime that made rapid inroads there and in much of the rest of the world.

In short, development in recent decades has come to overlap with globalization in the following sense: institutional changes in the global economy and financial system (described above) accompanied a gradual redefinition of "development" itself in the 1970s, with large institutions such as the World Bank shifting their focus from economic specialization within a national framework to specialization in a world economy; thus, for the Bank, development became "participation in the world market" (as stated in the World Bank's *World Development Report 1980*, quoted in McMichael 2000:111, 113). In addition, "the debt crisis shifted the terms of development from a national to a global concern. States still pursue development goals, but these goals have more to do with global positioning than with management of the national 'household'" (McMichael 2000:150).

The seismic economic and political changes associated with neoliberal globalization coincided with anthropology's turn away from macro-narratives, grand theory, and realist ethnography.

Toward a new political economy

To repudiate one's theoretical ancestors has been an anthropological tradition since Franz Boas's renunciation of 19th-century evolutionism.[33] Yet the precursor paradigms sometimes become caricatures or straw men in contemporary academic turf battles. Such appears to be the case with certain traditions of grand narrative that can be misleadingly equated with political economy broadly defined. Moreover, as Miller notes in his chapter below, "one of the main targets of criticism has become not so much political economy, but the way it had been developed by Marx, in particular through his use of Hegel." Carrier and Miller's 1998 volume signals a departure from earlier traditions in its subtitle "A New Political Economy." Similarly, many other contemporary approaches that might carry the political economy label do not actually embody the projected ghosts of naïve empiricism, Western teleologies, economic reductionism, or rigid structuralism.[34] To discard political economy carelessly, on the basis of outdated or misleading stereotypes, would be a costly move. This section suggests why that is the case, illustrating the remarkable potential of fresh political economy approaches and new syntheses in the contemporary anthropology of development and globalization.

In the 1970s, anthropologists influenced by dependency and world-system theories, peasant studies, and feminism often placed the culture-political economy relation at the center of their investigations. By the mid-1980s, an important shift had occurred in some quarters, where anthropologists increasingly avoided systematic analyses of political economy and the new economic neoliberalism in favor of fragmentary attacks on economic reductionism and cultural essentialism. Political economy continued to flourish in other quarters, however, as feminist scholars such as Micaela di Leonardo and linguist Susan Gal (among others) articulated important theoretical shifts in political-economic work away from the ahistorical verities propounded by the more mechanistic varieties of Marxism.[35]

In the 1990s, few anthropologists explicitly challenged neoliberal claims that most economic decision-making should be left to free markets rather than governments. On the other hand, neither did many explicitly address the opposite claim: that most economic decision-making should be left to states rather than markets. Yet, as Cooper (2001), Graeber (2002), Tsing (2000), and others suggest, anthropological analyses often appeared to take neoliberalism's premises for granted as they celebrated global "flows," fragmentation, the "indigenous," grassroots organizations, and cultural difference.[36] Instead anthropologists would be well placed to explore how markets and the corporations and state and supra-national institutions that influence and administer them actually work. Such analyses could demonstrate why contemporary economic globalization is not natural or inevitable but rather the outcome of contingent historical processes. A late-20th-century preference for focusing on flux and fragmentation rather than powerful economic actors perhaps reflected anthropology's traditional focus on small-scale phenomena. Did it also mirror the very market ideology ("freedom as choice") that had become so pervasive? We would argue, following Graeber, that the concern with "choice" and micro-phenomena, as well as the determination to reject grand narratives, distracts "attention away from the current attempt to impose the largest and most totalising framework in world history – the market – on just about everything" (Graeber 2002:1224).

Nearly lost from view is *variation* in the state's role in contemporary capitalist economies, as well as historical oscillations (even on the political Right) in faith in states or markets as agents of economic prosperity, democracy, and social justice. Before World War II the political Right favored strong states and was skeptical of the market. In the 1980s and 1990s, a new Right, claiming roots in classical liberalism (in the European sense of that term), celebrated the freedoms of the market and labelled the state a potential agent of tyranny. Now it is rarely recalled, as suggested above, that the most radical proponents of free-market solutions to social problems – Friedrich von Hayek and Milton Friedman, for example, – were, until the late 1970s, widely seen as eccentric extremists. Faith in the state's capacity to propel progressive social change, on the other hand, in the late 20th century was construed as a trait of the political Left. In early postwar development thought, a general consensus existed (which included socialists and capitalists alike) that it was necessary for the state to intervene in economies – whether to recover from the 1930s world depression, to rebuild Europe after the war, or to speed economic growth in Latin America.

When the postwar economic boom ended in the 1970s, the limitations of state-led development suddenly appeared obvious and a reanimated Right, invoking neoclassical economic theory, pushed for reducing the role of the public sector. Much as Polanyi had described 19th-century history as shaped by the tension between movement toward unregulated markets and a "countermovement" to "re-embed" the market in society (1957:130), the polarization between pro- and anti-market forces intensified in the late 20th century. By then the Left had been politically weakened while the Right had shifted to the offensive, attacking government safety nets, unions, and state regulation of airlines, energy, environment, air traffic control, railroads, and financial services. By the beginning of the 21st century, however, new security threats, economic crises, poor nations' debt burdens, and corporate scandals invited re-consideration of neoliberal market fundamentalism. It was no longer only those on the political Left who saw an urgent need for, among other things, more extensive government oversight and regulation of corporate accounting and pension fund management, or for debt relief for poorer nations, or new programs to mitigate the effects of two decades of IMF/World Bank-mandated structural adjustment in the Third World. Nor was it only those on the Left who believed that privatization of US airport security contributed to the security lapses that enable terrorist attacks, or that energy deregulation might contribute to unreliable power supplies, or that privatization of military procurement services made US forces in Iraq vulnerable to food and water shortages. Others, of course, in the spirit of Hayek and Friedman, believed such lapses signal the incompleteness rather than the failure of market de-regulation. For them, the neoclassical economic models had to be correct and, despite the tragic human costs of such experiments, getting prices and other market signals "right" was not only possible but desirable. Thus neoliberal economists believed the world should be made to test the models even if it meant rising economic inequality globally and within nations, accelerated environmental devastation, and erosion or removal of public-sector safety nets that once protected access to health care, food, and education for the citizenry, and particularly for the less well off. Polarizing rhetoric of market triumphalism leaves little political space for thoughtful debate of such issues.

To make development theory useful and interesting again, it must, as Leys argues in the chapter below, explore ways to subordinate markets to the social goals of the communities that markets serve. Expanding the practical ambitions of development theory in turn means revisiting and re-invigorating the agenda of classical political economy.[37]

Anthropologists' rejection of grand narratives, however, unwittingly accedes to the constriction of contemporary intellectual debate, and points to an urgent need, as Miller (1998:188) puts it, to "clarify connections between features of our world that too often seem like isolated fragments whose simultaneous existence is no more than fortuitous."[38] (See also Jonathan Friedman's chapter below, in Part III of this volume.) Daniel Miller offers an example of how to resurrect grand narrative through his analysis of consumption, in "A Theory of Virtualism" (reproduced in Part IV of this volume). Among his targets is the outsized influence of a particular paradigm within the discipline of economics, and the power of academic modellers to define economic policy through widely imposed programs such as the World Bank's and International Monetary Fund's structural adjustment reforms for developing nations during the 1980s and 1990s.[39]

The anthropology of development, like the rest of sociocultural anthropology, sometimes appears to fundamentally reject the re-combination of historical analysis with political engagement in the following sense: "The danger is that many... invok[e] power in the form of 'capitalism,' 'colonialism,' or 'the state' without actually analyzing its forms, relations, structures, histories, or effects. History as process... is actively rejected" (Roseberry 1996:91).

There are notable exceptions, such as the "regional modernities" approach of Agrawal and Sivaramakrishnan (2003), which retains a strong historical and ethnographic focus in the study of development, and which is informed as well by post-structuralism and post-colonialism. Roseberry (1996:89-90) suggests that in spite of its political claims, contemporary anthropology risks losing "the very attempt to analyze and understand the relations and structures of power in, through, and against which people live." Such an anthropology, he notes, requires histories of colonialism or capitalism, class analysis, processual analysis, ethnographic analysis, and grand narratives – none of which is sufficient on its own, but all of which (and more) are key elements in critical new theorizing. Silencing many of these approaches to power, history, and ethnography, Roseberry suggests, can only produce "anthropology-lite."

In sum, it is partly through the silencing of political economy (both classical and 20th-century debates on the political economy of development) that anthropologists during the 1980s and 1990s rarely engaged directly economic neoliberalism's central arguments. Although development has captured the imaginations of anthropologists, as well as states and others around the world, key economic landmarks in the recent development story – Bretton Woods, GATT, NAFTA, and the WTO – are surprisingly invisible in much recent anthropological work on development and globalization. The sometimes piecemeal critiques anthropologists have produced instead include innovative studies of cultural difference, transnationalism, gender, civil society, NGOs, political ecology, globalization, and consumption (among other topics). Many have emphasized the politics of knowledge and representation, culture as a site of class struggle, and the cultural shaping of relations of economic and political domination. Anthropology, as noted earlier, has not always downplayed political economy, and the discipline may be due for another theoretical pendulum swing back toward politics and economics and their inextricable historical connections to the cultural issues that have received so much recent attention. Among those producing innovative work along these lines is Sivaramakrishan, who observes:

> For the anthropology of development – a field already animated by the anthropological debates on nationalism, globalization, transnational flows, diasporic cultures, and most importantly the cultural analysis of modernity, postmodernity, and postcoloniality – there is, then, a doubly reinforced challenge to think beyond the study of discourse, representation, knowledge, narrative, and all other manners of cultural construction (2000:432-433).[40]

Anthropology offers powerful analytical tools for integrating culture, power, history, and economy into one analytical framework. Many of the contemporary contributions reprinted below signal the creative new possibilities of such approaches.

Additional under-explored questions more anthropologists might address include the following:

- The changing and contested boundaries of the concept of "market" itself, which even in the mid-19th century often referred to a specific physical location where particular types of goods were stored and traded (Moreno Fraginals 1985:11) and which only later assumed the metaphorical and deterritorialized qualities that increasingly adhere to it (see also Mitchell 2002).

- The persistence in the late 20th and early 21st centuries of "moral economies," comparable to those described by E. P. Thompson (1971) and James Scott (1976), which in country after country – and transnationally – have constituted a political obstacle to the imposition and implementation of pro-corporate free-market policies, whether a rise in bus fares, a privatization of a public utility company, or a global agreement on intellectual property rights under WTO auspices. (See also Jane Collins' chapter in Part V of this volume on erosion of moral economies under neoliberal globalization.)
- The invention and trading of new – and intangible – commodities such as derivatives, pollution credits or carbon secuestration instruments. This focus would complement innovative work on artefacts of cultural hybridity such as "world music" or immigrants' videos of their countries of origin.
- The efforts of grassroots groups, such as those anthropologists traditionally studied, to develop innovative forms of non-corporate, vertically integrated economic organization that permit retaining more of the wealth produced (or value-added) in local communities or that otherwise constitute an alternative to an unfavorable and perhaps exploitative insertion in a liberalized economy.

Promising anthropological territory can also be found in the innovative work of political scientist Tim Mitchell (2002), who notes the limitations of viewing the economy simply as a social construct or "an invention of the imagination." Instead he posits the economy "as a set of practices that puts in place a new politics of calculation" (2002:8); he calls attention to the transformation of the "processes of exchange that economists had always studied . . . into an object that had not previously existed . . . [which] made possible new forms of value, new kinds of equivalence, new practices of calculation, new relations between human agency and the nonhuman, and new distinctions between what was real and the forms of its representation" (2002:5). Promising new anthropological pathways also are opened in Graeber's (2001) imaginative work on an "anthropological theory of value" that avoids the limitations of reductionist economics paradigms and that links anthropology to social activism. These are only illustrative examples of market-related issues that have received insufficient attention. Institutional economists and historians have at times posed questions such as those listed above, but by the early 21st century anthropologists had only begun to probe the dominant faith in the magic of markets.

As market triumphalism came to dominate development thought during the 1980s and 1990s, globalization – especially in its non-economic guises – became an object of anthropological fascination. The next section examines the resultant interplay of anthropology, development, and globalization.

III   Anthropology's Contributions and Silences

Anthropology and globalization

Globalization, even more so than development, is a protean term, with distinct connotations for different people, a moving target that is not the same from one day to the next or in different locations or social situations. Globalization, like capitalism and modernity, is a "megatrope" (Knauft 2002:34). "For the executive of a multinational corporation," writes Néstor García Canclini,

'globalization' includes principally the countries where he operates, the activities he directs, and the competition he faces; for Latin American leaders whose trade is primarily with the United States, globalization is nearly synonymous with 'Americanization'. . . . For a Mexican or Colombian family with various members working in the United States, globalization refers to the close connection with events in the area of that country where their relatives live, which is different from what those Mexican or Colombian artists... who have a broad audience in the United States imagine as globalization (García Canclini 1999:12).

David Harvey points out that the term globalization was "entirely unknown before the mid-1970s" and that it then "spread like wildfire" when American Express used it to advertise the global reach of its credit card (Harvey 2000:12-13).[41] Anna Tsing comments that "globalism is multireferential: part corporate hype and capitalist regulatory agenda, part cultural excitement, part social commentary and protest" (Tsing, 2000:332). For Bourdieu, globalization is

a simultaneously descriptive and prescriptive pseudo-concept that has taken the place of the word "modernization," long used by American social science as a euphemistic way of imposing a naively ethnocentric evolutionary model that permits the classification of different societies according to their distance from the most economically advanced society, which is to say American society... (Bourdieu 2001:2).

For many anthropologists, globalization signifies accelerated flows or intensified connections – across national and other boundaries – of commodities, people, symbols, technology, images, information, and capital, as well disconnections, exclusion, marginalization, and dispossession (see Appadurai 1996; Ferguson 1999).

A growing literature on anthropology and globalization by the early 21st century exhibited four striking limitations: tendencies (a) to de-historicize globalization and to favor a "giddy presentism" (Graeber's term) or an exoticizing fascination with new manifestations of cultural hybridity; (b) to bypass or downplay the continuing role of nation-states as economic and political actors;[42] (c) to naturalize contemporary neoliberalism by, for example, treating global phenomena as deterritorialized, impersonal "flows";[43] and (d) to portray economic globalization as an inexorable or overly simplified and coherent set of forces and then to focus on how they are culturalized (Cooper 2001; Graeber 2002; Tsing 2000). Often the most comfortable niche for anthropologists discussing globalization has been to show how non-elites "creatively resist, appropriat(e), or reinterpret some apparently homogenizing influence imposed from above (e.g., advertising, soap operas, forms of labor discipline, political ideologies, etc.)" (Graeber 2002:1223). It is worth considering what this genre excludes and with what effects. For example, Inda and Rosaldo (2002:27) acknowledge as "important gaps" in their excellent anthology on *The Anthropology of Globalization* "transnational social movements, global religious communities, global cities, and transnational pollution," as well as the work of "precursor theorists" writing about the "political economy of culture" such as Eric Wolf, Sidney Mintz, June Nash, and Michael Taussig. The World Trade Organization (WTO) is not even mentioned in the index of any of the three recent volumes on globalization that Graeber (2002:1226) reviews – or, as he notes, "for that matter, some recent volumes that actually have pictures of the Seattle [anti-WTO] protests on their cover!"

The WTO, viewed by its detractors as part of an evil troika whose other two members are the World Bank and the International Monetary Fund, inspires popular campaigns, social movements, and imaginings that are central to understanding globalization, development, social change, and modernity. Anthropology should have much to contribute to the fiery debates about policies of the World Bank and International Monetary Fund and about the World Trade Organization's power, secrecy, lack of public accountability, and capacity to override laws passed democratically by sovereign nations. A few anthropologists and sociologists have begun to make these and similar institutions objects of ethnographic research (Goldman 2001; Grimm 1999; Harper 2000), but the linkages between their findings and those of scholars operating at higher levels of abstraction are tenuous. By the late 20th century, neither the ethnographers of the economic governance institutions nor the niche grand theorists of transnationalism and hybridity focused much on how their respective methodological approaches might limit understanding of globalization. The political role of anthropologists – many of whom work within the international financial institutions, particularly the World Bank – has similarly received only cursory attention (but see Davis 1999 and Fox's chapter in Part VII of this volume).

Whether globalization is new or not – or how new it is – is the subject of much debate. Deregulated global financial markets linked in real time, declining transport and communications costs, and increasingly significant multilateral institutions and agreements are clearly major changes during the 1980s and 1990s (see UNDP 1999; McMichael 2000). Some scholars nonetheless argue that globalization – particularly of commodities markets – has been around at least since 1492, if not longer (Amin 2001:16; Harvey 2000:21). Others see the period from 1870 to 1914 as a prior age of globalization – a time of laissez-faire policies well suited to an era of imperialism (Hirst 2000:108). Even in the 1860s, they suggest, submarine telegraphy cables, which linked intercontinental markets and permitted day-to-day price-making, were "a far greater innovation than . . . electronic trading today" (Hirst and Thompson 1996:3). In any case, labor was less mobile in the late 20th century – by some measures – than it was in the 19th, when passports were often unnecessary (Mintz 1998). International labor migration skyrocketed during the century after 1815, and France's barriers to African immigrants, for example, were much lower in the 1950s than in the 1970s (Cooper 2001:194). The foreign-born proportion of the US population was 14 percent in 1900 and only 11 percent one hundred years later, even after a period of sustained immigration. Furthermore, long-term migration "affects only about 1% or 2% of the world's population" (Lewellen 2002:9). The history of migration during the 19th century suggests to Mintz (1998) that the contemporary view of transnationalism as qualitatively different from earlier times is exaggerated, as is the notion that the contemporary mobility of people requires a new anthropology. In short, late-20th-century markets offer freer movement of goods and capital than of labor. The less common restrictions on migration during the 19th century meant that "labor's international mobility was more comparable to that of capital," while the present situation of "asymmetry between mobile capital (physical and human) and immobile 'natural' labor" is relatively recent (Rodrik 2003:382). That said, the world's population has grown enormously and recent decades have witnessed a net increase in absolute numbers of migrants (legal and illegal), as well as vastly more varied migration patterns. These changes attract increasing anthropological attention.

Whether globalization is old, new, or newly recognized, it is probably most useful to view the world economy as having passed through a globalizing phase from approximately 1870 to 1914, a deglobalizing period from about 1930 to 1980, and a renewed era of globalization since 1980 (see also Part III introduction). In any case, globalization and transnationalism have captivated scholarly imaginations, even if some scholars have been less than enthusiastic. Yet this infatuation recalls a similar obsession in the 1950s and 1960s with modernization – now widely seen as a failed development paradigm (Tsing 2000; Cooper 2001).

What is historically remarkable is the celebration of a particular form of globalization – economic neoliberalism – and the increasingly common tendency for tests of market viability to be taken for granted or naturalized in domains as disparate as academia, journalism, and art. An earlier generation of scholars saw the question of how market relations are extended to new domains and then naturalized as a defining feature of major historical transitions (Polanyi 1957; Thompson 1971). Today again anthropologists can help explain how ideological expressions of the "free-market" are naturalized and how they come to seem inevitable (if not necessarily legitimate). Yet anthropologists' attention often turns elsewhere. As Tsing indicates, "the possibility that capitalisms and governmentalities are themselves situated, contradictory, effervescent, or culturally circumscribed is much less explored" than the ways "self-consciously 'local' diversity is a form of resistance to . . . globalist capitalism and hypermodernist governmentality" (2000:339). Global, rather than simply local, diversity, demands attention and Tsing suggests it may be useful to abandon the familiar "distinction between 'global' *forces* and 'local' *places*" (Tsing 2000:352, emphasis in original). It may also be time to discard binaries of "local authenticity" and "global domination" (Cooper 2001:199).

Akhil Gupta's *Postcolonial Developments* (1998) is an example of recent anthropological studies that problematize the distinction between "the local" and "the global." This duality, he suggests, often depends on a naturalization – others might say, a forgetting – of the nation-state. Yet Gupta reminds us, "the global" is not simply that which is beyond the boundaries of the nation-state, and changing nation-state configurations profoundly shape how global forces affect "the local." Moreover, "the global" is not usually as deterritorialized as anthropologists and others assume, since it tends to be produced and propagated in a relatively small number of particular places. Sivaramakrishnan and Agrawal (2003) propose "regional modernities" as a useful analytical move beyond global/local oppositions, strict spatial connotations of region, and "a globalized, homogeneous vision of modernity that development is supposed to inscribe" – enabling us to understand patterns in the ways modernity is multi-locally produced (2003:4, 11, 13).[44] This approach also avoids any easy mapping of the global/local opposition onto that between domination and resistance (Sivaramakrishnan and Agrawal 2003:25).

Whether one views the end of the 20th century and start of the 21st as a time of market tyranny or market triumph, there is little doubt about the contemporary force of one economic model, one conception of economy (see Carrier and Miller 1998). Contemporary global capitalism "has gone to the extreme of converting the market into a kind of supreme natural law, ethically neutral, like the law of gravity" (De Rivero 2001:113). Yet one might ask if anthropologists' celebratory declarations of the end of the era of totalizing narratives draws attention away from the astonishing contemporary reach of economic neoliberalism (Graeber 2002:1224; Miller chapter 15 in this volume). Often forgotten is that the reproduction of this model occurs through actual institutions and processes and politics – and that there is nothing inevitable about it.

The most enthusiastic global promoters of free-market hype have been prone to a conspicuously selective application of free-market policies. In the United States, for example, the financial sector

> has enjoyed massive federal support that doesn't get the attention it deserves. . . . Since the early 1980s, you've had the federal government bailing out the people who held Latin American debt, the banks in Texas and Continental Illinois, and the savings and loan bailout. Then we went into the 1990s with the peso bailout in Mexico and Long-Term Capital Management. . . . And this is the crowd that will tell you about the purity of the markets and free enterprise. . . . So obviously the role of government is cherished by much of the free market crowd (Barsamian 2002:35).

So too the Pentagon is "a huge bureaucratic collective" and overall the Federal Government "administer(s) almost half the nation's wealth" (Hart 1992:215). US farm subsidies, textile quotas and steel tariffs have been major stumbling blocks in negotiating both bilateral free trade accords and further trade liberalization under the WTO.[45]

Conventional critical narratives about globalization – which contain much more than a grain of truth – define our era as one of flexible production, footloose capital, footloose factories, and corporations that demand great flexibility of their workers even as they offer them fewer guarantees of job security or retirement or health care benefits (see Harvey 1989; McMichael 2000; Klein 2002). Underpaid, disposable, perpetually temporary "McWork" jobs (Klein 2002:233) proliferate in the service sectors of affluent countries – a pattern that frequently breeds worker disloyalty. Many corporations meanwhile are engaged in two "races" – the "race to the bottom" where labor is cheap and regulations weak or unenforced, and the "race toward weightlessness," to outsource production, reduce payrolls, and produce the most powerful brand images (Klein 2002:4). Economic neoliberalism has – almost everywhere – brought declining corporate taxes and shortages of funds in the public sector for schools, health care, and other services. Its impacts include expanding informal economies, contract farming, ecotourism, toxic dumping, and struggles over environmental protections and access to land and other resources. It has also contributed to the sharpest economic inequalities the world has ever seen. Do anthropologists who write about globalization, transnationalism, development and modernity treat too much of this larger economic picture as given? Do empirical studies of globalization processes (described below) support the claims of the conventional narrative?

Economic globalization issues – now development issues – fuel highly energized social movements in many parts of the world (though more so in Latin America and Canada, for example, than in the United States). As globalization hype wears thin and as consumers in wealthier nations become aware of the abysmal working conditions and the negative health and environmental impacts of the global garment, coffee and other industries, growing numbers begin to feel complicit in corporate misdeeds, and consumer boycotts and anti-corporate activism spread (Klein 2002). The Biotic Baking Brigade throws pies in the faces of Bill Gates, Milton Friedman, and James Wolfensohn (Klein 2002:326) – just one example of attention-grabbing activist theatre. On US college campuses, an earlier political focus on issues of race, gender, sexuality and identity politics has broadened to include corporate power, labor rights, and environmental justice (Klein, 2002:xxi). On many campuses, students have mobilized anti-sweatshop campaigns against producers of apparel bearing university logos, and have promoted campaigns for living wages for campus workers such as janitors and cooks. Students have both devised and publicized many of the "semiotic bruises" suffered by Nike and other corporations as their logos and slogans have been parodied and subverted (Klein 2002:367). International anti-Nike movement slogans, for example, include "just don't do it", "Justice. Do it, Nike," "Nike – No, I Don't Buy It!" (Klein, 2002:366-369). In addition, there has been anti-Nike street theatre, giant puppets of Nike CEO Phil Knight with dollar signs for eyes, and a "twelve-foot Nike swoosh dragged by small children (to dramatize child labor)" (Klein 2002:367). The Gap, Shell, Disney, McDonald's and many other corporations have been targets as well. And youthful protesters at recent demonstrations against the World Bank and International Monetary Fund shouted slogans about controversial economic policies such as debt relief for poor nations, water privatization, and structural adjustment programs ("hey hey, ho ho, structural adjustment has got to go!"). Although the media often depict activists in the global movement for social justice as irrational "anti-globalizers," many of them actively reject the anti-globalization label and are more accurately characterized as against particular neoliberal economic policies (see Graeber's chapter in Part III of this volume).

In the Global South, the traditional focus of most anthropological research, small farmers, factory workers, shantytown dwellers, environmentalists, women and youth activists, and ethnic and sexual minorities have also forged links to their counterparts in other countries and joined struggles to preserve and extend various rights as part of the broader global justice movement. Struggles for land and housing, against discrimination and corporate domination, and in defense of the environment and public-sector health and utility systems increasingly form part of broader movements against neoliberal globalization and frequently involve alliances between constituencies in rich and poor countries. Yet anthropology has been slower than other disciplines such as political science and sociology to embrace research agendas centered on economic globalization, activist networks, and new social movements.

Globalization's effects of course are not uniformly negative; rather they can be double-edged, as illustrated by studies such as Chibnik's (2003) of Oaxacan wood carvings.[46] Global markets for these Mexican crafts have helped many Oaxacan families to improve their standard of living, and "even the worst-off artisans are better off than they were before the boom" of the past two decades (Chibnik 2003:239). The collapse of the market for inexpensive pieces in recent years, however, signals familiar local vulnerabilities to world market forces. Yet rural Oaxacans' diverse and flexible income strategies confer some resilience. Furthermore, there is no reason to assume the market for these wood carvings among tourists and others will disappear.

In other respects as well, globalization theory demands nuance. Theorists' claims about the demise of the welfare state, "footloose capital," and the "race to the bottom" have begun to receive increasing empirical scrutiny. Perhaps surprisingly, considerable evidence suggests that, at least for wealthy countries, interventionist state welfare policies provide benefits to capital (a healthy, educated workforce; growing productivity; political stability) that are sufficient to blunt the corporate "exit threats" frequently cited as a defining feature of contemporary globalization and as undermining the nation-state. Moreover, outside of poor nations, exposure to global markets actually spurs greater government spending on redistributive programs that compensate for market-generated inequalities (Garrett 2003). The situation in less wealthy countries, however, conforms more closely to the conventional view, since labor tends to be less qualified and often poorly organized or otherwise unable to engage in effective collective action (Rudra 2002). Yet even among poorer nations, there is enormous variation in the consequences of neoliberal policies. In short, such findings confirm new patterns of national difference in economic globalization processes that sometimes are presumed to be inevitably homogenizing – an analytical path that counters the tendency some have noted for "mapping the cultural to differentiation, and the economic to homogenization" (see Sivaramakrishnan and Agrawal 2003:8).

The "neoliberal" camp is itself divided, as noted above, and new debates about alternatives are emerging in centrist as well as more Left-leaning circles. Even vocal "pro-globalizers" such as Jagdish Bhagwati caution that globalization "needs appropriate governance," including "prudent monitoring and institutional reforms" to prevent the kind of financial and economic crisis East Asia suffered in the late 1990s (2001:7; see also 2004). Neoliberalism does not utterly lack mass appeal – for example, among countries that previously experienced heavy state intervention or suffered under violent and corrupt governments, where domestic entrepreneurs enjoy new opportunities afforded by privatization, and where workers are paid better wages in transnational rather than domestic factories (Lewellen 2002:19). Yet critics and advocates remain profoundly divided about whether economic globalization writ large is a force for social good – whether it alleviates or causes poverty, and whether it improves or undermines labor and environmental standards, health protections, gender equality, democracy, and human rights.[47]

We turn next to snapshots of a half-dozen vibrant anthropological topics whose connections – whether explicit or not – to pressing development and globalization issues invite further attention. These include NGOs and civil society; gender and population; culture; consumption; environment; and city and countryside. These thumbnail sketches highlight analytical contributions as well as silences. Our intent is to encourage imaginative new analytical turns in the era of economic neoliberalism.

NGOs and civil society

Since the 1980s, non-governmental organizations (NGOs) have played growing roles in mainstream and alternative development projects, large and small.[48] The reduction of the neoliberal state's social welfare programs, the sacking of intellectuals from downsized public universities and government agencies, and the crucial participation of civil society organizations in the democratization of countries in Africa, Latin America, and the formerly socialist countries, all fueled the NGO boom. The astonishing proliferation of such organizations, many of which are quasi-rather than non-governmental, and more transnational than "local," has had a rapid and profound impact on development theory and practice, as well as on grassroots movements for social change.

As the importance of supra-national governance institutions grew in the late 1980s and 1990s, NGOs and other civil society organizations became a constant presence at "parallel summits" held outside meetings of the World Bank, IMF, WTO, and the G7/G8 heads-of-state, as well as the 1992 Rio environmental conference, the 1995 Beijing women's conference, the 1996 Rome food security conference, and other international gatherings (Pianta 2001). US and European cooperation policies shifted toward an emphasis on funding citizens' groups that were often held up as scrupulous and efficient alternatives to the corrupt, bloated and ineffective public sectors that previously absorbed most foreign aid.

Of course NGOs are not necessarily more dependable and often are not as separate from state interests and personnel as the ideal type implies. Many European donor NGOs, for example, obtain most of their funding from their respective national governments or the European Union, which hardly makes them "non-governmental." Furthermore, "even when NGOs have not been part and parcel of the state in a new guise, they are not inherently preferable to it. NGOs sometimes have been tied to local parochialisms, are not necessarily technically qualified to assume tasks that have been foisted upon them, and often lack a national vision of development" (Mueller 2004:3). They provide new avenues of economic mobility for some, at times contributing to inequalities of power and wealth. Some are opportunists who spuriously claim to represent the poor or people in a particular ethnic category, in order to obtain foreign aid monies. NGOs have increasingly assumed responsibilities for delivery of services ranging from healthcare to agricultural extension, and have also become conduits for political demands initially articulated by social movements and other pressure groups.

Particular development strategies, such as the provision of micro-credit to community groups, have become closely associated with NGOs, suggesting that at times the form itself may drive the strategy (Robinson 2001). Historically situated studies such as Gill's (2000) on Bolivia show how neoliberalism changed the NGO landscape, with many such organizations shifting from political opposition to accommodation during a time of dramatic expansion in the number of NGOs. As international funding for NGOs increased in the mid- and late-1980s, competition for such external resources intensified, and new neoliberal NGOs in Bolivia pioneered initiatives that "relied on indebtedness and unwaged female labor to encourage entrepreneurialism, individualism, and competition" (Gill 2000:138).

Contrasting theoretical conceptions of how to bound "civil society" are often tied to distinct development agendas and views of democratization. Many concur that "civil society" is the associational realm between the household and the state, while others emphasize the emergence of a global civil society and transnational advocacy networks. Beyond these assumptions, however, two polar positions exist, separated by opposing views on whether to include economic actors – specifically, markets and firms – within "civil society." Those who argue for considering markets and corporations as part of the category typically back a neoliberal development agenda (an irony, given this position's roots in Hegel and Marx) which sees "civil society" as a domain outside of and morally superior to the state. They posit choice and freedom of association as fundamental characteristics of both the market and "civil society," making support for economic liberalization and "civil society" institutions not only entirely compatible, but complementary strategies for checking state power. Neoliberal theorists of civil society – and policymakers in donor institutions such as the US Agency for International Development – increasingly express reservations about many NGOs' unclear lines of accountability, which they contrast with the supposedly greater transparency of "democratic" states and "shareholder-accountable" corporations. Theorists who exclude the market and firms from "civil society," on the other hand, usually consider it a domain of associational life that attempts to defend autonomous collective institutions from the encroachments of *both* the market and the state. In comparison with neoliberal theorists, they tend to accord much greater analytical importance to how social inequality structures or limits political representation.

During the past two decades, the struggle between these divergent conceptions has played out in academia, bilateral and non-governmental funding agencies, supranational governance institutions, and the countries of the South. Proponents of neoliberal development often have favored strengthening legal institutions and elite lobbying groups as a way to facilitate market-driven approaches to growth, and to resolve social problems. They also often back compensatory programs targeted at population sectors or geographical regions that have suffered most from economic liberalization. Targeted anti-poverty projects, while sometimes helping to alleviate the most dramatic kinds of misery, usually have only limited political support, and critics charge that under neoliberalism they substitute for earlier welfare-state programs based on universal entitlements that enjoyed widespread backing. Supporters of alternative development strategies, on the other hand, often back organizations with a dual focus on income-generating projects for historically disadvantaged sectors of the population and on pressure-group tactics intended to create more profound structural change. The latter line of attack, favored by many European donor NGOs and bilateral cooperation agencies, has enabled grassroots organizations to reshape many development debates and policies.

Gender and population

Recent shifts in understanding the gendered dimensions of development are emblematic of civil society's growing influence on policymakers' debates. The "Women in Development" (WID) approach that accompanied the United Nations Decade for Women (1975–85) sought to address "male bias" by increasing female access to and participation in development programs (much as rural development programs had tried to compensate for "urban bias"). By the mid-1990s, however, at the insistence of an increasingly vocal international women's movement, mainstream development institutions recognized that the WID paradigm did little to address key concerns, such as unequal inheritance and property rights for men and women, domestic violence, men's abandonment of their children, or family planning and prevention of sexually transmitted diseases. Addressing these issues not only required male participation within a new "Gender and Development" framework (that largely superseded WID), but also presupposed fundamental modifications of existing practices of masculinity and femininity. Scholars such as Sylvia Chant and

Matthew Gutmann, however, note that recent Gender and Development policies have not fundamentally altered WID's emphasis on programs designed by and for women (see Chant and Gutmann's chapter in Part V of this volume). Thus Chant and Gutmann argue that development programs should incorporate "men as a gendered category in a feminist sense," with attention to unequal relations between men as well as between men and women.

These contemporary concerns should be viewed in relation to what was, not long ago, the virtual invisibility of a gender dimension in development studies. In 1970, Esther Boserup's *Women's Role in Economic Development* analyzed how European colonialism, changing gendered divisions of domestic labor, population density, rural–urban migration, technological innovations, and shifting labor markets affected women's status. Distinguishing between male and female farming systems (the latter typical of sub-Saharan Africa and parts of South and Southeast Asia), she suggested that women's subordination worsened as colonial administrations transferred land rights from women to men and encouraged agricultural modernization, plough agriculture, and export-oriented production. While Boserup was later criticized for equating modernization with industrialization and for overly optimistic assumptions about the liberating potential of mechanizing family labor, her pioneering effort to delineate the differential impacts of economic changes on men and women constituted a point of departure for almost all subsequent studies of gender and development.

Boserup's demonstration of how population density in agrarian societies affected women's status was also an early effort to bring much needed rigor to discussions about the relation between demographic change and economic development. Few themes related to development have been more controversial. In explaining rural poverty, the relative weight given to population pressure versus unequal distribution of resources such as land, the trade-off between investing in family planning or greater agricultural productivity, the consequences for fertility and child-rearing behavior of increasing women's access to education and participation in the labor force, and the role of improved health services in changing demographic patterns have all been raised as crucial considerations for development scholarship and policy-making.[49] While neo-Malthusian doomsday "population bomb" scenarios have long been considered simplistic and overly pessimistic, Panglossian assumptions that demographic growth is ipso facto good for development or that expanding productivity and output can keep pace with growing populations have ceased to have much of a following, even among intellectuals and planners in developing countries who earlier rejected neo-Malthusian approaches and family planning as "imperialist" impositions.[50] Indeed, scholars and planners of diverse views now consider sustainable population-resource balances and human capital investment as central features of any local or national program of development.

The demographic transition from high mortality and high fertility to low mortality and low fertility is widely seen as a characteristic of the most successful cases of national development (e.g., Taiwan in Asia and Costa Rica in Latin America). Improvements in women's educational levels, workforce participation and health have been both cause and effect of the demographic transition. At the same time, falling fertility and aging populations – with below-replacement growth rates – represent a major challenge for the long-term sustainability of pension and welfare-state programs in developed countries, particularly in western Europe, where a rising proportion of elderly retired people will have to be supported by a smaller proportion of younger employed workers. In such contexts, the extent to which immigrants and their children are absorbed into society and are granted the full rights and benefits of citizenship becomes a crucial factor not just in attenuating social tensions but in preserving extensive systems of entitlements.

Culture

Is underdevelopment a state of mind, an artifact of culture or values? Few anthropologists would agree, though many writings about development now reduce the spirit of capitalism to ahistorical cultural essences – a move that divorces culture from politics and economy in ways Weber and other classical theorists did not. During the 20th century, however, specialization and atomization in the social sciences and humanities accompanied growing divisions between approaches to social change based on economics and politics on the one hand, and those based on cultural values and beliefs on the other (Knauft 2002:10; see also Geertz's chapter in Part IV of this volume). Some recent scholarship attempts to bring these diverging strands together again, though of course *how* they are brought together (with what relative weights, reductionisms and determinisms) is itself contentious.

Mostly outside of anthropology, devotees of Rostowian modernization theory still view "traditional" culture as an obstacle to change, while other theorists have attributed economic dynamism – of the "Asian tigers," for example – to either Confucian values or long-established Asian forms of household organization.[51] How culture is connected to the spread of commodity exchange and cash is a theme with roots in classic works by scholars such as Georg Simmel and Thorstein Veblen and is a central concern as well in early-21st-century debates about globalization and the role of the imaginary in identity and social change. Simmel's *Philosophy of Money* (1990) first appeared in German in 1900, four years before Weber's *Protestant Ethic*. Simmel viewed money as the decisive psychological feature of his time and as a force that supplanted emotionality and made rational calculation pervasive in social life (1990:444–445). Like Marx and Weber, he saw money as encouraging individualism and anonymity and as destroying traditional forms of solidarity and community, although unlike them he devoted little attention to the distinction between a money economy and a capitalist one. Simmel's concern with the subjective experience of consumption and commodities – including the "extensive mental consumption" made possible by increased exposure to mass media (1990:455) – mark him as an early theorist of what later came to be called the imaginary. Veblen's *Theory of the Leisure Class* (1934) took a different tack, analyzing the "pecuniary emulation" and "conspicuous consumption" of Gilded Age elites who accumulated not for "want of subsistence or of physical comfort," but because they were competing in "a race for reputability on the basis of an invidious comparison" (1934:32).[52]

Contemporary anthropology's emphasis on culture as contested, flexible, fragmentary, deterritorialized, and contingent[53] is hard to reconcile with "culturalist" explanations of underdevelopment or Confucian capitalism, which tend to assume that people mechanically enact norms. Thus anthropologists often clash with their development agency employers, as well as with some political scientists and economists, when analyzing cultural aspects of development. Those political scientists and economists who incorporate culture into their analytic frameworks are more likely than anthropologists to treat culture as bounded, homogeneous, and coherent. They tend to quantify culture in the language of dependent and independent variables, reducing culture to discrete or isolable traits that can be calculated and compared with other factors. Without denying that norms influence behavior, many anthropologists focus on what norms or symbols individuals invoke in particular situations to justify or explain their actions – exploring the rich possibilities of contradictory or contested cultural imperatives, and their situational contingency. Development practitioners, on the other hand, demand simplifying models that travel well across national boundaries.

In the development industry, non-anthropologists often assume culture to be static unless influenced by "modern society," and in a stance that "echo(es) Malinowski's claim that anthropologists can help colonialists," the development industry calls upon social scientists to be "culture brokers" – "to understand and then handle cultural and social factors" (Crewe and Harrison 1998:43).[54] Thus the anthropologist is called in to explain to expatriate stove design specialists what supposed "cultural" barriers (whether presumed ignorance, irrationality, or blind adherence to "tradition") prevent many rural Kenyans or Sri Lankans from adopting a particular cookstove or chimney innovation (Crewe and Harrison 1998). Interestingly, the "targets" or "beneficiaries" of such projects themselves may express similar ideas about culture as a barrier, as they recycle or reformulate the developers' strong assumptions and prejudices about cultural rules driving practice. Savvy recipients of foreign aid quickly learn the "culture" of expatriate donors and project personnel. As is well known, foreign technologists often overlook or ignore local technological innovation, experimentation, and design successes. Instead outside engineers or designers assume that they must fill a local knowledge gap, and then work with anthropologists to overcome the presumed irrationality of local culture or tradition so that local people adopt the introduced technology. This outdated approach lives on in much (not all!) of the development industry. Why such assumptions and the old dichotomy between tradition and modernity survive is a question Crewe and Harrison consider in chapter 16 of this volume.

Recognizing the limitations of common assumptions about culture in development institutions, the World Bank in the early 2000s initiated a forum on culture and public action, and sponsored a June 2002 conference, one of whose outcomes is an interdisciplinary book (Rao and Walton 2004).[55] The Bank commissioned papers on culture and development by distinguished anthropologists such as Arjun Appadurai, Mary Douglas, Stephen Gudeman, and Keith Hart and invited comments from economists and others. This new World Bank initiative acknowledges the need to move beyond the misleading but still influential "culture of poverty" concept, or the notion that culture itself is an obstacle to economic development and poverty reduction. Cultural conservatism, after all – as Elizabeth Colson (1985) noted in her Malinowski Award lecture – "is more characteristic of bureaucracies than it is of people who are trying to make a living from agriculture, fishing, or small industry" (1985:195).

It remains a challenge for development agencies to avoid using anthropologists simply to enumerate existing cultural ideas and practices for planners, so that these may be mechanically contrasted with the perspectives of development institutions, without addressing the "analytical limitations and political repercussions of this highly reified and static view of culture" (Pigg 1997:263). As Pigg's research in Nepal illustrates, development plans do not simply "act on a stable field of indigenous understandings and practices," but rather development ideas enter social fields in which villagers "are already assuming and seeking certain kinds of relationships to development" and are viewing the latter "as a kind of social space to which programs give them access" (1997:281).

Supposed cultural conservatism or cultural difference maps onto ethnic identities and hierarchies, and these too figure in representations, whether official or social scientific, of putative differences in receptivity to development. Ethnic or cultural difference becomes an easy alibi for histories of regional economic and social inequalities and deprivation, as in the well-documented case of the San peoples of southern Africa (Sylvain 2002), or among Chinese minorities (Schein 2002:67). Peoples such as those termed San in southern Africa struggle for economic and social justice in a context where those struggles are often distorted as demands for "cultural preservation" (Sylvain 2002). Indigenous and minority rights movements complicate earlier assumptions about culture and development, individual and group rights, and what rights accompany indigenous or minority status.[56] Successful claims to local authenticity or indigenous identity in international arenas may confer significant material advantages, and thus encourage people to strategically deploy or re-invent cultural, ethnic, indigenous, or local identities. Thus "struggles over political and economic resources... become struggles over cultural representations" (Dove 1999:232). Cultural symbols are invoked as well by right-wing and conservative movements (such as anti-immigrant movements in Europe or Islamic fundamentalism), though anthropologists have been less likely to theorize movements that promote exclusivity, racism, or intolerance (see Edelman 2001:301-303). In short, ethnographic studies of identity or cultural politics, what it means to be "indigenous," and when essentialism is strategic or romantic (see Brosius 1999) place anthropologists at the center of development politics and practice – whether they claim "development" as their focus or not.

Consumption

Anthropology originally drew students to societies marked by the absence of modern consumer goods that signal development (see Miller 1995; Ferguson 1997). Hence the cartoons in "magazines such as *The New Yorker* and *Punch* (e.g., with stereotypical natives shown in a panic, accompanied by captions such as 'Put away the radio (or television or refrigerator) – the anthropologists are coming'" (Miller 1995:142). Economic anthropologists traditionally analyzed production, consumption and distribution in such societies, but accelerating consumerism during the 20th century had a powerful impact almost everywhere, whether in creating intense new desires or providing all sorts of novel paraphernalia to erstwhile "primitives" and peasants. Ethnographic studies of consumption have explored both the symbolic and material significance of goods that consumers desire (and indeed the symbolic/material opposition is itself problematic), and commodity as thing as well as commodity as fetish. Scholars differ in their assumptions about the normative dimensions of the spread of mass consumption and its effects on "local" cultures, and about processes of homogenization and differentiation. One finds a split between those who see emancipatory versus destructive forces in commodification and mass consumption, though anthropologists studying these phenomena in the 1990s were moving beyond such oppositions and instead exploring how processes of commodification differ from the assumptions of modernization models (Miller 1995:14).

Anthropology imaginatively extends consumption analysis far beyond expenditure figures, avoids exclusive reliance on methodological individualism and narrow rational choice assumptions, and re-inserts consumption in social processes and relationships.[57] Consumers can use commodities to create individual and collective identities, with culture providing the justification for (and indeed the very idiom for understanding) these social boundaries and controls, as discussed by Douglas and Isherwood (1996:xxiv), among others. Commodities are embedded in social relations in any economy, and analysts now often look beyond the gift/commodity dichotomy and its attendant evolutionary assumptions about a great divide between "the West and the rest" (see Alexander and Alexander 1991; Appadurai 1986; Carrier 1994, 1995; Miller 1997, among others). Much of the expanding ethnographic analysis of consumption focuses on the cultural politics of identity, desire, aesthetics, and the subjective and normative aspects of consumption in daily life. Many emphasize the agency, subjective experiences, and meanings attributed by consumers to commodities such as sneakers, soft drinks, jeans, televisions, VCRs, perfume, or CDs. Another focus of much recent anthropology is the "traffic in culture" through which objects produced for utilitarian, aesthetic or spiritual reasons by indigenous peoples are transformed into commodified art, then displayed and consumed in metropolitan centers by elites who seek to demonstrate their cosmopolitan sensibilities (García Canclini 1990; Myers 2002; Nash 1993; Price 1991). Scholars disagree about the extent to which consumers, especially those in poorer nations, are coerced and manipulated into new wants and needs. Foreign goods have been a source of fascination in diverse times and places, from the medieval European nobles who sought exotic spices or cane sugar to the New Guinea groups who famously prayed that cargo would fall from the sky.[58] A few scholars have examined how a preference for imported goods, especially among the affluent, may, in addition to its cultural impact, reduce investment and exacerbate balance-of-payments problems (see Orlove and Bauer 1997). Yet such studies, which integrate histories of consumption and macroeconomic effects, are rare. In much recent anthropological work on consumption, historical political economy is often downplayed or ignored – an ironic timing, given the increasing precariousness of consumption in many poorer nations (Hansen 2000:14).[59]

A recent striking exception to the elision of historical political economy is Hansen's (2000) study of Zambia's second-hand clothing trade, which explores the "work of consumption" and the agency of the consumer in a "cultural economy of judgment and style" that entails creative local appropriations of second-hand clothing that is donated by the West and then sorted and introduced into commercial circuits that link North and South. Hansen's analysis ranges from the practices and meanings consumers bring to bear on commodities (showing how Zambians work to "mak[e] the West's clothing their own"), and the effects of global and national economic and political liberalization on Zambia's garment trade – including those entities rarely seen in anthropological works: GATT and WTO. Other innovative recent work analyzes global and local dimensions of crafting meanings and markets for Oaxacan wood carvings (Chibnik 2003), and connections between altered (often worsening) conditions of production of commodities such as sugar or grapes in poorer nations and changing consumption preferences in wealthier industrialized nations. For example, examining grape production in northeastern Brazil, Collins (2000) uses the concept of commodity chains to explore the feminization of labor to meet changing quality standards in globalizing markets in "luxury" edibles such as grapes. Moving beyond models of local communities connected to abstract global forces, Collins's approach instead sheds light on specific social relationships that constitute the growing distance between points of production and consumption. Environmentalists point out that globalization has lowered prices and stimulated consumption, even as awareness grows that today's developed-country over-consumption pattern can only spread at great cost to the fragile ecology of the planet (Gardner et al. 2004). Social justice advocates in turn call wealthy consumers' attention to and sometimes organize boycotts of commodities sponsored by corporations but produced in poorer nations' sweatshops. That millions strive to acquire modern consumer goods "seals their participation in labor markets, even at a cost of long-distance migration, the separation of families, and the sense of earning less – for women, far less – than one's worth" (Schneider 2002:75).

Although scholars have rejected many elements of 1960s modernization theory, that paradigm's traditional/modern binaries are very much alive in everyday language and culture, especially in consumption practices, which can signal newly imagined futures, conformity, creativity, rebellion, subversion, or strategic image-making, among other possibilities. Consumer appearances, for example, have become so important that one finds so-called impostors who talk on toy cellular telephones, parade in supermarkets with luxury-filled carts they later abandon as they sneak out the door without buying anything, and people who suffer extreme heat in their cars rather than roll down the windows and reveal that they have no air conditioning (Galeano 2001).[60] Capital has always denied to many the dream of consumption, but in the era of neoliberal globalization the images that fuel the fantasy are ubiquitous, the "needs" more infinite, and the possibilities of realizing the dream still minimal or nonexistent for a vast share of the world's people.

Environment

The "ecological anthropology" and "cultural ecology" of the 1970s, which often rested on functionalist and exaggeratedly localistic assumptions, have ceded ground to "historical ecological" or "political ecology" approaches. The concerns of the latter often paralleled those of new environmentalist movements and non-governmental organizations working for "sustainable development." Political ecology links environment, development and social movements, often drawing on post-structuralist theory as well as political economy critiques of development (as in Peluso and Watts 2001).[61] Central to contemporary political ecology is how "cultural practices – whether science, or 'traditional' knowledge, or discourses, or risk, or property rights – are contested, fought over, and negotiated" (Watts 2000:259). Some politically disadvantaged groups, for example, appropriate state tools by turning to alternative or "counter-mapping" to formalize their claims to key local resources and territories (Peluso, chapter 20 in this volume; Hodgson and Schroeder 2002; Chapin and Threlkeld 2001). Anthropologists such as Emilio Moran (1998) have employed satellite remote sensing data to monitor changing land use practices in fragile environments, such as the Amazon; to develop famine early-warning systems in Africa; and to improve understanding of environmental history (see Leach and Fairhead's chapter in Part VI of this volume). The new approaches vary in method and focus, but usually eschew adaptation as a starting premise. Indeed, maladaptive processes have become a key concern, while other analyses contain implicit adaptationist assumptions discussed in an idiom of "sustainable development." Would environmental catastrophe result, for example, if five billion people in poor nations were to consume at the level enjoyed by the one billion who live in the wealthiest societies (De Rivero 2001:8)? In the early 21st century 12 percent of the world population living in North America and Western Europe account for 60 percent of global private consumption, while the one-third living in sub-Saharan Africa and South Asia account for a mere 3.2 percent (Gardner et al. 2004:5–6). Per capita production of solid wastes, greenhouse gases and other environmental contaminants is vastly greater in affluent societies. Can markets recognize costs – human or environmental – as well as they set prices (see Hawken 1993:75)? Is "sustainability" possible on a small or large scale, and what role does it imply for market forces, whether local or global (see Barkin 2001)? How have differing interpretations of "sustainability" shaped struggles over development policy?

Free-market enthusiasts challenge the notion of environmental crisis, sometimes questioning the scientific reality of global warming and ozone depletion, or simply suggesting that market forces can resolve environmental problems. Less orthodox economists such as Herman Daly (2001:267) emphasize that the economy cannot expand forever precisely because it is part of a "finite and nongrowing ecosystem." Daly proposes sustainable development policies, which demand, for example, that we reject standard neoclassical economic practices such as "counting the consumption of natural capital as income" (Daly 2001:268). He favors increasing taxation on "bads" such as resource throughput ("the matter-energy that goes into a system and eventually comes out")[62] and decreasing it on "goods" such as labor and income, and urges a shift from a globalist to a nationalist orientation to trade, capital mobility and export policies. Yet global financial institutions such as the World Bank, though they claim to support "sustainable" development, have little time for innovative economists such as Daly (who resigned from his World Bank position). By contrast, for some NGOs, grassroots movements, and those pursuing "alternatives to development" – those who challenge modernist Western development – sustainable development is a serious pursuit (e.g., Shiva 1989; Escobar 1995).

"Sustainable development" was initially defined in Gro Harlem Brundtland's UN-sponsored report *Our Common Future* as practices that satisfy the needs of our generation, without jeopardizing the possibilities for future generations to satisfy their needs (WCED 1987). This approach had become gospel by the time of the 1992 Rio Environment Conference. Yet "needs" – left undefined – proved to be one of several contentious aspects of the new paradigm, which the World Bank, multinational corporations and radical environmental movements all claim as their own.[63]

Some large corporations have coopted the notion of green development – a ploy that prompted CorpWatch to give out bimonthly Greenwash Awards to large oil, nuclear, biotechnology, and chemical "corporations that put more time and energy into slick PR campaigns aimed at promoting their eco-friendly images, than they do to actually protecting the environment."[64] In publicizing deceptive claims that might lead one to believe that "Shell will reverse global warming" or that Monsanto is our "best hope to eliminate hunger," CorpWatch's aim in part is to discredit corporate promotion of self-policing or voluntary measures as a substitute for legislation and regulation. These and other environmentalists have been a far more vocal lobbying group than social scientists, and the former now take on sociocultural as well as "physical" issues, observes former World Bank sociologist Michael Cernea (1995:344).

Anthropological studies of the environment and resource conservation focus less on economic policies, everyday politics, or new forms of multilateral governance than on indigenous rights, social constructions of nature, and debates between radical and mainstream environmentalists. Environmental stresses and resource conflicts have become a pressing post-cold war security issue, sometimes expressed as identity politics (Watts 2000:270–271). Yet political ecology until recently has been surprisingly silent about geopolitical questions such as regional integration, transnational governance and environmental security, and decentralized politics.

City and countryside

There are three principal reasons why theorists and policy–makers have historically considered the urban and rural dimensions of development to pose distinct challenges. First, terms of trade or the relative prices of industrial and agricultural goods constitute a source of contention in every society no matter how its economy is organized. Second, the always severe and now widening gap between urban and rural standards of living suggests that different development policies may be appropriate in the city and in the countryside. And third, rural poverty has – most notably in the post-World War II period – been a source of insurgency and social unrest and thus of anxiety for policy-makers and planners and of fascination for social scientists.

Since the advent of cities, no society has ever entirely resolved the tension over terms of trade between urban and rural areas or between consumers and producers of agricultural products. Is there to be cheap food and fiber for urbanites and manufacturers, or are farmers to receive better prices for their harvests? This fundamental dilemma of all economic systems – whether pre-capitalist, capitalist, socialist, or in-between – has been "resolved" in some times and places through political compromises or stalemates and in others through draconian dictates or powerful market forces. Its ubiquity and persistence speak to the continuing need to consider the specificities and interrelationships of city and countryside – and different sectors within each – in any vision of development.

Terms of trade were a principal issue in heated discussions over the Corn Laws in early-19th-century Britain. Passed in 1815, the Corn Laws prohibited grain exports when prices were high and encouraged them when prices were low. Cereals could only be imported when domestic prices were high. These measures artificially benefited landowners and increased the price of bread, which became a source of radical agitation. The 1846 repeal of the Corn Laws marked the end of protectionism in British agriculture, a defeat for the landed aristocracy and a victory for the rising class of industrialists, which had sought to reduce food prices for urban workers and thus lower their wage bill and diminish social unrest. Indeed, the campaign for repeal of the Corn Laws and, more broadly, for trade liberalization could be said to have boosted the careers of the second generation of classical political economists, particularly Ricardo and Malthus, both of whom sharpened their analytical and polemical skills as opponents of the protectionist and pro-aristocratic premises of the Corn Laws.

In the decade following the 1917 Bolshevik revolution, the relations between cities and countryside in the Soviet Union became a major source of strife and controversy, with terms of trade one of the central axes of dispute. Soviet leaders shifted from violent grain confiscations during the civil war that followed the revolution, to a "New Economic Policy" that provided peasants market incentives to produce food for the cities, to an expropriation plan that forcibly converted smallholders into either collective-farm members or employees of state farms. Bolshevik economist Evgenii Preobrazhensky formulated an influential "law" of "primitive socialist accumulation" that maintained that industrialization could only occur in a backward country such as the Soviet Union through "an exchange of values between large-scale [state-sector] and petty [peasant] production under which the latter gives more to the former than it receives" (Preobrazhensky 1971:224). In practice "non-equivalent exchange" meant the institutionalization of measures to extract surplus from the countryside to fuel rapid industrialization. As Stalin consolidated power in the late 1920s, dissenting voices, such as that of Nikolai Bukharin, who argued against anti-peasant policies and for generating demand for industrialization from an expanding consumer market, were sidelined and then silenced – as was Preobrazhensky himself, albeit ostensibly for different reasons (S. Cohen 1980:160–212).

The long-term decline in terms of trade that Raúl Prebisch viewed as undermining Latin American development in the 1950s (see above) has continued to afflict rural dwellers in the South. Producers of the main internationally traded agricultural commodities, in particular, have been hard hit by developed-country protectionism and, especially, by market gluts resulting from new highly productive technologies, shifts in US and European farm subsidy policies (which once emphasized land set-asides and supply management, but which after 1996 encouraged excess production for export) and the breakdown of other supply management mechanisms, such as the national export quotas established under the International Coffee Agreement (which collapsed in 1989). A recent Oxfam report on the impact of falling coffee prices asks, "How much coffee does it take to buy a Swiss Army knife?" In 1980, it took 4.171 kilograms, in 1990 the "price" rose to 6.941 kilos, in 2000 it reached 7.406 kilos, and in 2001 it jumped to a whopping 10.464 kilos (Gresser and Tickell 2002:13). The story is similar for most other farm products and for their relation to the jeeps, tractors, machetes, chemicals, fuel, and other manufactured goods that farmers require.

The huge disparities of wealth and income between city and countryside are a second reason why theorists and planners often conceive of development as having distinct urban and rural components or even of being afflicted by "urban bias" (Lipton 1977). Three-quarters of the 1.2 billion people classified as "extremely poor" (surviving on less than $1 per day) live in rural areas (IFAD 2001). Within most nations poverty rates are significantly higher in rural zones. Clearly, successful poverty-reduction policies must focus on rural areas where access to education, health care, technology, credit, and other services is most limited and where additional disadvantages stemming from remoteness condemn the poor to a Hobson's choice between a hardscrabble existence in the countryside and migration to urban slums. Because most societies are undergoing rapid urbanization, and rural areas frequently lose political clout in the process, one of the most compelling arguments for rural development programs of all kinds, apart from their possible intrinsic merits, is that they also help alleviate urban poverty by reducing migration to the cities or by better equipping migrants to survive. Nonetheless, national development plans often exacerbate historically unequal relations between city and countryside, whether this is understood as "urban bias" or "internal colonialism" (Lipton 1977; McMichael 2000:20–21; Stavenhagen 1969).

Rural development also assumed increasing urgency in the 1950s, 1960s and 1970s as nationalist and communist insurgencies spread and occasionally triumphed in various regions of Asia, Africa, and Latin America. These "peasant wars" were hardly the proletarian revolutions that traditional Marxists envisioned, but their insertion in cold-war geopolitical competition and their roots in longstanding rural poverty made them particularly troubling for Western policymakers.[65] Vietnam, in particular, transformed elite thinking about rural development, which in Indochina and elsewhere quickly became a pillar of counterinsurgency strategy or a preventive bulwark against potential revolutions. Robert McNamara, a key architect of US military strategy in Vietnam, went on in 1968 to spend more than a decade directing the World Bank, where he articulated a new approach towards poverty reduction aimed at "the poorest of the poor." The Vietnam War, together with the claims of Maoism about the revolutionary character of the peasantry, also contributed in the 1960s and 1970s to a new interest in "peasant studies" in the academy, both in Europe and North America and in South Asia and Latin America (Bernstein and Byres 2001).

The concerns of peasant studies and development studies were inextricably linked, not just because peasants were the majority of the population in most underdeveloped countries, but also because social scientists increasingly understood pre-existing agrarian structures to be causally related to political and development outcomes. While positing societal explanations for political-economic phenomena was not new, it re-emerged in the 1960s and after as part of the renewal of interest in non-sectarian Marxism and critical theory. Lenin, in *The Development of Capitalism in Russia* (1972), had sketched two possible roads to capitalism in agriculture: a "Junker" road, characteristic of Prussia and Poland, in which large capitalist farms emerged from feudal estates with a concomitant proletarianization of the labor force; and a "peasant" or "farmer" road, typical of western Europe, in which bourgeois revolutions had undermined feudalism and permitted the emergence of a sector of small and medium-size agricultural producers. The rediscovery and translation in the 1960s of the work of one of Lenin's arch-opponents, A.V. Chayanov (1986), stimulated a fresh wave of debate over whether social differentiation in the countryside produced distinct classes of wealthy and poor peasants or whether such differences resulted from the age and demographic composition of peasant households, with younger units having more dependents and fewer laborers and thus less wealth than older units.[66] Barrington Moore (1966), in a sweeping comparative study of England, France, Germany, Russia, the United States, China, Japan, and India, sought to explain the political-economic consequences of agrarian class relations – and especially the fate of reactionary rural elites – for the bourgeois democratic, capitalist authoritarian, and revolutionary socialist routes to modernity.[67] Robert Brenner (1976), posing the problem of the absence of an "indigenous" transition to capitalism outside of western Europe (although in terms entirely different than Weber's), compared Europe east and west of the Elbe, as well as France and England, and argued that class structures (property relations and surplus-extraction relations), once established, imposed strict limits on societies' long-term economic development.[68]

A cultural dimension was often missing from societal-based explanations for political-economic phenomena mentioned above. Political scientist James Scott insistently re-inserted this missing theme, which contributed to his substantial impact on anthropology in the English-speaking world. In an early work, Scott proposed that agrarian revolutions occurred not so much as a result of absolute immiseration but rather as a result of violations of the "moral economy" – peasant expectations developed over long historical time about "just prices" and what states and elites may claim and in turn must also provide in times of necessity (Scott 1976). Scott's discussion of the rural poor's understanding of justice implied an economy that was embedded in society and the product not just of market forces but of contention between antagonistic social groups. Later, in *Weapons of the Weak* (1985), he examined the micro-politics of class conflict, arguing that small acts of resistance (footdragging, gossip, petty theft), when taken together, significantly limited the types of economic relations and the intensity of exploitation that elites were able to impose. In *Seeing Like a State* (1998), Scott addressed the failures of grandiose, utopian, high-modernist development schemes, in cities and countrysides, and the ways authoritarian experiments in urban planning and rural development policies fail to understand and frequently obliterate or homogenize diverse local practices.

Anthropologists contributed to many of these debates, enriching both agrarian studies and understandings of development and, simultaneously, broadening the temporal, geographical, and intellectual scope of their traditional research practices.[69] Belatedly, they brought the state back into the analysis of local histories and cultures and also turned their lens on the state itself, no longer understood as an undifferentiated monolithic actor, but rather one composed of varied and sometimes competing actors and agencies with distinct bureaucratic interests and agendas (Edelman 1999; Gupta 1998; Nugent 1997). They also offered insightful analyses of urban informal economies and unofficial economic activities such as smuggling (Hart 1992; MacGaffey 1991), of the instabilities and opportunities that arise from interactions between formal and informal economies (Guyer 2004); and informal credit and cultural differences in conceptions of time, money, borrowing and lending (Shipton 1994, 1995). During the 1970s politicians and bureaucrats seized upon the informal economy as a "form of self-organized unemployment relief," and then in the 1980s it was promoted as "an image of popular creative energies finding expression in an unregulated market" (Hart 1992:218). That is, the informal economy concept "swung with" shifts in Western development ideologies. By the early 1990s, rampant economic informalization had moved close to the centers of power and had become a global phenomenon,

> embracing the international drugs traffic, bribery by multinational corporations, corrupt arms deals, tax evasion, smuggling, embezzlement by bureaucrats, peculation by politicians, offshore banking, "grey" markets, insider trading, the black market of communist regimes and organised crime, as well as such legitimate activities as small business, own account dealing and do-it-yourself (Hart 1992:218).

Finally, biotechnology occupies a central place in today's agrarian debates. Observers disagree, for example, about whether genetically modified crops are a solution to hunger and demographic pressure or an agent of "de-peasantization," privatization of germplasm, and agricultural industrialization (see Osgood 2001; Stone 2002; Magdoff et al. 2000; Gupta 1998; Shiva 2000; Tripp 2001). This is an area where anthropology can help to move the debate beyond the caricatures of agricultural systems put forward by both sides, and beyond the tendency to treat biotechnology as a monolithic entity (Stone 2003:618).

Most anthropologists no longer view urban and rural as separate "sectors" lodged in unilinear evolutionary trajectories.[70] Works such as Ferguson's *Expectations of Modernity*

(1999) illustrate how processes once assumed to be one-directional (urbanization, indus-trialization) now look much more complex, unpredictable, and reversible – challenging both academic and popular understandings of modernization. At least as significant as rural–urban migration in his Zambian study are frequent moves between urban jobs and shifting forms of economic and social connection between town-dwelling mineworkers and rural kin. Two decades earlier Colin Murray's (1981) landmark study in Lesotho innovatively analyzed the impact of urban labor migration on rural families. In much of Africa people are on the move between town and countryside, office job and farm, small business and outdoor market, constantly adjusting to rapid economic and political shifts, and careful to diversify their economic activities.

This mobility and economic diversification under conditions of economic uncertainty mean that many urban Africans' images of rural society are likely to be less removed from the realities of life in the countryside than were images of rural life enjoyed under the classical European processes of urbanization analyzed by Raymond Williams (1973). Ferguson (1992) explores this theme in Zambian images of town and countryside. As urban dwellers return to the Zambian countryside upon retirement or loss of employment, new tensions emerge between earlier images of an idealized, idyllic countryside, and the stark rural realities return migrants must confront. Ferguson (1992) remarks that some urban migrants forced by a weak Zambian economy to relocate to their "homes" in the countryside find the latter a place of impossible demands, treachery, witchcraft and selfishness. Macroeconomic shifts and cycles that propel migrants to and from the city are connected to reversible changes in the balance of power between cultural styles of cosmopolitanism and localism; thus the "golden hour" of urban cosmopolitan style in the 1950s and 1960s coincided with an economic expansion that enabled long-term urban settlement and attenuation of migrants' ties to the Zambian countryside (Ferguson 1999). In addition, as urban images of rural life become less rosy, the failings of the urban economy, Ferguson suggests, then "come to appear as attributable not to any external force, but to the internal moral faults of Zambian character" (Ferguson 1992:90). The latter theme resonates with colonial and post-colonial development ideologies that link development with personhood, implying that development "works for some kinds of people, and that, by implication, only personal transformations will make development work" (Karp 1992:10). Urban economic decline then may be experienced or rhetorically construed (by politicians, for example) as a matter of failed personal transformations. Such work illustrates the distinctive contributions offered by anthropology in linking analysis of culture, ideology, economy, subjectivity and personhood in studies of development and globalization.[71]

In sum, this section has illustrated the rich potential and accomplishments of an anthro-pology of development and globalization that both contributes to and benefits from studies of NGOs, civil society, gender, population, culture, consumption, environment, and rela-tions between city and countryside. Next we consider what happens when anthropologists actually work in development institutions. How are they received by their employers and by their anthropological and other colleagues? What challenges does this specialty pose to the discipline more broadly?

IV   Anthropologists in Development Institutions

Can anthropologists speak truth to power and still earn a living in the era of market liberalization? This question returns us to a distinction that invites fresh contemplation – namely that between development anthropology and its critical cousin, the anthropology of development. This section discusses the vanishing (but still disputed) boundary between these two anthropological subtypes, development anthropology's striking expansion since the 1970s, dilemmas of ethics and advocacy that development anthropology shares with the discipline more broadly, why lack of "local" knowledge is *not* the principal cause of development project failure, and how development anthropologists and anthropologists of development put their knowledge to work. The challenges they face in doing so combine with a larger disciplinary imperative to redefine anthropology's role in the public sphere, a theme taken up in the conclusion.

Development anthropology versus anthropology of development[72]

Again, *development anthropology*, in contrast to the anthropology of development, has been termed the work of practitioners who actually design, implement or evaluate programs of directed change, especially those intended to alleviate poverty in poor nations.[73] The *anthropology of development*, on the other hand, calls for a "radical critique of, and distancing from, the development establishment" (Escobar 1997:498; but cf. Gardner and Lewis 1996). Additional differences are as follows:

> While development anthropologists focus on the project cycle, the use of knowledge to tailor projects to beneficiaries' cultures and situation, and the possibility of contributing to the needs of the poor, the anthropologists of development centre their analysis on the institutional apparatus, the links to power established by expert knowledge, the ethnographic analysis and critique of modernist constructs, and the possibility of contributing to the political projects of the subaltern (Escobar 1997:505).

Why are these distinctions disputed? Even Arturo Escobar – once one of development anthropology's strongest critics – by 1997 suggested that any boundary between the anthropology of development and development anthropology is "newly problematic and perhaps obsolete" (1997:498).[74] For others, the divide has long been contested; for example, Bronislaw Malinowski (1961, quoted in Cernea 1995:340) wrote "unfortunately, there is still a strong but erroneous opinion in some circles that practical anthropology is fundamentally different from theoretical or academic anthropology."[75] Furthermore, the supposed boundary between anthropological theory and practice looks very different outside the United States (see below). In short, these two anthropological subtypes are historically contingent categories whose making and unmaking, as suggested earlier, may be more revealing than attempts to pin down definitions.

Anthropology's antinomies of realist epistemology and post-structuralism were sometimes mapped too readily onto the supposed contrasts between development anthropology and the anthropology of development. Scholars in both camps now take seriously the role of language and discourse in constituting – rather than simply reflecting – social reality. Few anthropologists today would consider development to be a neutral language that describes reality.

As an example of recent work that transcends what he earlier saw as a sharp boundary between development anthropology and the anthropology of development, Arturo Escobar (1997) calls attention to anthropologists such as Katy Gardner and David Lewis (see their chapter in Part VIII of this volume). Gardner and Lewis, he notes, draw on both practical development experience and a thorough understanding of the post-structuralist critique, and they are "crafting an alternative practice" that addresses dilemmas of poverty, environmental destruction, and globalization. Such work signals productive new engagements between anthropology and development – and most important, a new set of challenges to the entire discipline (see below). Norman Long (2001), similarly, has insisted on the need for both *theoretical models* aimed at understanding social change and *policy models* intended to promote development. He emphasizes as well the importance of transcending conventional "images" of intervention that are limited to discrete projects and isolated from evolving relations between social actors, including state institutions and officials.

As conventionally defined, development anthropologists work with programs carried out by *multilateral agencies* such as the International Monetary Fund, various United Nations agencies, regional development banks, and the World Bank group's International Bank for Reconstruction and Development and International Development Association; *bilateral agencies* such as the US Agency for International Development (USAID) or Britain's Department of International Development (formerly the Overseas Development Administration); *nongovernmental organizations* (NGOs) or nonprofit organizations such as Oxfam, Save the Children, or World Vision; and private consulting firms.[76] Some academic anthropologists work as part-time consultants for such agencies and others work for them full-time. Thus there is a tripartite division among academics who do *no* work for development agencies, those who *do*, and practicing anthropologists who have no university positions.

During the 1940s and 1950s, US anthropologists were relatively prominent in public policy circles and in the Truman administration's foreign aid planning, then nearly disappeared from development programs by 1970, and returned to them in significant numbers in the mid-1970s (Hoben 1982:351).[77] Since the 1970s, as development agencies became more interested in working directly with the poor and in addressing cultural and social (rather than simply technological) change, and as these agencies also became more bureaucratized, many new opportunities opened up for anthropologists interested in development work. The addition in 1975 of requirements for social soundness analyses in USAID project design[78] contributed to the growing demand for anthropological assistance in the development enterprise (Hoben 1982:358). USAID had just one full-time anthropologist in 1974, 22 by 1977, and 65 by the early 1990s (Hoben 1982:359; Nolan 2002:72).[79] Another one hundred or so anthropologists worked for USAID on short-term contracts (Hoben 1982:359). The World Bank hired its first anthropologist in the mid-1970s (while the World Health Organization did so in 1950) and by the mid-1990s the Bank had about 50–60 social scientists practicing development anthropology and sociology, with hundreds more hired as short-term consultants (Cernea 1995:341). A shrinking academic job market in the mid- and late 1970s propelled more anthropologists into development work. Thus by 1985, there were more anthropologists outside US academic institutions than within them, though by the mid-1990s the proportion of anthropology graduates working outside the academy seemed to have stabilized at 30 percent (Nolan 2002:69–70).

Anthropological participation in development of course is not just market-driven. Such work attracts individuals who believe they can help to alleviate human suffering or reduce the negative impact of – and sometimes help to end – policies with which they disagree.[80] Thus a larger justification for development anthropology is that the discipline needs spokespersons able to skillfully translate and mediate knowledge in public arenas. That implies moral involvement in critical contemporary issues – a stance advocated decades ago by Boas and Mead, and recently by scholars such as Scheper-Hughes (1995), as well as by senior development anthropologists such as Michael Horowitz and others during the 1990s (see Gow 2002:305; Bennett 1996; and chapters in this volume by Gardner and Lewis [chapter 27] and by Fox [chapter 23]). Thus some prominent development anthropologists such as Thayer Scudder and Kathleen Gough, and sociologist Norman Long became interested in development during their own "long-term field research that compelled them to take policy stands that often were unpopular to the development establishment" (Little and Painter 1995:603; see also Colson 1985).

Anthropologists not only need to "study up" (as Laura Nader suggested years ago); they also need to "move up" into more senior administrative and policy-making roles in development institutions, argues development anthropologist Riall Nolan (2002:261). Indeed, in addition to their familiar roles as culture brokers and data collectors, anthropologists have increasingly taken on responsibilities as project managers, team leaders, and policy-makers (Nolan 2002:247), though it remains more common for them to work on program assessment rather than the making of policy. Many occupy administrative rather than social science positions. USAID, for example, has "few – if any – career positions designated for anthropologists or social scientists generally, although as many as 75 people with graduate degrees in anthropology [were] employed by the agency" in the early 1990s (Little and Painter 1995:603).

Boundaries between development anthropology and academe are more rigid in the United States than in the United Kingdom, Scandinavia, or the Netherlands.[81] In the United Kingdom, prestigious interdisciplinary development institutes[82] have close ties to academic anthropology departments as well as to Britain's primary overseas development agency (the Department of International Development). Such interdisciplinary development programs are rare in the United States, and some noted ones have closed (such as Harvard's Institute for International Development and Stanford's Food Research Institute) or suffered serious funding cutbacks. Britain's Department of International Development sponsors a broader range of social science research (including peer-reviewed work) and more directly engages current theoretical scholarship than does its US counterpart, the Agency for International Development. And more so than in the United States, tight budgets in British universities encourage some scholars to pursue research topics that can be funded by development agencies. In a number of British universities, interdisciplinary development studies, with increasingly strong anthropological representation during the past decade or two, is a more established and prestigious field than it tends to be in the United States. Many UK universities now offer both MA and PhD programs in development studies. The institutional connections between UK academe and practical development work, and the high quality of these programs are reflected in stimulating publications by UK anthropologists who draw very effectively on both practical development experience and on contemporary social theory (see, for example, Cooke and Kothari 2001; Crewe and Harrison 1998 and their chapter in Part IV of this volume; Gardner and Lewis 1996 and their chapter in Part VIII of this volume; and Grillo and Stirrat 1997, among others).

Much more so than its British, Dutch, and Scandinavian counterparts, USAID blurs its research programs with its operational or program units, so that what the Agency for International Development funds as "research" is increasingly tied to its operational program exigencies – leaving little space for long-term, autonomous social science research and writing on large issues such as poverty, inequality and environmental degradation.[83] During the 1990s, USAID sharply reduced support for university-based social science research and subsequently relied increasingly on social scientists in consulting firms or NGOs (whose research agendas and professional credentials often differ sharply from those of scholars in universities or research institutes). Although the United States lacks the strong interdisciplinary development studies programs found in Europe, and although USAID less directly engages or funds theoretical research than does its British counterpart, the United States continues to produce many scholars of development.

The distinction between development anthropology and the rest of the discipline, or between policy and academic institutions, is less sharp or even absent in some Latin American nations and elsewhere than it is in the United States (Hewitt de Alcántara 1984). Little (2000) notes that "The polarization between theory and application, so evident in many US anthropology departments, is viewed as a luxury in many regions of the world, where scholars are actively engaged in policy debates and struggles regardless of their academic interests."

In the United States, the identity of development anthropology both shapes and is shaped by professional networks and organizations, such as the Society of Professional Anthropologists, the Washington Association of Practicing Anthropologists, and the National Association for the Practice of Anthropology (NAPA). NAPA, which had 716 members in 2002, formed as a subunit of the American Anthropological Association in 1984, defined its own code of ethics, and has produced a monograph series, among other activities. Members of these organizations conduct international development work as well as other types of activities in corporations, government entities and other agencies in the United States and elsewhere. Decades earlier (in 1941), the Society for Applied Anthropology was founded. It publishes a journal (*Human Organization*) and offers an annual Malinowski award to a distinguished practitioner.

In addition to these organizations, independent institutes and consulting firms in the United States also provide anthropological (and other) experts to the development industry. An example of the former is the nonprofit Institute for Development Studies, which was established in the mid-1970s, in Binghamton, New York, under the leadership of anthropologists David Brokensha, Michael Horowitz, and Thayer Scudder.[84] This institute has attracted funding from a wide array of institutions, including the World Bank, FAO, UNDP, USAID, the Ford Foundation, National Science Foundation, OECD, International Fund for Agricultural Development, World Conservation Union, and Inter-American Development Bank (Nolan 2002:257). The Institute for Development Anthropology not only coordinates the provision of social science expertise to development agencies, but it also has undertaken a broad range of research and training activities and has produced a large number of monographs, working papers, and a newsletter that includes research reports. It manages to be both critical of many development projects and determined to improve the capacities of development agencies to carry out more beneficial and environmentally sound projects. It has played a particularly strong role in training social scientists from poor nations and involving them in the institute's research programs.

Rethinking the critique of development anthropology

In sharp rebuttal to the development-anthropology history narrated above, a critique emerged in the early 1990s, and sparked counter-critiques. At the time, anthropologists such as Escobar (1991) urged us to look beyond development agencies' own benign rhetoric of "increased concern with the poor" in order to inquire more deeply into "the social and cultural configuration that this improved 'concern' entailed for the poor," and also to recognize that it was the increased visibility of the poor that enabled the anthropologist's visibility (1991:664). That is, attention was called to development as a Western, colonial, or imperial cultural construct. The "tight discourses" of USAID and the World Bank, in Escobar's view, are ideological operations that efface the "power that is inevitably linked to visibility" (1991:664). Thus the objectifying gaze of development institutions creates clients, labels, categories – such as "small farmers," "women" or "the environment" – visions that constitute apparatuses of power and social control, as well as means of transforming the conditions under which individuals live (Escobar 1995:155–156). When development anthropologists "interact with institutions, they inevitably inscribe local reality in terms of professional categories," even though they do "try to stay closer to local perceptions" (Escobar 1991:668). He urges anthropologists to explore how development institutions "shape the fields of thinking and action of both the anthropologist and his or her Third World clients" (Escobar 1991:668). Such an intellectual move, he suggests, then reveals how the development encounter – "with or without the participation of anthropologists – amounts to an act of cognitive and social domination" of the Third World (Escobar 1991:675).

While many scholars appreciate the intellectual richness and innovativeness of development discourse analysis, a number refute the notion of a monolithic development regime, noting the limitations of an approach that treats development agencies "as if they lacked internal conflict and struggle and as if they are not subject to the same real-life contingencies that shape every organization's behavior" (Little 2000:123).[85] Not all development discourses originate in Europe and North America, and development practices (even those lumped under the "neoliberal" rubric) display enormous variation. Resistance to development orthodoxies arises from both center and margins, as part of complexly intertwined transnational and local processes. Furthermore, development anthropologists were by no means blind to the ambiguities of their own positions within development agencies or to the workings of power, knowledge and ideology (see Gow 2002; Little and Painter 1995). Indeed many anthropologists working for development institutions wrestle with precisely the dilemmas Escobar (1991) highlights. Doing so may improve not only their bargaining power within the institutions that employ them (a motive Escobar criticizes) but also their effectiveness as advocates for the poor. Such advocacy transcends the supposed boundary between anthropology of development and development anthropology (see below). Thus Escobar (1997:498) later suggested that development anthropologists by the late 1990s were "articulating a powerful theory of practice for anthropology as a whole."

Early-21st-century anthropologists can no more easily avoid operating within the development framework than they could escape the colonial framework several decades ago. Thus Escobar's larger critique of development anthropologists' supposed failure to examine the "historically constituted character of development as a cultural system" extends to the discipline more broadly. Drawing explicit parallels between the colonial encounter (Asad 1973) and the development encounter, Escobar wonders how aware most anthropologists are of the effects of 'development' on the groups or situations they study (1991:676; see also Escobar 1997). "In the transition from the colonial to the development encounter, anthropology's historical awareness has left much to be desired," writes Escobar, as he urges consideration of development as a "chapter in the history of reason," part of the anthropological study of modernity (1991:659, 678). Many anthropologists, he notes, have been reluctant to consider seriously structures of power that have shaped the discipline, including "colonialism and neocolonialism, their political economy and their institutions," as well as the resulting asymmetrical and provisional intimacies of fieldwork, and the absence of any fundamental anthropological challenge to the inequalities of either the colonial world or the "development system" (1991:676–677).

Again, the "development system" in the early 21st century means economic neoliberalism and globalization – and, as we have noted, it is precisely the latter's historically contingent (rather than natural or inevitable) character that more anthropologists might engage directly (see also Miller's chapter in Part IV of this volume). Thus familiar criticisms of development anthropology may reveal more about the wider discipline's limitations than about those of development anthropologists. For example, anthropologists often are reluctant to study powerful institutions, preferring instead to study the local and the distant – for example, "indigenous movements and NGOs rather than government ministries and . . . local organizations of resistance rather than central organizations of repression" (Dove 1999:239–240). Such studies, Dove notes, "have served to denaturalize the social reality of local rather than central institutions" (1999:240). In short, are anthropologists today any more likely than their colonial predecessors to speak truth to power, to explicitly question their relationships to dominant institutions, or to critically historicize the present?

A sociologist who criticizes his own discipline on precisely those grounds is Loïc Wacquant, author of a number of essays in collaboration with Pierre Bourdieu. Wacquant writes that "U.S. sociology is now tied and party to the ongoing construction of the neoliberal state" and its "punitive management of the poor, on and off the street . . . . Either people are portrayed as maximizing computing machines pursuing their interests, or they're portrayed as symbolic animals that manipulate language and obey norms because they're members of a group."[86] To what extent may anthropologists today be captives of disciplinary modes of analysis that remove from critical scrutiny the institutional power, discourses and practices that undergird economic neoliberalism and growing material inequality?

Ethics and advocacy

The discipline has long debated ethical issues surrounding anthropologists' roles as advocates, brokers, spokespersons, historians, lobbyists, and expert witnesses. Such debates intensify at times of political controversy such as Project Camelot and the Vietnam War (Horowitz 1974; Wolf and Jorgensen 1970), but complex issues of power and knowledge – including when to speak truth to power – never disappear. All anthropologists – not just those working with development agencies – confront dilemmas of ethical and political responsibility.[87] We must weigh risks to interviewees and access to particular informants and field sites when we decide how to characterize or whether to mention at all matters such as corruption, human rights abuses, or political violence, and when we take on particular causes advanced by local NGOs or "indigenous" groups.[88] Also at issue, Little and Painter (1995:605) suggest, is "whether we accept responsibility for the fact that in any setting our work among the poor and in relatively poor countries rests on a position of power and privilege that shapes our findings and our very definition of what constitute problems for study."

Most challenging for any anthropologists (whether labelled development anthropologists or not) is to work as advocates for the people they study and to lobby for change (although this is considered more problematic in the US academy than it is elsewhere, in Latin America, for example). Advocacy and action anthropology may be distinguished, Chambers suggests, according to "who has control over a piece of work. . . . The parameters of advocacy work are generally determined by the anthropologist, while in action anthropology (in ideal terms) anthropologists make themselves available to appropriate clients who determine how anthropology might best contribute to their needs. . . . Both approaches are informed by the certainty that knowledge represents power. . . ." (1987:321). Collaborative research in turn often entails "joint authorship on the part of representatives of the community and participating anthropologists, and . . . in many cases a long-term commitment to a 'client' group." Advocacy work of course carries the risk that assisting some clients excludes or harms the interests of others.

A particular ethical challenge for development anthropologists is summarized by Nolan as follows:[89]

> Development anthropologists quickly learn that they, like other development specialists, are paid to do the client's bidding. Although paid specialists are allowed to complain a great deal, and sometimes are allowed to persuade those in power to see things differently, one basic rule remains: If we cannot persuade them, then we either fall into line or get out (2002:85).

Large organizations such as USAID and the World Bank prefer to move funds through the system quickly, and individuals within these institutions are rewarded for doing just that (rather than for actual project results). There is "a collusive web of relationships linking

agencies (and their oversight bodies), host country governments, and contract specialists
.... Often, completed projects are by definition successful ones, since they pave the way for
more projects – and more funding" (Nolan 2002:237).

Anthropologists in development agencies can easily become flies in the ointment, bearers
of unwelcome bad news that slows things down and makes life difficult for project
managers and others. Employers may sanitize anthropologists' reports in order to avoid
blocking the flow of funds through the agency pipeline. Thus anthropologists' task in these
agencies is not only to provide user-friendly data to their employers but also to persuade the
latter to act on that information, even when it challenges organizational norms and
standard practices, forces an unpopular change of course in an existing project or program,
or slows the disbursement of funds.[90] Anthropologists can help to propel changes in rules,
or in organizational culture – in other words institutional change to mandate the use of
anthropological knowledge (see Cernea 1995 for examples and references). Sometimes
they manage to exercise a modest influence on the theoretical underpinnings of key policy
frameworks, as in the debates within the World Bank over the concept of "social capital"
(Bebbington et al. forthcoming).[91] Anthropologists of course cannot shoulder this burden
alone, and indeed the development industry has spawned an array of NGOs and public
interest monitoring groups calling for new forms of accountability (see, for example, Fox
and Brown 1998; Clark et al. 2003).[92]

Putting anthropological knowledge to work

How can development anthropologists put disciplinary knowledge to work, and what
challenges do they face in doing so? Gow (2002) argues that this specialty is a moral project
– one based on strong ethical principles – the most effective contribution of which is to the
meaning of development, its vision of the "good society." In this view, development is
anthropology's moral twin rather than its evil twin (Gow 2002).

A vision of development as anthropology's moral twin points to a "need for critical
knowledge that explores the spaces between what we know and what can be done with that
knowledge" (Chambers 1987:322; see also R. Cohen 1986 and Collins 1986). How to
produce such knowledge about development – as a quest to reduce poverty and expand
people's choices – is fertile terrain both for development anthropology and the discipline
more broadly. What is at stake, as Fisher (1996:139) writes, "is not some simple war on
poverty and hunger, but the dignity and autonomy of individuals and cultures
[that] . . . have been treated as passive subjects of a set of unwanted interventions."

While anthropologists are trained to capture empirical complexity, particularity and
uncertainty, this is not the kind of knowledge development agencies can easily translate
into replicable policies and programs (see Roe's chapter in Part VII of this volume).
Anthropologists working in development institutions thus are challenged to present complex realities in narratives or stories as compelling and as intelligible to a wide audience as
those misleading classics such as the "tragedy of the commons."[93] They must persuade
their employers to design programs that do reflect local complexity, historical contingency,
economic constraints and priorities, and risk-taking strategies – even though development
agencies trying to achieve economies of scale with their funds tend to favor large projects,
with little design variation, which can be managed at a distance.

Anthropologists in development institutions also must negotiate disciplinary
hierarchies and stereotypes about "hard" and "soft" science, while operating as a distinct
minority whose findings and skills nonetheless are crucial. The economists and technical
experts such as engineers and agronomists, financial planners, and managers who dominate most development institutions often have little understanding of the professional skills

of anthropologists. Thus Cernea (1995:341), formerly a senior sociologist at the World Bank, refers to the "structural difficulties and sleep-robbing questions that we have confronted in introducing anthropological knowledge within an economic fortress." Some non-anthropologists assume that anthropological field investigations require no special training and can be done as easily by an agronomist or economist as by an anthropologist, and some scientists joke about anthropological data or field research as the collection of anecdotes. Thus anthropologists must explain and demonstrate the usefulness of their methods and approaches to non-anthropological colleagues.[94] In short, they must expend as much – often more – effort on institutional relationships as on the intellectual work of the field. In addition, as former USAID insider Hoben (1982:360) observes, career anthropologists in such an agency "face a difficult choice between remaining specialists who keep up their reading and contacts with other members of the discipline, or becoming 'generalists' with greater opportunities for upward mobility and influence."

The interdisciplinary teams so common in development work pose challenges to anthropologists, since the Euro-American tradition of our discipline emphasizes solo investigation and encourages us to question the assumptions underlying projects, models, and analytic approaches. (Team projects have been more central in the Mexican and other Latin American anthropological traditions.) Nonetheless, anthropologists have helped to create new multidisciplinary, team-based research approaches, such as rapid assessment procedures (RAP) and participatory rural appraisal (PRA), which define development goals and design and evaluate projects with the backing of target populations, increasingly referred to as "stakeholders" (see Nolan 2002:137–141).[95]

Cross-disciplinary collaboration between social and natural scientists was the focus of a Rockefeller Foundation program that offered two-year social science research fellowships in agriculture from the mid-1970s to the late 1990s. Under this program anthropologists (and other social scientists) conducted research with distinguished scientists in international agricultural research centers, a network of over a dozen prestigious institutes (known today as Future Harvest Centers) where scientists developed "green revolution" technologies and other agronomic innovations intended to improve crop production, reduce hunger, and promote sound management of natural resources.[96] Anthropologists conducting interdisciplinary research in these centers have contributed to the development of crop storage and other technologies that suit small farmers' circumstances (Rhoades 1984; Moock and Rhoades 1992; Dvorak 1993; Groenfeldt and Moock 1989); seed provision systems that meet new challenges of biotechnology and intellectual property protection (Tripp 2001);[97] emergency support for farmers who experience disasters such as the 1994 genocide in Rwanda (Sperling and Longley 2002); participatory plant breeding (Haugerud and Collinson 1990; Sperling and Berkovitz 1994);[98] improved understanding of the economy of changing gender relations among Senegambian rice farmers (Carney and Watts 1991); knowledge about agro-forestry and agrarian change in East Africa (Snyder 1996); understanding connections between child nutrition, intra-household income control, and labor patterns in Kenyan farm households (Rubin 1992, 1989); and how conflicting property regimes and political claims might prevent benefits of fish culture from accruing to the rural poor, especially landless women (Worby et al. 2002; Worby 1994).

A few among many anthropological contributions to practicing or understanding development include research on the social dynamics of food security (Pottier 1999) and long-term work on forced human resettlement – a process that affects some ten million people each year who are displaced by the construction of dams and urban infrastructure (Cernea 1995:349; see, for example, Scudder and Colson 1979; Cernea and Guggenheim 1993; Koenig 2001). Koenig and Diarra (1998) explore local environmental and agrarian consequences of a variety of policy changes from the 1970s to the 1990s in Mali, including effects of involuntary resettlement impelled by construction of the Manantali dam. McMillan (1995) provides a rich long-term study of planned settlement and voluntary migration in West Africa's Volta Valley that followed a successful international campaign against river blindness. Finally, one of the most intensively studied cases of intervention inspired by anthropologists is the Vicos project in Peru, which was initiated in the 1950s by Alan Holmberg at Cornell University, and which attempted to demonstrate the benefits of land reform by acquiring and transforming a hacienda, along with its population of resident peons (Babb 1985; Doughty 1987; Lynch 1981; Mangin 1979).

In spite of the expansion of both development anthropology and the anthropology of development in recent decades, there have been relatively few ethnographies of development projects.[99] As one development practitioner himself notes, we still "know very little – in an ethnographic sense – about how projects actually develop; about the way in which stakeholders at multiple levels negotiate meanings and outcomes with each other" (Nolan 2002:214).

What is known, but perhaps to little practical effect, is why most development projects fail. Indeed, fundamental criticisms of development projects have changed little over time. What is wrong with development has much less to do with simple incompetence or corruption or even lack of "local" knowledge than with institutional attributes:

> Although individuals within . . . [development] agencies may learn a great deal, this learning tends not to find its way into the organization. . . . the reason why large agencies do not learn is because they do not have to. Few agencies directly experience the effects of their plans, projects, and programs. Their internal operations, largely opaque to outsiders, are not particularly disposed to self-criticism or the discussion of failure. There are three broad reasons for this organizational inability to learn: the *paradigms* that dominate development work, the scripts or *development narratives* that this paradigm generates, and the collusive *structures* in which the development partners seem to be locked (Nolan 2002:233).

Anthropologists have contributed insightful analyses of these problems, including Roe (chapter 24, this volume) and Hoben (1995) on development institutions' need for simplifying "development narratives" or "blueprint development"; Ferguson (1990) on development as an "anti-politics machine" that emphasizes techno-managerial solutions; Hill (1986) on bureaucrats' misperceptions of peasant farmers; and many others. Ferguson (1990), for example, shows how a World Bank report transforms Lesotho into a generic "less-developed country" whose deficiencies are defined to correspond to the kinds of technical interventions development agencies can administer anywhere. The World Bank falsely casts Lesotho as a generic place of "primordial isolation," an aboriginal, ahistorical, "'traditional' society somehow untouched by the modern world" (Ferguson 1990:32) – an image that overlooks the country's long history of agricultural commercialization and migrant labor. Development discourse often naturalizes poverty, as in the construction of Egypt as object of development in USAID reports, whose narratives focus on nature, geography, and demography rather than on politics, power, and economic inequality (Mitchell 1991).

Such academic criticisms of development often have little impact on its practice. That may be partly because "so much of the criticism is damning, self-serving, and counterproductive" and offers no practical solutions, notes Gow (2002:300). On the other hand, the complexity, innovation, and self-critical tentativeness of anthropological analysis lose out to the simplicity, familiarity, and explicitness that are more digestible by development agencies (again, see Roe's chapter in this volume, as well as Dove 1999). Furthermore, anthropologists' dilemma is that "our research challenges what others want to believe;" we must find ways to persuade audiences to listen nonetheless – we must "become better political animals" (Colson 1985:193–194). Institutional conservatism, or development agencies' inability to learn and their unwillingness to shift course dramatically, contribute to the failure of many – perhaps most – development projects. Consultant economists find it no easier than anthropologists, for example, to alter the ideas and practices of the World Bank. A frank insider's account of struggles to do so is economist Peter Griffiths' (2003) book, *The Economist's Tale: A Consultant Encounters Hunger and the World Bank*. As Griffiths notes, "Workers in the aid industry have to bow to pressures from clients, consultancy firms, donor organizations and the whole aid system if they are to continue to work in aid" (2003:viii).[100] Ultimately, then, the limitations or failures of development anthropology "may say more about development and its problems than anthropology and its purported shortcomings" (Gow 2002:300). Whether development's shortcomings point to the necessity of alternatives *to* development (the post-development position) or to development alternatives is our final topic.

V Post-Development?

Development Alternatives, Alternatives to Development?

Recent development buzzwords – "participation," "partnership," "sustainability," "good governance" – respond to both current crises and earlier failures and shortcomings. Many argue, however, that these catchphrases too often merely dress up old and unsuccessful practices in new language. Crewe and Harrison (1998:69–90), for example, discuss the pitfalls (such as lingering inequalities and paternalism) of "partnership" in development rhetoric and practice. "Partnership," like so many other development domains, has been converted into a technical and managerial issue. The editors of another recent volume "challenge the participatory development orthodoxy" and term "participation" the "new tyranny" (Cooke and Kothari 2001).[101]

More fundamental questions – such as how to lessen increasingly grotesque inequities within and between societies or how to reduce unsustainable levels of consumption in the North – remain unresolved and would require structural transformations and political will beyond the capacity of existing agencies. Thus some scholars urge us to look beyond "development" as the answer to the "great questions of poverty, hunger and oppression" (e.g. Ferguson 1990:279–288 and Escobar 1995, 1997).[102] Many illustrate the usefulness of Foucauldian notions of power, analyzing, for example, how supposed empowerment (a current development buzzword) becomes subjection, and why it is that the more participatory rural development appraisals by interdisciplinary practitioner teams are, the more they conceal the power structures of local communities (Cooke and Kothari 2001:12, 139–152, 168–184). Among the larger dangers of today's conventional participatory development approaches are the capacity of the language of empowerment to "mask a real concern for managerialist effectiveness," naive assumptions about the "authenticity of motivations and behaviour in participatory processes," and the likelihood that "an emphasis on the micro-level of intervention can obscure, and indeed sustain, broader macro-level inequalities and injustice" (Cooke and Kothari 2001:14).

Advocates of "post-development" or alternatives to development exalt images of the "local" and sometimes romanticize or essentialize it.[103] In a reversal of modernization theory's assumption that "traditional" communities pose obstacles to change, some scholars and activists celebrate community as a valuable source of local or indigenous knowledge[104] and critique. They find hope in the "creative reconstitution" of social and economic life on the margins, in disengagement from market logic and creation of a "new commons," and in redefinition of needs to suit limited means (Esteva 1992:20–23).

Post-development approaches tend to view states as simply the agents of brutal or failed modernization (which they often are) rather than as vehicles of democratization and beneficial access to markets (which they can be as well). Such approaches raise questions about when "local" people might prefer a state that works for them rather than state withdrawal. As Watts (1998:92) notes, there is a danger in uncritically privileging "the local," "place," "culture," "the people," or "popular discourse from below" without acknowledging "the potentially deeply conservative, and occasionally reactionary, aspects of such local particularisms."[105] The politics of the local cannot be assumed to be benign or progressive. Neither do NGOs, the indigenous, or non-party politics necessarily offer transformative solutions to development dilemmas. In short, the limitations of some theorists' "yearning for a postdevelopment era" can be summed up as follows: "this yearning is unrealistic about the limits of pragmatic politics, ignores the historical consequences of similar aspirations for utopias, and remains unfair in assessing the multiple forms of development. . . . " (Sivaramakrishnan and Agrawal 2003:31).

Contrary to proclamations about its desired demise, in many parts of the world the idea of development remains a powerful aspiration – a hope that lives in spite of a justified loss of faith in particular policy prescriptions, well-founded critiques of ethnocentric measures of achievement or progress, and rejection of the environmentally destructive practices of wealthy nations. Indeed it is development goals – rather than their rejection – that often inspire social movements.[106] As Ferguson (1999:248) observes, "development" neither inaugurated the poverty and global inequalities its discourse organized, nor "can its demise be expected to make them suddenly disappear." The risk of celebrating a putative end of development is that "anti-development" critiques (Watts 1995, quoted in Ferguson 1999:249) could promote intellectual disengagement from increasingly brutal global inequalities. Instead we must work toward new conceptual apparatuses that take on these tragic problems. That demands more scholarly attention to the international financial and governance institutions (IMF, World Bank, WTO, UN) as well as critical analysis of states, NGOs, social movements, and "new, transnational forms of governmentality that need to be subjected to the same sort of critical scrutiny that has been applied to 'development' in the past" (Ferguson 1999:249). In addition, shifting the focus from development per se to poverty and inequality more broadly is one way for anthropologists to move forward, as Gardner and Lewis (1996:158) suggest.[107] These pressing agendas invite precisely those innovative blends of cultural, historical, and political economy analysis this essay is meant to encourage. They also invite new moral visions to frame anthropological engagement with the public sphere.

Conclusion

Two contrasting approaches to "development" and "underdevelopment" are encountered in the anthropological literature. One locates the concept of development squarely in the Enlightenment and the transition from feudalism to capitalism, the first period in history when it became possible to imagine spectacular advances in the productive forces that made progress possible. Another perspective, inspired by poststructuralist scholarship, analyzes "development" as a post-World War II discourse intended to justify the remaking of the "Third World" and suggests that "underdevelopment" – also primarily a discourse – originated in a 1949 speech by Harry Truman (Esteva 1988:665; Escobar1995:3; Kearney 1996:34; Sachs 1992:2).[108] Advocates of the first position see the second as ignoring both intellectual and economic history, overly focused on discourse, and insufficiently attentive to longstanding processes of exploitation. Proponents of the second tendency criticize supporters of the first approach for accepting an old "master narrative" about progress and for not acknowledging the utter failure of most 20th-century development efforts, whether carried out by states, multilateral institutions, or small NGOs. Some maintain that disillusion with development is so widespread that we have moved into a "post-development era."

But if not development, then what? To declare the development era over can only seem far-fetched to citizens of countries where the World Bank's and International Monetary Fund's unaccountable bureaucrats still largely define economic policies and where levels of poverty and inequality show no signs of diminishing. Alternatives imagined by post-development enthusiasts often remain just that – imaginary. They often accord social movements and popular mobilization, particularly at the local level, a central role in redefining collective needs and goals and in filling service provision gaps left by an uncaring, atrophied, and elite-dominated state apparatus. Nevertheless, while post-development advocates can point to a small number of success stories, it is doubtful that many of the small-scale local initiatives they favor can really be "scaled up" to the point where they resolve problems of widespread poverty and suffering. Moreover, this position typically fails to consider the implications for democratically elected representative institutions of making social movements or NGOs – which are sometimes as unaccountable as the international financial institutions – the protagonists of post-development.

In contrast, proponents of "another development" – that is, those who advocate development alternatives, rather than alternatives to development, have put forward a range of proposals, including "localization," "delinking" from the market, "fair trade," participatory budgeting, taxes on volatile capital movements, and a startling number of populist, nationalist and regional integration efforts to re-embed the economy in society (Cavanagh et al. 2002; Hines 2000; Patomäki 2001; Sandbrook 2003). They generally differ from post-development theorists in their continuing search for practical experiences that prove effective in raising living standards and that have potential for "scaling up." Often development alternatives are part of the practice of social movements, NGOs and other civil society organizations. As yet, however, apart from some tepid attempts to theorize a "third way" between capitalism and socialism, remarkably few in the development alternatives camp have tried to assert a role for a reinvigorated state as a vehicle for democratization, social justice, or even simply improved access to markets. And "third way" enthusiasts virtually never challenge the macroeconomic premises of neoliberalism (Giddens 1998; see also Giddens 2001). Many proponents of more radical development alternatives are caught in a different condnundrum than "third way" advocates. They rightly argue that social justice requires global institutions to regulate the global market. But since global institutions are dominated by pro-corporate elites, they fall back into a defense of national sovereignty as the only means of achieving a decent society – and this at a time when global neoliberalism is everywhere redefining and, in most cases, eroding the nation-state's capacity for autonomous decision making (Faux 2004:49).

Meanwhile, modernization theory's assumptions about supposed cultural obstacles to change remain alive and well among many development practitioners. And assumptions about "development," whether explicit or not, feature in the torrent of recent academic studies of "modernity." Yet contemporary anthropology often tends to de-historicize globalization, naturalize neoliberalism, and bypass the state in favor of the "local" or the transnational. Today's debates over globalization confirm that development is still hotly contested. Furthermore, as Graeber (2002:1223) suggests, globalization "has made the political role of anthropology itself problematic, in a way perhaps even more profound than the 'reflexive moment' of the eighties ever did." Development institutions that employ anthropologists typically assign them micro-interventions and culture broker roles, yet a genuine anthropology of development must analyze larger institutional practices and orientations that are more easily critiqued from afar. The economic and social forces that profoundly shape our era demand attention to states, international financial institutions, capital flows, political parties, regional groupings such as NAFTA and the European Union, and social movements. Writing effectively about these processes and about international financial and governance institutions while continuing to analyze local initiatives and responses to the market is as much a challenge today as it has ever been.

All of these dilemmas put new pressure on the deeply uneasy relationship between US academe and the public arena, and on distinctions between theory and practice. The theory/practice division is not an inevitable universal, but rather a recent historical product, and one that takes on quite varied national and local forms.[109] For example, until the 1960s, US social sciences were rooted in a "liberal belief in service for the public or common good" and were "supremely confident in the susceptibility of social problems to human intervention" (Anderson 2003:B7,8). The social and political upheavals of the 1960s revealed to US academics the contradictions of claiming both scientific standing and policy influence, Anderson argues, and academic gatekeepers in the United States came to equate policy interests with insufficient commitment to a discipline. That view was not shared, however, by social scientists in other parts of the world and their perspectives now infuse increasingly globalized American social sciences, which have experienced rising proportions of foreign scholars in US doctoral programs and faculties. In addition, US scholars are only beginning to understand the risks to life and livelihood faced by social scientists who live elsewhere under governments that fear them, declare their research treasonous; or imprison, torture, or harass them. Cernea (1995:342), for example, describes how sociology and anthropology were "ideologically banned" in post-war Romania and how during the 1960s in that country "[g]enuine fieldwork was ostracized, as it implied a threat to the establishment: the threat of deflating the ideological balloon with empirical evidence." Anthropology provokes similar fears in many poorer nations today – even when scholars do not explicitly mention its practical or policy implications.

With that global backdrop, recent American academic distinctions between practical and theoretical work can only appear parochial and limiting. Our uncertain era demands instead vigorous and imaginative new approaches to anthropology's role in the public sphere.[110] The discipline also "needs to clearly identify its inescapable interlocutors within the West itself" – whether cultural critics, rational choice theorists, historians, or World Bank or NGO officials (Trouillot 2003:137). This move is crucial, Trouillot argues, because identifying the interlocutors' premises allows us to identify the stakes, the public issues to which anthropological knowledge is profoundly relevant, instead of choosing scholarly comfort over risk and thus masking the wider public significance of the discipline's findings and debates.

Claims about the inevitability of market logic are everywhere (with academe no exception). Anthropologists are well placed to shine a bright light on the contingency – indeed the fragility – of that supposed logical necessity. In doing so, we can return to what Trouillot (2003:139) terms the "moral optimism that has been anthropology's greatest – yet underscored – appeal . . . because that is the side of humanity that we choose to prefer . . . and because anthropology as a discipline is the best venue through which the West can show an undying faith in the richness and variability of humankind" (see also Graeber 2001). We must look beyond "market arrogance," the notion of market choices as all the democracy we need,[111] and images of all people as "market citizens"[112] in hot pursuit of the next economic opportunity. Can anthropologists recover the discipline's moral optimism even though metanarratives are in decline and most development projects fail? It is time to think anew about intellectuals' role in the public sphere, and there is no topic more timely than the dream of enhanced well-being for the poor.

NOTES

1   Our names are in alphabetical order, to reflect equal co-authorship.

2   See Esteva (1988: 665). Crush (1995b: 2) writes that in "a recent spate of development diction-aries we sense an urgent, even desperate attempt to stabilize development and bring order out of ambiguity."

3   Social (rather than economic) goals of development were highlighted in the first World Summit for Social Development, held in Copenhagen in 1995. Anthropologists of course are interested in a variety of development goals, including environmental sustainability, poverty alleviation, literacy, equity, empowerment, and cultural identity. See also Sen (1999).

4   There are, however, important differences among scholars of development who draw on Foucault; Ferguson (1990, 1999) and Escobar (1995), for example, arrive at different conclu-sions about the power/knowledge regime of development and its implications for progressive change (see below). On limitations of Foucauldian and other poststructuralist approaches to development, see Agrawal (1996), Lewellen (2002), and Sivaramakrishnan and Agrawal (2003:25–35), among others.

5   On the other hand, one reviewer suggests that tales of development failure may be over-represented in scholarly literature; many development projects that are modest successes may receive little publicity.

6   On limitations of the notion of progress, see Cowen and Shenton's (1996: chapter 1) discussion of how ideas of progress and development were at various times connected to or separated from one another in the 19th and 20th centuries. See also Sahlins (1999) on anthropology's struggles with the Enlightenment.

7   Prominent development anthropologist Thayer Scudder (1999:359), for example, notes that it is a serious misconception to assume that those involved in "applied" anthropology do not do basic research.

8   Although evolutionary approaches have waned in sociocultural anthropology, evolutionary theory in the early 21st century was important for behavioral ecologists in anthropology and it was making a comeback in some social sciences (e.g., evolutionary psychology, ecological economics and use of evolutionary game theory in small-scale societies).

9   See Lewellen's (2002: 62) discussion of differences between development and globalization.

10 On this distinction, see discussion below and Escobar (1997:498), among others. The contrast is between "two broad schools of thought: those who favor an active engagement with develop-ment institutions on behalf of the poor, with the aim of transforming development practice from within; and those who prescribe a radical critique of, and distancing from, the development establishment." The former has been termed "development anthropology" and the latter the "anthropology of development." Yet by the late 1990s, Escobar notes, this distinction had blurred since a number of anthropologists were "experimenting with creative ways of articulat-ing anthropological theory and practice in the development field" (1997:498).

11 For histories of development theory and practice, see Arndt (1987), Cooper and Packard (1997), Cowen and Shenton (1996), Larraín 1989, Lewellen (2002), Leys (1996), Rist (1997), Robert-son (1984), and Watts (1995).

12 For an explanation of why this was so, see the chapter by Leys reprinted in this volume.

13 Several theorists, notably Esteva (1988) and Escobar (1995), view Truman's inaugural address as marking the invention of the concept of "underdevelopment" and the founding moment of an insidious development apparatus. The proximate derivations of the ideas in Truman's 1949 address, however, are clearly traceable to the Bretton Woods Conference, while the more remote origins of "development" and "underdevelopment" lie in Enlightenment thought, 19th-century Liberalism, and—in Latin America, early 20th-century populism (Cowen and Shenton 1996: 7–11; Edelman 1999:11–15). The Oxford English Dictionary dates the use of the word "devel-opment" to the mid-18th century (OED 1971: vol. I, 707–8). As Esteva (1988: 665) notes, until the mid-19th century the term often referred to the unfolding or unrolling of a vellum or parchment and, metaphorically, of a process.

14   Many have refuted the idea that development is simply a Western imposition, calling attention instead to the "immense evidence on the polyvocal, polylocal nature of development performances and appropriations" (Sivaramakrishnan and Agrawal 2003:29).

15   Similarly, Leys (1996:11, n. 22) notes "how little the U.S. modernization school establishment felt it necessary to respond to their critics, in spite of the effectiveness of the critique in sidelining modernization thinking outside the USA."

16   See McMichael (2000) for an overview of origins and outcomes of the 1980s debt crisis.

17   Cooper and Packard (1997:2–3) term this an "ultramodernist" approach to development.

18   The United Nations' Millennium Development Goals for the year 2015 (which included eradicating extreme poverty and hunger, achieving universal primary education, empowering women, improving health indicators, and ensuring environmental sustainability) were widely recognized as overly ambitious even as they were proclaimed to great fanfare in 2000.

19   Williamson is co-editor (with Pedro-Pablo Kuczynski) of a 2003 book titled *After the Washington Consensus*.

20   By the early 21st century, poverty alleviation itself had become a dominant buzzword, at risk of being a mantra that those seeking grants had to invoke in order to justify funding, but without necessarily signaling any deep shift toward programs that actually could alleviate poverty. Furthermore, some challenge the focus on deprivation as the "market-based representation of social life that neoliberal philosophy promotes and feeds upon," ignoring "the vast heterogeneity of economic restructuring" and obscuring the ways "people may be fashioning place-based responses to neoliberalism . . . in ways that indicate new directions in people's defense of their livelihoods, environments, and cultures" (Chase 2002: 12).

21   These arguments and others outlined in this paragraph and the next are drawn from a "Special Report on Global Economic Inequality," in the March 13, 2004 issue of the *Economist*, pp. 69–71, and from a rejoinder published in the *Economist* on April 10, 2004 by Martin Ravallion, who is research manager in the World Bank's Development Research Group.

22   Different results are obtained depending on whether one uses national-accounts data or household-survey data, as illustrated in a study (cited in the *Economist*, March 13, 2004, p. 70) by economist Angus Deaton ("Measuring poverty in a growing world (or measuring growth in a poor world)"—available at http://www.wws.princeton.edu/deaton/working.htm.

23   Foreign aid has never been politically popular in the United States, though surveys show that citizens greatly over-estimate the percentage of the federal budget allocated to foreign assistance. Legislative funding for foreign aid fluctuates over time, emerges from unstable coalitions, and tends to be "used selectively by the administration in power to pursue short-term foreign policy objectives that may conflict with long-term development goals" (Hoben 1982:352). In addition, different US government agencies may have conflicting aims in particular countries and programs, such as disposing of agricultural surpluses, securing strategic sea lanes, or creating markets for US manufacturers or service providers. Thus, program content and regional emphases shift over time.

24   The works of Colin Leys (excerpted in this volume, chapter 5) and Walter Rodney (1974) suggested that the dependency approach could be applied effectively in analyzing Africa.

25   Monopoly refers to a market structure in which there is a single seller, while monopsony refers to one in which there is a single buyer.

26   ECLA economists' and sociologists' use of the term "structuralist" should not be confused with the completely different meaning of the term in the "structuralist anthropology" of Claude Lévi-Strauss and his followers. Under ISI, as McMichael (2000:36) notes, "import controls reduced expensive imports of manufactured goods from the West and shifted resources into domestic manufacturing. Domestic industry was protected through tariffs and other barriers."

27   See LeClair and Schneider (1968) for an overview of the debate between formalists and substantivists in economic anthropology, and a compendium of the "classics" on this topic. Formalists drew on neoclassical economic theory and emphasized individual rationality and choice, while substantivists built upon Karl Polanyi's notion of the economy as embedded in both economic and non-economic institutions, or the economy as "instituted process."

28 On September 11, 1973, the Chilean Armed Forces under General Augusto Pinochet overthrew the elected, left-wing Popular Unity government of President Salvador Allende, ushering in a period of intense repression that only ended with the return of democracy in 1990.

29 See Brenner (1977) for a position that emphasizes the overlap between dependency and world-system theories.

30 In addition, the work of anthropologists informed the development studies of influential economists such as W. A. Lewis (1955) and Theodore Schultz (1964).

31 It also addressed the role of pariah capitalist or business-oriented diasporas (overseas Chinese, Jews, Levantine Arabs, and others) in linking many world regions to wider economic circuits. See also Curtin (1984).

32 Hayek had suggested, for example, that the election of the Labour Party would lead Britain down the road to totalitarianism (Polanyi Levitt 2000:4).

33 This sentence is a close paraphrase of Lewellen [2002: 44, quoting a table originally published in *Anthropology News*, titled "What's Hot, What's Not in Anthropology" (1999)]. As the table notes, the roster of dismissed and discredited theories includes "diffusionism, cultural evolutionism and neo-evolutionism (routinely, several times), group personality studies, and structural functionalism."

34 One reviewer suggested that these are less often seen as failings of political economy than of cultural evolutionism, cultural materialism, and Comtean positivism.

35 For example, see DiLeonardo (1998, 1991) and Gal (1989), as well as chapters by Friedman and Miller in this volume and discussion below of the latter two authors.

36 Similarly, geographer Michael Watts (1992:15) observes that "much anthropological work rooted in ethnographic and cultural relations tends to be as weak in situating local knowledge and meanings on the grand map of capitalism as geographers have been in struggles over meaning." Thus in theorizing global and local, the disciplines of anthropology and geography favor one another's silences, with anthropology focused on the "cultural and symbolic topography," "locally shared knowledges and practices," meanings, and subjectivity—precisely those areas geographer Watts finds "lacking in what passes for postmodern geography and contemporary social theory."

37 "Development studies' love affair with political economy and neoliberal economics is beginning to wane," the editors of a recent anthology on development approvingly declare. "Culture is coming back into the agenda, displaced by the centrality of the market over the last twenty years" (Haggis and Schech 2002: xiii). Such assertions probably reflect the institutional marginality of anthropology and cultural studies within the world of interdisciplinary development thought more than any profound shift away from political economy by mainstream or radical theorists.

38 See also Polier and Roseberry (1989) on the need to move beyond fragmentation and to explore historical and structural connections among social groups, institutions, states, ethnographic sites, and so on.

39 See also Escobar's (1995: chapter 3) "cultural critique of economics."

40 See also Sivaramakrishnan and Agrawal (2003) on the relationship between development and modernity, and on the concept of "regional modernities." These two scholars point to an "urgent need for the ethnographic, micro-historical, micropolitical turn in the study of development and regional modernities" (2003:47).

41 Held and McGrew (2003:1) date the use of the term to the "1960s and early 1970s."

42 See, for example, Sivaramakrishnan and Agrawal's (2003:37–42) discussion of the inattentiveness of much globalization analysis to the nation-state. They note that the nation-state is often seen as "besieged . . . by transnational flows of people, ideas and capital, and subnational challenges to its authority."

43 This naturalization, as Rosenberg (2000: 14) points out in *The Follies of Globalization Theory*, occurs in large part as a result of scholars being "cut off from the rich explanatory schemas of classical social theory"—especially the analysis of social classes.

44 Their analysis focuses on the "national variant of the regional . . . to show its suppleness," while recognizing that region of course "can refer to both subnational and supranational social and political formations" (Sivaramakrishnan and Agrawal 2003:7).

45   Market liberalization in agricultural commodities, for example, has been remarkably uneven, given the continuing high levels of trade-distorting subsidies provided to farmers in the United States, the European Union, and Japan. The WTO Agreement on Agriculture, for example, obliges poorer nations to open their borders to world trade, but African cotton farmers or Mexican maize farmers, for instance, cannot compete against heavily subsidized US cotton or maize production or survive the market gluts that such production generates.

46   See also Perry's (2000) analysis of why neoliberal policies and the emergence of rural weekly markets among Wolof small farmers in Senegal have fostered new forms of local reciprocity and strengthened old ones in ways that augment small farmers' economic security and enhance community life (contrary to assumptions that markets are an inevitable force of social dissolution). See Chalfin (2000) on how economic uncertainty under structural adjustment policies can be a key strategic resource for female traders in Ghana as they constitute markets, livelihoods and economic coalitions.

47   On the issue of whether free trade is associated with growing economic prosperity, for example, see Rodrik (2003) vs. T. N. Srinivasan and Bhagwati (http://www.columbia.edu/~jb38). Proposals for fairer and more democratic forms of globalization are offered by the World Commission on the Social Dimensions of Globalization (ILO 2004).

48   For background, see Fisher's (1997) anthropological review of the "politics and anti-politics" of NGO practices.

49   Important anthropological works include Durham (1982) on population pressure versus inequality, Harris and Ross (1987) and Ross (1998) on demand-for-labor approaches to understanding demographic change, and Greenhalgh (1995) on political, economic, and cultural influences on fertility behavior.

50   Population issues also are central to debates about genetically modified crops. The industry lobby for genetically modified crops plays the Malthus card as it warns about "current and future food shortages and the need for crop genetic modification to avert famine," while "critics of genetic modification stress that hunger in developing countries results from poverty rather than food shortage" and that genetic modification will worsen the "poverty behind hunger" (Stone 2002: 614, 616). Both sides, Stone argues, treat genetic modification as a monolithic entity—for example, obscuring differences between corporate and public-sector biotechnology.

51   Cf. Ong's (1999) critique of such assumptions.

52   Veblen saw economics as lacking cultural content and as "helplessly behind the times" compared with anthropology. As Gudeman (1992:283) points out, Veblen's critical view of US society "was often founded on the use of ethnography from other societies."

53   See, for example, Ortner (1999); Dirks et al. (1994); Gupta and Ferguson (1997); Appadurai (1996). On the integration of culture into development studies, see Schech and Haggis (2000).

54   Cernea (1995:350, n. 4) notes that while cultural analysis per se is an anthropological strength, what is objectionable is for development institutions to limit anthropologists to a cultural brokerage role focused only on the "minor aspects of language intermediation or other mechanics of 'development tourism' . . . while their competence on essential issues of social organization, stratification, ethnicity, and local institutions is not treated as indispensable to the job at hand."

55   See http://www.cultureandpublicaction.org for conference videos and proceedings, paper abstracts, commentaries, background materials, and additional web resources on this topic; see also UNESCO's Issues on Culture and Development pages (http://unesco.org/culture/development/), accessed March 21, 2004.

56   See Shipton (2003) on the origins and distribution of the idea of human rights in western European intellectual traditions, attempts to apply such ideas in Africa, and various African understandings of rights and duties. See the volume edited by Lund (1999) on development and rights.

57   Beyond the scope of this essay is an exciting array of recent works on media consumption, building in part on Appadurai's (1996) notion of ideoscapes. See, for example, two edited collections on the new field of anthropology and media: Ginsburg et al. (2002); and Askew and Wilk (2002).

58   See Schein (1999) for an analysis comparing early 20th-century cargo cults in the Pacific islands and consumerism in post-socialist China—as "two comparable moments of transnational commodity desire."

59   Carrier and Heyman (1997: 355) argue that "the anthropological literature on consumption is commonly synchronic and psycho-cultural, that it tends to see cultural variations within society as uni-dimensional, and that it tends to ignore or simplify inequalities and conflict." They urge more direct attention to "the ways that the structured meanings of objects shape, and are shaped by, the practical uses to which they are put and the social, political and economic processes in which they exist" (1997:370).

60   The term "impostor" in this context should not suggest that there are correct and incorrect uses of commodities, but rather that an anthropology of consumption includes attention to how people in different ethnographic contexts put commodities to varying uses, and what meanings they attach to those uses.

61   Environmental anthropology and cross-disciplinary specialties such as "political ecology" are vibrant growth areas (see Brosius 1999; Watts 2000). Political ecology also has its critics, such as Vayda and Walters 1999.

62   Daly (2001:270) writes that "It would be better to economize on throughput because of the high external costs of its associated depletion and pollution, and at the same time to use more labor because of the high social benefits associated with reducing unemployment.... As a bumper sticker slogan the idea is 'tax bads, not goods.'"

63   The summer 2003 issue of *Human Organization* included a symposium on sustainability and development anthropology, with an introductory overview by M. Priscilla Stone (2003). See Rich (1998) on the World Bank and environmentalism.

64   CorpWatch defines greenwash as "disinformation disseminated by an organization so as to present an environmentally responsible public image"; its website quotes Lewis Carroll: "But I was thinking of a plan to dye one's whiskers green." See www.corpwatch.org/campaigns/PCC.jsp?topicid=102 (accessed March 2003).

65   Several of the insurgencies that Wolf (1969) classified as "peasant wars" were not entirely or even largely made up of peasants (e.g., Cuba, Russia, and Algeria). However, the strong rural support for the Vietnamese communists and the recognition that in most poor countries peasants constituted the majority of the population were sufficient to trigger powerful Western anxieties.

66   Specialists on diverse world regions participated in this re-examination of the differentiation debate (see Bernstein and Byres 2001: 13–14; Deere 1995; Shanin 1972: 45–62).

67   Moore's approach generated great resonance, including in areas of the world he had not considered (see Huber and Safford 1995).

68   This raised a storm of controversy (see Aston and Philpin 1985).

69   William Roseberry was among the most astute anthropological analysts of this process (see Roseberry 1989, 1995). Outside of anthropology, economic historian Sara Berry's (1984, 1985, 1993) innovative analyses of agrarian "crisis," change, and property rights in Africa stimulated rethinking of these issues in several disciplines.

70   See A.F. Robertson (1984) on the misleading notion of "sectors" in development planning and problems with the practice of excising sectors such as agriculture for cross-country comparisons.

71   See also Sivaramakrishnan and Agrawal's (2003:43–45) discussion of the relationship between development and the fashioning of the self, or that between transformation of the self and of the nation.

72   This distinction goes back at least to the 1980s and is reflected in the title of volumes such as Brokensha and Little (1988).

73   For a historical review (from the late 1800s to the present) of the related category "applied anthropology" (a label many find misleading) see Nolan (2002: chapter 3), as well as Chambers (1987) and Gardner and Lewis (1996). For a history of anthropologists' roles in US development institutions between the mid-1940s and the early 1980s, see Hoben (1982). Other helpful works on the history of anthropological involvement in development include Bennett and Bowen (1988), de L'Estoile (1997), Green (1986), Grillo and Rew (1985), Hewitt de Alcántara (1984), Horowitz (1994), and Nolan (2002), among others. Nolan (2002) includes brief

descriptions of development projects and anthropologists' roles in them. For exploration of how "institutional practices such as the project cycle contribute to organizing the world, including the world of 'beneficiaries' (peasants, for example)," see Escobar (1991:667; 1995).

74 Escobar also suggests that "[d]evelopment anthropology and the anthropology of development show each other their own flaws and limitations; it could be said that they mock each other" (Escobar 1997:505).

75 On the relationship between development theory and anthropological practice, see also Little (2000); Little and Painter (1995), and Long and Long (1992), among others.

76 For descriptions of these four types of development agencies, see Nolan (2002:36–44). For an overview of anthropology and NGOs, see Fisher (1997). On USAID, see Hoben (1980 and 1982) and Tendler (1975). On the World Bank, see Finnemore (1997), Fox and Brown (1998), George and Sabelli (1994), Rich (1994), and Payer (1982).

77 AID's predecessor, the International Cooperation Administration (ICA) "was once the nation's largest employer of anthropologists" (Hoben 1982:354).

78 See Gow's (2002:304–305) discussion of contrasting views on the actual effects of anthropological social soundness analyses in AID and World Bank project design.

79 See Hoben (1980 and 1982:363–366) for examples of the substantive contributions of anthropologists to development work in various agencies and locations; see also Chambers (1987), Colson (1985), and Mair (1984), among others.

80 See Gow's (2002) analysis of development as anthropology's moral twin rather than its evil twin. He states that development anthropologists' "ethical concerns are not just an expression of self-righteous high-mindedness, but are rather an inheritance from the discipline's roots in the Enlightenment on the one hand and the continuing passage of 'enlightened' legislation by the United Nations and some of its specialized agencies on the other" (Gow 2002:300).

81 This paragraph draws on Maia Green's, Peter D. Little's, and K. Sivaramakrishnan's insights about the differences between development studies in the United States and United Kingdom, and between the United States and Scandinavia.

82 For example, the Institute of Development Studies at the University of Sussex; the Institute for Development Policy and Management at the University of Manchester; the Department of Development Studies at the School of Oriental and African Studies; Queen Elizabeth House at the University of Oxford; Development Studies Institute at the London School of Economics; and School of Development Studies at the University of East Anglia.

83 An exception is the Collaborative Research Support Program (CRSP) grants, which are mostly for agricultural research at US land grant universities.

84 See Brokensha (1986), Horowitz (1994), and Scudder (1988).

85 See also Sivaramakrishnan and Agrawal (2003), Derman and Ferguson (2000), Crewe and Harrison (1998), Pigg (1997), and Cooper and Packard (chapter 6 in this volume).

86 Quoted in "A Professor Who Refuses to Pull His Punches," *New York Times*, November 8, 2003, pp. B9, 11.

87 For example, see Bourgois (1990), Price (1998), and Scheper-Hughes (1995), among others. See also codes of ethics formulated by the American Anthropological Association (AAA) and Society for Applied Anthropology, and case studies of ethical dilemmas posted on the AAA website (www.aaanet.org). See Bennett's (1996) discussion of ethical issues in development anthropology.

88 On the latter issue, see Dove's (1999) analysis of issues of reflexivity, engagement, and the "need to counter rather than critique monolithic representations." Dove points to a crisis not of ethnographic representation but of ethnographic mis-representation, especially by states or political and economic elites whose misleading narratives he urges anthropologists to counter in ways that are not "self-critical, hesitant, and thus weaker than the representation that it opposes" (1999: 235). See Colson's (1985) Malinoswki Award lecture, which discusses the challenges anthropologists face in persuading officials to listen to information they may not find palatable.

89 See also Gow's (2002) critical analysis of ethical issues confronting development anthropologists, as well as Grillo and Rew (1985).

90 See Gow's (2002:303–304) discussion of examples where recommendations that "fly in the face of powerful political interests," offered by senior anthropologists such as William Partridge and Michael Horowitz, were accepted and where such advice was rejected by development agencies.

91 See Harriss (2001) for a critique of the World Bank's use of the idea of social capital.

92 A particularly vocal force (joined by some anthropologists) has been the environmental lobby, which now addresses sociocultural as well as resource issues. On the limitations and accomplishments of World Bank environmental reforms, see Rich (1998).

93 For an ethnographic case study of this issue in southern Africa, see Peters (1994). Other critical reassessments include McCay and Acheson (1987) and McCay (1998). As Little (2000: 124) notes, a 1979 report by Michael Horowitz (drawing on his long-term research on West African pastoralism), which appeared in a USAID publication series, was an "influential early publication that contributed to the common property debate" and challenged Hardin's notion of a tragedy of the commons.

94 Anthropologists often can increase their effectiveness in development institutions by acquiring technical and scientific expertise to complement their disciplinary training. Thus it is beneficial for an anthropologist working on pastoral development to learn about rangeland ecology and livestock management, for those working on agricultural projects to learn some crop science and agricultural economics, for those working on health issues to learn some epidemiology, and for those working on urban informal economies to learn some development economics. Economics is particularly important to all development anthropologists, as Cernea (1995:347) observes: "When anthropologists bypass economic variables . . . the resulting recommendations are embarrassingly naïve or directly erroneous." Expertise in statistics is also helpful.

95 See also Cooke and Kothari (2001), Green (2000), and our discussion elsewhere in this chapter of the critique of participatory development.

96 For a critical view of the science and politics of agricultural initiatives and knowledge production sponsored by the Rockefeller Foundation in less-developed nations such as Mexico, see Hewitt de Alcántara (1976) and Jennings (1988).

97 As Stone (2004:618) notes, growing corporate funding of public biotechnology research in networks such as the Future Harvest Centers means that "research agendas are in the balance," and here the impressive corpus of anthropological knowledge about complex agricultural systems could prove very valuable.

98 See the Participatory Research and Gender Analysis (PRGA) program co-sponsored by the Consultative Group on International Agricultural Research (CGIAR) and the International Development Research Center (IDRC) [CGIAR and IDRC 2004]; and Sperling and Loevinsohn (1997).

99 Ethnographies of development, loosely defined, include Benjamin (2000), Crewe and Harrison (1998), Ferguson (1990), and Tendler (1975), among others. Benjamin (2000) explores an Irish NGO's development interventions in agriculture, forestry, water supply, and family planning in Malangali, Tanzania, analyzing how a succession of development fads and fashions manufactured mostly in Europe and North America are "consumed" (understood and used) by the poor as well as by development planners, donors, and theorists. Sally Falk Moore (2001) offers a witty account of her experiences as a development consultant in West Africa.

100 Griffiths (2003:viii) goes on to write that "Like most of my colleagues, I try to do my best within the limits of what can be achieved. I suspect, though, that often I have acted within the limits of what is good for my career. Unless the aid industry tackles this problem, it will achieve as little in the future as it has in the past."

101 See also Green (2000) and the volume on participation and development knowledge edited by Pauline Peters (2000).

102 Ferguson (1999) later suggested a different approach to this issue, as discussed below.

103 See Haugerud (2003) on contradictory constructions of the local: as a residual category overtaken by development, as a haven of resistance against globalization, or as a historical or cultural construct; these notions of the local essentialize it, romanticize it, or erase it.

104   See Agrawal (1995) on limitations of the concept of indigenous knowledge.
105   See also Cooper and Packard (1997:36, n38).
106   For example, see Sinha (2003).
107   Cf. Chase 2002: 12, and note 20 above.
108   Escobar (1997:503) later wrote that "Even if its roots extend back to the development of capitalism and modernity—development has been shown to be part of an origin myth at the heart of occidental modernity—the late 1940s and 1950s brought with them a globalization of development and an explosion of institutions, organizations, and forms of knowledge all concerned with development."
109   On the historical contingency of the category "applied," see also Ferguson's discussion in chapter 7 of this volume of how "development" shifted from a theoretical to an applied topic in anthropology during the past century.
110   Three stimulating recent approaches to such questions include Graeber (2001), Di Leonardo (1998), and Trouillot (2003).
111   See Graeber (2001: xi).
112   See Chase (2002:6, 12).

REFERENCES CITED

Agrawal, Arun, 1995 Dismantling the Divide Between Indigenous and Scientific Knowledge. Development and Change 26: 413–439.

—— 1996 Poststructuralist approaches to development: Some critical reflections. Peace and Change 21(4): 464–477.

Alexander, Jennifer, and Paul Alexander, 1991 What's in a Fair Price? Price-setting and Trading Partnerships in Javanese Markets. Man 26(3): 493–512.

Althusser, Louis, and Etienne Balibar, 1970 Reading Capital. London: NLB.

Amin, Samir, 2001 Capitalismo, imperialismo, mundialización. In Resistencias mundiales: De Seattle a Porto Alegre, José Seoane and Emilio Taddei, eds., pp. 15–29. Buenos Aires: CLACSO.

Anderson, Lisa, 2003 The Global Reach of American Social Science. Chronicle of Higher Education, September 26, 2003: B7–B9.

Appadurai, Arjun, 1996 Modernity at Large: Cultural Dimensions of Globalization. Minneapolis: University of Minnesota Press.

—— 2000 Grassroots Globalization and the Research Imagination. Public Culture 12 (1): 1–19.

Appadurai, Arjun, ed., 1986 The Social Life of Things: Commodities in Cultural Perspective. Cambridge: Cambridge University Press.

Arndt, H.W.,1987 Economic Development: The History of an Idea. Chicago: University of Chicago Press.

Asad, Talal, ed., 1973 Anthropology and the Colonial Encounter. New York: Humanities Press.

Askew, Kelly, and Richard Wilk, 2002 The Anthropology of Media: A Reader. Malden, MA: Blackwell Publishers.

Aston, T.H., and C.H.E. Philpin, eds., 1985 The Brenner Debate: Agrarian Class Structure and Economic Development in Pre-industrial Europe. Cambridge: Cambridge University Press.

Babb, Florence, 1985 Women and Men in Vicos, Peru: A Case Of Unequal Development. In Peruvian Contexts of Change, William Stein, ed., pp. 163–209. New Brunswick: Transaction Books.

Baran, Paul A., and Paul M. Sweezy, 1966 Monopoly Capital: An Essay on the American Economic and Social Order. New York: Monthly Review Press.

Barkin, David, 2001 Neoliberalism and Sustainable Popular Development. In Transcending Neoliberalism: Community-Based Development in Latin America, Henry Veltmeyer and Anthony O'Malley, eds., pp. 184–204. Bloomfield, CT: Kumarian Press.

Barratt Brown, Michael, 1972 A Critique of Marxist Theories of Imperialism. In Studies in the Theory of Imperialism, Roger Owen and Bob Sutcliffe, eds., pp. 35–70. London: Longman.

Bebbington, Anthony, Scott Guggenheim, Elizabeth Olson, and Michael Woolcock, forthcoming, Exploring Social Capital Debates at the World Bank. Journal of Development Studies.

Beck, Ulrich, 2003 The Analysis of Global Inequality: From National to Cosmopolitan Perspective. *In* Global Civil Society 2003, Mary Kaldor, Helmut Anheier, and Marlies Glasius, eds., pp. 45–55. Oxford: Oxford University Press.

Benjamin, Martin, 2000 Development Consumers: An Ethnography of the "Poorest of the Poor" and International Aid in Rural Tanzania. Ph.D. Dissertation, Yale University.

Bennett, John, 1996 Applied and Action Anthropology: Ideological and Conceptual Aspects. Current Anthropology, Supplement, February: S23–S53.

Bennett, John, and John Bowen, eds., 1988 Production and Autonomy: Anthropological Studies and Critiques of Development. Lanham, MD: University Press of America/Society for Economic Anthropology.

Bernstein, Henry, and Terence J. Byres, 2001 From Peasant Studies to Agrarian Change. Journal of Agrarian Change 1(1): 1–56.

Berry, Sara, 1984 The Food Crisis and Agrarian Change in Africa. African Studies Review 27(2): 59–112.

—— 1985 Fathers Work for Their Sons. Berkeley: University of California Press.

—— 1993 No Condition is Permanent: The Social Dynamics of Agrarian Change in Sub-Saharan Africa. Madison: University of Wisconsin Press.

Bhagwati, Jagdish, 2001 Why Globalization is Good. Items and Issues 2 (3–4): 7–8. New York: Social Science Research Council.

—— 2004 In Defense of Globalization. Oxford University Press.

Bleaney, Michael, 1976 Underconsumption Theories: A History and Critical Analysis. New York: International Publishers.

Boserup, Esther, 1970 Women's Role in Economic Development. New York: St. Martin's Press.

Bourdieu, Pierre, 2001 Uniting Better to Dominate. Items & Issues (Social Science Research Council) 2 (3–4): 1–6.

Bourgois, Philippe, 1990 Confronting Anthropological Ethics: Ethnographic Lessons from Central America. Journal of Peace Research 27(1): 43–45.

Braudel, Fernand, 1972 The Mediterranean and the Mediterranean World in the Age of Philip ll, 2 vols. New York: Harper & Row.

Brenner, Robert, 1976 Agrarian Class Structure and Economic Development in Pre-Industrial Europe. Past and Present 70: 30–75.

—— 1977 The Origins of Capitalist Development: a Critique of Neo-Smithian Marxism. New Left Review 104: 25–92.

Brokensha, David W., 1986 IDA, the First Ten Years (1976–1986). Development Anthropology Network 4 (2): 1–4.

Brokensha, David, and Peter D. Little, eds., 1988 Anthropology of Development and Change in East Africa. Boulder and London: Westview Press.

Brosius, J. Peter, 1999 Analyses and Interventions: Anthropological Engagements with Environmentalism. Current Anthropology 40(3): 277–310.

Bulmer-Thomas, Victor, 1994 The Economic History of Latin America since Independence. Cambridge: Cambridge University Press.

Burawoy, Michael, ed., 2000 Global Ethnography: Forces, Connections and Imaginations in a Postmodern World. Berkeley: University of California Press.

Cardoso, Fernando Henrique, and Enzo Faletto, 1969 Dependencia y desarrollo en América Latina: ensayo de interpretación sociológica. Mexico: Siglo Veintiuno Editores.

Carney, Judith, and Michael Watts, 1991 Disciplining Women? Rice, Mechanization, and the Evolution of Mandinka Gender Relations in Senegambia. Signs 16(4): 651–81.

Carrier, James, 1994 Alienating Objects: The Emergence of Alienation in Retail Trade. Man 29(2): 359–380.

—— 1995 Gifts and Commodities: Exchange and Western Capitalism since 1700. London and New York: Routledge.

Carrier, James, and Josiah McC. Heyman, 1997 Consumption and Political Economy. Journal of the Royal Anthropological Institute 3: 355–373.

Carrier, James, and Daniel Miller, eds., 1998 Virtualism: A New Political Economy. Oxford and New York: Berg.

Castells, Manuel, 2000 End of Millenium, second edition. Volume III of The Information Age: Economy, Society and Culture. Oxford: Blackwell.

Cavanagh, John, Daphne Wysham, and Marcos Aruda, eds., 2002 Alternatives to Economic Globalization: A Better World is Possible. San Francisco: Berrett-Koehler Publishers.

Cernea, Michael, 1995 Malinowski Award Lecture: Social Organization and Development in Anthropology. Human Organization 54(3): 340–352.

Cernea, Michael M., and Scott E. Guggenheim, eds., 1993 Anthropological Approaches to Involuntary Resettlement: Policy, Practice, and Theory. Boulder: Westview Press.

CGIAR and IDRC [Consultative Group on International Agricultural Research and International Development Research Center], 2004 Participatory Research and Gender Analysis Program. <http://www.idrc.ca/seeds> (accessed March 17, 2004)

Chalfin, Brenda, 2000 Risky Business: Economic Uncertainty, Market Reforms and Female Livelihoods in Northeast Ghana. Development and Change 31: 987–1008.

Chambers, Erve, 1987 Applied Anthropology in the Post-Vietnam Era: Anticipations and Ironies. Annual Review of Anthropology 16: 309–337.

Chant, Sylvia, and Matthew C. Gutmann, 2001 Mainstreaming Men into Gender and Development: Debates, Reflections, and Experiences. London: Oxfam Working Papers.

Chapin, Mac, and Bill Threlkeld, 2001 Indigenous Landscapes: A Study in Ethnocartography. Arlington, VA: Center for the Support of Native Lands.

Chase, Jacquelyn, 2002 Introduction: The Spaces of Neoliberalism in Latin America. In The Spaces of Neoliberalism: Land, Place and Family in Latin America, Jacquelyn Chase, ed., pp. 1–21. Bloomfield, CT: Kumarian Press.

Chayanov, A.V., 1986 [1925] The Theory of Peasant Economy. Madison: University of Wisconsin Press.

Chibnik, Michael, 2003 Crafting Tradition: The Making and Marketing of Oaxacan Wood Carvings. Austin, TX: University of Texas Press.

Clark Dana, Jonathan Fox, and Kay Treakle, eds., 2003 Demanding Accountability: Civil Society Claims and the World Bank Inspection Panel. Lanham, MD: Rowman & Littlefield.

Cohen, Benjamin J., 1973 The Question of Imperialism: The Political Economy of Dominance and Dependence. New York: Basic Books.

Cohen, Ronald, 1986 Comment on "Smallholder Settlement of Tropical South America: The Social Causes of Ecological Disaster." Human Organization 45: 359–60.

Cohen, Stephen F., 1980 Bukharin and the Bolshevik Revolution. Oxford: Oxford University Press.

Collins, Jane, 2000 Tracing Social Relations in Commodity Chains: The Case of Grapes in Brazil. In Commodities and Globalization: Anthropological Perspectives, Angelique Haugerud, M. Priscilla Stone, and Peter D. Little, eds., pp. 97–109. Lanham, MD: Rowman & Littlefield.

—— 1986 Reply to Cohen. Human Organization 45: 360–62.

Colson, Elizabeth, 1985 Using Anthropology in a World on the Move. Human Organization 44(3):191–196.

Cooke, Bill, and Uma Kothari, eds., 2001 Participation: The New Tyranny? London and New York: Zed Books.

Cooper, Frederick, 2001 What Is the Concept of Globalization Good For? An African Historian's Perspective. African Affairs 100: 189–213.

Cooper, Frederick, and Randall Packard, 1997 Introduction. In International Development and the Social Sciences: Essays on the History and Politics of Knowledge, Frederick Cooper and Randall Packard, eds., pp. 1–41. Berkeley: University of California Press.

Cowen, M.P., and R.W. Shenton, 1996 Doctrines of Development. London: Routledge.

Crewe, Emma, and Elizabeth Harrison, 1998 Whose Development? An Ethnography of Aid. London and New York: Zed Books.

Crush, Jonathan, 1995 Introduction: Imagining Development. In Power of Development, Jonathan Crush, ed., pp. 1–23. London: Routledge.

Curtin, Philip D., 1984 Cross-Cultural Trade in World History. Cambridge: Cambridge University Press.

Daly, Herman, 2001 Policies for Sustainable Development. *In* Agrarian Studies: Synthetic Work at the Cutting Edge, James C. Scott and Nina Bhatt, eds., pp. 264–282. New Haven: Yale University Press.

Davis, Shelton H., 1999 Bringing Culture into the Development Paradigm: The View from the World Bank, Development Anthropologist 16(1–2): 25–31.

Deere, Carmen Diana, 1995 What Difference Does Gender Make? Rethinking Peasant Studies, Feminist Economics 1(1): 53–72.

de L'Estoile, Benoît, 1997 The "Natural Preserve of Anthropologists": Social Anthropology, Scientific Planning and Development. Social Science Information 36(2): 343–376.

DeMartino, George, 2000 Global Economy, Global Justice: Theoretical Objections and Policy Alternatives to Neoliberalism. New York: Routledge.

De Rivero, Oswaldo, 2001 The Myth of Development: Non-Viable Economies of the 21st Century. London and New York: Zed Books.

Derman, Bill, and Anne Ferguson, 2000 Writing Against Hegemony: Development Encounters in Zimbabwe and Malawi. *In* Development Encounters: Sites of Participation and Knowledge, Pauline E. Peters, ed., pp. 121–155. Cambridge, MA: Harvard University Press.

di Leonardo, Micaela, 1998 Exotics at Home: Anthropologies, Others, American Modernity. Chicago: University of Chicago Press.

—— 1991 Introduction: Gender, Culture, and Political Economy: Feminist Anthropology in Historical Perspective. *In* Gender at the Crossroads of Knowledge: Feminist Anthropology in the Postmodern Era, Micaela di Leonardo, ed., pp. 1–48. Berkeley: University of California Press.

Dirks, Nicholas B., Geoff Eley, and Sherry B. Ortner, eds., 1994 Culture/Power/History: A Reader in Contemporary Social Theory. Princeton: Princeton University Press.

Doughty, Paul L., 1987 Against the Odds: Collaboration and Development at Vicos. *In* Collaborative Research and Social Change, D.D. Stull and J.J. Schensul, eds, pp. 129–157. Boulder: Westview.

Douglas, Mary, and Baron Isherwood, 1996 [1979] The World of Goods: Towards an Anthropology of Consumption. London and New York: Routledge.

Dove, Michael, 1999 Writing for, Versus about, the Ethnographic Other: Issues of Engagement and Reflexivity in Working with a Tribal NGO in Indonesia. Identities 6(2–3): 225–253.

Durham, William H., 1982 Scarcity and Survival in Central America: Ecological Origins of the Soccer War. Stanford: Stanford University Press.

Dvorak, Karen Ann, ed., 1993 Social Science Research for Technology Development: Spatial and Temporal Dimensions. Oxford: CAB International on behalf of the International Institute of Tropical Agriculture with the support of the Rockefeller Foundation.

Economist, 2004 Special Report on Global Economic Inequality. The Economist, March 13, 2004: 69–71.

Edelman, Marc, 1999 Peasants Against Globalization: Rural Social Movements in Costa Rica. Stanford: Stanford University Press.

—— 2001 Social Movements: Changing Paradigms and Forms of Politics. Annual Review of Anthropology 30: 285–317.

—— Forthcoming. When Networks Don't Work: The Rise and Fall and Rise of Civil Society Initiatives in Central America. *In* Social Movements: A Reader, June Nash, ed. London: Blackwell.

Erlich, Paul R., 1968 The Population Bomb. New York: Ballantine Books.

Escobar, Arturo, 1991 Anthropology and the Development Encounter: The Making and Marketing of Development Anthropology. American Ethnologist 18(4): 658–682.

—— 1995 Encountering Development: The Making and Unmaking of the Third World. Princeton: Princeton University Press.

—— 1997 Anthropology and Development. International Social Science Journal 154: 497–515.

Esteva, Gustavo, 1988 El desastre agrícola: adiós al México imaginario. Comercio Exterior 38 (8) (Aug.): 662–72.

—— 1992 Development. *In* The Development Dictionary: A Guide to Knowledge as Power, Wolfgang Sachs, ed., pp. 6–25. London and New York: Zed Books.

FAO (Food and Agriculture Organisation of the United Nations), 2003 The State of Food Insecurity in the World 2003. Rome: Food and Agriculture Organisation.

Farmer, Paul, 2003 Pathologies of Power: Health, Human Rights, and the New War on the Poor. Berkeley: University of California Press.

Faux, Jeff, 2004 Without Consent: Global Capital Mobility and Democracy. Dissent 51(1) (Winter): 43–50.

Ferguson, James, 1990 The Anti-Politics Machine: Development, Depoliticization, and Bureaucratic Power in Lesotho. Cambridge University Press.

—— 1992 The Country and the City on the Copperbelt. Cultural Anthropology 7(1): 80–92.

—— 1997 Anthropology and Its Evil Twin: "Development" in the Constitution of a Discipline. *In* International Development and the Social Sciences: Essays on the History and Politics of Knowledge, Frederick Cooper and Randall Packard, eds., pp. 150–175. Berkeley: University of California Press.

—— 1999 Expectations of Modernity: Myths and Meanings of Urban Life on the Zambian Copperbelt. Berkeley: University of California Press.

Finnemore, Martha, 1997 Redefining Development at the World Bank. *In* International Development and the Social Sciences: Essays on the History and Politics of Knowledge, Frederick Cooper and Randall Packard, eds., pp. 203–227. Berkeley: University of California Press.

Firth, Raymond, 1981 Engagement and Detachment: Reflections on Applying Social Anthropology to Social Affairs. Human Organization 40(3): 193–201.

Fisher, William, 1997 Doing Good? The Politics and Antipolitics of NGO Practices. Annual Review of Anthropology 26: 439–464.

—— 1996 Review of Arturo Escobar's Encountering Development. American Ethnologist 23(1): 137–139.

Fox, Jonathan A., and L. David Brown, eds., 1998 The Struggle for Accountability: The World Bank, NGOs, and Grassroots Movements. Cambridge, MA: MIT Press.

Frank, Andre Gunder, 1969 Latin America: Underdevelopment or Revolution. Essays on the Development of Underdevelopment and the Immediate Enemy. New York: Monthly Review Press.

—— 1991 The Underdevelopment of Development, Scandinavian Journal of Development Alternatives 10 (3) (Sept.): 5–72.

Gal, Susan, 1989 Language and Political Economy. Annual Review of Anthropology 18: 345–367.

Galeano, Eduardo, 2001 Upside Down: A Primer for the Looking-Glass World. New York: Picador.

Garber, Peter M., 1993 The Collapse of the Bretton Woods Fixed Exchange Rate System. *In* A Retrospective on the Bretton Woods System: Lessons for International Monetary Reform, Michael D. Bordo and Barry Eichengreen, eds., pp. 461–494. Chicago: University of Chicago Press.

García Canclini, Néstor, 1990 Culturas híbridas: estrategias para entrar y salir de la modernidad. Mexico City: Grijalbo.

—— 1999 La globalización imaginada. Buenos Aires: Paidós.

Gardner, Gary, Erik Assadourian, and Radhika Sarin, 2004 The State of Consumption Today. *In* State of the World 2004, Linda Starke, ed., pp. 3–21. Washington, DC: Worldwatch Institute.

Gardner, Katy, and David Lewis, 1996 Anthropology, Development and the Post-Modern Challenge. London: Pluto Press.

Garrett, Geoffrey, 2003 Global Markets and National Politics. *In* The Global Transformations Reader, second edition, David Held and Anthony McGrew, eds., pp. 384–402. Cambridge: Polity.

Geertz, Clifford, 1956 Religious Belief and Economic Behavior in a Central Javanese Town: Some Preliminary Considerations, Economic Development and Cultural Change 4: 134–58.

—— 1962 Social Change and Economic Modernization in Two Indonesian towns: A Case in Point. *In* On the Theory of Social Change: How Economic Growth Begins, Everett E. Haven, ed., pp. 385–407. Homewood, IL: Dorsey Press.

—— 1963 Peddlers and Princes: Social Development and Economic Change in Two Indonesian Towns. Chicago: University of Chicago Press.

—— 1963 Agricultural Involution: The Process of Ecological Change in Indonesia. Berkeley: University of California Press.

George, Susan, and Fabrizio Sabelli, 1994 Faith and Credit: The World Bank's Secular Empire. Boulder: Westview Press.

Giddens, Anthony, 1973 Capitalism and Modern Social Theory: An Analysis of the Writings of Marx, Durkheim and Max Weber. Cambridge: Cambridge University Press.

—— 1998 The Third Way: The Renewal of Social Democracy. London: Polity Press.

——, ed., 2001 The Global Third Way Debate. London: Polity Press.

Gill, Lesley, 2000 Teetering on the Rim: Global Restructuring, Daily Life, and the Armed Retreat of the Bolivian State. New York: Columbia University Press.

Ginsburg, Faye D., Lila Abu-Lughod, and Brian Larkin, 2002 Media Worlds: Anthropology on New Terrain. Berkeley: University of California Press.

Godelier, Maurice, 1972 Rationality and Irrationality in Economics. New York: Monthly Review Press.

Goldman, Michael, 2001 The Birth of a Discipline: Producing Authoritative Green Knowledge, World Bank-style. Ethnography 2(2) (June): 191–218.

Gow, David, 2002 Anthropology and Development: Evil Twin or Moral Narrative? Human Organization 61(4): 299–313.

Grabel, Ilene, and Ha-Joon Chang, 2004 Reclaiming Development: An Alternative Policy Manual. London: Zed Books.

Graeber, David, 2001 Toward an Anthropological Theory of Value: The False Coin of Our Own Dreams. New York: Palgrave.

—— 2002 The Anthropology of Globalization (with Notes on Neomedievalism, and the End of the Chinese Model of the State). American Anthropologist 104(4): 1222–1227.

—— 2004 Fragments of an Anarchist Anthropology. Chicago: Prickly Paradigm Press.

Green, Edward C., ed., 1986 Practicing Development Anthropology. Boulder: Westview Press.

Green, Maia, 2000 Participatory Development and the Appropriation of Agency in Southern Tanzania. Critique of Anthropology 20(1): 67–89.

Greenhalgh, Susan, ed., 1995 Situating Fertility: Anthropology and Demographic Inquiry. Cambridge: Cambridge University Press.

Gresser, Charis, and Sophia Tickell, 2002 Mugged: Poverty in Your Coffee Cup. Boston: Oxfam America.

Griffiths, Peter 2003 The Economist's Tale: A Consultant Encounters Hunger and the World Bank. New York: Zed Books.

Grillo, Ralph, and Alan Rew, eds., 1985 Social Anthropology and Development Policy. London: Tavistock Publications.

Grillo, R. D., and R. L. Stirrat, 1997 Discourses of Development: Anthropological Perspectives. New York: Oxford University Press.

Grimm, Curt D., 1999 Anthropology at the U.S. Agency for International Development: Are the Best Years Behind? Development Anthropologist 16 (1–2): 22–25.

Groenfeldt, David, and Joyce L. Moock, eds., 1989 Social Science Perspectives on Managing Agricultural Technology. New York: Rockefeller Foundation and International Irrigation Management Institute.

Gudeman, Stephen, 1992 Markets, Models and Morality: The Power of Practices. In Contesting Markets: Analyses of Ideology, Discourse and Practice, Roy Dilley, ed., pp. 279–294. Edinburgh: Edinburgh University Press.

Gupta, Akhil, 1998 Postcolonial Developments: Agriculture in the Making of Modern India. Durham, NC: Duke University Press.

Gupta, Akhil, and James Ferguson, eds., 1997 Culture, Power, Place: Explorations in Critical Anthropology. Durham, NC: Duke University Press.

Guyer, Jane 2004 Marginal Gains: Money Transactions in Atlantic Africa. Chicago: University of Chicago Press.

Haggis, Jane, and Susanne Schech, 2002 Introduction: Pathways to Culture and Development. In Development: A Cultural Studies Reader, Susanne Schech and Jane Haggis, eds., pp. xiii–xxiii. Oxford: Blackwell.

Hansen, Karen, 2000 Salaula: The World of Secondhand Clothing and Zambia. Chicago: University of Chicago Press.

Hardin, Garrett, 1968 The Tragedy of the Commons. Science 162: 1243–48.

Harper, Richard, 2000 The Social Organization of the IMF's Mission Work: An Examination of International Auditing. In Audit Cultures: Anthropological Studies in Accountability, Ethics, and the Academy, Marilyn Strathern, ed., pp. 21–53. London: Routledge

Harris, Marvin, 1968 The Rise of Anthropological Theory. New York: Crowell.

Harris, Marvin, and Eric B. Ross, 1987 Death, Sex and Fertility: Population Regulation in Preindustrial and Developing Societies. New York: Columbia University Press.

Harriss, John, 2001, Depoliticizing Development: The World Bank and Social Capital. London: Anthem Press.

Hart, Keith, 1992 Market and State after the Cold War: The Informal Economy Reconsidered. In Contesting Markets: Analyses of Ideology, Discourse and Practice, Roy Dilley, ed., pp. 214–227. Edinburgh: Edinburgh University Press.

Harvey, David, 1989 The Condition of Postmodernity: An Enquiry into the Origins of Cultural Change. Cambridge, MA: Blackwell

—— 2000 Spaces of Hope. Berkeley: University of California Press.

Haugerud, Angelique, 2003 The Disappearing Local: Rethinking Global-Local Connections. In Ali Mirsepassi, Amrita Basu, and Frederick Weaver, eds., Localizing Knowledge in a Globalizing World: Recasting the Area Studies Debates, pp. 60–81. Syracuse, NY: Syracuse University Press.

Haugerud, Angelique, and Michael P. Collinson, 1990 Plants, Genes and People: Improving the Relevance of Plant Breeding in Africa. Experimental Agriculture 26: 341–362.

Hawken, Paul, 1993 The Ecology of Commerce: A Declaration of Sustainability. New York: Harper Collins.

Hayek, Friedrich A. von, 1994 [1944] The Road to Serfdom. Chicago: University of Chicago Press.

Heilbroner, Robert L., 1972 The Worldly Philosophers: The Lives, Times and Ideas of the Great Economic Thinkers, fourth edition. New York: Simon & Schuster.

Held, David, and Anthony McGrew, 2003 The Great Globalization Debate: An Introduction. In The Global Transformations Reader, second edition, David Held and Anthony McGrew, eds., pp. 1–50. Cambridge: Polity Press.

Helleiner, Eric, 1994 From Bretton Woods to Global Finance: A World Turned Upside Down. In Political Economy and the Changing Global Order, Richard Stubbs and Geoffrey R.D. Underhill, eds., pp. 163–175. New York: St. Martin's Press.

Hewitt de Alcántara, Cynthia, 1976 Modernizing Mexican Agriculture: Socioeconomic Implications of Technological Change 1940–1970. Geneva: UN Research Institute for Social Development.

—— 1984 Anthropological Perspectives on Rural Mexico. London: Routledge & Kegan Paul.

Hill, Polly, 1986 Development Economics on Trial: The Anthropological Case for a Prosecution. Cambridge and New York: Cambridge University Press.

Hilton, Rodney, ed., 1976 The Transition from Feudalism to Capitalism. London: NLB.

Hines, Colin, 2000 Localization: A Global Manifesto. London: Earthscan

Hirschman, Albert O., 1991 The Rhetoric of Reaction: Perversity, Futility, Jeopardy. Cambridge: Belknap Press of Harvard University Press

Hirst, Paul, 2000 The Global Economy: Myths or Reality? In The Ends of Globalization: Bringing Society Back In, Don Kalb, Marco van der Land, Richard Staring, Bart van Steenbergen, and Nico Wilterdink, eds., pp. 107–123. Lanham, Maryland: Rowman & Littlefield.

Hirst, Paul, and Grahame Thompson, 1996 Globalization in Question. Cambridge: Polity Press.

Hobart, Mark, 1993 Introduction: The Growth of Ignorance? In An Anthropological Critique of Development: The Growth of Ignorance, Mark Hobart, ed., pp. 1–30. London: Routledge.

Hoben, Allen, 1980 Agricultural Decision-Making in Foreign Assistance: An Anthropological Analysis. In Agricultural Decision Making: Anthropological Contributions to Rural Development, edited by Peggy Barlett, pp. 337–369. New York: Academic Press.

—— 1982 Anthropologists and Development. Annual Review of Anthropology 11: 349–75.

—— 1994 Paradigms and Politics: The Cultural Construction of Environmental Policy in Ethiopia. World Development 23(6): 1007–1021.

Hobson, J.A., 1965 [1902] Imperialism: A Study. Ann Arbor: University of Michigan Press.

Hodgson, Dorothy, and Richard A. Schroeder, 2002 Dilemmas of Counter-Mapping Community Resources in Tanzania. Development and Change 33: 79–100.

Horowitz, Irving Louis, ed., 1974 The Rise and Fall of Project Camelot: Studies in the Relationship Between Social Science and Practical Politics. Cambridge, MA: MIT Press.

Horowitz, Michael, 1994 Development Anthropology in the Mid-1990s. Development Anthropology Network 12(1–2): 1–14.

Hoselitz, Bert, 1952 Non-Economic Barriers to Economic Development. Economic Development and Cultural Change 1(1): 8–21.

Huber, Evelyn, and Frank Safford, eds., 1995 Agrarian Structure and Political Power: Landlord and Peasant in the Making of Latin America. Pittsburgh: University of Pittsburgh Press.

IFAD [International Fund for Agricultural Development], 2001 Rural Poverty Report 2001: The Challenge of Ending Rural Poverty. Oxford: Oxford University Press.

ILO [International Labor Organization], 2004 World Commission on the Social Dimension of Globalization, final report. Geneva: ILO. Available at <http://www.ilo.org/public/english/wcsdg/index.htm> (accessed March 31, 2004).

Inda, Jonathan Xavier, and Renato Rosaldo, eds., 2002 The Anthropology of Globalization: A Reader. London: Blackwell Publishers.

Jennings, B.H., 1988 Foundations of International Agricultural Research: Science and Politics in Mexican Agriculture. Boulder: Westview Press.

Karp, Ivan, 1992 Development and Personhood. Chicago: Red Lion Seminar, Northwestern University Program on African and African-American Studies. 23 pp.

Kay, Cristóbal, 1991 Reflections on the Latin American Contribution to Development Theory. Development and Change 22: 31–68.

Kearney, Michael, 1995 The Local and the Global: The Anthropology of Globalization and Trans-nationalism. Annual Review of Anthropology 24: 547–565.

—— 1996 Reconceptualizing the Peasantry: Anthropology in Global Perspective. Boulder: Westview.

Klein, Naomi, 2002 No Logo. New York: Picador.

Knauft, Bruce, 2002 Critically Modern: An Introduction. In Critically Modern: Alternatives, Alterities, Anthropologies, Bruce Knauft, ed., pp. 1–54. Bloomington: Indiana University Press.

Koenig, Dolores, 2001 Toward Local Development and Mitigating Impoverishment in Development-Induced Displacement and Resettlement. Report to the Refugee Studies Center, University of Oxford.

Koenig, Dolores, and Tieman Diarra, 1998 The Environmental Effects of Policy Change in the West African Savanna: Resettlement, Structural Adjustment and Conservation in Western Mali. Journal of Political Ecology 5: 23–52.

Korten, David C., 2001 When Corporations Rule the World, second edition. Bloomfield, CT: Kumarian Press and San Francisco: Berrett-Koehler Publishers.

Kristoff, Nicholas D., 1999 At This Rate, We'll Be Global in Another Hundred Years, New York Times 23 May, p. WK5.

Kuczynski, Pedro-Pablo, and John Williamson, eds., 2003 After the Washington Consensus: Restarting Growth and Reform in Latin America. Washington, D.C.: Institute for International Economics.

Laclau, Ernesto, 1971 Feudalism and Capitalism in Latin America. New Left Review 67: 19–38.

Larraín, Jorge, 1989 Theories of Development: Capitalism, Colonialism and Dependency. London: Polity Press.

LeClair, Edward E., and Harold K. Schneider, eds., 1968 Economic Anthropology: Readings in Theory and Analysis. New York: Holt, Rinehart and Winston.

Lenin, V. I., 1965 [1916] Imperialism, the Highest Stage of Capitalism: A Popular Outline. Peking: Foreign Languages Press.

—— 1972 [1899] The Development of Capitalism in Russia. In Collected Works, Volume 3. Moscow: Progress Publishers.

Lewellen, Ted, 2002 The Anthropology of Globalization: Cultural Anthropology Enters the 21st Century. Westport, CT and London: Bergin and Garvey.

Lewis, W.A., 1955 The Theory of Economic Growth. Homewood, IL: R. D. Irwin.

Leys, Colin, 1996 The Rise and Fall of Development Theory. Oxford: James Currey.

Little, Peter D., 2000 Recasting the Debate: Development Theory and Anthropological Practice. In The Unity of Theory and Practice in Anthropology: Rebuilding a Fractured Synthesis. Carole E.

Hill and Marietta L. Baba, eds., pp. 119–131. NAPA Bulletin 18. Washington, D.C.: American Anthropological Association.

Little, Peter D., and Michael Painter, 1995 Discourse, Politics, and the Development Process: Reflections on Escobar's "Anthropology and the Development Encounter." American Ethnologist 22(3): 602–616.

Lipton, Michael, 1977 Why Poor People Stay Poor: Urban Bias in World Development. Cambridge, MA: Harvard University Press.

Long, Norman, 2001 Development Sociology: Actor Perspectives. London: Routledge.

Long, Norman, and Ann Long, eds., 1992 Battlefields of Knowledge: The Interlocking of Theory and Practice in Social Research and Development. London: Routledge.

Lund, Christian, ed., 1999 Development and Rights: Negotiating Justice in Changing Societies. London: Frank Cass.

Luxemburg, Rosa, 1951 [1914] The Accumulation of Capital. London: Routledge & Kegan Paul.

Lynch, B. D., 1981 The Vicos Experiment, A Study of the Impacts of the Cornell-Peru Project in a Highland Community. Washington, D.C.: Agency for International Development.

MacGaffey, Janet, 1991 The Real Economy of Zaire: The Contribution of Smuggling and Other Unofficial Activities to National Wealth. Philadelphia: University of Pennsylvania Press.

Magdoff, Fred, J.B. Foster, and F.H. Buttel, eds., 2000 Hungry for Profit: The Agribusiness Threat to Farmers, Food, and the Environment. New York: Monthly Review Press.

Mair, Lucy, 1984 Anthropology and Development. London: Macmillan.

Malinowski, Bronislaw, 1929 Practical Anthropology. Africa 2(1): 22–38.

—— 1930 The Rationalization of Anthropology and Administration. Africa 3(4): 405–430.

—— 1961 The Dynamics of Culture Change. New Haven: Yale University Press. Reprinted 1976, Westport CT: Greenwood.

Malthus, Thomas Robert, 1872 An Essay on the Principle of Population, seventh edition. London: Reeves and Turner.

—— 1970 [1798 and 1830] An Essay on the Principle of Population and A Summary View of the Principle of Population. London: Penguin Books.

—— 1974 [1836] Principles of Political Economy. New York: A.M. Kelley.

Mangin, William, 1979 Thoughts on Twenty-Four Years of Work in Peru: The Vicos Project and Me. In Long-term Field Research in Social Anthropology, George M. Foster, Thayer Scudder, Elizabeth Colson, and R.V. Kemper eds., pp. 64–84. New York: Academic Press.

McCay, Bonnie, and James M. Acheson, eds., 1987 The Question of the Commons. Tucson: University of Arizona Press.

McCay, Bonnie J., 1998 Oyster Wars and the Public Trust: Property, Law, and Ecology in New Jersey History. Tucson: University of Arizona Press.

McClelland, David C., 1961 The Achieving Society. New York: D. Van Nostrand Company.

McMichael, Philip, 2000 Development and Social Change: A Global Perspective, second edition. Thousand Oaks, CA: Pine Forge Press-Sage.

McMillan, Della E., 1995 Sahel Visions: Planned Settlement and River Blindness Control in Burkina Faso. Tucson: University of Arizona Press.

Messer, Ellen, 1993 Anthropology and Human Rights. Annual Review of Anthropology 22: 221–249.

Miller, Daniel, 1995 Consumption and Commodities. Annual Review of Anthropology 24: 141–61.

—— 1997 Capitalism: An Ethnographic Approach. Oxford: Berg.

—— 1998 Conclusion: A Theory of Virtualism. In Virtualism: A New Political Economy, James G. Carrier, and Daniel Miller, eds., pp. 187–215. New York: Oxford.

Mintz, Sidney W., 1977 The So-Called World System: Local Initiative and Local Response. Dialectical Anthropology 2 (4) (Nov.): 253–70.

—— 1985 Sweetness and Power: The Place of Sugar in Modern History. New York: Viking Penguin.

—— 1998 The Localization of Anthropological Practice: From Area Studies to Transnationalism. Critique of Anthropology 18(2): 117–144.

Mitchell, Tim, 1991 The Object of Development: America's Egypt. In Power of Development, Jonathan Crush, ed., pp. 129–157. London and New York: Routledge.

—— 2002 Rule of Experts: Egypt, Techno-Politics, Modernity. Berkeley: University of California Press.

Moock, Joyce, and Robert Rhoades, 1992 Diversity, Farmer Knowledge and Sustainability. Ithaca, NY: Cornell University Press.

Moore, Barrington, 1966 Social Origins of Dictatorship and Democracy: Lord and Peasant in the Making of the Modern World. Boston: Beacon.

Moore, Sally Falk, 2001 The International Production of Authoritative Knowledge: The Case of Drought-Stricken West Africa. Ethnography 2(2): 161–189.

Moran, Emilio, 1998 The Development Encounter and Academic Anthropology. Development Anthropologist 16(1–2): 6–11.

Moreno Fraginals, Manuel, 1985 Plantations in the Caribbean: Cuba, Puerto Rico, and the Dominican Republic in the Late Nineteenth Century. In Between Slavery and Free Labor: The Spanish-Speaking Caribbean in the Nineteenth Century, Manuel Moreno Fraginals, Frank Moya Pons, and Stanley L. Engerman, eds., pp. 3–21. Baltimore: Johns Hopkins University Press.

Mueller, Susanne, 2004 Integrated Rural Development, Environmental Sustainability and Poverty Alleviation: Some Conventional Wisdoms Examined. Draft Discussion Paper of the United Nations Department of Economic and Social Affairs, 11 pp.

Murray, Colin, 1981 Families Divided: The Impact of Migrant Labour in Lesotho. Cambridge: Cambridge University Press.

Myers, Fred, 2002 Painting Culture: The Making of Aboriginal High Art. Durham, NC: Duke University Press.

Nash, June, ed., 1993 Crafts in the World Market: The Impact of Global Exchange on Middle American Artisans. Albany: SUNY Press.

Nash, Manning, 1966 Primitive and Peasant Economic Systems. Scranton, Pennsylvania: Chandler Publishing.

Neale, Walter C., and Anne Mayhew, 1983 Polanyi, Institutional Economics, and Economic Anthropology. In Economic Anthropology: Topics and Theories, Sutti Ortiz, ed., pp. 11–20. Lanham, MD: University Press of America.

Nolan, Riall, 2002 Development Anthropology: Encounters in the Real World. Boulder: Westview Press.

Nugent, David, 1997 Modernity at the Edge of Empire: State, Individual, and Nation in the Northern Peruvian Andes, 1885–1935. Stanford: Stanford University Press.

OED [Oxford English Dictionary], 1971 The Compact Edition of the Oxford English Dictionary. Oxford: Oxford University Press.

Ong, Aihwa, 1999 Flexible Citizenship: The Cultural Logics of Transnationality. Durham, NC: Duke University Press.

Orlove, Benjamin, and Arnold J. Bauer, 1997 Giving Importance to Imports. In The Allure of the Foreign: Imported Goods in Postcolonial Latin America, Benjamin Orlove, ed., pp. 1–29. Ann Arbor: University of Michigan Press.

Ortner, Sherry B., ed., 1999 The Fate of Culture: Geertz and Beyond. Berkeley: University of California Press.

Osgood, Diane, 2001, Dig It Up: Global Civil Society's Responses to Plant Biotechnology. In Global Civil Society 2001, Helmut Anheier, Marlies Glasius, and Mary Kaldor, eds., 79–107. Oxford: Oxford University Press.

Parsons, Talcott, 1937 The Structure of Social Action. New York: McGraw-Hill.

Patomäki, Heikki, 2001 Democratising Globalisation: The Leverage of the Tobin Tax. London: Zed Books.

Payer, Cheryl, 1982 The World Bank: A Critical Analysis. New York: Monthly Review Press.

Peet, Richard, and Michael Watts, eds., 1996 Liberation Ecologies: Environment, Development and Social Movements. London and New York: Routledge.

Peluso, Nancy, and Michael Watts, 2001 Violent Environments. Ithaca and London: Cornell University Press.

Perry, Donna L., 2000 Rural Weekly Markets and the Dynamics of Time, Space and Community in Senegal. Journal of Modern African Studies 38(3): 461–486.

Peters, Pauline, 1994 Dividing the Commons: Politics, Policy, and Culture in Botswana. Charlottesville and London: University Press of Virginia

——ed., 2000, Development Encounters: Sites of Participation and Knowledge. Cambridge, MA: Harvard University for Harvard Institute for International Development.

Pianta, Mario, 2001 Parallel Summits of Global Civil Society. *In* Global Civil Society 2001, Helmut Anheier, Marlies Glasius, and Mary Kaldor, eds., pp. 169–194. Oxford: Oxford University Press.

Pigg, Stacy 1997 "Found in Most Traditional Societies": Traditional Medical Practitioners between Culture and Development. *In* International Development and the Social Sciences: Essays on the History and Politics of Knowledge, Frederick Cooper and Randall Packard, eds., pp. 259–290. Berkeley: University of California Press.

Polanyi Levitt, Kari. 2000 The Great Transformation from 1920 to 1990. *In* Karl Polanyi in Vienna: The Contemporary Significance of The Great Transformation, Kenneth McRobbie and Kari Polanyi Levitt, eds., pp. 4–11. Montreal: Black Rose Books.

Polanyi, Karl, 1957 [1944] The Great Transformation: The Political and Economic Origins of Our Time. Boston: Beacon Press.

——1958 The Economy as Instituted Process. *In* Trade and Markets in the Early Empires, Karl Polanyi, Conrad Arensberg, and Harry W. Pearson, eds., pp. 243–70. Glencoe, IL.: Free Press.

Polier, Nicole, and William Roseberry, 1989 Tristes Tropes: Post-Modern Anthropologists Encounter the Other and Discover Themselves. Economy and Society 18(2): 245–262.

Portes, Alejandro, and A. Douglas Kincaid, 1989 Sociology and Development in the 1990s: Critical Challenges and Empirical Trends. Sociological Forum 4(4): 479–503.

Pottier, Johann, 1999, Anthropology of Food: The Social Dynamics of Food Security. Malden, MA: Polity Press.

Preobrazhensky, Evgenii, 1971 [1924] Peasantry and the Political Economy of the Early Stages of Industrialization. *In* Peasants and Peasant Societies, Teodor Shanin, ed., pp. 219–26. Harmondsworth, England: Penguin.

Price, David H., 1998 Cold War Anthropology: Collaborators and Victims of the National Security State. Identities 4(3–4): 389–430.

Price, Sally, 1991 Primitive Art in Civilized Places. Chicago: University of Chicago Press.

Rahnema, Majid, 1997 Towards Post-Development: Searching for Signposts, a New Language and New Paradigms. *In* The Post-Development Reader, Majid Rahnema and Victoria Bawtree, eds., pp. 377–403. London: Zed Books.

Rahnema, Majid, and Victoria Bawtree, eds., 1997 The Post-Development Reader. London and New York: Zed Books.

Rao, Vijayendra, and Michael Walton, eds., 2004 Culture and Public Action: A Cross-Disciplinary Dialogue on Development Policy. Stanford: Stanford University Press.

Rappaport, Roy, 1993 The Anthropology of Trouble. American Anthropologist 95(2): 295–303.

Ravallion, Martin, 2004 Economics Focus: Pessimistic on Poverty? The Economist, April 10, p. 65.

Redfield, Robert, 1941 The Folk Culture of Yucatan. Chicago: University of Chicago Press.

——1953 The Primitive World and Its Transformations. Ithaca: Cornell University Press.

Rhoades, Robert, 1984 Breaking New Ground: Agricultural Anthropology. Lima, Peru: International Potato Center.

Rich, Bruce, 1998 Mortgaging the Earth: The World Bank, Environmental Impoverishment and the Crisis of Development. Boston: Beacon Press.

Rist, Gilbert, 1997 The History of Development: From Western Origins to Global Faith. London: Zed Books.

Robertson, A.F., 1984 People and the State: An Anthropology of Planned Development. Cambridge: Cambridge University Press.

Robinson, Marguerite S., 2001 The Microfinance Revolution: Sustainable Finance for the Poor. Lessons from Indonesia. The Emerging Industry. Washington and New York: The World Bank and Open Society Institute.

Robinson, William I., 1997 Nicaragua and the World: A Globalization Perspective. *In* Nicaragua without Illusions: Regime Transition and Structural Adjustment in the 1990s, Thomas W. Walker, ed., pp. 23–42. Wilmington, DE.: Scholarly Resources.

Rocheleau, Dianne E., and Claudia Radel, 1999 Comment on J. Peter Brosius, Analyses and Interventions: Anthropological Engagements with Environmentalism. Current Anthropology 40(3): 296–297.

Rodney, Walter, 1974 How Europe Underdeveloped Africa. Washington: Howard University Press.

Rodrik, Dani, 2003 Has Globalization Gone Too Far? In The Global Transformations Reader, second edition, David Held and Anthony McGrew, eds., pp. 379–383. Cambridge: Polity.

Roe, Emery, 1999 Development Narratives, Or Making the Best of Blueprint Development. World Development 19(4): 287–300.

Roseberry, William, 1989 Anthropologies and Histories: Essays in Culture, History, and Political Economy. New Brunswick, N.J.: Rutgers University Press.

—— 1995 Latin American Peasant Studies in a "Postcolonial" Era. Journal of Latin American Anthropology 1(1): 150–177.

—— 1996 The Unbearable Lightness of Anthropology. Radical History Review 65: 73–93.

Rosenberg, Justin, 2000 The Follies of Globalization Theory. London: Verso.

Ross, Eric B., 1998 The Malthus Factor: Poverty, Politics and Population in Capitalist Development. New York: St. Martin's.

Rostow, W.W, 1960 The Stages of Economic Growth: A Non-Communist Manifesto. Cambridge: Cambridge University Press.

Rubin, Deborah, 1989 Interdisciplinary Research on Intercropping Sugarcane and Food Crops in South Nyanza, Kenya, in Social Science Perspectives on Managing Agricultural Technology, David Groenfeldt and Joyce L. Moock, eds., pp. 45–55. New York: Rockefeller Foundation and International Irrigation Management Institute.

—— 1992 Labor Patterns in Agricultural Households: A Time Use Study in Southwestern Kenya, in Diversity, Farmer Knowledge, and Sustainability, Joyce L. Moock and Robert Rhoades, eds., pp. 169–188. Ithaca, NY: Cornell University Press.

Rudra, Nita, 2002 Globalization and the Decline of the Welfare State in the Less-Developed Countries. International Organization 56(2): 411–445.

Sachs, Jeffrey D., 1999 Sachs Denounces IMF and HIPC; Calls for Debt Write-off, IMF to Get Out. Testimony for the House Committee on Banking and Financial Services, Hearing on Debt Reduction, June 15, 1999: <http://lists.essential.org/stop-imf/msg00144.html> (Accessed 2/10/04).

Sachs, Wolfgang, 1992 Introduction. In The Development Dictionary: A Guide to Knowledge as Power, Wolfgang Sachs, ed., pp. 1–5. London: Zed Books.

—— ed., 1999 The Development Dictionary: A Guide to Knowledge as Power. London and New York: Zed Books.

Sahlins, Marshall, 1999 What is Anthropological Enlightenment? Some Lessons of the Twentieth Century. Annual Review of Anthropology 28: i–xxii.

Sandbrook, Richard, ed., 2003 Civilizing Globalization: A Survival Guide. Albany: State University of New York Press.

Schech, Susanne, and Jane Haggis, 2000 Culture and Development: A Critical Introduction. Oxford, UK and Malden, MA: Blackwell Publishers.

Schein, Louisa, 1999 Of Cargo and Satellites: Imagined Cosmopolitanism. Postcolonial Studies 2(3): 345–375.

—— 2002 Market Mentalities, Iron Satellite Dishes, and Contested Cultural Developmentalism. Provincial China 7(1): 57–72.

Scheper-Hughes, Nancy, 1995 The Primacy of the Ethical: Propositions for a Militant Anthropology. Current Anthropology 36: 409–420.

Schneider, Jane, 2002 World Markets: Anthropological Perspectives. In Exotic No More: Anthropology on the Front Lines, Jeremy MacClancy, ed., pp. 64–85. Chicago: University of Chicago Press.

Schultz, Theodore, 1964 Transforming Traditional Agriculture. New Haven: Yale University Press.

Scott, James C., 1976 Moral Economy of the Peasant: Rebellion and Subsistence in Southeast Asia. New Haven: Yale University Press.

—— 1985 Weapons of the Weak: Everyday Forms of Peasant Resistance. New Haven: Yale University Press.

—— 1998 Seeing Like a State: How Certain Schemes to Improve the Human Condition Have Failed. New Haven: Yale University Press.

Scudder, Thayer, 1999 Malinowski Award Lecture: The Emerging Global Crisis and Development Anthropology: Can We Have an Impact? Human Organization 58(4): 351–364.

—— 1988 The Institute for Development Anthropology: The Case of Anthropological Participation in the Development Process. *In* Production and Autonomy: Anthropological Studies and Critiques of Development, John Bennett and John Bowen, eds., pp. 365–385. New York: University Press of America.

Scudder, Thayer, and Elizabeth Colson, 1979 Long-term Research in Gwembe Valley, Zambia. *In* Long-Term Field Research in Social Anthropology, George M. Foster, Thayer Scudder, Elizabeth Colson, and R.V. Kemper, eds., pp. 227–254. New York: Academic Press.

Sen, Amartya, 1999 Development as Freedom. New York: Alfred A. Knopf.

Shanin, Teodor, ed., 1972 The Awkward Class. Political Sociology of Peasantry in a Developing Society: Russia 1910–1925. Oxford: Clarendon Press.

—— 1983 Late Marx and the Russian Road: Marx and the Peripheries of Capitalism. New York: Monthly Review Press.

Shils, Edward, 1957 Political Development in New States. Gravenhage, Netherlands: Mouton.

Shipton, Parker, 1994 Time and Money in the Western Sahel: A Clash of Cultures in Gambian Rural Finance. *In* James Acheson, ed., Anthropology and Institutional Economics, pp.283–327. Lanham, MD: University Press of America, for the Society for Economic Anthropology.

—— 1995 Luo Entrustment: Foreign Finance and the Soil of the Spirits in Kenya. Africa 65(2):165–196.

—— 2003 Legalism and Loyalism: European, African, and Human "Rights". *In* At the Risk of Being Heard: Identity, Indigenous Rights, and Postcolonial States, Bartholomew Dean and Jerome M. Levi, eds., pp. 45–79. Ann Arbor: University of Michigan Press.

Shiva, Vandana, 1989 Staying Alive. London: Zed Books.

—— 2000 Stolen Harvest: The Highjacking of the Global Food Supply. Boston: South End Press.

Sikkink, Katherine, 1988 The Influence of Raúl Prebisch on Economic Policy-Making in Argentina, 1950–1962. Latin American Research Review 23 (2): 91–114.

Simmel, Georg, 1990 The Philosophy of Money, second enlarged edition. London: Routledge.

Sinha, Subir, 2003 Development Counter-Narratives: Taking Social Movements Seriously. *In* Regional Modernities: The Cultural Politics of Development in India, K. Sivaramakrishnan and Arun Agrawal, eds., pp. 286–312. Oxford and New Delhi: Oxford University Press.

Sivaramakrishnan, K., 1999 Modern Forests: Statemaking and Environmental Change in Colonial Eastern India. Stanford: Stanford University Press.

—— 2000 Crafting the Public Sphere in the Forests of West Bengal: Democracy, Development, and Political Action. American Ethnologist 27(2): 431–461.

Sivaramakrishnan, K., and Arun Agrawal, 2003 Regional Modernities in Stories and Practices of Development. *In* Regional Modernities: The Cultural Politics of Development in India. Stanford: Stanford University Press (and New Delhi: Oxford University Press).

Snyder, Katherine, 1996 Agrarian Change and Farmers' Land-Use Strategies Among the Iraqw of Northern Tanzania. Human Ecology 24(3): 315–340.

Soros, George, 2002 On Globalization. New York: Public Affairs-Perseus.

Sperling, Louise and Peggy Berkowitz, 1994 Partners in Selection: Bean Breeders and Women Bean Experts in Rwanda. Consultative Group for International Agricultural Research (CGIAR) Gender Paper, October 1994.

Sperling, Louise, and Michael Loevinsohn, eds., 1997 Using Diversity: Enhancing and Maintaining Genetic Resources On-Farm. Ottawa: International Development Research Center, online publication: <http://www.idrc.ca/en/ev-9290–201–1–DO_TOPIC.html>(Accessed March 21, 2004).

Sperling, Louise, and Catherine Longley, 2002 Editorial: Beyond Seeds and Tools: Effective Support to Farmers in Emergencies. Disasters 26(4): 283–287.

Stalin, Joseph, 1940 Dialectical and Historical Materialism. New York: International Publishers.

Stavenhagen, Rodolfo, 1969 Seven Erroneous Theses About Latin America. *In* Latin American Radicalism: A Documentary Report on Left and Nationalist Movements, Irving Louis Horowitz, Josué de Castro, and John Gerassi, eds., pp. 102–117. New York: Vintage.

Stiglitz, Joseph E., 2002 Globalization and its Discontents. New York: W.W. Norton.

Stocking, George W., Jr., 1968 [1965] On the Limits of "Presentism" and "Historicism" in the Historiography of the Behavioral Sciences. Journal of the History of the Behavioral Sciences 1(3) [1965]: 211–18; reprinted as chapter 1 of Stocking, Race, Culture, and Evolution: Essays in the History of Anthropology, pp. 1–12 (New York: Free Press, 1968).

Stone, M. Priscilla, 2003 Is Sustainability for Development Anthropologists? Human Organization 62(2): 93–99.

Sylvain, Renee, 2002 Land, Water, and Truth: San Identity and Global Indigenism. American Anthropologist 104(4): 1074–1085.

Tendler, Judith, 1975 Inside Foreign Aid. Baltimore: Johns Hopkins University Press.

Thompson, E. P., 1971 The Moral Economy of the English Crowd in the Eighteenth Century, Past & Present 50 (Feb.): 76–136.

Tripp, Robert, 2001 Seed Provision and Agricultural Development. London: James Currey.

Trouillot, Michel-Rolph, 2003 Global Transformations: Anthropology and the Modern World. New York: Palgrave Macmillan.

Tsing, Anna, 2000 The Global Situation. Cultural Anthropology 15(3): 327–360.

Turner, Terence, 1992 Defiant Images: The Kayapo Appropriation of Video. Anthropology Today 8(6): 5–16.

UNDP [United Nations Development Programme], 1999 Human Development Report 1999. New York: Oxford University Press.

—— 2001 Human Development Report 2001. New York: Oxford University Press.

Vayda, Andrew P., and Bradley B. Walters, 1999 Against Political Ecology. Human Ecology 27(1):167–179.

Veblen, Thorstein, 1934 [1899] The Theory of the Leisure Class: An Economic Study of Institutions. New York: The Modern Library.

Vincent, Joan, 1990 Anthropology and Politics: Visions, Traditions, and Trends. Tucson: University of Arizona Press.

Wallerstein, Immanuel, 1974 The Modern World-System: Capitalist Agriculture and the Origins of the European World-Economy in the Sixteenth Century. New York: Academic Press.

Watts, Michael, 1992 Capitalisms, Crises, and Cultures I: Notes toward a Totality of Fragments, in Reworking Modernity: Capitalisms and Symbolic Discontent, Allan Pred and Michael John Watts, eds., pp. 1–19. New Brunswick, NJ: Rutgers University Press.

—— 1993 Development I: Power, Knowledge, Discursive Practice. Progress in Human Geography 17: 257–272.

—— 1995 "A New Deal in Emotions": Theory and Practice and the Crisis of Development. In Power of Development, Jonathan Crush, ed., pp. 44–62. New York: Routledge.

—— 1998 Collective Wish Images: Geographical Imaginaries and the Crisis of Development. In Human Geography Today, Doreen Massey and John Allen, eds., pp. 85–107. Cambridge: Polity Press.

—— 2000 Political Ecology. In A Companion to Economic Geography, Eric Shepard and Trevor J. Barnes, eds., pp. 257–274. Malden, MA: Blackwell Publishers.

WCED [World Commission on Environment and Development], 1987 Our Common Future. Oxford: Oxford University Press.

Weber, Max, 1950 General Economic History. Glencoe, IL: Free Press.

—— 1958 [1904/1905] The Protestant Ethic and the Spirit of Capitalism. New York: Charles Scribner's Sons.

Wilk, Richard, 1990 Consumer Goods as Dialogue About Development. Culture History 7: 79–100.

Williams, Raymond, 1971 Marxism and Literature. Oxford: Oxford University Press.

—— 1973 The Country and the City. New York: Oxford University Press.

Williamson, John, 2002 What Should the World Bank Think about the Washington Consensus? The World Bank Research Observer 15(2): 251–264.

Wolf, Eric R., 1969 Peasant Wars of the Twentieth Century. New York: Harper and Row

—— 1982 Europe and the Peoples without History. Berkeley: University of California Press.

—— 2001 Pathways of Power: Building an Anthropology of the Modern World. Berkeley: University of California Press.

Wolf, Eric R., and Joseph G. Jorgensen, 1970 Anthropology on the Warpath in Thailand. The New York Review of Books 15(9) (Nov. 19): 26–35.

Worby, Eric, 1994 Hitting Hairs and Splitting Targets: Anthropological Perpsectives on Fish Culture Technology Transfer through NGOs in Bangladesh. Paper presented at the biannual conference of Rockefeller Foundation Post-Doctoral Fellows, Social Sciences in Agriculture. Addis Ababa, 14–18 November.

Worby, Eric, Z. Samina, and A. Opel, 2002 Social Dimensions of Fish Farming in Sharecropped Rice Fields. Grassroots Voice: A Journal of Development. Dhaka, Bangladesh.

World Bank, 1981 Accelerated Development in Sub-Saharan Africa: An Agenda for Action. World Bank: Washington, D.C.

Part I

Classical Foundations and Debates

Introduction

"Classics" constitute a problematic category. Our selection of articles for this section starts from the premise that a work may achieve canonical status for reasons ranging from the elegance of the prose to the coherence of the argument, from the prestige or institutional location of the author to the political resonance it generates among influential elites or restless masses. Whatever their origin, processes of canon formation too often lead to a facile association of a complex thinker with one big idea (Smith and "the invisible hand," for example). The articles in Part I include works from the Enlightenment to the mid-20th century by key theorists who have shaped later development debates – an admittedly "presentist" perspective (see Stocking 1968). In addition to the authors excerpted (Adam Smith, Karl Marx, Frederick Engels, Max Weber, and Karl Polanyi), this introduction discusses two other major figures: Thomas Malthus and David Ricardo.

Adam Smith, almost universally portrayed today as an unambivalent and prescient apostle of the free market, never really elaborated a coherent theory of development. In the 18th century, market relations still existed alongside vestiges of feudal societies. Smith's ideas about the wealth and poverty of nations mirrored his opinions about capitalists and aristocrats. For Smith, the differences between rich and poor nations, as well as between capitalists or merchants, on the one hand, and nobility on the other, hinged on differences between what he termed productive and unproductive labor (see his chapter below). Rich countries, in Smith's view reinvested a large proportion of the total social product in the production process; in poor countries, by contrast most of the social product was consumed in maintaining "unproductive hands." He was not specific about which "poor countries" he had in mind, but these clearly included "ancient" and "feudal" Europe, as well as a number of contemporary cities, such as Rome, Versailles, Madrid, and Vienna, where royal courts contributed to "idleness" and "frivolous" consumption. The wealth of London, Glasgow, and the Netherlands resulted from the "industry" of a productive labor force and an upper class that lived from profits on capital rather than rents.

Smith's claim that "great nations" are sometimes impoverished by "public prodigality" could be read as foreshadowing today's neoliberal attacks on "big government" or "unproductive spending." It is important to be cautious in treating Smith's late-18th-century work as a kind of sacred writ, laden with solutions to today's dilemmas. Historians of economic thought have shown that contemporary neoliberals have subtly converted Smith's famous "invisible hand" of Providence into an "invisible hand" of the market (Lubasz 1992; Hirschman 1991:15–16).

Rather than a totally convinced champion of market liberalism, Smith harbored many doubts. In *The Wealth of Nations* (first published in 1776) he railed against the greed of the powerful, declaring "All for ourselves, and nothing for other people, seems, in every age of the world, to have been the vile maxim of the masters of mankind." He was not averse, in some circumstances, to maintaining wages above market levels, since "Our merchants and master-manufacturers complain much of the bad effects of high wages in raising the price, and thereby lessening the sale of their goods both at home and abroad. . . . They are silent with regard to the pernicious effects of their own gains. They complain only of those of other people." Similarly, he feared that suddenly removing protectionist tariffs could result in "very considerable . . . disorder" (Smith 1976:III, 437; I, 110; IV, 491). Particularly in his earlier work (published in 1759), Smith levelled caustic criticism at the conspicuous consumption of the rich, calling the market a "deception which . . . keeps in continual motion the industry of mankind" by producing "trinkets of frivolous utility," such as "a toothpick, . . . an earpicker . . . [or] a machine for cutting the nails" (2000:263, 261).

Population dynamics have long been central to debates about development. Examples include the controversial role of population pressure on resources in the formation of ancient states or the destabilization of contemporary ones, the perennial argument between those who consider population growth a leading cause of poverty and theorists of demand-for-labor or human capital who emphasize inequality and the incentives that poor people have to reproduce (and that affluent people have not to), the place of the demographic transition in improving the status of women, the contentious struggle of women in pro-natalist societies (and elsewhere) for safe forms of contraception and abortion, and the ethics of other kinds of natality control (including coercive sterilization programs, infanticide, sex-selective abortion, and China's one-child policy).[1] The ideas of Thomas Malthus are always explicitly or implicitly present in these discussions, even two centuries after their initial formulation.

Malthus is best known for a simple idea expounded in 1798 in his "first essay," published anonymously after one of the earliest capitalist crises (Cowen and Shenton 1996:18). "Population," he said, "when unchecked, increases in a geometrical ratio. Subsistence increases only in an arithmetical ratio. A slight acquaintance with numbers will shew the immensity of the first power in comparison of the second" (Malthus 1970: 71). Demographic growth, in other words, will outstrip growth in food production unless slowed by "preventative" or "positive" checks. Malthus's admirers and critics have given "positive" checks – which included famines, disease, and the "barbarous practice" of exposing children to the elements – much more attention (Malthus 1970:89). "Preventative checks," which Malthus (who was an Anglican parson) saw as "vice" and among which he later included "moral restraint," were "the sort of intercourse which renders some of the women of large towns unprolific; a general corruption of morals with regards to the sex, which has a similar effect; unnatural passions and improper arts to prevent the consequences of irregular connections" (1970:250).

This puritanical and pessimistic outlook was part of a broader, reactionary vision. Malthus inveighed against "evil" progressive taxation, England's poor laws and the "disgusting passions" unleashed in the French Revolution (1872:421; 1970:121). While Malthus is most remembered for his alarmism about demographic explosion and agricultural stagnation, most of his *Essay on Population* was devoted to critiquing the Enlightenment belief in human perfectability held by such thinkers as the Marquis de Condorcet and William Godwin.

Given Malthus's enduring celebrity, it is perhaps surprising that his best-known idea – that population grows geometrically and agricultural production arithmetically – is not widely accepted. Malthus's critics note that he failed to foresee that improved technologies would boost food output and significantly reduce "positive checks" on population growth. Similarly, Malthus paid little attention to the age and sex structure of populations or to sexual or marriage practices, all central concerns of contemporary demographers. Nor did he anticipate the demographic transition from high fertility and high mortality to low fertility and low mortality, which has been observed in country after country.

Why does Malthus's "law" of population continue to attract attention? First, Malthus explained poverty in relation to his "law," rather than as an outcome of capitalist development, and he prescribed measures to ameliorate it like those that elites still favor, such as protecting private property and abolishing the Poor Laws (which provided low-wage jobs for the able-bodied, apprenticeships for children and cash handouts for those unable to work). Second, technological revolutions in agriculture cannot postpone indefinitely efforts to stabilize human populations. Third, Malthus's "law" has had extraordinary influence on a range of thinkers. Darwin attributed to a reading of Malthus's *Essay* his understanding of evolution through natural selection as a "struggle for existence" (Darwin 1958:42–43.). Spencer, the most influential social Darwinist and a key ideologue of 19th-century economic liberalism, echoed Malthus's attack on the poor laws, which helped "the worthless to multiply at the expense of the worthy" (Spencer 1961:94). More recently, Malthus's influence is evident in Hardin's (1968) "tragedy of the commons" thesis and Erlich's *The Population Bomb* (1968). The pessimism Malthus expressed in the "first essay" diminished over his lifetime and, in his treatment of public debt and business cycles, he is sometimes said to have anticipated Keynesianism.

Just as Adam Smith is represented today as an unequivocal advocate of free markets, David Ricardo is hailed for articulating the advantages of unfettered foreign trade and "comparative advantage." The latter doctrine held that each individual, region or nation ought to specialize in the production of those goods for which it was best endowed. But where Smith viewed markets as a harmonizing influence, with the "invisible hand" balancing the interests of buyers and sellers, Ricardo emphasized the unavoidable antagonisms that characterize all economics, notably the contradictory interests of town and country, industry and agriculture, and capitalists and landowners. Later economists referred to these contradictions as "terms of trade," a concept that became central to neoclassical theories of international commerce, as well as to dependency-oriented explanations of "unequal exchange" and "urban bias" (see the Introduction to this volume).

Liberal economists, Ricardo among them, waged a protracted campaign against Britain's early 19th-century Corn Laws (see Introduction to this volume) and protectionism, much of it marked by vitriolic attacks on the avaricious and parasitic British aristocracy. Nevertheless, the industrial interests that opposed the Corn Laws generally were not averse to protectionism in principle. The 1845 repeal of the Corn Laws marked a shift away from the protectionism that had enabled Britain to emerge as the first industrial power.

Ricardo's most succinct explanation of comparative advantage relied on a hypothetical example of trading Portuguese wine for English cloth (1975:77–93). Several aspects of this famous model deserve consideration. First, Ricardo understood the value of commodities as deriving from the labor "embodied" in them or required to make them. This was not an unusual position among political economists of his time but, like Marx's better known labor theory of value, it has no place in neoclassical theory, which explains comparative advantages instead as resulting from any difference in production costs – whatever the cause – for a particular item of trade. Second, the main units of analysis for Ricardo are nations, each with a distinct economy characterized by particular profit levels, labor costs, and commodity prices. While comparative advantage is often invoked now to encourage poor countries to specialize, it is only infrequently remembered that in the context in which the doctrine originated nations often had higher levels of self-sufficiency and autonomous decision-making capability than they do today. And third, Ricardo's example of the wine and cloth is indicative of a penchant for abstraction that runs throughout his work and that distinguishes him from political economists (e.g., Adam Smith) who argued more on the basis of historical data. Ricardo is widely credited with introducing model building into economics (Heilbroner 1972:99).

Comparative advantage is no longer understood in the same way as in Ricardo's day, but it remains a contentious topic.[2] Echoes of the Corn Law debates are present in today's arguments over "food sovereignty" and over whether agricultural price supports constitute "subsidies in restraint of trade," which would make them illegal under WTO rules. And the terms of trade between agriculture and industry – a central idea for Ricardo – remain a concern of policymakers and a focus of political struggle in virtually every economic system.

In 1848, just weeks before revolutions began to sweep the continent, Karl Marx and Friedrich Engels opened *The Communist Manifesto* with the famous declaration that "a spectre is haunting Europe – the spectre of communism" (1968:35). The *Manifesto* stands out among Marx and Engels' works for its eloquent, sonorous language, its passionate call for working-class organization, and its scathing descriptions of capitalism. The *Economic and Philosophic Manuscripts of 1844* may better describe Marx and Engels' view of human agency and Marx's *Grundrisse* or *Capital* may contain more detailed analyses of commodity fetishism and capitalist (and other) modes of production (1964, 1967, 1973; see also Engels 1972). But it is the *Manifesto* – probably the most widely read revolutionary pamphlet in history – that in the 19th century most contributed to gaining Marx's ideas a mass audience.

The *Manifesto* contains one of the most succinct outlines of Marx's theory of development. Four themes are central to the excerpt from the *Manifesto* included below: the ubiquity of class struggle, the social contradictions of each mode of production, capitalism as a force for dissolving tradition and generating technological advances, and the capitalist imperative to expand markets. Marx and Engels saw a social class as a group with a common relation to the means of production. In capitalist society, property owners and their proletarianized employees had an inherently antagonistic relation to each other as they struggled over the division of the social product. Previous societies, too, were distinguished by conflicts between social classes – lords and serfs, masters and slaves, and so on. Historical progress – equated in the *Manifesto* with movement from one mode of production to another – occurred as emergent social classes found they could not survive *as classes* under the existing order and transformed or overthrew it. Thus the capitalist class, chafing under a highly regulated feudalism, struggled to advance its interests and, in the process, ushered in a new era of bourgeois domination and free trade. Along with this reshaping of economic and political institutions, Marx and Engels said, the bourgeoisie effected a cultural revolution, "drowning" the "religious fervour and chivalrous enthusiasm" that legitimated noble rule under feudalism, insinuating the cash nexus even into "sentimental" family relations, and upending patriarchal relations (which they understood not simply as male domination – the way the term is often used today – but as the rule of all those who claimed authority based on hereditary or divine right).

The *Manifesto*'s discussion of modes of production is hardly the most sophisticated in Marx and Engels' work, but it is arguably the most influential. A mode of production, for Marx and Engels, consisted of relations of production and forces of production; the former were the social relations through which labor was mobilized and surpluses appropriated; the latter included the technological and scientific instruments and other material conditions with and upon which human labor acts. While Marx and Engels express a grudging admiration for the bourgeoisie ("It has accomplished wonders far surpassing Egyptian pyramids, Roman aqueducts, and Gothic cathedrals"), they also saw its need to constantly modernize and expand the forces of production and to amass large numbers of workers at each production site as ultimately bringing about cyclical crises and its own demise. Constant expansion was an imperative of capitalist economies, and occurred through both technological advance and competition and an extension of market relations to new spaces. But the combination of worker alienation and the concentration of huge numbers of workers in factories and mines could produce, in Marx and Engels' view, proletarian class consciousness and, ultimately, the overthrow of the bourgeoisie and the advent of socialism.

This picture of a succession of modes of production could be read as an evolutionary, Enlightenment-style "master narrative" or as an inexorable, teleological Hegelian process in which history advances toward a predetermined outcome. Such interpretations are not entirely wrong; Marx's thought was characterized by a tension between the positing of epochal, evolutionary processes and the recognition of contingent, historically specific forces.[3] Marx's dual role as scholar and militant suggests that he gave greater weight to the role of ideas and political struggle in history than is acknowledged by commentators who paint him as a crude economic determinist. Nonetheless, Marx and Engels' scheme of a succession of modes of production was simplified, first by Stalin (1940), then by pro-Soviet Communist Parties throughout the world, and eventually by French "structural" Marxists, notably Louis Althusser (Althusser and Balibar 1970) and his followers, who included several prominent cultural anthropologists (e.g., Godelier 1972; Meillasoux 1981; Rey 1976).

Ironically, over time, Marx increasingly questioned the certainty that slavery, feudalism, capitalism, and communism would succeed each other in lockstep fashion. Probably the clearest statement of his opposition to unilineal notions of progress was in his 1881 drafts of a letter to the Russian populist Vera Zasulich, who had inquired about his opinion regarding the fate under capitalism of the peasant commune (*mir* or *obshchina*, a pervasive institution in the countryside until well into the 19th century). The political question facing the populists was whether the rural commune could serve as a springboard for a direct transition to socialism, or whether the proletarianization of the peasantry and the dissolution of the *mir* were part of a necessary capitalist stage that would precede socialism. Marx (unlike later Russian Marxists) inclined toward the former position, suggesting a growing unease towards the end of his life about universal schemes of history (Shanin 1983).

The *Communist Manifesto*'s analysis of why the bourgeoisie needs "a constantly expanding market" has, in recent years, been employed to observe that many features of today's globalization are actually rather old or that Marx and Engels were extraordinarily prescient (Wood 1998; Katz 2001; Harvey 2000:22–40). There is little doubt that Marx and Engels' picture of a bourgeoisie that "must nestle everywhere, settle everywhere, and establish connections everywhere" has a remarkably contemporary ring. The destruction of national industries, the increasingly cosmopolitan character of consumption, and the use of cheap commodities to force "barbarian nations" into "civilization" are – shorn of their mid-19th-century Eurocentric language – all themes examined in this book and central to later discussions of development. Fascination with the contemporaneity of the *Manifesto*'s words, however, may too easily obscure two crucial elements: first, Marx and Engels saw expanding markets in large part as a means of competition between firms and nations and of resolving inevitable, periodic crises in the capitalist mode of production; and second, their apparent prescience with respect to some dimensions of change existed alongside a certain blindness to the persistence of others, especially nationalism ("national one-sidedness and narrow-mindedness become more and more impossible") and the ethnic intolerance and religious zealotry which proved to be of such significance in 20th-century world history.

One of the towering figures of early-20th-century social science, Max Weber was, like both Smith and Marx, concerned with the conditions that gave rise to capitalism in what he called "the modern Occident." Weber posited the existence of a variety of capitalisms – commercial, speculative, colonial, financial, and even "political" – characterized by a common profit-making orientation (Weber 1978:164–166). But his theory of capitalist development is nonetheless frequently represented as being limited to "the West" and as giving almost exclusive emphasis to religious factors. In *The Protestant Ethic and the Spirit of Capitalism*, his first major work, he posed "traditionalism" as a major obstacle to the spread of market relations and argued that "wherever modern capitalism has begun its work of increasing the productivity of human labor by increasing its intensity, it has encountered the immensely stubborn resistance of this leading trait of pre-capitalistic labor" (1958:60).[4] Contemporary scholarship – and punditry – that privileges "cultural" or "ideological" factors in development could be read as echoing Weber's concern with "rationalizing" institutions in order to transcend the heavy weight of "tradition." The same could be said of discussions today that try to explain capitalism's development in the West, and its apparent failure almost everywhere else, as a result of cultural predispositions or the entrepreneurial capacities unleashed in societies with legal systems that applied uniform yet minimal bureaucratic standards to the registration and mortgaging of property, the signing and enforcement of contracts, and the accountability of officials (e.g., Landes 1998; De Soto 2000).

In *The Protestant Ethic*, Weber suggested that Martin Luther's notion of the "calling" – a "life-task" set by God – provided, for the first time in history, a positive ethical framework for justifying individual accumulation through rational self-discipline, the severing of obligations to larger kin groups, and the abandonment of traditional notions about just price and wage levels. This "social ethic of capitalistic culture," which Weber characterized as "the earning of more and more money, combined with the strict avoidance of all spontaneous enjoyment of life," was both cause and effect of the extension of market relations to more and more areas of life (1958:53–54). Success on earth, in Calvinist-Protestant doctrine, was evidence of an individual's membership in the predestined "elect," who were bound for heaven. Yet Weber's specific claims about Calvinist Protestantism were considerably more complex and integrally linked to several of his other central concerns, notably bureaucracy, rationalization, and the nature of the state.

Weber believed that what energized the modern capitalist economy was not religious doctrine per se, but rational social actors, operating within a rationalized legal system that permitted individuals to weigh utility and costs and to feel confident about the security of their capital. "Rational", for Weber, did not mean "good", "just" or "right". Rather, the modern state and the firm were similar inasmuch as both operated according to formal, bureaucratic criteria rather than the personalistic or familial considerations that governed economic life in traditional societies. The frequently cited (and variously attributed) adage that Weber was arguing with "the ghost of Karl Marx" is thus only partly accurate. Diverse scholars sympathetic to Marxist approaches – from Georg Lukács (1971) to C. Wright Mills (1959), Eric Wolf (2001), and Anthony Giddens (1971) – acknowledge major intellectual debts to Weber, especially his analyses of political power and legitimacy. Other Marxists, including literary theorist Raymond Williams (1977) and anthropologist William Roseberry, echo key aspects of Weber's thought (though without explicit recognition) in analyzing how "ideas and meanings are themselves material products and forces" (Roseberry 1989:54).

Importantly, Weber's ideas about development were informed not just by his study of Protestantism, but by an inquiry into the sociology of religion that produced studies of several Asian spiritual traditions and ancient Judaism. The excerpt below from Weber's *General Economic History* (1950) suggests the complexity of his views about development, outlines his thesis about why Protestantism produced "the spirit of capitalism," and indicates why he believed other religious traditions contributed to different development outcomes.

Karl Polanyi – born in Vienna, raised in Hungary and later a refugee in Britain, Canada and the United States – began writing *The Great Transformation* (first published in 1944) against the background of the great depression, the rise of fascism and World War II. "Fascism," he declared, "like socialism, was rooted in a market society that refused to function" (1957:239). Polanyi's objective was to explain the demise of 19th-century liberalism and the rise and collapse of the "self-regulating market," and to formulate a broader critique of "market society" (he rarely used the term "capitalism"). As Fred Block (2003:282) points out, the two key claims of Polanyi's book – that "economy" is "embedded" in society and that land, labor and money are "fictitious commodities" – constituted a challenge to the assumption, shared by free-market liberals and Marxists, that "economy" – especially under capitalism – was an analytically autonomous entity with its own internal logic.

The economy, for Polanyi, was in every society – even "market society" – "embedded" in social institutions. Concretely, this meant that institutionalized mechanisms of intervention in the market – and not only or even primarily the class struggle emphasized by Marxists – shaped economic outcomes of all kinds and particularly systems of distribution (which in turn affected production systems, the starting point of most Marxist analysis). In articulating not only the human and financial, but also the environmental consequences of allowing "the market mechanism to be the sole director," Polanyi was in many respects unusually ahead of his time. Giving free rein to the market would, he said, cause "the demolition of society"; the perishing of human beings as "victims of acute social dislocation through vice, perversion, crime, and starvation"; as well as the defiling of neighborhoods and landscapes, pollution of rivers, and the destruction of "the power to produce food and raw materials.... Shortages and surfeits of money would prove as disastrous to business as floods and droughts in primitive society" (1957:73).

Polanyi's claim that land, labor, and money are "fictitious commodities," the central theme of chapter 4 below, is based on a definition of "*commodity*" that is narrower than most. For Polanyi, a true commodity was something *produced* for sale. Labor, in contrast, was simply "human activity which goes with life itself," land was originally part of nature, and money was "merely a token of purchasing power" (1957:72). The price of labor, until the late 18th or early 19th century, was not subject to the unfettered market, but to regulation by craft guilds or, in Britain, to the Poor Laws, which until their repeal in 1834 provided the indigent with a minimum of subsistence – in effect, a floor below which wages could not fall. Land, similarly, was "outside of commerce," whether because of feudal privileges or, in England, Common Law regulations on access to different kinds of property.

Polanyi's deployment of the term "fictitious" has much in common with today's post-modernists' use of "fiction" to mean, not a mendacious invention opposed to truth, but rather "something made or fashioned" – which, as James Clifford (1986:6) has pointed out, is the main connotation of the word's Latin root, *fingere*. Land and labor could become commodities, but only through this process of fashioning as human institutions and cultures changed. This emphasis on human agency – and the rejection of historical teleologies, "laws," and beliefs about the inevitability of progress – is another element of Polanyi's work that diverges from Marxism and that has a remarkably contemporary ring. If there were historical "dialectics" or "motors" of history, they involved ethical imperatives and a search for democratic alternatives to the tyranny of both totalitarianism and the market. Although he was born Jewish, as an exile in England he forged close relations with radical Christian groups and some analysts have even described *The Great Transformation* as "a Christian socialist manifesto" (Topik 2001:82, 84–85; Block 2003:278).

Polanyi's engagement with anthropology was evident throughout *The Great Transformation*, but particularly in the chapter on "Societies and Economic Systems" and in the notes on sources that accompanied it (1957:43–55, 269–273). Basing his work largely on the writings of Bronislaw Malinowski and Richard Thurnwald, he described how societies, in the Trobriand Islands and elsewhere, were organized not around market exchange but rather around reciprocity and redistribution. Non-market forms of distribution were also a central theme in Polanyi's second major work, *Trade and Markets in the Early Empires* (1957), co-edited with anthropologist Conrad Arensberg and economist Harry Pearson. It was this collection that formed a sort of charter for what became the "substantivist" school of U.S. economic anthropology, which insisted, following Polanyi, on the "embeddedness" of the economy in social institutions and which locked horns over the following two decades with an emerging school of "formalists" who believed in the applicability of neoclassical models even to non-market societies.[5]

A second wave of interest in Polanyi began in the 1990s, with the institution of biannual international conferences and an outpouring of new literature, including a new edition of *The Great Transformation* with a foreword by the former chief economist of the World Bank, Joseph Stiglitz, who had become an acerbic critic of neoliberalism. There is little doubt that this new interest reflects the great resonance of Polanyi's ideas in the era of globalization. As Stiglitz (2001:vii) indicates, "his arguments – and his concerns – are consonant with the issues raised by the rioters and marchers who took to the streets in Seattle and Prague in 1999 and 2000 to oppose the international financial institutions."

The classical theorists whose works are discussed above, especially those of the 18th and 19th century, are sometimes relegated to the "prehistory" of development thought, primarily because they concentrated on the economics of western Europe and North America rather than on the poorer countries (Arndt 1987:30–35). As we indicate in the volume Introduction and in Part II, however, their influence on the development debates and, in some cases, the anthropology of the second half of the 20th century was profound. Nor was their interest limited to the wealthy countries of the North. Most had significant concerns with other parts of the world, especially Asia, as well as comparative sensibilities that are part of what makes their works of continuing relevance even today.

NOTES

1 A useful, if partisan, overview is Harris and Ross 1987. See also, Ross 1998.
2 Porter (1990) has argued that "clusters" of related and supporting industries confer advantages on particular firms, nations or regions. He defines "vertical clusters" as groups of firms linked through buyer-seller relations. Horizontal clusters are made up of industries that produce for the same market, use related technologies, employ similarly skilled labor, or depend on the same natural resources.
3 On this and related themes, see Donham (1999, 1990) for a subtle reading of Marx (and contemporary theorists) in a cultural history of the Ethiopian revolution.
4 Compare this with Marx and Engels' (1968:38) assertion that in the bourgeois epoch "all fixed, fast-frozen relations, with their train of ancient and venerable prejudices and opinions, are swept away... All that is solid melts into air."
5 Anthropologists spilled a large amount of ink on this theoretical controversy. For a succinct summary of the key issues see LeClair and Schneider (1968).

REFERENCES CITED

Althusser, Louis and Etienne Balibar, 1970 Reading Capital. London: NLB.

Arndt, H.W., 1987 Economic Development: The History of an Idea. Chicago: University of Chicago Press.

Block, Fred, 2003 Karl Polanyi and the Writing of the Great Transformation. Theory and Society 32:275–306.

Clifford, James, 1986 Introduction: Partial Truths. In Writing Culture: The Poetics and Politics of Ethnography, James Clifford and George E. Marcus, eds., pp. 1–26. Berkeley: University of California Press.

Cowen, M.P., and R.W. Shenton, 1996 Doctrines of Development. London: Routledge.

Dalton, George, and Jasper Köcke, 1983 The Work of the Polanyi Group: Past, Present, and Future. In Economic Anthropology: Topics and Theories, Sutti Ortiz, ed., pp. 21–50. Lanham, MD: University Press of America.

Darwin, Charles, 1958 [1892] The Autobiography of Charles Darwin and Selected Letters. New York: Dover.

De Soto, Hernando, 2000 The Mystery of Capital: Why Capitalism Triumphs in the West and Fails Everywhere Else. New York: Basic Books.

Donham, Donald L., 1990 History, Power, Ideology: Central Issues in Marxism and Anthropology. Cambridge: Cambridge University Press.

—— 1999 Marxist Modern: An Ethnographic History of the Ethiopian Revolution. Berkeley: University of California Press.

Engels, Friedrich, 1972 Origin of the Family, Private Property and the State. New York: International Publishers.

Erlich, Paul R., 1968 The Population Bomb. New York: Ballantine Books.

Giddens, Anthony, 1971 Capitalism and Modern Social Theory: An Analysis of the Writings of Marx, Durkheim and Max Weber. Cambridge: Cambridge University Press.

Godelier, Maurice, 1972 Rationality and Irrationality in Economics. New York: Monthly Review Press.

Hardin, Garrett, 1968 The Tragedy of the Commons. Science 162:1243–1248.

Harris, Marvin, and Eric B. Ross, 1987 Death, Sex, and Fertility: Population Regulation in Pre-industrial and Developing Societies. New York: Columbia University Press.

Harvey, David, 2000 Spaces of Hope. Berkeley: University of California Press.

Heilbroner, Robert L., 1972 The Worldly Philosophers: The Lives, Times and Ideas of the Great Economic Thinkers, fourth edition. New York: Simon and Schuster.

Hirschman, Albert O., 1991 The Rhetoric of Reaction: Perversity, Futility, Jeopardy. Cambridge: Belknap Press of Harvard University Press.

Katz, Claudio, 2001 The Manifesto and Globalization. Latin American Perspectives 28(6) (Nov.): 5–16.

Kuhn, Thomas, 1962 The Structure of Scientific Revolutions. Chicago: University of Chicago Press.

Landes, David S., 1998 The Wealth and Poverty of Nations: Why Some Are So Rich and Some So Poor. New York: W.W. Norton & Company.

Leclair, Edward E., and Harold K. Schneider, eds., 1968 Economic Anthropology: Readings in Theory and Analysis. New York: Holt, Rinehart and Winston.

Lubasz, Heinz, 1992 Adam Smith and the Invisible Hand – of the Market? In Contesting Markets: Analyses of Ideology, Discourse and Practice, ed. Roy Dilley, pp. 37–52. Edinburgh: Edinburgh University Press.

Lukács, Georg, 1971 History and Class Consciousness: Studies in Marxist Dialectics. Cambridge: MIT Press.

Malthus, Thomas Robert, 1872 An Essay on the Principle of Population, seventh edition. London: Reeves and Turner.

—— 1970 [1798 and 1830] An Essay on the Principle of Population and A Summary View of the Principle of Population. London: Penguin Books.

—— 1974 [1836] Principles of Political Economy Considered with a View to their Practical Application, second edition. Clifton: Augustus M. Kelley Publishers.

Marx, Karl, 1964 Economic and Philosophic Manuscripts of 1844. New York: International Publishers.

—— 1967 Capital: A Critique of Political Economy, 3 vols. New York: International Publishers.

—— 1973 Grundrisse: Foundations of the Critique of Political Economy. New York: Penguin.

Marx, Karl, and Friedrich Engels, 1968 [1848] Manifesto of the Community Party. In Marx and Engels, Selected Works New York: International Publishers.

Meillasoux, Claude, 1981 Maidens, Meal and Money: Capitalism and the Domestic Economy. Cambridge: Cambridge University Press.

Mills, C. Wright, 1959 The Sociological Imagination. New York: Oxford University Press.

Polanyi, Karl, 1957 [1944] The Great Transformation: The Political and Economic Origins of Our Time. Boston: Beacon.

Polanyi, Karl, Conrad M. Arensberg, and Harry W. Pearson, eds., 1957 Trade and Markets in the Early Empires: Economies in History and Theory. Glencoe, IL.: Free Press.

Porter, Michael E., 1990 The Competitive Advantage of Nations. New York: Free Press.

Rey, Pierre-Philippe, 1976 Les alliances de classes: Sur l'articulation des modes de production. Suivi de Matérialisme historique et luttes de classes. Paris: François Maspero.

Ricardo, David, 1965 The Principles of Political Economy and Taxation. London: Dent.

Roseberry, William, 1989 Anthropologies and Histories: Essays in Culture, History, and Political Economy. New Brunswick: Rutgers University Press.

Ross, Eric, B., 1998 The Malthus Factor: Poverty, Politics and Population in Capitalist Development. New York: St. Martin's Press.

Shanin, Teodor, ed., 1983 Late Marx and the Russian Road: Marx and the Peripheries of Capitalism. New York: Monthly Review Press.

Smith, Adam, 1976 [1776] An Inquiry into the Nature and Causes of The Wealth of Nations. Chicago: University of Chicago Press.

—— 2000 [1759] The Theory of Moral Sentiments. Amherst, NY: Prometheus Books.

Spencer, Herbert, 1961 [1874] The Study of Sociology. Ann Arbor: University of Michigan Press.

Stalin, Joseph, 1940 Dialectical and Historical Materialism. New York: International Publishers.

Thompson, E. P. 1966 The Making of the English Working Class. New York: Vintage.

Topik, Steve 2001 Karl Polanyi and the Creation of the Market Society. In The Other Mirror: Grand Theory through the Lens of Latin America, Miguel Angel Centeno and Fernando López-Alves, eds., pp. 81–104. Princeton, NJ: Princeton University Press.

Weber, Max, 1950 General Economic History. Glencoe, IL: Free Press.

—— 1958 [1904/1905] The Protestant Ethic and the Spirit of Capitalism. New York: Charles Scribner's Sons.

—— 1978 Economy and Society: An Outline of Interpretive Sociology. Berkeley: University of California Press.

Williams, Raymond, 1977 Marxism and Literature. Oxford: Oxford University Press.

Wolf, Eric. R., 2001 Pathways of Power: Building an Anthropology of the Modern World. Berkeley: University of California Press.

Wood, Ellen Meiksins, 1998 The Communist Manifesto After 150 Years. Monthly Review 50(1) (May):14–36.

1

Of the Accumulation of Capital, or of Productive and Unproductive Labour

Adam Smith

There are Two Sorts of Labour, Productive and Unproductive

There is one sort of labour which adds to the value of the subject upon which it is bestowed: there is another which has no such effect. The former, as it produces a value, may be called productive; the latter, unproductive labour. Thus the labour of a manufacturer adds, generally, to the value of the materials which he works upon, that of his own maintenance, and of his master's profit. The labour of a menial servant, on the contrary, adds to the value of nothing. Though the manufacturer has his wages advanced to him by his master, he, in reality, costs him no expence, the value of those wages being generally restored, together with a profit, in the improved value of the subject upon which his labour is bestowed. But the maintenance of a menial servant never is restored. A man grows rich by employing a multitude of manufacturers: he grows poor, by maintaining a multitude of menial servants. The labour of the latter, however, has its value, and deserves its reward as well as that of the former. But the labour of the manufacturer fixes and realizes itself in some particular subject or vendible commodity, which lasts for some time at least after that labour is past. It is, as it were, a certain quantity of labour stocked and stored up to be employed, if necessary, upon some other occasion. That subject, or what is the same thing, the price of that subject, can afterwards, if necessary, put into motion a quantity of labour equal to that which had originally produced it. The labour of the menial servant, on the contrary, does not fix or realize itself in any particular sub-ject or vendible commodity. His services generally perish in the very instant of their performance, and seldom leave any trace or value behind them, for which an equal quantity of service could afterwards be procured.

Many Kinds of Labour Besides Menial Service are Unproductive

The labour of some of the most respectable orders in the society is, like that of menial servants, un-productive of any value, and does not fix or realize itself in any permanent subject, or vendible com-modity, which endures after that labour is past, and for which an equal quantity of labour could afterwards be procured. The sovereign, for example, with all the officers both of justice and war who serve under him, the whole army and navy, are unproductive labourers. They are the servants of the public, and are maintained by a part of the annual produce of the industry of other people. Their service, how honourable, how useful, or how necessary soever, produces nothing for which an equal quantity of service can afterwards be procured. The protection, secur-ity, and defence of the common-wealth, the effect of their labour this year, will not purchase its pro-tection, security, and defence for the year to come. In the same class must be ranked, some both of the gravest and most important, and some of the most frivolous professions: churchmen, lawyers, phys-icians, men of letters of all kinds; players, buf-foons, musicians, opera-singers, opera-dancers, &c. The labour of the meanest of these has a certain value, regulated by the very same principles which regulate that of every other sort of labour; and that of the noblest and most useful, produces nothing which could afterwards purchase or procure an equal quantity of labour. Like the declamation of the actor, the harangue of the orator, or the tune of the musician, the work of all of them perishes in the very instant of its production.

[...]

In the opulent countries of Europe, great capitals are at present employed in trade and manufactures. In the ancient state, the little trade that was stirring, and the few homely and coarse manufactures that were carried on, required but very small capitals. These, however, must have yielded very large profits. The rate of interest was nowhere less than ten per cent. and their profits must have been sufficient to afford this great interest. At present the rate of interest, in the improved parts of Europe, is no-where higher than six per cent. and in some of the most improved it is so low as four, three, and two per cent. Though that part of the revenue of the inhabitants which is derived from the profits of stock is always much greater in rich than in poor countries, it is because the stock is much greater: in proportion to the stock the profits are generally much less.

That part of the annual produce, therefore, which, as soon as it comes either from the ground, or from the hands of the productive labourers, is destined for replacing a capital, is not only much greater in rich than in poor countries, but bears a much greater proportion to that which is immediately destined for constituting a revenue either as rent or as profit. The funds destined for the maintenance of productive labour, are not only much greater in the former than in the latter, but bear a much greater proportion to those which, though they may be employed to maintain either productive or unproductive hands, have generally a predilection for the latter.

The proportion between those different funds necessarily determines in every country the general character of the inhabitants as to industry or idleness. We are more industrious than our forefathers; because in the present times the funds destined for the maintenance of industry, are much greater in proportion to those which are likely to be employed in the maintenance of idleness, than they were two or three centuries ago. Our ancestors were idle for want of a sufficient encouragement to industry. It is better, says the proverb, to play for nothing, than to work for

nothing. In mercantile and manufacturing towns, where the inferior ranks of people are chiefly maintained by the employment of capital, they are in general industrious, sober, and thriving; as in many English, and in most Dutch towns. In those towns which are principally supported by the constant or occasional residence of a court, and in which the inferior ranks of people are chiefly maintained by the spending of revenue, they are in general idle, dissolute, and poor; as at Rome, Versailles, Compiegne, and Fontainbleau. If you except Rouen and Bourdeaux, there is little trade or industry in any of the parliament towns of France; and the inferior ranks of people, being chiefly maintained by the expence of the members of the courts of justice, and of those who come to plead before them, are in general idle and poor. The great trade of Rouen and Bourdeaux seems to be altogether the effect of their situation. Rouen is necessarily the entrepôt of almost all the goods which are brought either from foreign countries, or from the maritime provinces of France, for the consumption of the great city of Paris. Bourdeaux is in the same manner the entrepôt of the wines which grow upon the banks of the Garonne, and of the rivers which run into it, one of the richest wine countries in the world, and which seems to produce the wine fittest for exportation, or best suited to the taste of foreign nations. Such advantageous situations necessarily attract a great capital by the great employment which they afford it; and the employment of this capital is the cause of the industry of those two cities. In the other parliament towns of France, very little more capital seems to be employed than what is necessary for supplying their own consumption; that is, little more than the smallest capital which can be employed in them. The same thing may be said of Paris, Madrid, and Vienna. Of those three cities, Paris is by far the most industrious: but Paris itself is the principal market of all the manufactures established at Paris, and its own consumption is the principal object of all the trade which it carries on. London, Lisbon, and Copenhagen, are, perhaps, the only three cities in Europe, which are both the constant residence of a court, and can at the same time be considered as trading cities, or as cities which trade not only for their own consumption, but for that of other cities and countries. The situation of all the three is extremely advantageeous, and naturally fits them to be the entrepôts of a great part of the goods destined for the consumption of distant places. [...]

Increase or Diminution of the Capital of a Country Consequently Increases or Diminishes its Annual Produce.

The proportion between capital and revenue [...] seems every-where to regulate the proportion between industry and idleness. Wherever capital predominates, industry prevails: wherever revenue, idleness. Every increase or diminution of capital, therefore, naturally tends to increase or diminish the real quantity of industry, the number of productive hands, and consequently the exchangeable value of the annual produce of the land and labour of the country, the real wealth and revenue of all its inhabitants. Capitals are increased by parsimony, and diminished by prodigality and misconduct. [...]

[...]

Parsimony, by increasing the fund which is destined for the maintenance of productive hands, tends to increase the number of those hands whose labour adds to the value of the subject upon which it is bestowed. It tends therefore to increase the exchangeable value of the annual produce of the land and labour of the country. It puts into motion an additional quantity of industry, which gives an additional value to the annual produce.

[...]

The prodigal perverts [savings] in this manner. By not confining his expence within his income, he encroaches upon his capital. Like him who perverts the revenues of some pious foundation to profane purposes, he pays the wages of idleness with those funds which the frugality of his forefathers had, as it were, consecrated to the maintenance of industry. By diminishing the funds destined for the employment of productive labour, he necessarily diminishes, so far as it depends upon him, the quantity of that labour which adds a value to the subject upon which it is bestowed, and, consequently, the value of the annual produce of the land and labour of the whole country, the real wealth and revenue of its inhabitants. If the prodigality of some was not compensated by the frugality of others, the conduct of every prodigal, by feeding the idle with the bread of the industrious, tends not only to beggar himself, but to improverish his country.

[...]

Great nations are never impoverished by private, though they sometimes are by public prodigality and misconduct. The whole, or almost the whole public revenue, is in most countries employed in maintaining unproductive hands. Such are the people who compose a numerous and splendid court, a great ecclesiastical establishment, great fleets and armies, who in time of peace produce nothing, and in time of war acquire nothing which can compensate the expence of maintaining them, even while the war lasts. Such people, as they themselves produce nothing, are all maintained by the produce of other men's labour. When multiplied, therefore, to an unnecessary number, they may in a particular year consume so great a share of this produce, as not to leave a sufficiency for maintaining the productive labourers, who should reproduce it next year. The next year's produce, therefore, will be less than that of the foregoing, and if the same disorder should continue, that of the third year will be still less than that of the second. Those unproductive hands, who should be maintained by a part only of the spare revenue of the people, may consume so great a share of their whole revenue, and thereby oblige so great a number to encroach upon their capitals, upon the funds destined for the maintenance of productive labour, that all the frugality and good conduct of individuals may not be able to compensate the waste and degradation of produce occasioned by this violent and forced encroachment.

[...]

Apart from increase or diminution of capital different kinds of expense may be distinguished. As frugality increases, and prodigality diminishes the public capital, so the conduct of those whose expence just equals their revenue, without either accumulating or encroaching, neither increases nor diminishes it. Some modes of expence, however, seem to contribute more to the growth of public opulence than others.

The revenue of an individual may be spent, either in things which are consumed immediately, and in which one day's expence can neither alleviate nor support that of another; or it may be spent in things more durable, which can therefore be accumulated, and in which every day's expence may, as he chuses, either alleviate or support and heighten the effect of that of the following day.

[...]

[...]

As the one mode of expence is more favourable than the other to the opulence of an individual, so is it likewise to that of a nation. The houses, the furniture, the clothing of the rich, in a little time, become useful to the inferior and middling ranks of people. They are able to purchase them when their superiors grow weary of them, and the general accommodation of the whole people is thus gradually improved, when this mode of expence becomes universal among men of fortune. In countries which have long been rich, you will frequently find the inferior ranks of people in possession both of houses and furniture perfectly good and entire, but of which neither the one could have been built, nor the other have been made for their use. [...] The marriage-bed of James the First of Great Britain, which his Queen brought with her from Denmark, as a present fit for a sovereign to make to a sovereign, was, a few years ago, the ornament of an ale-house at Dunfermline. In some ancient cities, which either have been long stationary, or have gone somewhat to decay, you will sometimes scarce find a single house which could have been built for its present inhabitants. If you go into those houses too, you will frequently find many excellent, though antiquated pieces of furniture, which are still very fit for use, and which could as little have been made for them. Noble palaces, magnificent villas, great collections of books, statues, pictures, and other curiosities, are frequently both an ornament and an honour, not only to the neighbourhood, but to the whole country to which they belong. Versailles is an ornament and an honour to France, Stowe and Wilton to England. Italy still continues to command some sort of veneration by the number of monuments of this kind which it possesses, though the wealth which produced them has decayed, and though the genius which planned them seems to be extinguished, perhaps from not having the same employment.

[...]

The expence [...] that is laid out in durable commodities, gives maintenance, commonly, to a greater number of people, than that which is employed in the most profuse hospitality. Of two or three hundred weight of provisions, which may sometimes be served up at a great festival, one-half, perhaps, is thrown to the dunghill, and there is always a great deal wasted and abused. But if the expence of this entertainment had been employed in setting to work masons, carpenters, upholsterers, mechanics, &c. a quantity of provisions, of equal value, would have been distributed among a still greater number of people, who would have bought them in penny-worths and pound weights, and not have lost or thrown away a single ounce of them. In the one way, besides, this expence maintains productive, in the other unproductive hands. In the one way, therefore, it increases, in the other, it does not increase, the exchangeable value of the annual produce of the land and labour of the country.

[...]

2

Manifesto of the Communist Party

Karl Marx and Frederick Engels

[...] The history of all hitherto existing society[1] is the history of class struggles.

Freeman and slave, patrician and plebeian, lord and serf, guild-master[2] and journeyman, in a word, oppressor and oppressed, stood in constant opposition to one another, carried on an uninterrupted, now hidden, now open fight, a fight that each time ended, either in a revolutionary reconstitution of society at large, or in the common ruin of the contending classes.

In the earlier epochs of history, we find almost everywhere a complicated arrangement of society into various orders, a manifold gradation of social rank. In ancient Rome we have patricians, knights, plebeians, slaves; in the Middle Ages, feudal lords, vassals, guild-masters, journeymen, apprentices, serfs; in almost all of these classes, again, subordinate gradations.

The modern bourgeois society that has sprouted from the ruins of feudal society has not done away with class antagonisms. It has but established new classes, new conditions of oppression, new forms of struggle in place of the old ones.

Our epoch, the epoch of the bourgeoisie, possesses, however, this distinct feature: it has simplified class antagonisms. Society as a whole is more and more splitting up into two great hostile camps, into two great classes directly facing each other – bourgeoisie and proletariat.

From the serfs of the Middle Ages sprang the chartered burghers of the earliest towns. From these burgesses the first elements of the bourgeoisie were developed.

The discovery of America, the rounding of the Cape, opened up fresh ground for the rising bourgeoisie. The East-Indian and Chinese markets, the colonisation of America, trade with the colonies, the increase in the means of exchange and in commodities generally, gave to commerce, to navigation, to industry, an impulse never before known, and thereby, to the revolutionary element in the tottering feudal society, a rapid development.

The feudal system of industry, in which industrial production was monopolized by closed guilds, now no longer suffices for the growing wants of the new markets. The manufacturing system took its place. The guild-masters were pushed aside by the manufacturing middle class; division of labor between the different corporate guilds vanished in the face of division of labor in each single workshop.

Meantime, the markets kept ever growing, the demand ever rising. Even manufacturers no longer sufficed. Thereupon, steam and machinery revolutionized industrial production. The place of manufacture was taken by the giant, Modern Industry; the place of the industrial middle class by industrial millionaires, the leaders of the whole industrial armies, the modern bourgeois.

Modern industry has established the world market, for which the discovery of America paved the way. This market has given an immense development to commerce, to navigation, to communication by land. This development has, in turn, reacted on the extension of industry; and in proportion as industry, commerce, navigation, railways extended, in the same proportion the bourgeoisie developed, increased its capital, and pushed into the background every class handed down from the Middle Ages.

We see, therefore, how the modern bourgeoisie is itself the product of a long course of development, of a series of revolutions in the modes of production and of exchange.

Each step in the development of the bourgeoisie was accompanied by a corresponding political advance in that class. An oppressed class under the sway of the feudal nobility, an armed and self-governing association in the medieval commune[3]: here independent urban republic (as in Italy and Germany); there taxable "third estate" of the monarchy (as in France); afterward, in the period of manufacturing proper, serving either the semi-feudal or the absolute monarchy as a counterpoise against the nobility, and, in fact, cornerstone of the great monarchies in general – the bourgeoisie has at last, since the establishment of Modern Industry and of the world market, conquered for itself, in the modern representative state, exclusive political sway. The executive of the modern state is but a committee for managing the common affairs of the whole bourgeoisie.

The bourgeoisie, historically, has played a most revolutionary part.

The bourgeoisie, wherever it has got the upper hand, has put an end to all feudal, patriarchal, idyllic relations. It has pitilessly torn asunder the motley feudal ties that bound man to his "natural superiors", and has left no other nexus between man and man than naked self-interest, than callous "cash payment." It has drowned out the most heavenly ecstasies of religious fervour, of chivalrous enthusiasm, of philistine sentimentalism, in the icy water of egotistical calculation. It has resolved personal worth into exchange value, and in place of the numberless indefeasible chartered freedoms, has set up that single, unconscionable freedom – Free Trade. In one word, for exploitation, veiled by religious and political illusions, it has substituted naked, shameless, direct, brutal exploitation.

The bourgeoisie has stripped of its halo every occupation hitherto honored and looked up to with reverent awe. It has converted the physician, the lawyer, the priest, the poet, the man of science, into its paid wage laborers.

The bourgeoisie has torn away from the family its sentimental veil, and has reduced the family relation into a mere money relation.

The bourgeoisie has disclosed how it came to pass that the brutal display of vigour in the Middle Ages, which reactionaries so much admire, found its fitting complement in the most slothful indolence. It has been the first to show what man's activity can bring about. It has accomplished wonders far surpassing Egyptian pyramids, Roman aqueducts, and Gothic cathedrals; it has conducted expeditions that put in the shade all former exoduses of nations and crusades.

The bourgeoisie cannot exist without constantly revolutionizing the instruments of production, and thereby the relations of production, and with them the whole relations of society. Conservation of the old modes of production in unaltered form, was, on the contrary, the first condition of existence for all earlier industrial classes. Constant revolutionizing of production, uninterrupted disturbance of all social conditions, everlasting uncertainty and agitation distinguish the bourgeois epoch from all earlier ones. All fixed, fast frozen relations, with their train of ancient and venerable prejudices and opinions, are swept away, all new-formed ones become antiquated before they can ossify. All that is solid melts into air, all that is holy is profaned, and man is at last compelled to face with sober senses his real condition of life and his relations with his kind.

The need of a constantly expanding market for its products chases the bourgeoisie over the entire surface of the globe. It must nestle everywhere, settle everywhere, establish connections everywhere.

The bourgeoisie has, through its exploitation of the world market, given a cosmopolitan character to production and consumption in every country. To the great chagrin of reactionaries, it has drawn from under the feet of industry the national ground on which it stood. All old-established national industries have been destroyed or are daily being destroyed. They are dislodged by new industries, whose introduction becomes a life and death question for all civilized nations, by industries that no longer work up indigenous raw material, but raw material drawn from the remotest zones; industries whose products are consumed, not only at home, but in every quarter of the globe. In place of the old wants, satisfied by the production of the country, we find new wants, requiring for their satisfaction the products of distant lands and climes. In place of the old local and national seclusion and self-sufficiency, we have intercourse in every direction, universal inter-dependence of nations. And as in material, so also in intellectual production. The intellectual creations of individual nations become common property. National one-sidedness and narrow-mindedness become more and more impossible, and from the numerous national and local literatures, there arises a world literature.

The bourgeoisie, by the rapid improvement of all instruments of production, by the immensely facilitated means of communication, draws all, even the most barbarian, nations into civilization. The cheap prices of commodities are the heavy artillery with which it forces the barbarians' intensely obstinate hatred of foreigners to capitulate. It compels all nations, on pain of extinction, to adopt the bourgeois mode of production; it compels them to introduce what it calls civilization into their midst, i.e., to become bourgeois themselves. In one word, it creates a world after its own image.

The bourgeoisie has subjected the country to the rule of the towns. It has created enormous cities, has greatly increased the urban population as compared with the rural, and has thus rescued a considerable part of the population from the idiocy of rural life. Just as it has made the country dependent on the towns, so it has made barbarian and semi-barbarian countries dependent on the civilized ones, nations of peasants on nations of bourgeois, the East on the West [. . . .]

The bourgeoisie, during its rule of scarce one hundred years, has created more massive and more colossal productive forces than have all preceding generations together. Subjection of nature's forces to man, machinery, application of chemistry to industry and agriculture, steam navigation, railways, electric telegraphs, clearing of whole continents for cultivation, canalization or rivers, whole populations conjured out of the ground – what earlier century had even a presentiment that such productive forces slumbered in the lap of social labor?

We see then: the means of production and of exchange, on whose foundation the bourgeoisie built itself up, were generated in feudal society. At a certain stage in the development of these means of production and of exchange, the conditions under which feudal society produced and exchanged, the feudal organization of agriculture and manufacturing industry, in one word, the feudal relations of property became no longer compatible with the already developed productive forces; they became so many fetters. They had to be burst asunder; they were burst asunder.

Into their place stepped free competition, accompanied by a social and political constitution adapted in it, and the economic and political sway of the bourgeois class.

A similar movement is going on before our own eyes. Modern bourgeois society, with its relations of production, of exchange and of property, a society that has conjured up such gigantic means of production and of exchange, is like the sorcerer who is no longer able to control the powers of the nether world whom he has called up by his spells. For many a decade past, the history of industry and commerce is but the history of the revolt of modern productive forces against modern conditions of production, against the property relations that are the conditions for the existence of the bourgeois and of its rule. It is enough to mention the commercial crises that, by their periodical return, put the existence of the entire bourgeois society on its trial, each time more threateningly. In these crises, a great part not only of the existing products, but also of the previously created productive forces, are periodically destroyed. In these crises, there breaks out an epidemic that, in all earlier epochs, would have seemed an absurdity – the epidemic of over-production. Society suddenly finds itself put back into a state of momentary barbarism; it appears as if a famine, a universal war of devastation, had cut off the supply of every means of subsistence; industry and commerce seem to be destroyed. And why? Because there is too much civilization, too much means of subsistence, too much industry, too much commerce. The productive forces at the disposal of society no longer tend to further the development of the conditions of bourgeois property; on the contrary, they have become too powerful for these conditions, by which they are fettered, and so soon as they overcome these fetters, they bring disorder into the whole of bourgeois society, endanger the existence of bourgeois property. The conditions of bourgeois society are too narrow to comprise the wealth created by them. And how does the bourgeoisie get over these crises? On the one hand, by enforced destruction of a mass of productive forces; on the other, by the conquest of new markets, and by the more thorough exploitation of the old ones. That is to say, by paving the way for more extensive and more destructive crises, and by diminishing the means whereby crises are prevented.

The weapons with which the bourgeoisie felled feudalism to the ground are now turned against the bourgeoisie itself.

But not only has the bourgeoisie forged the weapons that bring death to itself; it has also called into existence the men who are to wield those weapons – the modern working class – the proletarians.

In proportion as the bourgeoisie, i.e., capital, is developed, in the same proportion is the proletariat, the modern working class, developed – a class of laborers, who live only so long as they find work, and who find work only so long as their labor increases capital. These laborers, who must sell themselves piecemeal, are a commodity, like every other article of commerce, and are consequently exposed to all the vicissitudes of competition, to all the fluctuations of the market.

Owing to the extensive use of machinery, and to the division of labor, the work of the proletarians has lost all individual character, and, consequently, all charm for the workman. He becomes an appendage of the machine, and it is only the most simple, most monotonous, and most easily acquired knack, that is required of him. Hence, the cost of production of a workman is restricted, almost entirely, to the means of subsistence that he requires for maintenance, and for the propagation of his race [....]

Modern Industry has converted the little workshop of the patriarchal master into the great factory of the industrial capitalist. Masses of laborers, crowded into the factory, are organized like soldiers. As privates of the industrial army, they are placed under the command of a perfect hierarchy of officers and sergeants. Not only are they slaves of the bourgeois class, and of the bourgeois state; they are daily and hourly enslaved by the machine, by the overlooker, and, above all, in the individual bourgeois manufacturer himself. The more openly this despotism proclaims gain to be its end and aim, the more petty, the more hateful and the more embittering it is.

The less the skill and exertion of strength implied in manual labor, in other words, the more modern industry becomes developed, the more is the labor of men superseded by that of women. Differences of age and sex have no longer any distinctive social validity for the working class. All are instruments of labor, more or less expensive to use, according to their age and sex [....]

The lower middle class, the small manufacturer, the shopkeeper, the artisan, the peasant, all these fight against the bourgeoisie, to save from extinction their existence as fractions of the middle class. They are therefore not revolutionary, but conservative. Nay, more, they are reactionary, for they try to roll back the wheel of history. If, by chance, they are revolutionary, they are only so in view of their impending transfer into the proletariat; they thus defend not their present, but their future interests; they desert their own standpoint to place themselves at that of the proletariat [....]

Hitherto, every form of society has been based, as we have already seen, on the antagonism of oppressing and oppressed classes. But in order to oppress a class, certain conditions must be assured to it under which it can, at least, continue its slavish existence. The serf, in the period of serf-dom, raised himself to membership in the commune, just as the petty bourgeois, under the yoke of the feudal absolutism, managed to develop into a bourgeois. The modern laborer, on the contrary, instead of rising with the process of industry, sinks deeper and deeper below the conditions of existence of his own class. He becomes a pauper, and pauperism develops more rapidly than population and wealth. And here it becomes evident that the bourgeoisie is unfit any longer to be the ruling class in society, and to impose its conditions of existence upon society as an overriding law. It is unfit to rule because it is incompetent to assure an existence to its slave within his slavery, because it cannot help letting him sink into such a state, that it has to feed him, instead of being fed by him. Society can no longer live under this bourgeoisie, in other words, its existence is no longer compatible with society [....]

When, in the course of development, class distinctions have disappeared, and all production has been concentrated in the hands of a vast association of the whole nation, the public power will lose its political character. Political power, properly so called, is merely the organized power of one class for oppressing another. If the proletariat during its contest with the bourgeoisie is compelled, by the force of circumstances, to organize itself as a class; if, by means of a revolution, it makes itself the ruling class, and, as such, sweeps away by force the old conditions of production, then it will, along with these conditions, have swept away the conditions for the existence of class antagonisms and of classes generally, and will thereby have abolished its own supremacy as a class.

In place of the old bourgeois society, with its classes and class antagonisms, we shall have an association in which the free development of each is the condition for the free development of all.

NOTES

1 That is, all written history.
2 Guild-master, that is, a full member of a guild, a master within, not a head of a guild.
3 This was the name given their urban communities by the townsmen of Italy and France, after they had purchased or conquered their initial rights of self-government from their feudal lords.

3

The Evolution of the Capitalistic Spirit

Max Weber

It is a widespread error that the increase of population is to be included as a really crucial agent in the evolution of western capitalism. In opposition to this view, Karl Marx made the assertion that every economic epoch has its own law of population, and although this proposition is untenable in so general a form, it is justified in the present case. The growth of population in the west made most rapid progress from the beginning of the 18th century to the end of the 19th. In the same period China experienced a population growth of at least equal extent – from 60 or 70 to 400 millions, allowing for the inevitable exaggerations; this corresponds approximately with the increase in the west. In spite of this fact, capitalism went backward in China and not forward. The increase in the population took place there in different strata than with us. It made China the seat of a swarming mass of small peasants; the increase of a class corresponding to our proletariat was involved only to the extent that a foreign market made possible the employment of coolies ("coolie" is originally an Indian expression, and signifies neighbor or fellow member of a clan). The growth of population in Europe did indeed favor the development of capitalism, to the extent that in a small population the system would have been unable to secure the necessary labor force, but in itself it never called forth that development.

Nor can the inflow of precious metals be regarded, as Sombart suggests, as the primary cause of the appearance of capitalism. It is certainly true that in a given situation an increase in the supply of precious metals may give rise to price revolutions, such as that which took place after 1530 in Europe, and when other favorable conditions are present, as when a certain form of labor

organization is in process of development, the progress may be stimulated by the fact that large stocks of cash come into the hands of certain groups. But the case of India proves that such an importation of precious metal will not alone bring about capitalism. In India in the period of the Roman power, an enormous mass of precious metal – some twenty-five million *sestertii* annually – came in in exchange for domestic goods, but this inflow gave rise to commercial capitalism to only a slight extent. The greater part of the precious metal disappeared in the hoards of the rajahs instead of being converted into cash and applied in the establishment of enterprises of a rational capitalistic character. This fact proves that it depends entirely upon the nature of the labor system what tendency will result from an inflow of precious metal. The gold and silver from America, after the discovery, flowed in the first place to Spain; but in that country a recession of capitalistic development took place parallel with the importation. There followed, on the one hand, the suppression of the *communeros* and the destruction of the commercial interests of the Spanish grandees, and, on the other hand, the employment of the money for military ends. Consequently, the stream of precious metal flowed through Spain, scarcely touching it, and fertilized other countries, which in the 15th century were already undergoing a process of transformation in labor relations which was favorable to capitalism.

Hence neither the growth of population nor the importation of precious metal called forth western capitalism. The external conditions for the development of capitalism are rather, first, geographical in character. In China and India the enormous costs of transportation, connected with the decisively inland commerce of the regions, necessarily formed serious obstructions for the classes who were in a position to make profits through trade and to use trading capital in the construction of a capitalistic system, while in the west the position of the Mediterranean as an inland sea, and the abundant interconnections through the rivers, favored the opposite development of international commerce. But this factor in its turn must not be over-estimated. The civilization of antiquity was distinctively coastal. Here the opportunities for commerce were very favorable, (thanks to the character of the Mediterranean Sea,) in contrast with the Chinese waters with their typhoons, and yet no capitalism arose in antiquity. Even in the modern period the capitalistic development was much more intense in Florence than in Genoa or in Venice. Capitalism in the west was born in the industrial cities of the interior, not in the cities which were centers of sea trade. [...]

In the last resort the factor which produced capitalism is the rational permanent enterprise, rational accounting, rational technology and rational law, but again not these alone. Necessary complementary factors were the rational spirit, the rationalization of the conduct of life in general, and a rationalistic economic ethic.

At the beginning of all ethics and the economic relations which result, is traditionalism, the sanctity of tradition, the exclusive reliance upon such trade and industry as have come down from the fathers. This traditionalism survives far down into the present; only a human lifetime in the past it was futile to double the wages of an agricultural laborer in Silesia who mowed a certain tract of land on a contract, in the hope of inducing him to increase his exertions. He would simply have reduced by half the work expended because with this half he would have been able to earn twice as much as before (sic). This general incapacity and indisposition to depart from the beaten paths is the motive for the maintenance of tradition.

Primitive traditionalism may, however, undergo essential intensification through two circumstances. In the first place, material interests may be tied up with the maintenance of the tradition. When for example in China, the attempt was made to change certain roads or to introduce more rational means or routes of transportation, the perquisites of certain officials were threatened; and the same was the case in the middle ages in the west, and in modern times when railroads were introduced. Such special interests of officials, landholders and merchants assisted decisively in restricting a tendency toward rationalization.

Stronger still is the effect of the stereotyping of trade on magical grounds, the deep repugnance to undertaking any change in the established conduct of life because super-natural evils are feared. Generally some injury to economic privilege is concealed in this opposition, but its effectiveness depends on a general belief in the potency of the magical processes which are feared.

Traditional obstructions are not overcome by the economic impulse alone. The notion that our rationalistic and capitalistic age is characterized by a stronger economic interest than other periods is childish; the moving spirits of modern capitalism are not possessed of a stronger economic impulse than, for example, an oriental trader. [...]

If the economic impulse in itself is universal, it is an interesting question as to the relations under which it becomes rationalized and rationally tempered in such fashion as to produce rational institutions of the character of capitalistic enterprise.

Originally, two opposite attitudes toward the pursuit of gain exist in combination. Internally, there is attachment to tradition and to the pietistic relations of fellow members of tribe, clan, and house-community, with the exclusion of the unrestricted quest of gain within the circle of those bound together by religious ties; externally, there is absolutely unrestricted play of the gain spirit in economic relations, every foreigner being originally an enemy in relation to whom no ethical restrictions apply; that is, the ethics of internal and external relations are categorically distinct. The course of development involves on the one hand the bringing in of calculation into the traditional brotherhood, displacing the old religious relationship. As soon as accountability is established within the family community, and economic relations are no longer strictly communistic, there is an end of the naive piety and its repression of the economic impulse. This side of the development is especially characteristic in the west. At the same time there is a tempering of the unrestricted quest of gain with the adoption of the economic principle into the internal economy. The result is a regulated economic life with the economic impulse functioning within bounds. [...]

The typical antipathy of Catholic ethics, and following that the Lutheran, to every capitalistic tendency, rests essentially on the repugnance of the impersonality of relations within a capitalist economy. It is this fact of impersonal relations which places certain human affairs outside the church and its influence, and prevents the latter from penetrating them and transforming them along ethical lines. The relations between master and slave could be subjected to immediate ethical regulation; but the relations between the mortgage creditor and the property which was pledged for the debt, or between an endorser and the bill of exchange, would at least be exceedingly difficult if not impossible to moralize. The final consequence of the resulting position assumed by the church was that medieval economic ethics excluded higgling, overpricing and free competition, and were based on the principle of just price and the assurance to everyone of a chance to live. [...]

[...]

It is [...] necessary to distinguish between the virtuoso religion of adepts and the religion of the masses. Virtuoso religion is significant for everyday life only as a pattern; its claims are of the highest, but they fail to determine everyday ethics. The relation between the two is different in different religions. In Catholicism, they are brought into harmonious union insofar as the claims of the religious virtuoso are held up alongside the duties of the laymen as *consilia evangelica*. The really complete Christian is the monk; but his mode of life is not required of everyone, although some of his virtues in a qualified form are held up as ideals. The advantage of this combination was that ethics was not split asunder as in Buddhism. After all the distinction between monk ethics and mass ethics meant that the most worthy individuals in the religious sense withdrew from the world and established a separate community.

Christianity was not alone in this phenomenon, which rather recurs frequently in the history of religions, as is shown by the powerful influence of asceticism, which signifies the carrying out of a definite, methodical conduct of life. Asceticism has always worked in this sense. The enormous achievements possible to such an ascetically determined methodical conduct of life are demonstrated by the example of Tibet. The country seems condemned by nature to be an eternal desert; but a community of celibate ascetics has carried out colossal construction works in Lhassa and saturated the country with the religious doctrines of Buddhism. An analogous phenomenon is present in the middle ages in the west. In that epoch the monk is the first human being who lives rationally, who works methodically and by rational means toward a goal, namely the future life. Only for him did the clock strike, only for him were the hours of the day divided – for prayer. The economic life of the monastic communities was also rational. The monks in part furnished the officialdom for the early middle ages; the power

of the doges of Venice collapsed when the investiture struggle deprived them of the possibility of employing churchmen for oversea enterprises.

But the rational mode of life remained restricted to the monastic circles. The Franciscan movement indeed attempted through the institution of the tertiaries to extend it to the laity, but the institution of the confessional was a barrier to such an extension. The church domesticated medieval Europe by means of its system of confession and penance, but for the men of the middle ages the possibility of unburdening themselves through the channel of the confessional, when they had rendered themselves liable to punishment, meant a release from the consciousness of sin which the teachings of the church had called into being. The unity and strength of the methodical conduct of life were thus in fact broken up. In its knowledge of human nature the church did not reckon with the fact that the individual is a closed unitary ethical personality, but steadfastly held to the view that in spite of the warnings of the confessional and of penances, however strong, he would again fall away morally; that is, it shed its grace on the just and the unjust.

The Reformation made a decisive break with this system. The dropping of the *concilia evangelica* by the Lutheran Reformation meant the disappearance of the dualistic ethics, of the distinction between a universally binding morality and a specifically advantageous code for virtuosi. The otherworldly asceticism came to an end. The stern religious characters who had previously gone into monasteries had now to practice their religion in the life of the world. For such an asceticism within the world the ascetic dogmas of protestantism created an adequate ethics. Celibacy was not required, marriage being viewed simply as an institution for the rational bringing up of children. Poverty was not required, but the pursuit of riches must not lead one astray into reckless enjoyment. Thus Sebastian Franck was correct in summing up the spirit of the Reformation in the words, "you think you have escaped from the monastery, but everyone must now be a monk throughout his life."

The wide significance of this transformation of the ascetic ideal can be followed down to the present in the classical lands of protestant ascetic religiosity. It is especially discernible in the import of the religious denominations in America. Although state and church are separated, still, as late as fifteen or twenty years ago no banker or physician took up a residence or established connections without being asked to what religious community he belonged, and his prospects were good or bad according to the character of his answer. Acceptance into a sect was conditioned upon a strict inquiry into one's ethical conduct. Membership in a sect which did not recognize the Jewish distinction between internal and external moral codes guaranteed one's business honor and reliability and this in turn guaranteed success. Hence the principle "honesty is the best policy" and hence among Quakers, Baptists, and Methodists the ceaseless repetition of the proposition based on experience that God would take care of his own. "The Godless cannot trust each other across the road; they turn to us when they want to do business; piety is the surest road to wealth." This is by no means "cant," but a combination of religiosity with consequences which were originally unknown to it and which were never intended.

It is true that the acquisition of wealth, attributed to piety, led to a dilemma, in all respects similar to that into which the medieval monasteries constantly fell; the religious guild led to wealth, wealth to fall from grace, and this again to the necessity of re-constitution. Calvinism sought to avoid this difficulty through the idea that man was only an administrator of what God had given him; it condemned enjoyment, yet permitted no flight from the world but rather regarded working together, with its rational discipline, as the religious task of the individual. Out of this system of thought came our word "calling," which is known only to the languages influenced by the Protestant translations of the Bible. It expresses the value placed upon rational activity carried on according to the rational capitalistic principle, as the fulfillment of a God-given task. [. . .]

This development of the concept of the calling quickly gave to the modern entrepreneur a fabulously clear conscience, – and also industrious workers; he gave to his employees as the wages of their ascetic devotion to the calling and of co-operation in his ruthless exploitation of them through capitalism the prospect of eternal salvation, which in an age when ecclesiastical discipline took control of the whole of life to an extent inconceivable to us now, represented a reality quite different from any it has today. The Catholic and Lutheran churches also recognized and practiced ecclesiastical discipline. But in the Protestant ascetic communities admission to the Lord's Supper was conditioned on ethical fitness, which again was identified with business honor, while into the content of one's faith no one inquired. Such a powerful, unconsciously refined organization for the production of capitalistic individuals has never existed in any other church or religion, and in comparison with it what the Renaissance did for capitalism shrinks into insignificance. Its practitioners occupied themselves with technical problems and were experimenters of the first rank. From art and mining experimentation was taken over into science.

The world-view of the Renaissance, however, determined the policy of rulers in a large measure, though it did not transform the soul of man as did the innovations of the Reformation. Almost all the great scientific discoveries of the 16th and even the beginning of the 17th century were made against the background of Catholicism. Copernicus was a Catholic, while Luther and Melanchthon repudiated his discoveries. Scientific progress and Protestantism must not at all be unquestioningly identified. The Catholic church has indeed occasionally obstructed scientific progress; but the ascetic sects of Protestantism have also been disposed to have nothing to do with science, except in a situation where material requirements of everyday life were involved. On the other hand it is its specific contribution to have placed science in the service of technology and economics.

The religious root of modern economic humanity is dead; today the concept of the calling is a *caput mortuum* in the world. Ascetic religiosity has been displaced by a pessimistic though by no means ascetic view of the world, such as that portrayed in Mandeville's Fable of the Bees, which teaches that private vices may under certain conditions be for the good of the public. With the complete disappearance of all the remains of the original enormous religious pathos of the sects, the optimism of the Enlightenment which believed in the harmony of interests, appeared as the heir of Protestant asceticism in the field of economic ideas; it guided the hands of the princes, statesmen, and writers of the later 18th and early 19th century. Economic ethics arose against the background of the ascetic ideal; now it has been stripped of its religious import. It was possible for the working class to accept its lot as long as the promise of eternal happiness could be held out to it. When this consolation fell away it was inevitable that those strains and stresses should appear in economic society which since then have grown so rapidly. This point had been reached at the end of the early period of capitalism, at the beginning of the age of iron, in the 19th century.

4

The Self-Regulating Market and the Fictitious Commodities: Labor, Land, and Money

Karl Polanyi

[...] Never before our own time were markets more than accessories of economic life. As a rule, the economic system was absorbed in the social system, and whatever principle of behavior predominated in the economy, the presence of the market pattern was found to be compatible with it. The principle of barter or exchange, which underlies this pattern, revealed no tendency to expand at the expense of the rest. Where markets were most highly developed, as under the mercantile system, they throve under the control of a centralized administration which fostered autarchy both in the households of the peasantry and in respect to national life. Regulation and markets, in effect, grew up together. The self-regulating market was unknown; indeed the emergence of the idea of self-regulation was a complete reversal of the trend of development. It is in the light of these facts that the extraordinary assumptions underlying a market economy can alone be fully comprehended.

A market economy is an economic system controlled, regulated, and directed by markets alone; order in the production and distribution of goods is entrusted to this self-regulating mechanism. An economy of this kind derives from the expectation that human beings behave in such a way as to achieve maximum money gains. It assumes markets in which the supply of goods (including services) available at a definite price will equal the demand at that price. It assumes the presence of money, which functions as purchasing power in the hands of its owners. Production will then be controlled by prices, for the profits of those who direct production will depend upon them; the dis-

tribution of the goods also will depend upon prices, for prices form incomes, and it is with the help of these incomes that the goods produced are distributed amongst the members of society. Under these assumptions order in the production and distribution of goods is ensured by prices alone.

Self-regulation implies that all production is for sale on the market and that all incomes derive from such sales. Accordingly, there are markets for all elements of industry, not only for goods (always including services) but also for labor, land, and money, their prices being called respectively commodity prices, wages, rent, and interest. The very terms indicate that prices form incomes: interest is the price for the use of money and forms the income of those who are in the position to provide it; rent is the price for the use of land and forms the income of those who supply it; wages are the price for the use of labor power, and form the income of those who sell it; commodity prices, finally, contribute to the incomes of those who sell their entrepreneurial services, the income called profit being actually the difference between two sets of prices, the price of the goods produced and their costs, i.e., the price of the goods necessary to produce them. If these conditions are fulfilled, all incomes will derive from sales on the market, and incomes will be just sufficient to buy all the goods produced.

A further group of assumptions follows in respect to the state and its policy. Nothing must be allowed to inhibit the formation of markets, nor must incomes be permitted to be formed otherwise than through sales. Neither must there be any interference with the adjustment of prices to changed market conditions – whether the prices are those of goods, labor, land, or money. Hence there must not only be markets for all elements of industry,[1] but no measure or policy must be countenanced that would influence the action of these markets. Neither price, nor supply, nor demand must be fixed or regulated; only such policies and measures are in order which help to ensure the self-regulation of the market by creating conditions which make the market the only organizing power in the economic sphere.

To realize fully what this means, let us turn for a moment to the mercantile system and the national markets which it did so much to develop. Under feudalism and the gild system land and labor formed part of the social organization itself (money had yet hardly developed into a major element of industry). Land, the pivotal element in the feudal order, was the basis of the military, judicial, administrative, and political system; its status and function were determined by legal and customary rules. Whether its possession was transferable or not, and if so, to whom and under what restrictions; what the rights of property entailed; to what uses some types of land might be put – all these questions were removed from the organization of buying and selling, and subjected to an entirely different set of institutional regulations.

The same was true of the organization of labor. Under the gild system, as under every other economic system in previous history, the motives and circumstances of productive activities were embedded in the general organization of society. The relations of master, journeyman, and apprentice; the terms of the craft; the number of apprentices; the wages of the workers were all regulated by the custom and rule of the gild and the town. What the mercantile system did was merely to unify these conditions either through statute as in England, or through the "nationalization" of the gilds as in France. As to land, its feudal status was abolished only in so far as it was linked with provincial privileges; for the rest, land remained *extra commercium*, in England as in France. Up to the time of the Great Revolution of 1789, landed estate remained the source of social privilege in France, and even after that time in England Common Law on land was essentially medieval. Mercantilism, with all its tendency towards commercialization, never attacked the safeguards which protected these two basic elements of production – labor and land – from becoming the objects of commerce. In England the "nationalization" of labor legislation through the Statute of

Artificers (1563) and the Poor Law (1601), removed labor from the danger zone, and the anti-enclosure policy of the Tudors and early Stuarts was one consistent protest against the principle of the gainful use of landed property.

That mercantilism, however emphatically it insisted on commercialization as a national policy, thought of markets in a way exactly contrary to market economy, is best shown by its vast extension of state intervention in industry. On this point there was no difference between mercantilists and feudalists, between crowned planners and vested interests, between centralizing bureaucrats and conservative particularists. They disagreed only on the methods of regulation: gilds, towns, and provinces appealed to the force of custom and tradition, while the new state authority favored statute and ordinance. But they were all equally averse to the idea of commercializing labor and land – the pre-condition of market economy. Craft gilds and feudal privileges were abolished in France only in 1790; in England the Statute of Artificers was repealed only in 1813–14, the Elizabethan Poor Law in 1834. Not before the last decade of the eighteenth century was, in either country, the establishment of a free labor market even discussed; and the idea of the self-regulation of economic life was utterly beyond the horizon of the age. The mercantilist was concerned with the development of the resources of the country, including full employment, through trade and commerce; the traditional organization of land and labor he took for granted. He was in this respect as far removed from modern concepts as he was in the realm of politics, where his belief in the absolute powers of an enlightened despot was tempered by no intimations of democracy. And just as the transition to a democratic system and representative politics involved a complete reversal of the trend of the age, the change from regulated to self-regulating markets at the end of the eighteenth century represented a complete transformation in the structure of society.

A self-regulating market demands nothing less than the institutional separation of society into an economic and political sphere. Such a dichotomy is, in effect, merely the restatement, from the point of view of society as a whole, of the existence of a self-regulating market. It might be argued that the separateness of the two spheres obtains in every type of society at all times. Such an inference, however, would be based on a fallacy. True, no society can exist without a system of some kind which ensures order in the production and distribution of goods. But that does not imply the existence of separate economic institutions; normally, the economic order is merely a function of the social, in which it is contained. Neither under tribal, nor feudal, nor mercantile conditions was there, as we have shown, a separate economic system in society. Nineteenth-century society, in which economic activity was isolated and imputed to a distinctive economic motive, was, indeed, a singular departure.

Such an institutional pattern could not function unless society was somehow subordinated to its requirements. A market economy can exist only in a market society. We reached this conclusion on general grounds in our analysis of the market pattern. We can now specify the reasons for this assertion. A market economy must comprise all elements of industry, including labor, land, and money. (In a market economy the last also is an essential element of industrial life and its inclusion in the market mechanism has, as we will see, far-reaching institutional consequences.) But labor and land are no other than the human beings themselves of which every society consists and the natural surroundings in which it exists. To include them in the market mechanism means to subordinate the substance of society itself to the laws of the market.

We are now in the position to develop in a more concrete form the institutional nature of a market economy, and the perils to society which it involves. We will, first, describe the methods by which the market mechanism is enabled to control and direct the actual elements of industrial life; second, we will try to gauge the nature of the effects of such a mechanism on the society which is subjected to its action.

It is with the help of the commodity concept that the mechanism of the market is geared to the various elements of industrial life. Commodities are here empirically defined as objects produced for sale on the market; markets, again, are empirically defined as actual contacts between buyers and sellers. Accordingly, every element of industry is regarded as having been produced for sale, as then and then only will it be subject to the supply-and-demand mechanism interacting with price. In practice this means that there must be markets for every element of industry; that in these markets each of these elements is organized into a supply and a demand group; and that each element has a price which interacts with demand and supply. These markets – and they are numberless – are interconnected and form One Big Market.

The crucial point is this: labor, land, and money are essential elements of industry; they also must be organized in markets; in fact, these markets form an absolutely vital part of the economic system. But labor, land, and money are obviously *not* commodities; the postulate that anything that is bought and sold must have been produced for sale is emphatically untrue in regard to them. In other words, according to the empirical definition of a commodity they are not commodities. Labor is only another name for a human activity which goes with life itself, which in its turn is not produced for sale but for entirely different reasons, nor can that activity be detached from the rest of life, be stored or mobilized; land is only another name for nature, which is not produced by man; actual money, finally, is merely a token of purchasing power which, as a rule, is not produced at all, but comes into being through the mechanism of banking or state finance. None of them is produced for sale. The commodity description of labor, land, and money is entirely fictitious.

Nevertheless, it is with the help of this fiction that the actual markets for labor, land, and money are organized;[2] they are being actually bought and sold on the market; their demand and supply are real magnitudes; and any measures or policies that would inhibit the formation of such markets would *ipso facto* endanger the self-regulation of the system. The commodity fiction, therefore, supplies a vital organizing principle in regard to the whole of society affecting almost all its institutions in the most varied way, namely, the principle according to which no arrangement or behavior should be allowed to exist that might prevent the actual functioning of the market mechanism on the lines of the commodity fiction.

Now, in regard to labor, land, and money such a postulate cannot be upheld. To allow the market mechanism to be sole director of the fate of human beings and their natural environment, indeed, even of the amount and use of purchasing power, would result in the demolition of society. For the alleged commodity "labor power" cannot be shoved about, used indiscriminately, or even left unused, without affecting also the human individual who happens to be the bearer of this peculiar commodity. In disposing of a man's labor power the system would, incidentally, dispose of the physical, psychological, and moral entity "man" attached to that tag. Robbed of the protective covering of cultural institutions, human beings would perish from the effects of social exposure; they would die as the victims of acute social dislocation through vice, perversion, crime, and starvation. Nature would be reduced to its elements, neighborhoods and landscapes defiled, rivers polluted, military safety jeopardized, the power to produce food and raw materials destroyed. Finally, the market administration of purchasing power would periodically liquidate business enterprise, for shortages and surfeits of money would prove as disastrous to business as floods and droughts in primitive society. Undoubtedly, labor, land, and money markets *are* essential to a market economy. But no society could stand the effects of such a system of crude fictions even for the shortest stretch of time unless its human and natural substance as well as its business organization was protected against the ravages of this satanic mill.

The extreme artificiality of market economy is rooted in the fact that the process of production itself is here organized in the form of buying and selling. No other way of organizing production for the market is possible in a commercial society. During the late Middle Ages industrial production for export was organized by wealthy burgesses, and carried on under their direct supervision in the home town. Later, in the mercantile society, production was organized by merchants and was not restricted any more to the towns; this was the age of "putting out" when domestic industry was provided with raw materials by the merchant capitalist, who controlled the process of production as a purely commercial enterprise. It was then that industrial production was definitely and on a large scale put under the organizing leadership of the merchant. He knew the market, the volume as well as the quality of the demand; and he could vouch also for the supplies which, incidentally, consisted merely of wool, woad, and, sometimes, the looms or the knitting frames used by the cottage industry. If supplies failed it was the cottager who was worst hit, for his employment was gone for the time; but no expensive plant was involved and the merchant incurred no serious risk in shouldering the responsibility for production. For centuries this system grew in power and scope until in a country like England the wool industry, the national staple, covered large sectors of the country where production was organized by the clothier. He who bought and sold, incidentally, provided for production – no separate motive was required. The creation of goods involved neither the reciprocating attitudes of mutual aid; nor the concern of the householder for those whose needs are left to his care; nor the craftsman's pride in the exercise of his trade; nor the satisfaction of public praise – nothing but the plain motive of gain so familiar to the man whose profession is buying and selling. Up to the end of the eighteenth century, industrial production in Western Europe was a mere accessory to commerce.

As long as the machine was an inexpensive and unspecific tool there was no change in this position. The mere fact that the cottager could produce larger amounts than before within the same time might induce him to use machines to increase earnings, but this fact in itself did not necessarily affect the organization of production. Whether the cheap machinery was owned by the worker or by the merchant made some difference in the social position of the parties and almost certainly made a difference in the earnings of the worker, who was better off as long as he owned his tools; but it did not force the merchant to become an industrial capitalist, or to restrict himself to lending his money to such persons as were. The vent of goods rarely gave out; the greater difficulty continued to be on the side of supply of raw materials, which was sometimes unavoidably interrupted. But, even in such cases, the loss to the merchant who owned the machines was not substantial. It was not the coming of the machine as such but the invention of elaborate and therefore specific machinery and plant which completely changed the relationship of the merchant to production. Although the new productive organization was introduced by the merchant – a fact which determined the whole course of the transformation – the use of elaborate machinery and plant involved the development of the factory system and therewith a decisive shift in the relative importance of commerce and industry in favor of the latter. Industrial production ceased to be an accessory of commerce organized by the merchant as a buying and selling proposition; it now involved long-term investment with corresponding risks. Unless the continuance of production was reasonably assured, such a risk was not bearable.

But the more complicated industrial production became, the more numerous were the elements of industry the supply of which had to be safeguarded. Three of these, of course, were of outstanding importance: labor, land, and money. In a commercial society their supply could be organized in one way only: by being made available for purchase. Hence, they would have to be organized for sale on the market – in other words, as commodities. The extension of the market mechanism to the elements of industry – labor, land, and money – was the inevitable consequence of the introduction of the factory system in a commercial society. The elements of industry had to be on sale.

This was synonymous with the demand for a market system. We know that profits are ensured under such a system only if self-regulation is safeguarded through interdependent competitive markets. As the development of the factory system had been organized as part of a process of buying and selling, therefore labor, land, and money had to be transformed into commodities in order to keep production going. They could, of course, not be really transformed into commodities, as actually they were not produced for sale on the market. But the fiction of their being so produced became the organizing principle of society. Of the three, one stands out: labor is the technical term used for human beings, in so far as they are not employers but employed; it follows that henceforth the organization of labor would change concurrently with the organization of the market system. But as the organization of labor is only another word for the forms of life of the common people, this means that the development of the market system would be accompanied by a change in the organization of society itself. All along the line, human society had become an accessory of the economic system.

We recall our parallel between the ravages of the enclosures in English history and the social catastrophe which followed the Industrial Revolution. Improvements, we said, are, as a rule, bought at the price of social dislocation. If the rate of dislocation is too great, the community must succumb in the process. The Tudors and early Stuarts saved England from the fate of Spain by regulating the course of change so that it became bearable and its effects could be canalized into less destructive avenues. But nothing saved the common people of England from the impact of the Industrial Revolution. A blind faith in spontaneous progress had taken hold of people's minds, and with the fanaticism of sectarians the most enlightened pressed forward for boundless and unregulated change in society. The effects on the lives of the people were awful beyond description. Indeed, human society would have been annihilated but for protective countermoves which blunted the action of this self-destructive mechanism.

Social history in the nineteenth century was thus the result of a double movement: the extension of the market organization in respect to genuine commodities was accompanied by its restriction in respect to fictitious ones. While on the one hand markets spread all over the face of the globe and the amount of goods involved grew to unbelievable proportions, on the other hand a network of measures and policies was integrated into powerful institutions designed to check the action of the market relative to labor, land, and money. While the organization of world commodity markets, world capital markets, and world currency markets under the aegis of the gold standard gave an unparalleled momentum to the mechanism of markets, a deep-seated movement sprang into being to resist the pernicious effects of a market-controlled economy. Society protected itself against the perils inherent in a self-regulating market system – this was the one comprehensive feature in the history of the age.

NOTES

1 The practice of the market is twofold: the apportionment of factors between different uses, and the organizing of the forces influencing aggregate supplies of factors.
2 Marx's assertion of the fetish character of the value of commodities refers to the exchange value of genuine commodities and has nothing in common with the fictitious commodities mentioned in the text.

Part II

What Is Development? 20th-Century Debates

Introduction

Development theory is in deep trouble, argues political scientist Colin Leys in this section's first chapter. The practical ambitions of development theory have shrunk, Leys says, even though what is at stake is momentous: "nothing less than whether human beings can act, collectively, to improve their lot." Leys fears that the possibilities of change are small unless world market forces – the "free markets" of the neoliberal era – can be tamed and placed under democratic control, "under a new system of international and national regulation." New development theories must confront this issue, with grander ambitions, a return to development theory's classical origins, and more explicitness about political commitments than has been common since the 1950s, Leys argues. He offers a cross-disciplinary review of the history of development theory, accompanying changes in the world economy, and five principal lines of scholarly response to the crisis in development theory since the late 1980s. The latter approaches range from eclecticism to rational choice theory, dependency theory, and post-structuralism.

The history of the development concept itself is the focus of historians Frederick Cooper and Randall Packard's chapter. "An imagined future and a repudiated past rather than a carefully spelled out analysis of the present" are the starting point of development constructs, Cooper and Packard (1997:viii) note. The idea of development has appealed to leaders of both poor and wealthy nations, while the development process from the start has been "self-critical and subject to critiques." Cooper and Packard note what was new about the notion of development in the colonial world of the late 1930s and 1940s, and how formerly colonized peoples transformed the development concept in quite variable ways. They contrast that variability with alternative depictions of the supposed "emergence of a singular development discourse, a single knowledge-power regime" (the latter being the position of some "post-development" theorists, as discussed in this volume's Introduction). Cooper and Packard also emphasize the significance of the international networks through which development ideas circulate; the shifting capacities of powerful institutions such as the World Bank to disseminate and shape development orthodoxies; and the often unintended ways development knowledge is received, appropriated and transformed.

Development and anthropology make an uneasy pair. Development might even be considered anthropology's "evil twin," James Ferguson suggests in a provocative essay in this section. His chapter explores reasons for this ambivalent relationship, which is connected to "anthropology's historical role as the science of 'less developed' peoples" (as in the discipline's late-19th-century social evolutionist rankings of societies), and the field's subsequent attraction to and simultaneous distrust of models of progressive change.

The notion that development is an "applied" rather than a "theoretical" topic is, as Ferguson notes, both historically recent and different from the way development is categorized in other disciplines such as sociology and political science. The discipline's self-definition in the conventional academic division of labor (i.e., what distinguishes anthropology from political science and sociology, for example), Ferguson says, as well as its internal reward structure, continue to favor work in the "Third World" and in "small, rural, isolated, or marginal communities." He observes that "graduate students who wish to work in less traditionally anthropological sites report encountering significant difficulties in finding acceptance and legitimacy for their work, both within their graduate training programs, and in the arena of academic hiring once they complete their degrees." The concept of development sits astride this fundamental binary opposition between "us" and "them," "the West" and "the rest" – a duality that binds anthropology to its "evil twin." A forceful alternative, as discussed in this volume's Introduction, is that development is anthropology's moral twin (Gow 2002) rather than its evil twin.

REFERENCES CITED

Cooper, Frederick, and Randall Packard, 1997 Preface. *In* International Development and the Social Sciences, Frederick Cooper and Randall Packard, eds., pp vii–ix. Berkeley: University of California Press.

Gow, David, 2002 Anthropology and Development: Evil Twin or Moral Narrative? Human Organization 61(4):299–313.

5

The Rise and Fall of Development Theory

Colin Leys

[...] What is at stake is – or rather was, since the practical ambitions of 'development theory' have been progressively reduced over the years – nothing less than whether human beings can act, collectively, to improve their lot, or whether they must once again accept that it is ineluctably determined by forces – nowadays 'world market forces' – over which they have, in general, little or no control (and least of all those who need it most). Unfortunately, in spite of the importance of the question, 'development theory' has returned only partial and conflicting answers to it.

The First Theories of Development

To see why, it is useful to begin with an owl's eye view of human history over the past 10,000 years or so since settled agriculture first began to replace hunting and gathering. Agriculture required, but also made possible, an increased specialization of labour, and the development of state apparatuses capable of organizing the defence of cultivated land against outside aggressors and of assuring stability in the increasingly complex social and economic relations on which an agricultural society gradually came to depend. With the establishment of agriculture, then, the process of social evolution greatly accelerated relative to that which had occurred during the preceding 1.8 million years of human life on earth; but for a long time (we may suppose) the process was still sufficiently gradual, and sufficiently precarious at any given place and time, for it not to be felt as an acceleration by the people living through it.

The advent of capitalism in the fifteenth and sixteenth centuries, however, and above all

the advent of industrial capitalism in the late eighteenth century, forced the fact of human economic, social, political and cultural development on people's attention. Various thinkers, from Condorcet to Kant, began to conceive of a 'universal history' which would disclose the cumulative pattern and meaning of it all, and its ultimate destination; but the decisive innovators were, of course, Hegel and Marx. [...]

What makes Hegel and Marx true originators of development theory is that they recognized that it was the sudden acceleration in the rate of change that the establishment of capitalist production and bourgeois society had generated that made it necessary and possible to think of history in this way. Bourgeois society had to be understood historically if it was to be made rational (Hegel's idea), or superseded (Marx's); but this understanding, both of them realized, in which capitalist society was seen as the outcome of an evolutionary process stretching back into the mists of time, should also make possible an adequate understanding of earlier societies. Between them they inspired a vast subsequent output of theory-inspired historiography and historically based social science concerned with understanding the evolution of human life on earth as a structured totality.

The Emergence of 'Development Theory'

But this tradition of thought about development is not what most people have meant by the term 'development theory', which emerged in the 1950s to deal with a far narrower issue: namely, how the economies of the colonies of Britain, France, Portugal and other European powers, colonies comprising some 28% of the world's population, might be transformed and made more productive as decolonization approached, in the context of the still 'semi-colonial' condition of the former colonies of Latin America (accounting for a further 7%).[1] Understanding this unprecedented event, and gearing policy to these aims, unquestionably called for new theoretical work. But it is striking how little of this work drew on, or even related itself to, the existing body of theory about development that had been prompted by the original advent of capitalism itself.

There were three main reasons for this. First of all, the new 'development theory' had a very strong practical orientation: its aim was to provide grounds for immediate action. Even academic theorists – as opposed to those directly working for development agencies of one sort or another – were drawn to the field by a desire to do something for the peoples of the ex-colonies, and had an even higher degree of conscious commitment to intervention than is usual in most other branches of social science. This militated against philosophical dispassion and reflective self-criticism.

Secondly, the 'new nations' were a prime stake in the Cold War, so that theories of their development were unavoidably contaminated by this. Of course, most development theorists saw their work as science, not propaganda: few were interested in following the example of W.W. Rostow by subtitling any of their works 'A Non-Communist Manifesto'. But, whereas the early theorists of rising capitalism thought it essential to locate it in a broad conception of history, most Western theorists of development in the post-war years (and most of them were Westerners) avoided doing so because it meant, unavoidably, taking seriously the work of Marx, which at the height of the Cold War was not merely considered unscientific, but in the USA could easily cost you your job. As a result 'development studies' tended to be conducted, at least until the mid-1960s, as if they had no significant historical or philosophical roots or presuppositions; and while 'development theorists' were usually glad to affirm their strong normative reasons for being concerned with development, they rarely acknowledged the extent to which their thinking reflected their own political commitments.[2]

A third crucial conditioning factor in the birth of 'development theory' was the Bretton Woods financial and trading regime. These arrangements were designed to permit national governments to manage their economies so as to maximize growth and employment. Capital was not allowed to cross frontiers without government approval, which permitted governments to determine domestic interest rates, fix the exchange rate of the national currency, and tax and spend as they saw fit to secure national economic objectives. National economic planning was seen as a natural extension of this thinking, as were domestic and international arrangements to stabilize commodity prices. It is not a great oversimplification to say that 'development theory' was originally just theory about the best way for colonial, and then ex-colonial, states to accelerate national economic growth in this international environment. The goal of development was growth; the agent of development was the state and the means of development were these macroeconomic policy instruments. These were taken-for-granted presuppositions of 'development theory' as it evolved from the 1950s onwards.

For over ten years (i.e. from 1955 to the late 1960s) 'development theory' so conceived progressed with only modest excitement. Then, partly due to disappointment with the results of policies based on 'development theory' (especially in Latin America and India), and partly to the general reaction of the 1960s against all 'official' values and ideas, the theoretical temperature rose. The ahistorical, unself-critical and politically partisan nature of 'development theory' was put in question by critics on the 'left'; and one way to understand the heady debates that followed throughout most of the 1970s is as a struggle between those who tried to keep 'development theory' within its original parameters, and critics who were trying to extend them and place the issues back into the framework of the historically orientated and ethical tradition of general development theory founded by Hegel and Marx.

The full implications of doing this were, however, obscured for a long time by the fact that most of the critics also subscribed to a very practical, short-term, state-orientated conception of development (and in many cases were also influenced by Cold War partisanship). But the work of finally demonstrating the limitations of mainstream 'development theory' was not left to be accomplished by criticism alone. By the mid-1980s the real world on which 'development theory' had been premissed had also disappeared. Above all, national and international controls over capital movements had been removed, drastically curtailing the power of any state wishing to promote national development, while the international 'development community' threw itself into the task of strengthening 'market forces' (i.e. capital) at the expense of states everywhere, but especially in the

Third World. As a result most states could no longer be the prime movers of development that 'development theory' had hitherto always presupposed, and none of the alternative candidates (such as 'social movements' or 'communities') proposed by 'development theorists' as the field unravelled were very convincing.

[. . .]

Development Theories: Science and Discourses

The first formulations of development theory were the work of economists, all strongly influenced by the ideas of Keynes and the wartime and post-war practices of state intervention in the economy, including the perceived success of the Marshall Plan, which was in many ways a model for later ideas about 'aid'. They shared the broadly social-democratic ethos of the period, including its commitment to planning and its conviction that economic problems would yield to the actions of benevolent states endowed with sufficient supplies of capital and armed with good economic analysis. They produced what P.W. Preston has aptly called development theory's 'positivist orthodoxy'.[3] They wrote development plans for both newly independent countries and the not yet independent colonies of Africa, based on the idea of raising rural productivity and transferring underutilized labour out of agriculture into industry.

By the end of the 1950s, however, the original optimism that this approach would yield rapid results had begun to evaporate, and the limitations of development economics as a theory of development were beginning to be exposed. The failure of the Indian economy, in particular, to respond rapidly to this approach was attributed in part to the 'softness' of the Indian state, which seemed to lack the capacity to live up to the social-democratic ideal of a rational, firmly benevolent enforcer of the national interest and impose the necessary discipline on everyone from businessmen and landlords to small peasants. But this famous judgement, coming from Gunnar Myrdal and his associates (notably Paul Streeten, and later Dudley Seers), representing the 'left' (and most historically and sociologically sensitive) wing of development economics, signalled the existence of complex problems which lay beyond the conceptual and empirical scope of mainstream – i.e. neo-classical – economics. Marx had long ago grasped that states were, as he put it, but the 'official résumés' of civil society. In the first phase of development economics this had been forgotten. What was it

about these societies that made them unresponsive to the 'positivist orthodoxy'?

'Modernization theory' was an American response to this question. It was constructed by sociologists and political scientists involved in the rapidly expanding research and teaching programmes established by the US government to equip the country with the regional expertise it needed to exercise its new role as a superpower. These experts none the less found themselves largely excluded from policy-making roles in the US Agency for International Development (USAID) or the World Bank, the two most important aid agencies in the world, both headquartered in Washington; and modernization theory can be understood in part as their explanation of why the plans of development economists who monopolized these organizations so seldom worked. (They believed that in the transition from 'traditional' to 'modern' forms of social organization, already completed in the industrialized West, the complex interactions between social change and economic development, mediated by politics, could be traced with some precision, using 'structural-functional analysis' and a typology of social structures derived from Weber by Talcott Parsons.) [. . .]

Practically, the modernization theorists envisaged modern values being diffused through education and technology transfer to the 'élites' of the periphery. Some attention was paid to this idea in aid policies, especially through technical assistance and scholarship programmes, but on the whole its influence on policy was minor. The modernization school had a bigger impact on academic research, although this owed more to the important topics they opened up by their well-funded fieldwork – topics such as political parties, social movements and the dynamics of social change, whose study had not been encouraged by the former colonial authorities – than to their methodology. And, although the influence of Max Weber on their work was transmitted in the schematized form of Talcott Parsons's 'pattern variables', it had some valuable consequences; for example, some modernization research took seriously the persistence of precapitalist social relations and their cultural practices, issues that were largely neglected by the modernization school's critics in the 1970s.

But modernization theory suffered from defects closely connected with its leading exponents' place in the scheme of things. As Irene Gendzier has pointed out, they were mostly closely connected to the American state and accepted its purposes, including its intense preoccupation with combating communism.[4] Some modernization theorists were serious cold warriors – Gabriel Almond, Edward Shils, Lucien Pye and Samuel Huntington, for example – others merely accepted the Cold War and were content to see themselves as the 'liberal' wing of American development studies, believing that modernization would in any case bring democracy as well as economic growth. Very few at that time publicly questioned the identification of modernization studies with the aims of US foreign policy. In the 1950s and early 1960s the Central Intelligence Agency (CIA) regularly 'debriefed' US scholars returning from Third World fieldwork and the State Department frequently sought their advice. This situation also led to a 'symptomatic silence' about the social character of development, a silence cloaked, perhaps, by the doctrine of 'value-freedom'. It was implicit that the development under discussion was not socialist, but its capitalist character was not acknowledged either; it was just 'development', and was certainly not seen as prone to generate class formation and conflict, or as inherently uneven or crisis-ridden.

The shortcomings of modernization theory were first attacked where they were most plainly apparent – in Latin America, which had enjoyed formal independence for more than a century, but had still to enjoy the fruits that according to modernization theory ought long since to have flowed from it. Or, rather, they were attacked from within Latin America by the German-American Andre Gunder Frank, arriving in Chile from the USA in 1962, using the concepts of dependency and underdevelopment. [...] Even before the naïve optimism of much early modernization theory had been exposed by the end of the post-war boom and the deepening US involvement in Vietnam and other anticommunist ventures, Frank's polemical assaults, coinciding with the student revolt of the 1960s, had effectively demolished its pretensions to scientificity.

The early 1970s thus became – briefly – an era of dependency theory. Or, to be more accurate, in intellectual circles, especially among students in Europe and in ThirdWorld countries, dependency theory held the initiative; and eventually even the international 'development community' felt obliged to accommodate some of its perspectives: for instance, the International Labour Office's 1972 call for 'redistribution with growth' and the World Bank's adoption in 1973 of the principle of meeting 'basic needs' were both influenced by the (unacknowledged) impact of dependency thinking.

Dependency theory inverted many of the assumptions of modernization theory. It saw metropolitan policy as maleficent, not beneficent; inflows of foreign investment were seen as giving rise to much greater interest and profit outflows; 'modernizing élites' were really compradores, or lumpen-bourgeoisies, serving their own and foreign interests, not those of the people; world trade perpetuated structures of underdevelopment, rather than acting as a solvent of them. Capitalist development ('development' now had a label, at least for 'left' dependency theorists) offered nothing to the periphery; the solution lay in reducing links to the metropoles and bringing about 'autocentric' national economic growth.

[...] [Dependency theorists'] critique of official development thinking rested fundamentally on a pulling away from the short-term, ahistorical and uncritical perspectives of Western-produced, state-orientated development discourse, towards the perspective of a 'universal history'.

But they themselves also believed that the countries of the 'periphery' could somehow, through better theory and different political leadership, jump over the barriers placed in their way by history, and this gave rise to some key ambiguities in their thought: above all, their tendency to assume the availability of some unspecified alternative development path, more equitable and less painful, which was not – in the absence of stronger and more mobilized social forces at the periphery, and more sympathetic support from abroad – really available. This problem persisted, even when Frank's early version of dependency theory, according to which development was always systematically blocked at the periphery, had been generally abandoned in favour of the idea that, while it was always necessarily difficult, dependent on external forces and 'distorted' (Cardoso's famous 'associated dependent development'), development might none the less sometimes be possible.[5]

In sub-Saharan Africa, dependency theory was broadly accepted by many foreign Africanists and many, perhaps most, African social scientists, not to mention educated people in general, and especially the youth; but there was a further problem, that outside the Republic of South Africa the level of development in few countries had yet produced either a local 'national' capitalist class or a local labour movement (or indeed any other modern social movement) that had the capacity to lead national development along any alternative development path, even if such a path could be plausibly specified. As a moral critique of existing policy in Africa, dependency theory played a significant role. But, except in Nyerere's Tanzania, dependency thinking was not adopted as an explicit basis for policy, and the problems of Tanzanian socialism had many sources besides the inherent shortcomings of dependency theory.

In any case, it was not shortcomings revealed in practice that led to the most significant critiques of dependency theory. Critics from the right generally failed to make the effort needed to understand the Marxian *problématique* from which many of dependency theory's key ideas were drawn, so as to be able to make effective attacks on it (this was particularly evident in the attempts to use cross-national statistical data to prove, for example, that periphery country growth rates were not inversely related to trade links with the countries of the 'core'). The most damaging criticism came rather from the 'classical Marxist' left.

These critics were, ironically enough, probably the nearest thing we now have to 'traditional intellectuals', in Gramsci's sense of the term (i.e. a category of intellectuals not linked to either of the main contesting classes). [. . .] Writers like Geoffrey Kay, Giovanni Arrighi, Arghiri Emmanuel, Michael Cowen and Bill Warren often seemed to display the attachment of the political exile (in their case, exile from the academic and policy-making mainstream) to theory as such. While this had its disadvantages, it did enable them to make a trenchant critique of the eclecticism, populism and practical ambiguity of dependency theory: now for the first time 'development theory' of the post-war variety was squarely confronted from the perspective of the historical tradition of development theory derived from Hegel and Marx.

[. . .]

[The classical Marxist] argument that capitalist development of the periphery was a necessary prelude to socialism [was] not a political stance that appealed to many people on the left, inside or outside the Third World, who in any case did not believe it would happen. [. . .]

Marxist development theorists were also frequently attacked for being 'Eurocentric', especially for applying to backward societies categories like that of 'the working class', which did not apply there, and neglecting phenomena like ethnicity, which did. On the whole, this was a canard. The real issue was how far capitalist development was forming classes, and how far this cut across ethnic and other precapitalist solidarities. In practice, the empirical studies conducted by Marxist researchers were no more Eurocentric than those of their critics.

No, the real problem of the Marxists' contribution to development theory was not so much that their analysis was wrong; in many ways they appear in retrospect to have maintained a rather objective stance, relative to the various other schools, helped by the broad historical perspective and understanding of capitalist dynamics that they drew from Marx. Their crucial problem was rather that there were too few people in the Third World – and virtually none in tropical Africa – for whom the political and moral standpoint of their analysis (i.e. that people should struggle against capitalist development, while not expecting to transcend it until it had first been accomplished) made sense. Their perspective was, to say the least, very long-term, and offered no plausible line of immediate political action to improve matters. The fact that 'mainstream' development theory had consistently failed to produce results did not make the Marxist view any better in this respect.[6]

A more plausible political position was, of course, that of the neo-liberals, who did not believe that capitalism would give way to socialism and were only interested in accelerating its advance in the Third World.[7] They believed that what was blocking or retarding this was none of the things highlighted by all the theories so far discussed, but rather the whole idea of bringing about development through state intervention in the economy in the first place. This was the standpoint of P.T. (later Lord) Bauer, Deepak Lal, Bela Balassa, Ian Little and others, who represented in development theory the neo-liberal revolution that was taking place in the metropoles at the end of the 1970s, and who offered an intellectual justification for a new wave of market-orientated intervention by the World Bank and the International Monetary Fund (IMF). The older representatives of this current belonged to a small group of economists who opposed the post-war social-democratic consensus and who were, as a result, almost as exiled from the mainstream as the Marxists. [. . .] They argued that development was blocked by inflated public sectors, distorting economic controls and over-emphasis on capital formation.[8] Governments were part of the problem, not part of the solution; they were inefficient and often corrupt and hence parasitic, not stimulators of growth. The solution was to privatize the public sector, reduce the scale and scope of government spending and give up all policies, from exchange rate controls to subsidies and redistributive taxation, that altered any prices that would otherwise be set by the impersonal forces of the market.

As John Toye pointed out, the neo-liberals' success in relation to the Third World owed a good deal to the fact that they were ready to say openly what others in the 'development community' knew perfectly well but had (unlike the dependency theorists) been unwilling to say, out of an anxiety not to jeopardize relations between Third World governments and the development agencies for which they worked: namely, that these governments were never exclusively concerned to promote the development goals they were ostensibly committed to, and quite often were not committed to them at all.

There was also a strong core of justification for their criticisms of the public sector and of government practices in most Third World countries. But, as Toye has also shown, this common-sense criticism did not add up to a theoretical justification for the neo-liberals' claims about the benefits that would flow from an unrestricted market. These claims were very poorly supported with evidence, and were often prima facie implausible; they sprang rather from a deep ideological hostility to government in general, and especially to the legitimacy which the doctrine of state intervention gave to socialists or even social-democrats in office.

In any case it was not the shortcomings of the principal existing schools of development theory, serious as they were, that made possible the ascendancy of neo-liberalism (whose shortcomings were quickly revealed as no less serious). What made possible the triumph of neo-liberalism in mainstream development thinking was material, not ideal: the radical transformation in both the structure and the management of the world economy that had begun in the 1960s, and which finally seemed to offer the possibility of creating for the first time in history a truly unified global capitalist economy – and one regulated, if at all, only by institutions reflecting the interests of transnational capital. Neo-liberalism articulated the goals and beliefs of the dominant forces that stood to benefit from this process, and pushed it forward. Social-democratic parties and labour movements tried to resist it, but the 'new right' succeeded in neutralizing this resistance and initiating its own market-orientated project in one industrial country after another.[9] The 'development community', which was either part of the state apparatuses of these countries or depended critically on them for funding, was bound to come into line.[10]

But, although the 'develoment community' was loath to acknowledge it, the new global economic regime thoroughly undermined the foundations of development theory as it had hitherto been conceived.

The Real World of Development

The world in which Keynesian policy-making – and its offshoots, development economics and development theory – made sense had changed fundamentally. It is true that in some respects the world economy at the end of the 1980s was less integrated than it had been at the beginning of the century, and there were significant tendencies towards protectionism, offsetting those towards a single worldwide market. But, relative to the situation that existed between 1945 and the late 1960s, the changes were fundamental.

World trade as a share of world output had returned to the general level of 1913 (i.e. up from 7% of total gross domestic product (GDP) in 1945 to 15% in 1988); foreign direct investment had risen to account for significant shares of total investment (5–10% of capital stock) in most major economies, and about a third of all trade between countries had come to consist of the movement of goods between different national branches of one or another multinational company. The mutual dependence of national economies implied by these facts was significant (obviously, it is not necessary for half of a country's capital assets to be foreign owned for decisions taken in foreign countries to have a major impact on its fortunes); but even more striking was the internationalization of capital flows. Instead of merely financing world trade, by the end of the 1980s banks and non-bank financial institutions were dealing in currency exchanges, currency and commodity futures and so-called 'derivatives' of all sorts on a scale that not only dwarfed the conventional transactions needed for trade and investment, but made it impossible for the governments of even large economies to influence the value of their currency by intervening in the currency markets.

But in the meantime control of capital movements had in any case also been abandoned as a deliberate policy decision, promoted, above all, by the USA. As competition with other industrial countries intensified, the USA borrowed abroad and became the world's largest debtor nation. [. . .] In 1973, the Bretton Woods system of fixed exchange rates was abandoned altogether. This opened up new opportunities for international currency speculation and led to a new period of extreme instability in currency values and commodity prices, including the oil price increases of the 1970s and 1980s; these in turn led to vast new dollar balances being accumulated by the oil-exporting countries, and correspondingly vast expansions of borrowing, which drove up the total of international debt to previously unheard-of levels.

The abandonment of the post-war international trading regime was followed in 1979-80 by the abandonment of Keynesian economic policy in the Organization for Economic Co-operation and Development (OECD) countries, led by the UK and the USA. Deregulation in the USA and deregulation and privatization in the UK were accompanied by high interest rates. The governments of the other European industrial countries followed suit, either willingly or (in the case of France) because keeping interest rates significantly below those of other countries led to capital outflows that could no longer be prevented – 'Keynesianism in one country' was no longer practicable. Capital exports were formally deregulated in the UK in 1979 and *de facto* everywhere else by the mid-1980s. Then, at the end of 1993, the conclusion of the 'Uruguay Round' of the General Agreement on Tariffs and Trade (GATT) negotiations inaugurated a further extension of global free trade, including the formerly sacrosanct agricultural sector, while further reductions in the regulatory powers of most industrial country governments were imposed by the European Union's Single Market and Maastricht Treaties and the North American Free Trade Agreement.

These changes did not succeed in restoring growth rates to the levels achieved after the Second World War. From the late 1960s the average rate of growth of the OECD countries fell from the post-war level of 3–4% to around 2%. The developing countries inevitably followed suit, except that there was now a growing polarization among them. Besides the four East Asian newly industrialized countries (NICs) (which accounted for half of the entire Third World's exports of manufactures), in the 1980s China and, to a lesser extent, India began to grow faster, while the other developing countries slowed down – in the recession that began in the late 1970s their average growth rate declined and in 1983 even became negative. Lower growth rates in the OECD countries and intensified competition also adversely affected the Third World countries' terms of trade and interest rates. [...]

Most Third World countries, then, found themselves more vulnerable than at any time since they were first colonized. Their economies were least well placed to prosper in the new 'global' market place. Primary commodity exports, other than oil, became steadily less significant as manufacturing became less commodity-intensive, and the overall share of the Third World in world trade fell dramatically. Faced with stagnating economies, and with per capita incomes declining from levels at which many people could barely survive already, they responded by increased borrowing abroad until servicing the debt led to balance of payments difficulties so acute that they were forced to turn to the IMF. As a condition of further support the IMF and the World Bank then forced them to cut back government intervention in their economies, leaving these instead to be revived by the freer play of 'market forces'. This did not, of course, produce the anticipated results. Per capita incomes fell still further in all the affected countries (in sub-Saharan Africa, by over a quarter), while the debt-service burden (the proportion of export earnings spent on capital repayments and interest) of the 'low-income countries' (excluding China and India) rose from 11.8% in 1980 to 24.5% in 1992.[11] The overall effects are well summed up by Glyn and Sutcliffe:

The share of Africa, Asia and Latin America in world trade is now substantially lower than before 1913. This reflects a major decline in the relative importance of tropical raw materials in world trade ... This long-term structural reason for the decline ... has been joined in the period since 1973 by a major short-term crisis in many poorer countries ... [...]. The picture for international investment is rather similar. Between 1950 and 1980 the share of all foreign investment going to the Third World held roughly constant at about 25 percent. But after 1984 the share fell sharply to well under 20 percent ... [and] is very unequally distributed. It goes in significant quantities to only a few resource-rich countries and the newly industrialising countries (including China) while the so-called 'least developed countries' are increasingly excluded. In the second half of the 1980s this group received only 0.1 percent of all foreign investment ... Once again Africa and most of Latin America and some Asian countries are failing to participate in the growing globalisation of the rest of the world ... they are increasingly marginalised within the system of which they form a part.[12]

The story of the world economy under liberalization can, of course, be given a rosy gloss, as in the following excerpt from a *Washington Post* editorial:

> The rise of wealth in the late 20th century has been more sustained and more widespread than ever before in history... Economic growth is measured in dollars, but it translates into other and much more important things – better health and longer lives, less harsh physical labor, greater economic security. There are drawbacks, like development's threats to the environment and the dismaying tendency of governments to spend too much of their new wealth on weapons. But it is hardly Pollyannaish to say that the balance remains strongly in favor of the essential human values.[13]

Admittedly, to take this line involves overlooking the implications of many of the data reviewed in the last few paragraphs, not to mention the serious risk of conflicts within or between countries of the former 'First' or 'Second' Worlds as the impact of global competition drives whole districts, regions or even countries into permanent poverty, while others prosper. But for present purposes it does not really matter: even on the most optimistic view this picture leaves little or no room for 'development theory' as it used to be conceived.

The era of national economies and national economic strategies is past – for the time being, at least. With capital free to move where it wishes, no state (and least of all a small poor one) can pursue any economic policy that the owners of capital seriously dislike. Economic planning, welfare systems and fiscal and monetary policies all became subject to control, in effect, by the capital markets, signalled, in the case of Third World countries, by the conditions attached to IMF/World Bank lending – precisely the situation the Bretton Woods system was designed to prevent.[14] And in the Third World the whole thrust of recent IMF/World Bank policy, imposed through the conditions attached to almost two hundred structural-adjustment lending programmes and reinforced by bilateral lending consortia, has been to reduce still further the power of national governments to act as prime movers of development. Instead of reforming inefficient agencies, structural adjustment policies have tended to emasculate or eliminate them. Parastatals have been privatized, without thereby becoming more effective. It is hardly too much to say that by the end of the 1980s the only development policy that was officially approved was not to have one – to leave it to the market to allocate resources, not the state. In the World Bank's own ingenuous language, 'New ideas stress prices as signals; trade and competition as links to technical progress; and effective government as a scarce resource, to be employed sparingly and only where most needed.'[15]

Individual national governments – especially in the smaller underdeveloped countries, with which development theory used to be above all concerned – thus no longer have the tools at their disposal to manage their domestic economies so as to accelerate growth, foster industrialization and 'catch up', as development theory originally envisaged, and theories premised on their existence become irrelevant; for most of them Gunder Frank's comment was painfully accurate: 'Now neo-liberalism, post-Keynesianism, and neo-structuralism have... become totally irrelevant and bankrupt for development policy. In the real world, the order of the day has become only economic or debt crisis management.'

Most observers accept that significant parts of the former Third World, including most of sub-Saharan Africa, are more likely to regress than to advance in the new global economy; it is in the nature of an unregulated competitive system that this will happen. Not every country has the capacity to compete in the market; a few will succeed, while others will decline and some will collapse into civil war or anarchy. [...]

[...]

We can now see that the 1950s and 1960s were not 'normal' times but, on the contrary, a special interlude in the history of the worldwide expansion of capitalism in which 'development theory' could be born, but outside which it could not survive.

This is not to say that theorizing development is no longer possible or necessary; we need theoretical maps of our increasingly integrated world. But we can no longer assume, as all the principal varieties of 'development theory' have up to now, who the agents of collective action for change will be, or that means exist for them to accomplish anything. Perhaps states, acting singly or in groups, will rediscover the means, but this too must be part of the task of theory to establish. In the meantime, we must recognize that an era is closed, that development theory must return to its classical roots and that the relation between theory and practice that has been assumed hitherto (i.e. theory in the service of this or that existing or imagined coalition of political forces in control of a state) has been put radically in question.

'Development Theory' Faced with the End of its *Raison D'Être*

The authors of the World Bank's annual *World Development Reports* have dealt with the problem by ploughing ahead with an increasingly incoherent discourse of opposites: the state is needed, after all, but not too much, and only when the market doesn't work well; democracy is important but not if it leads to inappropriate demands for redistribution; and so on. Academic development theorists could hardly follow suit, but what could they do instead?

It was not until towards the end of the 1980s that the full significance of the changed environment began to be registered in the theoretical literature, although the drastic reduction in the official goals of development propounded by the World Bank and other agencies over the years had signalled it clearly enough. By the early 1970s the vision of 'catching up' (culminating, in Rostow's 1960 version, in a 'high mass-consumption' society, which implicitly included 'equity' and democracy) had already given way to more modest ambitions: 'redistribution with growth' – i.e. some reduction in inequality, but financed out of growth so that the better off in the developing countries might be less unwilling to agree to it – in a word, fewer illusions about democracy. And by the end of the 1970s redistribution had given way to just trying to meet the 'basic needs' of the poor, who, it seemed, would always be with us after all; the goal of equity had disappeared. Then came structural adjustment; to get growth, under-developed societies were to adjust themselves to the procrustean bed allocated to them by the market, and for this purpose even basic needs must be sacrificed.

By then, however, everyone was aware that things had radically changed and that 'development theory' was in deep trouble. Apart from neo-liberalism itself, five main lines of theoretical response can be identified. One has been to see the problem as essentially one of theory itself: there is a theoretical 'impasse', which must be overcome by better concepts and research. A second response might be called 'eclecticism as usual in the development community'. A third consists of further evolutions of dependency theory. A fourth response is to return to the unfinished agenda of Myrdal and the 'neo-institutionalists' of the 1960s – i.e., how to 'add' social and political dimensions on to the analyses of development economics – but

this time by analysing these dimensions in terms of rational choice theory. A fifth response, and the last to be considered here, is to renounce any commitment to development, seeking (often in the name of post-structuralism) merely to 'understand' what goes on.

Let us look briefly at these. [. . .]

'Development Studies' as a Substitute for 'Development Theory'?

In 1991 a group of left-inclined development theorists collaborated to produce an excellent volume, edited by Frans Schuurman, called *Beyond the Impasse: New Directions in Development Theory*.[16] The idea of an 'impasse' in critical development theory had been canvassed in various articles of the mid-1980s, including one by David Booth;[17] by 1991, however, Booth, in a leading contribution to the Schuurman volume, saw signs that the impasse was being overcome. In his view (strongly endorsed by Schuurman) empirical research had emancipated itself from the excessive generality, necessitarianism, teleology, class reductionism, dogmatism and other short-comings of Marxist-influenced development theory, and in doing so had begun to show a potential for fresh theoretical initiatives. New theory would be sensitive to the great diversity of situations in the Third World, would refuse to reduce complex and locally specific gender and other relations to relations of class, and would allow for the possibility of 'room for manoeuvre' at the 'micro' and 'meso' levels of action, as well as the 'macro' level, which had been the focus of previous development theory – without, however, abandoning the inherited agenda of political economy. It might also, Booth hoped, succeed in combining the study of the cultural meanings subjectively attributed to things by people with the study of those same things from an external or objective standpoint, in a way not achieved before: and it would try to be relevant to the concerns of those engaged in practical development work.[18]

Booth's starting-point – the enormous expansion of field research under the aegis of 'development studies' – was, of course, valid; and if we add to this the no less impressive accumulation of social research not necessarily conceived of as 'development studies' – including social and economic history and gender studies in Third World countries – both the volume and the quality have clearly outstripped what went before, frequently revealing the somewhat shaky empirical foundations of previous 'grand theory' as well. And Booth's characterization of this work as mostly free from some of the vices of earlier development thinking – reductionism, excessive generality and the rest – and as being much more varied in its interests, was also accurate. Women, local-level activity, ethnicity, religion and culture, for example, which all tended to be secondary in the earlier literature, are often foregrounded in more recent work, which also tends to show more concern for detail, sets higher standards of proof and is in many ways intellectually refreshing.[19]

But Booth's idea that new development theory will emerge autogenetically from the accumulating volume and density of all this work, through some spontaneous fusion with the concerns of previous political economy, is a different matter. On the one hand, these 'mini-narratives' (if one may so call them, in contrast to the old 'big meta-narratives' which it is now fashionable to disclaim) have implicit higher-level theoretical presuppositions that need to be made explicit (microfoundations imply macrostructures, as much as the other way round), and it would be surprising if these were found to constitute, so to speak spontaneously, a new and better theory of development. And, even more crucially, the construction of a new theory of development is necessarily a political task, involving political choices about whom (what social forces) the theory is for, to accomplish what ends and in what contexts. Conflicting political commitments were, after all, what ultimately inspired the powerful theoretical debates within 'development theory' in the 1970s, and any worthwhile renewal of development theory now depends on a renewed clarification of political presuppositions and purposes as well.

To put it another way, what is striking about the way Booth and his colleagues conceive of the 'impasse' and its transcendence is that it is so idealist, i.e. the origins and the solution of the problem seem to lie in theory itself. With the exception of a page in Schuurman's 'Introduction', little reference is made in the book to the changes in the real world that have undercut the original development project. [.... The authors] do not confront the thought that, so long as collective socio-economic interests are supposed to be the products of the action of market forces rather than goals of strategic state action, the domain of 'development theory' is radically changed, if not abolished; that what is left is simply a world economy whose effects are overwhelmingly determined by very powerful states and market actors, with at most minor modifications or delays brought about by

the actions of lesser states, social movements, communities or whatever, which do not have significant military or market power. Certainly, this thought may be mistaken, or at least exaggerated; but in that case a new theory of development must at least begin by showing why.

[...] Theory needs both a subject and an object, and the prerequisite of any new development theory that aims to be practical must surely be the analysis of the now deregulated global market and the social forces that dominate it, and then a definition of alternative social forces whose developmental needs cannot be met within this system, and which can be expected to struggle against it. Simply abjuring the alleged short-comings of the theories that were constructed in the period of the collectively regulated world economy of legally sovereign states, and accumulating ever more detailed and subtle empirical analyses of local and particular experiences, will not of itself answer this need; for that world economy is, as Hegel put it, a form of life that has become old, and which theory cannot rejuvenate but only understand.

Eclecticism as Usual in the Development Community?

The term 'development community' refers here to the network of people professionally concerned with development – the staff of 'donor' and recipient country development ministries, of multilateral 'aid' agencies, financial institutions and non-government organizations, and academic and non-academic consultants. It implies no disrespect to say that this community also constitutes an interest which has to adapt as best it can to constantly changing circumstances, rather like civil servants at the national level. There is a broad consensus about aims and possibilities, founded on development economics but honed by experience and the perspectives of other disciplines into a somewhat eclectic mixture capable of absorbing sometimes quite drastic changes in fashion or politics (witness, for example, the World Bank's successive accommodations, first to a mild touch of dependency, and then, within a decade, to neoliberalism); and then, when the need passes, reverting back to a more centrist stance. How has the development community responded to the new situation?

As an example we may take John Toye's widely acclaimed study, *Dilemmas of Development*, which I have already cited. Toye's book is well known as a trenchant critique of the neo-liberal dogma which gained ascendancy in the World Bank and IMF in the 1980s, but it is also quite a revealing statement of his own position. For, besides criticizing the neo-liberals, Toye also criticizes the old political economy ('left wing', in his terminology) to which neo-liberalism was a reaction. Toye treats 'left-wing' political economists in rather general terms, and even lumps them together as the exponents of what he calls 'the standard left view' (for example, of the state (pp. 121–22)), even though it is sometimes hard to think of any individual theorist who has actually subscribed to the view he describes; but what is interesting is that Toye seems to be at least as hostile towards them as to the neoliberals, and this draws attention to the fact that the ground Toye sees himself occupying is the sensible, reasonable, middle ground, in between these untenable extremes. What is the nature of this terrain?

The answer is not immediately obvious. Toye is a careful and penetrating critic of other theories, but the standpoint from which his criticism is made is not so clear. For instance, he explicitly subscribes to the following views, among others: 'global modernization' is 'inherently conflictual' because it is 'a human directed historical process' (p. 6); what is practicable and desirable is 'managed capitalism' (p. 10); in seeking to promote development we must avoid bringing preconceptions from outside, and see things through the eyes of poor people in the countries concerned (p. 40); and the recent economic retrogression in so much of the Third World 'appears to be a short-period interruption to a long period of buoyant growth' (p. 34).

Now, none of these ideas is self-evident. Why should human-directed historical processes be considered inherently conflictual, rather than inherently collaborative? What theory of history or human nature is involved here? On what grounds does it make sense to believe in 'managed capitalism' as an ideal, given capital's dramatically successful escape from management into the realm of the 'self-regulating' global market since the 1970s? On what grounds and in what circumstances are the perceptions of poor people to be respected, relative to other kinds of understanding? (What makes their thinking about economics important or valid, but not, for example, their ideas about the supernatural?) And from what theoretical stand-point does the retrogression of the last decade or more appear as a short-period interruption to growth, rather than as a long term, if not permanent, reversal?

Toye undoubtedly has answers to such questions. What is interesting is that he does not seem to feel the need to offer them; he does not defend his assumptions, eclectic and open to challenge as they are. [. . .]

[. . .] It is also worth reflecting on what Toye puts in place of the 'single desired social state' (another straw man – who on the right or the left has really advocated this?) that he rejects as a 'teleological' approach to development: 'what most people would say mattered ultimately', he suggests, 'is the ending of large-scale poverty . . . sickness, ignorance and premature death, not to mention the violence, ugliness and despair of daily life' (p. 36). Apart from the fact that this seems no less 'teleological' than any other goal of development, where do these values come from? Who are these 'most people' whose authority is being appealed to here, and who no longer care about equality or democracy? Is this 'common sense', in whose name theory, left and right, is attacked, anything other than the tradition of Western charity?

Dependency Theory in the 1990s

Dependency theory in its early sense of a general theory that sought to explain underdevelopment at the periphery as almost wholly the insuperably self-perpetuating effect of metropolitan capital probably has few remaining adherents. The NICs showed that structures of dependence might sometimes be overcome, while growing interdependence among even industrialized economies has made all dependence relative. However, dependency theory's focus on the many forms of acute dependence of small, open, ex-colonial economies on the powerful economic interests and states that dominate the financial and commodity markets in which they operate ('concrete situations of dependency') remains indisputably valid. [. . .]

[. . .] It is interesting to see how the changes that have occurred in the real world have been seen by one of dependency theory's most famous Western exponents, Andre Gunder Frank, who has described the changes in his own thinking in an autobiographical essay published in 1991.[20]

[. . .]

As the 1970s progressed, Frank [. . .] became convinced that not only was dependency theory devoid of any convincing alternative conception of development, but the whole idea of national development, which had been the *raison d'être* of development theory, was no longer tenable in the emerging conditions of a worldwide market. His historical work on the emergence of the capitalist world system led him to see all dreams of alternative development paths pursued by particular countries or regions 'delinked' from that system as illusory [. . .], while his work on the 'crisis' into which the world capitalist system had entered in the 1970s convinced him that for most of the Third World development within the system was also impossible. In particular, so long as Third World countries were paying on average about 6.5% of their gross national product (GNP) to service their debt, as he estimated was the case through much of the 1980s, there could only be 'development of underdevelopment', with '*dis*investment in productive infrastructure and human capital and with the loss of competitiveness on the world market'.

The theoretical position to which this led Frank was that the only useful object of study is 'world development', which sets the limits to whatever normative goals it makes sense to try to pursue, and that the only useful agents capable of pursuing such goals are 'particular groups or classes' (p. 54). Such goals, even if they can be achieved by such groups or classes, will be relative to the way world development currently affects the part of the globe they live in, a development that has been going on throughout recorded history:

> I now find the *same continuing world system*, including its center-periphery structure, hegemony-rivalry competition, and cyclical ups and downs has been evolving (developing?) for five thousand years at least . . . In this world system, sectors, regions and peoples *temporarily and cyclically* assume leading and hegemonic central (core) positions of social and technological 'development'. They then have to cede their pride of place to new ones who replace them. Usually this happens after a long interregnum of crisis in the system. During this time of crisis, there is intense competition for leadership and hegemony. The central core has moved around the globe in a predominantly westerly direction. With some zig-zags, the central core has passed through Asia, East (China), Central (Mongolia), South (India) and West (Iran, Mesopotamia, Egypt, Turkey) . . . Then the core passed on to Southern and Western Europe and Britain, via the Atlantic to North America, and now across it and the Pacific towards Japan. Who knows, perhaps one day it will pass all the way around the world to China. (pp. 56–57)

Development theory based on any idea of 'autonomous' national development, on any conception of 'de-linking', is, therefore, an illusion (p. 58). What is needed is 'a more rounded, dynamic and all-encompassing supply and demand side economics to analyse, if not to guide, *world* economic and technological development'. The significance of the words 'if not to guide' is not made clear: perhaps Frank is still faintly agnostic on the possibility of some form of world government emerging? [. . .]

'Most development for one group . . . comes at the expense of anti-development for others. They are condemned to dualistic marginalisation and/or to underdevelopment of development. That is what real world development really means' (pp. 58–60). And, since all existing models of development are inadequate, Frank pins his hopes only on radical democratization, based on the emerging strength of the hitherto neglected social groups, and especially women.

[. . .]

[. . .] At one time the success [of the NICs] was attributed by neo-liberals to the virtues of *laissez faire*, until the work of Hamilton, White, Amsden, Wade and others showed incontrovertibly that, if anything, the NICs' experience demonstrated the precise opposite, i.e. the necessity for forceful, systematic and sustained economic intervention by a strong, centralized state pursuing a coherent long-term development strategy.[21] This conclusion has now been swallowed, albeit with some difficulty, by the World Bank,[22] but its implications for 'development theory' have still to be fully digested in 'mainstream' circles.

[. . .]

Rational Choice and Development

One of the most influential reactions – at least in the USA – to the end of 'development theory's' *raison d'être* has been to try to build a new political economy of development in which the key to economic performance is seen as institutions that can be analysed in terms of rational choice theory.

This response makes sense in several ways. First, it involves going back to the problem raised by Myrdal and his colleagues in the 1960s – how to incorporate the obstacles posed by political and social phenomena into the analysis of economic development – but this time in a way that explicitly tries to stay within the assumptions of neo-classical or marginalist economics, that is unlike the neo-Weberians of the modernization school (not to mention Marxists or neo-Marxists), the 'new institutionalism' is supposed to rest on the assumption of rational individuals maximizing their utilities and nothing more, and should (in its most optimistic version, at least) be capable of being integrated with economics and modelled mathematically. Given the recent ascendancy of neo-classical economics in the 'development community', this has an air of political realism about it (and maybe – some people evidently hope – it can also endow political science with some of the economists' famous rigour).

Second, it holds out the prospect of dispensing with the Marxist phenomenology of classes and relations of production and other unclean entities, whose relevance to the problems of development cannot always be denied; in the choice-theoretic discourse all of these are reducible to special cases of a very small stock of extremely general concepts, such as institutions, organizations and their principals and agents.

[...]

The central idea of the 'new institutionalism' or 'new political economy' is that what makes for an efficient economy is a set of institutions that permit individuals to benefit personally from doing what will also serve the (material) interests of society as a whole. Thus, for instance, a system of land tenure that allows tenants to keep for themselves a significant part of any expanded output they produce through allocating extra resources of capital or effort to its production is more economically efficient than one which does not. This reasoning can be applied to taxation, the organization of central or local government, education, banking, marketing – in effect, to any social arrangements (even marriage law and custom). Conversely it is often possible to see, retrospectively, that the institutional structure has provided incentives for individuals to do things which were inimical to development; while prospectively it is often possible to imagine or even design institutional arrangements that will improve the social returns to the economic activity of individuals (which is, roughly, what management consultants are supposed to be concerned with when they are hired by the state).

But [...] we cannot explain in terms of the 'paradigm' how any particular set of institutions that existed in the past or exist today in a given country came into existence. For that we have to resort to a much wider, looser theory of social change of precisely the kind that most exponents of public choice theory are trying to dispense with. [...]

[...] So much of the problem of understanding social change is understanding what motivates collective action, and the results of centuries of study and reflection suggest very strongly that *there are not going to be any general, or any* simple,

answers. Any interesting answers have always been specific to historically well-studied places and times (the French Revolution, the nineteenth century labour movement in Europe), and have involved complex long-term and short-term interactions between individuals, groups, cultural practices and institutions of specific kinds (churches, constitutions, professions, communities, armies) – in short, they almost always involve the social whole. [...]

A second difficulty is the project's reductionism. For instance, the idea that developmentally significant change may be understood as being the result of the interaction between existing institutions and the organizations formed to achieve whatever goals the institutional structure makes possible and attractive is, obviously, a very general statement about the sort of relationship that Marx postulated between classes and property rights. Presumably the advantage of reformulating it in these terms is that it brings out the general characteristics, which any such hypothesis needs to have, in a way that does not prejudge what it will actually state. The difficulty is, however, that whatever plausibility the general statement has comes from the particular case, not from the abstract one, which looks like a tautology. [...]

Third, there is a closely related tendency [...] to argue that, because some aspect of observed reality can be modelled, that aspect is the determinative or key one. For instance, institutions are very broadly defined, in this literature, as systems of rules or norms constraining behaviour, which means that virtually all persisting social relations can be represented as institutions.[23] But then the claim that institutions 'are the underlying determinant of the long-run performance of economies' becomes an unhelpful truism – i.e. the pattern of social relations determines economic performance. [...]

But what about the determinative effects of all the other aspects of all the other kinds of institutions not susceptible of being modelled in this way? What about the effects of the passion aroused in religious movements, or the conservatism, loyalty, discipline, etc., embodied in cultural norms, or the reforming or revolutionary zeal generated by class or national feeling, all of which seem to have played no less crucial parts in determining economic performance at one time or another in history? They can be brought back in only by accepting that the claim that institutions are the 'underlying' determinant is true by definition. It is plausible that, other things being held constant, property laws will have important effects on economic performance. But the whole difficulty of understanding development [...] is that other things do not stay constant but continually interact with property rights and all other kinds of social relations in ways that cannot be comprised within any model as simple and one-sided as those of rational choice theorizing.

Thus, while rational choice undoubtedly has valuable contributions to make to specific issues in development – the work of Samuel Popkin on peasant farmers' behaviour is an excellent example – it does not point the way towards a new development theory for our times.

'Rethinking Third World Politics'

Assuming, that is, that we are still concerned with development. The response of some academics has been, on the contrary, to frankly abandon it. [...] It is interesting to see what is involved in abandoning any policy concerns, including any commitment to 'development', by examining the work of [...] Jean-François Bayart.

In his chapter entitled 'Finishing with the Idea of the Third World: The Concept of the Political Trajectory', Bayart outlines his concept of 'historicity', the idea that politics must always be understood as a moment in a complex and very long-term story.[24] This story can be understood, Bayart suggests, in three possible ways: as the story of a 'civilization' (in Braudel's sense), as the story of a system of inequalities (caste, class, age, etc.) or as the story of a culture – or as a combination of these. Out of people's experience of this past, or these pasts – pasts which, Bayart stresses, comprise external influences as well as forces endogenous to the country or region under study – they have constructed various 'discursive genres', in terms of which politics are understood: examples he gives include such widely differing genres of discourse as the British system of government (a discourse about representation, civil liberties, etc.), Islamic thought, and the 'world of the invisible' (the occult, witchcraft, etc.). People think in terms of these discourses, and politics are constrained by them while at the same time involving contestations between them. The analysis of politics must therefore, according to Bayart, try to link 'the collective work of the production of the state to the subjective interiority of its actors' (p. 68) by studying both the long-term historicity of a people, through which their political institutions have evolved, and the discourses through which

these institutions are participated in and understood today.

[...]

In contrast, Bayart offers a '*longue durée*' view of Africans as having over the centuries always been subordinate players in relation to the outside world, but players none the less, always engaged in a process of 'extraversion', in which they have sought to draw on resources or alliances available in the external environment in furtherance of their continuing internal competitions and conflicts.[25] [...] What is now going on, Bayart argues, is the construction of new historic blocs, 'rhizomatically' linked to the underlying societies (i.e. like shoots from a tuber) and clustering around the state, and actually combining elements that earlier theorists have tended to see as mutually exclusive and opposed to each other: traditional and modern élites, local and central élites, chiefs and civil servants, state and private-sector élites, etc. In Bayart's view, ethnicity, class and the rest are all interlinked in a 'reciprocal assimilation of élites', as the members of these élites collaborate with each other to profit as best they can from their dealings, with the world outside.

And so what earlier theorists saw as deformations or aberrations appear in Bayart's optic as more or less normal, and in truth functional. Even a deeply corrupt state can be seen as an integrative force; even military coups can be understood as modes of intervention to cool out élite competition which has become out of control and destabilizing (p. 154); even structural adjustment programmes may be seen as removing spoils from the control of parts of the historic bloc that the president might otherwise not be able to dominate adequately (pp. 225–26). [...]

As for the African masses, Bayart frequently asserts that they are not passive victims of external forces, that they make their own history; but the actual role he shows them playing is circumscribed so closely by their lack of capacity to act for themselves and by their desperate struggle for survival that they much more often seem complicit in the trends he describes. [...]

There is notable inconsistency in Bayart's account, in its oscillation between a sort of gruff realism about the post-colonial state and moral discomfort. For, where the modernization school expected the African élites to be modernizing and good, Bayart expects them to be what they are, interested in power, wealth and status at more or less any cost. His standpoint might seem Hegelian: history unfolds according to the cunning of reason, so that it makes no sense to shed tears for history's victims. To do so is inconsistent, and furthermore empty, since there is no way to intervene. But, unlike Hegel, Bayart does not subscribe to an 'objective idealism'. In his concept of history there is no higher purpose which people's suffering serves.

And this is what it means to try to study the Third World without any commitment. The work of those committed to 'development' had faults, but thanks to this commitment they all had some idea – however imperfect – of who they were writing for, and who might act in the light of what they wrote. Bayart's intended readers, on the other hand, seem to be ultimately just 'Africanists', capable of getting their minds round Africa's 'historicity', but with neither the power nor the wish to act historically. As with Toye's stance, this may have an air of being more 'realistic' than the stance of Marxists, dependency theorists or modernizers, but what does this amount to?

Bayart has evident affinities with post-structuralist discourse, according to which we can never know reality but can only make a variety of statements about it with varying degrees and kinds of usefulness. Among social scientists a frequent symptom of this idea is to lay stress on the complexity of everything and the way no one formulation ever fully captures it, a 'distancing effect' that certainly seems to play a part in Bayart's work. But, even within that discourse, something eventually is said, a choice of statements is made, a general account emerges. And then, it is fair to ask, from what standpoint is Bayart's ultimately quietist picture drawn? And for whom is it painted, if not for the aforementioned kleptocrats, whom it does not exactly celebrate, but does not condemn either?

Consistently, for someone uncommitted to any concept of development, Bayart makes a resolute separation of politics from economics and says virtually nothing about the relation between them. In his account of Africa, what matters is only how economic resources are appropriated to service the endless cycle of the reciprocal assimilation of élites. If at the end of the twentieth century many African countries are destined to suffer desertification, famine, crime and warlordism, or to undergo recolonization as vast refugee camps, is it of great importance in the *longue durée*? In practice, Bayart has been an active spokesman for African interests in French public debate. The stance outside or above the fray that he explicitly adopts in his thesis on historicity contradicts this, and it is this contradiction that repeatedly surfaces in these texts.

In Conclusion: Development, or the Fate of the Ancients?

These sketches of a few selected currents in contemporary writing about development (or, in the case of [. . .] Bayart, in reaction against development) are, of course, subjective and partial. Their point is to raise the question of what 'development theory' was and has become, and above all to try to clarify what seems to me to be at stake: namely, the urgent need to revive development theory, not as a branch of policy-orientated social science within the parameters of an unquestioned capitalist world order, but as a field of critical enquiry about the contemporary dynamics of that order itself, with imperative policy implications for the survival of civilized and decent life, and not just in the ex-colonial countries.

Since the late 1960s, the debate about 'development theory' has in fact been more and more clearly about the theory of global development that each one presupposed, although the participants have all too often not recognized, or not acknowledged, that this was the issue at stake. Today it has to be frankly confronted: what do 'the universal development of the productive forces' and a truly global relation of supply and demand, which the OECD governments and the international financial institutions have been labouring for almost two decades to realize, now imply for any individual project of 'development'? For whom, contemplating what goals and by what means, can a useful 'development theory' be constructed?

The scale on which these questions seem to oblige us to think is painfully vast, and may seem almost to threaten incoherence; but, if it was not impossible to have a theory of capitalism on a national scale, why should it be impossible to have one of capitalism on a global scale? The theories of Hegel or Marx (or Weber or Fukuyama, for that matter) are not incoherent, but just very large-scale and necessarily full of selective simpifications, speculative elements, debatable assumptions and 'middle-level' problems of all kinds. What is really incoherent is a 'development theory' that does not rest explicitly on as clear a general theory of world history, and of world capitalism in particular, as it is possible to have.

Such a theory must, evidently, indicate what is and is not possible for various potential actors, just as the Keynesian theory of global capitalism did at the birth of 'development theory'. On the basis of such a general theory, new development theories at a lower level of abstraction can then be formulated. These may be for states, for groups of states organized in regional or other organizations or for non-state agents of various kinds. The goals of development envisaged by these theories will depend on the actors for whom they are formulated and the scope for change that the theorist's preferred theory of world capitalism suggests exists for them. If, as I fear, it seems that not much scope for change exists – especially for small, severely underdeveloped countries – without a radical resubordination of capital to democratic control, development theory will have also to be about this, and agents capable of undertaking it.

This abstract conclusion seems to me preferable, in spite of its abstraction, to trying to breathe life back into any kind of 'development theory' whose illusory appearance of concreteness and 'practicality' depends on averting one's gaze from its lack of adequate foundations.

NOTES

1   Estimated from data in Colin McEvedy and Richard Jones, *Atlas of World Population History* (New York: Facts on File, 1978). Fifty years later, population growth had produced a situation where the 'developing countries' (including China) accounted for almost four-fifths of the world's population.

2   A striking illustration of this can be found in Gabriel Almond's contribution to the review of late modernization theory edited by Myron Wiener and Samuel P. Huntington, *Understanding Political Development* (Boston: Little, Brown, 1987), in which he represents the modernization school as 'objective' ('governed by professional criteria of evidence and inference') and its critics as mere propagandists (pp. 444–68 and especially 450 ff.).

3   P.W. Preston, *Theories of Development* (London: Routledge, 1982), Chapter 3, referring to the work of Harrod and Domar and their successors, 'exported' to the soon-to-be ex-colonies.

4   Irene Gendzier, *Managing Political Change: Social Scientists and the Third World* (Boulder: Westview, 1985). [...]

5   F.H. Cardoso, 'Dependency and Development in Latin America', *New Left Review* 74, 1972, pp. 83–95. [...]

6   For an engaging discussion of the spurious and self-interested demand often made by some members of the 'development community', that critical theorists of development should come up with an answer to the question of 'what is to be done?', see James Ferguson, *The Anti-Politics Machine: 'Development,' Depoliticization, and Bureaucratic Power in Lesotho* (Cambridge: Cambridge University

Press, 1990), pp. 279–88. Members of the 'development industry', he remarks, 'seek only the kind of advice they can take. One "developer" asked my advice on what his country could do "to help these people". When I suggested that his government might contemplate sanctions against apartheid, he replied, with predictable irritation, "No, no! I mean *development!*" The only "advice" that is in question here is advice about how to "do development" better' (p. 284).

7   The convergence of Marxist and neo-liberal thinking in terms of their analysis of global capitalism should not have surprised anyone who appreciated their shared intellectual roots in the thought of Smith and Ricardo, as Dudley Seers pointed out in *The Congruence of Marxism and Other Neo-classical Doctrines*, IDS Discussion Paper No. 13 (University of Sussex: Institute of Development Studies, 1978). [...]

8   Lord Bauer has outlined his early thinking in 'Remembrance of Studies Past: Retracing First Steps', in Gerald M. Meier and Dudley Seers (eds), *Pioneers in Development* (New York: World Bank and Oxford University Press, 1984), pp. 27–43. The general position of the neo-liberals is summarized and criticized by John Toye in *Dilemmas of Development*, op. cit., Chapters 3 and 4. See also Christopher Colclough, 'Structuralism versus Neo-liberalism: An Introduction', in C. Colclough and James Manor (eds), *States or Markets? Neo-liberalism and the Development Policy Debate* (Oxford: Clarendon Press, 1992), pp. 1–25.

9   [...] See Eric Helleiner, 'From Bretton Woods to Global Finance: A World Turned Upside Down', in Richard Stubbs and Geoffrey R.D. Underhill (eds), *Political Economy and the Changing Global Order* (Toronto: McClelland and Stewart, 1994), pp. 163–75.

10 The dependency of international agencies such as the World Bank and the IMF on the policy preferences of their major participating states is obvious, but the pressures [are] extended to the non-government organizations (NGOs) in the development field as well. [...]

11 Manfred Bienefeld, *Rescuing the Dream of Development in the Nineties*, Silver Jubilee Paper 10 (University of Sussex: Institute of Development Studies, 1991, p. 13). [...]

12 Glyn and Sutcliffe, 'Global But Leaderless?', The New Capitalist Order, *Socialist Register 1992* (London: Merlin Press, 1992), pp. 90–91.

13 'A World Growing Richer', *Washington Post* editorial in the *Manchester Guardian Weekly*, 26 June 1994. [...]

14 See Helleiner, 'From Bretton Woods to Global Finance', in Stubbs and Underhill (eds), op.cit., pp. 164–65.

15 This revealing formulation comes from the conclusions of the World Bank's review of 'the evolution of approaches to development' in its 1991 *World*

Development Report under the heading 'The Way Forward'. As the real consequences of structural adjustment became inescapably obvious towards the end of the 1980s, especially in Africa, official policy veered back towards an emphasis on the importance of the state, but without reconciling this with the continued official emphasis on the superiority of markets over state action – in a word, official policy became contradictory, as any thoughtful reader of the 1991 *World Development Report* can see.

16 Frans J. Schuurman (ed.), *Beyond the Impasse: New Directions in Development Theory* (London: Zed Books, 1993).

17 David Booth, 'Marxism and Development Sociology: Interpreting the Impasse', *World Development* 13/7, 1985, pp. 761–87. [...]

18 David Booth, 'Development Research: From Impasse to a New Agenda', in Schuurman (ed.), *Beyond the Impasse*, op. cit., pp. 49–76. [...]

19 For an exemplary review of a great deal of this work see Frederick Cooper, Florencia E. Mallon, Steve J. Stern, Allen Isaacman and William Roseberry, *Confronting Historical Paradigms: Peasants, Labor, and the Capitalist World System in Africa and Latin America* (Madison: University of Wisconsin Press, 1993).

20 Andre Gunder Frank, 'The Underdevelopment of Development', Special Issue of *Scandinavian Journal of Development Alternatives* 10/3, September 1991.

21 See Clive Hamilton, *Capitalist Industrialisation in Korea* (Boulder: Westview, 1986); Gordon White, *Developmental States in East Asia* (New York: St Martin's Press, 1987); Alice Amsden, *Asia's Next Giant: South Korea and Late Industrialization* (New York: Oxford University Press, 1989); and Robert Wade, *Governing the Market: Economic Theory and the Role of Government in East Asian Industrialization* (Princeton: Princeton University Press, 1990).

22 See *The East Asian Miracle: Economic Growth and Public Policy* (New York: Oxford University Press for the World Bank, 1993).

23 'Institutions are the rules of the game in a society, or, more formally, are the humanly devised constraints that shape human interaction' (North, *Institutional Change and Economic Performance* (Cambridge: Cambridge University Press, 1990), p. 3).

24 In James Manor (ed.) *Rethinking Third World Politics* (London: Longman, 1991), pp. 53–54.

25 Jean-François Bayart, *The State in Africa: The Politics of the Belly* (London: Longman, 1993).

6

The History and Politics of Development Knowledge

Frederick Cooper and Randall Packard

The last fifty years have witnessed the transformation of the political geography of the globe, as vast areas that were once known as "colonies" became "less developed countries" or "the third world." People in the declining empires, in the rival superpowers that now dominated international affairs, in the countries born of earlier decolonizations, and in the new nations of Africa and Asia had to rethink how the world was constituted. The idea of development – and the relationship it implied between industrialized, affluent nations and poor, emerging nations – became the key to a new conceptual framework. Unlike the earlier claims of Europe to inherent superiority or a "civilizing mission," the notion of development appealed as much to leaders of "underdeveloped" societies as to the people of developed countries, and it gave citizens in both categories a share in the intellectual universe and in the moral community that grew up around the world-wide development initiative of the post-World War II era. This community shared a conviction that the alleviation of poverty would not occur simply by self-regulating processes of economic growth or social change. It required a concerted intervention by the national governments of both poor and wealthy countries in cooperation with an emerging body of international aid and development organizations.

The problem of development gave rise to a veritable industry in the academic social sciences, with a complex and often ambiguous relationship to governmental, international, and private agencies actively engaged in promoting economic growth, alleviating poverty, and fostering beneficial social change in "developing" regions of the world. From Oxfam to the United States Agency for International Development to the World Bank

to rice research institutes in India to the World Health Organization, a diverse and complex set of institutions – funded with billions of dollars – has focused on research and action directed toward development. Meanwhile, people from developing countries have studied economics or public health in European or American universities, done stints in international organizations, attended international conferences, and staffed government and nongovernmental organizations in their home countries. Missions go out from agencies in the United States or Europe to investigate problems and set up projects and work with experts, bureaucrats, and politicians in "host" countries.

Such processes have created overlapping networks of communication within which ideas and theories of development have emerged, circulated, and been appropriated within a wide variety of institutional settings – from Washington to Dakar and back again. [. . .]

Thinking Critically About Development

The development process has from its inception been self-critical and subject to critiques. Most projects include an element of "evaluation." Development specialists have found old ideas to be wanting and have moved on to others.[1] For all the shifting fashions, it is possible to discern a wide – but far from universal – set of operating assumptions emerging since the 1940s, often considered to constitute a "development orthodoxy": that foreign aid and investment on favorable terms, the transfer of knowledge of production techniques, measures to promote health and education, and economic planning would lead impoverished countries to be able to become "normal" market economies.

More radical alternatives came from Latin American theorists of "underdevelopment" who argued that international exchange itself widens the gap between rich and poor. Such arguments actually reinforced development as a category, by insisting that there is a normal pattern of economic development which Latin American, African, or Asian countries fell "under." Marxist theorists (for example, Amin 1974, 1993; Mandel 1975) came from a different direction – moving from an analysis of production in capitalist societies to a consideration of capital accumulation on a global scale – but ended up in a similar place: while claiming that capitalism was making poor societies poorer, they insisted that another kind of directed social change could bring about prosperity and justice.

Particularly since the 1980s, two quite distinct sets of critics have rejected the entire developmentalist framework. One set might be called ultramodernist. It consists of economic theorists who insist that the laws of economics have been proven valid, that the invisible hand of the market allocates resources optimally. Therefore, there is only economics, not development economics. When governments or outside agencies try to make the market work better, they introduce distortions which make it work worse. The free market does not guarantee equality of outcome, they say, but it produces as optimal an allocation of resources as is possible.[2]

A second set is postmodernist. This group sees development discourse as nothing more than an apparatus of control and surveillance. Development is but one of a series of controlling discourses and controlling practices – a "knowledge-power regime" – that has emerged since the Enlightenment, the extension of a universalizing European project into all corners of the globe. That most development projects fail – a point post-modernists and ultramodernists agree on – actually reinforces developmentalism, they say, for the failure defines a "target population" bounded from the rest of humankind by its aboriginal poverty, ignorance, and passivity, and hence by its need for the intervention of knowledgeable outsiders (Escobar 1995; Apffel Marglin and Marglin 1990; Sachs 1992; Nandy 1988; Crush 1995).

The ultramodernist and the postmodernist critiques actually have a lot in common, especially their abstraction from the institutions and structures in which economic action takes place and which shape a power-knowledge regime. The ultramodernists see power only as a removable distortion to an otherwise self-regulating market. The postmodernists locate the power-knowledge regime in a vaguely defined "West" or in the alleged claims of European social science to have found universal categories for understanding and manipulating social life everywhere.

James Ferguson (1990) points to a way of analyzing development as a controlling discourse while locating it in a specific set of international and national apparatuses. The state in "less developed countries" and international agencies such as the World Bank each find a role by accepting each other's: the national government allocates development resources and portrays itself as the agent of modernity, while outside agencies legitimately intervene in sovereign states by defining their services as benevolent, technical, and politically neutral. Both are content with development as a process which depoliticizes and disempowers local populations; both portray poverty as "aboriginal," disconnected from the history which gave rise to unequal access to resources; both are content with an expertise-driven structure of development; both are reinforced by failure as much as success. Ferguson's study opens the possibility of an ethnographically and historically situated analysis of development institutions, where the ability to deny or provide funds intersects with the ability to define what kinds of knowledge are or are not acceptable.

Locating power does not show that it is determinant or that a particular discourse is not appropriable for other purposes. That development interventions are both technical and moral renders them subject to critique through research findings and theoretical revision and to debate within the framework of universal rights and global citizenship upon which the development regime draws. Within poor countries, states' attempts to portray themselves as development agents do not immunize them from having their populist rhetoric thrust back upon them or prevent a debate on what is and what is not development. The marvelous ambiguity of the word development – eliding in a single concept notions of increased output and improved welfare – does not in itself prevent debates over its meanings, within and across national boundaries. What at one level appears like a discourse of control is at another a discourse of entitlement, a way of capturing the imagination of a cross-national public around demands for decency and equity.

The strange convergence of free market universalists and anti-universalist critics thus leaves a great deal to be discussed: of all the ways to conceptualize political and moral issues in international relations, how do some emerge while others are marginalized? to what extent are the terms of development discourses susceptible to becoming the basis of popular mobilization or of claims on national elites or international institutions?

[...] Postmodernists accuse developers of imposing an undesired modernity, while free marketeers denounce the nihilism of the postmodernists and the statism of the more orthodox; people working in the trenches of development projects insist that they do practical work, that they need coherent and reasonable frameworks through which to make day-to-day decisions, and that the problems of sickness and poverty which they address are not going to be helped by sweeping evocations of "community values" or "getting prices right." No side in these tussles has a monopoly of virtue, and all have something to gain by a more introspective, contingent view of the terrain upon which these battles have taken place.

Development, over the last half century, has been a framework for debate. But those debates have not taken place on level ground: some ideas have had the backing of powerful institutions and others have not. At times, conditions in the world economy have widened the possibilities of policies that could be tried, at others times alternatives have been narrowed. Social science theorizing and projects in Africa, Asia, and Latin America; funding priorities; and projects in the field have had ambiguous relations: the extent to which academic social science responds to the kinds of knowledge that political institutions demand of it and the degree to which social science helps to define what kinds of problems are recognized and deemed to be solvable are important and quite open questions. Learning does take place within institutions, but it is far from clear that ideas about eradicating poverty or disease have been influential merely because they were good.

Social scientists and development practitioners – and their ambivalent relationship to one another – should be as much the subject of investigation as the cultures and histories of African, Asian, or Latin American peoples. They are all part of a complex encounter. [...] Studying "up," as anthropologists call it, is difficult: any study of the powerful focuses on people and institutions with power to exclude themselves from the realm of the discussible. Yet it is far from clear that such power is absolute or that the people involved consider that they have something to hide. [...]

[...]

How different fields of inquiry claim authority, police the boundaries of professionalism, and position themselves in relation to governments and foundations has been the subject of a rich and growing body of literature. Of all the social sciences, anthropology has probably worried the most over how it constitutes the object of its analysis, debating what constitutes "ethnographic authority" and how that authority is related to the structure of power in colonial and postcolonial societies (Clifford and Marcus 1986). Economics – the most self-consciously "hard" of the social sciences and the one which has tended the most to claim "development" as its territory – seems the least likely territory for such explorations. Yet Donald McCloskey, in *The Rhetoric of Economics* (1985), opens up such a possibility. This conservative, Chicago-school economist shows elegantly that an economic argument is fundamentally an exercise in persuasion. [...]

The "conversation" about development is an extraordinarily extensive one, taking place all over the world, involving people from numerous cultural origins. Development experts are a very cosmopolitan community, a kind of "new tribe" (Hannerz 1990) involving the diverse staffs of institutions like the World Bank and giving rise to linkages – cemented by the languages of expertise – between developed and developing countries. Development language is simultaneously universalistic and pliable. Yet this phenomenon gives rise to a series of questions not fully developed by McCloskey and his colleagues: who is excluded from a conversation, and on what grounds? How are rhetorics defined historically and what are the processes within communities of experts that determine which rhetorics are deemed convincing and which are not? We need to take equally seriously the institutional and discursive mechanisms which made the transnational conversation possible and those which reproduced inequality within it. This calls for the kind of careful examination that puts institutions and ideas in the same frame, that looks not only at rhetoric but at historical and social processes [...]

This perspective leads to questions of how discourses and practices are bounded: is there a clearly definable "mainstream" of meanings and representations and an established repertoire of actions – from the report of the visiting mission to "strategic planning" to technical assistance – that developers consistently draw on? How does the professonalization of a discipline and the creation of institutions engaged with development distinguish the persons and ideas included within acceptable practice from those labeled as marginal, as pedants, or as quacks?

[...] There is great theoretical uncertainty in the development field and even less awareness of how policy-makers and development practitioners define the economic and social problems on which they work. And yet the world has fifty years of experience with development initiatives in Asia, Africa, and Latin America. The lessons of this experience have not been fully assimilated. Pressing human problems are at issue, and the question remains whether we can appreciate the complexity of social processes and the elusiveness of our categories for analyzing them without becoming paralyzed.

Development in History

Many of the activities that now fall under the rubric of development – as well as the ethos of directed progress – have a long history. [...] In mid-nineteenth-century Europe, theorists – Friedrich List most notable among them – and political leaders in "late industrializing nations" debated the need for national policies to catch up. The creole elites of Latin America since at least the early nineteenth century have wondered whether they should model their economic and cultural aspirations on European bourgeoisies or emphasize their distinctiveness; follow ideas of laissez-faire or pursue specifically national approaches to economic growth; join the "progressive" causes of their era, such as abolishing slavery, or defend their own way of doing things against outside pressure.[3] For intellectuals and social scientists in Europe – and those defining themselves in relation to Europe – the idea of development provided a way of narrating world history, but not necessarily a rationale for acting upon that history.

The form of the development idea that captured the imagination of many people across the world from the 1940s onward had quite specific origins – in the crisis of colonial empires. That colonial states were supposed to facilitate exports had long been a given, but only through investments expected to bring a rapid return. France and Britain both had firm doctrines of colonial financial self-sufficiency – each colony was supposed to pay its own way – in the name of which long-term initiatives to improve colonial infrastructure were repeatedly rejected. What was new in the colonial world of the late 1930s and 1940s was that the concept of development became a framing device bringing together a range of interventionist policies and metropolitan finance with the explicit goal of raising colonial standards of living.[4]

From colonial empires to less developed countries

[...] The colonial development effort had quite a different effect: it provided a means by which imperial powers could reconcile themselves to their loss of power, while maintaining a connection with their ex-colonies and a continued sense of their mission in shaping their future. Declining imperial powers were caught in an ambivalence that has attached itself to development ideas ever since: were they a description of ongoing, self-propelled models of social change, or blueprints for action?

[...] The colonizer's conceit that "other" people needed to adopt new ways of living was internationalized, making development simultaneously a global issue and a concern of states. The standard of living of a poor Bengali became an issue debatable at Geneva as well as Dacca, while the terms of such a discussion (per capita income or other national statistics) reinforced the centrality of the national unit's economic role even as it opened up its performance to international examination. The development concept was crucial to all participants to rethink unequal relationships in the era of decolonization. Yet the historical trajectory that brought the different nations of the world to this point framed development in a particular way: former colonial officials were holding before themselves a future in which their conception of economic behavior could be a model for the world, while African and Asian leaders were eager to look away from their colonial past. Neither side was looking very clearly at the present, where complex yet dynamic forms of production and exchange presented opportunities and constraints.

[...] By the late 1940s [...] American economic leaders became increasingly skeptical that they could wait for the benefits of opening more areas to the market. The shift away from market-driven development was encouraged by the expanding threat of communism, with its supposed appeal to the world's poor. It was in this context that Harry Truman announced in 1949 that the United States would undertake an effort to mobilize "our store of technical knowledge in order to help [the people of underdeveloped nations] realize their aspirations for a better life." In doing so he took development out of the colonial realm and made it a basic part of international politics.

The growing convergence of U.S. and European interests around the need to generate development through technical assistance programs played an important role in fostering the creation of a series of international organizations during the late 1940s and early 1950s. Founded in the context of European reconstruction and the Bretton Wood agreements in the late 1940s, the World Bank and International Monetary Fund expanded their field of action from financing European recovery and financial stability in the 1940s to fostering international development in the 1950s. Equally important was the United Nations system of development organizations – the Food and Agricultural Organization, the World Health Organization, UNICEF, UNESCO, and the UN's Expanded Programme of Technical Assistance. The creation of these multilateral agencies contributed to the internationalization of development. Although the administration of these organizations was initially dominated by Europeans and Americans and debates within the organizations reflected specific national interests, the organizations served to de-emphasize such interests and make the case that a prosperous, stable world was a shared goal (Lumsdaine 1993). And the increasing presence of "developing" nations in the United Nations organization made it easier for their leaders to insert their conceptions of development into debates, even as western-controlled institutions funded projects and multinational corporations exercised great power over capital flows.

Different developments?

One cannot appreciate the power of the development idea without realizing that the possibility that modern life and improved living standards could be open to all, regardless of race or history of colonial subjugation, was in the 1950s a liberating possibility, eagerly seized by many people in the colonies. Development gave African and Asian leadership a sense of mission, for they were positioned to assimilate the best that Europe had to offer while rejecting its history of oppression and cultural arrogance. These elites positioned themselves to broker relationships among diverse societies, world markets, and international organizations.
[...]
We thus need to see the engagement of people in former colonies with the development concept in dynamic terms. They had already turned the post-1930s version of colonial development into claims

for material welfare and political power, so that the development framework turned into something quite different from what it originally was supposed to be. From the Bandung conference of 1955 onward, a "third worldist" conception of social justice emerged, built around claims for a larger share of the world's resources to be devoted to the poorest countries without compromising the latter's sovereignty. [...]

In different countries, there emerged important variations on the development theme which did not necessarily accept the idea of North–South interaction as naturally beneficial to both parties or of development as an act of generosity of the rich to the poor. It is thus too simple to assert the emergence of a singular development discourse, a single knowledge-power regime. The appropriations, deflections, and challenges emerging within the overall construct of development – and the limits to them – deserve careful attention.

It is a mark of the power and the limits of the development framework that emerged out of the crisis of colonial empires that it was both embraced and reshaped by policymakers and social scientists from Latin America, a century beyond its own decolonization. For Latin American elites, the development framework offered new terms for articulating grievances in regard to the trade, investment, and financial policies of domineering economic partners and opened a new arena in which they could assert leadership, both abroad and at home. [...]

Meanwhile, newly independent India experimented with combinations of Soviet planning models and capitalist production in ways that reveal points of convergence as well as the clear contradictions of the opposed visions of societal transformation and economic growth. India's experience revealed as well the possibilities – and the tensions – of combining an explicitly progressive, western-influenced notion of development (associated particularly with Nehru) with a conception of Indian history (symbolized by Gandhi) which stressed the virtues of tradition and simplicity [...]. Yet [...] this dichotomy oversimplifies the complex political debates that took place from the 1930s onward: critics of the "modern" nation-state could become enthused about the possibilities of "science" or economic planning, while the most vigorous developmentalists often saw themselves as doing what was necessary to preserve the distinctiveness of Indian culture.

What was striking about the 1940s was how much was open for debate: the usefulness of specific colonial institutions or social structures, the specific aspects of what was "western" or "Indian" that were to preserved, emulated, rejected, or changed. The Indian National Congress attached itself to development as a national project even before the British government had made up its mind about the colonial variant, and after 1947 India set itself the task not only of building a nation, but also an economy relatively insulated from foreign investment and control. [...] National development had its achievements, not least of which was the creation of a knowledge-building apparatus, so that India not only was capable of managing its economy but contributed some of the most important figures to the economics profession worldwide. India has also produced a strong attack on the very idea of development and fora, like *Economic and Political Weekly*, where different viewpoints clash at a high level of sophistication. [...] Struggles do not line up neatly between the friends and foes of development, between "modernity" and "community," but engage differences in a more nuanced manner and involve people who have been immersed as deeply in international organizations and communication as in local social movements.

Africa was the latest of the late developers, the least able to generate its own academic knowledge. Yet African political leaders and intellectuals also pushed a distinct view of economic development, one less oriented than the conventional view toward a generic "developed economy" and more focused on the communitarian roots of African economies. [...]

The heterodoxy of development theory in the last half century implies neither randomness nor equality: certain sets of ideas and theories have gained prominence at particular periods of time, while others have been excluded from international debates. [...] Within particular domains the development construct has become a framework that rationalizes and naturalizes the power of advanced capitalism in progressivist terms – as the engine bringing those on the bottom "up" toward those who are already there. [...] This very framework became a basis for claims and mobilization, clashing with often powerful forces intent on containing or suppressing such initiatives. [...] The contents of such a discourse shifted within institutions and gave rise, in various situations, to orthodoxy, heterodoxy, and ambivalence in social science disciplines. Disciplinary knowledge could variously give coherence and depth to elites' world views, bring out the complications of development prescriptions, or point to fundamental flaws in policy frameworks and underlying biases in public discourse. [...] The point is not to decide whether or not development discourse is truly hegemonic, but to examine projects of building and fracturing hegemonies: how financial, political, and discursive power was deployed, how such projects were contested within their own terms and through efforts to redefine the terrain of debate, and how one can find where room for maneuver remains in international institutions and in the numerous sites where development initiatives encounter the complexity of particular social struggles.[5]

Demarcating a new terrain for academic inquiry

[...]

Anthropology, as James Ferguson shows here, has been skeptical of the idea of development and deeply caught up in it. Its place in the division of labor among mid-twentieth century social sciences was based both on a theoretical stance that stressed the integrity of individual societies and a methodological one that stressed fieldwork and hence the complexity of particular instances. Yet anthropology had never quite got over its older evolutionist perspective on societies, and by the 1930s many of its practitioners were drawn to models of progressive change that could liberate Africans from the racial oppression they observed around them. Hence anthropology's deep ambivalence about development: welcoming yet distrusting social and economic progress, worrying about the damage change might inflict on diverse cultures yet acknowledging the misery of the present. When development institutions asked anthropologists to contribute their culturally specific knowledge to projects, anthropologists found at the same time job opportunities, a chance to insert their sensitivities into projects and to validate the usefulness of their discipline, and a danger of becoming immersed in a system of deploying knowledge within which they would have a secondary role (see also Escobar 1995 for a biting critique of anthropology's encounter with development). Anthropology – as several contributions to the workshops made clear – has at least complicated the social sciences' picture of development, showing its unpredictable effects, raising fundamental questions about the clash of cultures, and pointing to the possibility of ethnographic analysis of the development apparatus itself.

[...]

One can see the tension between the contextualizing fields (history, anthropology) and the universalizing fields (economics), as well as the more profound tension inherent in the relationship of social science and policy and the fact that abstract theory and empirical research both arise in concrete situations, in relation to funding possibilities and distinct knowledge communities with their own prestige systems. Carl Pletsch (1981) argues that the Cold War strongly shaped the way in which the kinds of knowledge asserted by the colonial "experts" gave way to different disciplinary domains: the realm in which universalistic social sciences actually had relevance, mainly the West (where sociology, political science, and economics reigned supreme) versus the nonwestern exceptions (given over to anthropology, history, and new area studies centers focusing on Africa, Asia, or Latin America) versus the exceptions who had nuclear weapons (demanding the special expertise of Kremlinologists and Sinologists).

From the side of organizations doing practical work, tensions over knowledge are equally profound. Such institutions may assert power through their command of technical expertise and insist on academic qualifications for their personnel yet complain that the economists coming out of universities are taught "ingenious models" that give "a hopelessly oversimplified view of how economies really work" (Coats 1986: 127). Ambitious economists from western countries may find the developing world too confusing, too unpredictable to be a place to build a career, while economists from India or Pakistan find the international development apparatus attractive (Rosen 1985: 230–33). Global development efforts seem to require replicability, yet taking an integrated approach to social and economic change demands deep local knowledge (Lewis 1988: 7). Project design demands prediction; investigation frequently points to uncertainty.

Development brings out such tensions in a particularly vivid way: it makes distinctions among human beings; it raises questions of when suffering is to be observed and when it is to be remedied; and it cannot escape questions of when the intervention of knowledge-bearing people brings about constructive change or when it merely demeans those who cannot claim such knowledge.

If different disciplines have tried to take pieces of social change and give them analytic precision, it is not clear that a kind of evolutionism – a desire to make "traditional" people into something else – has gone away despite all the criticism such perspectives have received within different social sciences. The 1950s and 1960s were the heyday of modernization theory, a social science approach that purported to demonstrate that change in one domain of life implied comprehensive reconfiguration, leading virtually to the creation of a new sort of person – rational instead of superstitious, oriented toward achievement rather than status. Modernization theory has been effectively discredited, but the ethos behind it lies behind less comprehensive approaches to development.[6] [. . .] The idea of creating a new person is much older than development policies; it goes back to missionaries, in a sense the first NGOs to work in colonized regions. The idea of making a new person was downplayed in Africa as colonial governments came to realize how little control they had over such a process: in the 1920s colonial governments claimed to favor change within existing cultural traditions while the anthropology of the 1930s tended toward cultural conservationism. But the development drive of the 1940s brought to the fore once again the possibility of reconstructing Africans or Asians in all aspects of their beings, this time in a way that was as attractive to leaders of newly independent countries as it was to social scientists eager to chart the movement from tradition to modernity.

The flip side of the new person being created was the categorization of the person who had not made the transition: the "indigenous person," the "traditional" person, the "community," the "village," the "local" – generic categories that collapsed the variety and complexity of life in particular locations into a single word [. . .]. The very importance in development programs of defining a "target population" has tended to bring evolutionism back in, whether explicitly or inexplicitly [. . .]. And as Pigg points out, the "local" intermediaries working with international development projects were particularly likely to want to see themselves as new people, distinguished from the constraints and backwardness of village life, even when overseas development personnel were trying to stress their own cultural sensitivity.

Critics of development interventions are as likely as proponents to reify the categories of traditional and modern, of "community" and "West," giving the category of community positive value instead of negative. Historically, however, the two sides are more deeply imbricated in each other than such a dichotomous suggestion implies.[7] Development initiatives came about as much through the initiatives of impoverished workers in Jamaica as those of visionaries in London. The most powerful organizations in the world have seen their initiatives fail because they did not resonate in a local context. As development policies oscillate from basic needs to participation to getting prices right to sustainability – and perhaps back again – it is not clear that the determinants of these policies are as independent of what goes on at the grassroots as they appear to their authors or their critics to be. Nor are villages homogeneous or harmonious entities: some people within them may find in initiatives from outside a way to get ahead, a way to get away from an oppressive local landlord or patriarchal authority.

Development in the 1940s was a framing device through which colonial regimes tried to respond to challenges and reassert control and legitimacy, but it was a device that could itself be challenged and seized, used for different ends by a Nehru or by an ambitious young man in a remote village. The dialectic of control and contestation is an ongoing one, and after fifty years of development initiatives, the objectives and strategies – as well as the ethical implications and material effects – of development are still being debated (Dasgupta 1993).

Ideas, Institutions, and Contexts: Sticky Thinking and Shifting Paradigms

Much development knowledge is down to earth – agricultural technologies, methods of keeping government accounts – and institutions are often eager to portray development knowledge in such terms. Yet development is fundamentally about changing how people conduct their lives, and the very claim to technical knowledge is itself a political act.

While the frame of development has opened up intense struggles over means and ends, not all ideas or positions have held the same valence or power. At certain moments and in certain places there has been a broad convergence of thinking about development around certain models or theories. Some of these convergences have had long lives, while others have been more fleeting, emerging at one moment as orthodoxy and then losing support to a new paradigm. In some cases – as with current interest in sustainable agriculture or market-led development – earlier paradigms reemerge.

[...]

The transmission and circulation of development knowledge

The fact that a new orthodoxy emerges within powerful institutions does not by itself explain the wider acceptance of this orthodoxy. It is necessary to examine as well the processes by which development knowledge circulates.

In part the ability of powerful institutions to disseminate ideas arises from their place at the center of development finance. Money talks. Yet this materialist explanation overlooks the specific networks of communications through which ideas circulate internationally. The power of an institution like the World Bank is based as well on its position within overlapping global networks of research, communication, and training. The Bank's employment of a small army of researchers, recruited internationally from developing and developed countries, produces masses of country and project review documents filled with statistical data which are disseminated globally. The recruitment of academics from developing countries to work for short stints in the Bank and the support of training programs for mid-level bureaucrats contributes as well to the dissemination of the Bank's ideas. [...]

Yet even with their financial and communication power, the knowledge-shaping power of institutions varies over time. The World Bank's influence on the creation of development orthodoxies, as Thomas Biersteker suggested (1993 [...]), has been mediated by shifts in the global economy. The availability of credit in the 1970s made it worthwhile for national governments or international agencies to mount efforts for interventionist development programs – paying and empowering a wide range of experts – but the credit squeeze of the 1980s made it seem as if doing anything other than leaving things to the market had to buck financial pressure as well as strong arguments from well-situated economists. Much of the current rhetoric about structural adjustment programs is about the absence of alternatives, while critics of such policies try to get the idea of alternatives back in. In fact, some states have been better able than others to hold off structural adjustment programs; any explanation of their differential acceptance and impact must consider national politics as well as the power of international institutions.

The successful transmission of ideas emanating from powerful development organizations was also fostered by global political shifts. The end of the Cold War narrowed development options by discrediting socialist alternatives. The absence of both financial and ideational options has narrowed the space within which the governments of developing countries can make policy choices. It is perhaps historically significant that the earlier postwar push for market-led development was short circuited by the rising fear of communist expansion and the need for more interventionist development, while the second coming of market-driven development – and the willingness of leaders in the United States and elsewhere to accept whatever consequences the market may have – became politically feasible, in part, through the demise of communism.

The strong stress on market discipline sits rather uneasily with the other major trend among the powerful development institutions: their concern with "governance" and the imposition of political conditions – some form of democratization – on the provision of aid. Compelling as many of the critiques of government corruption, clientalism, and incompetence are, it is not clear that imposed austerity helps to build political capacity. More important, looking at this new trend in historical perspective makes it look less new. The insistence on "good government" reproduces much that was previously said about the "good economy": a bland assertion that the West has defined objective standards for others to meet, a generalized set of categories (elections, multiple parties) that define those standards, irrespective of the actual debates that might be going on in specific contexts over how more people might acquire meaningful voice in their own lives.

The reception and appropriation of development knowledge

While development ideas may spread out from key institutions, they may not be simply accepted or replicated. They may be transformed or appropriated in ways that were unintended. [...]

How does one analyze stickiness within the reception of development ideas? Language is often stickier than policies. Gillian Feeley-Harnik [has] argued that deeply held images, developed out of specifically American experience with "taming" the wilderness, have a deep, often subliminal, effect on the way issues like conservation and population control are talked about, and which remain powerful even as immediate policy issues shift. The concept of community participation is an ideal which is applied to a wide range of programs, even when that participation is diluted of influence or empowerment. Words like "overgrazing" convey images of conservation problems as rooted in the behavior of "target" populations – making it easy to ignore the social processes that gave rise to these problems.[8] Concepts like sustainability and participation become a kind of shorthand, distilling complex and in many cases

highly problematic processes. In this way they are part of a range of template mechanisms through which development institutions function.

[...]

Issues of gender present a striking instance in which a social category both opens up and bounds a complex set of issues. Both academic social scientists and activist organizations have insisted that the majority of the world's poor are women, that women do much of the world's farming, and that the concrete manifestation of industrial development is often the entry of women into extremely low-paid jobs. Yet much writing about development codes women as "traditional" and sees men as the agents of transformation. The program of Women in Development is a response to these critiques, yet this sort of response risks compartmentalizing the problem, as if action directed toward women could be an "add on" to a development process otherwise unchanged. A more radical approach, Gender and Development, focuses instead on the subordination of women and thus forces examination of power and patriarchy. Some writers (for example Shiva 1988) insist that a feminist approach should lead to a rejection of the development framework altogether, as a patriarchal project leading to the appropriation of ever more finite resources – notably water and forests – that only diminish the kind of sustenance-oriented economic activity in which women are most often engaged in practice and which they symbolize ideologically. This argument approaches from a feminist standpoint the rejection of science and development as projects of an oppressive modernity that have come from certain scholar-activists as a critique of imperialism (for example Nandy 1988). But feminist theory has been at least as critical of the substitution of generalized conceptions of "women" for analysis of gender politics in specific instances, and some feminists argue for a complex engagement with the details of development processes and careful discussion of how they can be altered (Moser 1993; Agarwal 1992). All this hardly exhausts the possibilities of analysis of gender, and one of the achievements of the past two decades has been a wealth of research that reveals the fluid and contested nature of gender relations in a variety of situations. The most difficult challenge is to turn such investigation into programmatic initiatives that address the specific circumstances of women without essentializing the category of gender.

Templates, cultural paradigms, and generic representations of the "indigenous" are not about to disappear. Large-scale organizations need to simplify; funding cycles demand replicable project designs. When USAID and other organizations tried to focus on small projects to avoid the problems of giganticism for which past development efforts were rightly criticized, they needed approaches that did not demand deep situational analyses for each project. Academic social scientists should not be dismissive of such difficulties. The historian's or anthropologist's concern with context and complexity is neither more nor less separable from a self-serving professionalism than the development practitioner's concern with the replicability of project design, the desire for stable decision-making frameworks, and the need for a quick and readily graspable analysis of the specificity of each case in which action is being taken. Nor does one get to the bottom of such issues by attributing them to the developer's apparent conceit of remaking the world in the name of modernity: "indigenous" societies are as socially constructed as developers' world views, with parallel tendencies to leave much of social life out of focus, to obscure the operations of power and hierarchy. Development paradigms – from the orthodox to the radical – have at least thrown different frameworks into relation to each other, drawing attention to the fact that at the local level as much as at the global one, what exists is not necessarily what has to be.

Such considerations underscore the need for a frank and far-reaching examination of the politics of development, beyond the general tendency of large organizations to behave in certain ways or of scientific paradigms to be resistant to contradictory evidence. Power entails both arrogance and limits. Agencies working in developing countries delve into local political and economic complexities at their own peril. It is politically more judicious to explain the destruction of the rain forest in Brazil or soil erosion in the West African Sahel in terms of a "tragedy of the commons" model than to analyze the political and economic forces which drive farmers in both regions to expand cultivation into environmentally fragile areas (Peters 1994). Highlighting these forces might embarrass and alienate local national governments and imply interventions which are politically unacceptable to them. Conversely, focusing narrowly on the age-old deficiencies of a "target" population may facilitate the cooperation of an international agency intent on accomplishing something within the limits of the status quo and a national bureaucracy interested in acquiring outside resources to distribute and in perpetuating a view of economic problems as being amenable to

the sort of expertise the bureaucracy shares with knowledgeable outsiders (Ferguson 1990).

Academic disciplines as much as development institutions work through paradigms and other template mechanisms which are resistant to change, and the way they select future practitioners often works to exclude rather than encourage forms of knowledge which challenge the discipline's core assumptions. Economics, for instance, operates through the construction of models which by their very nature work to stabilize assumptions used for decision making. [...] In anthropology, Ferguson's argument that development anthropologists are too compromised by the practicality of what they do to achieve high status within the discipline is paralleled by the danger that their research is too painstakingly specific to be at the core of development projects.

Perhaps the most important question of all concerns the knowledge that is generated and disseminated within Latin America, Africa, and Asia (Long and Long 1992). Rosen (1985: 233) argues that the greatest contribution a development effort can make is not so much the concrete projects that result, but the building up of institutions – including the training of local economists – who can "examine, analyze, and suggest solutions for the problems of their own country." Such expertise would also be able to examine, reject, or modify "expert" advice coming from outside. [...] But capacities vary greatly: India or Argentina is far better able to participate in such dialogues than Sierra Leone or Burma. An undesirable effect of antistate, promarket bias in current development programs is losing focus on the fact that education and research require a complex infrastructure and expensive, if not immediately productive, investment.

The issue is deeper than this. The power of western science may be felt even when the institution doing that science is located in Asia. Recently, many development practitioners have acquired a new respect for what is called "indigenous technical knowledge." Yet the very category suggests that such knowledge can be neatly bounded from knowledge of the more universal sort; Africans or Asians are assumed to know certain things by virtue of their birth and culture, whereas the rest of us know certain things by virtue of having gone to the trouble of learning them. [...]

Yet concepts of the "indigenous" or the "local" can be politically useful even when they are referring to political and social relationships far less bounded than the terms suggest. It is often in the name of "indigenous rights" that movements – which sometimes connect the allegedly local with national intellectuals in a capital city and support organizations around the world – make a coherent and compelling case for why a dam should be considered harmful or why forestry policy should be made by those affected. While the leaders of such movements may gain stature by linkages to international NGOs as much as by support of a "community," it is by demonstrating the power of the local that they make a case.

It is not hard to deconstruct the modes of discursive power. It is much harder to discover how discourse operates within institutions. One point on which there was wide agreement at the workshops was how little we actually know about the way institutions – from small NGOs to the World Bank – actually operate. [. . .] In North America, we know even less about the distinct forms of organization, the political issues, and the relations with former colonies that characterize the European Economic Community, Scandinavia, or Japan (see Gendarme 1995). We tend to think of NGOs as a category whose mere existence shows that "civil society" is working to counter the state's dominance of development initiatives, but we also tend to treat those organizations in generic terms, not exploring their varied ideologies, organizational forms, and relations to state mechanisms. The subtle interplay of national policy, foundations with the financial resources to shape intellectual inquiry, and the operations of programs in the field deserves further study. [. . .] The momentous events of recent years that cast Eastern Europe into a realm of "transition" and "development" raises questions that have long needed more attention in Africa, Latin America, and Asia: how to understand specific dynamics of change without taking the end point for granted (Verdery 1996; Stark 1996).

After all is said, we are still left with dilemmas intrinsic to the enormous inequalities of wealth, power, and access to knowledge in the world: the desperate nature of problems versus the imperiousness of proposed solutions, the specific social relations and struggles in each situation versus the dangers of paralysis before vast and varied problems, awareness of the ways in which global and national structures condition exploitation and impoverishment versus the political dangers of too close an examination of precisely those sorts of issues.

Uses and Dangers: Development as Discourse and Practice

To argue, as we have been doing, that the development concept can be located in historical conjunc-tures and that it can be understood in relation to intellectual trends, shifts in global economic structures, political exigencies, and institutional dynamics has important implications for debates about the future. It lends a certain skepticism to assumptions that current fashions – such as "getting prices right" or "sustainability" – represent the triumph of one model over another. The record of the past suggests that theories that seem to be conquering the world are part of shifting patterns, perhaps even a cyclical alternation between approaches that are laissez faire and growth-oriented versus those that are politically interventionist and equity-oriented. [. . .] [Recent work] encourage(s) skepticism over whether "the market" can be neatly opposed to "the state" or to "policy interventions"; once one starts to talk about real markets they turn out to be as messy, as filled with blockages and contradictions, as the real states whose failings have become all too familiar. Market mechanisms, state mechanisms, kinship mechanisms, and other kinds of social organizations are not pristinely separated from one another [. . .]. We are also skeptical of the argument that development represents an instance of the tyranny of modernity, of colonialism by other means, for the history which shows the colonial origins of development initiatives and the development construct is also a history of how that concept was mobilized and deflected for other ends. People around the world are in some way *engaged* with far-reaching structures of power, and those engagements take more varied and complex forms than acquiescence or resistance. Denunciations of modernity or evocations of community are not going to make multinational corporations or representatives of the World Health Organization go away. The question is how deeply the implications of interactions can be discussed, and how wide the range of possibilities for affecting those interactions can be broadened [. . .].

The development framework, as it has existed in the past half century, has excluded many questions that are quite germane to questions of poverty, power, and change. In public contexts, institutions like the World Bank cannot talk too much about the power relations within the sovereign states with which they work. But critics of the World Bank don't necessarily want those questions probed either, for condemnation of Bank-type interventions are often set against notions of "community" or "social movement" that might not look so positive if subject to scrutiny.[9] Neither "universality" nor "community" has a monopoly of virtue, or of evil. What is important is the relationship of the two categories [...]. People living within situations of oppression or exploitation – by local tyrants, by multinational corporations, by local patriarchs, by greedy bureaucrats – have the possibility of attaching their cause to something beyond their own borders, of turning rhetoric of human rights, of self-determination, of cultural integrity to political use. Development rhetoric represents one possible framework in terms of which causes can be mobilized. The point is not that development – any more than a list of universal human rights – itself offers answers, but that it shapes possibilities for political mobilization that cross differences of culture, nationality, and geography.

[...]

It is as true now as it was fifty years ago that most of what contributes to productive investments (or destructive exploitation) comes not from "projects" devised in the name of development, but from the operations of local entrepreneurs, multinational corporations, banks, and parastatals. Yet the very fact that a development question exists points to the limitations of capitalist development: it is precisely because large areas of the world are poor and are not contributing to the generation of surplus value that there is a development problem which cannot be reduced to analysis of the immanent logic of capitalism.

Interventionist policies have been advocated on the grounds that they would bring more people into the sphere of capitalist production, to the mutual benefit of the people involved and of capitalists. Now, the argument is being made by ultra-modernist critics of development economics that one should leave the entire problem to the undistorted market. It is far from obvious that doing that would work any better than it did on the eve of the first wave of colonial development interventions in the 1940s. Arguments that the market works better than planned interventions are thus misspecified – it is not clear that this dichotomy corresponds to economic organization in either developed or undeveloped societies. But such arguments remain powerful ideological statements: they imply that certain parts of the world will be rewarded by world markets if they do well, while others can be written off if they do badly. That is what the end of the development era would mean: to narrow issues that can be the objects of fruitful debate.

Fifty years of development initiatives and development rhetoric have laid before the world's population the knowledge that conditions of mal-nutrition and ill health exist around the world and the insistence that all of us are implicated and complicit in that fact. Poverty in all corners of the world has become a discussible issue – an issue around which profound disagreements may exist, which pose dangers of objectification of "victims," and which may create privileged domains of operation for the entrepreneurs of poverty eradication. Debate over such issues keeps open the possibility that local movements can mobilize around pressing issues and make their cause a wider one. Capitalism is no more likely to have brought all the world's population into useable relations of production and consumption in the year 2000 than it did in 1900. It is certain that poverty and inequality will remain, but whether they will remain issues that can be fruitfully debated, within and across state boundaries, is less clear. The issues that have been at the center of the development framework can be ignored, but they will not go away.

NOTES

1 For a concise review of the succession of theories in economics, see Arndt (1987).
2 Such an argument has gone from dissent to dominance. See Bauer (1972) and Lal (1985).
3 Robert Shenton and Michael Cowen have argued that development should in fact be seen as a quintessentially nineteenth-century construct. [...]
4 The obvious point that economic growth and institutional change took place even where developers did not consciously try to bring it about has been emphasized by defenders of the free market (Bauer 1984) and Africanists who want to show that Africans were themselves agents of progress (Chauveau 1985).
5 Some critics of development write as if identifying a "development discourse" shows it to be hegemonic and as if deconstructing that discourse automatically destroys its legitimacy. Discourses are studied in relation to other discourses. People working in the trenches have good reason to believe that something is missing here. For examples of the linguistic critique of development, see Moore and Schmitz (1995), Sachs (1992), and Crush (1995).
6 Although the inability of modernization theory to deal with the conflictual nature of change, its teleological conception of modernity, and its reduction of "tradition" to an ahistorical foil is widely acknowledged, there are attempts to resurrect it, notably through concepts like "civil society" and "governance," put forward as new stand-ins for the old teleology. See Barkan (1994) and more generally Apter and Rosberg (1994).

7   Such approaches to development are similar to the dichotomous views that have become influential in colonial states, in works ranging from Fanon to James Scott (1990) to Subaltern Studies (Guha and Spivak 1988): the "autonomy" of the "subaltern" or the "hidden transcript" of subaltern discourse is starkly separated from colonial discourse. For arguments for an interactive, nonbinary approach see Cooper (1994) and Cooper and Stoler (1997). [. . .]

8   Literatures exist about labeling (Wood 1985), development narratives (Roe 1991), and development discourse (Apthorpe 1986, Moore and Schmitz 1995). Deconstructing the power relations behind "keywords" may give the misleading impression that the messages they seem to convey are what is received by their audience (a problem, for example, with Sachs 1992).

9   Some critics would like to see initiatives for change coming from social movements rather than from a global framework like development (Escobar 1995). This begs the key question: what distinguishes a "good" social movement, which expands the opportunities for human fulfillment, from a "bad" one, which imposes one sort of particularism on other people? Both are social movements, and implicitly the critic is imposing some sort of general criteria of human progress on them – in short coming back into the same sort of universalizing discourse that they criticize in the development concept. Escobar and others are making a quite valid effort to look for a more modest, more culturally specific, less universalistic "we" implied in the idea that "we can make a better world" than the more totalizing versions of the development framework. Yet their solution no more resolves the tensions of universal and particular than does the development concept – which is also amenable to nuance and recognition of the tensions it embodies. [. . .]

REFERENCES

Agarwal, Bina. 1992. "The Gender and Environment Debate: Lessons from India". *Feminist Studies* 18: 119–57.

Amin, Samir. 1974. *Accumulation on a World Scale.* Translated by Brian Pearce. New York: Monthly Review Press.

——. 1993. *Itinéraire Intellectuel.* Paris: L'Harmattan.

Apffel Marglin, Frederique, and Stephen Marglin, ed. 1990. *Dominating Knowledge: Development, Culture, and Resistance.* Oxford: Clarendon Press.

Apter, David E., and Carl G. Rosberg, eds. 1994. In *Political Development and the New Realism in Sub-Saharan Africa.* Charlottesville: University Press of Virginia.

Apthorpe, Raymond. 1986. "Development Policy Discourse". *Public Administration and Development* 6: 377–89.

Arndt, H. W. 1987. *Economic Development: The History of an Idea.* Chicago: University of Chicago Press.

Barkan, Joel. 1994. "Resurrecting Modernization Theory and the Emergence of Civil Society in Kenya and Nigeria". In *Political Development and the New Realism in Sub-Saharan Africa,* edited by David Apter and Carl G. Rosberg, 87–116. Charlottesville: University Press of Virginia.

Bauer, P. T. 1972. *Dissent on Development.* Cambridge, Mass.: Harvard University Press.

——. 1984. "Remembrances of Studies Past: Retracing First Steps". In *Pioneers in Development,* edited by Gerald Meier and Dudley Seers, 27–43. New York: Oxford University Press.

Biersteker, Thomas J. 1993. "Evolving Perspectives on International Political Economy: Twentieth Century Contexts and Discontinuities". *International Political Science Review* 14: 7–33.

Chauveau, J. P. 1985. "Mise en valeur coloniale et développement: Perspective historique sur deux exemples ouest-africains". In Boiral et al. 1985, 143–66.

Clifford, James, and George Marcus, eds. 1986. *Writing Culture.* Berkeley: University of California Press, 1986.

Coats, A. W., ed. 1986. *Economists in International Agencies: An Exploratory Study.* New York: Praeger.

Cooper, Frederick. 1994. "Conflict and Connection: Rethinking Colonial African History". *American Historical Review* 99: 1516–45.

Cooper, Frederick, and Ann Stoler, eds. 1997. *Tensions of Empire: Colonial Cultures in a Bourgeois World.* Berkeley: University of California Press.

Crush, Jonathan, [ed.]. 1995. *Power of Development.* London: Routledge.

Dasgupta, Partha. 1993. *An Inquiry Into Well-Being and Destitution.* Oxford: Clarendon Press.

Escobar, Arturo. 1995. *Encountering Development: The Making and Unmaking of the Third World.* Princeton: Princeton University Press.

Ferguson, James. 1990. *The Anti-Politics Machine: Development, Depoliticization and Bureaucratic Power in the Third World.* Cambridge: Cambridge University Press.

Gendarme, René. 1995. "La coopération de l'Europe et de l'Afrique: Histoire d'une espérance déçue". *Mondes en Développement* 23, 92: 15–33.

Guha, Ranajit, and Gayatri Chakrovorty Spivak, eds. 1988. *Selected Subaltern Studies.* New York: Oxford University Press.

Hannerz, Ulf. 1990. "Cosmopolitans and Locals in World Culture". In *Global Culture: Nationalism, Globalization and Modernity,* ed. by Mike Featherstone, 237–52. London: Sage.

Lal, Deepek, 1985. *The Poverty of Development Economics.* Cambridge, Mass.: Harvard University Press for the Institute of Economic Affairs.

Lewis, John P., ed. 1988. *Strengthening the Poor: What Have We Learned?* New Brunswick, NJ: Transaction Books.

Long, Norman, and Ann Long, eds. 1992. *Battlefields of Knowledge: The Interlocking of Theory and Practice in Social Research and Development*. London: Routledge.

Lumsdaine, David Holloran. 1993. *Moral Vision in International Politics: The Foreign Aid Regime, 1949–1989*. Princeton: Princeton University Press.

Mandel, Ernest, 1975. *Late Capitalism*. Translated by Jores de Bres. London: New Left Books.

McCloskey, Donald. 1985. *The Rhetoric of Economics*. Madison: University of Wisconsin Press.

Moore, David B., and Gerald J. Schmitz, eds. 1995. *Debating Development Discourse: Institutional and Popular Perspectives*. New York: St. Martin's Press.

Moser, Caroline O. N. 1993. *Gender Planning and Development: Theory, Practice and Training*. London: Routledge.

Nandy, Ashis, ed. 1988. *Science, Hegemony and Violence: A Requiem for Modernity*. Delhi: Oxford University Press.

Peters, Pauline. 1994. *Dividing the Commons: Politics, Policy and Culture in Botswana*. Charlottesville: University of Virginia Press.

Pigg, Stacy. 1997 "Found in Most Traditional Societies: Traditional Medical Practitioners Between Culture and Development". In *International Development and the Social Sciences: Essays on the History and Politics of Knowledge* edited by Frederick Cooper and Randall Packard, 259–90. Berkeley: University of California Press.

Pletsch, Carl E. 1981. "The Three Worlds, or the Division of Social Scientific Labor, Circa 1950–1975". *Comparative Studies in Society and History* 23: 565–90.

Roe, Emery M. 1991. "Development Narratives, or Making the Best of Blueprint Development". *World Development* 19: 287–300.

Rosen, George. 1985. *Western Economists and Eastern Societies*. Baltimore: Johns Hopkins University Press.

Sachs, Wolfgang, ed. 1992. *The Development Dictionary: A Guide to Knowledge as Power*. London: Zed Books.

Scott, James. 1990. *Domination and the Arts of Resistance: Hidden Transcripts*. New Haven: Yale University Press.

Shiva, Vandana. 1988. *Staying Alive: Women, Ecology and Development*. London: Zed.

Stark, David. 1996. "Recombinant Property in East European Capitalism". *American Journal of Sociology* 101: 993–1027.

Verdery, Katherine. 1996. *What Was Socialism, and What Comes Next?* Princeton: Princeton University Press.

Wood, Geof. 1985. "The Politics of Development Policy Labelling". *Development and Change* 16: 347–73.

7

Anthropology and Its Evil Twin: "Development" in the Constitution of a Discipline

James Ferguson

Development Knowledge and the Disciplines: A Research Agenda

[...] It seems more and more that our thinking about an object, development, that once seemed familiar (with its recognizable political economic logic, its manifest ideological motivations, its worrisome deleterious effects) must now take the form less of a set of convictions or conclusions than of a series of unanswered, but answerable, questions. Where did this bulwark of mid- to late-twentieth-century common sense come from? How did it end up taking the form that it did? What are the dynamics through which it is changing, and what political strategies might be effective in opposing, disrupting, or reforming it?

[...]

A familiar academic conceit would have it that key ideas are developed and tested by "theorists" in academia before gradually diffusing outward into various "real world" applications. Development practitioners, in contrast, appear more likely to believe that important development ideas tend to be hammered out in practice, and that academic theory is largely irrelevant to what they do. The actual situation, however, may be more complicated than either of these folk models would allow.

A historical view reveals that models and theories developed within academic settings have been far from irrelevant to "real world" development practice, although they have not always been applied and used in the way that their academic originators might have wished. At the same time, though, it is clear that relations between different academic and nonacademic sites for the produc-

tion of both knowledge and theory have been complex and multidirectional. In anthropology, for instance, no one could deny that academic theories of "functioning systems" and "social equilibrium" guided both the practice of applied anthropologists in colonial Africa, and the formulation of certain official ideas and policies pertaining to "colonial development." At the same time, however, one would be obliged to recognize that the applied research initiatives taken up in the 1940s and 1950s by the Rhodes-Livingstone Institute, for instance, helped in turn to shape the theoretical agenda of British academic anthropology. [...]

What is more, it seems clear that the nature of such relations between academic forms of theory and knowledge and those used in development settings varies both over time and across disciplines. [...] As I will show, the idea that development is an applied issue and not a theoretical one is a fairly recent addition to the stock of anthropological common sense. In other disciplines, meanwhile, the issue appears to be posed quite differently. For political science and sociology, for instance, development appears to be an issue not so much for applied researchers as for "area studies" or "international" specialists – a distinction that has little force in anthropology, where everyone is an area studies specialist.

The kinds of relations that link the academic disciplines to the production and circulation of development knowledge and theory therefore require to be studied with some specificity, taking into account the distinctive configurations of the different disciplines, as well as changing relations over time. Such a project might be important not only as a way of furthering our understanding of the world of development and how it works, but also as a way of understanding our own positions as academics who seek to have some effect on that world. How, for instance, are we to understand the real importance and efficacy of academic critique in the politics of development? Considering how central the project of critique is to many academics who work on development we have remarkably little understanding of what it actually accomplishes. Clearly critique is not as all-powerful a force as we might like to believe. (Consider only how little difference the academic-theoretical destruction of "modernization theory" seems to have had on the practices of many development agencies, where practitioners assure us it remains alive and well.) Yet it is equally clear that what happens in the domain of academic critique is not wholly cut off from the wider world, either. What kinds of flows exist, linking academic theories and knowledges to the world of agencies, policies, and practical politics? What does this mean for the tactics of a critical intellectual activity that seeks to participate in the crucial political struggles surrounding the governing and managing of what has come to be called "the Third World"?

This paper does not seek to answer these questions, but to begin work on one small part of a larger research agenda that might do so. By looking at some of these issues in the context of one discipline, it contributes to a larger project that would systematically investigate the relations between the ideas and practices of development and the disciplinarily configured knowledges of the social sciences.

For the case of anthropology, I will argue, the disciplinary relation to development has been both especially difficult and especially central, thanks to anthropology's historical role as the science of "less developed" peoples. While the underpinnings of such a conception in social evolutionist theory were largely eroded during the course of the twentieth century, the place of anthropology in the academic division of labor (and thus its academic-political need for distinctiveness vis-à-vis sociology, history, political science, etc.) has continued to give "the anthropological" a special relation to the "less developed." In particular, I will try to show that the marked antipathy of much mainstream anthropology for development, as well as the sharp separation of an applied development anthropology from a theoretical academic sort, may be taken as signs not of anthropology's critical distance from development but of its uncomfort-

able intimacy with it. I will suggest that insofar as the idea of a distinctively anthropological domain of study remains linked (if only implicitly) to ideas of development and its lack, a truly critical stance toward development will require a willingness to question the disciplinary identity of anthropology itself.

The Concept of "Development" and the Theoretical Foundations of Anthropology

[W]e owe our present condition, with its multiplied means of safety and of happiness, to the struggles, the sufferings, the heroic exertions and the patient toil of our barbarous, and more remotely, of our savage ancestors. Their labors, their trials and their successes were a part of the plan of the Supreme Intelligence to develop a barbarian out of a savage, and a civilized man out of this barbarian.

Lewis Henry Morgan, closing lines of *Ancient Society* (1877:554)

The origins of anthropology as a discipline are conventionally traced to the late nineteenth century, and to such "founding father" figures as Lewis Henry Morgan in the United States and E. B. Tylor in Britain. The dominant conception that such thinkers elaborated, and the key idea that gave to anthropology its early conceptual coherence as a discipline, was the idea of social evolution. [...] The social evolutionists insisted that what they called "savages" and "civilized men" *were* fundamentally the same type of creature, and that if "higher" forms existed, it was because they had managed to evolve out of the "lower ones" (rather than vice-versa, as degeneration theory had it).

The project for the new field of anthropology was to trace the different stages of this progression, and to use observations of "savage" and "barbarian" peoples as evidence that would fill in what the earlier stages of human history had been. Thus did nonwestern peoples end up construed as living fossils whose history and experience "represent, more or less nearly, the history and experience of our own remote ancestors when in corresponding conditions" (Morgan 1877: vii). On the one hand, [...] this was a vision of a kind of human unity. But on the other, of course, it was a device of differentiating and ranking different contemporary societies according to their level of evolutionary development, since (in spite of the best laid plans of the Supreme Intelligence) "other tribes and nations have been left behind in the race of progress" (1877: vi).

The idea of "development" was, of course, central to this conception – indeed, Tylor was able to refer to the social evolutionist position simply as "the development theory" (Tylor 1884: 90–91). Development was the active principle according to which new and higher stages of human society might emerge out of older and more simple ones: the driving motive force in human history. The circular logical move from a perceived directionality in history (e.g., a perception that complex civilizations arose from simpler ones) to the imputation of a teleological force that had caused it (i.e., the idea that such "advances" are *caused* or *explained* by a universal principle or "law" of social evolution) cast doubt upon the scheme's explanatory power, as anti-evolutionist critics quickly pointed out. But the idea that human history was animated by a single great principle of directional movement – evolutionary "development" – provided an extraordinarily powerful narrative device for those who would tell a single, unified, and meaningful story of "Mankind." The metaphor of "development" invited, too, a fusing of the idea of evolutionary advance with the developmental maturation of an organism or person, thus facilitating the persistent slippage between the contrasts primitive/civilized and child/adult that played a key role in ideologies of colonialism.

[...] There are three key principles embedded in nineteenth-century social evolutionism [...]. First, there is the central idea that different societies are to be understood as discrete individuals, with each society making its way through the evolutionary process at its own pace, independently of the others. Second is the insistence that although each society is in some sense on its own, all societies are ultimately heading toward the same destination; in this sense, human history is one story, not many. Finally, the social evolutionary schemes posited that differences between human societies were to be interpreted as differences in their level of development. If other peoples differed from the western standard, it was only because, "left behind in the race of progress," they remained at one of the prior developmental levels through which the West had already passed. Taken together, these three principles frame a formidable and durable vision of human history and human difference, "a vast, entrenched political cosmology" (Fabian 1983: 159) that has been of enormous consequence both in anthropology and in the wider world.

Within anthropology, the evolutionary schemes of nineteenth-century theorists like Morgan and Tylor are generally taken to have been definitively refuted in the early twentieth century, most of all by the work of the American relativist and culture historian Franz Boas and his students. In the wake of their devastating criticisms of the empirical adequacy of the nineteenth-century evolutionary schemes, the emphasis on sorting societies according to their level of evolutionary development largely dropped out of anthropology in the first half of the twentieth century. Both in the United States and in Britain,[1] though in different ways, a critique of speculative evolutionism was followed by moves to relativize ideas of progress and development. From whose point of view could one society be seen as "higher" than another, after all? Evolutionism came to be seen not only as empirically flawed, but as ethnocentric as well. The task, instead, came to be seen as one of understanding each unique society "in its own terms," as one of many possible ways of meeting human social and psychological needs (Malinowski), or as one "pattern of culture" (Benedict), one "design for living" (Kluckhohn) among others.

At one level, such shifts did mark a clear break with evolutionist ideas of development: nonwestern cultures, in the new view, were no longer to be understood as "living fossils" trapped in evolutionary stages through which the West itself had already passed. Different societies now really were different, not just the same society at a different stage of development. Yet the break with evolutionism was less complete than it is often made to appear. It is significant, for instance, that mid-twentieth-century relativist approaches (whether Boasian/American or functionalist/British) preserved the old evolutionist idea that different societies were to be conceived as individuals.[2] Even more striking, perhaps, is the way that postevolutionist approaches preserved the grand binary distinction between primitive and modern societies, and accepted that anthropologists' primary specialization would remain the study of primitive societies. No longer would different primitive societies be placed on a ladder and ranked against each other; all were now equally valid, forming whole culture patterns (US) or functioning systems (UK) worth studying in their own right. But they were still seen as a distinctive class set apart from, and in some sense prior to, "modern," "western," "civilized" society. [...]

[...] The idea of an evolutionarily primitive state, prior to the contaminations of "development," remains remarkably central to a certain idea of both what anthropologists study, and to whom they owe their political loyalties. Insofar as an explicitly nonevolutionist anthropology through most of the twentieth century continued to be construed as the study of (as Levi-Strauss would still have it) "small populations" who "remain faithful to their traditional way of life," the anthropological object continued to be defined within the terms of a plainly evolutionary dualism that insistently distinguished between a developed, modern "us" and a not-yet-developed, primitive "them."[3]

"Development" Becomes "Applied"

"They are too modern. They probably all wear pants."
A senior British Africanist, ca. 1969, to Sally Falk Moore, explaining why a study of the "modernizing" Chagga of Tanzania would be of merely applied, rather than theoretical, interest.

Anthropologists had, of course, long recognized the existence of a set of issues surrounding the interactions of "primitive" peoples with a modern industrial world that encroached upon them. Some early twentieth-century diffusionists had emphasized such connections (Vincent 1990: 119–25), and even the most ahistorical sorts of "salvage anthropology" were obliged to recognize the impact of such things as capitalism and colonialism, if only so that their distorting effects could be filtered out in the reconstruction of hypothetical "pre-contact" social and cultural forms (Tomas 1991, Stocking 1991). It was also recognized early that anthropology might claim a place for itself in the world of practical affairs (and, not incidentally, a share of the funding pie) by providing scientific advice on the nature of such processes. [...] Malinowski call[ed] for a "Practical Anthropology," which would be an "anthropology of the changing Native" and "would obviously be of the highest importance to the practical man in the colonies" (1929: 36). As Stocking has noted, such appeals to practical application were key to the establishment of British anthropology in the 1930s, especially through the securing of Rockefeller Foundation funding (Stocking 1992: 193–207, 255–75; see also Kuklick 1991). In the United States, meanwhile, applied work on change and acculturation flourished

in the 1930s and 1940s, as the discipline's emphasis turned away from "salvage anthropology" and toward domestic social problems, poverty, and the war effort (Vincent 1990: 152–222, Stocking 1992: 163–68; see Gupta and Ferguson, 1997).

There are two observations that might be made about such work. First, although the connection may appear self-evident to the late-twentieth-century reader, the idea of development does not seem, in this period, to have been considered especially central to the question of the impact of western expansion on peripheral or colonized peoples. The operative concepts, instead, were "acculturation" and "assimilation" (especially in the United States) and "culture contact" and (later) "social change" (mostly in Britain). The old idea of evolutionary development, after all, had referred to an internal and immanent societal process, analogous to the autonomous development of an organism; the question of the impact one society might have on another was of quite another order. And such evolutionist theories of society were in any case out of favor at this time, on both sides of the Atlantic. In this context, the theoretical concept of development seems to have had very little to do with discussions of social change, acculturation, and applied anthropology.

Second, it is important to note that although studies of culture contact and culture change enjoyed some significant visibility in the field during the 1930s and 1940s, they failed to achieve dominance, or even full legitimacy, within the discipline. [...] There does not seem to be any intrinsic reason why social change and culture contact should not themselves have been considered theoretical topics. How did such issues come to be seen as primarily *applied* concerns in the first place?

As I have argued elsewhere (Gupta and Ferguson, 1997), the ascendancy of a distinctively localizing, "peoples and cultures" style in anthropology was tied to the rise of fieldwork as a hegemonic and disciplinarily distinctive method. With the Malinowskian revolution in fieldwork methodology (which was really only consolidated in the 1930s) came a newly strengthened expectation that a scientific anthropological study would be a comprehensive account of "a people," "a society," "a culture" – in short, an *ethno*-graphy, an account of a whole social or cultural entity, ethnically defined. Within such an optic, the central theoretical agenda concerned the description and comparison of "whole societies" characterized by their distinctive "social systems" (UK) or "cultural con-figurations" (US). When societies left this state of wholeness through processes of change imposed from without, they also threatened to leave the domain of anthropology, in a process that was generally considered to be of great practical im-portance, but limited theoretical interest.[4] [...]

Development, decolonization, modernization

A major geopolitical restructuring, and with it a new burst of social engineering, reconfigured the political and institutional landscape of the social sciences in the years following World War II. [...] Cooper (1997) has recently begun to excavate the origins of a global project of "development" from within the postwar planning of the colonial empires (see also Cooper 1996). One important early finding of this work is that, in the process of decolonization, a strategically vague story about development came to provide an ambiguous char-ter both for retreating colonial bureaucrats *and* for ascendant nationalist rulers [...]. This charter, a broad vision that came to be shared by a wide set of transnational elites, framed the "problems" of the "new nations" in the terms of a familiar (at least to those schooled in nineteenth-century anthropol-ogy) developmentalist story about nations (con-ceived, again, as individuals) moving along a pre-determined track, out of "backwardness" and into "modernity."[5]

It was within the terms of this narrative, of course, that a host of "development agencies," programs of "development aid," and so on, were conceived and put into place in the years following World War II (Escobar 1995). One of a number of consequences of this development was that funding and institutional positions became in-creasingly available for those with the sorts of expertise considered necessary to bring about the great transformation. The world of academic knowledge could hardly have remained un-affected. Not surprisingly, the first discipline to feel the effects of the new order was economics, and a recognized subfield of "development eco-nomics" appeared swiftly in response to the post-war initiatives (Hirschman 1981, Seers 1979). But how did this historical conjuncture affect the prac-tices of anthropologists?

As experts on "backward peoples," anthropolo-gists were clearly well positioned to play a role in any project for their advancement. In the past, anthropologists had often been openly hostile toward social and cultural change, seeing it as a destructive force that might wipe out fragile cul-tures before they could be properly recorded and studied by ethnographers. Yet development in the postwar era was linked to a much more optimistic mood, and to a universalizing political project of democratization and decolonization (see Cooper, 1996). The new notion of progress was linked not simply to western expansion or emulation, as in the nineteenth century, but to a specifically *inter-national* conception in which formerly "primitive" peoples might proudly "emerge" into the modern world and take their seat at the table of the "family of nations" (Malkki 1994). Where anthropo-logical liberalism had once been most comfortable arguing that nonmodern "others" had function-ing, well-adapted social and cultural orders of their own, the times more and more called for a different argument: that "natives" could just as well, given a little time (and perhaps a little help), participate in the modern world on equal terms (see Wilson and Wilson 1945; Mead 1956).

Such impulses are particularly well illustrated in the work of the Rhodes-Livingstone Institute in (then) Northern Rhodesia. Set up as an applied research institute to provide useful information to government and industry, it is often cited as an early example of anthropological engagement with problems of industrialization, migrant labor, and other "modern" issues (Werbner 1984, Brown 1973). Animating such work was an opti-mistic conception of an emerging modern Africa, and a commitment to showing that Africans were successfully adapting to urban, industrial condi-tions. Against conservative and racist arguments that Africans did not belong in "white" towns on a permanent basis, and would always remain primi-tive villagers at heart, anthropologists sought to show that African migrants were settling more permanently in town (Wilson 1941–1942), that they were developing new modes of urban social interaction there (Mitchell 1956), and arriving at new political structures suited to their new needs (Epstein 1958). Such accounts retained some traces of the old anthropological suspicion that economic and cultural assimilation to western ways was not necessarily a welcome development, and they emphasized the ethnographically particu-lar details of a process that resisted being neatly fitted into a simplistic, universal developmental narrative. But however messy it might be, they left no doubt that what they called "the industrial revolution in Africa" was an epochal, historically progressive force that would ultimately bring Af-ricans into the modern world. Portraying with sympathy and approval the emerging new class of "modern," westernized, urban Africans (as Magubane [1971] has charged), the Rhodes-Livingstone Institute anthropologists positioned themselves not, in the traditional anthropological style, as the chroniclers of the vanishing old ways, but as the defenders of the right of Africans to enjoy the modern new one.[6] (See Ferguson 1990.)

As decolonization proceeded, the social sciences became more and more concerned with the problems of the development of new nations. In the process, the anthropological concern with social and cultural change became increasingly linked with the idea of development, and (especially in the United States) with modernization theory as elaborated in other disciplines (notably Political Science and Sociology). "Social change" was now to be understood as "development," the evolutionist connotations of the old nineteenth-century term being newly appropriate to the mood of the times. Indeed, ideas of linear stages that would have been quite familiar to Morgan began to reappear in surprisingly explicit ways in modernization theory (see Hymes 1972: 28–30). Theoretically, ideas of social evolution began to become respectable again in American anthropology (starting with Leslie White in the 1940s, and continuing through the 1950s and 1960s, with figures like Service, Sahlins, and Harris). But even anthropologists with no explicit allegiance to neo-evolutionist theory began to bend their work in the direction of modernization.[7] Indeed, it is striking how many American anthropologists trained in a cultural relativist tradition that explicitly rejected evolutionist schemes of stage-wise progressions were by the early 1960s signing on uncritically to such dubious modernization schemes as Walt Rostow's *The Stages of Growth* (1960), offering as a distinctive anthropological contribution the locating of cultural obstacles to economic "take-off" (for a sophisticated example, see Geertz 1963a, 1963b).

If the earlier anthropological shift from evolutionism to relativism had resulted in the issue of developmentalist progressions being turned "from an explicit concern into an implicit theoretical assumption" (Fabian 1983: 39), the postwar era begins to see a shift back to explicit concern. [...] Increasingly, the question becomes, how do "traditional societies" become modern? And how can they be helped (or made) to make this transition? But, significantly, this question has become linked less to abstract theoretical speculation than to explicit programs of directed social change. The grand project that Morgan (in the passage quoted at the opening of this essay) saw as reserved for

"the Supreme Intelligence" – "to develop ... a civilized man out of this barbarian" – was now understood to be a job for the merely mortal intelligence of anthropologists.

For Morgan, of course, the question of how societies developed from one evolutionary level to the next was nothing if not a theoretical one: his typology of developmental stages aimed at nothing less than the explanation of both human history and human diversity. Even for evolutionism's relativist and functionalist critics, as I have argued, the distinction between "primitive" and "modern" societies was a theoretically motivated one. But with the new project of official modernization, issues of development came increasingly to belong (as had the earlier issues of "acculturation" and "social change") less to the academic world of theory (which remained largely devoted to comparing and generalizing about "primitive societies") than to a domain of practical, policy-oriented work on problems of contemporary economic transitions. "Development" had become "applied."

Academic anthropology in the 1950s and 1960s mostly kept its distance from such applied issues of development. The "theoretical" work that earned high status in the academic world was largely centered on comparing and generalizing about societies and cultures conceived as separate and autonomous individuals, whether the subject matter was kinship, social structure, or culture and personality. In this larger context, the change-oriented work of the Rhodes-Livingstone Institute was indeed exceptional. Yet, even in this case, it is noteworthy that the Rhodes-Livingstone anthropologists who had the greatest impact on academic anthropology were not those working on urbanization and industrialization (e.g., Clyde Mitchell, who came to be appreciated more by sociologists than by anthropologists, or Godfrey Wilson, whose *Essay on the Economics of Detribalization in Northern Rhodesia* was not widely appreciated until much later). The greatest academic influence, instead, was exerted by figures like Max Gluckman and Victor Turner, whose best-known works on the Lozi and Ndembu respectively remained in the classical anthropological mold of the ahistorical, rural, "tribe" study. Studying "modernizing" peoples might well be of considerable applied or policy significance, as the senior Africanist quoted at the top of this section conceded. But a study of people (men?) who "probably all wear pants" could hardly be central to the more prestigious arena of anthropological theory, built as it was upon the description and comparison of societies as little contaminated by development as possible.

Neo-Marxist critique

A major disruption of the received anthropological wisdom regarding development and modernization came with the rise of dependency theory and a set of neo-Marxist critiques of both modernization theory and traditional anthropology. The nature of these critiques is well known. [. . .]

The context for the neo-Marxist critique was significantly shaped by the social and political upheavals of the 1960s. Developments in the wider world (especially the rising tide of Third World nationalism and anti-colonial wars of liberation) combined with political upheavals on western university campuses to impress upon anthropologists the need to give more attention to questions of social change, domination, and colonialism. [. . .] By the 1970s, both disciplinary and national borders seemed to have softened: French structural Marxism (as elaborated by philosophers such as Louis Althusser, as well as by anthropologists such as Claude Meillassoux and Pierre-Philippe Rey), as well as Latin American dependency theory and Wallersteinian world system theory, began to make their way into the Anglo-American anthropological mainstream. The old functionalist orthodoxy began to splinter, as history, political economy, and colonialism began to gain new legitimacy as bonafide anthropological topics.

For anthropology's relation to development, the most significant aspect of the turn to Marxism and political economy in the 1970s was its profound challenge to two key pillars of anthropology's inherited developmentalist cosmology. First, and perhaps most profoundly, the new critical anthropology rejected the picture of the world as an array of individual societies, each moving through history independently of the others. This, as I suggested above, was a vision that was largely shared by the nineteenth-century evolutionists and their twentieth-century critics, who disagreed about whether the different tracks all headed in the same direction, but accepted the idea of different and separate tracks.[8] In place of this conception, anthropologists influenced by dependency theory, neo-Marxist modes of production theory, and world system theory, began to insist that differences between societies had to be related to a common history of conquest, imperialism, and economic exploitation that systematically linked

them. Supposedly traditional practices and institutions, rather than being relics of a pre-capitalist past, might instead be interpreted as products of, or reactions to, processes of capitalist penetration, the articulation of modes of production, or world-system incorporation. And poverty, rather than an original condition, might be a *result* of such processes. Instead of being simply "*un*developed" (an original state), the Third World now appeared as actively "*under*developed" by a first world that had "underdeveloped" it (thus Walter Rodney's influential title: *How Europe Underdeveloped Africa*).

This brings us to the second pillar of developmentalist thought that was brought into question in this period: the assumed identity of development with a process of moral and economic progress. Neo-Marxists insisted that what was called "development" was really a process of *capitalist* development: the global expansion of the capitalist mode of production at the expense of existing pre-capitalist ones. And the outcome of such a process might not be "real development," in the sense of a better life for people in the Third World, at all. Development (really, capitalist development), then, might not be "Progress" in any simple way; indeed, for poor peasants, it was likely to make life much worse. The benign moral teleology of the development story (a central feature of nineteenth-century anthropology and 1960s "modernization theory" alike) was radically called into question.

These two breaks with anthropology's developmentalist heritage were of fundamental importance. Indeed, they provide an invaluable point of departure for those who would restructure anthropology's disciplinary relation to development. However, as with the relativists' rejection of nineteenth-century social evolutionism, it is important to recognize not only what the critics were rejecting of the development story, but what they were willing to retain of it as well. It is evident, for instance, that for neo-Marxism, world history still had the character of an evolution, with the march of the capitalist mode of production leading in a linear, teleological progression toward a future that would culminate (if only after a long process of struggle) in socialism. There remained, too, a tenacious attachment to the idea of what was again and again spoken of as "*real* development" (in the name of which "mal-" or "under-" development could be denounced). And if capitalism could not deliver the "real development" goods, neo-Marxism was prepared to promise that socialism could – and even, all too often, to endorse the exploitation of peasant producers by radical Third World states in the name of "socialist development."

"Development Anthropology"

It is ironic, but probably true; that the very popularity within anthropology of the radical, neo-Marxist critiques of orthodox development and modernization theory in some ways set the stage for a new era of closer collaboration between anthropologists and the organizations and institutions charged with implementing capitalist development policy. If nothing else, the radical critiques made it more legitimate, and more intellectually exciting, to study issues of development in the context of an increasingly radicalized and politicized discipline. At a time when university-based scholarship was under pressure to demonstrate its relevance, and when anthropology was particularly challenged to show that it had something to say about change, not just stasis, and about the modern world, not just the "tribal" one, a politically engaged and theoretically challenging approach to development had considerable appeal. For anthropologists in graduate school during the 1970s, "underdevelopment" became an increasingly hot topic.

At the same time, the wider institutional context was changing quite dramatically. Driven by an awareness of the failures of conventional development interventions, and perhaps also motivated by the apparent successes of communist insurgencies in mobilizing poor peasants (especially in Asia and Latin America), mainstream development agencies began to place a new emphasis on the "basic needs" of the poor, and on the distinction between mere economic growth and "*real* development," understood in terms of such measures of human welfare as infant mortality rates, nutrition, and literacy. The World Bank, under the leadership of Robert McNamara [. . .], and later the United States Agency for International Development (USAID), under a congressional mandate to channel aid to the poor, began to direct more attention to the "soft," "social" side of development policy, and to turn more readily to social sciences other than economics. This conjunctural moment, fitting nicely with an employment crisis in academic anthropology, gave rise to a burst of anthropological interest in development, and a new, recognized subfield of anthropology, "development anthropology." (See Hoben 1982, Escobar 1991 for reviews of the period).

Many anthropologists thus came to development with a strong sense of theoretical and political purpose, determined to bring anthropological knowledge to bear on the great problems of poverty, exploitation, and global inequality. As Escobar (1991) has argued, however, work in development anthropology gradually came to be more and more adjusted to the bureaucratic demands of development agencies, at the expense of its intellectual rigor and critical self-consciousness. In spite of anthropology's long-standing claims of sensitivity to local perceptions, and its principled rejection of ethnocentrism, Escobar's review concludes that development anthropology has for the most part "done no more than recycle, and dress in more localized fabrics, the discourses of modernization and development" (Escobar 1991: 677). Significantly, as this adjustment of anthropologists to the demands of development agencies was proceeding, the strong links with theory that had characterized a more radical anthropology of development in the 1970s gradually weakened. The theoretical engagement with structural Marxism and radical underdevelopment theory – which had once linked such mundane empirical concerns as the dynamics of rural African household structure with the most abstract sorts of theoretical debates (e.g., the Althusserian critique of empiricist epistemology) – slowly slipped from view almost entirely, and with it the idea of a theoretically ambitious anthropology of development. Within academic anthropology, development anthropology came to be seen as a low-prestige, "applied" subfield – recognizably anthropological in its grass-roots focus and vaguely populist commitments, but commonly understood to have little to do with mainstream anthropological theory.

Within development agencies, meanwhile, development anthropology was not faring much better. The distinctive disciplinary emphasis on the particularity and specificity of local conditions made it easy enough for the development anthropologist to serve up post-hoc criticism of failed projects (which quickly became a kind of anthropological specialty). But given the institutional needs of development bureaucracies, the anthropological talent for demonstrating the complexity of development problems (and for disclaiming certainty in offering prescriptions) could hardly compete with the universalistic, context-independent projections and prescriptions so confidently dispensed by the economist or the agronomist. Like the challenges to neoclassical orthodoxy generated from within economics [. . .], anthropological critiques have made little headway in the policy sphere – not because they lack policy implications, but because those implications are complex, context-dependent, and entail uncertainty. In spite of on-and-off rhetorical commitments to such apparently anthropological principles as "indigenous knowledge," "popular participation," and "local decision-making," development agencies have mostly allowed anthropologists only a very marginal position, with little influence on policy formation (Hoben 1982, Chambers 1987, Escobar 1991, Gow 1993).

Anthropology and Its Evil Twin, or, Why "Development" Is Not Welcome in the House of Anthropology, and Why It Just Won't Leave

Anthropologists, for the most part, have taken post–World War II "development" for granted; they have accepted it as the normal state of affairs and have thus contributed to its naturalization. How unanthropological, one might say, to accept an entire historically produced cultural field without probing its depths.

Arturo Escobar, "Anthropology
and the Development Encounter"

For many anthropologists, there are few things more alarming than applied anthropology.

Glynn Cochrane,
Development Anthropology

Well, which is it? Has anthropology been guilty of an uncritical acceptance of development, as Escobar would have it? Or has anthropology spontaneously rejected development, fleeing in alarm at the very idea, as Cochrane insists? The answer, curiously, is that it has done both at the same time. On the one hand, Escobar is surely right: development anthropology has plodded along as a subfield in a way that even its own practitioners insist is characterized by a striking lack of self-consciousness or critical awareness (Chambers 1987, Gow 1993, Redclift 1985). Largely oblivious to current theory and historically grounded criticism alike, development anthropology seems hardly to care if its most central assumptions are regarded as untenable or worse in the wider discipline. Indeed, as one practitioner has recently noted, development anthropologists "have studiously avoided defining the principal objectives of

development" (Gow 1993: 382), and have been conspicuously uninterested in the larger theoretical and historical issues that development interventions raise. In the absence of attention to such issues, Gow points out,

> the anthropologist can easily become a practitioner of the "quick fix" approach, engaged in relieving the more visible symptoms of "underdevelopment", but in the process inadvertently running the risk of strengthening the very forces responsible for the conditions it seeks to alleviate (1993: 382).

Yet Cochrane, in the second of the quotations paired above, also has a point: academic anthropology has indeed looked upon development anthropology and other applied sub-fields with disdain and discomfort, leading one commentator to suggest that "the meaning of applied anthropology is to be found in its rejection by those in the mainstream of the subject" (Grillo 1985: 9). Development anthropologists commonly report being treated by academics "with a certain aloofness, if not passive contempt" (Gow 1993: 381). Nor is this reaction a particularly recent one. An academic skepticism of anthropological participation in "development" goes back at least to Evans-Pritchard (1946; see also Firth 1938), and the eminent academic anthropologist, Edmund Leach, was only echoing a widespread sentiment within the discipline when he remarked (in an introductory textbook), "I consider 'development anthropology' a kind of neo-colonialism" (1982: 50).

Development anthropologists are, of course, acutely aware of the way that such attitudes leave them "isolated from those programs and individuals generally regarded as leaders in constructing and teaching anthropological theory" (Little and Painter 1995: 603). Indeed, some development anthropologists report feeling "doubly damned" – by the prejudices of academic anthropologists, who see them as second-rate anthropologists at best, cynical hacks at worst; *and* by those of development professionals, who see them as the local representatives of a romantic, softheaded, and obstructionist discipline (Gow 1993). But development anthropologists, of course, have their own disdain for academic anthropology, which they see as irresponsibly detached from the practical problems and struggles of real people, and sometimes so preoccupied with "theoretical" issues of "texts," "discourses," and "cultural construction" as to be unreadable by most Third World colleagues, with little to say about real-world solutions to global tragedies like poverty and violence (Little and Painter 1995: 605).

The result, then, is a field that is divided between those who retain a characteristically anthropological antagonism toward "development" (based chiefly in the academy) and those who have embraced the development world, only to find themselves marginalized and sometimes scorned in the anthropological field at large. What are we to make of this stark opposition, even antagonism, between an applied, development anthropology, and an academic, theoretical sort? And why, as Grillo (1985: 9) has asked, "does anthropology, more than any other social science, appear to make such heavy weather of this distinction?"

To answer this question, we must begin by observing that academic anthropology itself continues to be defined in disciplinary terms that are in some ways continuous with its nineteenth-century roots as the science of the less developed. Indeed, in this sense, development (or its absence), far from defining a mere subfield within the discipline, continues to be at the heart of the constitution of anthropology itself.

Evolutionist ideas have been surprisingly durable in anthropology, as authors such as Fabian (1983) and Thomas (1989) have pointed out. Indeed, it is difficult to read the annual program of the American Anthropological Association meetings (littered as it still is with allochronic papers on this or that "traditional society") without suspecting that Tylor may have been right that aspects of a culture may persist as "survivals" long after they have ceased to fulfill any real function. But surely the anthropological romance of the primitive *is* an anachronism? In the wake of at least two decades of vigorous internal critique – first along the lines of political economy, later via a critique of representation – anthropology can surely not *still* be in the thrall of its old developmentalist metanarratives?

To some extent, to be sure, anthropology's disciplinary object has indeed been transformed, and anthropologists now are routinely concerned with questions of history and transformation, with the way local communities are linked to a wider world, and with a host of nontraditional substantive questions. The extent to which such a restructuring has taken place, however, has been limited by a number of factors. Perhaps the most important of these is the way that what anthropologists do, and what will be taken to be "anthropological," is determined by the conventional division of academic labor between the social scientific disciplines. What distinguishes anthropology from sociology, political science, and other fields continues, in practice, to be largely a matter of the kinds of societies or settings that they study.[9] Anthropologists, in practice (at least those who are trained and hired by "leading departments"), continue to work mostly in the Third World, and to specialize disproportionately in the study of small, rural, isolated, or marginal communities. Indeed, graduate students who wish to work in less traditionally anthropological sites report encountering significant difficulties in finding acceptance and legitimacy for their work, both within their graduate training programs, and in the arena of academic hiring once they complete their degrees ("All very interesting, but what's the *anthropological* angle?"). Anthropologists today are expected, it is true, to address questions of the transformation of local communities, and of linkages with wider regional and global processes; but it remains the case that it is a particular *kind* of people we are interested in seeing change, and a particular kind of local community that we seek to show is linked to that wider world.

The idea of "the local," in fact, has come to assume a remarkably prominent place in anthropology's disciplinary self-definitions. Where once anthropology studied "the savage," "the primitive," "the tribal," "the native," or "the traditional," today we are more likely to say that anthropologists study "the local." More and more, anthropology seems to be defined as a kind of attentiveness to "local knowledge" (Geertz 1983), or a field that specializes in the study of "local people" in "local communities" (thus, not incidentally, a sort of study that must be carried out "in the field"). Such a definition does make it possible to study a wider range of phenomena than did the older conception of "primitive" or "traditional" societies. But the difference may be easily overstated. After all, even if it is true that all social processes are in some sense local, it is also clear that, in normal anthropological practice, some problems, some research settings, even some people, are more local than others. A California real estate office, for instance, could surely serve as a site for anthropological, participant-observation research; but would this sort of local site be as local (and thus as anthropological) as, say, a New Guinea village? Certainly, all would politely agree that the anthropologist studying the real estate office was still doing anthropology, but would such work provide the foundation for a successful academic career? Disciplinary hiring practices – which (as I have suggested elsewhere [Gupta and

Ferguson, 1997]) rely heavily on authenticating experience in "the field" (archetypically not only "local," but muddy, tropical, disease-infested, and so on) – make such an outcome unlikely.

Insofar as a certain opposition of "us" and "them," "the West" and "the rest," continues to inform the constitution of anthropology as an academic discipline, the concept of development must retain a special salience, sitting as it does astride this venerable binary opposition. For the kind of societies and settings that anthropologists typically study and the kind they do not are separated precisely by development (those that have not experienced development are most anthropological; those that are "developed" are least; and those in between, "developing," are in the middle of the spectrum of anthropological-ness). Indeed, it is clear not only that anthropologists have mostly studied in "less developed countries," but also that they have tended to study "less developed" categories of people within those countries (indigenous native peoples in Brazil, "tribal" and "hill people" in Southeast Asia, foragers in southern Africa, and so on). Likewise, when anthropologists work in the "developed world," they tend to study the poor, the marginalized, the "ethnic" – in short, the Third World within. Indeed, anthropologists in the West usually work in settings that might also make good sites for "community development programs." In all these cases, too, those who lack "development" are those who putatively possess such things as authenticity, tradition, culture: all the things that development (as so many anthropologists have over the years agreed) places in peril.

We are left, then, with a curious dual organization binding anthropology to its evil twin: the field that fetishizes the local, the autonomous, the traditional, locked in a strange, agonistic dance with the field that, through the magic of development, would destroy locality, autonomy, and tradition in the name of becoming modern. Anthropology is left with a distinct resentment of its evil twin, Development; but also with a certain intimacy, and an uneasy recognition of a disturbing, inverted resemblance. How often have western anthropologists "in the field" felt the unsettling need to distinguish themselves, in their forays among the "less developed," from those other white folks one is likely to meet out in "the bush" – the "development people" who (like those other alter egos, the missionaries), are "others" who resemble a little too closely the anthropological self (indeed, for whom one might oneself be mistaken)? [. . .]

Like an unwanted ghost, or an uninvited relative, development thus continues to haunt the house of anthropology. Fundamentally disliked by a discipline that at heart loves all those things that development intends to destroy, anthropology's evil twin remains too close a relative to be simply kicked out; "after all," anthropology says to itself, "these issues, even if theoretically suspect, are of great practical importance." Thus we end up with an "applied" subfield ("development anthropology") that conflicts with the most basic theoretical and political commitments of its own discipline (hence its "evil"); yet which is logically entailed in the very constitution of that field's distinctive specialization (hence its status as "twin" to a field that is always concerned with the "less," the "under," the "not-yet" . . . developed). A twin that can seemingly never be embraced, accepted, or liked; but which just won't leave.

To move beyond this impasse will require a recognition that the extraordinarily tenacious vision of a world divided into the more and less "developed" has been, and in many ways continues to be, constitutive of the anthropological domain of study. Critiques of development, however necessary they may be, and however effectively they may be articulated,[10] will not be sufficient to solve the Jekyll-and-Hyde-like conflict between development and anthropology, or applied and academic types of anthropological knowledge (as if an academically based critique of development could simply overturn it, and thus do away with the division). On the contrary, so intimately intertwined is the idea of development (and its lack) with the idea of anthropology itself, that to be critical of the concept of development requires, at the same time, a critical reevaluation of the constitution of the discipline of anthropology itself. Anthropology cannot throw the evil twin out of the house, because the twin remains a part of itself, if only in a repressed and ill-acknowledged way.

Conclusion

The larger question of the relations linking development knowledge to the academic disciplines of the social sciences, with which I began, cannot be answered in any general way; a better understanding will await a good deal of quite detailed and specific work on the subject. But if the case of anthropology suggests anything of importance for this larger project, it is that the shape of development knowledge is not unrelated to the shape of disciplinary knowledges. Insofar as this is true, it may be suggested that in order to truly transform the kinds of knowledge that participate in questions of global politics and policy, it may be necessary to start by transforming the shapes of our disciplinary knowledges. If so, some immediate intellectual tasks may be closer to hand, and less utopian, than railing, from within our academic disciplines, against the development monster outside (as we patiently explain, yet again, to an audience of the already-converted, why structural adjustment hurts Africa's poor...). A real reconfiguration of the epistemic terrain that makes most academic work so irrelevant and powerless in its encounter with development may require, at least as a beginning, that we engage in some foundational work on our own disciplinary houses.

NOTES

1   Throughout this paper, I concentrate on anthropology as it developed in the United States and Britain (including some significant influences from the French tradition), while ignoring other regional and national traditions in anthropology that may well be significantly different. Such a choice is justified by the global hegemony that Anglo-American anthropology has undoubtedly enjoyed, but it is not meant to foreclose the possibility that the relationship of anthropology to "development" may be differently configured elsewhere. [...]

2   This is an idea that the early Boasian emphasis on diffusion in some ways called into question, but which emerged strongly in the more developed relativisms of Benedict and Mead and was quickly written into the collective "peoples and cultures" common sense of the emerging discipline.

3   There is an interesting study to be done of the search by mid-twentieth-century anthropology for a coherent analytic object, as various attempts were made to explain what distinguished "primitive" societies (or those which anthropologists could legitimately claim as their own distinctive object) from others. [...]

4   Among the most significant exceptions to this general trend were the anthropologists affiliated with the Rhodes-Livingstone Institute.

5   As Chatterjee (1986) has argued, the new nationalist elites did not for the most part challenge this Eurocentric picture, but concentrated instead on speeding the progression that it implied, building "modern" nations out of "backward" ones. See also Ludden 1992 [...].

6   The Rhodes-Livingstone Institute anthropologists' conception of their own work as a defense of the urban African against racist colonial conservatism helps to explain the shock and disbelief with which they responded to Magubane's attack (see the comments appended to Magubane 1971). [...]

7   In fact, there seems to have been surprisingly little interest on the part of U.S. neo-evolutionists in the modernization projects of the 1950s and 1960s. This may be, in part, explained by the general alignment of the evolutionism of this period with a cold-war Left politics, in what some have seen as a sort of shadow dance with a politically taboo, and not very well understood, Marxism – it being one of the more surprising accomplishments of McCarthyism to have turned Morgan (the corporate railway lawyer) into a surrogate for Marx.

8   Early twentieth-century diffusionism, both in the United Stated and in Britain, challenged this conception. But with the rise of functionalism and the quest for whole, functioning societies, diffusionism's concerns with history and culture contact were marginalized, only to be rediscovered in a different form many decades later (Vincent 1990: 119–25; see. also Gupta and Ferguson, 1997).

9   The other main point of distinction, the unique anthropological emphasis on fieldwork, is not unconnected to the question of "kind of society," as Akhil Gupta and I have recently argued (Gupta and Ferguson 1997).

10 I have in mind here Escobar's important review of "development anthropology" (1991), which convincingly dissects the failings and limitations of the subfield, but does not go very far toward connecting these in any systematic way with what seem to me a related set of failings and limitations of "mainstream" anthropology – thus letting us academics, as it were, off the hook all too easily.

REFERENCES

Brown, Richard. 1973. "Anthropology and Colonial Rule: The Case of Godfrey Wilson and the Rhodes-Livingstone Institute, Northern Rhodesia". In *Anthropology and the Colonial Encounter*, edited by T. Asad, 173–97. London: Ithaca Press.

Chambers, Erve. 1987. "Applied Anthropology in the Post-Vietnam Era". *Annual Review of Anthropology* 16: 309–37.

Chatterjee, Partha. 1986. *Nationalist Thought and the Colonial World: A Derivative Discourse?* London: Zed.

Cochrane, Glynn. 1971. *Development Anthropology*. New York: Oxford University Press.

Cooper, Frederick. 1997, "Modernizing Bureaucrats, Backward Africans and the Development Concept," pp. 64–92 in International Development and the Social Sciences, edited by Frederick Cooper and Randall Packard, Berkeley: University of California Press.

Cooper, Frederick. 1996. *Decolonization and African Society: The Labor Question in French and British Africa*. Cambridge: Cambridge University Press.

Epstein, A. L. 1958. *Politics in an Urban African Community*. Manchester: Manchester University Press.

Escobar, Arturo. 1991. "Anthropology and the Development Encounter: The Making and Marketing of Development Anthropology". *American Ethnologist* 18, no. 4: 658–82.

——1995. *Encountering Development: The Making and Unmaking of the Third World*. Princeton: Princeton University Press.

Evans-Pritchard, E. E. 1946. "Applied Anthropology". *Africa* 16: 92–98.

Fabian, Johannes. 1983. *Time and the Other: How Anthropology Makes Its Object*. New York: Columbia University Press.

Ferguson, James. 1990. "Mobile Workers, Modernist Narratives: A Critique of the Historiography of Transition on the Zambian Copperbelt". *Journal of Southern African Studies* 16, no. 3: 385–412; 16, no. 4: 603–21.

——1994. *The Anti-Politics Machine: "Development", Depoliticization, and Bureaucratic Power in Lesotho*. Minneapolis: University of Minnesota Press.

Firth, Raymond. 1938. *Human Types*. London: T. Nelson and Sons.

Geertz, Clifford. 1963a. *Peddlers and Princes: Social Development and Economic Change in Two Indonesian Towns*. Chicago: University of Chicago Press.

——1963b. *Agricultural Involution: The Process of Ecological Change in Indonesia*. Berkeley: University of California Press.

——1983. *Local Knowledge: Further Essays in Interpretive Anthropology*. New York: Basic Books.

Gow, David D. 1993. "Doubly Damned: Dealing with Power and Praxis in Development Anthropology". *Human Organization* 52, no. 4: 380–97.

Grillo, Ralph. 1985. "Applied Anthropology in the 1980s: Retrospect and Prospect". In *Social Anthropology and Development Policy*, edited by R. Grillo and A. Rew, 1–36. New York: Tavistock.

Gupta, Akhil, and James Ferguson, 1997. "Discipline and Practice: "The Field" as Site, Method, and Location in Anthropology". In *Anthropological Locations: Boundaries and Grounds of a Field Science*, edited by A. Gupta and J. Ferguson. 1–46. Berkeley: University of California Press.

Hirschman, Albert O. 1981. "The Rise and Decline of Development Economics". In *Essays in Trespassing*, 39–65. Cambridge: Cambridge University Press.

Hoben, Allen. 1982. "Anthropologists and Development". *Annual Review of Anthropology*. 11: 349–75.

Hymes, Dell. 1972. "The Use of Anthropology: Critical, Political, Personal". In *Reinventing Anthropology*, edited by D. Hymes, 3–79. New York: Pantheon.

Kuklick, Henrika. 1991. *The Savage Within: The Social History of British Anthropology, 1885–1945*. Cambridge: Cambridge University Press.

Leach, Edmund, 1982. *Social Anthropology*. New York: Oxford University Press.

Little, Peter D., and Michael Painter. 1995. "Discourse, Politics, and the Development Process: Reflections on Escobar's *Anthropology and the Development Encounter*". *American Ethnologist* 22, no. 3: 602–616.

Ludden, David. 1992. "India's Development Regime". In *Colonialism and Culture*, edited by Nicholas B. Dirks, 247–88. Ann Arbor: University of Michigan Press.

Magubane, Bernard. 1971. "A Critical Look at Indices Used in the Study of Social Change in Colonial Africa". *Current Anthropology* 12: 419–31.

Malinowski, Bronislaw. 1929. "Practical Anthropology". *Africa* 2, no. 1: 22–38.

——1930. "The Rationalization of Anthropology and Administration". *Africa* 3, no. 4: 405–430.

Malkki, Liisa. 1994. "Citizens of Humanity: Internationalism and the Imagined Community of Nations". *Diaspora* 3, no. 1: 41–68.

Mead, Margaret, 1956. *New Lives for Old: Cultural Transformation – Manus, 1928–1953*. New York: Morrow.

Mitchell, J. C. 1956. *The Kalela Dance*. Rhodes-Livingstone Paper, no. 27. Manchester: Manchester University Press.

Moore, Sally Falk. 1994. *Anthropology and Africa*. Charlottesville, Virginia: University of Virginia Press.

Morgan, Lewis Henry. 1877. *Ancient Society*. New York: Henry Holt and Company.

Redclift, M. R. 1985. "Policy Research and Anthropological Compromise: Should the Piper Call the Tune?". In *Social Anthropology and Development Policy*, edited by R. Grillo and A. Rew, 198–202. New York: Tavistock.

Rostow, W. W. 1960. *The Stages of Growth: A Non-Communist Manifesto*. Cambridge: Cambridge University Press.

Seers, Dudley. 1979. "The Birth, Life, and Death of Development Economics". *Development and Change* 10:707–19.

Stocking, George W., Jr. 1992. *The Ethnographer's Magic and Other Essays in the History of Anthropology*. Madison: University of Wisconsin Press.

——, ed. 1991. *Colonial Situations: Essays on the Contextualization of Ethnographic Knowledge*. Madison: University of Wisconsin Press.

Thomas, Nicholas, 1989. *Out of Time: History and Evolution in Anthropological Discourse*. Cambridge: Cambridge University Press.

Tomas, David. 1991. "Tools of the Trade: The Production of Ethnographic Knowledge in the Andaman Islands". In *Colonial Situations*, edited by G. Stocking, 75–108. Madison: University of Wisconsin Press.

Tylor, Edward Burnett, 1884. "How the Problems of American Anthropology Present Themselves to the English Mind". *Transactions of the Anthropological Society of Washington* 3:81–95.

Vincent, Joan. 1990. *Anthropology and Politics: Visions, Traditions, and Trends*. Tuscon, Ariz.: University of Arizona Press.

Werbner, Richard P. 1984. "The Manchester School in South-central Africa". *Annual Review of Anthropology* 13: 157–85.

Wilson, Godfrey. 1941–1942. *An Essay on the Economics of Detribalization in Northern Rhodesia, Parts One and Two*. Rhodes-Livingstone Papers 5–6. Manchester: Manchester University Press.

Wilson, Godfrey, and Monica Wilson. 1945. *The Analysis of Social Change*. Cambridge: Cambridge University Press.

Part III

From Development to Globalization

Introduction

The dramatic emergence of neoliberal globalization as the late-20th century's dominant development discourse and policy was discussed in this volume's Introduction. Brief introductory essays of this sort often aim to produce a sense of coherence about a particular domain of inquiry, but contemporary "globalization" debates – and the phenomena they seek to describe – hardly lend themselves to this objective. First, the proliferation of "G-literature" is such that by 2002 there were at least four books titled *Globalization and Its Discontents* – all without appropriate apologies to Sigmund Freud or, in the case of the most recent three, to the authors of the previous volumes.[1] The market for books with "global" titles seems boundless – not as dynamic as the "dot.com" boom of the 1990s, but surely one of academia's growth industries of the moment. And second, because different scholars often have distinct referents in mind when they employ the G-word, it is hard to escape Ronaldo Munck's conclusion that it "is a term which has undergone a conceptual inflation in recent years and has now been devalued. It can mean anything, everything or nothing" (Munck 2000:84).

Despite its ambiguities, we believe that "globalization" remains a useful category if one takes the following analytical steps to make the term more precise. The first is *periodization*. Historical eras vary in the degree of cross-border capital movements and market openings (see editors' Introduction to this volume). The period from the late 19th century to World War I was one of significant liberalization of international trade and finance, but it was followed by a "deglobalizing" period from the 1930s through the 1960s when many national economies, including the most powerful ones, turned inward and established strong public sectors, high tariffs, controls on capital movements, and fixed currency exchange rates. The latter practices were particularly widespread during the heyday of the Bretton Woods agreement from the end of World War II until around 1970. As discussed in this volume's Introduction, the post-1970 breakdown of Bretton Woods ushered in another era of renewed economic liberalization (or neoliberalism) that today is widely considered synonymous with "globalization." Part of the periodization process for any scholar involves decisions about what features of a new period are substantially distinct from those of earlier periods and how these might be measured (see Sutcliffe and Glyn 2003). As with other aspects of globalization, the issue of whether globalization is new is, we believe, only worth discussing if it is done with great precision about both antecedent and current conditions.

A second analytical move toward greater specificity is to delineate contrasting doctrines or political positions regarding the liberalization of global trade and finance (and perhaps movements of people or other aspects of what some consider part of "globalization"). There is, obviously, no single appropriate way to do this; different approaches serve different analytical objectives. Some authors (e.g., Held and McGrew 2003) see "globalists" and "sceptics" on opposite sides of a "great globalization debate" over key concepts, the contemporary significance (or lack of it) of nation-states, cultural hybridization versus heightened national identity, and the degree of autonomy possible in the global economy for regional economic blocs (e.g., Mercosur, NAFTA or the European Union). Others, analysing positions on trade, distinguish between "supporters," "regressives" (who favor globalization if it benefits their interests), "isolationists," "reformers" (who believe in humanizing globalization), and "alternatives" (who seek space for new models in competition and alongside the dominant one) (Said and Desai 2003:66; see also Lee 2003:331). Others dissect the logical premises of "globalization theory," arguing that its claims manifest confusion between cause and effect, or "*explanans*" and "*explanandum*" (Rosenberg 2000).

The readings in Part III indicate an important shift in anthropology and in the anthropology of globalization. Increasingly, scholars find the discipline's traditional methodological focus on directly observable local phenomena to be completely inadequate for addressing key questions about social and cultural change in the late 20th and early 21st centuries. Although this was the case earlier as well, it was only a small minority of social anthropologists, notably Eric Wolf and Sidney Mintz, who analytically engaged larger social fields. The move to transcend single-site, local-oriented studies is still characteristic of a minority within the discipline, but it is a growing minority that rides a broader wave of intellectual discontent with the foundations of anthropological research practice.

Jonathan Friedman's chapter below demonstrates a willingness to confront head on macro-processes of accumulation in the world economy that are more often analyzed by political scientists or economists. Yet in classic anthropological fashion he deftly relates the challenges globalization poses for developmentalist, modernist nation-states to the worldwide increase in "rooted," ethnic and nationalist forms of identity and violence, as well as to rising inequality and the formation of new, cosmopolitan elites and transnational criminal networks. Jean Comaroff and John Comaroff depart, like Friedman, from an analysis of global capitalism, which they see as driven less significantly by production than by new forms of consumption (see also Part IV below). They also discuss distinctive features of today's transnational elites, criminal and legitimate, and demonstrate that the business scandals that have rocked financial markets and the resurgence of "occult economies," based on magic and the commodification of human bodies, are similar inasmuch as they elevate market imperatives ("the spirit of neoliberalism") to new heights where human dimensions are lost from view. David Graeber, an anthropologist and a prominent global justice activist, debunks misconceptions about the "anti-globalization" movement, arguing that it is a product of – and in some ways enthusiastic about – globalization, and that it represents an effort to struggle for and to reinvent anti-authoritarian forms of democracy and consensus.

The devastation of New York City's financial district in the September 11, 2001 terrorist attacks highlighted significant features of the global economy even as it led to the "re-nationalizing" and de-privatizing of security controls and increased measures to limit or watch over international movements of people, money and goods. All of these trends could be interpreted as running counter to the logic of neoliberal globalization. Saskia Sassen's chapter describes a "sharply asymmetrical yet interdependent world" in which a few malevolent individuals with a modest budget could make the global economy sputter and stall and where specific places – a handful of "global cities" – remain strategic places despite all the rhetoric about deterritorialized flows, information technology, and footloose electronic money.

NOTE

1 These are Burbach et al. (1997), Sassen (1999), McBride and Wiseman (2000), and Stiglitz (2002). Freud's original 1930 title (*Das Unbehagen in der Kultur*) is not as artful as *Civilization and Its Discontents*, which must be credited to Joan Riviere, his first English translator (Strachey: 1962: 6).

REFERENCES

Burbach, Roger, Orlando Núñez, and Boris Kagarlitsky, 1997 Globalization and its Discontents: The Rise of Postmodern Socialisms. London: Pluto Press.

Held, David, and Anthony McGrew, 2003 The Great Globalization Debate: An Introduction. *In* The Global Transformations Reader, 2nd edition, David Held and Anthony McGrew, eds., pp. 1–50. Cambridge: Polity Press.

Lee, Simon, 2003 The Political Economy of the Third Way: The Relationship Between Globalization and National Economic Policy. *In* The Handbook of Globalization, Jonathan Michie, ed., pp.331–343. Cheltenham, UK: Edward Elgar.

McBride, Stephen, and John Richard Wiseman, eds., 2000 Globalization and Its Discontents. New York: Palgrave Macmillan.

Munck, Ronaldo, 2000 Labour in the Global: Challenges and Prospects. *In* Global Social Movements, Robin Cohen and Shirin M. Rai, eds., pp.83–100. London: Athalone Press.

Rosenberg, Justin, 2000 The Follics of Globalization Theory. London: Verso.

Sassen, Saskia, 1999 Globalization and Its Discontents: Essays on the New Mobility of People and Money. New York: New Press.

Said, Yahia and Meghnad Desai, 2003 Trade and Global Civil Society: The Anti-Capitalist Movement Revisited. *In* Global Civil Society 2003, Mary Kaldor, Helmut Anheier, and Marlies Glasius, eds., pp.59–85. Oxford: Oxford University Press.

Stiglitz, Joesph E., 2001 Foreword. *In* The Great Transformation: The Political and Economic Origins of Our Time, Karl Polanyi, pp.vii–xvii. Boston: Beacon Press.

—— 2002 *Globalization and its Discontents*. New York: Norton.

Strachey, James, 1962 Editor's Introduction. *In* Civilization and Its Discontents, Sigmund Freud, pp.5–9. New York: Norton.

Sutcliffe, Bob and Andrew Glyn, 2003 Measures of Globalization and their Misinterpretation. *In* The Handbook of Globalization, Jonathan Michie, ed., pp.61–78. Cheltenham, UK: Edward Elgar.

8

Globalization, Dis-integration, Re-organization: The Transformations of Violence

Jonathan Friedman

[...] One of the most explosive developments in the world economy that has often been signaled as a novelty is the enormous expansion of financial markets. Their massive development is, of course, an important phenomenon to understand. Since the beginning of the 1980s, financial assets have been increasing 250 percent faster than the "aggregate GDP of all the rich industrial economies" (Sassen 1996:40). The current global financial markets are estimated to be worth about $75 trillion and the statistic has risen to $83 trillion in 1999, that is, three and a half times the OECD's aggregate Gross Domestic Product (GDP) (Sassen 1996:41; Sassen 2000:3). In contrast with world cross-border trade, $6 trillion and foreign direct investment, $5.1 trillion is truly astonishing. While it is debatable to what extent this is the product of the successful struggle of capital against the nation–state, it is not debatable that technological changes have made the movement of capital an instantaneous process in which sensitivity to conditions of accumulation has increased logarithmically. If this increase is related to the general trend in the growth of fictitious capital in periods of declining profitability of industrial production, it might be suggested that the current growth of finance capital (generated in the West) combines such tendencies with a new information technology that raises the rate of speculative turnover exponentially, thus accounting for the appearance of "global glut."

Globalization need not be an evolutionary stage of world history. There may indeed be tendencies to the establishment of worldwide institutional arrangements, of which the United Nations is but one example. But such tendencies have occurred in the past only to be replaced by opposite tendencies.

The Recent History of Globalization in the World System

Globalization is a phase within the pulsation of the global system. We need only to return to the turn of this century to get an idea of the salience of this phenomenon as historical rather than world evolutionary. Globalization is not new at all, according to many who have actually researched the question. While there is much debate, there is also an emergent consensus that the world is no more globalized today than it was at the turn of the century. [...]

Foreign direct investment, which was a minor phenomenon relevant to portfolio investment, reached 9 percent of world output in 1913, a proportion that was not surpassed until the early 1990s (Bairoch and Kozul-Wright 1996:10). Openness to foreign trade was not markedly different in 1993 than in 1913. In the 1890s the British were very taken with all the new world products that were inundating their markets (Briggs and Snowman 1996), cars, films, radio, X-rays, and light bulbs.

By the late twentieth century trade was booming, driven upward by falling transport costs and by a flood of overseas investment. There was also migration on a vast scale from the Old World to the New.

Indeed, in some respects the world economy was more integrated in the late nineteenth century than it is today. The most important force in the convergence of the nineteenth century economies was mass migration, mainly to America. In the 1890s, which in fact was not the busiest decade, emigration rates from Ireland, Italy, Spain, and Scandinavia were all above forty per thousand. "The flow of people out of Europe, 300,000 people a year in mid-century, reached 1 million a year after 1900. On top of that, many people moved within Europe. True, there are large migrations today, but not on this scale" (*Economist* 1997–1998).

[...]

The period from 1880 to World War I was followed by a period of deglobalization and re-gionalization in the global system, one that was not reversed until the 1950s, a reversal that has accelerated in the 1970s until the present. There is already evidence today that the world is again beginning to regionalize strongly into three major zones, APEC, NAFTA, and EU. Of course the system has historically increased in size. Of course there is technological speedup and increasing cap-acities for movement. But it is not at all clear that such changes have led us to the threshold of a new era in human history, even if it might well be argued that "time-space" compression in itself may ultimately transform the very conditions of operation of the global system. Instead of either celebrating or castigating globalization, we would do better to try and grasp the potential trajectories and tendencies in contemporary historical change.

The Regional Shift

Whether or not one conceives global process in terms of shifting accumulation or the formation of a new globalized economy, there is a de facto emergence of a new powerful economic region. And in spite of the current crisis, there is no doubt that there has been a redistribution of shares in the world economy in favor of the Asian Pacific.

The fact is that as nation-states exist, the level of welfare is still a national phenomenon, that is, the degree to which capital investment tends to con-centrate in one place or another. It is this clustering that makes it possible for Porter (1990) to argue for a comparative advantage of nations in an era of globalization. In 1956 the United States had forty-two of the top fifty corporations, a clear sign of hegemony over world production. In 1989 that number had dropped to seventeen. Europe as a whole has a larger number (twenty-one) of the fifty top firms today than the United States.

This would imply that the globalization of cap-ital is a temporally delimited phenomenon or phase within a larger system rather than a general evolutionary phenomenon. It would in this case be related to the breakup of hegemonies, a process of fragmentation and decentralization of accumula-tion of wealth in the larger system. Now in the contemporary situation there are clear markers of this process. While production and export have increased unabated since the 1960s, the developed market economies decreased their share of total world production from 72 to 64 percent while developing countries more than doubled. Between 1963 and 1987 the United States saw a decrease in its share of world manufacturing from 40.3 per-cent to 24 percent. Japan increased its portion from 5.5 percent to 19 percent in the same period. West Germany was stable around 9 percent to 10 percent, but the United Kingdom declined from 6 percent to 5 percent to 3.3 percent. France, Italy, and Canada also declined somewhat in this period (Dicken 1992:27), and while there were quite sig-nificant increases in Spain, Brazil, and India, the Asian NIC countries have been the major benefac-tors of the decentralization of capital accumula-tion and especially of manufacturing (Dicken 1992:27).

Countries such as Hong Kong, Taiwan, Korea, and China have moved up rapidly in rank on the list of manufacturing export nations at the same time as the leading advanced economies have lost ground in this arena, some such as the United Kingdom and the United States, by significant amounts.

And it is the center that is the target market for this new production. [...] The process is one where exported capital produces products that are reimported to the center. The trend here is toward increasing competition, decentralization, and a clear shift of capital accumulation to the East (Bergesen and Fernandez 1995:24). The model for this argument is that rapid multination-alization of capital is a general process in periods of hegemonic decline.

That we are heading toward an increasingly integrated world, a globalized economy, is cer-tainly a tendency in economic terms, but it does not necessarily mean that we are entering a new kind of world. The world of transnational capital and accompanying transnational institutions, clubs, classes, and elites is certainly a part of the globalization process, but this does not account for the changes in regional distribution of accumu-lation and power in the world. Globalization, in other words, does not mean unification or even integration in any other way than coordination of world markets. TNCs are, in important respects, the agents of decentralization of wealth rather than its geographical concentration.

[. . .]

Parameters of Globalization I: Horizontal Fragmentation

The decline of hegemony of the advanced industrial centers has led to a process that I have previously described in terms of fragmentation. It relates the decline of modernist identification to an increase in "rooted" forms of identity, whether regional, indigenous, immigrant-ethnic or national. If the modernist nation-state is based on the identification of a subject population with a national project that defines its members, in principle, in terms of equality and political representativity, and which is future oriented and developmentalistic, when this project loses its power of attraction, its subjects must look elsewhere. The modern nation-state is founded upon a massive transformation of the world system in which a homogenizing, individualizing, and democratizing process in the center is combined with and dependent upon a hegemonic expansion in the rest of the world, the formation of a center–periphery organization. The modernist state is one in which the ethnic content of the nation is usually secondary to its function as a citizenry-based development project, in which cultural assimilation is a necessary by-product of the homogenization of regional and ethnic differences that might weaken the unity of the national project. The decline of hegemony is also the decline in the unifying force of its mechanisms of identification. Those who were partly integrated and stigmatized move to establish themselves and those who were totally assimilated must search for new forms of collective belonging. This leads to a range of cultural identifications that fragment and ethnify the former political units, from ethnic to religious to sexual, all in the vacuum left by a vanishing future.

Indigenous populations have increased in size since the mid-1970s, not as a matter of biology but of identity choice. It is estimated that there are 350 million indigenous people and they have become increasingly organized as well as winning a series of battles over land and cultural autonomy.

Subnational regionalism is also on the increase and forms, for example, a powerful lobby in Europe today, aiming for a combination of a strong centralized Europe and a decentralized nation-state. This has, like indigenous movements, been developing since the mid-1970s.

Migration is again a massive phenomenon in a destabilized world. But immigrants no longer come to their new countries simply to become good citizens. On the contrary, the ethnification of such groups has led to a strong tendency to diasporization and to a cultural politics claiming recognition in the public sphere. In some cases this has led to a fragmenting of a former national unity. That is, rather than becoming assimilated to declining nation-states such groups maintain and develop transnational identities, cultures, and social existences.

National identity has become increasingly ethnified in this period as well in parallel with the ethnification of immigrants. This is expressed in the emergence of nationalist movements, and xenophobic ideologies that are themselves partially generated by economic crisis and downward mobility (see next section).

This process cannot be understood without placing it in the context of a weakened nation-state structure as a specific form of relation between people and their representative governmental bodies. The decline of modernism is very much a product of the weakening of the nationalizing component of the state machine, its tendency in the 1970s toward bankruptcy and general insecurity largely a result of the accelerating mobility of capital and taxable income. The transformation of the state is an issue in itself to which we must return. What is crucial here is that the focality of the state in identity formation is giving way to competing identities from indigenous, regional, and migratory populations. The latter has also entailed a decentralization of resources within the state, along broadly ethnic lines, and an increasing division of powers, between the state as representative of the nation and the subgroups that tend to displace it. This might be understood as a temporary phenomenon. Certainly with respect to immigration earlier periods of our history are filled with debates concerning assimilation versus weaker forms of integration or even the formation of more loosely federal structures (Kallen 1924). On the other hand situations in which the subgroups themselves were so organized are rare, and there was nothing like the strong multiethnic tendency that predominates today. From quite early on in the century, assimilation became the absolutely dominant policy in the United States, just as it was simply taken for granted in Europe. Assimilation was not only about the absorption of newcomers, but of the continuous homogenization of all sorts of cultural differences. [...] Contemporary ethnic fragmentation is merely an aspect of a much broader cultural fragmentation including gender, age, religion, and most of the other cultural categories that constitute modern society.

It is worth noting the difference between previous tendencies to multiethnicity at the turn of the century and the current situation. In the earlier period, while there were, as we said, debates on the reconstitution of society in multicultural terms, the same kind of debate was not present in Europe where assimilation was simply taken for granted. Europe was still organized around the combination of a strongly mono-ethnic/civil state and a colonial world structure in which coming to the metropolis was interpreted as social mobility, an increase in status implying a will to assimilate to the superior. This was structured strongly enough to be more or less obvious to nationals as well as immigrants, regionals, and indigenous peoples. While there were clearly differences in the constitution of nation-states, such as the jus sanguinis of Germany and the jus soli of France, the process of assimilation was powerful in all cases. The high proportion of Polish laborers in German industrial development did not deter their eventual absorption into German national identity. The legal processes and cultural processes were not, of course, equivalent, and there was clearly both physical and psychological violence involved. While the conditions of assimilation are difficult to ascertain, I would argue that the ideological situation in earlier parts of the century was strongly nationalist while this situation has become reversed in the past decades. This reversal or ideological inversion is an important aspect of the general situation. Gitlin (1995) has argued for the same identity shift in the United States. Earlier in the century, immigrants came to become part of the country whereas today they come to remain part of their countries of origin. Immigration in the current situation harbors strong tendencies to diasporization. The latter must be understood in terms of a set of practices in which identification with a homeland is the basis for the organization of cultural, economic, and social activities that transgress national borders.

Globalization, Inversion, and Horizontal Polarization

It is important to note that it is not immigration itself that is the basis of ethnification but of the articulation of migration and social integration. In a period of declining hegemony, then, migration leads to ethnification, enclavization, and diaspora formation. The two arenas where ethnification is evident is in the public political discourses and struggles for recognition of such groups and in the ethnic formation of underclasses in the different national states. In virtually all western countries of Europe, there has been a significant increase in criminalization within marginalized ethnic groups. In Europe such groups are primarily immigrants. In Canada, the United States, and Australia they are primarily black and indigenous populations. The parallels, however, are noteworthy.

There is a change in the view and also the activities of minority populations. West Indians in the late 1960s and 1970s were not associated with crime in the United Kingdom. [...]

Similarly, in other parts of Europe, immigrants tended to integrate into the larger national arena. This does not imply that there were no conflicts, but that in the process of accommodation, the cultural hierarchy between national versus immigrant was clearly established. This situation began to be reversed from the late 1970s. The same people have now become ethnically stronger, and opposed to integration.

[...]

The tendencies for certain minorities to become parts of underclass or marginalized zones in a period of increasing cultural identification creates a highly ambivalent and cathected situation for those involved. Marginalized zones are increasingly integrated into nonnational sodalities. The latter provide conditions of reproduction in economic and cultural terms that the nation-state has not been able to afford. The result is the formation of oppositional identities that become increasingly transnational.

Parameters of Globalization II: Vertical Polarization

While cultural and social fragmentation is occurring with various degrees of confrontation and violence in the former hegemonic regions of the world system, there is another process that has been discussed widely. Class stratification in the old centers is on the increase and often in quite astounding proportions, not least in the old centers of the world system. This is not, of course, a simple process and is definitely not limited to a combination of impoverishment and the enrichment of a capitalist class. The stratification process includes significant elites connected to public institutions, international bureaucracies, and professional classes all of whom depend in varying degrees on tax funds, their speculative growth, and other sources of income that have been in one way or another transferred to the public sphere. I have referred to this earlier in my work as the global pork barrel phenomenon (Friedman 1997), which plays an important role in consolidating global class identities and novel cultural discourses. The economic parameters of this process in the old centers of the world system are well known through variations on a number of common themes. Countries like Sweden with a low level of class differentiation and countries like the United States with much higher levels, have experienced the same transformational vectors in the past decade, vectors that are common properties of a global dynamic. While the wealth ratio of richest to poorest in Sweden is 2.7 as opposed to 5.9 for the United States, the same kinds of changes have occurred. These are the economic vectors discussed in the first part of the chapter; the combination of global shift, speedup, and the changing composition of capital. The United States has experienced the clearest example of this kind of change where downward mobility since the 1970s has been a constant. Flexible labor regimes have expanded, leading to a larger proportion of working poor. Incomes have stagnated or declined and mobility has become increasingly limited. In Europe unemployment has reached alarming proportions. In Sweden it was above 12 percent in the mid- to late 1990s and has now declined, primarily due to public sector spending and make-work programs. While there is current evidence of a slight reversal of these trends they in no way match the economic growth rates of 2 to 4 percent that are their basis. In other words there appears to have been a structural shrinkage of the work force that is only offset in countries like the United States where there are large-scale low-wage service sectors.

The actual situations of populations vary significantly according to the degree of welfare. And the latter are very much products of the way in which the national arenas are constituted. At one extreme there is a cultural minimal state, which is approximated in the United States, where individualism and a sacred private sphere have entailed a certain disinterested tolerance for cultural difference as long as it is not politicized. In continental Europe, on the other hand, the nation-state has a much stronger cultural character and multiculturalism there appears as a serious threat to a former social contract that has always been considerably weaker in the United States. Public

economics are clearly expressive of the different natures of the nation-state. In Europe the percentage of the population below the poverty line that is raised above that threshold by government transfers is between 40 percent and 60 percent with the Scandinavian countries approaching 100 percent. The equivalent figure for the United States is 0.5 percent. The United States sports an official poverty rate of more than 15 percent for the nation as a whole, jumping to considerably more than 20 percent in some states. If one calculates in terms of families and raises the income to $25,000, which might be a more adequate definition of the threshold of subsistence adequacy, then the figure rises to 28 percent (Hacker 1997:229). More important, with an unemployment rate below 5 percent, there's a considerable population of working poor. In both Europe and the United States the rate of ghettoization has been extreme and the formation of underclasses has been the formation of marginalized minorities as well, whose unemployment rates are often several times higher than those of the native born or more often those identified as "real nationals." Here of course there is a significant difference between polar extremes such as Sweden where in the relatively well-off welfare supported ghettos, unemployment reaches 90 percent or more, and states like California where entire industries are dependent on the influx of undocumented immigrants.

Downward mobility and deindustrialization have been accompanied by an upward mobility in the upper echelons of society. It is reflected in reports of enormous incomes among the capitalist elite as well as increasing incomes among political and cultural elites. The spate of scandals concerning credit cards, double salaries, long vacationlike "official" trips, and nightclub visits by politicians has led to a generalized crisis of confidence in the political elites. This crisis of accountability expresses an increasing rift between elites and the "people." The former along with capitalists, who were always in such a position, have been assimilated into a global circuit of relations with similarly placed people, so that elite interests have become forged into a class for itself in many ways. The European Union has become a kind of supranational and weakly accountable political organ that makes increasing numbers of decisions that affect national-level political situations. The real salaries of Union officials are considerably higher than those at the national level. And as there is no clearly defined social project, careers in themselves have become the modus vivendi of this massive reorganization of European political elites.

This kind of development at the regional and international level has produced new kinds of experiences for those involved. A person with such a career is very bound to his or her peers in the system. Representativity becomes less important than position itself. And the position may be imbued with a new moral posture. The cosmopolitan is promoted to a new kind of legitimacy. It is increasingly associated with a series of agendas that may contradict those of the nation-state itself. [. . .]

The New Age is the age of democracy, multiculturalism, and globalization. It is interesting to consider the reversal of perspectives in which a formerly nationalist elite, which may have seen "the people" as a motley foreign mixture, [. . .] identifies itself as hybrid/multicultural and views "the people" as dangerous purists.

Cosmopolitan Discourses and Ideological Hegemony

The formation of new globalizing elites is the social foundation of the increasing hegemony of celebratory globalization. Vertical polarization has characterized most of the societies of the West. It unites a number of political and cultural elites and links them to an economic project of transnational solidarity among such elites that sometimes mistake themselves for the "international community." [. . .] The former implicit relation of representativity that united national elites with the "people" began to fracture as early as the 1970s in some countries, that is, during the same period as the nation-state began to weaken financially and multiculturalism began its contemporary career. [. . .]

And the notion of *classes dangereuses* was reborn (Julliard 1997:204). If the elite could be said to have been "captured" in the earlier phase of the welfare state, it has now been liberated. The product of this freedom is the production of a new set of discourses. Chief among these is multiculturalism and hybridity. The latter is a logical product of a real experience of the world from the top. A "We Are the World" encompassment of humanity is not a new perspective. It can be found in the proclamations of the Freemasons, various representatives of the British Empire, as well as in the more recent discourses of the Mount Pelerin Society and the World Economic Forum. The logic of this discourse is one that reduces the national population to an ethnic group among many and that seeks to replace national identity by pluralism. It is significant that pluralism was the core of

colonial rule. J. S. Furnivall, one of the foremost analysts of colonial society, stated the case as follows:

> In tropical dependencies there was no common social will to set a bar to immigration, which has been left to the play of the economic forces. The plural society arises where economic forces are exempt from control by social will.
>
> (Furnivall 1948:306)

Cosmopolitanism in this sense implies the capacity to distance oneself from one's place of origin and to occupy a higher position above a world in which indigenous, national, and migrant populations all inhabit an enriched cultural territory. Cultural difference is consumed in the form of cultural products, from cuisine to art, and is, of course, the stuff for innumerable festivals and dinner parties. Difference is appropriated into the lives of the elites and becomes a kind of furnishing of their existences. The embodiment of the world's diversity becomes a new kind of self-representation. This is not merely the way the world is represented by postcolonial intellectuals, by the international media, and by other cultural elites; the language of this New Age is firmly anchored in the international business community and its own cultural producers. [. . .]

[. . .]

[. . .] Academics, artists, media "intellectuals," and others who identify themselves as the new "travelers," have been instrumental in the production of discourses of transnationalism and hybridity, border crossing, and a number of "anti-essentialist" representations of reality. These have been employed extensively, sometimes in political projects, such as those of self-proclaimed multicultural states. In Australia, perhaps the most immigrant-dense country in the world, the government some years ago launched a multicultural policy program and a book called *Creative Nation* that was meant to recreate unity out of increasing diversity. An apocryphal story is that on one occasion a representative literary scholar went to talk to a group of Aboriginal artists and intellectuals, presumably to entice them into the new multicultural project. He went on for some time about how *mixed* the Aborigines were as a population and that any other view of themselves was tantamount to *essentialism*, that favorite word of cultural studies. When he was through, an older man rose and looked the hybridist straight in the eyes and said, "Listen, mate! I'm an essentialist and if you don't like it you can bugger off!"

There is clearly a conflict between hybridizing elites and those who identify as indigenous.

Canada, another state that has declared itself multicultural, has faced similar opposition from Indians who refuse to be classified as just another ethnic minority. They are the First [Nations], and this, of course, is more than cultural distinctiveness. It is about rights to land and political autonomy.

There is little evidence that hybridity works on the ground. Attempts to establish "biracial" identity in the United States have had an interesting development. The biracial movement is primarily a middle-class activity and it contains a strong strategy of distinction making in which class mobility leads to attempts to separate oneself from a preceding, in this case, lower-status identity. The polarizing attractor in this is "whiteness." The logical contradiction in this kind of identification lies in the interstice between individual and collective identity. Every individual has a specific genealogy and is thus a very particular mixture. Collective creole identities in the past have always and continue to be closed ethnic identities, indistinguishable, in this sense, from nonmixed identities. The biracial movement split some years ago when Asian biracials protested the dominance of African Americans. The new group took on the title, *Hapa* Forum, *hapa* being the Hawaiian word for "half." This is a normal product of the above contradiction. Any attempt to form a collectivity must also create boundaries and raise issues concerning the particular constituents of that identity. Hybrid identity only works as a discourse, as an individual identity or in situations where the specificity of the hybridity can be ignored. It is thus most suitable for elites where the only commonality of the identity is that it is positioned above the fragmenting multiethnic world below.

Paradoxes of Globalization

What is often summarized by the term globalization is, in this analysis, a complex process of double polarization, of cultural fragmentation, and of the formation of transnational networks: economic, social, and cultural. These flows interact with the fragmentation process, often splitting it by creating microclasses. The example of the Maori is of importance here. The Maori indigenous movement made important inroads into New Zealand politics in the 1970s and 1980s. This led to numerous concessions, both cultural and economic. The restoration of tribal lands led ultimately to the establishment of "tribal capitalism" (Rata 1997) in which the tribal units were able to run fisheries while maintaining their conical clan structures. This created a new hierarchy of control within the tribal units since those closest to the central lineages were those who controlled the capital. The Maori today control a third of New Zealand's fisheries, but in an unequal way. More seriously, those Maori who do not have genealogical access to tribal land remain in their urban slums. They make up between 40 and 50 percent of the Maori population. Thus the Maori success story has created a class division within the group that did not exist previously. Throughout the world NGOs are helping to create similar kinds of divisions. The same kind of class division occurred historically among the Sami, between the small minority of reindeer owners and those who had been cut off from this livelihood and lost their territorial rights. There is also a considerable skim-off within the Fourth World that has created a traveling class of tribal representatives based largely around UN organs as opposed to those who stay home. Now this new class does not partake of a hybrid ideology as such, but they might be seen as minor actors in the multiculturalization of the world in which the hybrid encompassers occupy the apex. The interaction of globalization and fragmentation consists in driving a class wedge through the ethnic groups themselves, leading to a whole new set of internal conflicts. [. . .] There are international consultant firms today that specialize in what they call the "sovereignty business," specialized, that is, in milking the funds that are destined for indigenous groups.

At the same time indigenization has been a powerful factor of identification among the marginalized populations and underclasses of the declining hegemons. The ideologies of the New Rights in Europe, and militia groups in the United States are evidence of this. Many of these groups have strongly indigenous ideologies, invoking antiuniversalism, local autonomy, nationhood over citizenship, "tribal" religion, and antimodernist holism. [. . .]

These tendencies [. . .] are not isolated from one another. They all interact on the Internet and are thoroughly embedded in the world systemic processes that we have discussed, the combined and seemingly contradictory phenomena of increasing cultural fragmentation in substantial parts of the world at the same time as there is an apparent increase in global unity in the form of communication, capital flows, and global elite formation. These simultaneities are organized by a single nexus of global political economic processes and form the basis for the differential identity politics that are sometimes referred to in terms of "globalization," the globalization of the local and the localization of the global. The latter metaphors, however, are not expressions of cultural processes in themselves but aspects of more powerful forces of local/global articulation. Class and ethnicity, vertical and horizontal polarization, are the two contradictory patterns that emerge from the dynamics of globalization.

[. . .]

Global Process and the Structuring of Violence

The process referred to by the term globalization results in a double polarization of the kind sketched above. In social terms it implies massive dislocation in the lower reaches of the global arena, not least in those zones that are party to hegemonic decline either directly or as peripheries. As the Western state relinquishes its national responsibilities, welfare declines seriously and perilous zones appear in the large urban areas. These zones are constituted by downwardly mobile nationals, second- and third-generation immigrant workers and newly arrived immigrants, products of the larger disorder in the weak links of the system. These weak links are the areas in which imperial orders such as the Soviet Union have collapsed or where peripheral postcolonial states have disintegrated, phenomena that are systematically connected to the transformation of the West as these areas were related via the import of funds and capital and now via the export of people. These are zones of ethnification, the privatization of the state, of warfare and banditry. The process of fragmentation has not been a particularly peaceful one. In 1993, for example, there were fifty-two major violent conflicts in the world in forty-two countries, the most severe conflicts being in Eastern Europe, Central Asia, and Africa. Half of these conflicts had been under way for more than a decade (UNRISD Report 1995:15). This is very different than the previous decades of the Cold War when there was a simpler division and a much stronger degree of control in the world system. [. . .]

The fragmentation of these larger units is not merely a process of disintegration since the fragments themselves are integrated into larger networks of trade in drugs, arms, and people. And the fragmentation does not apply only to political, ethnic, or regional units. It penetrates into the basic social fabric, dissolving kinship and even nuclear family sodalities, producing, as in parts of Africa, a population of youths who are expelled from a larger context of sociality, of social integration, and of life cycle expectations. The capital circulating in such networks reinforces the fragmentation insofar as the fragments are linked to raw materials or other sources of wealth, including the funds to acquire weapons. For example, the liberation of young men from family structures combines with the political and economic projects of petty bosses in the form of the proliferation of private militias supplied with arms from international networks, drug sales, and the control of local resources such as diamonds or oil. In terms of the organization/disorganization of social worlds there is much to be asked and to be learned. The kinds of violence that are most salient are located in the arenas produced by the process of disintegration of larger unities. There is a violence of lumpenproletarianization in many of the word's urban zones. There is the ethnic violence that is related to sociocultural fragmentation and there is the violence related to both of these that consists in the formation of transnational criminal networks. The role of state violence should not be underplayed here, but it should be noted that this violence, for example in Africa, is not part of a project of national integration but of control over resources by privatized elites. The state has become an actor with its own special interests that are not related to the function of representing a larger population.

[. . .]

The gamut of conflict harboring potential violence occurs primarily on the fault lines of larger social fields of which there are several kinds today. There are fault lines caused by fragmentation. [. . .] But there are also the fault lines of transnational organizations themselves. These can be summarized by transnational associations such as politically and economically organized diasporas and organizations that have specialized in living off the larger disorder in the system. Diasporas create new fault lines at local levels to the extent that they represent fragmentation within larger state societies. They have and are accused of activities that are incompatible with the maintenance of the nation-state.

[. . .]

There is an important difference between identity-based conflict and the violent activities of global networks, but both represent the violence that comes of disintegration of larger territorial homogeneities and/or hierarchical orders.

[. . .]

REFERENCES

Bairoch, P., and R. Kozul-Wright. 1996. "Globalization Myths: Some Historical Reflections on Integration, Industrialization and Growth in the World Economy." UNCTAD Discussion Paper no.113.

Bergesen, A. and R. Fernandez. 1995. "Who Has the Most Fortune 500 Firms?: A Network Analysis of Global Economic Competition, 1956–1989." *Journal of World Systems Research* 1, no. 12. http://csf.colorado.edu/wsystems/jwsr.html.

Briggs, A., and D. Snowman, 1996. *Fins de Siècle: How Centuries End, 1400–2000*. New Haven, Conn.: Yale University Press.

Dicken, P. 1992. *Global Shift: The Internationalisation of Economic Activity*. London: Chapman.

Economist. 1998. "The Century the Earth Stood Still," December 20, 1997–January 2, 1998, 71–73.

Friedman, J. 1997. "Global Crises, the Struggle for Cultural Identity and Intellectual Pork-Barreling: Cosmopolitans, Nationals and Locals in an Era of Dehegemonisation." In *The Dialectics of Hybridity*. Edited by P. Werbner, 70–89. London: Zed Press.

Furnivall, J. S. 1943. *Colonial Practice and Policy*. Cambridge, U.K.: Cambridge University Press.

Gitlin, T. 1995. *The Twilight of Common Dreams: Why America Is Wracked by Culture Wars*. New York: Holt.

Hacker, A. 1997. *Money: Who Has How Much and Why*. New York: Scribner.

Juillard, J. 1997. *La faute des élites*. Paris: Gallimard.

Kallen, H. 1924. *Culture and Democracy in the United States*. New York: Arno.

Porter, M. 1990. *The Competitive Advantage of Nations*. New York: Macmillan.

Rata, M. 1997. "Global Capitalism and the Revival of Ethnic Traditionalism in New Zealand: The Emergence of Tribal Capitalism." Ph.D. diss., University of Auckland.

Sassen, S. 1996. *Losing Control? Sovereignty in an Age of Globalisation*. New York: Columbia University Press.

——. 2000. "Economic Globalization and the Redrawing of Citizenship." In *Globalization, the State and Violence*, Edited by Jonathan Friedman (Lanham, MD: Rowman & Littlefield).

UNRISD Report. 1995. *States of Disarray: The Social Effects of Globalization*. London: Banson.

9

The Globalization Movement: Some Points of Clarification

David Graeber

A great deal of nonsense has been written about the so-called antiglobalization movement – particularly the more radical, direct action end of it – and very little has been written by anyone who has spent any time inside it. As Pierre Bourdieu noted, the neglect of the movement by North American academics is nothing short of scandalous. Academics who for years have published essays that sound like position papers for large social movements that do not in fact exist seem seized with confusion or worse, highminded contempt, now that real ones are everywhere emerging. As an active participant in the movement as well as an anthropologist, I want to provide some broad background for those intellectuals who might be interested in taking up some of their historical responsibilities. This essay is meant to clear away a few misconceptions.

The phrase "antiglobalization" movement was coined by the corporate media, and people inside the movement, especially in the non-NGO, direct action camp, have never felt comfortable with it. Essentially, this is a movement against neoliberalism, and for creating new forms of global democracy. Unfortunately, that statement is almost meaningless in the US, since the media insist on framing such issues only in propagandistic terms ("free trade," "free market") and the term neoliberalism is not in general use. As a result, in meetings one often hears people using the expressions "globalization movement" and "antiglobalization movement" interchangeably.

In fact, if one takes globalization to mean the effacement of borders and the free movement of people, possessions and ideas, then it's pretty clear that not only is the movement a product of globalization, but that most of the groups involved in it –

particularly the most radical ones – are in fact far more supportive of globalization in general than supporters of the International Monetary Fund or World Trade Organization. The real origins of the movement, for example, lie in an international network called People's Global Action (PGA). PGA emerged from a 1998 Zapatista *encuentro* in Barcelona, and its founding members include not only anarchist groups in Spain, Britain and Germany, but a Gandhian socialist peasant league in India, the Argentinian teachers' union, indigenous groups such as the Maori of New Zealand and [indigenous federations] of Ecuador, the Brazilian landless peasants' movement and a network made up of communities founded by escaped slaves in South and Central America. North America was for a long time one of the few areas that was hardly represented (except for the Canadian Postal Workers Union, which acted as PGA's main communications hub until it was largely replaced by the internet). It was PGA that put out the first calls for days of action such as J18 and N30 – the latter, the original call for direct action against the 1999 WTO meetings in Seattle.

Internationalism is also reflected in the movement's demands. Here one need look only at the three great planks of the platform of the Italian group Ya Basta! (appropriated, without acknowledgement, by Michael Hardt and Tony Negri in their book *Empire*): a universally guaranteed "basic income," a principle of global citizenship that would guarantee free movement of people across borders, and a principle of free access to new technology – which in practice would mean extreme limits on patent rights (themselves a very insidious form of protectionism). More and more, protesters have been trying to draw attention to the fact that the neoliberal vision of "globalization" is pretty much limited to the free flow of commodities, and actually increases barriers against the flow of people, information and ideas. As we often point out, the size of the US border guard has in fact almost tripled since signing of NAFTA. This is not really surprising, since if it were not possible to effectively imprison the majority of people in the world in impoverished enclaves where even existing social guarantees could be gradually removed, there would be no incentive for companies like Nike or The Gap to move production there to begin with. The protests in Genoa, for example, were kicked off by a 50,000-strong march calling for free immigration in and out of Europe – a fact that went completely unreported by the international press, which the next day headlined claims by George Bush and Tony Blair that protesters were calling for a "fortress Europe."

In striking contrast with past forms of internationalism, however, this movement has not simply advocated exporting Western organizational models to the rest of the world; if anything, the flow has been the other way around. Most of the movement's techniques (consensus process, spokescouncils, even mass nonviolent civil disobedience itself) were first developed in the global South. In the long run, this may well prove the most radical thing about it.

Ever since Seattle, the international media have endlessly decried the supposed violence of direct action. The US media invoke this term most insistently, despite the fact that after two years of increasingly militant protests in the US, it is still impossible to come up with a single example of someone physically injured by a protester. I would say that what really disturbs the powers-that-be is that they do not know how to deal with an overtly revolutionary movement that refuses to fall into familiar patterns of armed resistance.

Here there is often a very conscious effort to destroy existing paradigms. Where once it seemed that the only alternatives to marching along with signs were either Gandhian non-violent civil disobedience or outright insurrection, groups like the Direct Action Network, Reclaim the Streets, Black Blocs or Ya Basta! have all, in their own ways, been trying to map out a completely new territory in between. They're attempting to invent what many call a "new language" of protest combining elements of what might otherwise be considered street theater, festival and what can only be called nonviolent warfare (nonviolent in the sense adopted by, say, Black Bloc anarchists, of eschewing any

direct physical harm to human beings). Ya Basta! for example is famous for its *tuti bianci* or white overalls: elaborate forms of padding, ranging from foam armor to inner tubes to rubber-ducky flotation devices, helmets and their signature chemical-proof white jumpsuits. As this nonviolent army pushes its way through police barricades while protecting each other against injury or arrest, the ridiculous gear seems to reduce human beings to cartoon characters – misshapen, ungainly but almost impossible to damage. (The effect is only increased when lines of costumed figures attack police with balloons and water pistols or feather dusters.) Even the most militant – say, eco-saboteurs like the Earth Liberation Front – scrupulously avoid anything that would cause harm to human beings (or for that matter, animals). It's this scrambling of conventional categories that so throws off the forces of order and makes them desperate to bring things back to familiar territory (simple violence): even to the point, as in Genoa, of encouraging fascist hooligans to run riot as an excuse to use overwhelming force.

Actually, the Zapatistas, who inspired so much of the movement, could themselves be considered a precedent here as well. They are about the least violent "army" one can imagine (it is something of an open secret that, for the last five years at least, they have not even been carrying real guns). These new tactics are perfectly in accord with the general anarchistic inspiration of the movement, which is less about seizing state power than about exposing, delegitimizing and dismantling mechanisms of rule while winning ever-larger spaces of autonomy from it. The critical thing, though, is that all this is only possible in a general atmosphere of peace. In fact, it seems to me that these are the ultimate stakes of struggle at the moment: a moment that may well determine the overall direction of the 21st century.

It is hard to remember now that (as Eric Hobsbawm reminds us) during the late 19th century, anarchism was the core of the revolutionary left – this was a time when most Marxist parties were rapidly becoming reformist social democrats. This stituation only really changed with World War I, and of course the Russian revolution. It was the success of the latter, we are usually told, that led to the decline of anarchism and catapulted Communism everywhere to the fore. But it seems to me one could look at this another way. In the late 19th century people honestly believed that war had been made obsolete between industrialized powers; colonial adventures were a constant, but a war between France and England on French or

English soil seemed as unthinkable as it would today. By 1900, even the use of passports was considered an antiquated barbarism.

The 20th century (which appears to have begun in 1914 and ended sometime around 1989 or '91) was by contrast the most violent in human history. It was a century almost entirely preoccupied with either waging world wars or preparing for them. Hardly surprising, then, as the ultimate measure of political effectiveness became the ability to create and maintain huge mechanized killing machines, that anarchism quickly came to seem irrelevant. This is, after all, the one thing that anarchists can never, by definition, be very good at. Neither is it surprising that Marxism (whose parties were already organized on a command structure, and for whom the organization of huge mechanized killing machines often proved the only thing they were particularly good at) seemed eminently practical and realistic in comparison. And could it really be a coincidence that the moment the cold war ended and war between industrialized powers once again seemed unimaginable, anarchism popped right back to where it had been at the end of the 19th century, as an international movement at the very center of the revolutionary left?

If so, it becomes more clear what the ultimate stakes of the current "anti-terrorist" mobilization are. In the short run, things look very frightening for a movement that governments were desperately calling terrorist even before September 11. There is little doubt that a lot of good people are about to suffer terrible repression. But in the long run, a return to 20th-century levels of violence is simply impossible. The spread of nuclear weapons alone will ensure that larger and larger portions of the globe are simply off-limits to conventional warfare. And if war is the health of the state, the prospects for anarchist-style organizing can only be improving.

I can't remember how many articles I've read in the left press asserting that the globalization movement, while tactically brilliant, has no central theme or coherent ideology. These complaints seem to be the left-wing equivalent of the incessant claims in the corporate media that this is a movement made up of dumb kids touting a bundle of completely unrelated causes. Even worse are the claims – which one sees surprisingly frequently in the work of academic social theorists who should know better, like Hardt and Negri, or Slavoj Zizek – that the movement is plagued by a generic opposition, rooted in bourgeois individualism, to all forms of structure or organization. It's distressing that, two years after Seattle, I should even have to write this, but someone obviously should: in North America especially, this is a movement about reinventing democracy. It is not opposed to organization; it is about creating new forms of organization. It is not lacking in ideology; those new forms of organization are its ideology. It is a movement about creating and enacting horizontal networks instead of top-down (especially, state-like, corporate or party) structures, networks based on principles of decentralized, nonhierarchical consensus democracy.

Over the past 10 years in particular, activists in North America have been putting enormous creative energy into reinventing their groups' own internal processes to create a viable model of what functioning direct democracy could look like, drawing particularly, as I've noted, on examples from outside the Western tradition. The result is a rich and growing panoply of organizational forms and instruments – affinity groups, spokescouncils, facilitation tools, break-outs, fishbowls, blocking concerns, vibes-watchers and so on – all aimed at creating forms of democratic process that allow initiatives to rise from below and attain maximum effective solidarity without stifling dissenting voices, creating leadership positions or compelling people to do anything to which they have not freely consented. It is very much a work in progress, and creating a culture of democracy among people who have little experience of such things is necessarily a painful and uneven business, but – as almost any police chief who has faced protestors on the streets can attest – direct democracy of this sort can be remarkably effective.

Here I want to stress the relation of theory and practice this organizational model entails. Perhaps the best way to start thinking about groups like the Direct Action Network (which I've been working with for the past two years) is to see it as the diametrical opposite of the kind of sectarian Marxist group that has so long characterized the revolutionary left. Where the latter puts its emphasis on achieving a complete and correct theoretical analysis, demands ideological uniformity and juxtaposes a vision of an egalitarian future with extremely authoritarian forms of organization in the present, DAN openly seeks diversity: its motto might as well be, "if you are willing to act like an anarchist in the present, your long-term vision is pretty much your own business." Its ideology, then, is immanent in the antiauthoritarian principles that underlie its practice, and one of its more explicit principles is that things should stay that way.

There is indeed something very new here, and something potentially extremely important. Consensus process – in which one of the basic rules is that one always treats others' arguments as fundamentally reasonable and principled, whatever one thinks about the person making it – in particular creates an extremely different style of debate and argument than the sort encouraged by majority voting, one in which the incentives are all towards compromise and creative synthesis rather than polarization, reduction and treating minor points of difference like philosophical ruptures. I need hardly point out how much our accustomed modes of academic discourse resemble the latter – or even more, perhaps, the kind of sectarian reasoning that leads to endless splits and fragmentation, which the "new new left" (as it is sometimes called) has so far managed almost completely to avoid. It seems to me that in many ways the activists are way ahead of the theorists here, and that the most challenging problem for us will be to create forms of intellectual practice more in tune with newly emerging forms of democratic practice, rather than with the tiresome sectarian logic those groups have finally managed to set aside.

10

Globalization After September 11

Saskia Sassen

It is a material truth, whatever the moral ramifications, that new interstate collaboration,
multilateral networks, and global capitalism have
tied the world tighter. No matter how far away
geographically, we in the rich countries can no
longer fully escape or ignore poverty, wars, and
disease in the global south, because once an infrastructure for cross-border transactions is set up, it
will be used also for purposes other than those
originally intended. Affluent nations may or may
not take responsibility for aspects of life in newly
opened-up countries of the global south; either
way, life in those areas will inevitably affect us
through the many new linkages created through
globalization. Those relationships constrain us
in ways we might not have envisioned, but they
also offer us opportunities we might not have
thought of.

Governments have had to re-enter domains from
which they had withdrawn. Forms of openness
that had come to be considered crucial for a global
economy – such as those enabling international
business travel – are now subject to new physical
and psychological restrictions that may hamper
worldwide commerce and investment. We are
seeing a renationalizing of governments' efforts to
control their territory after a decade of "denation-
alizing" national economies. But we are also seeing
new types of cross-border government coalitions in
legal, policing, and military arenas.

In the long run, September 11 will not have
halted or permanently reversed globalization, but
that day did change the US approach to it. In less
than one hour, caution came to be capital's
new escort.

In discussing interconnectedness, perspective
matters. From a global, northern viewpoint,

three sometimes-overlapping features of globalization stand out.

One is unintended consequences. International
financial channels can be used to launder money as
well as for investment. Worldwide people channels can be used by terrorists and drug dealers as
well as for business travelers and tourists.

The second is the way in which informal connections piggyback on formal ones. Consider how
global trade has brought with it pests and diseases
to countries where they had been eradicated or
never seen. For instance, within the last several
years, a shipment of rubber tires introduced the
encephalitis-producing Nile mosquito to the
global north.

The third is the way interconnections affect us
psychologically, making migration more plausible
to those who seek greater opportunity or freedom.
Nations might become beacons or villains in our
minds, but they're also becoming less absolute
entities in the way we consider identity. More
people than ever before, for example, now hold
dual nationality. While there is no precise count,
more nations – for instance, recently, Mexico – are
allowing it. Of the 22 million-plus immigrants
legally admitted to the United States from 1961
to 1997, 16.3 million (75 percent) are from countries that allow dual or multiple citizenship.

These three aspects of globalization collide in
daunting ways, such as the booming black-market
trafficking in people. Even as the global north experienced a "decade of unprecedented peace and
prosperity," in the language of our leaders, a growing number of countries in the south experienced
accelerated indebtedness and unemployment,
and deteriorating health, social services, and
infrastructure. In 1998, those conditions fueled,

according to figures from the United Nations, the trafficking of 4 million people from poor to rich countries, producing a profit of $7-billion for criminal groups.

As the north has increasingly pressured the south to open up its economies to foreign corporations and foreign investment, a good 20 percent of the population in many of these countries have seen their income rise, at least for several years. But that leaves out the 80 percent who have become poorer. Over all, southern nations have become poorer and ever more dependent on remittances from immigrants to the north, remittances estimated at an annual $70-billion in the last several years. That gives southern nations less and less incentive to manage legal and illegal emigration. The north's emphasis on competitiveness drives southern nations to cut health, education, and social budgets, hampering development and further fueling legitimate and unsanctioned emigration. It is a vicious cycle.

Given such connections, how could poverty, war, and disease in the south not reach deep into the north over the bridges global capital has built?

In this context, we must recognize forms of violence less visible than crashes of planes into buildings. For instance, there's the debt trap. A deeply indebted country is not the same as a deeply indebted company. The debt eventually indirectly traps wealthy nations through the explosion in illegal trafficking in people, drugs, and weapons; the re-emergence of once-conquered diseases; and the further devastation of fragile ecosystems. Some 50 countries are now recognized as hyperindebted and unable to redress the situation. But while hyperdebt was once the plague solely of poor countries, the case of Argentina demonstrates debt's contagion to middle-income nations, as does Indonesia's increasingly troubled economy.

Argentina has defaulted on $132-billion in debt, the largest default ever for a government. International financial institutions, most notably the International Monetary Fund, have had limited success dealing with hyperdebt crises. We need to do some radical rethinking about how to handle this global explosion of hyperindebtedness.

The bitter but conventional medicine of rescheduled payments is no longer effective. Most extreme-debtor nations will simply be unable to pay off their loans in full under current conditions. The key ratio of debt service to gross national product in many of these countries exceeds sustainable limits. Consider, for instance, that in Latin American debt crises of the 1980s,

the debtor nations generally had a debt-service-to-GNP ratio of 42 percent; that ratio for recent Asian debtor nations has been about 28 percent. In contrast, current African debtor nations have a ratio of roughly 123 percent.

The IMF generally asks debtor nations to pay 20 to 25 percent of their export earnings toward debt service. In comparison, in 1953, the Allies canceled 80 percent of Germany's war debt and only insisted on 3 to 5 percent of export earnings going toward debt service. Similar favorable terms were given to Central European countries after communism.

Few poor countries can avoid trade deficits. Of 93 low and moderate-income countries, only 11 had trade surpluses in 1998. Poor countries would like to export more, and are striving to through organizations such as the new African Trade Insurance Agency, which supports exports to, from, and within Africa. Such specialized and focused efforts hold promise, but they can only make a limited difference as long as wealthy nations are, in effect, milking poorer ones dry.

That the global north is increasingly feeling the effects of rising debt, poverty, and disease in the global south is a complex macro-level asymmetry. September 11 demonstrated a micro-level asymmetry, but one with devastating consequences: the capabilities of "bricolage" terrorists to take on superpowers. The affluence that globalization has made possible in some regions has been accompanied by an increased vulnerability. Whether wealth and material sophistication inspire terrorist violence is a matter for continuing debate. What's clear is that wealth and sophisticated infrastructures offer insufficient protection against bombs loaded with carpenter nails, elementary nuclear devices, and "homemade" biological weapons, not to mention computer hackers and hijackers.

A third type of asymmetry caused by the broad, delicate web of financial and technological conduits is the diminutive scale of resources needed to make the global economic engine sputter, if not stall. The glaring example, of course, is the relatively low price of the attack on the World Trade Center and its enormous damage to the US and global economies. The Al Qaeda network is understood to have operated in more than 60 countries with, at most, half-a-billion dollars in available capital before the United States-led war on terrorism began in late September. That's not a lot of money when you consider that, according to the Forbes 2001 list, 29 of the richest individuals in the world each have fortunes worth over $10-billion, and that the global capital market was estimated at $68-trillion before September 11. The funds mobilized by the Al Qaeda network to set up operatives in 60 countries, or the $2-million estimated cost of the September 11 attack, are on a minute order of magnitude in comparison with the global economic system. And yet they represent a massive threat to the normal functioning of the most powerful countries in the world.

To be sure, there are positive types of asymmetries. Because of the global news media, a single tortured body can justly spark international outrage. War-crime tribunals can pursue the guilty no matter where they might have committed misdeeds or where they might be living. Universal jurisdiction allows judges in countries with the enabling legislation to sue even powerful former or current heads of state accused of crimes against humanity.

But over all, recent events have shown the international socioeconomic pall a well-organized act of destruction can cast in our sharply asymmetrical yet interdependent world. Much, though by no means all, global business has come to thrive increasingly on deregulation and privatization. But the terrorists' use of the financial system, along with money laundering and tax evasion by drug barons and other criminal groups, all suggest the limits of liberalization and privatization, and the need to re-insert governments in the global financial system.

I am not calling for a reversion to earlier state-centered control, but for multilateral and international measures along the lines of the recent antiterrorist financial clampdown jointly carried out by the United States and the European Union. They are attempting to widen the clampdown through the Financial Action Task Force, the world's main anti-money-laundering body, and its 31 member countries. Governments will be asked to create legal powers to freeze terrorists' assets, not only within mainstream banking, but also in money-service businesses. The latter is more problematic since it includes well-established and largely licit systems such as the *hawala* system – Islam's version of the correspondent banking of medieval Europe's Lombards.

Governments are also being pushed to resume subsidizing airlines and other social and business mainstays; offering Keynesian-style fiscal and monetary stimuli; and taking over sensitive private sectors, such as airport security. There are many positive sides to this; the main risk is that subsidies will go to a few very large and rich corporations.

After a decade of believing that markets could encompass more and more social domains, we must now accept that markets cannot take care of everything. Governments will have to govern a bit more. That shouldn't mean a return to old practices – countries' surrounding themselves with protective walls. It will require multilateralism and radical innovations.

Those innovations will be felt everywhere, but they will be felt most in what I call global cities, largely in electronic markets. Most of the value produced in the global economy revolves around financial transactions. The 2000 values of global trade (about $8 trillion) and of foreign direct investment flow (about $1 trillion) are minimal compared with the value of internationally traded derivatives ($68 trillion).

If financial transactions are largely electronic and international – globally circulating, dematerialized instruments – then why should the devastation of a square mile in lower Manhattan have disrupted the global financial system as severely as it did?

The language of globalization and information technology deceives us. It suggests that the electronic action is divorced from specific places. Yet a closer examination shows to what extent much of what we call the global economy takes place in a network of cities that handle most of the financial transactions and assets under management. Twenty-five cities in the world account for about 80 percent of assets under management. New York, London, Tokyo, Singapore, Hong Kong, Zurich, Geneva, Frankfurt, and Paris account for 85 percent of the foreign-currency market, the most globalized of all markets, in a world with more than 150 different currencies. A small number of cities account for most global exports of corporate accounting, legal, advertising, telecommunications, and other such services used by companies and markets for their global operations. New York and London are the leading exporters of such services in the world.

Why is activity involving electronic dematerialized capital so geographically concentrated? As firms and markets globalize their operations, their central coordination and planning become more complex, subject to increasingly variable and unpredictable conditions – financial, political, regulatory, and so on. These tasks are now so complex and specific that firms often prefer to contract out such services rather than hiring all the needed specialists as full-time, in-house personnel. Moreover, those specialized contractors rely on each others' expertise. A financial-services firm, for instance, needs access to accounting and legal talent, software designers, and economic-forecasting experts. The quality and efficiency of these contractors are crucial.

The contractors function best in an intense milieu of concentrated expertise and experience – in other words, New York, London, Frankfurt, Paris, Amsterdam, Hong Kong, Barcelona, Sydney, Sao Paulo, Bombay, and other such cities. They are the Silicon Valleys of global finance. One of the great ironies of the information age is that social connectivity is as important in many of the most strategic and complex sectors as technical connectivity. And cities are prime environments, enabling that social connectivity.

What went down with the devastation of lower Manhattan's square mile was one of the two most-strategic centers of global finance, London's City being the other. It was New York's global-city function that came to a standstill in the immediate aftermath of the attacks. That was enough to produce alarm, disorientation, doubt, and paralysis in the markets. Much of global finance, especially in leading sectors, is about transactions rather than simply money flows – the management of transactions and the creation of new instruments to do so. [...] On September 11, those capabilities were brought to a standstill. A key part of the international financial brain stopped delivering. Because speed and decisiveness have become so

vital to the world economy, a standstill of a week is devastating. And because New York is a major node and we are so interdependent, the repercussions were felt worldwide.

After September 11, many companies left lower Manhattan for Connecticut and New Jersey and won't return. But my forecast is that the top executives – those most involved with high-level innovations and speculative investments – will have to come back. The large financial-services firms, like Goldman Sachs, that had about 10,000 employees in lower Manhattan do not need that many there – just a few hundred top personnel. In many ways, before September 11, there was an inertia. Brutal as it sounds – and, of course, no one would want such a catalyst – the horrible destruction forces firms into a far tighter set of locational choices.

In addition to the top-level financial-service professionals, new sectors, such as new media, will seize the opportunity to move to lower Manhattan. In the '80s, after the so-called third-world-debt crisis, the large commercial banks and insurance companies left that area, making room for small, lively upstarts in finance. We can expect new types of hybrid businesses, ones that we cannot even foresee, to move in, the way software developers, hybrids in the '80s, became an established sector in the '90s.

That dynamic characterizes the fearsome vitality of globalization. By the time you're able to describe it, it's already something new. Therein lies our constant challenge in steering, and humanizing, it.

11

Millennial Capitalism and the Culture of Neoliberalism

Jean Comaroff and John L. Comaroff

[...]

The global triumph of capitalism at the millennium, its Second Coming, raises a number of conundrums for our understanding of history at the end of the century. Some of its corollaries – "plagues of the 'new world order,'" Jacques Derrida (1994: 91) calls them, unable to resist apocalyptic imagery – have been the subject of clamorous debate. Others receive less mention. Thus, for example, populist polemics have dwelt on the planetary conjuncture, for good or ill, of "homogenization and difference" (e.g., Barber 1992); on the simultaneous, synergistic spiraling of wealth and poverty; on the rise of a "new feudalism," a phoenix disfigured, of worldwide proportions (cf. Connelly and Kennedy 1994). For its part, scholarly debate has focused on the confounding effects of rampant liberalization: on whether it engenders truly global flows of capital or concentrates circulation to a few major sites (Hirst and Thompson 1996); on whether it undermines, sustains, or reinvents the sovereignty of nation-states (Sassen 1996); on whether it frees up, curbs, or compartmentalizes the movement of labor [...]; on whether the current fixation with democracy, its resurrection in so many places, implies a measure of mass empowerment or an "emptying out of [its] meaning," its reduction "to paper" (Negri 1999: 9; Comaroff and Comaroff 1997). Equally in question is why the present infatuation with civil society has been accompanied by alarming increases in civic strife, by an escalation of civil war, and by reports of the dramatic growth in many countries of domestic violence, rape, child abuse, prison populations, and most dramatically of all, criminal "phantom-states" (Derrida 1994: 83; Blaney and Pasha

1993). And why, in a like vein, the politics of consumerism, human rights, and entitlement have been shown to coincide with puzzling new patterns of exclusion, patterns that inflect older lines of gender, sexuality, race, and class in ways both strange and familiar (Gal 1997; Yúdice 1995). Ironies, here, all the way down; ironies, with apologies to Jean-Paul Sartre, in the very soul of the Millennial Age.

Other features of our present predicament are less remarked, debated, questioned. Among them are the odd coupling, the binary complementarity, of the legalistic with the libertarian; constitutionality with deregulation; hyperrationalization with the exuberant spread of innovative occult practices and money magic, pyramid schemes and prosperity gospels; the enchantments, that is, of a decidedly *neo*liberal economy whose ever more inscrutable speculations seem to call up fresh specters in their wake. Note that, unlike others who have discussed the "new spectral reality" of that economy (Negri 1999: 9; Sprinker 1999), we do not talk here in metaphorical terms. We seek, instead, to draw attention to, to interrogate, the distinctly pragmatic qualities of the messianic, millennial capitalism of the moment: a capitalism that presents itself as a gospel of salvation; a capitalism that, if rightly harnessed, is invested with the capacity wholly to transform the universe of the marginalized and disempowered (Comaroff 1999a).

All this points to another, even more fundamental question. Could it be that these characteristics of millennial capitalism – by which we mean *both* capitalism at the millennium and capitalism in its messianic, salvific, even magical manifestations – are connected, by cause or correlation or copresence, with other, more mundane features of the contemporary historical moment? Like the increasing relevance of consumption, alike to citizens of the world and to its scholarly cadres, in shaping selfhood, society, identity, even epi-stemic reality? Like the concomitant eclipse of such modernist categories as social class? Like the "crises," widely observed across the globe, of reproduction and community, youth and masculinity? Like the burgeoning importance of generation, race, and gender as principles of difference, identity, and mobilization? The point of this essay lies in exploring the possibility of their interconnection; even more, in laying the ground of an argument for it.

[. . .]

Specters, Speculation: Of Cons and Pros

Consumption, recall, was the hallmark disease of the eighteenth and nineteenth centuries, of the First Coming of Industrial Capitalism, of a time when the ecological conditions of production, its consuming passions (Sontag 1978; cf. Comaroff 1997), ate up the bodies of producers. At the end of the twentieth century, semiotically transposed, it is often said to be the "hallmark of modernity" (van Binsbergen and Geschiere n.d.: 3), the measure of its wealth, health, and vitality. An overgeneralization, maybe, yet the claim captures popular imaginings and their representation across the earth. It also resonates with the growing Eurocultural truism that the (post)modern person is a subject made with objects. Nor is this surprising. Consumption, in its ideological guise – as "consumer*ism*" – refers to a material sensibility actively cultivated, for the common good, by Western states and commercial interests, particularly since World War II. It has even been cultivated by some non-capitalist regimes: In the early 1990s, Deng Xiaoping advocated "consumption as a motor force of production" (Dirlik 1996:194).

In social theory, as well, consumption has become a prime mover (van Binsbergen and Geschiere n.d.: 3). Increasingly, it is *the* factor, *the* principle, held to determine definitions of value, the construction of identities, and even the shape of the global "ecumene."[1] As such, tellingly, it is the invisible hand, or the Gucci-gloved fist, that animates the political impulses, the material imperatives, and the social forms of the Second Coming of Capitalism – of capitalism in its neoliberal, global manifestation. Note the image: the invisible hand. It evokes the ghost of crises past, when liberal political economy first discerned the movements of the market beneath swirling

economic waters, of "free" enterprise behind the commonweal. Gone is the deus ex machina, a figure altogether too concrete, too industrial for the "virtualism" (Carrier and Miller 1998) of the post-Fordist era.

As consumption became the moving spirit of the late twentieth century, so there was a concomitant eclipse of production; an eclipse, at least, of its *perceived* salience for the wealth of nations. This heralded a shift, across the world, in ordinary understandings of the nature of capitalism. The workplace and labor, especially work-and-place securely rooted in a stable local context, are no longer prime sites for the creation of value or identity (Sennett 1998). The factory and the shop, far from secure centers of fabrication and family income, are increasingly experienced by virtue of their erasure: either by their removal to an elsewhere – where labor is cheaper, less assertive, less taxed, more feminized, less protected by states and unions – or by their replacement at the hands of nonhuman or "nonstandard" means of manufacture. Which, in turn, has left behind, for ever more people, a legacy of irregular piecework, of menial "workfare," of relatively insecure, transient, gainless occupation. Hence the paradox, in many Western economies, of high official employment rates amidst stark deindustrialization and joblessness. In the upshot, production appears to have been superseded, as the *fons et origo* of wealth, by less tangible ways of generating value: by control over such things as the provision of services, the means of communication, and above all, the flow of finance capital. In short, by the market and by speculation.

Symptomatic in this respect are the changing historical fortunes of gambling. The latter, of course, makes manifest a mechanism integral to market enterprise: It puts the adventure into venture capital. Financial risk has always been crucial to the growth of capitalism; it has, from the first, been held to warrant its own due return. But, removed from the dignifying nexus of the market, it was until recently treated by Protestant ethics and populist morality alike as a "pariah" practice. Casinos were set apart from the workaday world. They were situated at resorts, on reservations and riverboats: liminal places of leisure and/or the haunts of those (aristocrats, profligates, "chancers") above and beyond honest toil. Living off the proceeds of this form of speculation was, normatively speaking, the epitome of immoral accumulation: the wager stood to the wage, the bet to personal betterment, as sin to virtue. There have, self-evidently, always been different cultures and mores of betting. However, the activity –

whether it be a "flutter" on the horses or a domestic card game, on a sporting contest or an office pool – has generally been placed outside the domain of work and earning, at best in the ambiguous, nether space between virtue and its transgression. Over a generation, gambling, in its marked form, has changed moral valence and invaded everyday life across the world. It has been routinized in a widespread infatuation with, and popular participation in, high-risk dealings in stocks, bonds, and funds whose fortunes are governed largely by chance. It also expresses itself in a fascination with "futures" and their downmarket counterpart, the lottery. Here the mundane meets the millennial: "Not A LOT TO TOMAR, OW!" proclaims an ironic inner-city mural in Chicago [. . .], large hands grasping a seductive pile of casino chips, beside which nestles a newborn, motherless babe. This at a moment when "gambling [is] the fastest growing industry in the US," when it is "tightly woven into the national fabric," when it is increasingly "operated and promoted" by government.[2]

Life itself has become the object of bookmaking; it is no longer the sole preserve of the "respectable" insurance industry, of its abstract argot of longevity statistics and probability quotients. A recent article in *Newsweek* sports the headline "Capital Gains: The Lottery on Lives": "In America's *fin de siècle* casino culture, no wager seems *outré*. So how about betting on how long a stranger is likely to live? You can buy part or all of his or her insurance policy, becoming a beneficiary. Your gamble: that death will come soon enough to yield a high return on the money you put up. The Viatical Association of America says that $1 billion worth of coverage went into play last year."[3] A much better bet, this, than the sale of the Savior for thirty pieces of silver. Inflation notwithstanding.

In the era of millennial capitalism, securing instant returns *is* often a matter of life and death. The failure to win the weekly draw was linked with more than one suicide in Britain in the wake of the introduction of national lottery in 1994; in 1999, the *India Tribune* reported that one of the biggest central Indian States, Madya Pradesh, was "caught in the vortex of lottery mania," which had claimed several lives.[4] Witnesses described "extreme enthusiasm among the jobless youth towards trying their luck to make a fast buck," precisely the kind of fatal ecstasy classically associated with cargo cults and chiliastic movements (Cohn 1957). More mundanely, efforts to enlist divine help in tipping the odds, from the Taiwan-

ese countryside to the Kalahari fringe, have become a regular feature of [. . .] "fee-for-service" religions (Comaroff 1999a). These are locally nuanced fantasies of abundance without effort, of beating capitalism at its own game by drawing a winning number at the behest of unseen forces. Once again, that invisible hand.

The change in the moral valence of gambling also has a public dimension. In a neoliberal climate where taxes are anathema to the majoritarian political center, lotteries and gaming levies have become a favored means of filling national coffers, of generating cultural and social assets, of finding soft monies in times of tough cutbacks. The defunct machinery of a growing number of welfare states, to be sure, is being turned by the wheel of fortune. With more and more governments and political parties depending on this source for quick revenue fixes, betting, says George Will, has "been transformed from a social disease" – subjected, not so long ago, to scrutiny at the hands of Harvard Medical School – "into social policy."[5] Once a dangerous sign of moral turpitude, "it is now marketed almost as a 'patriotic duty.'"[6]

Put these things together – the explosion of popular gambling, its legitimate incorporation to the fiscal heart of the nation-state, the global expansion of highly speculative market "investment," and changes in the moral vectors of the wager – and what has happened? "The world," answers a reflective Fidel Castro, has "become a huge casino." Because the value of stock markets has lost all grounding in materiality, he says – anticipating a point to which we shall return – their workings have finally realized the dream of medieval alchemy: "Paper has been turned into gold."[7] This evokes Susan Strange (1986: 1–3; cf. Harvey 1989: 332; Tomasic and Pentony 1991), who, in likening the Western fiscal order to an immense game of luck, was among the first to speak specifically of "casino capitalism": "Something rather radical has happened to the international financial system to make it so much like a gambling hall. . . . [It] has made inveterate, and largely involuntary, gamblers of us all." Insofar as the growth of globalized markets, electronic media, and finance capital have opened up the potential for venture enterprise, the gaming room has actually become iconic of capital: of its "natural" capacity to yield value without human input (Hardt 1995: 39), to grow and expand of its own accord, to reward speculation.

And yet crisis after crisis in the global economy, and growing income disparities on a planetary scale, make it painfully plain that there is no such thing as capitalism sans production, that the neoliberal stress on consumption as the prime source of value is palpably problematic. If scholars have been slow to reflect on this fact, people all over the world – not least those in places where there have been sudden infusions of commodities, of new forms of wealth – have not. Many have been quick to give voice, albeit in different registers, to their perplexity at the enigma of this wealth: of its sources and the capriciousness of its distribution, of the mysterious forms it takes, of its slipperiness, of the opaque relations between means and ends embodied in it. Our concern here grows directly out of these perplexities, these imaginings: out of worldwide speculation, in both senses of the term, provoked by the shifting conditions of material existence at the turn of the twentieth century.

We seek, here, to interrogate the *experiential* contradictions at the core of neoliberal capitalism, of capitalism in its millennial manifestation: the fact that it appears both to include and to marginalize in unanticipated ways; to produce desire and expectation on a global scale (Trouillot 1999), yet to decrease the certainty of work or the security of persons; to magnify class differences but to undercut class consciousness; above all, to offer up vast, almost instantaneous riches to those who master its spectral technologies – and, simultaneously, to threaten the very existence of those who do not. Elsewhere (Comaroff 1999b) we have argued that these contradictions, while worldwide in effect, are most visible in so-called postrevolutionary societies – especially those societies that, having been set free by the events of 1989 and their aftermath, entered the global arena with distinct structural disadvantages. A good deal is to be learned about the historical implications of the current moment by eavesdropping on the popular anxieties to be heard in such places. How do we interpret the mounting disenchantment, in these "liberated zones," with the effects of hard-won democracy? Why the perceptible nostalgia for the security of past regimes, some of them immeasurably repressive? Why the accompanying upsurge of assertions of identity and autochthony? How might they be linked to widespread fears, in many parts of Eastern Europe and Africa alike, about the preternatural production of wealth?

The end of the Cold War, like the death of apartheid, fired utopian imaginations. But liberation under neoliberal conditions has been marred by a disconcerting upsurge of violence, crime, and disorder. The quest for democracy, the rule of law, prosperity, and civility threatens to dissolve into strife and recrimination, even political chaos, amidst the oft-mouthed plaint that "the poor cannot eat votes or live on a good Constitution."[8] Everywhere there is evidence of an uneasy fusion of enfranchisement and exclusion; of xenophobia at the prospect of world citizenship without the old protectionisms of nationhood; of the effort to realize modern utopias by decidedly postmodern means. Gone is any official-speak of egalitarian futures, work for all, or the paternal government envisioned by the various freedom movements. These ideals have given way to a spirit of deregulation, with its taunting mix of emancipation and limitation. Individual citizens, a lot of them marooned by a rudderless ship of state, try to clamber aboard the good ship Enterprise. But in so doing, they find themselves battling the eccentric currents of the "new" world order, which short-circuit received ways and means. Caught up in these currents, many of them come face to face with the most fundamental metamorphosis wrought by the neoliberal turn: the labile role of labor in the elusive equation connecting production to consumption, the pro to the con of capitalism.

[. . .]

Labor's Pain: Producing the Class of 2000

The emergence of consumption as a privileged site for the fabrication of self and society, of culture and identity, is closely tied to the changing status of work under contemporary conditions. For some, the economic order of our times represents a completion of the intrinsic "project" of capital: namely, the evolution of a social formation that, as Mario Tronti (1980: 32) puts it, "does not look to labor as its dynamic foundation" (cf. Hardt 1995: 39). Others see the present moment in radically different terms. Scott Lash and John Urry (1987: 232–33), for instance, declare that we are seeing not the denouement but the demise of organized capitalism, of a system in which corporate institutions could secure compromises between management and workers by making appeals to the national interest. The internationalization of market forces, they claim, has not merely eroded the capacity of states to control national economies. It has led to a decline in the importance of domestic production in many once industrialized countries – which, along with the worldwide rise of the service sector and the feminization of the workforce, has dispersed class relations, alliances, and antinomies across the four corners of the earth. It has also put such distances between sites of production and consumption that their articulation becomes all but unfathomable, save in fantasy.

Not that Fordist fabrication has disappeared. There is a larger absolute number of industrial workers in the world today than ever before (Kellogg 1987). Neither is the mutation of the labor market altogether unprecedented. For one thing, Marx (1967: 635) observed, the development of capitalism has always conduced to the cumulative replacement of "skilled laborers by less skilled, mature laborers by immature, male by female" – also "living" labor by "dead." As David Harvey (1989: 192–93) reminds us, the devaluation of labor power has been a traditional response to falling profits and periodic crises of commodity production. What is more, the growth of global markets in commodities and services has *not* been accompanied by a correspondingly unrestricted flow of workers; most nation-states still try to regulate their movement to a greater or lesser extent. The simultaneous "freeing" and compartmentalizing of labor [. . .] is a tension long endemic to capitalism.

Nonetheless, Harvey insists, if not in quite the same terms as Lash and Urry (1987), that the current moment *is* different: that it evinces features that set it apart, fracturing the continuing history of capital – a history, Engels once said, that "remain[s] the same and yet [is] constantly changing" (quoted by Andre Gunder Frank [1971: 36]). Above all, the explosion of new markets and monetary instruments, aided by sophisticated means of planetary coordination and space-time compression, have given the financial order a degree of autonomy from "real production" unmatched in the annals of political economy (cf. Turner n.d.: 18). The consequences are tangible: "Driven by the imperative to replicate money," writes David Korten (1996: 13; [. . .]), "the [new global] system treats people as a source of inefficiency": ever more disposable. [. . .] The market and its masters, an "electronic herd" (Friedman 1999) of nomadic, deterritorialized investors, appear less and less constrained by the costs or moral economy of concrete labor.

If capital strives to become autonomous of labor, if the spatial and temporal coordinates of modernist political economy have been sundered, if the ontological connection between production and consumption has come into question, what has happened to the linchpin of capitalism: the concept formerly known as class?

Denunciations of the concept, Fredric Jameson (1999: 46–47) laments, have become "obligatory."

Even for Marxists. This in spite of the fact that class names an "ongoing social reality," a persistently active dimension of "post-Cold War maps of the world system." He is, moreover, unconvinced by claims that it no longer makes sense of the transnational division of labor; nor is he persuaded that gender, race, and ethnicity are more constitutive of concrete experience in the contemporary moment. For Jameson, gender and race are too easily reconciled with the demands of liberal ideology, with its solutions to social problems, with the sorts of politics it proffers. Class, finally, remains more intractable and more fundamental. Thus Tom Lewis (1999: 151): the failure to recognize it as "the most effective subject position" through which to organize against racism and sexism is "particularly regrettable."

But surely the matter runs deeper than this? Subject positions are multiply determined, shaped less by political expediency than by the compelling truths of sense and perception. As Jameson himself notes (1999: 49), "Nothing is more complexly allegorical than the play of class connotations across the . . . social field." Our task, surely, is to examine how consciousness, sentiment, and attachment are constituted under prevailing conditions; why class has become a less plausible basis for self-recognition and action when growing disparities of wealth and power would point to the inverse [. . .]; why gender, race, ethnicity, and generation have become such compelling idioms of identification, mobilizing people, both within and across nation-states, in ways often opposed to reigning hegemonies.

Once again, this problem is hardly new. There has long been debate about the two big questions at the nub of the historical sociology of class: Why do social classes seem so seldom to have acted for themselves (*für sich*)? And why have explicit forms of class consciousness arisen relatively infrequently, even under the worst of Fordist conditions (see, e.g., Wallerstein 1972: 173; Comaroff and Comaroff 1987)? Complex, poetically rich, culturally informed imaginings have always come between structural conditions and subjective perceptions – imaginings that have multiplied and waxed more ethereal, more fantastic, as capitalist economies have enlarged in scale. Neither the absolute increase in industrial workers across the globe nor the fact that 70 percent of the population in advanced capitalist societies "structurally belong to the working class" (Lewis 1999: 150–51) dictates that people will experience the world, or act upon it, in classic proletarian terms.

Quite the opposite. As we have already said, the labile relation of labor to capital may have intensified existing structures of inequality, but it is also eroding the conditions that give rise to class opposition as an idiom of identity and/or interest. Key here is the dramatic transnationalization of primary production (this by contrast to trade in raw materials and finished products, which has long crossed sovereign borders; see Dicken 1986: 3). A world-historical process, it is having profound effects on the configuration, and the cognition, of social relations of production everywhere: (1) By undermining the capacity of states to sustain economies in which "production, plant, firm and industry were essentially national phenomena" (Hobsbawm 1979: 313), it renders obsolete the old system of bargaining in which labor and capital could negotiate wages and conditions within an enclaved territory (Lash and Urry 1987: 232–33; see above); (2) by subverting domestic production in industrialized countries, it encourages the cutting of labor costs through casualization, outsourcing, and the hiring of discounted (female, immigrant, racinated) workers, thereby either making blue-collar employees redundant or forcing them into the menial end of the service sector; (3) by widening the gulf between rich and poor regions, it makes the latter – via the export of labor or the hosting of sweatshops and maquiladoras – into the working class of the former; and (4) by reducing proletarians everywhere to the lowest common denominator, it compels them to compete with little protection against the most exploitative modes of manufacture on the planet.

To the extent, then, that the nation-state is, as Aijaz Ahmad (1992: 318) says, "the terrain on which actual class conflicts take place," it follows that the global dispersal of manufacture is likely to fragment modernist forms of class consciousness, class alliance, and class antinomies at an exponential rate. It is also likely to dissolve the ground on which proletarian culture once took shape and to disrupt any sense of rootedness within organically conceived structures of production. Already, in many places, there has been a palpable erosion of the conventional bases of worker identity. Thus, while it is possible to argue, with Terence Turner (n.d.: 25; cf. Cox 1987: 271), that transnational flows of capital and labor have replicated "internal" class divisions on an international scale, existing relations among labor, place, and social reproduction – and, with them, the terms of class conflict itself – have been thoroughly unsettled for now.

While the contours of the global proletariat are ghostly at best – and while middle classes seem everywhere to be facing a loss of socio-economic security, their center ground ever shakier [. . .] – a transnational capitalist class is taking more and more tangible shape. Here, again, there are questions of nuance about the old and the new: international bourgeoisies are, arguably, as old as capitalism itself. Dependency theorists have long insisted that they were a critical element in the making of modern European states and their national economies; also that their exploitation of colonial wealth was indispensable to the development of the Western metropoles. The new transnational capitalist elite – its frequent-flier executives, financiers, bureaucrats, professionals, and media moguls – may appear to be the planetary version of those older cosmopolitan bourgeoisies, its cadres centered in the imperial capitals of the world. But, as Leslie Sklair (1998: 136–37) argues, this new elite is distinctive in several ways. Above all, its interests are vested primarily in globalizing forms of capital: capital whose shareholder-driven imperatives are related to any particular local enterprise, metropolitan or colonial. Hence, while its business ventures might loop into and out of national economies, this does not, as Saskia Sassen (n.d.) stresses, make them "national" enterprises. The entrepreneurial activities of this class are conceived in terms of markets, monetary transactions, and modes of manufacture that transcend national borders. They seek to disengage from parochial loyalties and jurisdictions, thus to minimize the effects of legal regulations, environmental constraints, taxation, and labor demands.

Decontextualization, the distantiation from place and its sociomoral pressures, is an autonomic impulse of capitalism at the millennium; crucial, in fact, to its ways and means of discounting labor by abstracting itself from direct confrontation or civic obligation. The poor are no longer at the gates; bosses live in enclaved communities a world away, beyond political or legal reach. Capital and its workforce become more and more remote from each other. Here is the harsh underside of the culture of neoliberalism. It is a culture that, to return to our opening comment, re-visions persons not as producers from a particular community, but as consumers in a planetary marketplace: persons as ensembles of identity that owe less to history or society than to organically conceived human qualities.

[. . .]

The paradox of class at the millennium, in sum, must be understood in these terms. Neoliberalism aspires, in its ideology and practice, to intensify the abstractions inherent in capitalism itself: to separate labor power from its human context, to replace society with the market, to build a universe out of aggregated transactions. While it can never fully succeed, its advance over the "long" twentieth century has profoundly altered, if unevenly in space and time, the phenomenology of being in the world. Formative experiences – like the nature of work and the reproduction of self, culture, and community – have shifted. Once-legible processes – the workings of power, the distribution of wealth, the meaning of politics and national belonging – have become opaque, even spectral. The contours of "society" blur, its organic solidarity disperses. Out of its shadows emerges a more radically individuated sense of personhood, of a subject built up of traits set against a universal backdrop of likeness and difference. [. . .]

[. . .]

Occult Economies and New Religious Movements: Privatizing the Millennium

A striking corollary of the dawning Age of Millennial Capitalism has been the global proliferation of "occult economies." These economies have two dimensions: a material aspect founded on the effort to conjure wealth – or to account for its accumulation – by appeal to techniques that defy explanation in the conventional terms of practical reason; and an ethical aspect grounded in the moral discourses and (re)actions sparked by the real or imagined production of value through such "magical" means. It is difficult, of course, to quantify the presence of the occult – and, therefore, to make any claim to its increase. As we note above, finance capital has always had its spectral enchantments, its modes of speculation based on less than rational connections between means and ends. Both its underside (the pariah forms of gambling of which we spoke a moment ago) and its upper side (a fiscal industry, embracing everything from insurance to stock markets) have been rooted, from the first, in two inscrutables: a faith in probability (itself a notoriously poor way of predicting the future from the past) and a monetary system that depends for its existence on "confidence," a chimera knowable, tautologically, only by its effects. Wherein, then, lies the claim that occult economies are presently on the rise?

In the specific context of South Africa, we have demonstrated (Comaroff 1999a, 1999b) that there has been an explosion of occult-related activity – much of it violent, arising out of accusations of

ritual killing, witchcraft, and zombie conjuring – since the late apartheid years. These also include fantastic Ponzi schemes, the sale of body parts for "magical" purposes, satanic practices, tourism based on the sighting of fabulous monsters, and the like. Here middle-class magazines run "dial-a-diviner" advertisements, national papers carry headline articles on medicine murders, prime-time television broadcasts dramas of sorcery, and more than one "witchcraft summit" has been held. Patently, even here we cannot be sure that the brute quantum of occult activity exceeds that of times past. But what *is* clear is that their reported incidence, written about by the mainstream press in more prosaic, less exoticizing terms than ever before (Fordred 1999), has forced itself upon the public sphere, rupturing the flow of mediated "news." It is this rupture – this focus of popular attention on the place of the arcane in the everyday production of value – to which we refer when we speak of a global proliferation of occult economies.

It is not difficult to catalogue the presence of occult economies in different parts of the world. In West Africa, for example, Peter Geschiere (1997), among others, has shown how zombie conjuring is becoming an endemic feature of everyday life, how sorcery and witchcraft have entered into the postcolonial political economy as an integral element of a thriving alternative modernity, how magic has become as much an aspect of mundane survival strategies as it is indispensable to the ambitions of the powerful (see also Bastian 1993). Nor is all of this based in rural situations or among poor people. In South Africa a recent case involved a well-known physician: she was "turned into a zombie" by a "Nigerian devil-worshipper," who, having rendered her insensate, took a large sum of money from her bank account.[9] By labeling the accused a Nigerian devil worshipper, the report ties the menace of the satanic to the flow of immigrants across national borders.

Nor is this only an African phenomenon. In various parts of Asia occult economies thrive, often taking surprising turns [. . .]. In Thailand – where fortune-telling has been transformed by global technology and e-mail divination has taken off – one "traditional" seer, auspiciously named Madam Luk, reports that her clients nowadays ask three questions to the exclusion of all others: " 'Is my company going broke?' 'Am I going to lose my job?' and 'Will I find another job?' "[10] In the United States, too, the fallout of neoliberal capitalism is having its impact on magical practice. There is, for instance, a growing use ("seeping into the grassroots" of the US heartland and taking its place beside other millennial pursuits) of tarot readings as a respectable form of therapy – described by the director of the Trends Research Institute as a low-cost "shrink in the box."[11] By these means are psychology, spirituality, and fortune-telling fused.

Sometimes dealings in the occult take on a more visceral, darker form. Throughout Latin America in the 1990s, as in Africa and Asia, there have been mass panics about the clandestine theft and sale of the organs of young people, usually by unscrupulous expatriates (Scheper-Hughes 1996). Violence against children has become metonymic of threats to social reproduction in many ethnic and national contexts, the dead (or missing) child having emerged as the standardized nightmare of a world out of control (Comaroff 1997). There, and in other parts of the globe, this commerce – like international adoptions, mail-order marriage, and indentured domestic labor – is seen as a new form of imperialism, the affluent North siphoning off the essence of poorer "others" by mysterious means for nefarious ends. All of which gives evidence, to those at the nether end of the global distribution of wealth, of the workings of insidious forces, of potent magical technologies and modes of accumulation.

That evidence reaches into the heart of Europe itself. Hence the recent scares, in several countries, about the sexual and satanic abuse of children (La Fontaine 1997); about the kidnapping and murder of street "urchins," most recently in Germany by "Russian gangs," for purposes of organ harvest and export; about the alleged "trafficking in women [especially] from . . . nations of the former Soviet bloc" for prostitution, labor, and other "personal services" in Western Europe, the Americas, Japan, and China.[12] Again, the United States is not exempt from anxieties over the pilfering of human bodies and body parts for profit. Note, for just one extreme instance, the urban myth that traversed the Internet in 1997 about the secret excision of kidneys, by apparently incredible means, from business travelers.[13]

In other contexts, the occult concentrates itself in purely financial dealings. Thus there seems to have been an extraordinary intensification of pyramid schemes lately, many of them tied to the electronic media. These schemes, and a host of scams allied with them – a few legal, many illegal, some alegal – are hardly new. But their recent mushrooming across the world has drawn a great deal of attention – partly because of their sheer scale and partly because, by crossing national borders and/or registering at addresses far from

the site of their local operation, they insinuate themselves into the slipstream of the global economy, thereby escaping control. Recall the ten or so whose crash sparked the Albanian revolution early in 1997, several of which took on almost miraculous dimensions for poor investors. One pyramid manager in Albania, according to the *New York Times*, was "a gypsy fortune teller, complete with crystal ball, who claimed to know the future."[14] Even in the tightly regulated stock markets of the United States, there has been a rise in illegal operations that owe their logic, if not their precise operation, to pyramids: another *New York Times* report attributes this to the fact that investors are presently "predisposed to throw dollars at get-rich-quick schemes." Six billion dollars were lost to scams on the New York Stock Exchange in 1996.[15] These scams also bring to mind others that arise from a promiscuous mix of scarcity and deregulation, among them, the notorious Nigerian-based "419," a truly transnational con that regularly traps foreign businessmen into signing over major assets and abets large-scale, amazingly intricate forms of fraud (Apter 1999); also the Foundation for New Era Philanthropy, a US pyramid created "to change the world for the glory of God." On the basis of a promise to double their money in six months, its founder, John Benett, persuaded five hundred nonprofit organizations, Christian colleges, and Ivy League universities to invest $354 million.[16] The line between Ponzi schemes and evangelical prosperity gospels is very thin indeed.

All of these things have a single common denominator: the allure of accruing wealth from nothing. In this respect, they are born of the same animating spirit as casino capitalism; indeed, perhaps they *are* casino capitalism for those who lack the fiscal or cultural capital – or who, for one or another reason, are reluctant – to gamble on more conventional markets. Like the cunning that made straw into gold (Schneider 1989), these alchemic techniques defy reason in promising unnaturally large profits – to yield wealth without production, value without effort. Here, again, is the specter, the distinctive spirit, of neoliberal capitalism in its triumphal hour.

[. . .]

NOTES

1   "Ecumene" refers to a region of "persistent cultural interaction and exchange" (Kopytoff 1987: 10; cf. Hannerz 1989: 66).

2   George F. Will, Hooked on gambling: Other comment, *International Herald Tribune*, 26–27 June 1999, 8.

3   Jane Bryant Quinn, Capital gains: The lottery on lives, *Newsweek*, 15 March 1999, 55. "Viaticals" are insurance policies bought from the terminally ill, especially those in the late stages of AIDS.

4   Lottery mania grips Madya Pradesh, many commit suicide, *India Tribune* (Chicago), 2 January 1999, 8.

5   Will, Hooked on gambling. On the Harvard Medical School study, see Brett Pulley, Compulsion to gamble seen growing, *New York Times*, 7 December 1997, 22.

6   Michael Tackett and Ted Gregory, Gambling's lure still a divisive issue, *Chicago Tribune*, 20 May 1998, 3. The words quoted are those of James Dobson, president of Focus on the Family, a Christian media ministry. They echo observations made by a range of witnesses for the US National Gaming Impact Study Commission, set up in 1996 to study the effects of gambling.

7   Fidel Castro, Castro: World has become a huge casino, *Sunday Independent* (Johannesburg), 6 September 1998, 4; the article is a transcript of a speech given to the South African Parliament.

8   Ebrahim Harvey, Spectre of capitalism haunts ANC, *Mail and Guardian* (Johannesburg), 29 October-4 November 1999, 43.

9   Mzilikazi Wa Afrika, "I was turned into a Zombie": Doctor says she endured eight days of torment after a devil-worshipper lured her into a trap, *Sunday Times* (Johannesburg) [Extra], 11 July 1999, 1.

10 Uli Schmetzer, Letter from Bangkok: Thai seers dealt reversal of fortune, *Chicago Tribune*, 18 November 1997, 4.

11 Connie Lauerman, "Got a problem? Pick a card: Tarot has moved out of the occult realm – to become the low-cost "Shrink in a box," *Chicago Tribune*, Tempo Section, 4 December 1997, 1, 13.

12 There have been countless stories in British tabloids about the sexual and satanic abuse of children. For an especially vivid one, see Brian Radford, Satanic ghouls in baby sacrifice horror, *News of the World* (London), 24 August 1997, 30–31. Its two subtitles – Cult is cover for pedophile sex monsters and They breed tots to use at occult rites – reflect well the moral panic to which they speak. On the kidnapping of German children for these purposes, see Children killed for their organs, *Sunday World* (Johannesburg), 31 October 1999, 10; the report, based on German secret service documents from Berlin, originated with Reuters. The quotation about the trafficking in women is in Vladimir Isachenkov, Enslaving women from former Soviet bloc is widespread, *Santa Barbara News-Press*, 8 November 1997, A8; see also Denis Staunton, Couple on trial for child torture offer, *Guardian* (London), 8 August 1997, 13.

13 According to this urban myth, the telling of which is always accompanied by authenticating detail, the victim is offered a drink at an airport – New Orleans appears to be a favorite – and awakes in a hotel bath, body submerged in ice. A note taped to the wall warns him not to move, but to call 911. He is asked, by the operator, to feel carefully for a tube protruding from his back. When he finds one, he is instructed to remain still until paramedics arrive: His kidneys have been harvested.

14 Edmund L. Andrews, Behind the scams: Desperate people, easily duped, *New York Times*, 29 January 1997, 3. See also Celestine Bohlen, Albanian parties trade charges in the pyramid scandal, *New York Times*, 29 January 1997, 3.

15 See Leslie Eaton, Investment fraud is soaring along with the stock market, *New York Times*, 30 November 1997, 1, 24. Eaton also notes that these scams have been facilitated "by the rise of low cost telecommunications and...the internet."

16 Charity pyramid schemer sentenced to 12 years, *Chicago Tribune*, 23 September 1997, 6.

REFERENCES

Ahmad, Aijaz. 1992. *In theory: Classes, nations, literatures.* New York: Verso.

——. 1999. Reconciling Derrida: "Specters of Marx" and deconstructive politics. In Sprinker 1999.

Apter, Andrew. 1999. IBB = 419: Nigerian democracy and the politics of illusion. In *Civil society and the political imagination in Africa: Critical perspectives*, edited by John L. and Jean Comaroff. Chicago: University of Chicago Press.

Barber, Benjamin R. 1992. Jihad vs. McWorld. *Atlantic Monthly*, March: 53–65.

Bastian, Misty L. 1993. "Bloodhounds who have no friends": Witchcraft and locality in the Nigerian popular press. In *Modernity and its malcontents: Ritual and power in postcolonial Africa*, edited by Jean and John L. Comaroff. Chicago: University of Chicago Press.

Blaney, David L., and Mustapha Kamal Pasha. 1993. Civil society and democracy in the Third World: Ambiguities and historical possibilities. *Studies in Comparative International Development* 28, no. 1: 3–24.

Carrier, James G., and Daniel Miller, eds. 1998. *Virtualism: A new political economy.* Oxford: Berg.

Cohn, Norman Rufus Colin. 1957. *The pursuit of the millennium: Revolutionary millenarians and mystical anarchists of the middle ages.* London: Secker and Warburg.

Comaroff, Jean. 1997. Consuming passions: Nightmares of the global village. In *Body and self in a post-colonial world*, edited by E. Badone, special issue, *Culture* 17, no. 1–2: 7–19.

——. 1999a. Occult economies and the violence of abstraction: Notes from the South African postcolony. *American Ethnologist* 26: 279–301.

——. 1999b. Alien-nation: Zombies, immigrants, and millennial capitalism. *CODESRIA Bulletin*, 3/4: 17–28.

Comaroff, John L., and Jean Comaroff. 1987. The madman and the migrant: Work and labor in the historical consciousness of a South African people. *American Ethnologist* 14: 191–209.

——. 1997. Postcolonial politics and discourses of democracy in southern Africa: An anthropological reflection on African political modernities. *Journal of Anthropological Research*, 53 no. 2: 123–46.

Connelly, Matthew, and Paul Kennedy. 1994. Must it be the rest against the West? *Atlantic Monthly*, December: 61–84.

Cox, Robert W. 1987. *Production, power, and world order: Social forces in the making of history*. New York: Columbia University Press.

Derrida, Jacques. 1994. *Specters of Marx: The state of debt, the work of mourning, and the new international*, translated by Peggy Kamuf. New York: Routledge.

Dicken, Peter. 1986. *Global shift: Industrial change in a turbulent world*. London: Harper and Row.

Dirlik, Arif. 1996. Looking backwards in an age of global capital: Thoughts on history in Third World cultural criticism. In *Pursuit of contemporary East Asian culture*, edited by X. Tang and S. Snyder. Boulder, Colo.: Westview Press.

Fordred, Lesley. 1999. Narrative, conflict, and change: Journalism in the new South Africa. Ph.D. diss., University of Cape Town.

Frank, Andre Gunder. 1971. *Capitalism and underdevelopment in Latin America: Historical studies of Chile and Brazil*. Harmondsworth, U.K.: Penguin.

Friedman, Thomas L. 1999. *The Lexus and the olive tree*. New York: Farrar, Straus and Giroux.

Gal, Susan. 1997. Feminism and civil society. In *Transitions, environments, translations*, edited by J. Scott, C. Kaplan, and D. Keats. New York: Routledge.

Geschiere, Peter. 1997. *The modernity of witchcraft: Politics and the occult in postcolonial Africa*. Charlottesville: University of Virginia Press.

Hannerz, Ulf. 1989. Notes on the global ecumene. *Public Culture* 1: 66–75.

Hardt, Michael. 1995. The withering of civil society. *Social Text*, no. 45: 27–44.

Harvey, David. 1989. *The condition of postmodernity: An enquiry into the origins of cultural change*. Oxford: Blackwell.

Hirst, Paul, and Grahame F. Thompson. 1996. *Globalization in question: The international economy and the possibilities of governance*. Cambridge: Polity Press.

Hobsbawm, Eric J. 1979. The development of the world economy. *Cambridge Journal of Economics* 3: 305–18.

Jameson, Fredric. 1999. Marx's purloined letter. In Sprinker 1999.

Kellogg, P. 1987. Goodbye to the working class? *International Socialism* 2, no. 36: 105–12.

Kopytoff, Igor. 1987. The internal African frontier: The making of African culture. In *The African frontier*, edited by I. Kopytoff. Bloomington: Indiana University Press.

Korten, David. 1996. *When corporations rule the world*. East Hartford, Conn.: Kumarian Press.

La Fontaine, Jean S. 1997. *Speak of the devil: Allegations of satanic child abuse in contemporary England*. Cambridge: Cambridge University Press.

Lash, Scott, and John Urry. 1987. *The end of organized capitalism*. Madison: University of Wisconsin Press.

Lewis, Tom. 1999. The politics of "hauntology" in Derrida's *Specters of Marx*. In Sprinker 1999.

Marx, Karl. 1967. [1867]. *Capital: A critique of political economy*, vol. 1. New York: International Publishers.

Negri, Antonio. 1999. The specter's smile. In Sprinker 1999.

Sassen, Saskia. 1996. *Losing control? Sovereignty in an age of globalization*. New York: Columbia University Press.

——. n.d. Cracked casings: Notes towards an analytics for studying transnational processes. Manuscript.

Scheper-Hughes, Nancy. 1996. Theft of life: The globalization of organ stealing rumors. *Anthropology Today* 12, no. 3: 3–11.

Schneider, Jane. 1989. Rumpelstiltskin's bargain: Folklore and the merchant capitalist intensification of linen manufacture in early modern Europe. In *Cloth and human experience*, edited by A. Weiner and J. Schneider. Washington: Smithsonian Institution Press.

Sennett, Richard. 1998. *The corrosion of character: The personal consequences of work in the new capitalism*. New York: W. W. Norton.

Sklair, Leslie. 1998. The transnational capitalist class. In Carrier and Miller 1998.

Sontag, Susan. 1978. *Illness as metaphor*. New York: Farrar, Straus and Giroux.

Sprinker, Michael, ed. 1999. *Ghostly demarcations: A symposium of Jacques Derrida's* Specters of Marx. London: Verso.

Strange, Susan. 1986. *Casino capitalism*. Oxford: Blackwell.

Tomasic, Roman, and Brendan Petony. 1991. *Casino capitalism? Insider trading in Australia*. Canberra: Australian Institute of Criminology.

Tronti, Mario. 1980. The strategy of refusal. *Semiotext(e)* 3: 28–36.

Trouillot, Michel-Rolph. 1999. Close encounters of the deceptive kind: The anthropology of the state in the age of globalization. Paper presented on the occasion of the fiftieth anniversary of the founding of anthropology at Stanford University, 9–10 April.

Turner, Terence. n.d. Globalization, the state, and social consciousness in the late twentieth century. Manuscript.

Van Binsbergen, Wim, and Peter Geschiere. n.d. Call for papers for an international conference on Commodification and Identities – *The Social Life of Things* Revisited, Amsterdam, 10–14 June 1999.

Wallerstein, Immanuel. 1972. Social conflict in post-independence black Africa: The concepts of race and status group reconsidered. In *Racial tensions in national identity*, edited by E. Campbell. Nashville, Tenn.: Vanderbilt University Press. Reprinted in *The capitalist world economy*, by I. Wallerstein. Cambridge: Cambridge University Press, 1979.

Yúdice, George. 1995. Civil society, consumption, and governmentality in an age of global reconstruction. *Social Text*, no. 45: 1–25.

Part IV

Consumption, Markets, Culture

Introduction

Why have some contemporary theorists become newly skeptical about the dismissal of "grand narratives"? Why do notions of culture as a barrier to change persist in the development industry, and what are the challenges of blending cultural and economic analysis? When powerful institutions such as the World Bank invent new commodity categories, what are the local consequences? What spaces of consumer desire and development are emerging in post-socialist China? These and other questions about consumption theory, culture and markets are the focus of articles in Part IV.

"I had danced for rain: I got a flood," writes Clifford Geertz in the chapter reprinted below, where he reflects critically on two decades of intense debate sparked by his classic 1963 book, *Agricultural Involution*. Before Geertz emerged as a prominent advocate of symbolic anthropology, his research (as noted in this volume's Introduction) engaged two key issues of modernization theory: "tradition" as an impediment to change and "take-off" as a precondition for economic growth. Geertz's *Agricultural Involution* – a foundational work of ecological anthropology – described how irrigated rice terraces on Java, Indonesia's largest and most densely populated island, could absorb greatly increased labor inputs "almost indefinitely" when populations grew. This capacity "to work one more man in without a serious fall in per capita income" was, Geertz (1963:35, 80) indicates, "ultimately self-defeating," since it inhibited industrialization and economic diversification. Notable in Geertz's 1984 reevaluation of *Agricultural Involution* are his skepticism about both modernization theory's notion of "take-off," and about Marxist predictions of increasing class differentiation within the Javanese peasantry. Indeed he finds little value in models of social change "in which everyone ends up a class warrior or a utility maximizer." Instead he insists that analyzing social change requires "an understanding of the passions and imaginings that provoke and inform it," rather than a focus on economic processes alone, or a "pulverization of village social structure into numbers."

The power of the World Bank or USAID to define what counts as a "traditional" or "nontraditional" export product in Africa and elsewhere profoundly shapes the opportunities and incomes of farmers. Yet, as Little and Dolan observe in their chapter below, the category of "nontraditional commodity" (NTC) is full of contradictions and varies both within and across national boundaries. Business entrepreneurs and politicians, they note, sometimes petition government authorities to reclassify commodities as nontraditional exports in order to receive subsidies or credits. In the era of neoliberal structural adjustment, Little and Dolan write, "millions of dollars of third world development funds now chase NTC (nontraditional commodity) programs in hopes of diversifying exports, increasing trade revenues, and enhancing the private sector." What kinds of agrarian changes – such as shifts in investment patterns, gender relations, labor conditions, and self-provisioning – follow when farmers are "restructured" under an economic reform program that emphasizes NTCs? Little and Dolan explore this topic historically and ethnographically in The Gambia (a small nation in West Africa), situating their study in relation to global transformations in commodity systems, trade, and development agendas.

Louisa Schein's chapter addresses post-socialism (also see Verdery's chapter in Part VIII below) and the anthropology of consumption. What happens, Schein asks, when corporations and the Chinese state propagate a "rich culture of consumerism" in a society in which few have the means to consume and where, in some ethnic minority regions, the advertised commodities are not even available at all? The rapid transformation of China from socialism to a dynamic if authoritarian capitalism (with some hybrid and vestigial socialist features) removed most of the earlier system of universal entitlements to public-sector health care and other services. The state, however, has now insured that satellite TV will reach even the most remote and impoverished households. This new guarantee, Schein says, created over one billion "consumers-in-training" in a "space of ever-renewed desire." Longing for a television thus becomes an impetus for development, as families scheme about how to raise the cash necessary for the purchase and then dream of emulating the lifestyles they see, especially on foreign programs. This phenomenon, which economists might relate to "pent-up demand" and which Schein terms "cultural developmentalism," has wider repercussions in the Chinese economy. Indeed, free-market reform in China is officially thought to depend not just on exports (a view common in the United States), but on the "promiscuous contact with media and commodities" that fuels domestic demand. Schein points out that new consumption patterns go hand-in-hand with unprecedented levels of inequality, and that this may limit the extent to which consumption in China is employed to fashion novel individual and group identities.

Daniel Miller helped to pioneer anthropological studies of consumption. In chapter 15 below he maintains that even though Hegel's and Marx's views of history as an inexorable process were clearly mistaken, anthropologists' recent disdain for "grand narratives" is in many ways misplaced, since the homogenizing tendencies in today's capitalism (for example, a global capitalist class) need to be understood with models that acknowledge their universality (David Graeber makes a similar point in his chapter in Part III). At the same time, Miller points to a contradiction that earlier critics of capitalism rarely perceived. People consume objects that express their individual or group identity, repudiating or negating in this expression of individuality and specificity the homogenizing forces typically highlighted by critics of capitalism and globalization. Some (e.g., Klein 1999) argue that mass consumption is considerably less creative and autonomous than Miller suggests, and that it often reflects corporate manipulation of consumers. Graeber (2004:99–100) proposes that anthropological rhetoric about "creative consumption," or consumption as a means of establishing one's particular identity, disturbingly comes to echo the very ideology of global capitalism. For Miller one of the most striking aspects of consumption is what he terms its "virtualism" – the modeling of the consumer by corporate interests and public-sector auditors in ways that shape and limit the possibilities that consumer has of consuming. Thus, as Miller observes, "the people and institutions proclaiming the inevitability of the market, from economists and politicians downwards, do so in the name of the consumer," and economic theory creates a chimera – the virtual consumer (rather than representing "flesh-and-blood consumers"). More broadly, "virtualism" refers to the power that models exercise in economic policy-making, where decisions are made in accordance with esoteric neoclassical abstractions rather than in relation to concrete, measurable needs. Indeed, Miller writes, "where the existing world does not conform to the academic [economist's] model, the onus is not on changing the model, testing it against the world, but on changing the world, testing us against the model." Miller's chapter also echoes Polanyi's (chapter 4) in its discussion of how nature becomes alienated as private property and, like Harper's chapter in Part VII, describes how auditing is (ironically) an ever-growing feature of today's free-market capitalism, where trust has to be certified rather than earned.

Emma Crewe and Elizabeth Harrison, as noted in this volume's Introduction, are among a cluster of innovative anthropologists in the United Kingdom whose work blurs the boundary between the anthropology of development and development anthropology. Their scholarship is informed by critical and post-structuralist theory, as well as by substantial experience working in development agencies. In the chapter below, they explore why ideas about "traditional culture" as a barrier to change persist in the development industry. Assumptions linking traditionalism to supposedly backward psychological or cultural dispositions are accompanied by tendencies for development agencies to confine anthropologists they hire to culture broker roles. Yet some development workers who perceive culture as a barrier view it as a domain to be protected rather than as an impediment to be overcome. Challenging gender relations, in this view, might risk a social upheaval or at least the failure of projects predicated on a conventional male-female division of labor. Crewe and Harrison write that "the idea that culture is worth protecting when gender is involved is inconsistent when set beside other social transformations brought about by development" – such as changes in class or caste relations that are intended to "make poorer people richer." As this and other chapters in Part IV illustrate, culture remains a fiercely contested domain in development theory and practice.

REFERENCES CITED

Geertz, Clifford, 1963 Agricultural Involution: The Processes of Ecological Change in Indonesia. Berkeley: University of California Press.
Graeber, David, 2004 Fragments of an Anarchist Anthropology. Chicago: Prickly Paradigm Press.
Klein, Naomi, 1999 No Logo. New York: Picador.

12

Agricultural Involution Revisited

Clifford Geertz

1

When I began, more than thirty years ago, to study Indonesia, indigenous cultural traditions were thought by all but a handful of economists, and probably by most anthropologists, to be a simple obstacle to social change, and especially to that particularly wished-for sort of social change called 'development'. The traditional family, traditional religion, traditional patterns of prestige and deference, traditional political arrangements were all regarded as standing in the way of the growth of properly rational attitudes towards work, efficient organisation, and the acceptance of technological change. Breaking the cake of custom was seen as the pre-requisite to the escape from poverty and to the so-called 'takeoff' into sustained growth of *per capita* income, as well as to the blessings of modern life in general. For the economists, the thing to do with the past was abandon it; for the anthropologists, to study it before it was abandoned, and then perhaps to mourn it.

In the Indonesian case, this general attitude did not long survive direct encounter with the place. As Western economists began to flow into Jakarta, from the early 1950s, as advisors, researchers or teachers, the fact that traditional patterns were not only deeply rooted but extraordinarily various and would not yield easily to advanced notions was made brutally apparent to them. The advisers were ignored, the researchers could not find reliable numbers on anything, the teachers found their students seriously unprepared. And when, a bit later, Indonesians began to be trained abroad in modern economic theory, only to return to the proliferating tensions of the late Sukarno period, when virtually every cultural difference in the so-

ciety was ideologically dramatised, the search for a view of the relation between established life ways and social transformation more adequate than 'the more you have of the one the less you have of the other' grew almost desperate.

The anthropologists (like the economists, predominantly American at that time), being the supposed 'experts' on traditional culture and about the only scholars, aside from a few Dutch philologists, operating outside Jakarta, were, naturally enough, looked to for help. But there were some serious problems.

In the first place, there were, in those early post-Independence days (the formal transfer of Sovereignty took place in the last week of 1949), very few of us – hardly more than a half dozen. Most of us, furthermore, were engaged in a single project centred on a town-village complex in eastern central Java. Worse, none of us was particularly concerned with 'development' as such. Dissertation-conscious graduate students that we all were, we were absorbed with the standard concerns of anthropology (or of anthropology professors): kinship, religion, village organisation, agricultural technique, language, exchange relations. Most of our methodological reflections, such as they were, were given over to the rather more immediate question, to us at least, of how to conduct ethnographic research in a complex civilisation with two millennia of recorded history, a highly differentiated social structure, an extraordinary level of artistic and intellectual accomplishment, and a vast population; a type of work then just getting under way in our still largely tribe and island oriented discipline. And finally, as none of us had much more than the normal college course in economics, we were rather unsure, to put it mildly, how to go about trying to be of use in making Indonesia 'modern', even if we so desired – which, distrusting the growth ethos as ethnocentric at best, imperialist at worst, we were very far from sure that we did.

The most immediate result of this non-meeting of minds between development-oriented economists and ethnographically oriented anthropologists was a sort of inverse version of the culture-as-obstacle view. As anthropological studies began to appear, in various types of barely legible pre-publication versions, they were eagerly combed – not only by economists but by political scientists, sociologists, and those anthropologists who had been brought to see the necessity of change by their encounter with mass poverty – for beliefs and practices that might aid, or be somehow brought to aid, 'modernisation'. [...] People began to talk about 'The modernity of tradition', 'The advantage of backwardness', and 'The Muslim ethic and the spirit of capitalism'.

I go into all this [...] in order to convey a sense of the immediate setting in which the main lines of debate over the relationships between Indonesia's astonishingly variegated cultural inheritance and its even more astonishingly persistent directions of change, arose and crystallised. That debate cannot be understood without some knowledge of how it took form, what it was in response to, who took part in it, what *idées reçues* it was seeking to overcome, and how shamelessly *ad hoc* it was.

It was developed, not in the halls of academe by systematic theorists, divided into sects and questioning one another's methodological premisses, ideological commitments or human sympathies (that came later), but in the field, by active researchers primarily concerned with instant matters and grateful for any leads from any quarter which might aid them in comprehending in any way a society whose complexity and depth they found overwhelming. [...]

It soon became apparent to those of us who did begin to feel the necessity of thinking seriously about the question, 'Whither Indonesia?' (even if still not persuaded that the answer was, or ought to be, 'To where we are now') that neither the culture-as-obstacle nor the culture-as-stimulus view was going to do. Both these views saw local beliefs and values as external to the processes of institutional change, impalpable forces, psychological perhaps, slowing it down here, speeding it up there, distorting it in this regard, rationalising it in that. [...] Whatever the country was doing, it was changing; and apparently it had been, in about

the same sort of way, for a very long time. Whatever it was changing to, it was but another version, perhaps one even less 'developmental', of what it was; and it looked to be doing so for a fairly long time to come.

As far as I was concerned, the massive social fact that seemed to render arguments about whether communal land tenure, the 'closed corporate village', ascetic mysticism, ascriptive hierarchy, higgling trade, or Quranic fatalism were or were not 'good for development' grandly beside the point was the enormous population density of the core areas of Indonesia and especially, of course, of the core of cores, central Java. [...] Any discussion of culture and change in Indonesia that did not have the past, present, and future of Javanese demography constantly before it would hardly be worth much. [...]

At the same time, I was hardly inclined to take a Malthusian view, within which the whole matter reduced to a question of Christian arithmetic: the abstinent prosper, the indulgent starve. What I felt was needed was the placing of Indonesian, especially rural Javanese, demographic history, in the context of the cultural forms which had surrounded it at the various stages of its course. Some of these forms, however altered, surrounded it still, and some, doubtless even further altered, seemed likely to go on surrounding it, at least for that developmentalist dream-time, the foreseeable future. Accordingly, I wrote, in the late fifties and early sixties, a short, rather schematic, rather argumentative book, *Agricultural involution: the processes of ecological change in Indonesia*, which, whatever its worth, certainly launched the sort of discussion I wished to see launched.[1] Praised and derided, used and misused, passionately dissected and aimlessly invoked, 'the involution thesis' has probably been the most extensively, if not always the most perceptively, debated theoretical idea in Indonesian studies since the second world war.[2] I had danced for rain; I got a flood.

2

The argument of *Agricultural involution* is structurally quite simple. But as this has not prevented a fair amount of the secondary presentation of it from getting important aspects of it seriously wrong, whether for tendentious reasons (White 1983) or out of mere incomprehension (Collier 1981; Knight 1982), let me restate its essentials in a breathless and unshaded, synoptic paragraph – a schema schematised.

Indonesia is not merely very heavily populated, but the internal distribution of the population is radically skewed, Java having about nine per cent of the land area and (1961) nearly two-thirds of the people; and this situation is of long duration and extended prospect. The capacity of terraced wet rice agriculture, concentrated mainly on Java, to absorb increasing labour inputs per hectare while keeping per capita output at constant or very slowly declining rates, a capacity lacking in the shifting cultivation, 'swidden' regimes of much of Sumatra, Borneo, The Celebes, and the eastern islands, has made this pattern possible. These rising levels of labour intensification were themselves enabled by the ecological characteristics of rice terraces, by a wide range of tenurial, technological, and work organisational developments, and by extensive reworkings of traditional peasant culture and social structure. The earliest stages of this process are impossible to trace circumstantially, but the systematic imposition by the Dutch of forced export crop cultivation (indigo, coffee, tobacco, and, most critically, sugar) from about 1830 powerfully accelerated it, as well as creating a (relatively) capital intensive enclave economy within the peasant economy, the connections between the two being generally symbiotic though hardly symmetrically beneficial. The ultimate result (ca. 1950) was, on the peasant side, 'involution'. This term was borrowed from the American anthropologist, Alexander Goldenweiser, who devised it to describe culture patterns which, like Gothic architecture or Maori carving, having reached a definitive form, continued nonetheless to develop by becoming internally more complicated. Javanese agriculture particularly, but Javanese social life more generally, maintained itself in the face of a steadily rising population and increasing colonial pressure by such an internal complexification, to the point that by the middle of this century a terrible impasse had come into being: an extremely large and still growing labour force, a weakening capacity to absorb it into traditional agriculture through involutional processes (even Maori carving runs out of space between the lines), and a small encapsulated, and job-poor industrial sector. On the one side, rural class polarisation of the sort found in many third world countries – even neighbouring ones such as the Philippines – was inhibited; but on the other, so was the steady reduction of the proportion of the labour force employed in agriculture that has been characteristic of development in Europe and North America. The book closed with some comparative remarks about Japan's rather different agrarian history (different, that is, from both

European and Indonesian) that I still think enlightening but which hardly anyone else seems to have grasped the point of, some whistlings in the dark about the future, and a plea for carrying forward the diagnosis of the Indonesian malaise 'beyond the analysis of ecological and economic processes to an investigation into the nation's political, social and cultural dynamics'. (1963: 154)

There were, of course, a number of other matters touched on in the book: the incipient, but ill-fated moves toward smallholder export agriculture in some parts of the so-called 'Outer Islands' during the 1920s; an analysis of swidden and wet rice terracing in ecosystem terms; a critique of both environmental determinism and the evasive response to it called 'possibilism'; a discussion of the changing strategies of colonial exploitation – trade monopoly, forced cultivation, corporate farming – on Java. But these have not much entered into the debate, perhaps because it has been, left, right, and centre, so intensely economistic in its tenor; a point I will make a great deal of in what follows. Also, some of the questions on which the book has stimulated controversy – when involution really set in; the causes, indeed the reality, of the nineteenth century 'population explosion'; the precise nature of the interaction between Dutch and Javanese agricultural technologies – seem to me empirical issues of some moment, however one might want to phrase them, but not ones whose resolutions are likely to contribute all that much towards either weakening or strengthening its central thesis. In any case, they are matters for specialists, quarrels about quarrels, and cannot be entered into here.[3] What I do want to enter into is the degree to which the call to situate the general inquiry in its cultural context has been heeded, and with what effect.

The short and brutal answers to these questions are: 'not much' and 'very little'. My own main disappointment with most of the reactions to the book – with those that are 'for' as well as those that are 'against' – is that they interpret it independently of the rest of my Indonesian work on religion, stratification, politics, bazaar trading, village organisation, family structure, etc., rather than as a prolegomena to that work, which it was intended to be. [. . .] The book has come to be regarded as rather a sport; an unaccountable lapse from my general, supposedly dreamy, approach to things. [. . .] The bulk of the involution debate has taken precisely the sort of turn the book was written expressly to forestall: that is, toward 'economism'.

'Economism' is a useful, if unlovely, term of art whose diffusion to English-speaking anthropology from French we owe perhaps as much to Marshall Sahlins (1976) as to anyone. It is the view that the moving forces in individual behaviour (and thus in society, which is taken to be an aggregate of individual behaviours or some stratificational arrangement of them) are those of a need-driven utility seeker manoeuvring for advantage within the context of material possibilities and normative constraints: 'the home-bred economizing of the market place...transposed to the explication of human society' (1976: 86). Man (and, in her own place, Woman) the strategiser, manipulating 'means-ends relations [within] an eternal teleology of human satisfactions' (1976: 85), takes the centre and most of the rest of the social stage. Custom, convention, belief, and institution are but *mise-en-scène*, the particular setting within which the universal drama of boundless desires and scarce fulfilments or, in the Marxist version, productive forces and class interests, is played out.

So far as the involution debate is concerned, 'economism' has led to what one might call the re-externalisation of cultural (or sociocultural) matters reminiscent of the culture-as-barrier *v.* culture-as-stimulus framework from which the discussion sought to escape in the first place. Now, however, the alternatives tend to be culture-as-mystifying-ideology (Alexander & Alexander 1982; Gerdin 1982; Lyon 1970) or culture-as-forceless-trapping (Collier 1981; Miles 1979; Robison 1981): collective illusion concealing (one is never quite sure from whom, although one can be sure it is not the analyst) the mechanics of power and exploitation, or collective poetry which makes nothing happen. Down deep, culture is shallow; society runs on the energies of want.

More concretely, there have been (simplifying madly a cluttered landscape of creed and theory) two main expressions of this general approach to the issues posed by Java's (and thus Indonesia's) resilient predicament: one centred around mode-of-production conceptions of one sort or another, stemming of course from Marxist perspectives transmogrified by structuralism; the other centred around rational action models, stemming from Neoclassical perspectives softened with populist sentiments.

3

The mode of production approach has concerned itself with the incorporation of Java into the world economy and, particularly, with the impact of the so-called 'Capitalist' on the so-called 'Asiatic' Mode of Production. (Or 'Tributary', or 'Mercantile', or 'Feudal': as is usual in Marxist polemic, whose form is a good deal more stable than that of either Marxist theory or Marxist praxis, types tend to multiply and distinctions to proliferate to the point where each participant ends up a party of one, at least as anxious to dispatch rival comrades as bourgeois enemies.[4]) Matters are cast on a resolutely grand and abstract scale, a dialectic of mega-concepts heavily annotated with opportune mini-facts, assembled from here, there and elsewhere, rather in the manner of a lawyer's brief – a tendency reinforced by the appearance of World Systems Theory with its cores, semiperipheries, dependencies, dominations, global divisions of labour, and other triumphant categories. [...]

The main problematic (as its adherents would be likely to call it) animating this way of addressing the issues raised by the involution thesis, is this. Has or has not Indonesian history, and again especially Javanese history, consisted, from quite early on – say, 1511, or 1602, or 1755, or 1830 (all resonant dates in Indonesian history) – of a progressive, step by irresistible step, encroachment of the logic of capitalism upon that of indigenous society such that that society has been fairly thoroughly transformed into a commoditised, class-polarised, 'dependent' system, a peripheral outlier of a formerly colonial, now neocolonial hierarchical world economy whose apex is, in Geoffrey Hainsworth's (1982: 9) mocking phrase, 'most likely located in the New York Board Room of the Chase Manhattan Bank'? Most (Knight 1982; Elson 1978*a*, 1978*b*; White 1983; Aass 1980; Alexander & Alexander 1978; van Niel 1983), though with differing degrees of assurance and for somewhat differing reasons, rather think that it has. Some, also with varying confidence and for varying reasons (Tichelman 1980; Mortimer 1973; Fasseur 1975; Onghokham 1975; Slamet 1982; Robison 1982; Kahn n.d.), rather think that it has not. The difference of opinion is not, of course, whether such an impact has occurred and been extremely significant; no one, from any perspective, has ever denied that. It is whether the force of that impact has been such as to overwhelm Javanese rural society and 'reconstitute' its peasantry in Capitalist, Man and Master terms, or whether it has been insufficiently massive or too specifically focused to overcome the 'Asiatic' constraints proper to that society, the immanent logic of the 'Tributary' or the 'Mercantile' or the 'Feudal' Mode of Production.

According to this way of thinking, the characteristic mark of capitalism is a fundamental opposition between the owners of the means of production and wage labourers, alienated from such ownership, while the characteristic mark of the Asiatic Mode of Production is one between patrimonial or feudal tribute-takers and the kin- and community-bound primary producers from whom the tribute is taken. Historical and sociological arguments therefore focus on the degree to which, at any point and generally, the first of these exploitative conditions displaces the second.

In particular, one scans the history of rural Java for signs of the implantation of a monetised market economy conjoining privately managed property to formally free labour because, from the relative presence or absence of this, everything else in some sense follows. [. . .] The economism, the hegemony of 'larger forces', lingers on.

Those who believe that at least the nineteenth- and twentieth-century history of Java [. . .] consists of the progressive class polarisation of the peasantry in rural capitalist/rural proletarian terms argue as follows. The incursion of Western forms of enterprise, especially plantation enterprise, and Western goods, especially consumption goods, individualised, or perhaps 'familised', the supposedly communal village economy to such an extent that those marginally better placed in that economy markedly increased their material position at the expense of those marginally less well placed, until a proper gulf appeared between them. A little more land, a little greater integration into regional trade networks, a little better placement in the village political hierarchy, and the passage to country-style *embourgeoisement* was launched, never after to be more than temporarily arrested. Or, to change the idiom, that necessary figure in the Marxist agrarian romance, The Kulak, was born.

Or invented. Some of the elements of this picture are reasonably easy to establish; but not, in my opinion and that of some others (Kahn n.d.; Mackie n.d.), the picture as a whole. [. . .]

The question that arises for this view is, of course, where, if this process of kulakisation has been gathering force for a century or more, all the kulaks are. If the members of the Javanese rural elite have been so exquisitely capitalistic, why aren't they rich? As we shall see, there are those who argue that such primitive accumulators, ruthlessly rationalising production, commoditising labour, and appropriating wealth, are at last, in the past decade or so, coming into being, providing, to quote Robison (1982, 57), 'a powerful

landlord/kulak class which constitutes a significant strategic basis of political support for the [Suharto regime]'. But even if that is the case (and, as we shall see, it is possible to have reservations here also), it is extremely difficult to trace a continuous history of such a forming class over the colonial and early post-Independence periods.[5] Indeed, in so far as such a history can be traced at all, it seems quite discontinuous, a series of weak, incipient movements, local spasms soon swallowed up in the general immiseration, gradual, diffuse and unrelenting, of Javanese village society.

What evidence there is seems to indicate that the overall pattern of small, very gradually declining average farm size, with a comparatively narrow, markedly downwardly skewed distribution, maintained itself from at least the beginning of the last century to at least the middle of this. The Alexanders' (1982) summary of the situation, if not the interpretation ('structural realities' *v.* 'ideological dreams') they place upon it, seems to me as close to indefeasible as one can get in the shadow-facts and floating-numbers world of Javanese rural history: [. . .] "Although the average farm size at the time of Independence was [thus] very small, it does not appear to represent a significant decline from some higher level." [. . .]

Against this general background – the gradual miniaturisation of a farming system lilliputian to start with – farmers of a dimension and disposition sufficient to qualify as proper kulaks, to the degree that they appear at all, seem but bubbles in the stream, local, fragile and evanescent, soon engulfed by the central current. If one looks hard enough, especially along hospitable coasts (Knight 1982), around enterprising sugar mills (Elson 1978b), in late developed interior regions (van Doorn & Hendrix 1983) or migrant settled frontier ones (Geertz 1965), and during particular times (export booms, crop revolutions, administrative florescences), one finds a few proprietary heads beginning to appear above the subsistence mass, but when one looks back again, after the boom has receded, the crop pattern restabilised, or the regime re-routinised, they are gone.[6] Poverty lasts, and indeed proliferates; landlords don't.

The reasons for this 'non-reproduction of a landlord class' (Alexander & Alexander 1982: 603) – to stay in the idiom – given by capitalist-transformation theorists, when they recognise the fact at all, are largely *ad hoc*, strained, and thoroughly undeveloped, which is about the best one can do when cultural phenomena are neglected, or pushed off into a mystifying ideology in favour of economistic analyses. [...]

The problem is again that the placing of cultural matters outside social process as but deceptive metaphors for changing economic relationships leaves one helpless to understand even those relationships, never mind the metaphors, to which no real attention is given anyway. The externalisation of Javanese (or Indonesian) moral, political, practical, religious and aesthetic ideas, the conceptual frame within which Javanese (or Indonesians) perceive what happens to them and respond to it, ends not with the discovery of the 'real', material determinants of change, nor with the restoration of the 'hegemony' of economics over society (Alexander & Alexander 1982: 615), but with a disjunction between them that neither the most desperate of speculations nor the most determined of dogmas can paper over. Whatever happened in pre-Independence Java – involution, class formation, or anything else – it did not consist in the progressive working out of 'the logic of capitalism', and it did not take place in a cultural vacuum.

4

This comes to a head and finds its practical point, of course, in assessments of the present situation. Whatever may or may not have happened around Pasuruan in the 1850s, Tulungagung in the 1920s, or Kediri in the 1950s, there has emerged a strong current of opinion that holds that something else is happening now – that the long awaited rural capitalist has, like some inverse Messiah, at last arrived, this time to stay, and involution, if it ever did exist, is over, as is perhaps the past in general. Here, it has been mostly agricultural economists (and their anthropological fellow travellers) with an essentially Neoclassical rather than a Marxist conception of how the rich get richer and the poor poorer who have been in the vanguard, though the contrast is far from absolute. [...] This is particularly so since the rise of Suharto's 'New Order' has induced a pervasive sense of moral dissatisfaction, mounting at times to outrage, among the overwhelming majority (myself included) of independent observers of Indonesia, whatever their political persuasions (for a useful sampling, see Anderson & Kahin 1982). Present injustices, unlike past ones, tend to drive people who would otherwise not much agree with one another into each other's arms.

The difference in the general atmosphere within which students of Indonesia, foreign or domestic,

now prosecute their studies and the one within which those of us who worked in the fifties prosecuted ours is so great as to be difficult to overestimate. [...] I say [this] to draw attention again to the fact that the substance of, in this case, the involution debate – what is genuinely at issue after the appeals to methodological gods are stripped away – cannot be effectively grasped without some understanding of the contexts within which positions are formed, research conducted and polemics launched.

To write, even about rice growing, population pressure, or land tenure, just after a successful political revolution seems to have opened up a vast range of new possibilities is one thing; to write about them just after the ignominious collapse of a hyper-populist regime, a great popular massacre and the installation of an anti-populist Government seem to have closed them up again, is quite another. The question is whether the transformation in what I can again only call 'the general atmosphere' has led to a tendency to misinterpret what is now happening in rural Java: to see a continental shift where there is but a collection of marginal adjustments to a persisting, if accelerating, erosive process. The difference between my critics and myself (or at least *one* of the differences) is that I rather think that it has.

Those who see such a continental shift find its moving causes not in mode-of-production abstractions such as 'capitalism', but in particular technical innovations, and in novel employment practices directly induced by such technical innovations, which have, in good factors-of-production style, 'resulted in shifts in the relative "economic bargaining position" of landowners, near-landless, and landless groups' in favour of landowners (Sinaga & Collier 1975: 21). Everything, from the introduction of small Japanese-made rice hullers, increasing substitution of the sickle for the famous 'finger-knife' in reaping, and the spread of lease-out commercial harvesting, to the fertilisers, insecticides, and 'miracle seeds' of the Green Revolution, is working to strengthen the strong and weaken the weak in the intensified price bargaining over the distribution of Java's (and Indonesia's) agricultural product. The cold winds of the free market in commoditised land, labour, and capital are now blowing through the landshort, labour-bloated, capital-thin village economy, little hindered by established practice or moral constraint, certainly not by fellow-feeling. Growth (about 4 per cent. a year since the midsixties [Booth & McCawley 1981; *cf.* Pauuw 1983]) is being purchased at the expense of equity.

The two most persistent themes in this sort of analysis are large scale labour displacements and the radical rationalisation (or, perhaps better, deculturalisation) of economic relationships. The introduction of labour saving innovations, even if limited, into a rural economy in which landlessness or near-landlessness runs on the average around twenty percent (Montgomery & Sugito 1980) and in the worst cases to 75 per cent or more (Stoler 1977a; cf. White 1976b: 127; Penny & Singarimbun 1973), drastically reduces employment opportunities and enables those who do have workable farms, even if miniscule, to deal with agricultural workers in strenuously iron law terms.[7] The Ricardian paradise, swelling rents and subsistence wages, finds an Asian home.

The construction of this picture rests mainly on extensive, highly focused, spot-survey type observation, almost all of them quantitative, plus a great deal of notional arithmetic, rather than on long-term, intensive and systematic, 'multiplex', community studies directed toward uncovering how village life is holistically put together. That is, it rests on what I have elsewhere called 'divergent' as opposed to 'convergent' data:

> By convergent data I mean descriptions, measures, observations, what you will, which are at once diverse, even rather miscellaneous, both as to type and degree of precision and generality, unstandardized facts, opportunistically collected and variously portrayed, which yet turn out to shed light on one another for the simple reason that the individuals they are descriptions, measures, or observations of are directly involved in one another's lives; people, who in a marvellous phrase of Alfred Schutz's, 'grow old together'. As such they differ from the sort of [divergent] data one gets from polls, or surveys, or censuses, which yield facts about classes of individuals not otherwise related: all women who took degrees in economics in the 1960s; the number of papers published on Henry James by two-year periods since World War II. (Geertz 1983:156)[8]

There is, of course, no general argument favouring one of these sorts of data over the other. Both have their uses; for some purposes they complement one another; and it is possible to get things precisely or vaguely wrong, employing either of them. But the sharp turn towards the divergent data approach does raise serious questions about the adequacy of interpretations of the contemporary scene in rural Java which flow from such a 'what you count is what you get' sort of analysis. When you are dealing with, to quote myself again (1983: 157) 'communities of multiply connected individuals in

which something you find out about A tells you something about B as well, because having known each other too long and too well, they are characters in one another's biographies', number crunching – tables, graphs, ICORs, and Gini Coefficients – may not be enough.

In any case, the estimating, categorising, counting, summing, 'percentifying', and row-and-column showing forth of things, the wild intensity of which cannot really be appreciated without looking at the studies themselves, has not resulted in much of a consensus about what is or isn't going on in rural Java so far as social change is concerned.[9]

Differences in estimates of the amount of labour displaced by mechanical hullers rise as high as an order of magnitude (Timmer 1973; Collier, Colter, et al. 1974; Timmer 1974), a small figure in astronomy, perhaps, but rather a large one in the social sciences. The percentage of the 'destitute' in rural Java (i.e. those consuming less than 180 kg of rice-equivalent a year) is claimed on the one hand to have markedly risen in recent years (Sajogyo; cited in Bose 1982) and on the other to have, about as markedly, fallen (Meesook; cited in Bose 1982). One calculator can argue that the technological innovations of the Green Revolution have radically 'widened the [income] gap between small peasants and ... big farmers' (Hüsken 1982b: 8); a second that 'the majority of the Indonesian people have benefited, in terms of material living standards, from the economic growth of [recent] years, though no doubt in an unequal degree' (Arndt 1975: 83); a third that 'there is no persuasive evidence that Indonesia's relatively egalitarian income distribution has significantly changed since 1965' (Papanek 1980: 65); a fourth that, urban Java aside, between 1970 and 1976, 'a decline in absolute poverty occurred' and 'the poor were able to increase their real expenditure more rapidly than the rich' (Pauuw 1983: 249). [...]The pulverisation of village social structure into numbers and the setting aside of cultural factors altogether as something for Islamologists, mythographers, and shadow-play enthusiasts to deal with seems to lead not to increased precision but to ascending indeterminacy.

5

Only the recontextualisation of Javanese and Indonesian economic processes within Javanese and Indonesian life as concretely enacted, the de-externalisation of culture, can reduce this indeterminacy, however slightly, and deliver answers we can have some faith in, however modest. It is not economic analysis itself that is the problem, any more than it is quantification. It is economism: the notion (to which, in fact, anthropologists, at least in Indonesia, seem rather more susceptible these days than do economists) that a determinate picture of social change can be obtained in the absence of an understanding of the passions and imaginings that provoke and inform it. Such understanding is inevitably limited. [...] But without it there is nothing but polemic, schematicism and endless measurements of amorphous magnitudes: history without temper, sociology without tone.

If the debates that have arisen around 'the involution thesis' are ever to be properly adjudicated and, at least, some reasonable determination made as to whether the present crisis in the Indonesian rural economy is one of incremental immiseration (as the returns from agriculture are distributed ever more thinly across the swelling rural population) or whether it is one of a classic, have and have-not confrontation (monopolisation of the means of production, dispossession of the working class), we shall have to know a great deal more about the concrete particulars of social life than we are likely to get from global categories, divergent data and, if I may say so, the processed sentiments of evangelical social theories. Nor is it only the particulars of peasant life, in the narrow sense, that need to be uncovered, but those of commerce and artisanry, of state-society relationships, of religious differentiation and aesthetic transformation, and much else as well.

This is not a counsel of perfection. It is not necessary to know everything to know anything. Nor is it a counsel of despair. There are other forms of dynamism than those Marxists and Liberals have already thought of, as well as other forms of disaster. It is merely a plea for us to begin again to look for answers to our questions where the answers might conceivably be. The shamelessly *ad hoc* grappling with the whole grand conglomeration of social practices, the willingness to take factual or analytical instruction from whatever direction it might come, and above all the determination to situate processes of change within local ways of going at life that marked the first phases of 'developmental theorizing' in Indonesia may have lacked a certain rigour and certainly lacked a sufficient precision. But, at least, they did not confine us to searching for lost coins only where the light was, and they did not imagine that it was advantage that made the world go round.

The case is particular, but the point is general. Whatever one may think of omega point models of social change, in which everyone ends up a class warrior or a utility maximiser (and I, obviously, think very little of them), there is no chance of analysing change effectively if one pushes aside as so much incidental music what it is that in fact is changing: the moral substance of a sort of existence. The Renaissance, the Reformation, the Enlightenment and the Romantic Reaction made the modern world as much as trade, science, bureaucracy and the Industrial Revolution; and, indeed, vast changes of social mind, they made it together. Whatever happens in Asia, Africa, and Latin America – Rough Beasts or New Forms of Architecture – it will, you can count on it, involve comparable passages, comparably vast.

NOTES

1   Geertz (1963).
2   Among the discussions (book reviews aside), pro, con, or uncertain, of the involution thesis, see: Wertheim (1964); Penny (1966); Yengoyan (1966); Lyon (1970); Larkin (1971); Penny & Singarimbun (1972); Sajogyo (1972–73); Utrecht (1973); White (1973); Sievers (1974); Hinkson (1975); van den Muijzenberg (1975); Polak (1976); Sajogyo (1976); Temple (1976); White (1976a); 1976b; Collier, Hadikoesworo et al., (1977); Stoler (1977a, 1977b); Alexander & Alexander (1978); Elson (1978a; 1978b); May (1978); Mubyarto (1978); Stoler (1978); Alexander & Alexander (1979); Hüsken (1979); Miles (1979); van Doorn (1980); Hüsken & van Schaik (1980); Kano (1980); Sherman (1980); Tichelman (1980); Zimmerman (1980); Collier (1981); Alexander & Alexander (1982); Gerdin (1982); Hüsken (1982a); Knight (1982); Mubyarto (1982); Alexander (1983), White (1983); van Niel (1983); Kahn (n.d.); Mackie (n.d.); Strout (n.d.) [...] The debate has also spilled beyond the border of Indonesia to southeast Asia more generally: see Scott (1976); Popkin (1979); cf. Brow (1976). [...]
3   In order to avoid the charge of evasion concerning these questions, and because White (1983), has seen fit to assemble polemicised versions of them in order to dismiss me as (exchangeable terms for him, apparently) a 'Parsonian', an 'infuriating' *littérateur*, and a peddler of 'imperialist software' – 'Geertz-bashing' as he winningly calls it – let me merely indicate, without argument, my present views on them. (And so as not to be misunderstood, I should remark that White's intellectual vulgarity is not generally characteristic of the involution debate, which has for the most part been conducted, from infra-red to ultraviolet, on a high and serious level; some of my most persistent critics (the Alexanders 1978, 1979, 1982,

for example) have been consistently fair, temperate and scholarly.)

1) As to whether the involution process got firmly under way during the pre-colonial period (Mubyarto 1982; May 1978), the *cultuurstelsel* ('Culture' or 'Cultivation System') period (Geertz 1963) or the 'Corporate Plantation/Ethical System' period (Tichelman 1980) I confess myself still partial to my original position. [. . .]

2) As for the causes of the population 'explosion', I find the arguments of White (1973) and Alexander (1983) for a 'labour demand theory of population', which sees the 'explosion' to be a result of Dutch pressures on the peasant labour force, in turn causal of altered reproductive practices, intriguing, speculative and unconvincing (cf. Geertz 1973). On the other hand, I would now be more inclined to doubt (with Widjojo 1970 and van der Walle 1973; cf. White 1976*b*: 60–1) a proper 'explosion' at all in contrast to a general, more or less steady rise, than I was in 1963. The history of Indonesian population dynamics, and most especially of their micro-dynamics, before 1930 remain obscure and will probably stay that way no matter how many just-so stories about lactation and post-partum sex taboos the 'labour demand' theorists can contrive to tell.

3) On the interaction of Dutch and Javanese production modes, especially in sugar, I find a number of the points made by recent historical research (Elson 1978*b*; Alexander & Alexander 1978; van Niel 1983) enlightening and usefully corrective; others (particularly ones which attribute to me positions I never held, such as that 'the ecological requirements of sugar cane are identical to those of wet rice' or that 'sugar cane technology was deliberately developed . . . by the capitalists to conform to the ecological requirements of irrigated paddy' (Sajogyo 1976)) much less so. The general 'adverse symbiotic' characterisation seems, in any case, to stand largely undamaged. Indeed, in some ways it seems to have been strengthened by exacter specification than I was able to give it.

Finally, 4) one other supposed correction to the involution thesis – the importance of housegardening in local agricultural production (Stoler 1978), was in fact mentioned in the original formulation (Geertz 1963: 96, n. 41), and indeed, as pointed out there, had been stressed and quite thoroughly investigated by the Dutch agricultural economists, well before the second world war (for a summary, see Terra 1946). Similar remarks can be made concerning my supposed neglect of dry field cultivation (Stoler 1978; cf. Geertz 1963: 91–4, 101, 106, 145).

4 For a critical discussion and an historically global application of 'mode of production' theory, see Wolf (1982), esp. pp. 73–100, 400–4.

5 Quantitative arguments here are extremely tricky to make – trickier than most of the class-polarisation theorists, who rely very heavily upon them, often seem to realise, though the usual caveats are entered and ignored. Not only are the numbers unreliable as such, many of them having been made up in some administrative office or other for purposes more rhetorical than analytic, but the great complexity of proprietary institutions within the historic Javanese [. . .] local community [. . .] makes the application of familiar measures of rural inequality based on a fee-simple view of ownership often quite misleading. [. . .]

6 As a number of people have pointed out in self-induced puzzlement (Alexander & Alexander 1982; Mackie n.d.; van Niel 1983; White 1983), I myself (Geertz 1965; 40–3, 49–51) discussed the appearance of a nascent, though soon undermined 'rural middle class of slightly larger landholders' (p. 42) during the sugar boom of the 1920s in the eastern Central Javanese Subdistrict (Pare) where I did most of the field research that gave rise to the involution idea. As in this case, it was the collapse of the sugar boom in the thirties depression that most instantly undercut this 'capitalist' development in village society, the tendency has been to regard its stultification as an ungeneralisable historical accident. But the point is (and the ungrasped point of my discussion was) that it is an ungeneralisable historical accident that keeps happening over and over again in diverse places. [. . .] A series of scattered sociological hiccoughs – small noises, soon dispersed – do not, however, an 'agrarian transition' (White 1983) make, much less 'a pervasive growth of capitalist relations and purposes' (Knight 1982: 147). What they make, given a Java in the 1970's in which probably less than one per cent of the landholdings are more than five hectares (Booth & Sundrum 1981: 184), and virtually none are more than nine (Kahn, n.d.: 25), is a howling counterfactual question.

7 [. . .] Discussions of the effect of (and rationales for) alternative cut-off points – and indeed of the robustness of measures in general – are largely absent from this literature (for a partial exception, see Montgomery & Sugito 1980). [. . .]

8 Even in those few cases in which polarisation arguments are based on extended-residence village studies (White 1976*b*; Gerdin 1982), the studies involved consist less in an attempt to determine the overall order of social relationships and the cultural forms that sustain it, than the mobilisation of quantifiable fact into objectivised categories – wealth, income, employment, work hours, labour efficiency, household expenditure, calorie consumption. They are rather more in the nature of mini-surveys than they are community ethnographies: it is magnitudes that are wanted, not pictures; findings not portrayals. For an exception, yet somewhat in tension with my own views, see Hefner (1983).

9 For examples of runaway quantophrenia, calculating everything from 'fodder eaters per household' in six

southern hamlets to 'net mending costs per year' for small *v.* medium sized perahu operators in a north coast fishing village, see White (1976*b*); (Birowo, Collier *et al.* 1974). Aside from doubts as to the possibility of obtaining reliable estimates of matters such as these by means of point-blank questions to panel-sampled peasants by intrusive investigators, my objection to much – *not all* – of this sort of work is the seeming lack of recognition of the fact that, as probabilities do not add but multiply, the chance that an extended string of calculations connected together by estimated conversion ratios, *ceteris paribus* assumptions, and various other postulated magnitudes will culminate in an accurate conclusion is vanishingly small. It is not quantification that is the problem (for some careful, less thesis-driven, and technically more sophisticated studies that have at least heard of instrument effects and error estimates, see Montgomery & Sugito 1980; Strout n.d.), but the making of very soft data look very hard by casting it into numerical rhetoric.

REFERENCES

Aass, S. 1980. The relevance of Chayanov's macro theory to the case of Java. In *Peasants in history: essays in honour of Daniel Thorner* (eds) E. Hobsbawm *et al.* Calcutta: Oxford Univ. Press.

Alexander, J. & P. Alexander 1978. Sugar, rice and irrigation in colonial Java. *Ethnohistory* 25, 207–23.

——— & ——— 1979. Labour demands and the 'involution' of Javanese agriculture. *Social Analysis* 3, 22–44.

——— & ——— 1982. Shared poverty as ideology: agrarian relationships in colonial Java. *Man* (N.S.) 17, 597–619.

Alexander, P. 1983. Labor expropriation and fertility: population growth in nineteenth-century Java. In *Culture and reproduction* (ed.) W. P. Handwerker. New York: Academic Press.

Anderson, B. & A. Kahin (eds) 1982. *Interpreting Indonesian politics: thirteen contributions to the debate* (Corn. mod. Indon. Proj., int. Rep. 21). Ithaca.

Arndt, H. 1975. Development and equality: the Indonesian case. *WldDev.* 3, 77–90.

Bernstein, R. 1983. *Beyond objectivism and relativism*. Philadelphia: Univ. of Pennsylvania Press.

Birowo, A., W. Collier *et al.* 1974. Employment and income in coastal villages of the north coast of Java. Agro-Economic Survey of Indonesia, unpublished.

Boeke, J. 1948. *The interests of the voiceless Far East: introduction to oriental economics*. Leiden: Institute of Pacific Relations.

——— 1953. *Economics and economic policy of dual societies*. Haarlem: Tjeenk Willink.

Booth, A. & P. McCawley 1981. The Indonesian economy since the mid-sixties. In *The Indonesian economy during the Suharto era* (eds) A. Booth & P. McCawley. Kuala Lumpur: Oxford Univ. Press.

Booth, A. & R. Sundrum 1981. Income distribution. In *The Indonesian economy during the Suharto era* (eds) A. Booth & P. McCawley. Kuala Lumpur: Oxford Univ. press.

Bose, S. 1982. Has economic growth immiserised the rural poor in Indonesia? A review of conflicting evidence. In *Village-level modernization in southeast Asia* (ed.) G. Hainsworth. Vancouver: Univ. of British Columbia Press.

Brow, J. (ed.) 1976. *Population, land and structural change in Sri Lanka and Thailand* (Contrib. Asian Stud. 9), Leiden: E. J. Brill.

Collier, W. 1981. Agricultural evolution in Java: the decline of shared poverty and involution. In *Agriculture and rural development in Indonesia* (ed.) G. Hansen. Boulder: Westview Press.

———, J. Colter *et al.* 1974. Choice of technique of rice milling on Java: a comment. *Bull. Indon. econ. Stud.* 10, 106–20.

———, H. Hadikoesworo *et al.* 1977. *Income, employment and food systems in Javanese coastal villages*. Athens, Ohio: Ohio Univ. Press.

Doorn, J. van 1980. Javanese society in regional perspective: some historical and sociological aspects. Rotterdam: Erasmus University (CASP).

——— & W. Hendrix 1983. The emergence of a dependent economy: consequences of the opening up of West Prinangan, Java, to the process of modernisation. Rotterdam: Erasmus University (CASP 9).

Dunn, J. 1983. Social theory, social understanding, and political action. In *Social theory and practice* (ed.) Christopher Lloyd. Oxford: Univ. Press.

Ellen, R. 1982. *Environment, subsistence and system: the ecology of small-scale social formations*. Cambridge: Univ. Press.

Elson, R. 1978*a*. *The cultivation system and 'agricultural involution'* (Wk. Pap. 14, Cent. SE. Asian Stud.). Melbourne: Monash University.

——— 1978*b*. The impact of government sugar cultivation in the Pasuruan area, east Java, during the cultivation system period. *Rev. Indon. Malays. Stud.* 12, 26–55.

Fasseur, C. 1975. *Kultuurstelsel en koloniale Baten: de nederlandse exploitatie van Java, 1840–1860*. Leiden: E. J. Brill.

Geertz, C. 1963. *Agricultural involution; the processes of ecological change in Indonesia*. Berkeley: Univ. of California Press.

——— 1965. *The social history of an Indonesian town*. Cambridge, Mass.: MIT Press.

——— 1973. Comments on White. *Hum. Ecol.* 1, 237–9.

——— 1983. *Local knowledge: further essays in interpretive anthropology*. New York: Basic Books.

Gerdin, I. 1982. *The unknown Balinese: land, labour and inequality in Lombok* (Acta Univ. Gothob.). Göteborg: Univ. Press.

Hainsworth, G. 1982. Beyond dualism? Village-level modernisation and the process of integration into national economies in southeast Asia. In *Village-level modernization in southeast Asia* (ed.) G. Hainsworth. Vancouver: Univ. of British Columbia Press.

Hefner, R. W. 1983. The problem of preference: economic and ritual change in highlands Java. *Man* (N.S.) **18**, 669–89.

Hinkson, J. 1975. Rural development and class contradiction on Java. *J. contemp. Asia* **5**, 327–36.

Hüsken, F. 1979. Landlords, sharecroppers and agricultural labourers: changing labour relations in rural Java. *J. contemp. Asia* **9**, 140–51.

——1982*a*. Regional diversity in Javanese agrarian development: variations in the pattern of involution. In *Focus on the region in Asia* (eds) O. v.d. Muijzenberg *et al.* (CASP). Rotterdam: Erasmus University.

——1982*b*. Peasants and policy in colonial and postcolonial Java: the underlying continuity (Wk. Pap. 10), Amsterdam: Univ. of Amsterdam, Anthropologisch-Scoiologisch Centrum.

——1983. Kinship, economics and politics in a central Javanese village (unpublished)

——& A. van Schaik 1980. Regionale variaties op het involutie-patroon (CASP). Rotterdam: Erasmus University.

Kahn, J. S. n.d. Indonesian peasants after the demise of involution: critique of a debate (unpublished).

——& J. Llobera 1981. Towards a new Marxism or a new anthropology? In *The anthropology of pre-capitalist societies* (eds) J. Kahn & J. Llobera. London: Macmillan.

Kano, H. 1980. The economic history of a Javanese rural society: a re-interpretation *Dev. Econ.* **18**, 3–32.

Knight, G. R. 1982. Capitalism and commodity production in Java. In *Capitalism and colonial production* (eds) H. Alavi *et al.* London: Croom Helm.

Larkin, J. 1971. The causes of an involuted society: a theoretical approach to rural southeast Asian history. *J. Asian Stud.* **30**, 755–95.

Lyon, M. 1970. *Bases of conflict in rural Java*. Berkeley: Center for South and Southeast Asia Studies.

Mackie, J. n.d. Property and power in new order Indonesia. Draft of AAS paper, 1983 meetings.

McPherson, M. 1983. Want formation, morality and the interpretive dimension of economic inquiry. In *Social science as moral inquiry* (eds) N. Haan *et al.* Berkeley: Univ. of California Press.

May, B. 1978. *The Indonesian tragedy*. London: Routledge & Kegan Paul.

Mears, L. 1961. *Rice marketing in the Republic of Indonesia*. Jakarta: Pembangunan.

Miles, D. 1979. The finger knife and Ockham's razor: a problem in Asian culture history and economic anthropology. *Am. Ethnol.* **6**, 223–43.

Montgomery, R. & T. Sugito 1980. Changes in the structure of farms and farming in Indonesia between census, 1963–73: the issues of inequality and near-landlessness. *J. SE. Asian Stud.* **11**, 348–65.

Mortimer, R. (ed.). 1973. *Showcase state: the illusion of Indonesia's 'accelerated modernisation*. Sydney: Angus & Robertson.

Mubyarto 1978. Involusi pertanian dan pemberantasan kemiskinan: kritik terhadap Clifford Geertz. *Prisma* **2**, 55–63.

——1982. The fixation of agricultural policy in Indonesia: an historical perspective. In *Village modernization in southeast Asia: the political economy of rice and water* (ed.) N. Hainsworth. Vancouver: Univ. of British Columbia Press.

——*et al.* 1983. Problems of rural development in central Java: ethnomethodological perspective. *Contemp. SE. Asia* **5**, 41–52.

Muijzenberg, O. van den 1975. Involution or evolution in central Luzon? In *Current anthropology in the Netherlands* (eds) P. Kloss & H. Calessen. Rotterdam: Netherlands Sociological & Anthropological Society.

Niel, R. van 1983. Nineteenth-century Java: variations on the theme of rural change. Southeast Asian Social Studies Association Conference Paper, Ohio Univ., Athens.

Onghokam 1975. The residency of Madiun: Priyayi and peasant in the nineteenth century. Thesis, Yale University.

Papanek, G. 1980. Income distribution and the politics of poverty. In *The Indonesian Economy* (ed.) G. Papanek. New York: Praeger.

Pauuw, D. 1983. Recent economic trends in Indonesia. *J. SE. Asian Stud.* **14**, 248–9.

Penny, D. 1966. The economics of peasant agriculture: the Indonesian case. *Bull. Indon. econ. Stud.* **5**, 22–44.

——& M. Singarimbun 1973. *Population and poverty in rural Java: some economic arithmetic from Srijarjo* (Corn. int. agr. Dev. Monogr. **41**). Ithaca.

Polak, A. 1976. Agrarian development on Lombok: an attempt to test Geertz's concept of agricultural involution. *Trop. Man* **5**, 18–45.

Popkin, S. 1979. *The rational peasant: the political economy of rural society in Vietnam*. Berkeley: Univ. of California Press.

——1981. Culture, politics, and economy in the political history of the new order. *Indonesia* **31**, 1–29.

——1982. The transformation of the state in Indonesia. *Bull. concerned Asian Scholars* **14**, 48–60.

Sahlins, M. 1976. *Culture and practical reason*. Chicago: Univ. Press.

Sajogyo 1972–3, Modernisation without development in rural Java. FAO paper.

——1976. Kata pangantar: per tanian, landasan tolak bagi pengembangan bangsa Indonesia. Introduction to the Indonesian translation of Geertz 1963: *Involusi pertanian Indonesia*. Jakarta: Bhratara.

Scott, J. 1976. *The moral economy of the peasant*. New Haven: Yale Univ. Press.

Sherman, G. 1980. What 'green desert'? The ecology of Batak grassland. *Indonesia* **29**, 143–8.

Sievers, A. M. 1974. *The mystical world of Indonesia: culture and economic development in conflict*. Baltimore: Johns Hopkins.

Sinaga, R. & W. Collier 1975. Social and regional implications of agricultural development policy, Presented at the South East Asian Agricultural Economics Association in Balikpapan, Indonesia.

Slamet, I. 1982. Cultural strategies for survival: the plight of the Javanese (CASP 5). Rotterdam: Erasmus University.

Stoler, A. 1977a. Rice harvesting in Kali Loro: a study of class and labor in rural Java. *Am. Ethnol.* **4**, 678–98.

——1977b. Class structure and female autonomy in rural Java. *Signs* **3**, 74–89.

——1978. Garden use and household economy in rural Java. *Bull. Indon. econ. Stud.* **14**, 85–101.

Strout, A. n.d. Agricultural involution and the green revolution on Java. Agro-Economic Survey, draft report.

Temple, G. 1976. Mundurnya involusi Pertanian: migrasi, kerja dan pembagian pendapatan di Jawa. *Prisma* **April**, 18–29.

Terra, G. 1946. Tuinbouw. In *De landbouw in den Indischen Archipel*, vol. 2a (eds) C. van Hall & C. van der Koppel. The Hague: Van Hoeve.

Tichelman, F. 1980. *The social evolution of Indonesia: the Asiatic mode of production and its legacy.* The Hague: Martinus Nijhoff.

Timmer, C. 1973. Choice of technique in rice milling on Java. *Bull. Indon. econ. Stud.* **9**, 57–76.

——1974. Choice of technique in rice milling on Java: a reply. *Bull. Indon. econ. Stud.* **10**, 121–6.

Utrecht, E. 1973. American sociologists in Indonesia. *J. contemp. Asia* **3**, 39–45.

Vollenhoven, C. van 1925. *De Indonesiër en zijn grond.* Leiden: Univ. Press.

Walle, E. van der 1973. Comments on Benjamin White's 'Demand for labor and population growth in colonial Java.' *Hum. Ecol.* **1**, 241–9.

Wertheim, W. 1964. *East west parallels: sociological approaches to modern Asia* The Hague: van Hoeve.

White, B. 1973. Demand for labor and population growth in colonial Java. *Hum. Ecol.* **1**: 217–36, **2**: 63–5.

——1976a. Population, employment and involution in rural Java. *Dev. Change* **7**, 267–90.

——1976b. Production and reproduction in a Javanese village. Thesis, Columbia University.

——1983. 'Agricultural involution' and its critics: twenty years after Clifford Geertz (Wk. Pap. Ser. 6). The Hague: Institute of Social Studies.

Widjojo Nitisastro 1970. *Population trends in Indonesia.* Ithaca: Cornell Univ. Press.

Wolf, E. 1982. *Europe and the people without history.* Berkeley: Univ. of California Press.

Yengoyan, A. 1966. Ecological analysis and traditional agriculture. *Comp. Stud. Soc. Hist.* **9**, 105–17.

Zimmerman, G. 1980. Landwirtschaftliche Involution in staatlich geplanten indoenischen Transmigrationsprojekten. *Geiss. geogr. Schr.* **48**, 121–8.

13

Nontraditional Commodities and Structural Adjustment in Africa

Peter D. Little and Catherine S. Dolan

Introduction

Fifteen kilometers south of Banjul, the West African capital city of The Gambia, a woman gardener stoops in the blistering sun to harvest the last of her green chili peppers. Her produce will fulfill a contract with a large export company. On the other side of the continent, 50 kilometers north of Nairobi, Kenya, a similar scenario unfolds. A peasant farmer is busily sorting her recent harvest of French green beans, packing the highest quality produce into cartons labeled "Marks and Spencer," the trademark of the popular London-based retailer. The less attractive produce is stuffed in plastic bags destined for the hotel markets of Nairobi, or ferried back to smallholder farms and fed to livestock. As in The Gambia and other African countries, the exportable produce from Kenya will go to an international airport, and then be shipped more than 5,000 kilometers to Europe, where within twenty-four hours it will embellish the shelves of grocery stores and produce stands. This process embodies a complex set of global power relations, institutional actors, and consumer demand(s) that is ambiguously labeled the "nontraditional" commodity trade.

What is a nontraditional commodity (NTC)? Barham and his colleagues, in their study of nontraditional agricultural exports in Latin America, offer a threefold typology for examining commodity types and markets:

First, an export can be nontraditional because it involves a product that has not been produced in a particular country before, such as snowpeas in Guatemala. A second type of nontraditional export is a product that was traditionally produced for domestic production but is now being

exported, like various tropical fruits. Finally, the term can refer to the development of a new market for a traditional product, such as exporting bananas to the Soviet Union. (1992, 43)

As the authors demonstrate, however, the definition encompasses larger social and political contexts, of which the physical product is merely one element. The classification process and its language reflect global changes that are closely associated with neoliberal trade policies and the structural adjustment programs of the past decade. In short, a definition cannot be divorced from the power relations embedded in the World Bank and other investment groups that largely determine what is classified as a nontraditional commodity. The taxonomic exercise has considerable consequences, since millions of dollars of third world development funds now chase NTC programs in hopes of diversifying exports, increasing trade revenues, and enhancing the private sector (Barham et al. 1992; Meerman 1997; World Bank 1989). Part of what it means to be restructured, therefore, is played out through the discourse and power relations that designate some peasants as nontraditional commodity growers and others as traditional commodity farmers.

In practice, the NTC concept is rife with contradictions and uncertainties because what constitutes a nontraditional export changes both within and across national boundaries. For example, under the US Agency for International Development (USAID) trade program in Ghana, the yam, a tuber crop with a lengthy history in West Africa, is classified as a nontraditional export while cocoa, an industrial commodity introduced by the British in the past century, is considered a traditional export product. The contradictions are even more striking in East Africa; in Uganda coffee and cotton are labeled as traditional products, but maize and some local bean varieties qualify as nontraditional commodities because they have not been exported to overseas markets in the past. The whole range of so-called specialty crops the World Bank (1989) has strongly endorsed – including "exotic" produce (e.g., mangoes), high-value horticultural products (e.g., French beans and cut flowers), and spices – fall mainly into the nontraditional category. The distinctions are often blurred, however; business entrepreneurs and politicians have been known to petition the government (usually an export promotion unit established by the World Bank or another outside agency) to have a certain product reclassified as a nontraditional export in order to receive a subsidy or credit. Thus, with one stroke of a pen, a banker or planner can reclassify an entire commodity regime, its farmers, and its traders into a grouping worthy of investment and promotion, potentially instigating agrarian changes and struggles that have widespread implications (as discussed below).

This chapter examines nontraditional commodity production and trade in Africa, addressing both the ideology (discourse) and practice (farming) of this activity. It goes beyond work such as that by Barham and his collaborators (1992), by arguing that the nontraditional commodity business creates opportunities for private capital (both international and domestic) to reconfigure African agriculture. Although the local impact of this phenomenon has been documented in some Latin American countries, with unsettling results (Paus 1988; Stonich 1991; Carter et al. 1994), the topic is relatively new for economic anthropologists working in Africa (see Dolan 1997; Little and Watts 1994). Using a recent case study of nontraditional exports in The Gambia, this chapter explores what it is like for a group of farmers to be restructured under an economic reform program that emphasizes NTCs.

Theory and Concepts

To theorize about NTCs, we draw on the work of scholars such as Friedland (1984), who [...] recognizes that each commodity is associated with specific conditions of labor, processing, and marketing from the point of production to consumption. International capital enters particular commodity systems at different points in the chain, reconfiguring their technical requirements.

Such interventions might include investment in new forms of refrigeration and processing. Commodity-specific characteristics influence [...] particular commodity systems, since labor, processing, and marketing demands are not universal. For instance, green tea must be processed within eight hours after harvest, sugarcane requires a moisture threshold for crushing, and vegetables must meet certain standards (quality, size, and taste) to be exportable. [...] In this chapter, we draw on insights of Friedland and others (Friedmann 1987; McMichael 1994; McMichael and Myhre 1991; Watts 1994) who have used a commodity systems approach to examine recent changes in global agricultural trade.

From a nonmaterialist perspective, Appadurai's (1986) work is helpful in conceptualizing the cultural dimensions of commodities. The introduction to his book, *The Social Life of Things: Commodities in Cultural Perspective*, includes three points that are useful to analysis of NTCs. First, he shows that the values attached to certain commodities reflect power relations that often circumscribe local communities producing for global markets; local producers and consumers "are intimately tied to larger regimes of value defined by large-scale polities" (Appadurai 1986, 30). Although his analysis emphasizes European monarchies' valuation of commodities, the ways medieval European monarchs and courts shaped production by defining goods such as silk rugs as "royal" items are similar to international capital's influence on what types of commodities (e.g., specialty produce) third world producers emphasize.

Second, Appadurai's schema highlights the importance of larger – often hidden – knowledge relations that characterize commodities. In our case an NTC embodies substantially more than the particular knowledge of an agricultural commodity; it carries with it a set of knowledge relations about private sector investment, the restructuring of state policies in the South, and neoliberal trade philosophy. This knowledge is not shared between the point of consumption (the North) and the workplace (the South) of commodity production, since what is "read into the commodity" varies sharply across positions in global trade (Appadurai 1986, 41). Without necessarily comprehending the nonlocal context of her actions, the Gambian gardener mentioned earlier is part of a larger agenda that aims to fundamentally restructure African economies.

A third significant element of Appadurai's discussion is the notion that, like all social things, commodities experience distinct life cycles. These sequences reflect complex historical and political relations that go beyond changing conditions of supply and demand. As Mintz (1985) has so eloquently demonstrated, even sugar was at one time an exotic commodity that only graced the tables of royalty and rich merchants. As sugar became more widely available and culturally acceptable to the masses, it was transformed into a necessity. There are myriad examples of the conversion of a nontraditional or exotic commodity into a common or "humble" one (the latter term is Appadurai's [1986, 40]). Illustrations include bananas and pineapples; both are important tropical export products that have been transformed from exotic to common commodities during this century. Some vegetables categorized as exotic, such as French beans and chili peppers, are now so widespread in European markets that they might be destined for relabeling.

While this chapter acknowledges the power of symbols and discourse, they can only account for part of the NTC production story. The rest emerges from the farm fields and often harsh labor conditions and relationships that characterize this activity.

Historical Context

The 1980s witnessed a rapid increase in low-income farmers' participation in NTC production. As prices of classical export crops such as sugar and cocoa declined during that decade, many farmers, who were actively encouraged by governments and development agencies, pursued high-value, "niche" crops such as spices and certain vegetables. In The Gambia, for example, the share of groundnuts in total foreign exchange earnings fell from 45 percent in the early 1980s to 12 percent in 1991–1992 (Hadjmichael, Rumbaugh, and Verreydt 1992). Confronted with declining incomes from traditional export commodities, governments and international development agencies initiated campaigns to diversify export production among smallholders and other producers. The campaigns entailed significant alterations in the organization of smallholder production and marketing, including the promotion of agribusiness and contract farming (see Little and Watts 1994). Such changes are part of larger transformations in global commodity systems and trade; high-value exports and foods have partly compensated for declining traditional export incomes in much of the third world, including Africa. Many policymakers view these structural changes in agriculture as optimal solutions

for resolving agricultural and trade dilemmas faced by the poorest countries (World Bank 1989).

Growth in nontraditional exports during the past fifteen years is best illustrated by examining the global fresh fruit and vegetable (FFV) industry, which has involved strong participation by both agribusiness firms and smallholders. Growing demand for fresh produce in northern countries, particularly Japan, as well as technical innovations in refrigerated storage and transportation (Watts 1994, 37) have increased fresh fruit and vegetable trade, which grew annually by more than 9 percent from 1965 to 1985 (Islam 1990, cited in Watts 1994, 37). According to Watts (1994, 37), when processed fruits and vegetables are included, the global fruit and vegetable trade represents "the fourth most important commodity group in world agricultural trade." Although a few key countries such as Mexico and Thailand account for most of the growth in horticultural exports, African agriculture is affected nonetheless by the boom. Watts (1994, 39) remarks on the continent's surge in exports:

> Between 1976 and 1988 sub-Saharan Africa's horticultural exports doubled.... By the 1990s they were third in value, in excess of tea, cotton, and tobacco and only trailing coffee and cocoa. [...] In all of these cases, contracting and subcontracting arrangements were central to the dispersion and growth of the horticultural industry worldwide.

Most of Africa's horticultural produce goes to Europe, where demand for African produce is especially strong in the winter months when the region's own production of fruits and vegetables is limited. Countries such as South Africa and Kenya, whose air connections to Europe are frequent and generally reliable, have a significant advantage over most other African nations where international air traffic is minimal. Trade statistics demonstrate South Africa's and Kenya's overwhelming dominance in African horticultural exports.

Growth in nontraditional exports has accompanied changes in the economic policies of developing countries and international donor agencies. During the 1980s, when African governments confronted threats of national bankruptcy and depleted foreign exchange reserves, a radically different approach to development emerged (or reemerged, some might say). The new paradigm advocated private-sector development with an emphasis on export-led growth, monetary and fiscal reform, and government deregulation in agricultural production and marketing. Structural adjustment programs (SAPs) imposed by the International Monetary Fund (IMF) and the World Bank became part of the new development agenda, and nontraditional export activities were central to reforms that promoted export diversification. These programs included expansion of niche-market exports such as spices, flowers, and specialty fruits and vegetables. The need for production and marketing flexibility and perceived failures of the state in agricultural export ventures became justifications for a private-sector–led strategy (see World Bank 1981, 1989).

In Africa, the notion of a nontraditional commodity took on powerful associations. [...] While production and trade in traditional export commodities symbolize the old statist policies and "backward-looking" programs of agriculture, the NTC business is seen as progressive, export-driven, and entrepreneurial. In short, NTC production signifies the necessary replacement of Africa's previous parastatal-controlled agriculture by market-savvy private actors (including transnational companies), fiscally conservative budget reformers, and true believers in the benefits of global commerce.

The International Finance Corporation (IFC) and other international and bilateral donors have been important sources of funding for export diversification projects. USAID alone now supports more than twenty-five export diversification programs.[1] In sub-Saharan Africa, where structural adjustment programs exist in more than 80 percent of the countries, the promotion of NTC exports is tied closely to austerity measures that often provoke political instability. The Economic Recovery Programme (ERP) introduced in The Gambia in 1985, one of the most far-reaching programs on the continent, included strong fiscal and other incentives to encourage both private firms and farmers to invest in niche-market activities. Here, as elsewhere, government helped to establish an export promotion council within the country and has promoted international trade shows to solicit markets for the country's exports. The Gambian export promotion council planned to depict a ripe mango and egg-plant on its brochures, with the caption: "The Gambia means more than beautiful beaches and friendly people."[2]

Nontraditional Commodities in The Gambia

The Gambia is a small country of just 1.1 million people on the West African coast (Kakoza et al.

1995). Its annual per capita income of less than US\$300 places it among the twenty poorest countries in the world. It inherited a British colonial structure centered on control of the Gambia River, a wedge in French-controlled Senegal. At independence, The Gambia's private sector included mostly Europeans and other non-Africans. As in so many newly independent states, the government quickly moved to gain control over lucrative export commodities that had benefited Africans very little. Before the ERP, The Gambia adopted a policy of direct intervention in agricultural production and trade of groundnuts, the country's main export crop, and established a state marketing board to ensure government profits from this commodity.

Under the ERP, donor aid was to transform The Gambia into the "Gateway to West Africa" (Kakoza et al. 1995, 3). [...] Foreign aid accounted for more than 50 percent of the operating budgets of many Gambian government ministries, and one product (groundnuts) accounted for more than 40 percent of agricultural export earnings. Given such high dependence on foreign aid, it is not surprising that The Gambia became one of the first African countries to succumb to World Bank and IMF structural adjustment programs. Indeed, by the end of the 1980s it was heralded as one of the most successful cases of structural adjustment on the continent, with a reduced budget deficit, a growing export portfolio, and an environment conducive to private foreign investment (Jabara 1990; Radelet and McPherson 1995). The rationale for the 1994 coup, however, included public disenchantment with corruption and poor results of the privatization program, which incited public demonstrations.

Before the coup, President Sir Dawda K. Jawara and his party were very committed to economic reform. [...] By the early 1990s, however, the country faced a major budget deficit and unprecedented corruption. The Jawara government's failure to address corruption "increased the public perception that ordinary Gambians were being asked to sacrifice in the name of reform, while Jawara allowed his colleagues to reap the benefits" (Grindle and Roemer 1995, 315).

The Nontraditional Commodity Drive

By the mid-1980s NTC promotion had taken hold in The Gambia as the country attracted transnational investment and emerged as an important regional exporter of horticultural produce to Europe. [...] The Gambia exported horticultural products before the 1980s as well, but the volume was minimal. Investment in NTCs was partly a response to decline in the world price of groundnuts, historically the mainstay of The Gambian economy. Despite widespread official enthusiasm for the NTC subsector (see *Task Force ... 1993*), annual earnings remained below US$10 million in 1994.

[...] Horticultural exports [...] are almost entirely under the control of a few private companies and individuals. The government has eliminated export taxes on horticultural produce and tariffs on certain inputs and, with donor funding, has subsidized infrastructure and marketing services for export firms. Some of the NTC export farms received funding from the IFC, the Commonwealth Development Corporation (United Kingdom), and the African Development Bank (the latter is financed by the World Bank, USAID, and several other Western institutions). Nonetheless, exporters believe that the government and international aid donors have done very little for them.[3]

The Gambia's most important horticultural exports, in order of importance, are eggplant, mangoes, chilies, okra, green beans, a range of Asian vegetables (e.g., kerela and dudhi), and flowers. Most Gambian produce exports go to the United Kingdom, though other European countries import these products as well. The Gambia's export trade has particularly targeted the United Kingdom's ethnic markets that serve the growing Southeast Asian immigrant community. [...]

The productive and institutional arrangements of export horticulture incorporate Gambian farmers into international agro-food systems. Export horticulture trade and production systems are quite diverse, ranging from discrete traders to large-scale corporations. Market concentration is increasing; since 1989 the proportion of total horticultural exports accounted for by the two largest firms has grown by an estimated 30 percent. [...]

Reality at the Workplace

The supermarket chains in Europe know nothing about farming or the needs of farmers. They only want a certain size and color of vegetable and think that a farmer should be able to produce this every time. They think our farms are like factories where we can turn out a bean of 10 centimeters every time. Farming is not like factory

work. (Gambian farmer and exporter, 4 May 1994)

The exporters ask us to grow chilies and to harvest them when they are green. Then they don't come to pick them up and pay us. We have a lot of problems with these exporters. There is no local market for green chilies so we will not grow them unless we have a written contract. (Gambian gardener, 18 February 1993)

Who is involved in the production and export of horticultural products? What realities underlie an industry so many organizations have praised? When horticultural exports began to take off in the mid-1980s, policymakers hoped that village small-holders and members of communal gardens,[4] especially women growers, would benefit from this boom. Even some local nongovernmental organizations (NGOs) jumped on the NTC bandwagon: it has been assumed "that vertical integration by vegetable producers is more desirable than other market interventions" (Sumberg and Okali 1987, cited in Daniels 1988, 32).

[...] Some local villagers do grow produce for export firms, but their numbers have declined since the 1980s. [...] More than 90 percent of export produce is grown directly on export farms, using hired laborers, rather than by small-scale gardeners. Until the 1994 coup, however, official rhetoric stressed the importance of small farmers in NTC activities and suggested that they benefited immensely from export diversification and market reforms.[5]

Horticultural export production in The Gambia is practiced in several types of production units: communal or village gardens, household or "backyard" gardens, and export or large farm units. A fourth category of vegetable producer recently emerged in sizable, peri-urban villages, where the small export producer (owner of two to six irrigated hectares) is typically a male who also has an urban job. These farms are referred to as "small commercial farms" and should be distinguished from both the larger export (commercial) farms and the smaller local gardens (communal or household). While they represent a relatively small percentage of total producers (less than 1 percent), they are favored by some horticultural firms who contract them for production and provide a means to participate in the export trade.

Most communal and household vegetable producers are women who engage in such production after the rice growing season ends in November. [...] Communal gardens, found in most peri-urban settlements around the capital city of Banjul, are usually 2 to 15 hectares, with approximately 5 hectares per communal garden allocated to vegetable production.

Export farms range in size from about 10 to 400 hectares, but most of their owners control additional uncultivated land. They rely almost solely on laborers hired from neighboring countries or nearby villages and urban centers. Field and farm managers supervise this labor. Most of these farms use motorized boreholes, and some have recently introduced sprinkler irrigation systems. They also depend on improved seed varieties, fertilizers, and pesticides, and incur much higher capital costs per land unit than do other farms.

In 1993 there were about fifteen export farms in the peri-urban areas, as was the case in 1988 (Daniels 1988). The average size of export farms, however, was much larger in the early 1990s than it was in the late 1980s. [...] This expansion further diminished the smallholder sector and ignited local resentment. [...]

Approximately 20 percent of Banjul's peri-urban export farms are vertically integrated into the marketing and investment operations of larger overseas companies, which allows the firms to substantially reduce production costs in the fresh produce trade. These firms include subsidiaries of parent companies operating in Europe that provide financial, technical, and marketing services. [...] Although large farms confront some of the same problems that other horticultural enterprises encounter (such as air cargo and storage constraints), they hold a competitive advantage over most producers, as confirmed by their better trade and financial performances.

Labor recruitment is critical to the operation of export farms, as well as to smallerscale producers of horticulture. An important institutional mechanism in The Gambia for acquiring labor is contract farming, a phenomenon that has strong roots in neoliberal economic policies (see Little and Watts 1994). [...]

Labor Relations and Contract Farming

Contract farming involves at least three types of production arrangements: communal gardens, small commercial growers, and export farmers. Peasants are involved in the NTC export trade as contracted outgrowers (a form of "waged" labor) or by working directly for export farms or firms. As mentioned, their role as contract farmers has declined in recent years; as a result, some peasants

now work as unskilled laborers (for minimal wages) for large export farms.

Contracting with communal gardens

Many exporters we interviewed in 1993 relied initially on communal gardens for procuring export produce while they were developing their own farms. [...] As the farm sector grew in the late 1980s and early 1990s – aided by liberal land policies and concessions (Roth et al. 1994) – attention shifted from small-scale gardeners to large export farms. [...]

Data from communal gardeners point to a similar trend. [...] Exporters prefer to use communal gardens to grow labor-intensive crops, such as chilies, and to use small commercial growers for other crops, such as Asian vegetables.

Exporters usually do not deal directly with individual members of communal gardens; rather, they work through the scheme management committee. An agreement, which usually does not entail a written contract, is made with the scheme committee itself and specifies the amount of land to be allocated to each contracted crop and the inputs the exporter will supply [...]. Payment typically occurs after the exporter is reimbursed, which means farmers may wait four to six weeks for compensation. In practical terms, then, gardeners actually provide credit and subsidize large-scale exporters.

In addition to payment delays, exporters frequently reject gardeners' produce, leaving the scheme with crops it cannot sell locally. [...] Women growers also complain about low prices and the labor intensity of growing many of the contracted crops. They argue that the local market – especially sales to tourist hotels – is more reliable and lucrative than growing for export.

Exporters, however, explain the decline of contract growing very differently. Their most frequent complaint about contracting with communal gardens is the problem of convincing growers to begin work on their gardens before December; most communal gardeners do not start work on export crop production until after they have harvested their rice in November. By the time they harvest their first vegetable crop in late January or February, the winter export season is well under way. A related difficulty is that of coordinating harvest schedules to meet export market demands. Exporters frequently complain that despite agreements to harvest at a certain date, gardeners may be delinquent because of other agricultural demands or social obligations, such as funerals or weddings. On more than one occasion in 1993 exporters contended that they could not fill orders or meet commitments for air cargo space because vegetables were not harvested on time.

Finally, exporters complain about the need to work through scheme committees to reach agreements on crops and prices. Although some would prefer to contract directly with individuals, many farmers prefer the current arrangement because it reduces their own liability under the contract and they do not want to work directly with exporters. Exporters rarely mention lack of high-quality vegetable production as a reason for not relying on communal gardens. Nevertheless, as long as export farms can acquire large tracts of land in peri-urban areas and the cost of farm labor remains relatively low, communal gardeners' participation in the export business is likely to diminish further.

Contracting with small commercial growers

In recent years a small but important class of commercial growers who concentrate almost exclusively on market production has emerged. In contrast to other vegetable growers, most of these producers are males who have significant sources of nonfarm income, including government positions in Banjul. [. . .] These small commercial producers contract with export farms to grow crops such as eggplants, French beans, and Asian vegetables. In return for selling their produce at an agreed price, exporters provide them with seeds, fertilizer, and, in some cases, diesel fuel.

In contrast to communal gardens, this category of contract farming appears to be increasing in importance. [. . .] In some respects they operate like mini-export farms, relying on hired farm managers and labor, and using expensive farm inputs. But rather than exporting directly, they grow under contract for large export firms that sell the produce overseas.

Contracting with other export farms

In addition to exporting their own produce, more than 40 percent of all export farms – especially the small enterprises – grow export crops, usually under contract, for the two largest export farms. Nearly one-third of export farms sell most of their export-quality produce through one large farm in The Gambia that is owned by a transnational firm with an import subsidiary in the United Kingdom.

This trend is increasing as smaller firms find it difficult to establish viable overseas market contacts and to secure air cargo space. [. . .] One of the smaller export farmers recalled in 1993 a recent instance when they had to "feed their cattle French beans" because they could not secure adequate cargo space and the local market was unable to absorb the produce.[6] Acquiring cargo space often involves a series of "rent payments" to airport employees. Small export farmers are willing to sell produce at lower prices under contract to avoid these transport and marketing problems.

Waged Laborers

Employment on large farms often is tied to the original land agreements between owners and village authorities. Because NTC activities are concentrated in the Banjul region, where population and land values are highest, "surplus" land is not easy to acquire. With government intervention, large farmers either acquired land by having it officially "titled" by local government authorities or by leasing it from villages. Land titling – especially in export agricultural zones – was encouraged under the structural adjustment program. Not coincidentally, those who acquired titles for large plots often held important political positions. When an exporter approached a village to acquire land for NTC activities, he or she frequently arranged with the *alkalo* (chief) to employ local laborers in return for use of the land. Interviews with several *alkalo* suggested that the hiring of villagers was the main reason that they agreed to these transactions.[7] At least one-quarter of such informal arrangements became an integral part of land acquisitions. In return for hiring villagers, a company was allowed access to landholdings that in some cases exceeded 100 hectares.

The employment-for-land deals, however, did not always produce stable relationships. Disputes over land both in the horticultural and coastal tourist areas were frequent and on more than one occasion villagers vehemently protested to the government about land deals. [. . .]. "We have let the large farmers use our land to grow their crops, but they have not hired our people as they promised. When they do so they pay us wages that are lower than we can earn working on a local farm."[8] Outside laborers are brought in for a number of reasons: (1) they are not "involved with local politics" and do not complain to local chiefs; (2) local peasants – who have their own farms – sometimes refuse to work on export farms, or do not reliably adhere to a rigid work regime; and (3) outside laborers are willing to work for very low wages, thereby deflating compensation levels for other laborers.

On large farms [. . .] wages are no higher than payments on local food farms and in some cases they are lower. Horticultural employment is seasonal, with most unskilled laborers being laid off during the summer months. Since employment on large farms tends to be a strategy of last resort for local laborers, other options, such as small-scale gardening and trading, are more lucrative.

Our survey data on wage laborers and employment show that most employment involves casual, low-paying positions at or below the minimum wage; skilled positions tend to go to non-Gambians. [. . .]

There is a salient gender division of labor on export farms. Women are hired for the more exacting tasks of planting, weeding, and picking; men engage in field preparation, irrigation work, and packing – tasks that hold less significance for the final product. [. . .] Work conditions are very difficult and shifts of up to ten hours are not uncommon in peak months. [. . .]

There are virtually no time-series data for employment on export farms, but some changes seem to have occurred since the 1980s. First, employment has been increasingly concentrated among the two largest horticultural companies, which in 1993 accounted for about 76 percent of total employment in the sample. [. . .]

The lack of alternative employment opportunities in rural and peri-urban areas and the displacement of small farmers (potential laborers) by the expansion of export farms may help to explain low wages. [. . .] Low levels of compensation suggest it is unlikely that living standards of most employees on NTC enterprises improved during the boom years.

Under one donor agency's program the consulting firm of a well-known transnational agribusiness firm studied the Gambian horticultural subsector and made recommendations on how to improve it (Cargill Technical Services, Ltd, 1994). The firm recommended that no export farm with less than US$1.5 million in start-up costs and 100 hectares of irrigated NTCs should be encouraged, which would effectively eliminate all but one of the country's exporters. [. . .] Noting that most labor in The Gambia is employed on a daily basis, the report states that "It would significantly improve productivity if piecework payment was introduced" (Cargill Technical Services, Ltd., 1994, 65). Most local chiefs have resisted piece-

rate payment ("it is not the local custom"), a form of labor relations that can be highly exploitative in the competitive horticultural market. (For a case of this in Kenya, see Little in Little and Watts, 1994.) Caught up in the NTC fever and its expectations, the Gambian government did not dispute the international consultants' conclusions, although many local entrepreneurs strongly contested their findings about farm size and capital requirements.

Conclusion

This chapter has combined economic and cultural analyses of nontraditional commodities by examining the social, symbolic, and material relations that embody the nontraditional export trade. The wide disparity between the official discourse of NTC production and its actual practice should not be surprising to most who have studied commodity relations in poor countries. NTCs are a powerful symbol of European hegemony, suggesting images such as cut flowers gracing the tables of an affluent couple. NTCs in The Gambia, however, have done little to improve the material welfare of farmers; NTC activities involve fewer farmers, yield smaller incomes, and incur greater risks than development agencies would like us to believe. As we have illustrated here, something as small as an "exotic" vegetable entails a set of global relations, symbols, and labor processes that encompass bankers, peasants, and large bureaucracies. The process discussed in this chapter is merely one example of a historical pattern described by Appadurai (1986) in which the affluent define the conditions and values of commodities produced by the poor.

[. . .]

NOTES

1 Personal communication with USAID official, The Gambia, 9 May 1994. From Peter Little's field notes.
2 Author's interview with Gambian government officials involved in export promotion. From Peter Little's field notes.
3 Peter Little's field notes.
4 These are irrigated gardens that have been established on communal land allocated to a group of farmers (usually women) by a chief. They have been the "favorite project" of many NGOs and some development agencies who have invested considerable funds in them.
5 In a recent study of Gambian traders we found that even these quintessential private-sector actors feel

they have benefited very little from market reform programs (Little and Dolan 1993).

6   Gambian exporter. Interview by Peter Little, Sere-kunda, The Gambia, 16 February 1993.

7   Most large farm owners did not consider insecure land rights to be a problem, probably because they knew that the state could be invoked in cases where chiefs tried to repossess land on behalf of villagers.

8   Local elder. Interview by Peter Little, Pirang village, The Gambia, 19 May 1993.

REFERENCES

Appadurai, Arjun. 1986. Introduction: Commodities and the Politics of Value. In Arjun Appadurai, ed., *The Social Life of Things: Commodities in Cultural Perspective*. Cambridge: Cambridge University Press.

Barham, Bradford, Mary Clark, Elizabeth Katz, and Rachel Schurman. 1992. Nontraditional Agricultural Exports in Latin America. *Latin American Research Review* 27(2): 43–82.

Cargill Technical Services, Ltd. 1994. Farm Strategies Study: Fruits/Vegetables and Flowers in The Gambia: Interim Report. Oxfordshire, U.K.: Cargill Technical Services.

Carter, Michael, Bradford Barham, and Dina Mesbah. 1994. Agroexport Booms and the Rural Resource Poor in Chile, Guatemala, and Paraguay. Unpublished manuscript. Department of Agricultural Economics, University of Wisconsin at Madison.

Daniels, Lisa. 1988. The Economics of Staggered Production and Storage for Selected Horticultural Crops in The Gambia. Master's thesis, Department of Economics, University of Wisconsin at Madison.

Dolan, Catherine. 1997. Tesco Is King: Gender and Labor Dynamics in Horticultural Exporting, Meru District, Kenya. Ph.D. diss., Department of Anthropology, State University of New York, Binghamton, N.Y.

Friedland, William. 1984. Commodity Systems Analysis. *Research in Rural Sociology* 1: 221–235.

Friedmann, Harriet. 1987. The Family Farm and the International Food Regimes. In Teodor Shanin, ed., *Peasants and Peasant Society*. Oxford: Blackwell.

Grindle, Merilee, and M. Roemer. 1995. Insights from the Economic Recovery Program for Sub-Saharan Africa. In Steven Radelet and Malcolm McPherson, eds., *Economic Recovery in The Gambia: Insights for Adjustment in Sub-Saharan Africa*. Cambridge, Mass.: Harvard University Press.

Hadjmichael, Michael T., Thomas Rumbaugh, and Eric Verreydt. 1992. *The Gambia: Economic Adjustment in a Small Open Economy*. International Monetary Fund (IMF) Occasional Paper 100. Washington, D.C.: IMF.

Islam, Nurul. 1990. *Horticultural Exports of Developing Countries: Past Performances, Future Prospects, and Policy Issues*. Research Report No. 80. Washing-ton, D.C.: International Food Policy Research Institute (IFPRI).

Jabara, Cathy. 1990. *Economic Reform and Poverty in The Gambia: A Survey of Pre-and Post-ERP Experience*. Washington, D.C.: Cornell University Food and Nutrition Policy Program.

Kakoza, J., R. Basanti, T. Ehrleck, and R. Prem. 1995. *The Gambia—Recent Economic Developments*. IMF Staff Country Report No. 95/123. Washington, D.C.: IMF.

Little, Peter D., and Catherine Dolan. 1993. *Horticultural Production and Trade in the Peri-Urban Area of Banjul, The Gambia*. Binghamton, N.Y.: Institute for Development Anthropology.

Little, Peter D. and Michael J. Watts, eds., 1994. *Living under Contract: Contract Farming and Agrarian Transformation in Sub-Saharan Africa*. Madison: University of Wisconsin Press.

McMichael, Philip, ed. 1994. *The Global Restructuring of Agro-Food Systems*. Ithaca, N.Y.: Cornell University Press.

McMichael, Philip, and David Myhre. 1991. Global Regulation versus the Nation-State: Agro-Food Systems and the New Politics of Capital. *Capital and Class* 43: 83–105.

Meerman, Jacob. 1997. *Reforming Agriculture: The World Bank Goes to Market*. Washington, D.C.: The World Bank.

Mintz, Sidney. 1985. *Sweetness and Power*. New York: Basic Books.

Paus, Eva, ed. 1988. *Struggle Against Dependence: Non-Traditional Export Growth in Central America and the Caribbean*. Boulder, Colo.: Westview Press.

Radelet, Steven, and Malcolm McPherson. 1995. Epilogue: The July Coup d'Etat. In Steven Radelet and Malcolm McPherson, eds., *Economic Recovery in The Gambia: Insights for Adjustment in Sub-Saharan Africa*. Cambridge, Mass.: Harvard University Press.

Roth, Michael, Ben Carr, and Jeff Cochranc. 1994. *Land Rights and Intra Household Employment and Resource Use in the Peri-Urban Area of Banjul, The Gambia*. Madison, Wisc.: Land Tenure Center.

Stonich, Susan. 1991. The Promotion of Non-Traditional Exports in Honduras. *Development and Change* 22: 725–755.

Sumberg, James E., and Christine Okali. 1987. *Workshop on NGO-Sponsored Vegetable Gardening Projects in The Gambia: A Report and Summary*. Banjul, The Gambia.

Task Force on the Formulation of a National Industrial Policy. 1993. Banjul, The Gambia: Ministry of Trade, Industry, and Employment.

Watts, Michael J. 1994. Life Under Contract: Contract Farming, Agrarian Restructuring, and Flexible Accumulation. In Peter D. Little and Michael J. Watts, eds., *Living under Contract: Contract Farming and Agrarian Transformation in Sub-Saharan Africa*. Madison: University of Wisconsin Press.

World Bank. 1981. *Accelerated Development in Sub-Saharan Africa: An Agenda for Action*. Washington, D.C.: The World Bank.

———. 1989. *Sub-Saharan Africa: From Crisis to Sustainable Growth*. Washington, D.C.: The World Bank.

14

Market Mentalities, Iron Satellite Dishes, and Contested Cultural Developmentalism

Louisa Schein

Snapshots of Consumerism

Andrea Koppel of CNN perches above Beijing in the midst of the much-anticipated 1997 summit visit of Chinese President Jiang Zemin to key landmarks of state, history and capitalism in the US.[1] Koppel is reporting on the Chinese economy with the familiar and always only thinly masked emphasis on market prospects for Americans. The camera surveys sumptuous goods displayed in sparkling Beijing department stores as she comments that here you can have 'almost anything your heart desires'. As the viewer is shown washing machines and fashionable clothes expensive enough to be enclosed in individual plastic coverings, she exclaims: 'What's remarkable is the number of people who have money to spend!'

But how many are we talking about? The careful eye notices that most 'customers' in these shops are pictured *browsing* through luxury goods, not handing over their meagre earnings at the cash registers. Indeed, what strikes the visitor to department stores in China's shiny urban hubs is the proportion of people who can be seen enjoying the commodity space of these temples to consumerism without ever purchasing anything. As the Asian economic crisis took hold on the mainland in December 1997, the American press struck a note of alarm: Asians were failing to live up to their reputation as the world's most promising consumers.[2] Calculations were made about the potential impact on the American economy, and astonishment was registered that buyers were failing to meet the grand expectations set out for them upon their enmeshment in the global econ-

omy. By the decade's end, there were consumption booms taking place all over the country, but market experts still saw the effort of breaking into the Chinese market as primarily one of what we might call the 'interpellation' of the consuming subject, the pedagogical program of inculcating very particular desires for acquisition rather than expectation of actual purchases. How can we make sense of the aggressive propagation of a rich culture of consumerism not commensurable with the exchange practices of acquiring commodities for money?

Transforming Prestige

The craze for children's 'Transformer' toys that swept China's affluent cities in 1989 illustrates eloquently the dilemmas posed by desires that exceed the means of new consumers.[3] Captivated by a Hasbro television cartoon series featuring the Transformer characters that had been broadcast during New Year and Chinese Spring Festival in Beijing, Shanghai and Guangzhou, urban children developed a wild craving to possess the toys regardless of the financial resources of their parents. Alarmed stories of parental anguish accumulated as debates emerged in the Chinese press about this latest form of commodity enslavement:

A boy of four or five was rolling about on the ground, shouting 'I want it, I want it'. The father tried to drag him up, saying 'that thing costs a hundred yuan or more, buy it and we won't eat this month' . . . all rushed to the toy counter. Some took out the money and paid. Others hesitated because of the high prices. But children refused to leave accusing their parents of being liars. . . . - Can those who cannot afford them get away with it? 'No.' The 'little master', who is too young to be considerate, sees classmates playing [with Transformers] and cannot help but ask for them. . . . Those who don't have Transformers will easily develop a sense of inferiority.[4]

For those whose skinny wallets have excluded them from acquiring newfangled commodities, there has indeed been envy and frustration – heralding perhaps the rise of a newly demarcated class system within China. The comparison between schoolmates, the sense of inferiority, and the pressure experienced by parents chronicled in the Transformer craze all point to the emergence of everfiner calibrations of social stratification indexed through key objects or styles of consumption. But in the interior – in, for instance, the southwest of China where I did fieldwork – there is also another form of exclusion. The majority of goods promoted in the slick – and often erotically charged – advertising that penetrates mountains and deserts through television, radio and print are simply not distributed there.

Purchasing 101

Kaili is a newfangled city, established with the founding of the capital of the Miao and Dong autonomous prefecture of Southeast Guizhou in 1956. Inhabiting the small metropolis are some minorities and a majority of Han, many of whom are families relocated from other parts of China during the Maoist years. From the perspective of Miao and Dong peasants in the region, Kaili is a shopping town – despite the fact that the purchasing power of most means meagre acquisitions. On a brisk December morning in 1999, I stumbled on a form of shopping I had not even begun to imagine. A small lane led off one of Kaili's main streets and, at 7.30 a.m., bustled with the activity of more than twenty street vendors. Making their way through the smoke and steam that issued from coal-burning fires on which were cooked all manner of morning delicacies, were the shoppers. None was more than 8 or 9 years old.

My eyes began to focus on the goods for sale. In addition to fried patties of sticky rice, dough and meats, there were toys and sweets, enticingly arranged on tables as low as a foot high. There were stickers and paper dolls, plastic guns and model airplanes. There were colourful pens and tiny notebooks, marbles and rubber stampers. And there was the merchandise of fandom – play money and paper cut-outs adorned with the images of famous movie stars. The lane was the approach to the elementary school and a lively business would be done until the bell rang at eight o'clock.

Clutching small bills in their fists, backpacks over their shoulders, and most of them unchaperoned by parents, children as young as 3 years old perused the offerings like the savviest of consumers. They had every intention of making purchases, but only if the product was right. A boy of 7 walked away from every table because they did not have the model in the series of eight that his collection still lacked. A girl of 9 wanted a pen, and it had to be blue. After selecting the style she liked, she asked the vendor to assemble a new one for her to try. He loaded a fresh ink cartridge, explained that they were replaceable, and offered it to her to test out. When she thought it didn't work, the vendor, struggling to assert the authority of his adulthood over the power of her cash, called her bluff: 'You don't know how to write [with it]!' He demonstrated, she tried it out and, satisfied but surly, tossed 1.50 yuan on the table.

Not every child bought something that day, but the vendors assured me that the children all did so with regularity, when they found the right choice. Some parents, I was told, gave their kids two yuan a day for personal shopping. Very few accompanied their offspring on their purchasing adventures. Special edibles had also been designed for juvenile delectation – little squirts of decorative cake icing in tiny covered plastic dishes with miniature spoons, or fried dough on a stick dipped in chocolate icing with rainbow sprinkles. By 1999, then, Kaili had fostered a youthful consumer sector and was sustaining it with affordable trinkets made ever so accessible to those with minimal mobility and limited means. Only a few years earlier, however, I had experienced Kaili as a site of shortcoming.

Colour Codes

Scattered through the primary and middle schools and in the remaining state offices situated in Xijiang – the Miao community in which I did long-term field-work – were a collection of urban-educated Miao young people who routinely lamented their having been dispatched back to the countryside to work after a few sweet years of metropolitan privilege. In 1993, one of these, whom I shall call Chang, struggled to teach rudimentary English to local students who were themselves, as native speakers of Miao, struggling just with mastering Mandarin Chinese. Learning

English in the city had meant for her learning about the ways of the West, coming to crave its affluence as emblematised by its modes of femininity. She accessed this world through the medium of Chinese popular magazines which were stacked high on a large bookshelf in her room. Among these were *Fiating* (*Household*) and *Fiating Yisheng* (*Family Doctor*), the latter of which included an article in the psychology section on knowing the inner secrets of your spouse's heart. Fashion magazines abounded in her collection, including *Shizhuang* (*Fashion*), *Shanghai Fuzhuang* (*Shanghai Fashion*), and *Findai* (*Golden Age*). All were replete with images of Western women. She had also added to her collection an American catalogue of an ear-ring discounter given to her by a Japanese photographer passing through town.

Knowing that she was an accomplished seamstress, I asked Chang to show me the clothing that she had made for herself. Reluctantly, she pulled garments out of her wardrobe, including a red suit with a skirt and a navy one with a miniskirt. But she dismissed all these, explaining that she hadn't been able to make the stylish set (*tao*) that she wanted for teaching. Although she was welcome to borrow her aunt's sewing machine any time, she couldn't produce her dream outfit until she could obtain the colour of fabric she preferred. She had searched at the local market, in the country seat, even in the little metropolis of Kaili where she had done her teacher training. One would have thought you could get anything in the city of Kaili, but not that longed-after and elusive hue. I asked what colour it was that she was holding out for, and without hesitation she pulled a well-worn style magazine off the shelf. Flipping through effortlessly, she located the object of her frustrated desire. A coiffed and groomed woman strode across the page in a trim business suit of radiant coral pink, exuding femininity and inspiring envy through every finely tailored seam of her lushly styled ensemble. Chang, consigned to her spectral role of yearning, could only imagine places far away where women, whether Chinese or foreign, could realise their personal fashion dreams.

Media Transport

One chill Autumn night in 1988, when peasants in the village of Xijiang huddled close inside their homes to dodge the cold, I called upon a family who had recently acquired a TV. It was a rare occurrence that riveted them to the fuzzy black-and-white screen – the broadcast of a full-length Australian feature film. That evening the choice was *Crocodile Dundee* (1986), dubbed in Mandarin. We watched in fascination. After many months of fieldwork, I found myself as captivated as they were by images of a goofy Australian country boy discovering the complexities of New York City. The comical narrative of his wide-eyed encounter with the quintessence of metropolitan sophistication, mediated by an affluent, very blonde, urban American woman, invited Chinese viewers into a fantasy of travel and self-transformation. Tacitly, we projected ourselves into the film in our disparate roles, imagining what it would be like were I to introduce my Miao friends to the Big Apple. It was with resignation, however, that we admitted to ourselves that the television offered us nothing more than the thickest materials for exploring fantasy, for the hopes for these villagers of travelling abroad were nothing more than that.

Iron Satellite Dishes

A new flower, one could say, has bloomed in every village of the Southeast Guizhou Miao countryside. It is white, sometimes the height of a two-storey house, and was planted by the government. Although most people don't know what it is called, its roots extend underground, creeping out to every household. In tandem with the removal of so many other state guarantees – of social welfare, employment, and development funding – what the state *has* guaranteed in the late 1990s is satellite television reception for every village. In many villages of the Miao countryside, cable has been laid to every home, even though many households lack the resources to purchase televisions.

In the Xijiang of 1999, I am told, 60 per cent of households have televisions, 20 per cent of which are colour. Ten per cent are said to have purchased VCDs. This string of upgrades, from black-and-white to colour television, then to VCD, is closely keyed to status and understood in a progressivist fashion as a sequence that each house will follow as soon as it acquires the means. In the meantime, those who are not yet media-equipped go to neighbours' houses to watch at night. Gone are the video houses that used to project tapes for paid viewing in the early 1990s. In their place, rental shops for VCDs are beginning to spring up. Xijiang's movie theatre burned down a few years ago and has not been rebuilt. The local government has ceased to project entertainment films on great white sheets hung on the façade of the schoolhouse for all to see on starry nights. The privatisation of media consumption proceeds apace: not only has public viewing been replaced by domestic viewing, but as soon as people acquire the means, they shift from reception of state-channelled broadcasts to the personally chosen VCDs that are the rage across the countryside.

Xijiang's Culture Station, which used to organise public events, movie screenings and dances, has been eliminated. In 1999, what the state supports is a tourism office – which aids outside visitors in finding and photographing local colour – and a broadcasting station. Here a government employee works from 8 a.m. to 2 a.m., making sure that the transmission of nine channels from satellite dish via cable into homes goes smoothly, maintaining and installing cable hookups, and playing three movies a day on a dedicated tenth channel. The people's favourite shows, one of these employees reports, are news and movies. Other viewers tell me that they benefit from technical agricultural information shows as well.

A Bewildering Carnival of Consumption Lack

I stage this bewildering sequence of spatial and temporal jump cuts to illustrate the disorientation that uneven marketisation brings about in sites such as the Miao countryside. While children in Beijing, Shanghai or Guangzhou scrambled to buy up toys they had learned to love from television, most rural Miao perceived media-hyped commodities as elements of a distant culture travelled to only through television. The Miao mountains are, without doubt, spaces of lack (*cha*), ones in which consumption practices have been little transformed in two decades of Dengist reform. While ever-enhanced media technologies parade more and more glamorous and expensive desirables across their surfaces, the goods available at the periodic market in Xijiang have changed little.

What could Xijiang inhabitants buy by the end of the 1980s, if they could muster the cash? Offerings were decidedly mundane, sharply disjunctive with the luxury glitz of the metropolis where the monied quested after DVDs, beepers, body-building machines or even apartments, and more and more extravagant forms of entertainment. The majority of shops featured a sampling of useful household items along with a few edible dry goods. While staple foods were culled directly from the fields and prepared in the home, the stores offered such supplements as instant milk powder, peanuts, sunflower seeds, noodles, sweetened biscuits, beer and cooking oil. Everyday household goods included washcloths, mosquito coils, soaps and de-

tergents, flashlights, batteries, cooking pots and utensils, basins, fabric, clothing, shoes, thread, needles, thimbles, safety pins, baskets, bicycle pumps, hinges, light bulbs, light switches, wire, firewood, toothpaste, toothbrushes, hairbrushes, combs, cigarettes, matches, lighters, padlocks, envelopes, pens and pencils, 'sanitary paper' for menstruation, vegetable seeds, mats for drying rice, and handkerchiefs. Luxury items, on the other hand, according to local classifications of value, included: ping pong balls, Pepsi, balloons, film, hair oils, playing cards, beads, ear-rings and bracelets, scarves, make-up, hand mirrors, stockings, perfume and bras. In the burgeoning category of luxury goods, as the list shows, were a preponderance of enhancements to women's beauty. Notably, among all the newfangled commodities glutting the Chinese market, these were the ones that, despite being classed by locals as luxurious, were desired enough that they would sell in Xijiang.

By 1999, a decade later, there were a few additions. A wider range of clothing was purveyed by itinerant pedlars from Hunan, and some local Miao, who rotated their wares within the regional circuit of periodic markets. There was a wider range of interior decorating paraphernalia, such as posters or lush Chinese paintings mounted in frames together with mirrors or clocks. Beauty products had proliferated, with many hues of lipstick, sumptuous lotions and foreign-branded shampoos. But aside from this handful of specialty items, goods in Xijiang stayed about the same.

What changed was the promotional media, the electrifying sense of offering and access that advertising – and its sidekick, lush programming – generates. What I want to foreground here is the tension between goods and media as two aspects of consumption. It must be emphasised that Chinese commodity envy is highly conditioned, not simply by media but more specifically by advertising. After enforcing a ban on product advertising, which began in the mid-1960s and continued throughout the Cultural Revolution into the late 1970s, the Chinese government began permitting radio and television ads in 1979. In 1982, Central Chinese Television gave CBS Productions 320 minutes of airtime for commercials in exchange for 60 hours of US television programming – a move that opened the floodgates for the visibility of foreign products.[5] The advertising industry expanded from less than 10 state-run agencies in 1980 to almost 7,000 mostly non-state agencies in 1987.[6]

By 1987, China's 81,000 ad industry employees were doing business with 966 Chinese newspapers, 1,788 magazines, 300 radio stations, and 360 television stations, which the then Chinese Ministry of Radio, Film and Television estimated reached more than 68 percent of China's billion-plus population. These were the kind of mass market statistics that ad men could only dream of in the outside world.[7]

Receiving the commercials, of course, is one thing; buying the advertised products, as I've said, is quite another. Aware that much of what ads proffer is economically out of reach for most Chinese audiences, authorities frame the function of advertising instead as 'educational and informational'.[8] High-visibility instances of super-spending are orchestrated and showcased by the state itself, with the subtext that most will be witnesses to consumption rather than its agents. The use value of goods is superseded not necessarily by exchange value but by their more elusive numinosity. In a telling literalisation of the magic of the commodity, post offices in the early 1990s auctioned off numbers for cell phones that were deemed lucky because of containing multiple eights. The number 900–888 went for 18,000 yuan in Dalian, while another containing four eights went for 50,000 yuan in Chongqing.[9]

In a manner so resoundingly critiqued by Horkheimer and Adorno in the West, this fledgling culture industry tutors Chinese consumers-in-training to live in the space of ever-renewed desire.[10] It is a space that, in the late twentieth century, occupies more and more of the globe. [...]

In theories developed for Western capitalism, what is effected by media, communications, and the promiscuous circulation of signs promoting goods is a system that has been described in terms of the desire for desire itself. In the inevitability of unfulfilment lies another kind of sensual pleasure – that of a delicious longing that replicates itself over and over. This state of resigned longing is coupled with enjoyable spectatorship; indeed the pleasure of watching is the condition for the maintenance of the unsated state of desire. Pleasure is to be derived from viewing alone. [...]

When Chinese television advertising began, in the 1980s, to replace utilitarian work objects (such as machinery for sale to state work units) with luxurious products for the home (such as dishwashers, toys and cosmetics), there was a particular Chinese valence to this promiscuous communication – a pointed renunciation of the Maoist collective work ethic and a celebration of newly-privatised domestic space. When global media and commodities gushed into China with the reform era's gradual lifting of restrictions, the passion to consume them derived in part from the fact that they had been prohibited for so many decades. One of the ways in which Chinese consumerism is distinctive is that, with the very gradual relaxing of state controls under reform, the commodities and lifestyles emblematised by foreigners were admired at a considerable distance and as alteric to the state. Hence, the medium of their display, the media messages beamed in from afar, were treasured simply for their presence. This, I think, is one of the reasons why unsatisfied commodity desire has such resiliency in China: since even the images of commodities and consumerism were forbidden during the austere years of the Cultural Revolution, they have a greater potential to be consumed as ends in themselves. To even gaze at objects sealed in glass cases, to peruse fashions arranged artfully on Madonna's MTV body, or to know that with sufficient funds one might have no other obstacle to purchasing a car or a pirated pornographic video, was a very significant form of access in and of itself, a circumvention of that state power that had protectively closed cultural borders for decades.

From TV to VCD and Other Dilemmas of Post-Socialist Market Desire

In Guizhou's Miao highlands, a legacy from the Maoist era of revolution-making media outreach has irrevocably shaped current practices of media reception. For decades, Miao peasants had laboured at agriculture on mountain terraces, returning to their villages to the sound of the morning and evening 'broadcasts' transmitted by the state over a public address system so loud that it penetrated all homes with news and announcements, in the flat, usually garbled, and Beijing-accented voices of central organs of information. As I've said, in Xijiang, the local authorities would occasionally project an educational film, on a topic such as fire prevention or revolutionary history, on to a huge white sheet mounted on the outdoor façade of the schoolhouse. A movie theatre was unlocked periodically so that the state-run Culture Station could show a feature film circulated, by government approval, to the rural areas. The mid-1980s saw the advent of television in some Miao areas, but electricity was erratic and transmission towers were always failing, so that it was only sometimes that peasants could catch a fuzzy black-and-white programme or two broadcast from the provincial station.

By 1999, all this had changed. At mid-decade, some of China's leaders had visited Miao areas, and, as the story goes, shocked at the abject level of poverty, they decided to intensify development of communications and transport. Policies of economic privatisation proceeded apace, and little changed in terms of fiscal support for economic development in the villages. What was changed, under a policy now referred to as *Kaifa Xibu*, or Opening the West, was the effort exerted by the state to bring television and roads to minority villages, so as to accelerate an overhaul of peasant consciousness toward market mentalities (*shichang sixiang*). Among the five top priorities for a development plan for the Mashan area of Guizhou, for instance, were not only improvement of basic living conditions, economic development and population control, but also connecting every village by satellite and by road.[11] TV, like the PA system before it, was to have an educative function, but now it was to socialise remote peoples to the consumption desires and profit-making schemes essential to the market transformation.

While central fiscal policy has retracted most guarantees of secure state employment or of social welfare for needy families, then, what *is* guaranteed is the government-installed satellite dish. Now that cable has been laid to every home in many Miao villages, the desire to purchase televisions is itself described as a potential spur to development: with cable access so close at hand, and nine channels now reliably received, the Miao are seen as more prone to seek economic schemes to raise the cash that will enable them to bring 'the world' into their households. The impact of avid television reception is indexed by the following: while decades of formal public address did little to propagate *putonghua* among Miao villagers, in 1999 almost anyone I spoke with, of any age or gender, could understand 'standard' oral Mandarin with ease. The current regime, in effect, has delegated the work of national linguistic standardisation to the more muted modalities of the mediated popular domain. Yet, while the state strives to foster through media the market's grip on the minds of minority peasants, another change is under way, one which throws this scheme radically into question.

In the finely calibrated system of consumption prestige throughout China, the technology of choice is, more recently, not the television but the VCD. By 1999, 10 per cent of households in Xijiang had already purchased a player and two shops had opened to rent VCDs to villagers. This leads to an unresolved empirical/theoretical area in thinking through cultural privatisation in post-Mao China. Assuming that television does indeed have a transformative effect on minority market consciousness, what difference might it make if media consumption shifts from the network programming – glutted with commercials that tutor consumers-in-training to long for new goods, set alongside morality tales about good entrepreneurs who make it rich on their own initiative – to VCD viewing in which programmes are selected by the viewer? Soap opera-type dramas, music videos and martial arts action shows appear to be gaining as the favoured fare for VCD viewers in the Miao countryside. To what extent might this process constitute the state's loss of access to the peasants it aims to marketise? How significant is it that, whereas in rural areas such as the Miao countryside what are transmitted from the satellite dish are exclusively domestic channels, the VCD market includes all manner of legal and pirated CDs *from abroad* in addition to domestic products? Is privatisation of consumption here tantamount to internationalisation of content? Such internationalisation of viewing content, of the type described by Arjun Appadurai, Mayfair Yang and others, holds the potential for social imaginings that exceed Chinese borders.[12] It can precipitate what I have called 'imagined cosmopolitanism' – a yearning for participation in a chimeric boundariless world of material abundance and supranational identities.[13]

Market Mentality as the Endpoint of Cultural Developmentalism

What I refer to as 'cultural developmentalism' is the notion, now widespread in China, that promiscuous contact with media and commodities will incite that much-hyped market *sixiang* on which the success of economic reform is thought to rest. Framed in the language of modernisation (*xiandaihua*), development (*fazhan*) and advancement (*xianjin*), the Miao and other commentators on them describe the process by which transformations in Miao culture and traditions will eventuate in prosperity. Here the burden of self-improvement devolves on to the non-Han peasantry in the form of an all-too-familiar discourse of mental progress. The Miao and other minorities will learn from the Han to be economically energetic, proactive and innovative, *and* to be duly consuming. Yet the uneven process of development that has structured not only China's actual economy but also its reform ethos, in practice *scripts* consumption shortfalls for remote minorities and others among the poorer rural peoples. In a passage strikingly resonant with the current Chinese scene, transnational communications analysts Mattelart, Delcourt and Mattelart describe this logic:

> the consumption model created by the transnational system demands, for anyone really to benefit from it, an income accessible to only 20 or 30 percent of the population. Thus the system of commercialisation, the system of production, and the system of communications all play a complementary role within the transnational framework by promoting a model of social inequality. The main patterns to emerge from the installation of new technologies in countries like Brazil show that, far from democratising access to cultural goods, they reinforce segregations and consolidate hierarchies.[14]

The hierarchy that is being elaborated in the Chinese consumerist order is one with deep roots in China's historical practices of *ethnic* hierarchical ordering. Cultural difference – as opposed to state policy or regional disparity – is purveyed as the key alibi for economic disparity. And with minorities, the recuperated version of this excuse amounts to a diagnosis of such groups as the Miao as being culturally impeded from grasping the means – ends equation of market activity and consumption prowess.

[...]

Conclusion: To Purchase Is to Sinicize?

Deliberations over cultural alternatives for development framed the process as one inexorably about time and time management as well as about values. Miao advocates for a particular Miao version of modernisation not only defied the characterisation of their people's mentality as irremediably *luohou* (backward), insisting instead that they were as capable as any of modernising impulses. When it came to making marketisation happen, what they emphasised was the challenges of production – the efficiency and economy required to venture into something like cash-cropping, and what impact it would have on labour-intensive time-honoured practices, from hairstyles to embroidery to rituals. What remained uninterrogated in these considerations was the very distinct impacts of production's mirror, the long tentacles of the culture of consumption as it reached into households all over the Miao countryside.

The current historical juncture, for the Miao and for China, leaves unanswered questions about the transformative effects of marketisation in the domain of consumerist desire. If alternative modernities and resistances to cultural developmentalism are beginning to be articulated now, are discourses of alternative modalities of consumption soon to follow? Certainly, popular culture studies in the West have shown that consuming can be a rich terrain for the fashioning of difference, for the carving out of style niches emblematic of ethno-racial groups in multi-ethnic societies. Is it conceivable that Miao villagers would embark on market ventures or garner cash through wage labour on the coast and then elaborate ways of spending their earnings that expressed distinctive Miao sensibilities?

I wonder, though, if the prevailing conditions of maldistribution and material lack in Miao China can allow for any forms of self-defining consumption. Moreover is there to be found in the consumerism being propagated in China these days a culture of conformity, one that confers prestige only through lockstep-style practices? What I mean to interrogate here is the underlying assumption that consumers are always questing after differences, that they are seeking (or have been induced to seek) to produce particularised selves or distinctive cultural communities. The implication in these arguments is that the multiplication of ever-proliferating modalities of the self is somehow an inevitable outcome of the late-century consumerist order. The case of Chinese consumerism may contravene this scenario in critical and divergent ways. Michael Dutton has suggested that in China consuming may actually demonstrate newfound membership in recuperated collectivisms.[15] For the Miao, consuming, and even modes of desiring, may be such potent implements for demonstrating a generic modernity over and against an ethnicised and devalued backwardness, that forging particularities in the style domain may be a remote and secondary concern. Until it becomes clearer on what cultural authority the valorisation of the market rests, it will be difficult to see how those still at its ragged edges are negotiating their relationship with this particular aspect of post-socialist China identity politics.

NOTES

1   The description here is a synopsis of a segment of *The Toughest Summit*, aired on CNN on October 28, 1997, during the visit of Chinese President Jiang Zemin to the US.

2 The *New York Times*, December 14, 1997, p. 12.

3 The following account is based on the discussion in Bin Zhao and Graham Murdock, 'Young Pioneers: children and the making of Chinese consumerism', *Cultural Studies*, vol. 10, no. 2, 1996, pp. 201–17.

4 Quoted in ibid., p. 211.

5 Leslie Sklair, *Sociology of the Global System*. Baltimore: Johns Hopkins University Press, 1991, p. 200.

6 Orville Schell, *Discos and Democracy: China in the Throes of Reform*. New York: Anchor, 1989, p. 344.

7 Ibid., p. 344.

8 Sklair, *Sociology of the Global System*, p. 201.

9 See account in David S. G. Goodman, 'The People's Republic of China: the Party-state, capitalist revolution and new entrepreneurs', in Richard Robison and David S. G. Goodman, eds, *The New Rich in Asia: Mobile Phones, McDonalds and Middle Class Revolution*. London: Routledge, 1996, pp. 225–42.

10 Max Horkheimer and Theodor W. Adorno, 'The culture industry: enlightenment as mass deception', in Horkheimer and Adorno, *The Dialectic of Enlightenment*. New York: Continuum, 1972 (1944), pp. 120–67.

11 Offices of the Guizhou Chinese Communist Party and the Guizhou Provincial Government, 'Guanyu Jiakuai Mashan, Yaoshan Diqu Fupin Kaifa Bufa de Tongzhi' (Memo on accelerating steps for poverty relief and development in the Mashan and Yaoshan regions), August 5, 1994, pp. 56–7.

12 Arjun Appadurai, *Modernity at Large: Cultural Dimensions of Globalization*. Minneapolis: University of Minnesota Press, 1996; Mayfair Mei-hui Yang, 'Mass media and transnational subjectivity in Shanghai: notes on (re)cosmopolitanism in a Chinese metropolis', in Aihwa Ong and Donald Nonini, eds, *Ungrounded Empires: The Cultural Politics of Modern Chinese Transnationalism*. New York: Routledge, 1997, p. 288.

13 Louisa Schein, 'Of cargo and satellites: imagined cosmopolitanism', *Postcolonial Studies*, vol. 2, no. 3, 1999, pp. 345–75.

14 Armand Mattelart, Xavier Delcourt and Michele Mattelart, 'International image markets', in Simon During, ed., *The Cultural Studies Reader*. London: Routledge, 1993, pp. 435–6.

15 In a discussion of fashion, Dutton takes issue with the notion that reform in China heralds individualism: 'many consumers in China do not operate with the notion of individuality that underpins even the most mass-produced of fashion products in the West. For these Chinese, fashion is not constructed to mark out one's individuality, but to mark out one's success. Success is made verifiable through the notion of correct choice. Success means choosing a coat that everyone else is wearing, for to see others in the same coat, dress, trousers or shirt is not a sign of social disgrace, but a mark of wisdom and affluence.... The Chinese, in this one crucial respect, have never really changed out of their Mao suits.... The Mao suit, like Maoism itself may well be simply a more recent refashioning of much deeper, unconscious commitments to a notion of a collective whole', Michael Dutton, *Streetlife China*. Cambridge: Cambridge University Press, 1998, p. 274.

15

A Theory of Virtualism: Consumption as Negation

Daniel Miller

[...]

A Defence of Grand Narrative

I want to tell a story. It is a particular kind of story, a grand narrative. With the rise of postmodernism and an academic sensitivity to cultural differences and pluralism over the past two decades, one of the main targets of criticism has become not so much political economy, but the way it had been developed by Marx, in particular through his use of Hegel. This tradition of political economy as grand narrative was rejected and replaced by many new areas of academic concern. These included cultural studies, literary studies, some branches of psychoanalysis (such as Lacanian) and a topic that will play a central role in this story, consumption.

Most of those interested in consumption saw it as a means to escape from the sins of grand narrative. This is because it implied a concern with the diverse fields of practice within which what otherwise might seem homogeneous phenomena, such as goods, services or media, become fragmented into the plural communities of consumption: different audiences might read the same text in opposing ways. It provided evidence not just for globalisation or homogeneity, but also for regional and local diversity. All of this is very welcome. My story has a somewhat perverse ambition, however, which is to use consumption in order to return to the tradition of a grand narrative. For a moment I put aside issues of diversity in order to see if there is any general direction in which history could be said to be moving.

The grand narrative, in its debt to Hegel, had many features that are now unpopular: it homogenised history as a normative sequence; it por-trayed history as moving in a particular direction; it was idealist in that it weighed history against explicit concepts of rationality. I believe Hegel was prescient. While many of these features may not have been justified for his time, they may be rather more appropriate for our time. It is, thus, ironic that this tradition is being attacked at the very moment when history itself is coming into line with its own story. In making this claim I do not mean that history has an intrinsic direction, and certainly I do not avow a Western conceptualisation of progress. Rather I wish to suggest that today, rather more than at the time in which Hegel lived, there exist forces of such power and global reach that certain trends have become ubiquitous, and hence that we can talk meaningfully, perhaps for the first time, about history's having a direction.

Hegelians have always looked for dialectical features within historical processes. Briefly, they take all cultural phenomena as inherently contradictory processes, with a contradiction that creates its own subject. Humanity successively establishes new objective forms and institutions, for instance law or money. These create the possibility of new abstract and universalistic concepts, while at the same time generating more particularistic difference. At each cycle we reach a point when such forms and institutions become so autonomous from us, their creators, so driven by their own logic, that they become highly oppressive and dangerous to us. We need, therefore, to return to an understanding, which Hegel saw as a philosophical understanding, that these are indeed our own creations and that potentially we can expand ourselves by bringing them back to us, dialectically transcending the distance between universality and particularity, transforming them into that which strengthens rather than diminishes our humanity.

Marx exemplified these ideas. However, he moved the focus from philosophy to a series of material changes that had, indeed, achieved new forms of abstraction on the one hand, and particularity on the other. Of these, the most extreme example was capitalism. Marx focused on the growth of an autonomous logic to capitalism based on the original alienation of nature as private property. Capital had become a relentlessly-abstract force devoted to its own expansion, a force that threatened to destroy all cultural traditions and tear society apart in that quest. It produced a system in which commodities were not recognised as human creations, but had become enslaved to the autonomous logic of expanding capital. Marx represented this not as a consequence of immutable laws, but as a stage in the story of history. Since that time, many versions of dialectic theory have arisen, but those that are the more teleological and historical have fared less well than those that use the dialectic to create a relational perspective on social life (for a recent account, see Harvey 1996: 46–113).

From a dialectical perspective, it is clear that the one thing Marx would not be if he were alive today is a Marxist, since his sense of history was such that statements made in one century had to be superseded by a new understanding appropriate to the next historical moment. In short, Marx today, if he were to be consistent, would not be searching for capitalism, but for some different yet equivalent force relevant to the end of the twentieth century. He would expect that, if communism were not the end of history, then capitalism should have been superseded by some new, even more abstract and alienating, historical movement. One aim, then, in telling a story in this chapter should be to bring Marx up to date.

[. . .]

A Story

The narrative has unfolded much as might have been predicted, which is to say, in ways that Marx did not predict. Today we see something very different from the capitalist society that Marx experienced and described. In most regions, our lives are dominated by much more than simply our niche in the circulation of capital. Homogeneity exists at some levels, such as the global capitalist class [. . .]. However, the diversity of society that the ethnographer encounters is a complete repudiation of the homogenisation of society under early capitalism. We would expect there to be a diversity of routes constituting any such negation: trade unions in one place, the state in another. The result today is that we have many different forms of capitalist societies, unless, of course, you believe the postmodernist mantra that all current diversity is simply superficiality.

As ethnographers we experience cultural difference as profound. One cause of these differences is the regional inequality that is created by capitalism as a global system. As the literature on world-systems demonstrated, often development in some areas has been secured through underdevelopment in others. In other regions it has been localisation, rather than globalisation, that has led to capitalism's being subject to increasing contextualisation: German capitalism has many elements that distinguish it from that of Japan, and both are quite distinct from plantation systems in South America. The degree to which this has historically proved to be the case could hardly be clearer, in that we live in a marvellous period when the fastest-growing version of capitalism is the Chinese Communist variety (Smart 1997). If so, our grand narrative is a story not without some quite good jokes.

If China and South Asia do achieve high growth rates and, rather more doubtfully, find means to spread the benefits that accrue, then the more progressive elements of this story would seem to apply to the majority of the world population, though the large number of gaps forbids any simple evocation of a concept of progress. For now, this story could be characterised as a clear taming of capitalism only for segments of populations within the countries that are most developed. In as much as this represents a historical tendency, then it probably achieved its fullest extent in Scandinavia in the 1960s, where powerful states achieved what I believe to be an unequalled ability to create from capitalism a machine for the service of human welfare through extremely tight forms of state control. We expect no perfection on this earth, and such state control may have had its less noble side, as in evidence for the use of eugenics under Swedish social democracy. Even so, though capitalist, these were genuinely welfare states, and Scandinavian social democracy serves as an example of where history might have led us. I take these states as a benchmark that can be used in order to critique any counter-trends that may be discerned today, an actual, historical benchmark, and hence better than fanciful ones like utopian communism, against which we all stand equally condemned.

Scandinavia shifts our understanding of what capitalism could become. Instead of intrinsic contradictions between capitalist and worker, the region showed that states can create structures in which workers, either as partners or as holders of pensions and other assets, can become aggregate capitalists who retain an interest in profits being converted into mass welfare. Workers there enjoyed vast wealth and services previously not imaginable. The speed with which such transformations might take place are astonishing. There have been few more evocative portraits of the hell on earth that early capitalism could be than *Hunger*, in which the Norwegian novelist Knut Hamsun (1921) portrayed Oslo around 1900. By comparison, oil-rich Norway today provides its citizens with benefits that are prodigious.

Changes in the organisation of states and economies can only achieve a negation of early capitalism if they are matched by processes that enable people to draw from capitalism forms that can be used to enhance ordinary life. In my first attempt to contribute a footnote to this story (Miller 1987), I argued that even though institutions such as the state were crucial in these processes, there was one phenomenon above all that most fully expressed this historical negation, and this was consumption. My argument was that the very abstraction and universalism embodied in capitalism was most fully negated in a force that it had created, but that expressed with the greatest eloquence the possibilities of particularity and diversity brought down to the level of ordinary human practice, the very forms of experience that capitalism as abstraction had destroyed. Consumption plays this role theoretically and sometimes in actuality. It is here that the smallest social groups, even individuals, confront objects that, in their production, express the very abstraction of the market and the state. Yet, through purchase and possession, people can use those objects to create worlds that strive to be specific and diverse precisely because we wish to escape from our sense of alienation from the vast institutions of the market and the state.

For example, I found that impoverished householders on government housing estates in London used the potential of gender as exchange (between male DIY labour and female expertise in interior aesthetics) in order to create transformations in goods and services (specifically their kitchens) that made the development of their social relations the direct negation of the stigma attached to their situation at the lowest end of state services and market provision (Miller 1988). In more affluent circles it seemed to me that even the most critical and ascetic of the academics amongst whom I worked enjoyed in their daily consumption goods ranging from the services of restaurants to the latest forms of word processor, summer holidays and devices intended to help in securing the safety of children, goods that, when generalised as mass consumption, were clearly being voted for in practice even when they were to be condemned in theory; and they did not seem to regard themselves as superficial or passive in their enjoyment. If our academic perspectives are in any way to remain consistent with our private lives, then we have to acknowledge the benefits of capitalist commodities that accrue to those who can afford them.

[...] The contradictions within capitalism expressed as the opposed interest of capitalist and worker had become ameliorated when, by the middle of the twentieth century, ordinary workers achieved material benefits on a par with the capitalists of a century before. This need imply no change in the logic of capitalism itself, a highly amoral system of capital reproduction that offers little opportunity for the self-construction of the species being as the young Marx understood it. Similarly, powerful states and bureaucracies, essential to the construction of equality through complex tax and redistribution systems, had their own logic of dehumanising anonymity. Although necessary to achieve such objectives, these too are not appealing sources of identity, particularly after seeing how they were aestheticised by some fascist and communist states to become the focus of identity.

Consumption as negation is not, of course, accomplished through the mere accumulation of material forms. Rather, it requires the long-term process by which consumers appropriate goods and services in direct repudiation of the massive and unattractive institutional forces of capitalism, the state and, increasingly, science, which had created these goods. Only consumption as a process provides the flexibility and creativity that allow societies, small groups and even individuals to return to that act of self-construction of the species being that is the definition of human culture within dialectical theory. In a word, this century has shown that it is in consumption, and not, as Marx had argued, in production, that commodities can be returned to the world as the embodiment of human potentiality.

After outlining this model, I sought to characterise and exemplify these processes. Contrary to most writings on the subject, I have always believed that consumption is primarily a social achievement, not an individual one; that it is a cultural process that is hardly ever about individuals or subjectivities. My main example (Miller 1994, 1997) has been based on consumption and identity in Trinidad. I have tried to show how Trinidadians historically represent the extremes of capitalist alienation as slaves, as indentured labourers and as Third World migrants without local history or roots. I then explored their consumption of key symbols of alienation: Christmas, Coca-Cola, transnational corporations and the like. By contrast with the orientation of most academic writings, I have tried to show how, in consumption, these symbols of alienation become the very instruments through which the specificity of Trinidadian identity has been created as the negation of their historical legacy of alienation: Trinidadian Christmas; a black, sweet drink from Trinidad; Trinidadian-owned transnational corporations. My most recent ethnographic work on shopping in North London points in the same general direction (Miller 1998). Shopping has very little to do with individuals, with hedonism or even with materialism; it can be better understood as a ritual parallel to the structure of ancient sacrifice that is devoted to the construction of key relationships and the objectification of devotional love.

I do not mean these examples to imply that all consumption negates capitalism or the state. Rather, I present them to illustrate how, at one moment in history, it has the potential to do so. As part of a dialectical story, consumption may stand as the moment of negation of capitalism as the most powerful form of oppressive abstraction developed by humanity. But if it is to remain contemporary, a grand narrative constantly has to be re-written. If consumption has been used to counteract the effects of capitalism that Marx described, then I suspect Marx himself would be searching for what might be called the negation of the negation. There should be some new force emerging that is based on the contradictions of these earlier forces, perhaps the contradictions of consumption, a force that is now creating another institutional embodiment of human creativity as abstraction that will come to replace capitalism, a force that necessarily will be more extreme than capitalism, more abstract and more dehumanising, until it in turn can be negated. Marx today would surely be searching for this emergent formation.

I suggested that the high point in the taming of capitalism is to be found, not today, but twenty years ago in Scandinavian social democracy. Seen from the perspective of Western states, the last twenty years can only be regarded as regressive. We see a decline in the movement towards greater equality, a decline in faith in the welfare state, a decline in the sense of the progressive potential of consumption, a potential explored most visibly in the 1960s, with its explosion of creativity in music, clothing, life-styles and so forth. This regression is conceded even by those most in favour of classic economic perspectives. Just before Christmas 1997, the *Economist*, a periodical renowned for its neo-classical economics and opposition to the state, included a small note, 'Rising tide, falling boats'. It reported that in the United States the family income of the richest fifth of the population had increased by 30 per cent since the late 1970s, while the income of the poorest fifth had declined by 21 per cent, leaving the income of the former 19.5 times higher than the income of the latter. Further, in all but one state during this period, the income of the middle fifth had also fallen.

It does not take a great deal of imagination to translate these figures into human experiences: a wealthy community for whom the additional increases merely add to monies that are almost beyond their ability to spend, but that front claims about the country as a whole becoming 'richer'; while the poor, for whom every small shift represents a major constraint on their ability to realise their goals and values, have seen a terrifying fall in their ability to participate meaningfully in their own society. Similar things are likely to be happening elsewhere. South Asia and the east coast of China have seen the rise of a formidable middle class; but there are suggestions from the hinterlands that both areas face a rise in inequality comparable to that in the United States. For any perspective with even a smidgen of concern for human welfare, then, we live in regressive times. Why did this happen? What were the grounds for this reversal in our recent history? How do they serve to negate the progressive potential of consumption?

Economics beyond Capitalism

If the aim is to rise above the trees and attempt to discern the shape of the woods, then Trinidad offers a useful perspective precisely because it is situated on a periphery, where power tends to divest itself of some of its disguises (Gledhill 1994). Trinidad is in a curious situation. The constraints imposed on the major companies that had developed in order to exploit the island were based almost entirely on nationalism, given teeth by the 1973 oil boom, rather than any form of socialism. As a result there had been a clear local taming of capitalism, to some extent reversed in the recession that followed the decline in the price of oil. Capitalism in contemporary Trinidad had become surprisingly localised, including some powerful local transnational corporations that were starting to become complementary, rather than antagonistic, to state welfare politics. Trinidad was no ideal society, but this was a clear step up from colonialism, let alone from slavery.

This progressive process is currently being undermined, and, I suspect, negated, because of the arrival of structural adjustment. [...] Structural adjustment is based on a series of models that were devised by economists working within some of the key institutions that were set up following the epochal meeting at Bretton Woods. These models, fostered most notably by the IMF and the World Bank, are purely academic, in the sense that they seem to pay no attention to local context. The measures for ending protectionism and abolishing currency control imposed on Trinidad would have been more or less the same if this had been Nigeria or the Ukraine. These sometimes fit the interests of capitalist corporations, but surprisingly often do not. This is because they are not the product of capitalism as an institutional practice of firms, or even a direct reflection of the interests of powerful countries, even the United States (though this is often claimed). I would argue instead that they are simply idealised and abstract models that represent the university departments of economics engaged in academic modelling.

[...] Economics is not the 'theory' of working capitalism, which has had to remain thoroughly engaged and performative, while economics has not. So, while capitalism as a process by which firms seek to increase capital through manufacture and trade has become increasingly contextualised, complex and often contradictory (Miller 1997), another force has arisen that has become increasingly abstract. This force takes the shape of academics, paid for by states and international organisations and given the freedom to rise above context to engage in speculative modelling. While Marx had to tease out the abstract logic of capitalism, today the greater abstraction of academic economics is quite transparent and constantly confirmed by its practitioners. Social scientists may not think of academics as particularly powerful; but then *they* are not economists.

While capitalism engages with the world and is thus subject to the transformations of context, economics remains disengaged, so that structural adjustment in Trinidad could be not one iota Trinidadian. This is because economics has the authority to transform the world into its own image. Where the existing world does not conform to the academic model, the onus is not on changing the model, testing it against the world, but on changing the world, testing us against the model. The very power of this new form of abstraction is that it can indeed act to eliminate the particularities of the world. If we examine its details we find that all the changes that Trinidad was being asked to make were to remove what the economists call 'distortions'. For example, Trinidad was required to end subsidies to local companies because these distort the market in which those companies operate, making it deviate from the economist's ideal of the free market. [...] This imposed remodelling of reality is by no means limited to developing countries.

[...]

Virtualism

But in whose name is this being done? By what right do economists have this authority, this manifest power in the world? If this story is to remain consistent, then the answers to these questions must approximate the negation of the negation. That is, they must relate to the same force, consumption, that has emerged as the vanguard of history in its negation of capitalism as oppression. This is exactly what we find. The people and institutions proclaiming the inevitability of the market, from economists and politicians downwards, do so in the name of the consumer. Indeed, the whole point of the market is that it is supposed to be the sole process that can bring the best goods at the lowest prices to the consumer, the ultimate beneficiary. It is in the name of the consumer that distortions in the market, whether caused by government, trade unions or even actual consumers, are to be eliminated, for these prevent the realisation of that ideal state that best benefits the consumer.

The unique ability of the pure, free market to benefit the consumer is fundamental to economics, as presented in its primary textbooks. Thus, Sloman (1994: 1) notes that the main concern of economics is production and consumption, the latter being 'the act of using goods and services to satisfy wants. This will normally involve purchasing goods and services.' In an ideal free market, 'competition between firms keeps prices down and acts as an incentive to firms to become more efficient. The more firms there are competing, the more responsive they will be to consumer wishes' (1994: 21). Similarly, Stiglitz (1993: 30) says:

> This model of consumers, firms, and markets is *the basic competitive model*. Economists generally believe that, to the extent that it can be duplicated by market systems in the real world, the competitive model will provide answers to the basic economic questions of what is produced and in what quantities, how it is produced, and for whom it is produced that result in the greatest economic efficiency.

This is related to the principle of consumer sovereignty, that individuals are the best judges of what is in their own interests (1993: 191).

With the hindsight of history, a dialectical perspective makes this look almost inevitable. Since it was consumption as an expression of welfare that was the main instrument in negating the abstraction of capitalism, the move to greater abstraction had to supplant consumption as human practice with an abstract version of the consumer. The result is the creation of the virtual consumer in economic theory, a chimera, the constituent parts of which are utterly daft, as Fine has pointed out in several works (Fine 1995, Fine and Leopold 1993). Indeed, neo-classical economists make no claim to represent flesh-and-blood consumers. They claim that their consumers are merely aggregate figures used in modelling. Their protestations of innocence are hollow, however, because these virtual consumers and the models they inhabit and that animate them are the same models that are used to justify forcing actual consumers to behave like their virtual counterparts. Just as the problem with structural adjustment is not that it is based on academic theory but that it has become practice, so the problem with the neo-classical consumer is the effects that the model has on the possibilities of consumer practice. In some kind of global card trick, an abstract, virtual consumer steals the authority that had been accumulated for workers in their other role as consumers.

Auditing and Virtualism

The rise and power of economic theory as manifested in the authority of economic institutions such as the IMF and the World Bank is the primary example what here will be called virtualism; but it is by no means the only one. If the power of these institutions is part of a larger movement in history,

then we can expect to see many parallel trends. The second candidate for virtualism is only too familiar to academics. In this case the ethnographic fieldworker need not stray much beyond the staff common room in order to accumulate the relevant evidence. If these last twenty years have indeed been the negation of the negation, then the cold winds of these changes should be felt even in such notoriously stuffy environments. In Britain, as in many other countries, the previous decades had seen an expansion of higher education, as also of medicine and welfare more generally. While hardly perfect, for inequalities certainly had not been eliminated, those decades clearly were improvements on the preceding era. More people were coming into education and the purpose of education was moving from esoteric research *per se* to giving students and others understanding, as well as knowledge.

In the last twenty years this movement has started to reverse, for what seems at first to be a rather curious reason. British academics bore each other endlessly with complaints about how they should spend their time in teaching or research, but actually seem to spend more and more of their time dealing with the paperwork generated by a variety of new institutional requirements that go under the common name 'auditing'. Paperwork once measured in pages is now measured by weight: teaching audits, research audits, audits of courses that may receive grants. These and too many others are the bane of academic life.

Academics will always grumble; but there has been a major shift in the use of time, confirmed by considering other institutions, such as the health service or local government. There has been a vast expansion of auditing, a curious result of a Thatcherite drive that, I suggest, sincerely believed in limiting centralisation and bureaucracy. Yet by its own actions, it increased substantially the resources going to management and homogenising bureaucracy. This contradiction between intention and result indicates that this historical process can not be understood as some simple expression of political will.

Auditing cannot be seen in isolation, but is part of the growth of 'new public management' (Power 1994: 15), which stresses the definition of goals and the competition for resources within the organisation. Private companies have created a parasite that is equally bloodthirsty in the various forms of management consultancy, on which firms that describe themselves as 'cash-strapped' will spend huge sums. The growth of these consultancies is part of what Thrift (1997) calls 'soft capitalism' and what Salaman (1997) calls 'the new narrative of corporate culture'. These are based on an abstracted discourse that is likely to prove just as detrimental to these willing victims as the audit explosion is to public organisations. [. . .]

[. . .]

In whose name are these audits, consultancy reports and cost – benefit calculations required? They claim their legitimacy from what Keat, Whiteley and Abercrombie (1994) call *The Authority of the Consumer*. All these procedures are justified on the grounds that they benefit the consumer, whether as the actual recipient of the services or as the taxpayer getting value for money. This explains the sad, ironic comments about how those who once were students or patients are now consumers of health or educational services. Indeed, it is hard to imagine what political authority is left today that is not reducible to this hegemonic rhetoric of the consumer. Even the central state is becoming a consumer democracy.

So, benefit to the consumer is crucial to the legitimacy of the set of processes that I have called 'auditing'. Indeed, much of the announced benefit of health and education audits is the idea that they will destroy the privileged autonomy of older bureaucracies and allow the emergence of the consumer citizen, the appropriate judge of whether what is being offered is really of benefit (Walsh 1994). But just as Marx saw a sleight of hand in commodity fetishism, there is plenty of illusion here. One of the main reasons that governments have favoured auditing is that it justifies, in the name of consumer benefit, cutting costs. However, most commonly cutting costs is achieved by cutting services to consumers. Furthermore, as MacLennan (1997) points out, the same logic that enables auditors to act in the name of consumers reduces the ability of citizens to dispute those actions, to protest that there are important criteria other than value for money, supposedly the ultimate consumer good. In sum, policies justified in the name of the consumer citizen become the means to prevent the consumer from becoming a citizen, from determining the priorities of expenditure in the public domain.

Thus it appears that auditing is a sign of a shift to political virtualism. As Power notes (1997: 49),

the executive arm of modern states raises funds through the legislature for mandated programmes. As supreme audit bodies have grown in significance, political accountability to the electorate has been more explicitly supplemented, if not displaced, by managerial conceptions of accountability embracing the need to deliver value for money.

Certainly the languages of governance seem to be shifting in a virtualist direction. Books that used to be about capitalism, a phenomenon imagined as being in a certain time and space, today are almost always about the market, which inhabits the timeless and space-less realm of economic models. Rose (1996) makes a related point, arguing that political considerations of 'society' increasingly have been replaced by 'community', an imagined entity that lends itself to virtualist treatment. In a sense, though, none of these are quite as problematic as what accounting does to the consumer, precisely because in this case there is no similar shift in language. The virtual consumer is simply called a consumer, so that the displacement of actual consumers leaves no trace.

The background to this narrative was an earlier argument that consumption as a practice is a negation of capitalism, and not an expression of it (Miller 1987). So, in turn, the present argument is that auditing is not what it claims to be, an expression of consumption or of the authority of the consumer. Rather, it is a negation of consumption, a negation of a negation. After all, the academic complaint is that auditing leads to deteriorating teaching and research, since the time available to spend on actual persons and projects is eaten away by the demands of auditing itself. Although there may be token consumer representation, auditing is primarily a managerial exercise that is allied to a strict market logic of cost and benefit. The paradox is that, while consumption is the pivot upon which these developments in history spin, the concern is not the costs and benefits of actual consumers, but of what we might call virtual consumers, which are generated by management theory and models. To the degree that virtual consumers come to displace actual consumers, resources that might have been used to turn abstract capital into welfare are moving backwards, fuelling the still more abstract models that are generated academically and in the institutions of auditing.

My argument, thus, is that structural adjustment in Trinidad and the rise of auditing in Britain are symptomatic not of capitalism, but of a new form of abstraction that is emerging, a form more abstract than the capitalism of firms dealing with commodities. If we need a new term for this historical period, then we might consider 'virtualism', because it rests on replacing consumers with virtual consumers.

[. . .]

REFERENCES

Fine, Ben 1995. From Political Economy to Consumption. In Daniel Miller (ed.), *Acknowledging Consumption*, pp. 127–163. London: Routledge.

Fine, Ben, and Ellen Leopold 1993. *The World of Consumption*. London: Routledge.

Gledhill, John 1994. *Power and Its Disguises*. London: Pluto Press.

Hamsun, Knut 1921. *Hunger*. New York: Knopf.

Harvey, David 1989. 1996. *Justice, Nature and the Geography of Difference*. Oxford: Basil Blackwell.

Keat, Russell, Nigel Whiteley and Nicholas Abercrombie (eds) 1994. *The Authority of the Consumer*. London: Routledge

MacLennan, Carol 1997. Democracy under the Influence: Cost–Benefit Analysis in the United States. In James G. Carrier (ed.), *Meanings of the Market: The Free Market in Western Culture*, pp. 195–224. Oxford: Berg.

Miller, Daniel 1987. *Material Culture and Mass Consumption*. Oxford: Basil Blackwell.

—— 1988. Appropriating the State on the Council Estate. *Man* 23: 353–372.

—— 1994. *Modernity: An Ethnographic Approach*. Oxford: Berg.

—— 1995. Introduction. In D. Miller (ed.), *Acknowledging Consumption*, pp. 1–57 London: Routledge.

—— 1997. *Capitalism: An Ethnographic Approach*. Oxford: Berg.

—— 1998. *A Theory of Shopping*. Cambridge: Polity Press.

Power, Michael 1994. *The Audit Explosion*. London: Demos.

—— 1997. *The Audit Society*. Oxford: Oxford University Press.

Rose, Nicholas 1996. The Death of the Social? Re-Figuring the Territory of Government. *Economy and Society* 25: 327–356.

Salaman, Graeme 1997. Culturing Production. In Paul DuGay (ed.), *Production of Culture/Cultures of Production*, pp. 235–272. London: Sage.

Sloman, John 1994. *Economics*. New York: Harvester-Wheatsheaf.

Smart, Alan 1997. Oriental Despotism and Sugar-Coated Bullets: Representations of the Market in China. In James G. Carrier (ed.), *Meanings of the Market: The Free Market in Western Culture*, pp. 195–225. Oxford: Berg.

Stiglitz, Joseph 1993 *Economics*. New York: W. W. Norton and Co.

Thrift, Nigel 1997. The Rise of Soft Capitalism. *Cultural Values* 1: 29–57.

Walsh, Kieron 1994. Citizens, Charters and Contracts. In Russell Keat, Nigel Whiteley and Nicholas Abercrombie (eds), *The Authority of the Consumer*, pp. 189–206. London: Routledge.

16

Seeing Culture as a Barrier

Emma Crewe and Elizabeth Harrison

[...]

While rational motivation is assumed to direct people towards maximizing gain, there is a prevalent view that 'traditional culture' relies on something far less reasonable. The idea of traditions holding people back has a persistence across the development industry. 'Developers' talk and write about the traditional way of life, the traditional relationship between husband and wife, traditional skills, the traditional three-stone fire, and traditional farming practices. This traditionalism is partly attributed to economic or ecological conditions, but is often conceived of as being linked to a psychological or cultural disposition that is in some sense backward and prevents people from embracing modernity. For example, an FAO Chief Technical Adviser writes:

> Unfortunately, many of the factors which determine the ability to climb up the ladder are largely beyond the scope of specific energy development progammes. Among these are household income and size, climate, settlement size and – let's be realistic – culture and tradition to a large extent (Hulscher 1997: 12).

Another FAO study describes the process of modernization in rather more complex terms:

> Such changes have affected urban life in many countries far more directly than rural society. The capitals are already integrated into the world economy. Their rural hinterlands depend on them for imported commodities and for centralized services based on export revenues. However, the villages are often far behind, not only in economic benefits, but also in the change in value-orientations that characterize what may be called a modern society. This is not because villages are isolated. Nor does it mean a breakdown in social integration between urban and rural members of families...But a differentiation is taking place between people of more modern orientation, with more education and/or ambition, and those with less (Hayward 1987: 3).

This characterization of culture implies stasis, unless a culture is influenced by 'modern society'. Other cultures are portrayed as absolute and given, and their characteristics subject to identification and possibly subsequent modification. Kinship, 'norms', 'taboos', and other aspects of social relations are treated as fixed, often in relation to 'modern' and flexible values. Echoing Malinowski's claim that anthropologists can help colonialists (1927: 40–1), social scientists are still used by development agencies to understand and then handle cultural and social factors. For the promoters of technologies, such as fish-farming or improved stoves, the practices associated with them are influenced by a social context that can be delineated and separated from the particular entity we (they) are interested in. The perception involves a simple process and unidirectional causation: cultural rules drive practice. In this way, gaps in knowledge, social obligation, reciprocity, and levelling mechanisms are seen as factors that influence whether or not the technology is 'adopted', rather than mental constructs developed partly by the 'developers' themselves. It is true that beneficiaries give expression to such ideas, but they are in part a reformulation of the developers' ideas about cultural rules.

So, 'local' people in Africa and Asia are seen as slow to adopt new technology partly because of 'cultural barriers'. These are portrayed in two ways: (a) as barriers derived from ignorance, and (b) barriers created by cultural rules. The following explanation by a technician stresses ignorance:

> An evaluation indicated that the replacement of the traditional ovens did not work successfully, basically because of social barriers. The new oven design worked well in the laboratory and was easily constructed by traditional oven builders, who supplied most of the households with ovens. However, despite many promotion activities, there was no awareness and concern about the need to save fuel and the new oven was not utilized economically (Usinger 1991: 7).

It is, therefore, natural to argue that it is the role of the promoters of the technology to assist in filling the knowledge gap. Although difficult to overcome, the problem is seen as essentially a technical one. Its solution is found in developing appropriate extension methods and technologies suitable to local conditions. If ignorance of the 'locals' is stressed, an aspect of this barrier is also acknowledged to be a failure on the part of the 'developers' themselves. For example, there have been attempts to introduce aquaculture to environments where people are not used to or are not keen on eating fish, or to introduce new stoves that burn fuel not available in that area. Attempts to improve understanding often entail an appreciation of the need to avoid earlier blunders.

The second category of barriers, those created by cultural rules, is seen as much more immovable. Broadly speaking, it is about the role of 'social control': this may include social obligation, reciprocity, and levelling mechanisms. In this sense, culture is a barrier to development in much the same way as it was when the language of 'primitive customs' was current. The potentially inhibiting role of cultural rules concerning accumulation, reciprocity, and appropriate behaviour has been widely noted (Ruddle 1991; Nash 1986; Hayward 1987). It is suggested that 'in many societies worldwide, levelling mechanisms are fundamental in controlling the individual and in functioning to maintain social status ranking' (Ruddle 1991: 12).

In 'developing' or 'traditional' societies, such mechanisms are expected to be particularly influential. Thus an individual who invests too much time and energy in economically productive activities as opposed to meeting social obligations is likely to be regarded as a deviant who must bear social costs. The nature of the costs will vary from theft and social ostracism to witchcraft accusations. The net result, however, is perceived to be

the same: reluctance to adopt new technologies and inability to continue using them after adoption. For example, aquaculture, with its potentials for accumulation and image of modernity, is thought to be subject to such pressures. A frequently cited example comes from Malawi, where apparently belief in witchcraft is so strong that small-scale farmers, including fish-farmers, dare not produce more than their peers for fear of being bewitched (ICLARM/GTZ 1991). In these accounts, 'traditional' and 'modern' are regularly contrasted. Particular beliefs and behaviour are presented as being internal to the village and in opposition to those from outside, and standing independently of people's interpretation and use of them. Little or no attention is paid to explaining why and how in particular situations beliefs and actions are labelled by actors themselves as traditional or modern.

This outlook is not really surprising. 'Tradition' and 'culture' are associated in people's minds with anthropology, and as an anthropologist you are expected to understand them. As Holy and Stuchlik (1983) point out, however, the assumption of norms having a compelling effect on behaviour is still implicitly entertained in many anthropological analyses, despite the common phenomenon of people violating rules to which they verbally subscribe. They argue that social life should not be treated as an entity with a definite (though changing) form. Rather, analysis should focus on the ways in which norms are given force when people invoke them or disregard them in their actions: 'the basic question is not whether the action is norm conforming or norm breaking, but which norms, ideas and reasons were invoked by the actors for the performance of the action' (Holy and Stuchlik 1983: 82).

'Culture' as a barrier is not, however, always seen as an impediment to be circumvented. Development workers, expatriate or national, sometimes explicitly state that they should not interfere with the 'traditions' of a culture. Within some agencies, this is particularly the case when it comes to gender relations. It is often argued that by challenging gender relations, outsiders disrupt the 'traditional' ways of an alien culture. The imposition of their values could possibly precipitate an unacceptable social upheaval. In some contexts, the social order within 'traditional' cultures is implicitly perceived to be closer to nature than 'modern' societies, and therefore governed by what some would describe as natural laws, which might include male dominance. Certainly it is often deemed to be inappropriate to question a gender division of labour where tasks such as fuel provision and cooking are designated as female, even when this critically affects the outcome of a fuel conservation or stove project. [...] There are some unlikely alliances between such views and those of opponents to the supposed imposition of Western feminism from within these countries.

The idea that culture is worth protecting when gender is involved is inconsistent when set beside other social transformations brought about by development. It is taken for granted by many that development rearranges class relations – the purpose of many projects is, rhetorically at least, to make poorer people richer. Even caste relations, which tend to be portrayed as a traditional cultural system, can be fair game. For example, Intermediate Technology project staff have related with pride that one project in Sri Lanka challenges the caste system because lower-caste potters employ higher-caste labourers. They dismiss gender concerns, in contrast, as cultural and irrelevant to their work with technology.

If the simplistic traditional culture versus modernity dichotomy is misleading, why does it survive? In some ways it is useful for development planners. It conceals many social processes – for example, how social phenomena are continually re-created, negotiated, and changeable. Nevertheless (or maybe therefore), it does help provide a framework for making difficult decisions. With limited resources, both project staff and development planners are increasingly faced with a dilemma. Given that you are unable to work with all farmers, which ones do you work with – those who are poorest or those who are more likely to make a 'success' of whatever venture is being promoted? The distinction between tradition and modernity thus fulfils two functions. It is a simplifying device for those who identify themselves with mainly technical issues and require a straightforward explanation of failure. It is also potentially a tool for overcoming the tricky problem of choosing which farmers to work with.

REFERENCES

Hayward, P., 1987, 'Socio-cultural aspects.' In ALCOM, Socio-Cultural, Socio-Economic, Bio-Environmental, and Bio-Technical Aspects of Aquaculture in Rural Development, ALCOM GCP/INT/436/SWE.1, Harare.

Holy, L. and M. Stuchlik, 1983, Actions, Norms and Representations: Foundations of Anthropological Inquiry. Cambridge: Cambridge University Press.

Hulscher, W.S., 1997, The fuel ladder, stoves and health. Wood Energy News vol. 12, no. 1, Regional Wood Energy Development Programme in Asia, Bangkok.

ICLARM/GTZ, 1991, The Context of Small Scale Integrated Aquaculture Systems in Africa: A Case Study of Malawi. Manila: ICLARM.

Malinowski, Bronislaw, 1927, The life of culture. In G.E. Smith et al. (eds), The Diffusion of Controversy. New York: Norton.

Nash, C., 1986, Observations on International Technical Assistance to Aquaculture. Rome: FAO.

Ruddle, K., 1991, The impacts of aquaculture development in socio-economic environments in developing countries: towards a paradigm for assessment. In R. Pullin, ed., Environment and Aquaculture in Developing Countries. ICLARM Conf. Proc. 31. Manila: ICLARM.

Usinger, J., 1991, Limits of technology transfer. Boiling Point, no. 26, Intermediate Technology Development Group, Rugby.

Part V

Gender, Work, and Networks

Introduction

Development policies are rarely, if ever, gender-neutral (see, for example, Benería and Sen 1986; Deere 1995; Gladwin 1991; Spring 2000). Institutions that intervene in development, as Sylvia Chant and Matthew Gutmann point out in chapter 17 below, often have patriarchal structures. And the societies in which the interventions occur typically favor men over women in access to resources and property rights, and in terms of prestige and personal autonomy. Since the 1970s, when the role of Women in Development first became a major concern, "gender" has implicitly referred to women, even though in the strict sense of the word it pertains to a *relation* between socially defined masculine and feminine categories. Chant and Guttmann argue that men must be incorporated into gender and development programs for two main reasons: gender relations are changing rapidly in most parts of the world and, for gender interventions to be effective they cannot only target women. In many parts of the world, rising female workforce participation and reduced employment prospects for un- or semi-skilled male workers have led to major shifts in the balance of power within households (Safa 1995). Problems such as domestic violence, Chant and Guttman maintain, must be addressed both by attending to the victims and the potential or actual perpetrators and by formulating development policies that reduce gender inequality and that have positive impacts on both men and women. Their contribution discusses how the assumption that "gender" means "women" had a number of perverse effects, such as male resentment of women's favored access to micro-credit programs and a neglect of key health problems that disproportionately affect men, including high-risk behavior and violence, vehicular and work accidents, and cardiovascular illness. The latter problems are, they suggest, closely connected to prevailing notions of masculinity. Essential to the success of gender and development programs, therefore, is the involvement of men-as-men or men as a gendered category.

In the works of E. P. Thompson and James Scott, "moral economy" referred to the beliefs, traditions, and emotions that surround relations between dominant and subordinate groups, whether in the labor or grain markets or in conflicts over notions of justice and customary practices, such as gleaning in fields, hunting in woods, or having right of way across properties (Thompson 1971, 1991; Scott 1976). Jane Collins, in chapter 18 below, examines how globalization has eroded moral economic assumptions and practices, specifically workers' possibilities of making claims on their employers. She documents a large textile operation's move from Virginia to Mexico which would appear to be a prototypical case of the corporate "race to the bottom." Collins is less interested in analyzing footloose capital, however, than in how the globalization of labor markets affects workers and their communities. Corporations are not only more mobile than ever before, but mobility, Collins maintains, has allowed them to replace the paternalistic, multi-dimensional, moral economic relationships that they once had with their employees with unidimensional, purely market-based relationships. Workers, on the other hand, face increasing difficulties in constructing knowledge about deterritorialized employers and have had to find "new ways of communicating information and imagining solidarity" across national borders.

In the 1980s and 1990s, the rise of "civil society" generated tremendous excitement among development practitioners and activists in the human rights, environmental, peace, women's, and minority rights movements. They saw civil society organizations as the motor of democratization in Eastern Europe and Latin America and as a dynamic emerging force for grassroots development and empowerment worldwide. Annelise Riles takes a more hard-nosed approach to the transnational networks of non-governmental organizations that have achieved growing prominence internationally and in the nations where their component groups are based. In a study of the Pacific women's groups that attended the 1995 Beijing United Nations Women's Conference, she finds that network processes of knowledge production often have a disturbingly circular character and emphasize the diffusion of certain kinds of imagery and organizational forms at the expense of serving their claimed constituencies.

Anthropologists and other social scientists have long debated the role of NGOs in development (Fisher 1997; Florini 2000; Gill 2000) and have warned about the "NGO-ization" of social movements (Alvarez 1998). Riles takes the critique a step further, calling attention not just to the romanticism of some NGO claims, but to the ways network activists learn to speak primarily to each other while largely neglecting the grassroots organizations that they claim to represent. Hers is a sobering analysis and while social scientists, foundation officers and development practitioners have informally related similar stories *sotto voce* for many years, Riles is among the first to articulate what many have whispered but few have had the courage to put in writing.

REFERENCES CITED

Alvarez, Sonia E., 1998 Latin American Feminisms "Go Global": Trends of the 1990s and Challenges for the New Millennium. *In* Cultures of Politics/Politics of Cultures: Re-Visioning Latin American Social Movements, Sonia E. Alvarez, Evelina Dagnino, and Arturo Escobar, eds., pp.293–324. Boulder, CO: Westview.

Benería, Lourdes, and Gita Sen, 1986 Accumulation, Reproduction, and Women's Role in Economic Development: Boserup Revisited. *In* Women's Work: Development and the Division of Labor by Gender, Eleanor Leacock and Helen I. Safa, eds., pp. 141–157. South Hadley, MA: Bergin & Garvey.

Deere, Carmen Diana, 1995 What Difference Does Gender Make? Rethinking Peasant Studies. Feminist Economics 1(1): 53–72.

Fisher, William F., 1997 Doing Good? The Politics and Antipolitics of NGO Practices. Annual Review of Anthropology 26: 439–464.

Florini, Ann M., ed., 2000 The Third Force: The Rise of Transnational Civil Society. Washington, DC: Carnegie Endowment for International Peace.

Gill, Lesley, 2000 Teetering on the Rim: Global Restructuring, Daily Life, and the Armed Retreat of the Bolivian State. New York: Columbia University Press.

Gladwin, Christina H., ed., 1991 Structural Adjustment and African Women Farmers. Gainesville: University Presses of Florida.

Safa, Helen I., 1995 The Myth of the Male Breadwinner: Women and Industrialization in the Caribbean. Boulder, CO: Westview.

Scott, James C., 1976 The Moral Economy of the Peasant: Rebellion and Subsistence in Southeast Asia. New Haven: Yale University Press.

Spring, Anita, ed., 2000 Women Farmers and Commercial Ventures: Increasing Food Security in Developing Countries. Boulder, CO: Lynne Rienner.

Thompson, E. P., 1971 The Moral Economy of the English Crowd in the Eighteenth Century. Past & Present 50 (Feb.): 76–136.

—— 1991 Customs in Common. New York: New Press.

17

"Men-streaming" Gender? Questions for Gender and Development Policy in the Twenty-first Century

Sylvia Chant and Matthew C. Gutmann

Introduction

Gender and Development (GAD) policies encompass a broad range of approaches and interventions, but to date have largely been associated with programmes established by women for women. This is despite the fact that, in theoretical terms, GAD is concerned with gender relations, and therefore with men as well as women. [. . .]

'Male-blindness' in practical applications of gender and development policy is in part a legacy from the early years of the United Nations Decade for Women (1975–85), when the 'WID' (Women in Development) movement emerged as the first step in a struggle against a seemingly universal 'male bias' in development programmes. WID aimed to see women integrated into development on an equal basis as men, notwithstanding that the tactic of concentrating exclusively on women failed to shake the patriarchal foundations of mainstream development thought and practice. Other identifiable reasons for men's relegation to the periphery of gender and development include the concern to ringfence for women the relatively small amount of resources dedicated to gender within the development field, worries about male hi-jacking of a terrain that women have had to work very hard at to stake out, lack of acknowledgement and understanding regarding men as gendered beings, the pragmatic difficulties of incorporating men in projects that have long been aimed primarily or exclusively at women, and last, but not least, an apparent lack of interest on the part of men in gender and development in general

and working with men on gender issues in particular [. . .].

Yet, it has become increasingly clear that a 'women-only' approach to gender planning is insufficient to overturn the patriarchal structures embedded in development institutions, and to redress gender imbalances at the grassroots in any fundamental way. This has prompted moves to 'mainstream' gender, such that instead of integrating gender into pre-existing policy concerns, attempts are made 'to *transform* mainstream policy agendas from a gender perspective' (Kabeer and Subrahmanian, 1996: 1, emphasis in original; [. . .]). Increasingly inscribed in principle, if not necessarily in practice, the process of mainstreaming entails the re-working of structures of decision-making and institutional cultures such that gender becomes a central rather than a peripheral issue. Theoretically, at least, mainstreaming also calls for men to be more involved both at operational and project levels. As observed by Rathgeber (1995: 212), planning for change in women's lives clearly entails changes for men, with structural shifts in male–female power relations being 'a necessary precondition for any development process with long-term sustainability' [. . .].

The fact that much of the impetus for men's involvement in development work originates with women – both at the grassroots level and in development agencies – indicates more than simply a lack of interest on the part of men in GAD. More significantly it points to a certain reluctance among both men and women in GAD work to engage with various core issues and problems that gave rise to gender and development frameworks in the first place. In this paper we address several of these conceptual and operational obstacles, basing our discussion in part on interviews with over 40 representatives from nearly 30 development organizations, agencies, foundations and consultancies in Britain and the USA in 1999. These interviews were conducted as part of research commissioned by the Latin America and Caribbean Division of the World Bank [. . .].

How far is GAD from WID?

To the extent that gender still largely is equated with women alone, the move from Women in Development to Gender in Development has really changed very little. The concept of including men in development work is undoubtedly more systematic as policy rhetoric than as actual practice. Nonetheless, the fact remains that many aspects of men's beliefs and behaviour cannot be understood if they are not viewed in the context of gender relations between men and women and among men themselves. If many women and some men have been subordinated because of gender identities and discriminatory practices, it necessarily follows that men have been the instigators of these forms of inequality. In addition, in development programmes to date, there has been a notable lack of interest, especially among male development workers, in working with men on gender issues such as those involved in the issues of reproductive health, education and violence. Among other problems there has emerged a debate regarding the prudence of promoting men's involvement in issues primarily centring around proclaiming and defending 'men's rights', in contrast to efforts aimed more at the incorporation of men in already existing projects conceived and executed under the aegis of feminist leaders.

Men as a human category have always been present, involved, consulted, obeyed and disobeyed in development work. Yet men as a gendered category in a feminist sense – involving unequal power relations between men and women and between men – have rarely been drawn into development programmes in any substantial way. While many development analysts and policy makers believe that more work with men should be conducted under the Gender and Development umbrella, there is far less consensus as to how this should be done, and the extent to which this should become a component element within development work around gender issues.

Why Should Men Be Incorporated in Gender and Development Operations?

Although to date there seems to be something of a hiatus between the imperative of 'mainstreaming' gender and the actuality of 'men-streaming' gender and development, there are two pressing sets of reasons why more dedicated efforts might be made to realizing the latter. One is the increasingly widespread recognition that, without men, gender interventions can only go so far. The second is that gender roles, relations and identities have been undergoing considerable upheaval in recent years [. . .]. This has created both a space and a need for men to be brought more squarely into the frame of gender and development work.

To deal with the latter set of issues first, while it cannot be refuted that, for reasons relating to gender, most women continue to face greater social and economic disadvantages than their male counterparts, habitual emphasis (by design or default) that men benefit from development in ways which women do not, gives the very misleading impression that men's power and privileges are uniform, fixed and universal [. . .]. As summed-up by Sweetman (1998): 'women are not always the losers'.

This has become increasingly apparent during the last ten years in which there has been growing talk of 'men in crisis', 'troubled masculinities' and 'men at risk', and where particular groups such as young lower-income males have been noted as especially vulnerable to insecurity and marginalization [. . .]. In various parts of the South, particularly in Latin America and the Caribbean, and to a lesser extent in Southeast Asia, male youth are beginning to fall behind their female counterparts in rates of educational attainment, and have more difficulty obtaining employment (see Kaztman, 1992; Corner, 1996; Lumsden, 1996; Chant and McIlwaine, 1998). Male concerns about being unable to provide for wives and children are also noted in various parts of sub-Saharan Africa (see Morrell, 2001; Obote Joshua, 2001).

Declining prospects for assuming the economic responsibilities attached to the widely idealized male role of 'breadwinner' have not only undermined men's status and identities, but are also linked with men's marginalization within, if not detachment from, conjugal family households (Moore, 1994; Escobar Latapí, 1998; Güendel and González, 1998; Silberschmidt, 1999). This, in turn, has been exacerbated by shifts in domestic power relations as women have entered the labour force in rising numbers and become increasingly enabled to take charge of their own domestic arrangements [. . .]. Rising emphasis in social policy on female household heads, and the intensification of social problems such as crime and violence, have been important corollaries of these trends (Sweetman, 1997: 4; Moser and McIlwaine, 1999).

Despite prevailing cultural norms that define men's familial responsibilities as revolving around their breadwinner capacities, in many parts of the world patriarchal family units dependent primarily or exclusively on male incomes are declining, and ideological challenges to traditional gender relations overall are growing. In this context, researchers are exploring the differential impact on men and women of recent and dramatic transformations in labour markets (see Safa, 1995, 1999; Gutmann, 1998, 1999). For instance, in Mexico, Agustín Escobar Latapí (1998: 123) has sought to 'understand the restructuration of men's lives that began with the broader economic and social restructuration . . .', as well as to gain a richer appreciation in terms of gender analysis and power distinctions of these larger macro-level processes.

The issue of men's shifting responsibility for providing financially for their families relates in turn to a more general relationship between gender and a host of related social divisions such as class, ethnicity and age. These relationships may be, and should be, made explicit. For example, in many societies in which poverty alleviation programmes and women's participation in microenterprise efforts have been underway for years, men's breadwinner status has been roundly challenged, with severe repercussions for both men and their families. Vijayendra Rao, an economist at the World Bank whom we interviewed in our survey, described the ramifications of a programme in South Asia:

. . . in a micro-credit programme, there's some evidence that men are using women as a conduit for bringing resources into the family. And there's resentment that only women can bring resources to the family. In a programme I was involved in six to seven years ago, men would ask, 'Why isn't there anything for me?' 'Why is there only help available for the women?' And these are valid questions. They didn't have access to credit, but we were giving it to women when the men were better educated and perhaps in a better position to take the information we provided them and be productive. There was a lot of confusion about what it was we were trying to do and there were a lot of conflicts that arose inadvertently. (Interview with Vijayendra Rao, economist, World Bank, Washington DC, 20 July 1999.)

Flowing in part from such changes is a range of 'lifestyle' factors such as domestic violence which has added to a widely noted increase in ill-health among men as well as women in developing countries. Male violence against women is in some respects better analysed than male violence against other men. Throughout the world, laws and penalties are becoming stricter, and therapy and assistance for women and children are growing. Though still badly underfunded, programmes designed to assist women who are victims of domestic abuse now have a long history, and many of the elements involved in providing shelter and counsel to these women are better understood. With respect to male-on-male violence, however, aside from many commonplace assumptions regarding the relationship between masculinity, testosterone and violent proclivities, there is still too little scholarly research and even less programmatic work on this problem.

Male gendered violence against men, motivated by homophobia, for example, provides a separate set of data for which reliable statistics are rarely available (see Rivera Fuentes, 1996). The issue of men and violence is further complicated because, although men and masculinity are clearly implicated, gender research no longer relies on the simplistic foundation that universally equated men with violence and women with peace. Still, the key problem that remains for development workers is not so much analytic as practical: how to engage men as well as women in work around crucial questions such as rape and sexual coercion, male homicide and gang activities. Greig *et al.* (2000: 4–5) write more generally about the importance of practical efforts around engaging men in development work and their relation to overall goals of gender equality:

Examining masculinity and the role it plays in the development process is not simply an analytical exercise, but has widespread implications for the effectiveness of programmes that seek to improve economic and social outcomes in virtually every country . . . Gender equality is not only an end in itself, but also a necessary means to achieving sustainable human development and the reduction of poverty.

Identifying a Problem Is Not Enough to Resolve It

To note that there is a preponderance of males who are perpetrators of violence does not resolve the questions as to *why* this might be the case nor *what* may be done to relieve the situation. Efforts aimed at resolving these problems must incorporate the understanding that men-as-men are themselves engendered and (that) they in turn engender others. Those involved in homicides (and suicides) are in most of the world men, and vehicular accidents, too, tend to affect men at far higher rates than women. Along with road accidents, work injuries and cardiovascular illness (Jiménez, 1996; Barker, 1997: 5–6; Pineda, 2000), men in many parts of the South also have disproportionate rates of infection from sexually transmitted diseases such as HIV / AIDS (Campbell, 1997). In part this is a result of same-sex sex among men and the climate of homophobia which prevails in many parts of the world that greatly hinders prevention and treatment efforts from the top levels of government down to those most plagued by this [. . .] illness. Nonetheless, the primary vector for HIV transmission in most parts of the world is heterosexual men, and HIV is today spreading faster among women than men, primarily through heterosexual sexual relations, both between spouses and between female sex workers and their clients. Further, although the spread of AIDS stems in large part from unprotected sexual liaisons of men with other men, as well as with women, the fact that men are currently 80% of a global total of 6–7 million injecting-drug users is also significant (Foreman, 1999: 128).

The extent to which men's 'risk behaviour' reflects the expectations encoded in formerly dominant/predominant masculinities or is a response to the progressive unseating of patriarchal power structures is unclear, but there is mounting evidence that men's fears and insecurities are growing. In the Kisii District of Western Kenya, for example, men are observed to be 'left with a patriarchal ideology bereft of its legitimising activities and not able to fulfil new roles and expectations' (Silberschmidt, 1999: 173). This also applies in northwest Costa Rica, where men's increasingly tenuous position with the household and the labour market is widely perceived to have been exacerbated by recent legislative and policy initiatives in women's interests. These include laws and programmes strengthening women's access to property, to social welfare, to the exercise of personal rights and to the elimination of domestic violence. Men feel that these measures have made them increasingly redundant in women's lives, especially given women's rising levels of employment (Chant, 2000b). In some cases men have broken the veil of silence traditionally surrounding male admissions of vulnerability, and are seeking help. As observed by Barker (1997: 4):

> Worldwide, men largely derive their identity from being providers or 'breadwinners', and lack ideas, or alternative gender scripts, to find other meaningful roles in the family in this changing economic environment. Research worldwide reports that men are confused about their roles in the family and about the meanings of masculinity in general and are requesting opportunities in which to discuss and deal with these changes.

Quite apart from men's growing needs for attention and assistance in their own right, it could also be dangerous for women and children if such needs are neglected. Castells (1997: 136) and Foreman (1999: 14), amongst others, observe that individual and collective anxiety over the loss of male power is provoking increases in male violence and psychological abuse. Alcoholism and marital strife are also on the increase (Barker, 1997). The United Nations Educational, Scientific and Cultural Organisation (UNESCO) further adds that where men lose power and status and are unable to enjoy their traditional entitlements, women may be the main victims [. . .] (UNESCO, 1997: 6).

With respect to violence brought about through war and national conflict, it is important to have projects that reach not just men in general, but more particularly young men, and that these projects engage them in programmes that include as a central component the examination of what it means to think and behave as men in particular social contexts in the twenty-first century. In addition to these larger questions it is also essential that more mundane problems such as alcoholism, and even the widespread reluctance of men in many countries to seek medical assistance until it is 'too late', also be addressed systematically. In their own right and in relation to the lives and health of women, the gendered aspects of men's customary behaviour have pervasive implications for the lives of whole societies (see UNICEF, 1997).

The Problem of Women-Only Interventions

If a 'crisis of masculinity' provides one set of justifications for thinking men into gender and development, the previously mentioned fact that women-only approaches have their problems is another. As Färnsveden and Rönquist (1999: 90) write:

The recent focus on men and masculinities opens up possibilities for an increased male interest for participation in GAD, since – all of a sudden – men's interest and positions are at stake when discussing gender issues. However, men still need to be encouraged to become involved in gender work, since women still feel that they have an epistemological privilege when discussing, and working with, gender issues. Here lies a great challenge for both men and women in the future work for promoting gender equality.

One major consequence of excluding men from GAD projects is that this can give rise to the emergence or aggravation of hostilities between men and women at the grassroots and to the blocking or sabotage of moves to enhance women's lives and livelihoods. An analysis of women's income-generating projects in Honduras, Greece and Kenya by Safilios-Rothschild (1990), for example, indicated that projects aimed at raising women's access to income in situations where men have difficulty being bread-winners were often unsuccessful. Men facing pressures of long-term employment insecurity responded to what they regarded as 'threats' posed by improvements in women's economic status by taking over projects, by controlling the income generated and/or, as a further backlash, increasing their authority and control within the home (see also Gutmann, 1998).

Aside from deliberate responses on the part of men to being 'left out', a major consequence of male exclusion from gender projects is the likelihood of women ending up with greater workloads and responsibility than they can actually take on. As summed-up by Sweetman (1997: 2), a focus on women alone can lead to 'overload and exhaustion'. Targeting women has become a particularly favoured route to economic and developmental efficiency since the onset of debt crises and neoliberal restructuring in the 1980s. Yet in Costa Rica, for example, evidence suggests that the increasing emphasis in social policy, and particularly in poverty alleviation programmes, on female heads of household can drive men still further from assuming familial responsibilities (Chant, 2000b). Lack of male involvement can also mean that benefits of such women-only projects may be seriously constrained. The first programme for female heads of household established by the [José María] Figueres administration in Costa Rica in 1996 had arguably less impact than it would otherwise have done had it included men. Despite proposals for a male-inclusive 'Re-socialization of Roles' component in the programme, this was dropped on grounds that it would be too difficult to execute. Instead, workshops on rights, self-esteem and so on were restricted to women who continued having to deal with unsensitized men in their personal lives, and with patriarchal structures in both private and public arenas (Budowski and Guzmán, 1998). The limited effectiveness of this approach was such that some women made specific requests to local programme organizers that their menfolk should participate (Chant, 2000a).

In other contexts, a push from the grassroots by women to involve men in gender work has already translated into practice, such as in the Nicaraguan NGO CISAS (Centro de Información y Servicios de Asesoría en Salud) (see Sternberg, 2001), and the Mexican NGO 'Salud y Género'. At the inception of the latter in 1992, Salud y Género worked on health promotion with women. Subsequently, however, its operations broadened to include men in response to the need to work holistically as opposed to compartmentally [with] respect [to] health problems with gendered causes and outcomes, such as alcoholism, violence and sexuality (de Keijzer, 1998). This also incudes working on masculinity itself as a risk factor. Indeed, acting as if men are irrelevant and that men do not have gender can impose demands on women that are impossible to fulfil and/or have serious implications. If men are not incorporated into gender and development work, the implicit assumption will be that women should continue to be largely if not solely responsible for problems relating to such issues as domestic violence and contraception. With respect to health, for instance, in addition to the need to address male-specific problems such as prostate and testicular cancer, the goal of educating men about reproductive health is premised on the notion that involving men with their partners in taking responsibility for safe sex, contraception and health care decisions more generally is essential if persisting inequalities are to be tackled. Making education and discussion about subjects such as condom use and vasectomies central to gender and development work will, or at least should, imply the central participation of men.

In addition to these considerations, Wood and Jewkes (1997: 45) note that ignoring men belies misplaced assumptions, for example, about women's ability to 'control their bodies and thereby achieve and sustain sexual health'. Such assumptions are perhaps particularly serious as far as female genital mutilation and AIDS and other sexually transmitted diseases are concerned (UNICEF, 1997; Foreman, 1999; Wasser, 2001). As identified by a representative of the International Planned Parenthood Association, in our interview survey, for example:

You could treat a woman every day for a sexually-transmitted disease and, if her partner has it and doesn't get treated, then he just keeps reinfecting her. So, in epidemiological terms, it doesn't make sense to keep wasting medication on women. (Interview with Judith Helzner, Director of Sexual and Reproductive Health, International Planned Parenthood Federation, Western Hemisphere Region, New York, 11 June, 1999.)

Leading on from this, it is obvious that incorporating men as well as women could make gender interventions more relevant to people's daily lives, and thereby enhance their chances of success. Moreover, in a longer-term perspective, active efforts to engage men in gender projects could help not only to dismantle gender inequalities, but make men bear greater responsibility for change. For example, a UNICEF project in Zambia for prevention and control of maternal and congenital syphilis sought to break the cycle of recurrent syphilis infection by encouraging men to seek treatment. This led to a jump from 6–8% to 60–80% of male partners attending the Maternal and Child Health (MCH) clinic in the interests of their children being born healthy (UNICEF, 1997: 32). Another UNICEF project in Vietnam, on child health, reached men through the Vietnam Women's Union to educate them in basic health prevention measures for infants and children. The initiative not only led to the participation of 47,000 men, but also to a 60% increase in the use of oral rehydration salts, and to immunization reaching a level of 90% in less than one year (UNICEF, 1997: 32). Another example is provided by 'Stepping Stones', a pilot project in Uganda that consisted of training young men around HIV/AIDS awareness, gender issues, and communication and relationship skills. This resulted in a decline in domestic violence and alcohol consumption after only 16 months of participation (Large, 1997: 28).

Ways to Include Men in Gender and Development

One important strategy to increase male participation and responsibility may be to bring more male staff into gender-related development work. In various cultural contexts, for example, it seems that men are more likely to listen to men, including when it comes to talking gender [...]. In the context of gender training in East Africa, for example, Obote Joshua (2001: 38) notes that '...a female trainer has a "less legitimate" voice than the men she is training, notwithstanding her education and knowledge'. Although male gender trainers may initially be perceived with disdain or mistrust on the part of other men, on balance they are more likely to be successful in communicating and gaining acceptance of new and alternative notions about gender (Obote Joshua, 2001: 38). The East African experience is also found in reproductive health programmes in Bangladesh, where the government has attempted to educate influential male religious leaders about the benefits of family planning in the hope that this will persuade more men to use and/or allow their wives to use, contraception (Neaz, 1996). Similarly, in Nicaragua, the NGO 'Puntos de Encuentro' has developed programmes and workshops among men to prevent male violence against women (Montoya Tellería, 1998).

[...]

Summarizing from diverse experiences throughout the world to date, there is no automatic organizational format for approaching these issues. In some contexts, such as in health and reproductive health programmes, men-only and women-only clinics seem to have been most effective, while in others the reverse has proved to be the case. Flexibility is crucial in providing substantial, and at times differential, access to facilities. Among men – for instance in Ghana (see International Planned Parenthood Federation [IPPF], 1996) – some pilot programmes designed to involve men in educational and health care initiatives have been launched inside factories. Yet, as noted by Wegner et al. (1998: 2),

...policymakers, programme managers, health care workers and other types of providers can block male involvement. This may occur because of conservative cultural and political values, the conventional wisdom that men are not interested in reproductive health matters or simply the assumption that family planning is a woman's responsibility.

Aside from the desirability of stepping up male inclusion as clients and personnel in gender and development programmes, building a critical mass of gender-sensitive male staff within development agencies more generally could have a domino effect, and work towards the destabilization of patriarchy in institutional cultures. Difficult though some of these questions might be, we know that, in general terms, the equation of gender with women has produced a weak, marginalised and under-funded sector, especially where gender issues are dealt with by specialised female-only or female-dominated units [. . .]. In the longer term, therefore, some 'de-feminization' of gender planning could result in greater resources for gender and development, and more enthusiastic and sustained commitment to the reduction of gender inequalities [. . .]. As Foreman (1999: 35) has suggested: 'The challenge of the future is to create societies where women's strength achieves its full potential without relegating men to insignificance'.

Given [. . .] that men as well as women have problems with 'gender culture' (White, 1994: 108), especially during an era now widely identified as one of 'male crisis', the idea that men might be able to shake-off the straitjacket of 'hegemonic masculinity' may be decidedly appealing. ('Hegemonic masculinity' is defined by Robert Connell (1997: 186) as an idealized, dominant, heterosexual masculinity, constructed in relation to women and to subordinated masculinities, and closely connected to the institution of marriage.) As Foreman (1999: 14) has summarized: 'Masculinity brings with it privileges and, in many societies, freedoms denied to most women. Such privileges, however, impose burdens'. Renegotiating gender may be especially desirable for those men who suffer domination, homophobia and other forms of discrimination and violation from other men [. . .]. This also applies to those who are caught up in acts of violence and/or armed conflict as a result of social and ideological pressures surrounding manhood [. . .].

Paradoxically, however, as Sarah White (2000: 35) observes, too often in discussions of masculinity there is a tendency to lose sight of some of such larger life-and-death issues:

In fact, there is a clear asymmetry in the way that men and women are approached in much of the gender literature. 'GAD for women' is robustly materialist, concentrating on social relations particularly as they define rights and responsibilities in work, consumption and households. That is, it has not been characterised by the exploration of female subjectivities. 'GAD for men' is by contrast much more individualistic and personal, much more preoccupied with the self.

One might argue that a key rationale for such an emphasis on male subjectivities stems from attempts to gain support for GAD by appealing to narrowly conceived notions of men's self-interests. That is, by endeavouring to avoid altogether the issue of gender inequality, the challenge of transforming oppressive social relations might be most appropriately addressed. Having said this, such assumptions feed roundly into what Cornwall (2000: 21) has termed the 'problematic male' discourse, whereby oppositions between men and women – which pose the former as useless, irrelevant, parasitic and so on, and the latter as either victims or heroines – are taken as a norm, regardless of context or intra-group heterogeneity. In addition, constructions of Third World men as 'idle' and 'irresponsible' can also be used to serve wider North-South political agendas, such as justifying why neoliberal reforms are not working (see Whitehead (2000) on the 'lazy man' in African agriculture).

Conclusions

Although there is considerable uncertainty regarding how exactly to go about including men as gendered constituencies in gender and development, many professionals would like to see debates and practice taken forward [. . .]. More specifically, our own survey of gender and development practitioners indicated that a strong desire to include men in GAD work was shared by all but a handful of our 41 respondents [. . .]. As articulated by one of our interviewees:

I think it's really positive that there is a strong push now to looking at men. For political reasons it's vital, and for practical reasons as well. Because we all know stories about how projects have been undermined because men were excluded from them. (Interview with Helen O'Connell, Education and Policy Coordinator, Oneworld Action, London, 8 July 1999.)

The field of gender initiatives with men is currently led primarily by organizations concerned with family planning, health and/or domestic violence, but our survey also indicated that gender work in education, family and youth, micro-credit programmes and employment-generating schemes is also likely to benefit from broadening out the traditional focus on women [. . .]. Clearly there is widespread support for finding ways to truly incorporate men in gender and development work generally. Yet without a doubt, too few practical efforts have been made to achieve this goal. There is a real need to clarify the means by which to accomplish the myriad tasks involved in such an endeavour as well as to develop a detailed series of policy goals that can actually lead to the greater involvement of men-as-men in development projects.

The concern that women will disappear from development work once the floodgates are opened to men is prevalent among many providers. As Muneera Salem-Murdock of USAID stated in her interview:

The reason – and this really comes from experience – that we keep focusing on women, is because experience has really taught us that if you do not focus, if you do not underline, if you do not specify, then more frequently than not they tend not to be considered at all. And you cannot do development without half the society... When we need to focus on men in GAD, I would welcome that time, because that means not only have women achieved equality, but they have surpassed it. And I would be more than happy to focus specifically on men if they are the underclass. Absolutely. Until that time, however, there's no need to focus specifically on men. (Interview with Muneera Salem-Murdock, USAID, Washington DC, 7 June 1999.)

The study of men and masculinities in both academic and development settings is in its true infancy. Inspired in large measure by feminist scholarship and advocacy, the fact is that, regardless of widespread popular opinions on the subject, we have relatively little systematic knowledge of men and their gendered beliefs and practices [...]. While important tactical issues remain to be worked out, and the process can in no way be fast-tracked, it is entirely conceivable that 'men-streaming' gender could become a critical tool in 'mainstreaming' gender (Chant and Gutmann, 2000). This, in turn, could help to sustain, and extend [into the twenty-first century and beyond] the gains made [thus far] by GAD advocates and practitioners [...].

REFERENCES

Barker, G. 1997: Emerging global trends related to the role of men and families. Briefing notes for a Brown Bag Discussion organised by the Chapin Hall Center for Children at the University of Chicago, October.

Budowski, M. and Guzmán, L. 1998: Strategic gender interests in social policy: empowerment training for female heads of household in Costa Rica. Paper prepared for the International Sociological Association XIV World Congress of Sociology, Montreal, 26 July–1 August.

Campbell, C. 1997: Migrancy, masculine identities and AIDS: the psychosocial context of HIV transmission on the South African gold mines. *Social Science and Medicine* 45(2), 273–81.

Castells, M. 1997: *The power of identity*. Oxford: Blackwell.

Chant, S. 1997: *Women-headed households: diversity and dynamics in the developing world*. Houndmills, Basingstoke: Macmillan.

Chant, S. 2000a: From 'woman-blind' to 'man-kind': should men have more space in gender and development? *IDS Bulletin* 31(2), 7–17.

Chant, S. 2000b: Men in crisis? Reflections on masculinities, work and family in northwest Costa Rica. *European Journal of Development Research* 12(2), 199–218.

Chant, S. and Gutmann, M.C. 2000: *Mainstreaming men into gender and development: debates, reflections, and experiences*. Oxford. Oxfam.

Chant, S. and McIlwaine, C. 1998: *Three generations, two genders, one world: women and men in a changing century*. London: Zed.

Connell, R.W. 1997: *Gender and power: society, the person and sexual politics*. Standford: Stanford University Press.

Corner, L. 1996: *Women, men and economics: the gender-differentiated effects of macro-economics*. New York: UNIFEM.

Cornwall, A. 2000: Missing men? Reflections on men, masculinities and gender in GAD. *IDS Bulletin* 31(2), 18–27.

de Keijzer, B. 1998: *El Varón como Factor de Riesgo, Familias y Relaciones de Género en Transformación: Cambios Trascendentales en América Latina*. Mexico City: Population Council/EDAMAX.

Escobar Latapí, A. 1998: Los hombres y sus historias: reestructuración y masculinidad en México. *La Ventana* 5, 122–73.

Färnsveden, U. and Rönquist, A. 1999: Why men? A pilot study of the existing attitudes among SIDA's staff towards male participation in the promotion of gender equality in development. Unpublished Masters dissertation, Peace and Development Research Institute, Göteborg University, Sweden.

Foreman, M. 1999: *AIDS and men: taking risks or taking responsibility*. London: Panos Institute.

Greig, A., Kimmel, M. and Lang, J. 2000: *Men, masculinities and development: broadening our work towards gender equality*. Monograph No. 10. New York: UNDP/GIDP.

Güendel, L. and González, M. 1998: Integration, human rights and social policy in the context of human poverty. In UNICEF, editor, *Adolescence, child rights and*

urban poverty in Costa Rica. San José: UNICEF/
HABITAT, 17–31.

Gutmann, M.C. 1996: *The meanings of macho: being a
man in Mexico City*. Berkeley, CA: University of California Press.

Gutmann, M.C. 1998. *Mamitis* and the traumas of development in a *Colonia Popular* of Mexico City. In
Scheper-Hughes, N. and Sargent, C., editors, *Small
wars: the cultural politics of childhood*. Berkeley,
CA: University of California Press, 130–48.

Gutmann, M.C. 1999: A manera de conclusión: solteras
y hombres, cambio e historia. In González de la
Rocha, M., editor, *Divergencias del modelo tradicio-
nal: hogares de jefatura femenina en América Latina*.
Mexico City: CIESAS, 163–72.

International Planned Parenthood Federation (IPPF)
1996: *Africa link: just for men: involving men in
sexual and reproductive health programmes*. London:
IPPF.

Jiménez, R. 1996: Adiós al patriarca. In Instituto Lati-
namericano de Naciones Unidas para la Prevención y
Tratamiento del Delincuente (ILANUD), *Construc-
ción de la identidad masculina*. San José: ILANUD,
43–46.

Kabeer, N. and Subrahmanian, R. 1996:
*Institutions, relations and outcomes: framework and
tools for gender-aware planning*. Discussion Paper
No.357. Brighton: Institute of Development Studies
University of Sussex.

Kaztman, R. 1992: Por qué los hombres son tan irre-
sponsables? *Revista de la CEPAL* 46, 1–9.

Large, J. 1997: Disintegration conflicts
and the restructuring of masculinity. In Sweetman, C.,
editor, *Men and masculinity*. Oxford: Oxfam, 23–30.

Lumsden, I. 1996: *Machos, maricones and gays: Cuba
and homosexuality*. Philadelphia/London: Temple
University Press/Latin America Bureau.

Montoya Tellería, O. 1998: *Nadando contra corriente:
buscando pistas para prevenir la violencia masculina
en las relaciones de pareja*. Managua: Puntos de
Encuentro.

Moore, H. 1994: *Is there a crisis in the family?* Occasional Paper 3, World Summit for Social Development.
Geneva: UNRISD.

Morrell, R. 2001: The times of change: men and masculinity in South Africa. In Morrell, R., editor, *Changing
men in Southern Africa*. Pietermaritzburg/London:
University of Natal Press/Zed, 3–37.

Moser, C. and McIlwaine, C. 1999: A guideline on conceptual and methodological issues for designing and
analysing the results of participatory urban appraisals,
PUAs, in the context of violence. Mimeo. Washington
DC: LCSES, World Bank.

Neaz, A. 1996: Converting Bangladesh's influential religious leaders. In International Planned Parenthood
Federation (IPPF), *Challenges: men's needs and responsibilities*. London: IPPF, 38–40.

Obote Joshua, M. 2001: Gender training with men: experiences and reflections from East Africa. In Sweetman, C., editor, *Men's involvement in gender and*

development policy and practice. Oxford: Oxfam,
35–43.

Pineda, J. 2000: Partners in women-headed households:
emerging masculinities. *European Journal of Development Research* 12(2), 72–92.

Rathgeber, E. 1995: Gender and development in action.
In Marchand, M. and Parpart, J., editors, *Feminism/
postmodernism/development*. London: Routledge,
204–20.

Rivera Fuentes, C. 1996: Todas locas, todas vivas, todas
libres: Chilean lesbians 1980–95. In Reinfelder, M.,
editor, *Amazon to Zami: towards a global lesbian
feminism*. London: Cassell, 138–51.

Safa, H. 1995: *The myth of the male breadwinner:
women and industrialization in the Caribbean*. Boulder, CO: Westview.

Safa, H. 1999: *Women coping with crisis: social conse-
qences of export-led industrialization in the Dominican Republic*. North-South Agenda Paper No. 36.
Miami FL: North-South Center, University of
Miami.

Safilios-Rothschild, C. 1990: Socio-economic determinants of the outcomes of women's income-generation in
developing countries. In Stichter, S. and Parpart, J.,
editors, *Women, employment and the family in the
international division of labour*. Houndmills, Basingstoke: Macmillan, 221–28.

Silberschmidt, M. 1999: 'Women forget that men are the
masters': gender, antagonism and socioeconomic
change in Kisii District, Kenya. Uppsala: The Nordic
Africa Institute.

Sternberg, P. 2001: Challenging machismo to promote
sexual and reproductive health: working with Nicaraguan men. In Sweetman, C., editor, *Men's involvement in gender and development policy and practice*.
Oxford: Oxfam, 59–67.

Sweetman, C. 1997: Editorial. In Sweetman, C., editor,
Men and masculinity. Oxford: Oxfam, 2–6.

Sweetman, C. 1998: 'Sitting on a rock': integrating men
and masculinities into gender and development. Paper
presented at ESRC Seminar 'Men, Masculinities and
Gender Relations in Development', Development Project and Planning Centre, University of Bradford, 8–9
September.

Sweetman, C., editor, 2001: *Men's involvement in gender
and development policy and practice: beyond rhetoric*.
Oxford: Oxfam.

UNICEF [United Nations Children's Fund] 1997: *The
role of men in the lives of children*. New York:
UNICEF.

UNESCO [United Nations Educational, Scientific and
Cultural Organisation 1997]: *Male roles and masculinities in the perspective of a culture of peace*. Report,
Expert Group Meeting, Oslo, Norway, 24–28 September. Paris: UNESCO.

Wasser, N. 2001: Male involvement in perpetuating and
challenging the practice of female genital mutilation in
Egypt. In Sweetman, C., editor, *Men's involvement in
gender and development policy and practice: beyond
rhetoric*. Oxford: Oxfam, 44–51.

Wegner, M.N., Landry, E., Wilkinson, D. and Tzanis, J. 1998: Men as partners in reproductive health: from issues to action. *Family Planning Perspectives* 24(1), 1–9.

White, S. C. 1994: Making men an issue: gender planning for the other half. In MacDonald, M., editor, *Gender planning in development agencies: meeting the challenge.* Oxford: Oxfam, 98–110.

White, S. C. 2000: 'Did the Earth move?' The hazards of bringing men and masculinities into gender and development. *IDS Bulletin* 31(2), 33–41.

Whitehead, A. 2000: Continuities and discontinuities in political constructions of the working man in rural Sub-Saharan Africa: The 'lazy man' in African agriculture. *European Journal of Development Research* 12(2), 23–52.

Wood, K. and Jewkes, R. 1997: Violence, rape and sexual coercion: everyday love in a South African township. In Sweetman, C., editor, *Men and masculinity.* Oxford: Oxfam, 41–46.

18

Deterritorialization and Workplace Culture

Jane L. Collins

Anthropologists have long understood that labor markets are social and cultural constructions, deeply embedded in local institutions and practices. When workers and employers struggle over the terms and conditions of labor, these power-charged negotiations are never simply market transactions. They draw on rhetorical strategies, habits, and traditions that are familiar to, if not endorsed by, both groups. They involve provisional agreements about what constitutes justice, what is a fair distribution of rewards and efforts, and how the parties should behave toward one another. These "moral economies" of the workplace provide the grounds on which one group makes claims on another and the language for framing those claims (Scott 1976; Thompson 1971). They are not closed and immutable systems, but open, communicative frameworks susceptible to innovations of many kinds (Jones 1983).

In this article, I ask the question: What happens to these moral economies and their rhetorical frameworks when the labor market in question is redrawn to include workers in vastly different national settings? The context for raising these questions was my ethnographic research conducted with workers and managers at a Virginia knitwear firm. The company, in operation since 1937, was the primary employer in a small southern town. It made the transition from old-fashioned mill, to a modern publicly owned corporation in the 1980s, to a unionized workforce in 1994. Buffeted by the competitive pressures that devastated the US textile and apparel industries in the 1990s, the firm sought to reshape work regimens at the same time that it moved some stages of production to Mexico and Jamaica. Through observations and inter-

views conducted in 1999, I sought to document the ways that workers and managers understood these changes.

In December 1999, the firm declared bankruptcy and its 4,300 workers lost their jobs. I documented the response of workers to this event. At the same time, I felt that I was missing part of the story. Following Marcus's (1995) suggestion that globalization may require multisited ethnography, I arranged for a brief period of research in Aguascalientes, Mexico, to observe and interview in a (still-functioning) factory where the Virginia firm had subcontracted its sewing operations.

The research in Virginia revealed that the dense, complicated, and profoundly ambiguous rhetoric and relationships that had structured the paternalist labor practices of the firm's first 57 years in Virginia had not simply evaporated. The emergent moral economy of the union period continued to be leavened by residual norms and expectations from the era of paternalism. But, more importantly, the transition to contractually governed work rules for which workers had struggled never quite occurred. The moment of union triumph (1994) was also a moment of triumph for neoliberal trade policies (the North American Free Trade Agreement [NAFTA]) and a moment in which unregulated consolidation in the retail sector was driving clothing prices down. Facing the competitive pressures unleashed by these events, the company ignored the union. Understanding that their jobs were at stake, there was little that workers could do in response. Global economic forces eroded the old ways that the Virginia workers could make claims on the firm, at the same time that they undermined the new basis for claims making that the union sought to establish. In Mexico, workers found themselves employed by a corporation with no ties to their community beyond a simple labor market transaction. Because of the practice of subcontracting, they did not know the name of the firm for which they were producing sweatshirts, where it was located, or who ran it. In addition, the Virginia-based firm had no legal responsibility for the conditions of their work.[1]

I argue that it is possible to understand communities of workers in both of the sites described here in terms that Appadurai (1990) has called "deterritorialization." Unlike the immigrant workers to whom theories of spatial dislocation have been previously applied (Lavie and Swedenburg 1996; Ong 1999; Sassen 1998) the individuals described here do not leave home. Rather, it is the mobility of firms and their construction of radically deracinated production processes that break apart relations between workers and their employers within the localized spaces where social reproduction occurs. Strategies of corporate relocation and subcontracting make it difficult for workers to know their employers and, in many cases, even to know whom their employers are.

My argument is not that deterritorialization is an inevitable part of economic globalization. Globalization is not like gravity. It is actively constructed and struggled over by actors in a multitude of locations. As the social movements that have coalesced around trade negotiations and the World Trade Organization (WTO) have emphasized, these struggles are not over whether the global economy should expand but over how it should be regulated; not over whether expansion is good or bad, but over who gains and who loses as a result of specific investments and regulations.

Deterritorialization is one way that firms can structure their relationships in the places where they do business. Ethnographers and geographers have sometimes characterized these relationships as the "erosion of locality" (Beynon and Hudson 1993; Peck 1996; Storper and Walker 1989). They have emphasized the diminishing investments that mobile firms make in locations where they have factories and the reduction of multistranded employment contracts to single-stranded wage transactions. It is a strategy of minimizing long-term commitments and investments, maintaining labor as a variable cost, and enhancing the flexibility of the firm at the expense of workers' security.

To take advantage of cheap labor, globally organized firms can rely on strategies other than deterritorialization. Some companies have developed ways of mobilizing local social networks to recruit and control workers. McKay (2001) has described the ways that electronics firms in the Philippines use kin-based recruitment strategies and screening of workers to insure a docile labor force. They may require referrals from local officials, who then assume responsibility for the workers' behavior (and to whom the workers then owe votes at election time). [. . .]

Neither deterritorialization nor localization are unambiguously good or bad for workers. They are different strategies or styles of recruiting and managing labor and as such they constitute distinct environments within which workers must struggle for autonomy, labor rights, respect, and fairness. [. . .] The networks of relations that sociologists are fond of calling "social capital" can have a dark side. [. . .] Certain kinds of connectedness can entrench inequalities and reproduce existing power relationships, making it more difficult for workers to act on their own behalf. A critique of deterritorialization is thus not a lament for an imputed golden age of close-knit communities – what Rosaldo has called "imperialist nostalgia" (1985). It is an attempt to describe one complex of social relations, work practices, and rhetoric that is fairly prominent in communities where production is for global markets.

Finally, deterritorialization is not a one-sided assault on workers and their communities. It is an ambiguous process within which workers struggle in different ways for power and autonomy. Localization strategies can be oppressive in making workers responsible for the behavior of their kin and community members and in establishing patronage relations that can be deeply exploitative. Sometimes workers struggle against such networks of connectedness, seeking more democratic and regularized procedures. Where corporations operate in bureaucratized and inhumane ways, however, workers may struggle for more personalized procedures and rules, preferring the strictures of paternalism to having no recourse and no room for negotiation (Wright 1997).

Ong has observed that anthropological articulations of the global and the local often construe "the global as political economic and the local as cultural" (1999:4). They miss the political and economic content of everyday life – both the ways in which lives are structured by large political and economic happenings and the ways in which people enact politics in their workplaces and neighborhoods and practice economics in daily living. In this article, I echo Ong in seeking an approach to understanding "people's everyday actions as a form of cultural politics embedded in specific power contexts" (1999:5), and I seek to extend understanding of the discourses and cultural frames that shape power relations in the workplace. As workers find themselves participating in a labor market that is global in scope, their fate is suddenly linked to individuals in other nations with whom they share neither a language nor a workplace culture. To characterize this process as the "erosion of locality" is to suggest that the social relations of workplace and community are irreparably lost. To conceptualize it as deterritorialization allows for the possibility that new, transnational forms of locality can emerge to "socialize" the actions of firms and foster community among workers.

Neoliberalism and Locality

In the popular imagination, the effects of globalization on workers in the developed countries are most often gauged by numbers of jobs lost or gained. There has been less attention to the question of how participation in an increasingly global labor market affects the institutions and practices of the workplace and the neighborhoods and communities where workers live. Workplace communities in the 1980s and 1990s were affected by two important developments. The first was a casualization of employment relations, in which long-term jobs with benefits were increasingly replaced with part-time and short-term jobs, which were often arranged through a sub-contracting agency. This trend not only had a tendency to inhibit relationships among workers, but it meant that many workers had no direct, contractual relationship with their employers. [. . .]

A second trend affecting workers and their communities in the 1980s and 1990s was the increased mobility of firms. According to *Site Selection Magazine*, Internet transactions, high-speed telecommunications, and fiber optic lines that allow the linkage of operations in diverse locations enabled corporate relocation within the United States to more than double from 1996 to 2000 (*New York Times* 2000:24). The movement of labor-intensive operations offshore, or the off-loading of those operations to subcontracted firms in other countries increased as well. The new mobility of firms has created a situation in which workers and their employers relate to place in different ways. [. . .]

This situation places workers at a disadvantage in their negotiations with employers. Burawoy has argued that it gives rise to a particular politics of

production that he calls "hegemonic despotism" (1985:150). He suggests that corporate mobility has created a situation in which the "tyranny of the overseer over individual workers has been replaced by the tyranny of capital mobility over the collective worker... the fear of being fired is replaced by the fear of capital flight, plant closure, transfer of operations and plant disinvestment" (1985:150). This fear creates a situation in which workers not only demand less from their employers, but also accept pay cuts, irregular hours (forced overtime when the company needs them, temporary layoffs when it does not), smaller benefits packages, and reduced enforcement of health and safety regulations. It has led workers to back away from unions. Long-lasting ties between employers and communities are lost, and corporate investment in the local environment is diminished.

Some researchers have argued that, while deepening internationalization has pulled workers apart by stretching production systems across borders and introducing a new level of competition among workers, it also binds these workers together in common international production systems, often under a single employer (Moody 1997:36). This is the situation in the case examined here, where the erosion of locality in one place was tied in complex ways to the establishment of a spatially dispersed production process linking workers in the United States and Mexico. While corporate officials plan and execute these spatially dispersed activities, a central task for workers is to construct knowledge of what the firm is producing in different locations, where inputs are coming from, and where products are sold. Building solidarity and a common agenda across spatially dispersed communities requires new ways of both communicating information and imagining community.

Paternalism as Moral Contract: Race, Gender, and "Family" in a Southern Knitwear Firm

The firm that came to be known as Tultex Corporation was founded in 1937 in the wake of a wave of unrest in the textile industry. [. . .] What led William Pannill to start a textile venture under such conditions was the allure of new knitting machines. Pannill had worked in cotton mills in North Carolina before moving north in 1903 to learn this new technology, which was first applied to hosiery production. He returned south to the small town of Martinsville, Virginia, in 1937 with the goal of setting up a factory that would produce knitted goods for other purposes. [. . .]

The new knitting mills were the most desirable sources of employment for textile workers in the 1930s. [. . .] Pannill did not build his knitting mill in an isolated hamlet that included housing for workers; instead, he took over an abandoned cotton mill in the growing town of Martinsville, Virginia, where he employed the wives and daughters of local furniture workers and rural women and men who had access to automobiles.

The firm was a family enterprise from the start. Pannill turned his new company—Pannill Knitting—over to his son-in-law, Michael Sale, soon after founding it. After three years, Sale passed on the firm, which he had renamed Sale Knitting, to his brother-in-law (the husband of another of Pannill's daughters), William Franck. The Franck family—first William and later his son John—retained ownership of the company until it went public in the 1980s. The elder Franck was able to obtain lucrative contracts for producing underwear for the military during World War II and emerged from the war with a thriving business.

In 1971, Sale Knitting merged with a diversified New York apparel firm—the Henry J. Tully Company, changing its name first to the Tully Company and, in 1976, to Tultex. The new firm that resulted was a vertically integrated operation that performed all tasks from the manufacture of yarn to the packing of finished clothing. Workers spun yarn; knit it into fabric; dyed or bleached it; fleeced it; and cut, sewed, labeled, and packaged the final product. Most of the work was done in Martinsville, but some sewing and yarn manufacturing took place in seven smaller plants in rural Virginia and North Carolina.

In the 1980s, when the market for sportswear and athletic apparel soared, Tultex soared with it. [. . .] When the firm went public in that decade, it had nearly 6,000 employees. From the 1970s through 1990s, it acquired several smaller firms that produced related products or inputs. [. . .] In December 1997, the firm was designated an "all-star" by *Apparel Industry Magazine.* [. . .] Its sales [. . .] in that year placed it among the top 30 US apparel firms (*Fairchilds Textile and Apparel Financial Directory* 1999).

Tultex brought a measure of prosperity and stable jobs to the otherwise poor region where it operated. [. . .]

It was a somber testimony to the competitive pressures facing the US apparel industry in the 1990s that, by December 1999, the firm had declared bankruptcy and laid off its 4,300 workers.

[. . .] The state faced massive unemployment claims, and local services were overwhelmed with demands, especially since the layoffs came during the coldest time of the year and in the midst of the December holiday season. City and county officials organized job fairs and short-term loan programs. They also put together a package of incentives for new industry that included free land for any company that would make a substantial capital investment. News services across the country picked up the story of the "Free Land for Jobs" program, and it was covered by Dan Rather on the Saturday Evening News.

A series of public hearings was held as Tultex's bankruptcy proceeded, in which workers voiced first their hurt and astonishment and, later, their determination to pursue claims as creditors against the company for severance pay, unpaid bonuses, vacation pay, and contributions to pension plans. Public outrage was fueled by news of the large payments made to top company executives in the last six months of operation and by the hefty severance packages that top managers were requesting from the bankruptcy judge. Meanwhile, the Virginia State Legislature debated and ultimately rejected a bill that would have provided emergency benefits to laid-off workers. (Virginia State Legislature 2000).

For 57 of its 62 years, Tultex had operated on a model of paternalism. Paternalism has been described by historians of the southern textile industry as a system that united white workers and their employers in a conservative and racialized consensus. Paternalistic mill owners sought to model their relationships with workers after that of a father dealing with his children. [. . .]

Historians of the southern United States disagree about whether paternalism ultimately had any value for workers. [. . .] In part, the debate reflects the different positions of the scholars who write about the institution, but it also derives from the fact that paternalism was many things in many places and times, continually being reworked to adapt to new conditions. [. . .]

As the primary employer in the town of Martinsville and surrounding counties, Tultex exerted a powerful influence over local politics and governance. It also scrupulously maintained a public face of good will and largesse. [. . .] Tultex cultivated the idea that what was good for the firm was good for the community and for workers, but it always retained the right to determine what that "good" was.

The enforcement of norms and expectations, and reciprocal but unequal duties, was facilitated

by dense webs of kinship within the firm. [...]
Family connections were not simply a way for the
firm to exercise control over workers, however. It
was the practice throughout the decades for line
bosses to be promoted up from the ranks of
workers. This meant that line bosses shared networks of kinship with other employees. Thus, they
could often be held accountable for tyrannical
workplace discipline through social networks outside the firm (Hall et al. 1987:96).

Because relationships within the firm were multistranded and face-to-face, there was a general
understanding that management could ask
workers for "help" in hard times. Workers could
be asked to work overtime to meet a deadline, to
defer a raise in times of economic difficulty, and to
tolerate layoffs in slow periods. There was also an
expectation that worker complaints would remain
internal to the firm. When a malfunctioning fork-
lift spewed carbon monoxide into one of Tultex's
small sewing plants in 1994, causing 60 workers
to pass out, employees came to work the next day
and none filed claims against the company despite
the fact that several experienced long-term health
effects. In return for their forbearance in this case,
workers felt that they were entitled to job security,
continuing (if slow) improvement in wages and
conditions, and treatment as individuals. [...]

As many analysts of the southern United States
have pointed out, racial segregation was a key
element of the paternalist system in the mills up
until the 1960s (Boyte 1972; Genovese 1976;
Janiewski 1991). One had to be white to be a
member of the "mill family" and they offered
racial exclusivity as part of the "wages of whiteness" (Roediger 1991). [...] As in most southern
mills, the majority of workers at Tultex were
female, so that rhetoric of racial segregation was
gendered, with the firm claiming to provide a safe
and respectable work environment for white
women workers. [...] Before this time, black
workers performed a number of nonproduction
jobs such as groundskeeping, loading and
unloading operations, and janitorial tasks.

After the Civil Rights Act of 1964, integration at
Tultex began slowly, but picked up speed in the
1970s. By the 1980s, African American workers
had come to form the majority in the plant. Once
hired, black workers were not drawn into the
social networks of paternalism that governed
everything from work assignments, to overtime,
to shift rotations. [...] They did not, or could not,
look to personal ties to white managers as a way to
insure fair treatment. At least in part for this
reason, black workers at Tultex were among the

earliest and most enthusiastic supporters of the
union.

Attempts to bring a union to Tultex had begun
in the 1970s, and workers waged seven membership drives before finally achieving success in
1994. [...] The union's success in 1994 could be
attributed, in part, to actions taken by Tultex in
the early 1990s in response to a series of bad years.
A slowdown in the market for sweatwear coincided with an increase in cotton prices and generalized deflation in the apparel sector. There was
growing pressure to lower labor costs as more and
more of the firm's competitors moved operations
(or subcontracted) overseas. Tultex responded by
laying off workers, closing down its sewing plants,
and moving those operations to Mexico and Jamaica. It then announced wage cuts and ended its
contributions to workers' pension plans.

All of these actions were seen by white workers
as violations of the paternalist contract. [...] In
an interview with me, a union organizer
[remarked] "They were changing in the 1990s to
a public corporation, and they changed the basis
on which they do business.... Before that Franck
would say 'give me another chance ... I built this
company with you.' And they would, but I think
they played the family card one time too many."

This sense of betrayal, or violation of an implicit
contract, was less marked among black workers
who, because they had been largely excluded from
personalized ties with (white) managers, had never
harbored illusions of the firm as "family." Most of
the firm's black employees saw the union, rather
than ties to management, as the best chance for
improved wages and working conditions. Frederickson (1985) has argued that the growth in mili-
tancy of southern textile workers since 1965 is a
direct result of the organizing activities of black
women. [...]

The fact that black workers had been excluded
from networks of patronage and had long experienced discrimination in things like job assignments, shift rotations, and access to overtime
meant that much of what they sought from the
union was standardization and fairness in work
procedures. Both black and white women workers
also wanted access to the full range of jobs in the
plant, including higher-paid positions that they
had been excluded from in a rigid, if somewhat
arcane, division of labor. The contracts that were
negotiated in 1995 and 1998 specified the rules for
every aspect of advancement and work assignment
in great detail. Establishing a culture in which the
rules mattered was a more difficult task. When
workers grieved violations in the first years of the

union they were not only attempting to redress unfairness that affected them as individuals but fighting a battle to replace the racially inflected personalism of the preceding period with habits of attention to democratically established rules and procedures.

The emergent rhetoric of contract associated with the 1994 union drive coexisted with the well-established rhetoric of paternalism. Both union and firm argued that they had the greater good of the community at heart and portrayed the other party as seeking narrow financial gain. [...]

[...] In the process of negotiating the first union contract with Amalgamated Clothing and Textile Workers Union (ACTWU) in early 1995, the firm reorganized itself to accommodate the new contractually governed practices of the union era. It raised prices to accommodate the higher wage bill, established rules for promotion, shift rotation, layoffs, and grievance procedures, and established an employee-management committee to address productivity issues.

The era of paternalism had left a mixed heritage. As a managerial style, it blended consent with force, but as a rhetoric, it provided workers with certain resources. [...] The ideology of firm as family went both ways and allowed workers to hold managers accountable for behavior that appeared uncharitable or self-interested. [...] It was these social and rhetorical resources that constituted "locality" in the mid-1990s.

The "Stretch-Out" in the Era of Globalization

At Tultex, the era of the union coincided exactly with growing pressure on the firm to globalize production. The cost-cutting measures that angered workers enough to make them vote for the union were the firm's first response to a complex set of competitive pressures that severely lowered corporate earnings in the 1990s. Consolidation in the retail sector increasingly allowed the firm's buyers to set prices.[2] [...] Apparel firms relied increasingly on overseas contractors to lower their labor costs. The passage of NAFTA in 1994 opened new opportunities to produce and subcontract in Mexico. Firms that were able to globalize their production strategy were better able to meet retailers' demands for deflationary pricing. Tultex could move its sewing operations overseas, but it could not easily transfer its more complex and capital-intensive knitting and dyeing operations. Moving some operations offshore required that the firm reorganize its tightly integrated vertical production process.

Because the coming of the union coincided with these pressures, there was no era of labor peace at Tultex. There was no period in which the union was simply a means to press claims, defend rights, and achieve gains in salary and benefits. [...] Union meetings served as a venue for workers to try to understand the forces that were undermining their position. During the union's first year, the firm closed two sewing shops, moving the work to owned and contracted sewing facilities in Mexico. It combined cuts in the number of hours employees could work each week with new productivity measures that increased stress for workers on the job.

Workers in textile mills have waged a battle against the stretch-out since the first days of the industry, although the term dates to the 1920s. The *stretch-out* referred to the practice of increasing the number of looms or spinning machines for which workers had responsibility. [...] Workers chafed under the new routines, striking in Greensboro, South Carolina; Elizabethton, Tennessee; and other locations. As one worker at Cone Mills expressed it: "Hundreds of folks go to jail every year... for doing things not half so bad or harmful to their fellow man as the stretch-out" (Terrill and Hirsch 1978:178).

The stretch-out introduced at Tultex in the 1990s had a new twist. In classic speedups, managers often reset piece rates in order to hold salaries more or less constant – so that workers did not realize a net gain from their higher productivity. At Tultex, a large proportion of workers in the plant were on piece rate or "incentive pay," and since rates were established by union contract, increasing the number of machines should have offered the potential for higher earnings. The stretch-out of the 1990s did not simply involve giving workers responsibility for more of the same machines, however. Managers were experimenting with new team-based approaches and with multitasking. The new approaches placed workers in different jobs on different days, or at different times of the day, or forced them to perform a combination of tasks simultaneously. This slowed workers down to the point that they could not make their "normal" rate at the same time that it vastly increased stress on the job. Researchers have warned of the disadvantage workers experience if piecework is combined with multitasking. [...]

For workers at Tultex, the combination of increased stress and lower earnings was painful. The company had (re)introduced the 12-hour day in the early 1980s, and workers performed these shifts in a complex schedule of four days on, three days off, keeping the plant running 24 hours a day. The lengthy days only exacerbated the stress of the new routines. As one young man from the knitting department complained in a union meeting in 1999, [...] "We're working harder and losing money on a daily basis." He reported that when he questioned his supervisors about his rate of pay, their answers were unsatisfactory: "They throw a bunch of numbers at you that are above your head. They say you're making more money. But you look in your wallet and see that you're not."

Chatting informally with workers after a union meeting, I found that many people concurred with this assessment of things. The 50-year-old President of the union, who had been at the plant for 18 years, said that his son-in-law could occasionally work fast enough to make money under the new system, but that he was "too old to work that hard now." Doris, who had worked as a knitter for 20 years, said, "When I started out, I worked six knitting machines and now I work 11 and a half on two floors. We have to walk further to keep check on all the machines. The walking makes it hard. And we have to carry much more yarn. Each cone is ten pounds, and we carry three at a time. A human body's not meant to carry like that all day long." [...]

The union encouraged workers to file grievances in cases like these. There was a widespread perception among union members, however, that the grievance procedures had ceased to work after the first few years. [...] In this climate, personalism and managerial impunity reasserted themselves. Workers told stories in their union meetings about having been laid off for filing a grievance. One said that his supervisor "shrank two of his creels" (frames that hold bobbins in a knitting machine) when he filed a complaint. This action required him to use smaller bobbins and to change them more frequently, increasing the difficulty of his work and slowing him down. When someone suggested that he grieve that action as harassment, he replied, "She told me if I did, she would shrink all my creels!" One woman summarized the situation: "There's not a grievance been won in fleece knitting in the last two years. They say, 'Your union is crap. Your union is so weak it can't do nothing.'"

For workers in the 1920s, the response to the stretch-out had been to go on strike. Workers at Tultex not only had a "no-strike" clause in their union contract, but they were painfully aware that jobs in the industry were being moved out of the country at a rapid pace. [...] A busload of 120 Tultex workers had traveled to Washington, DC, in 1993, where they visited the offices of members of Congress to encourage them to support anti-sweatshop legislation. [...] As one young man said: "We went to Washington to protest sweatshops. But third-floor knitting is a sweatshop now."

This was not simple irony, however. Hegemonic despotism – the threat of job loss – had unraveled the fabric of "unequal rights and obligations" between workers and the firm. The union's bargaining position was undermined by the fact that the boundaries of the labor market were no longer local. That market now included thousands of nonunionized workers in Mexico and other parts of the world. [...] The politically constructed "economic realities" of free trade were visible enough. Perhaps, in the end, it was Tultex's rootedness in place that prevented it from moving offshore quickly enough, ultimately leading to its bankruptcy.

When Tultex filed bankruptcy, workers were devastated. [...] An employee said, "It makes you feel like 14 years of your life are wasted" (Cawley 2000). "They just dumped us out like we were nothing," another added (Cox News Service 2000).

Union members had organizational structures that allowed them to share information, however. In the first days after the announcement of bankruptcy, this was information about job fairs, loan programs, and other kinds of assistance available to former workers. Later, these same networks were used to establish a creditor group to press claims against the company for back pay, vacation pay, and pension funds. Workers organized to attend public meetings with former company executives, with officials from the US Department of Labor, and with representatives of the US Bankruptcy Court. When Tultex executives argued that other priorities might come before worker claims, the union obtained information about executive pay and severance packages that were being negotiated with the bankruptcy judge and brought it to the attention of the local press. Reminiscent of incidents in the 1920s, when workers faced with the stretch-out obtained and published the tax returns of their employers (Simon 1991:91), workers dusted off the rhetoric of mutual obligation to suggest that managers were taking more than their fair share. One worker noted, "I feel disgusted, I feel it's ridiculous that salary people are getting the bonuses and all of the people doing the work aren't getting anything" (*Martinsville Bulletin* 2000).

Reconstructing Workplace Communities

[...]

Tultex employees struggled for nearly 20 years to replace the habits and practices of paternalism with the more democratically distributed rights and responsibilities of the union. The day-to-day practice of these new rights and responsibilities were also locally grounded – they took place in interactions with shop floor representatives, in membership meetings, regional workshops, picnics, holiday parties, canvassing, solidarity marches, and visits to local and national political representatives. At the moment of union success, however, new economic pressures were changing the shape of the industry. [...] Once it became feasible for firms to move their operations, competitive pressures made it imperative. The spatial framework for decision making shifted from the region to the globe, the time horizon from the long term to the next few years. As one Tultex executive said, "It was a race between us and our competitors to see who could get their sewing operations to Mexico first....If you weren't there, you were out of business."

If labor relations at Tultex were too embedded in place-based relationships and too encumbered by contract to give managers the flexibility they needed to lower the wage bill, what did labor relations in those alternative low-wage locations look like? In March of 2000, a research assistant for this project traveled to Aguascalientes, Mexico. [...] She spoke with local officials and leaders of the textile and apparel industry and visited several garment factories there, including one plant that had produced sweat-shirts for Tultex prior to its bankruptcy and that continued producing these items for Hanes, Sara Lee, and other US firms. This plant housed 60 sewing operators in a dark and cramped warehouse in the central city. Workers assembled garments from fabric that had been knitted, dyed, and cut in the United States. Under the terms of NAFTA, these items made of US materials could be re-imported into the United States without payment of tariffs.

Managers at the plant were attempting to improve the quality of their product through introducing in-line, as well as final, inspections. Shirts were checked by inspectors as the seamstresses produced them, and a "history of defects" was compiled for each worker. Workers' productivity and quality ratios were graphed and posted by their workstations. While these attempts to increase efficiency through "Taylorist" methods seemed to be effective, efforts to implement methods of teamwork and multitasking – like those that had troubled workers in Virginia – had apparently failed.[3] [...] Workers had been unwilling to accept a system of task sharing that slowed down piecework or that linked their wages to the rates of others. Through complaints and productivity declines, workers were able to convince managers to replace the "modular system" with the previous straight-line method.

There are many accounts of work in Mexican *maquilas*, a number of which discuss the politics of shop floor production.[4] Within apparel maquilas, in particular, high rates of labor turnover initially created an impediment to workplace community. By the mid-1980s, labor shortages forced managers to abandon practices of hiring primarily young, unmarried girls and to hire more married women. The average age of the workforce increased, along with the tenure of the average worker (Tiano 1994:80). In most contemporary maquilas, management at the level of the shop floor is personalistic. Line bosses know workers' family situations and bend rules for loyal employees, but they also discipline and fire workers with relative impunity. At higher levels of management, decisions about wages, conditions of work, and factory location are made by expatriates using decision criteria established by corporate headquarters (Fernández-Kelly 1983; Iglesias Prieto 1997; Ruiz and Tiano 1987; Tiano 1994; Wright 1997). The success of workers in Aguascalientes in rejecting new team-work regimens demonstrates the ability of workers to negotiate issues with line and plant managers. [...] More work remains to be done on the rhetoric and vocabularies that structure workers claims in these cases, how differences in institutional form and corporate hierarchy affect the ability of workers to make claims and have them heard, and how workers can obtain the information they need to press claims further up the corporate hierarchy.

Workers in Martinsville experienced job loss as their wages became too costly in a labor market the boundaries of which expanded to include places where workers made in a day what they made in an hour. In Aguascalientes, workers gained jobs selling their labor to corporations that had no ties to the community beyond that labor market transaction. The industry's structure of subcontracting made it difficult for them to know the name of the company that would sell their handiwork, the history of that firm, or the location of corporate headquarters. By law, the contracting firm had no responsibility for their working conditions or wages.

These are 21st-century dilemmas that can perhaps best be understood as dilemmas of deterritorialization. While workers of previous eras had to construct shared understandings and solidarity out of sometimes-fractious communities, under neoliberal production regimes workers must often create community itself before they start to construct solidarity. It is not just the greater mobility of corporations that has changed, but the ways in which firms associate with the places where they do business: the reduction of multistranded relationships with a specific place to single-stranded economic relationships in space (Harvey 1989).

In the 1990s, part-time work, subcontracting, and corporate relocation all challenged the ability of workers to establish lasting and meaningful ties to their employers and their peers. One of the challenges of the antisweatshop movement that emerged in that period, for example, was to help workers figure out who their employers actually were, since the subcontractors who supervised them did not make larger decisions about the production process or conditions of labor. The Justice for Janitors movement in Los Angeles visited the dispersed work sites where cleaning staff worked alone at night to provide them with information about the company that contracted their services and about the union; organizers then followed up with home visits. Bronfenbrenner has argued that spatially dispersed production systems require a new model of union organizing that utilizes grassroots campaigns, house calls, and intensive personal contact (1993:379). The renewed emphasis of some parts of the labor movement on "social movement unionism" (Moody 1997; Tufts 1998) represents an attempt to reground workplace issues within larger community concerns and to develop alliances among groups working for different social causes.

But while these efforts seek ways to reconnect workers and reestablish their grounds for communicating with and making claims on employers, they do not deal with the difficulties of constructing such community transnationally. Unions such as Union of Needletrades, Industrial, and Textile Workers (UNITE) have invested a good deal of effort in educating workers about the way that

the globalization of the industry affects their jobs. [...] It encouraged workers to see the connections between free trade and job loss, and between poor labor conditions in developing nations and corporate relocation. But such understandings may have only reinforced a sense of competition among workers in spatially separated locations. Wills (1996) has argued that local political traditions can be translated across space through the movement of workers and through demonstration effects. Activists in the antisweatshop movement of the 1990s, working through nongovernmental organizations, used Internet connections to uncover and transmit information about corporate organization to apparel factory workers. But at the moment, there are few examples of how such community building operates.

Ironically, experiments in transnational organizing have had more success in linking consumers and producers than in linking workers in the United States and Europe with their peers elsewhere. In the apparel industry, the National Labor Committee received significant media attention when it brought to the United States a young girl who had worked in a factory in El Salvador, producing Kathie Lee Gifford's line of Wal-Mart clothing. The girl's account helped consumers understand more about the conditions under which their clothing was made (Ross 1997). The exposure of sweatshops in Los Angeles revealed how subcontracting obscures responsibility for working conditions, prompting movements for reforming the law to hold branded marketers of apparel accountable for labor conditions in the factories that produce their clothing (Bonacich and Appelbaum 2000). Creating new networks for sharing such information may not resolve perceived conflicts of interest between workers in the United States and their counterparts elsewhere, but it is the first step in developing the kind of deterritorialized community where such issues can be addressed.

In a period when so much anthropological attention is focused on cultural flows across borders, hybridity, creolization, and transnational cross-fertilization, there has been relatively little attention devoted to transnational labor organizing. Workers in southern Virginia and Mexico can drink the same brands of soft drink, enjoy some of the same films, and wear T-shirts with the same logo. What they cannot yet do is share their concerns about labor practices that increase their stress on the job. They cannot act together to prevent their employers from playing each against the other to discipline and rein in their demands. They cannot engage their employers in a discussion about how the actions of the firm will affect their health or the well being of the communities over the long term. New transnational economic flows alter the institutions and practices of the workplace in ways that require workers to develop new rhetorical resources and new forms of resistance. What contestatory frameworks are available to replace the moral economies of paternalism and the besieged contractual economies of the union? How can workers reestablish sociality and reciprocity as a feature of work – building new transnational territorialities? And what new practices can link workers across national boundaries and help them address their shared employers based on their common concerns?

The case presented here suggests that spatially dispersed production regimes and casualized bonds between employers and workers erode the local conventions and practices that formerly structured and, to some extent, regulated employment. In so doing, they have profoundly altered the ways that class relations are experienced. In Martinsville, that erosion was felt intensely by workers in the months prior to the firm's bankruptcy, as their former strategies of making and pressing claims were rendered ineffective by the firm's new global logic of production. In Mexico, production arrangements in new apparel factories denied workers the kinds of knowledge, information, and multifaceted face-to-face contact that would have allowed them to make claims on the firm that employed them. While workers could (sometimes successfully) exert pressure on their immediate supervisors, subcontracting firms could also lose contracts for failing to implement recommended practices.

Anthropologists are learning a great deal from research on diasporic communities and the ways that they retain and recreate bonds across geographic distance (cf. Lavie and Swedenburg 1996; Ong 1999). Potentially, the same tools could be turned to the understanding of new deterritorialized forms of work. In the ways described here, these arrangements undermine the ambiguous moral economies that formerly structured the day-to-day experience of class for workers and their employers. At the same time, in ways that remain to be studied, they potentially link workers in different parts of the world to each other.

NOTES

1 In 1999, the US District Court for the Southern District of New York, in *Lopez v. Silverman*, found that an apparel manufacturer may be jointly liable for a contractor's failure to pay overtime to its employees. The court examined liability in the context of "joint employment doctrine," which is being tested in other economic sectors, such as janitorial work and agriculture. The case sent shock waves through the apparel industry and is under appeal (see *Bobbin Magazine* 1999).

2 In 1990, 20 firms controlled 38 percent of the apparel market. By 1998, the share of these retailers had increased to 47 percent. Among department stores in 1999, the six largest companies captured nine out of every ten consumer dollars spent (*Apparel Industry Magazine* 1999; *Women's Wear Daily* 1998).

3 Taylorism refers to the methods of scientific management developed by Frederick Winslow Taylor in the first decades of the 20th century.

4 Maquilas are plants run by foreign investors in Mexico under the terms of specific programs established by the Mexican government.

REFERENCES CITED

Appadurai, Arjun, 1990 Disjuncture and Difference in the Global Economy. Public Culture 2(2):1–24.

Apparel Industry Magazine, 1999 Apparel's "Big Six" Retailers Grab a 90% Share. Apparel Industry Magazine (June). Electronic document, http://www.aimagazine.com/archives/ 0699/jun99stor3.html, accessed October 7.

Beynon, Huw, and Ray Hudson, 1993 Place and Space in Contemporary Europe: Some Lessons and Reflections. Antipode 25(3): 177–190.

Bobbin Magazine, 1999 Labor Forum: Labor Law Liability – Where Does the Buck Stop? Lopez Case Shakes U.S. Manufacturer – Contractor Paradigm. Bobbin Magazine (April) 1999:64.

Bonacich, Edna, and Richard Appelbaum, 2000 Behind the Label: Inequality in the Los Angeles Apparel Industry. Berkeley: University of California Press.

Boyte, Harry, 1972 The Textile Industry: The Keel of Southern Industrialization. Radical America 6(2):4–49.

Bronfenbrenner, Kate L., 1993 Seeds of Resurgence: Successful Union Strategies for Winning Certification Elections and First Contracts in the 1980s and Beyond. Ph.D. dissertation, School of Industrial and Labor Relations, Cornell University.

Burawoy, Michael, 1985 The Politics of Production: Factory Regimes Under Capitalism and Socialism. New York: Verso.

Cawley, Jon, 2000 Tultex Head Fields Question from Rowdy Crowd. Roanoke Times, January 12. Electronic document, http://www.newslibrary.com/deliverccdoc.asp? SMH=143612, accessed February 14.

Cox News Service, 2000 In Their Hometown, Econimic Change Means Hard Times. Cox News Service, April 2. Electronic document, http://www.coxnews.com/washingtonb... 04-02-00SWEATSHIRTCAPITAL0402. htm, accessed June 21, 2001.

Fairchild's Textile and Apparel Financial Directory, 1999 Fairchild's Textile and Apparel Financial Directory. New York: Fairchild's Books and Visuals.

Fernández-Kelly, Maria Patricia, 1983 For We Are Sold, I and My People: Women and Industry in Mexico's Frontier. Albany: State University of New York Press.

Frederickson, Mary, 1985 "I Know Which Side I'm On": Southern Women and the Labor Movement in the Twentieth Century. In Women, Work and Protest: A Century of U.S. Women's Labor History. Ruth Milkman, ed. Pp. 156–180. Boston: Routledge and Kegan Paul.

Genovese, Eugene D., 1976 Roll, Jordan, Roll: The World the Slaves Made. New York: Random House.

Hall, Jacquelyn Dowd, James Leloudis, Robert Korstad, Mary Murphy, Lu Ann Jones, and Christopher Daly, 1987 Like a Family: The Making of a Southern Cotton Mill World. New York: Norton.

Harvey, David, 1989 The Condition of Postmodernity. Cambridge: Basil Blackwell.

Hurd, Richard, and William Rouse, 1989 Progressive Union Organizing: The SEIU Justice for Janitors Campaign. Review of Radical Political Economics 21(1):70–75.

Iglesias Prieto, Norma, 1997 Beautiful Flowers of the Maquiladora: Life Histories of Women Workers in Tijuana. Michael Stone, trans. Austin: University of Texas Press.

Janiewski, Dolores, 1991 Southern Honor, Southern Dishonor: Managerial Ideology and the Construction of Gender, Race and Class Relations in Southern Industry. In Work Engendered. Ava Baron, ed. Pp. 47–69. Ithaca: Cornell University Press.

Jones, Gareth Stedman, 1983 Languages of Class: Studies in English Working Class History, 1832–1982. New York: Cambridge University Press.

Lavie, Smadar, and Ted Swedenburg, eds., 1996 Displacement, Diaspora and Geographies of Identity. Durham, NC: Duke University Press.

Marcus, George, 1995 Ethnography in/of the World System: The Emergence of Multi-Sited Ethnography. Annual Review of Anthropology 24:95–117.

Martinsville Bulletin, 2000 Judge Cuts CEO's Request for Severance. Martinsville Bulletin, February 10. Electronic document, http://www.martinsvillebulletin.com/ ttx47.htm,accessed July 19, 2001.

McHugh, Cathy L., 1988 Mill Family: The Labor System in the Southern Textile Industry. New York: Oxford University Press.

McKay, Steven, 2001 Securing Commitment in an Insecure World: Power and the Social Regulation of Labor in the Philippine Electronics Industry. Ph.D. dissertation, Department of Sociology, University of Wisconsin.

Moody, Kim, 1997 Workers in a Lean World: Unions in the International Economy. New York: Verso.

New York Times, 2000 Renewed Corporate Wanderlust Puts Quiet Brake on Salaries. New York Times, July 24: A1.

Ong, Aihwa, 1999 Flexible Citizenship: The Cultural Logics of Transnationality. Durham, NC: Duke University Press.

Peck, Jamie, 1996 Work-Place: The Social Regulation of Labor Markets. New York: Guilford Press.

Roediger, David R., 1991 The Wages of Whiteness: Race and the Making of the American Working Class. New York: Verso.

Rosaldo, Renato, 1985 Imperialist Nostalgia. Paper presented to American Ethnological Society, Toronto, Ontario, May 10.

Ross, Andrew, ed., 1997 No Sweat: Fashion, Free Trade and the Rights of Garment Workers. New York: Verso.

Ruiz, Vicki L., and Susan Tiano, eds., 1987. Women on the U.S.–Mexican Border: Responses to Change. Boulder, CO: Westview.

Sassen, Saskia, 1998 Globalization and Its Discontents: Essays on the New Mobility of People and Money. New York: New Press.

Scott, James C., 1976 The Moral Economy of the Peasant: Rebellion and Subsistence in Southeast Asia. New Haven, CT: Yale University Press.

Simon, Bryant, 1991 Choosing between the Ham and the Union: Paternalism in the Cone Mills of Greensboro, 1925–30. In Hanging by a Thread: Social Change in Southern Textiles. Jeffrey Leiter, Michael D. Schulman, and Rhonda Zingraff, eds. Pp. 81–100. Ithaca: Cornell University Press.

Storper, Michael, and Richard Walker, 1989 The Capitalist Imperative: Territory, Technology and Industrial Growth. New York: Basil Blackwell.

Terrill, Tom E., and Jerrold Hirsch, 1978 Such as Us: Southern Voices of the Thirties. Chapel Hill: University of North Carolina Press.

Thompson, Edgar P., 1971 The Moral Economy of the English Crowd in the 18th Century. Past and Present 50: 76–136.

Tiano, Susan, 1994 Patriarchy on the Line: Labor, Gender and Ideology in the Mexican Maquiladora Industry. Philadelphia: Temple University Press.

Tufts, Steven, 1998 Community Unionism in Canada and Labor's (Re)Organization of Space. Antipode 30(3):227–250.

Virginia State Legislature 2000 Virginia State Bill 763. The Textile Workers Relief Act, January 2000.

Wills, Jane, 1996 Geographies of Trade Unionism: Translating Traditions across Space and Time. Antipode 28(4):352–378.

Women's Wear Daily, 1998 Seminar Focus: Megafirm's Clout. Women's Wear Daily, March 26: 14. 2001 Factory Jobs Continue to Decline. Women's Wear Daily, July 9:2.

Wright, Melissa, 1997 Crossing the Factory Frontier: Gender, Place and Power in the Mexican *Maquiladora*. Antipode 29(3): 278–302.

19

The Network Inside Out

Annelise Riles

[...]

Networks and networklike forms of analysis have captured the collective imagination across a span of contemporary disciplines and purposes. In international law and international relations theory, for example, networks as observable institutional organizations of governments and NGOs are widely viewed as more flexible, more progressive, more sophisticated forms of international action, which hold out the hope of success where the state system has failed (e.g., Jönsson 1986; Brysk 1993). Liberal institutions such as the Ford Foundation have invested heavily both in research into the study of networks and in the establishment of networks of human rights activists, women's rights advocates, and environmentalists (Sikkink 1993: 420). One such foundation-supported network [is] Asia-Pacific Women in Politics, which, in January 1994, was launched and funded by the Asia Foundation, an international aid agency closely tied to the US government [...]. As described to me by its Fiji "focal point," however, the Network might raise questions for the democratic principles it is thought to implement:

> I think maybe for us we just decided to call it a network, because it is just limited to that, it's a loose, not so formal organization, sort of thing ... [in] an organization, then you have to be accountable to an executive or to a council or to a board or something like, which we are not. Each of us is just accountable to our Asia Foundation, which is funding in our country.

Nevertheless, networks, in the liberal international relations view, can serve as conduits for the flow not only of information but of enlightenment. Sikkink, for example, notes that they serve "as carriers of human rights ideas" (1993: 437). Documents and documentation processes play a key role in this process: Sikkink offers as an example of an international network success story the "documentation" of abuses by human rights networks, which pass their documents on to the US State Department for inclusion in yet another document genre, the US annual human rights report (422).

If the vision of political change presented here seems askance, the process-oriented aspect of the vision, with its emphasis on the implicit political and cultural impact of daily social practices, is highly reminiscent of sociological analysis: "Every report, conference, or letter from the network underscores an alternative understanding: the basic rights of individuals are not the exclusive domain of the state but are a legitimate concern of the international community" (Sikkink 1993: 441). Drawing upon the sociologist Nicholas Luhmann's systemic theory of social organization as autopoesis (e.g., 1985), the legal scholar Günther Teubner has embraced the Network as a corporate organizational form. The Network, Teubner argues, is "not *between*, but *beyond* contract and organization" (1993: 42) because of its self-organizing quality. It possesses the capability of internally distinguishing and calibrating opposing elements and demands such as variety against redundancy, hierarchy against egalitarian ad hoc arrangements, or collectivity against individual autonomy so that each network transaction leaves the system transformed (48–49): "self-referential circles loop together in such a way as to form new elements which constitute a new system" autonomous from the previous one (43). The international law and international relations theorist Anne-Marie Slaughter appeals to these same networked powers when she argues that in the "real new world order"

> [t]he state is not disappearing, it is disaggregating into its separate, functionally distinct parts. These parts – courts, regulatory agencies, executives, and even legislatures – are networking with their counterparts abroad, creating a dense web of relations that constitutes a new, transgovernmental order. (1997: 184)

Networks, in other words, are systems that create themselves.

The Network's claim to spontaneous, collective, and internally generated expansion and its ability to create systems that preserve the heterogeneous quality of their elements imbues its extension and enhancement with a certain normativity. Its existence is a good in itself. No one, it would seem, could possibly be "against" networks (whether or not they achieve other ends), for the Network is simply a technical device for doing what one is already doing, only in a more efficient, principled, and sophisticated way. When states or organizations can reach consensus about nothing else, they always can agree to "strengthen information networks." In this sense, the Network form is the opposite of political motive, strategy, or content. The seemingly universal appeal of networks, furthermore, is enhanced by the fact that networks are imagined as fragile entities: they are easily interrupted or destroyed by the cessation of funding, the waning of commitment, the creation of an alternative network, the ineffectiveness of the "links," or the inappropriate actions of the focal points. Networks must be created, sustained, and made to expand, and this need enlists collective interest and commitment to Action.

In its parody of social scientific analysis, moreover, the Network plays on academic sentimentality about finally having found a "people" who speak our language, who answer our questions on our own terms. It appeals to our collective fantasy about linking up with our subjects and finding in the "data" exactly what we set out to find. The idea of the Network, as the term is used here and by the subjects of this study as a form that supersedes analysis and reality, might also be imagined to borrow from the reflexive turn in the social sciences – from the notion that there is no longer such a thing as dependent and independent variables, that causes and effects are all mutually constituted in an endless feedback loop.

Social scientists' captivation with the Network in all its dimensions belies a rapprochement between institutional politics and social scientific analysis and perhaps even a collective responsibility for the borrowing of social scientific models to new globalizing effects. We academics are all inside the Network in one way or another – we are skilled in the ways of funding applications [. . .]; we are members of "networks" of various kinds; and often we even participate in the policy arena. The Network also opens up opportunities for continuing existing projects in different guise. In their review of social movements scholarship, Simons, Mechling, and Shreier conclude that "whatever the political consequences of the protests of the 1960s and early 1970s, they surely yielded scholarly progress" (1984: 840). The dominant mode of analysis [. . .] has shifted from critique to networking.

Before we pronounce the Network as the new panacea, however, it may be worth considering what it leaves out. Although in Beijing there was perhaps more agreement than ever before, this may have been because there was more that could not be said and did not even need to be excluded or argued over in the sound bite atmosphere engendered precisely by the aura of inclusiveness, the effort to give every voice its thirty seconds of airing. [. . .]

[. . .]

Fact Finding and the Form of Global Politics

International lawyers have long understood that to assert the existence of an international system is to bring it into existence (Kennedy 1987). However, in "information" and its networks there is a "new" and even more effective tool than the rhetoric and doctrine that academics once used with these assertions. A small example will illustrate the device: in 1995, the UNDP issued a document entitled *Human Development Report* (UNDP 1995) containing statistical indicators that ranked UN member states according to the relative "status of women" in each. Fiji's relatively low ranking according to this "gender-related development index" caused considerable debate in the local press and was often cited by NGOs and government officials in speeches and documents. The competitive possibilities engendered by the simplicity of numerical ranking caught the attention of institutional participants in a way that admonitions or appeals to violations of international law had not. In its emphasis on Action through information gathering, then, the Beijing Conference was emblematic of a growing trend.

International law is increasingly governance by *fact*, as fact-finding becomes one of the principal competencies of the UN and other intergovernmental institutions. The efficacy of the secretary-general over the last decade is often credited largely to the frequent and effective use of the office's fact-finding powers, for example. Since 1987, the office includes an Office for Research and the Collection of Information, which creates data banks, monitors potential emergencies, and produces weekly information bulletins. Christiane Bourloyannis, of the Codification Division of the UN Office of Legal Affairs, brushes aside member states' concerns about the infringement of such policies on national sovereignty, noting that in the end efficient information gathering is in the interest of all member states "[i]n the contemporary era of communication, in which information often is the determinant of power" (Bourloyannis 1990: 669). The UN's fact-finding activities likewise have become the contemporary site of co-operation and conflict between international organizations and NGOs (Steiner 1991: 66). The International Monetary Fund's governance of the developing world is accomplished through its fact-finding missions and reports as much as through the leverage of its purse strings (Harper 1998). A considerable literature in international politics analyzes the institutions of the European Union as a network – a "flexible and dynamic" entity that "receives a much higher level of commitment from its members" and is thus more sophisticated than an international organization (Keohane and Hoffman 1991: 10; cf. Börzel 1997). The European Union Council Regulation establishing the European Environmental Agency in 1990 likewise specifies that its tasks are

> To provide the member states and the Community with information; to collect, record and assess data on the state of the environment; to encourage harmonization of the methods of measurement; to promote the incorporation of European environmental information into international monitoring programmes; to ensure data dissemination; to co-operate with other Community bodies and international institutions.
>
> (Majone 1997: 263)

Under such conditions, "the environment," "women," or "culture" exist to be documented, exist *because* they are documented.

The standardization of informational processes is increasingly tantamount to the Rule of Law. The International Organization for Standardization, an organization of governments and international institutions based in Geneva and in consultative status with all the major UN bodies, is only one example. Since its founding in 1947, it has been devoted to producing international standards for information exchange. The organization has published ten thousand different kinds of communication standards; among the most influential is an official set of public information symbols, artifacts of graphic design empirically tested to demonstrate their intelligibility to people of different cultures. Old debates about the legal basis of international institutions, of their authority to act in the absence of the express consent of states, which have plagued international law since its inception (Hall 1880; Wheaton 1866; Franck 1988; Falk 1970), find themselves swept aside by the benign objective of information sharing and by the expediency of the call to Action.

Policy studies scholars now routinely argue that "indirect, information-based modes of regulation" that depend on powers of "persuasion" rather than compulsion are "actually more in tune with current economic, technological and political conditions" (Majone 1997: 264). The emphasis is on providing information about market and other forms of risk to private parties in cases of environmental problems, for example, rather than on banning a certain kind of high-risk activity outright, and this privatization of government is understood as a more compassionate form of governmentality – "persuasion" rather than "compulsion" (266–67). Majone adds that in order for this strategy to succeed, however, international agencies must enter into "networks" that will ensure that, like individuals in a team, the agencies have an incentive to uphold their commitments and professional standards (272).

The rationale for global governance by fact is a familiar one [. . .]: the possibilities for measurement, comparison, or gridlike equivalency that inhere in the informational form – however metaphorical its relationship to the Real – prompt member states to action and engender *commitment* in a way that the doctrinal and political bases of international law have consistently failed to do. UN Secretary-General Boutros Boutros-Ghali appealed to these possibilities on the occasion of International Women's Day 1994:

> To examine the situation of women . . . is to provide both a yardstick, and a measure, of progress. We can see from the situation of women in a society whether power and entitlements are distributed fairly. We can see from women's health statistics, or from information about women's

educational attainments, how developed a society really is.

(INSTRAW and UNIFEM 1995)

To an anthropological mind, this ranking of societies according to a parallel ranking of the "situation of women" is perhaps disturbing. Yet, if we are to understand such comments ethnographically, we must read them as classic enlistments of the *form* of information, an effort to prompt the member states to action and commitment through an appeal to the yardstick, the measurement, the competitive possibilities of fact.

Unlike the designs of an early era of modernist activism, which aimed to transcend "real" distances and differences of culture, therefore, in the Network the question of transcultural efficacy is internal to the form. As we have seen, these forms displace the global/local with something far more mundane and in so doing foreclose the question of "cultural difference," at least for the moment of · their apprehension. This effect of design is by no means simply a bureaucrat's trick. The reappearance of battle shields among the Wahgi of the Western Highlands of Papua New Guinea, after years of disuse following European pacification, has seen the addition to the shield designs of words, numbers, and graphic images from advertisements that are "significant *by virtue* of being graphical marks" (O'Hanlon 1995: 481). These graphics literally precede social groups in the imagined battles for which the shields are made. Graphics, for the Wahgi, then, are what is intelligible even to one's enemies; they are a face to the outside, a universal language.

By now, it will be no surprise that this turn to the facts in international law accompanies a turn away from midcentury realism "back to formalism, general rules and judicial processes, a formalism which, however, had always been latent in realism itself" (Koskenniemi 1995: 11). Whether in negotiation or fact-finding, therefore, design now precedes agreement, an earlier era's way of transcending so-called cultural difference. Indeed, a system of international law grounded in consent now seems almost quaintly outmoded in comparison with the designs that elicit commitment and desire even as they internally generate the very cultural difference they transcend. Again, to critique such forms for the worldview latent in the facts would miss the point, for the character of the device is something much more powerful: the manufacture of desire through mundane "technicalities," the activating power of unnoticed forms.

Such patterns, which seemingly extend everywhere, might raise new questions about the place of academic analysis and critique. At the close of "The work of art in the age of mechanical reproduction," Benjamin considers the mass appeal and political uses of film. Noting that "reproduction [of film technology] is aided especially by the reproduction of masses" in patterns of parades and demonstrations that provided an image for such films ([1955] 1973: 243, n. 21), Benjamin concludes that through endlessly reproducible aesthetic devices such as film "Fascism sees its salvation in giving these masses not their right, but instead a chance to express themselves. . . . The logical result of Fascism is the introduction of aesthetics into political life" (234). The politics of early-twentieth-century propaganda films lay precisely in the opportunities generated by the form and the way in which the form enlisted *commitment*, demanded participation. The designs of the UN world conferences, with their endless cycles of inputs, might serve as a perfect example of a form in which everyone gets a chance, and nothing more than a chance, at self-expression (cf. Balkin 1992).

Benjamin's solution lay in "politicizing art" – the Marxist call to political critique alluded to in chapter 4 and the Bauhaus call to high modernist activism through design. Yet the conferences described here pose a dual challenge to this call. On the one hand, in the ultimate victory of this modernist project of universal design, the UN conferences subvert critique of the aesthetics of politics by rendering it impossible to imagine a political life without "aesthetics." Conversely, in the world conferences [. . .] we find design already "politicized" and even generating political commitment from within.

Of course, it is easy to see nonliberal politics as all about matters of form. As Benjamin and others have noted, fascism made of aesthetics an explicit question since the problem for critics was always how to explain the collective and irrational behavior that fascism engendered (Falasca-Zamponi 1997). The forms of liberal rationalism, and its accompanying humanism (Malkki 1996), are more difficult to bring into view. Martin Jay describes a second tradition of critique, associated with Paul de Man and Terry Eagleton, which understands the "aesthetic ideology" of fascism as the *completion* of the politics of liberal reason rather than its opposite (Jay 1993: 75–76). In this view, "aesthetics is attacked not because it is formally cold and antihumane, but rather because it is human-all-too-human" (77).

To put the point in other terms the forms of liberal rationalism are impervious to critique because they point not to themselves but to the gaps within the form, and beyond, to the Real: the point in President Clinton's justification is the terrorist, not the Network, and the same could be said of the place of "Women" in the networks I have described. Moreover, the forms considered here cleverly exploit our collective expectations that matters of rational agreement are not matters of form and vice versa and in so doing shade the forms that supersede and displace agreement itself.

International law and politics in the mode of information, then, represent not so much a revolution of norms as a perfection of form. What is interesting is the way form generates consensus where content and doctrine could never do so. One of the features most commented upon by delegates to the Beijing Conference and NGO Forum from Fiji and elsewhere who had attended previous women's conferences was the comparatively high degree of "consensus" on the "issues." Where delegates at previous meetings had been acrimoniously divided over whether structural adjustment or Palestinian liberation were in fact "women's issues" (Fraser 1987: 2; Jacquette 1995), at this meeting Fiji's participants in the academic women's networks from "the South" who had led the fight for the expansion of what counted as women's issues at previous conferences found, to their own surprise, that most of the European and North American attendees at their sessions were in fact converts to their position (cf. Anand 1996). [...]

[...]

All of the forms considered here share another feature. As abstract graphic designs, they can be large or small while keeping the same form, and they provide no clues as to their scale, no internal means of evaluating their "size" or their "significance." The extension of the Network or the replication of the pattern of the *Platform for Action* structure into a newsletter in Fiji did not alter the pattern, for example. The same is true of percentages, indicators, and all the other forms of statistical data that brought "women" into view. The patterned relationship among members keeps its form whatever their size, that is, whatever their (external) reference points may be.

Ironically, it was the figures' internal failures that enabled this optical effect of variation in scale. The gaps within the Matrix, for example, engendered a desire for the figure's completion, and it was this apprehension of the figure's internal lack that generated the desire to fill in the gaps that

in turn brought the Network diagram to the foreground. The uses of statistics as a "yardstick," in the UN secretary-general's term, for the status of women made of women (and UN governance) a coherent category by shielding the limitations of the numbers from view. To critique the statistics for what was left out, then, as anthropologists might feel compelled to do, ultimately would miss the point, for the "lack" is already well appreciated by the statistics' users. [...] Strathern has noted the information loss that accompanies academics' shifts from analysis at one level of scale to another (1991: 95). The point is that such failure is internal to the form and is also the engine of its ultimate effectiveness, the means of turning inside out and thus stimulating the momentary apprehension of depth.

We now can understand better what the forms that generate the global share. Such forms leave room for infinite flexibility in their relationship to whatever might lie beyond and ultimately only signify the Real, as the outside, within the parameters of the design. Both perfectly complete and utterly vacuous, forms such as facts and matrices, brackets full of text, or numbers and networks enable viewers to share everything and nothing, as does, for example, "knowing the facts." As such, the celebration of humanity as commonality and difference enacted at the UN Fourth World Conference on Women is the ideal design for a new global politics.

"It was living inside *Time* Magazine!" one friend repeatedly said of the experience of serving as a Fiji government delegate to the Beijing Conference. She proceeded to describe the diversity of events and cultures all around her there, and the experience of becoming the subject of global news, as an example of being at the center of things. The experience of encompassment within a magazine's patterns of words and graphics no doubt is a common encounter with the forms that define "the global." Where the forms exploit their own internal spaces to produce the effect of being all around us, it is no wonder that much of the exhaustion that pervades our understanding of the literature on transnationalism and globalization derives from a sense that analysis has no further room to expand.

REFERENCES

Anand, Anita. 1996. Beijing: Exhausting, frustrating, exciting. *Indian Journal of Gender Studies* 3:127–32.

Balkin, J. M. 1992. What is postmodern constitutionalism? *Michigan Law Review* 90 (7): 1966–90.

Benjamin, Walter. [1955] 1973. The work of art in the age of mechanical reproduction. In *Illuminations*, trans. Harry Zohn. London: Fontana.

Börzel, Tanja A. 1997. What's so special about policy networks? An exploration of the concept and its usefulness in studying European governance. European Integration Online Papers 1, 16. http://eiop.or.at/eiop/texte/ 1997-016a.htm.

Bourloyannis, M.-Christiane. 1990. Fact-finding by the secretary-general of the United Nations. *New York University Journal of International Law and Politics* 22:641–69.

Brysk, Alison. 1993. From above and below: Social movements, the international system, and human rights in Argentina. *Comparative Political Studies* 26(3): 259–85.

Falasca-Zamponi, Simonetta. 1997. *Fascist spectacle: The aesthetics of power in Mussolini's Italy.* Berkeley: University of California Press.

Falk, Richard. 1970. *The status of law in international society.* Princeton: Princeton University Press.

Franck, Thomas M. 1988. Legitimacy in the international system. *American Journal of International Law* 82:705–59.

Fraser, Arvonne S. 1987. *The U.N. Decade for Women: Documents and dialogue.* Boulder and London: Westview.

Hall, William E. 1880. *International Law.* Oxford: Clarendon.

Harper, Richard H. R. 1998. *Inside the IMF: An ethnography of documents, technology, and organisational action.* San Diego: Academic.

Jacquette, Jane S. 1995. Losing the battle/winning the war: International politics, women's issues, and the 1980 Mid-Decade Conference. In *Women, politics, and the United Nations,* ed. Anne Winslow. Westport, Conn.: Greenwood.

Jay, Martin. 1993. *Force fields: Between intellectual history and cultural critique.* New York: Routledge.

Jönsson, Christer. 1986. Interorganization theory and international organization. *International Studies Quarterly* 30:39–57.

Kennedy, David. 1987. *International legal structures.* Baden-Baden: Nomos Verlagsgesellschaft.

Keohane, Robert O., and Stanley Hoffmann. 1991. Institutional change in Europe in the 1980s. In *The new European Community: Decisionmaking and institutional change,* ed. Robert O. Keohane and Stanley Hoffmann. Boulder: Westview.

Koskenniemi, Martti. 1995. International law in a postrealist era. *Australian Year Book of International Law* 16:1–19.

Majone, G. 1997. The new European agencies: Regulation by information. *Journal of European Public Policy* 4(2): 262–75.

Malkki, Liisa H. 1996. Speechless emissaries: Refugees, humanitarianism, and dehistoricization. *Cultural Anthropology* 11(3): 377–404.

O'Hanlon, Michael. 1995. Modernity and the "graphicalization" of meaning: New Guinea highland shield design in historical perspective. *Journal of the Royal Anthropological Institute* (n.s.) 7 (1):469–93.

Sikkink, Kathryn. 1993. Human rights, principled issue-networks, and sovereignty in Latin America. *International Organization* 47:411–41.

Simons, Herbert W., Elizabeth W. Mechling, and Howard N. Schreier. 1984. The functions of human communication in mobilizing for action from the bottom up: The rhetoric of social movements. In *Handbook of rhetorical and communication theory,* ed. Carroll C. Arnold and John Waite Bowers. Boston: Allyn and Bacon.

Slaughter, Anne-Marie. 1997. The real new world order. *Foreign Affairs* 76 (5): 183–97.

Steiner, Henry J. 1991. *Diverse partners: Non-governmental organizations in the human rights movement.* Cambridge: Harvard Law School Human Rights Program.

Strathern, Marilyn. 1991. *Partial connections.* ASAO Special Publications, no. 3. Savage, Md.: Rowman and Littlefield.

Teubner, Gunther. 1993. The many-headed hydra: Networks as higher-order collective actors. In *Corporate control and accountability,* ed. Joseph McCahery, Sol Picciotto, and Colin Scott. Oxford: Clarendon.

United Nations Development Program (UNDP). 1995. *Human development report.* Washington, D.C.: United Nations.

United Nations International Research and Training Institute for the Advancement of Women (INSTRAW) and United Nations Fund for Women (UNIFEM). 1995. *Women and the UN, 1945–1995.* New York: United Nations.

Wheaton, Henry, 1866. *Elements of international law.* 8th ed. Boston: Little, Brown.

PART VI

Nature, Environment, and Biotechnology

Introduction

Forests, often imagined as untamed natural spaces, are also sites of state attempts at classification and control, and foci of commercial competition and extraction. Some offer hiding places for "outlaws" or opposition political forces, as well as vital medicinal plants, firewood, and spiritual sanctuaries. Official mapping of forest resources is, as Nancy Peluso indicates in chapter 20 below, "an intrinsically political act" – one that can prompt alternative or "counter" mapping. That is what occurred in late-20th-century Kalimantan, Indonesia, where local activists studied by Peluso used sketch maps (counter-maps) "to delineate and formalize claims to forest territories and resources their villages have traditionally managed." Some of them, she notes, match their sketch maps to official maps and to points on the Global Positioning System (GPS). Peluso explores two different counter-mapping strategies in Kalimantan: one organized by "expatriate anthropologists and geographers working through organizations such as the Worldwide Fund for Nature and the Ford Foundation, and the other initiated by local NGOs who sometimes contract international experts to make maps of village territories" (1995:384). She critically assesses counter-mapping as a political tool for inventing and reinventing "traditions" and customary law, and the attendant drawbacks and gains for local people of such strategies.

The West African forests that are the focus of James Fairhead and Melissa Leach's chapter[1] constitute a landscape that officials have routinely "misread" or drawn false conclusions about for more than a century. Those landscape misreadings, Fairhead and Leach argue, assume that there has been anthropogenic deforestation – rather than regeneration – in a forest-savannah transition zone in Guinea. Their own evidence is drawn from a rich array of sources: oral history, ethnographic research, aerial photographs extending back to the 1950s, satellite images, and landscape descriptions found in archives dating from 1893. Yet Guinean forestry staff displayed "incredulous reactions" when presented with Fairhead and Leach's data; the 1952 and 1990 air photographs, for example, led local staff to "a sceptical search for ways to render the comparison invalid." Similarly surprising research results elsewhere in West Africa, they note, "have simply been disbelieved and dismissed." They find that international rhetoric about environmental crisis, global biodiversity loss, and desertification has less appeal for villagers, who are supposedly enduring environmental crisis, than for local and national officials who are well aware of the kinds of programs that satisfy foreign donors. Fairhead and Leach discuss how misleading narratives about forest loss also are entailed in processes of ethnic distinction, and how they shape development policies and criminalize successful local production practices, such as hunting, fishing, felling trees, and burning fields. Their analysis calls attention to the casual landscape readings and discursive processes that condition the production of authoritative knowledge about development, and the stock narratives development agencies prefer partly for reasons of expediency (see also Roe's chapter in Part VII below).

Technological revolutions and their impact on society and development are a long-standing anthropological interest, but in recent decades the range of relevant concerns has expanded exponentially. Increasingly, social and cultural anthropologists have investigated fields as diverse as informatics, new reproductive technologies, alternative energy sources, nuclear weapons design, biotechnology, and the evolution of new diseases (Franklin and Ragone 1997; Gusterson 1996; Lindenbaum 2001; Stone 2002). And as market forces increasingly shape scientific research, connections between science studies and development studies have grown.

Hilary Cunningham examines one aspect of a broader trend, the commercialization and politicization of genetic research and, more broadly, of intellectual property. As her chapter describes in detail, the creation in the early 1990s of first the Human Genome Project and then the Human Genome Diversity Project provoked a storm of controversy, particularly as scientists associated with the latter effort applied for and received a patent of a cell line from a man from a Papua New Guinea group that enjoys an unusually high level of immunity to leukemia and related illnesses. Cunningham argues that this and similar moves to privatize life forms raise profound issues of ethics, North–South power asymmetries, and anthropologists' relations to power and to the frequently powerless people whom they study.

NOTE

1   The article reprinted here is a distillation of arguments Fairhead and Leach develop in their 1996 book *Misreading the African Landscape*, and in their film "Second Nature."

REFERENCES

Fairhead, James and Melissa Leach, 1996 Misreading the African Landscape: Society and Ecology in a Forest-savanna Mosaic. Cambridge: Cambridge University Press.

Franklin, Sarah and Helena Ragone, eds., 1997 Reproducing Reproduction: Kinship, Power, and Technological Innovation. Philadelphia: University of Pennsylvania Press.

Gusterson, Hugh, 1996 Nuclear Rites: A Weapons Laboratory at the End of the Cold War. Berkeley: University of California Press.

Lindenbaum, Shirley, 2001 Kuru, Prions, and Human Affairs: Thinking about Epidemics. Annual Review of Anthropology 30:363–385.

Peluso, Nancy, 1995 Whose Woods Are These? Counter-Mapping Forest Territories in Kalimantan, Indonesia. Antipode 27(4):383–406.

Stone, Glenn Davis, 2002 Both Sides Now: Fallacies in the Genetic-Modification Wars, Implications for Developing Countries, and Anthropological Perspectives. Current Anthropology 43(4):611–630.

20

Whose Woods Are These? Counter-Mapping Forest Territories in Kalimantan, Indonesia

Nancy Lee Peluso

Forests are repositories of great wealth and eco-logical importance; politically, they are much more than that. Forests are often located in critical spaces that states want to control: international border areas as well as zones which might be deemed "sensitive" because of either their polit-ical-ecological importance or sociological com-position. Historically, forests have also been the outposts of "outlaws" and "outcasts" and the base for many an opposition force to imperialistic powers – from 10th century "China" to 14th cen-tury Java to 20th century Peru and Vietnam (Men-zies, 1992). Forest mapping was embraced early by emerging European states, first for establishing political boundaries and later for management (Kain and Baigent, 1992:132, 210).

Mapping of forest resources is therefore an in-trinsically political act: whether drawn for their protection or production, they are drawings of a nation's strategic space. [...] Forest maps have been an important tool for state authorities trying to exclude or include people within the same spaces as forest resources; maps increase state control over spaces which are sources of social unrest and valuable resources (Menzies, 1992). Mapping facilitates large-scale accumulation strategies that work to forest dwellers' disadvan-tage, and consolidates state control over politic-ally sensitive areas such as border zones (Girot and Nietschmann, 1993).

This paper examines the origins, implementa-tion, and implications of forest mapping in two different forms in Kalimantan, Indonesia. In Indo-nesia, forest maps have been an important tool of state land managers and supporting international institutions, such as the FAO, the World Bank, Worldwide Fund For Nature, and the Inter-national Union for the Conservation of Nature. In response to two decades of intensive industrial timber exploitation and the Indonesian govern-ment's superseding of customary forest rights through official planning and mapping efforts, an alternative or "counter" mapping movement has begun. Local activists, with international and sometimes government assistance of various sorts, are using sketch maps to delineate and for-malize claims to forest territories and resources their villages have traditionally managed. In some cases they are matching their sketch maps to points on the Global Positioning System (GPS) and the official Indonesian forest planning maps using sophisticated software (Sirait, et. al; 1994; Momberg, 1994).

The goal of these efforts is to appropriate the state's *techniques* and *manner of representation* to bolster the legitimacy of "customary" claims to resources. The practical effect is far-reaching: the use of maps and a highly "territorialized" strategy redefines and reinvents customary claims to stand-ing forest resources and harvestable products as claims to the land itself. The case accordingly emphasizes the dynamic nature of customary and statutory forest law, both of which can be re-invented as new "traditions" when changing polit-ical economies and technologies permit (Hobsbawm and Ranger, 1983). The case also raises some questions about the control of power when NGOs and other local groups utilize high technology empowerment strategies.

[...]

The Politics of Mapping

Maps...exert a social influence through
their omissions as much as by the features
they depict and emphasize
(J. B. Harley, 1992).

Much of the "politics of mapping" theory is based
on local/national histories in early modern and
contemporary Europe and in the colonized "New
World" (including the USA and Canada, with
some attention to Europeanized Latin American
localities). It accordingly fails to capture the distinctiveness of contemporary Third World mapping politics. The most intensive state mapping
initiatives arrived on the "scenes" of the Third
World with global capitalism firmly entrenched
and in advanced stages, particularly in the "tiger-
ish" economies of East and Southeast Asia. The
advanced stage of mapping technology at which
both national mappers and local "counter-
mappers" have entered the game is also relevant
insofar as using the new tools both raises the stakes
of resource mapping and offers new political openings for resource users. These factors combine to
make this episode in the political economy of mapping exciting, timely, and precedent-setting.

[...] If maps can be seen as one of many "authoritative resources" that states mobilize to consolidate their own power (Giddens, 1984, cited in
Harley, 1988:279), then local groups' appropriation of the technology of mapping may help to
counterbalance or at least offset the previous monopoly of authoritative resources by the state or
capital. [...] Just as inclusion and exclusion are
powerful political tools used by states and state-
legitimated organizations to control and allocate
resource access (Harley, 1988, Menzies, 1992),
local groups can claim power through mapping
by using not only what is on a map, but what is
not on it. One effect of having multiple maps of a
single forest, for example, could be to challenge the
accuracy of a "standard" map used for planning.

An important element of such a challenge to state
authority to create maps is the re-insertion of
people on resource maps. Individual home-steads,
settlements, and villages are routinely excluded
from maps of private and state land holdings. [...]

Not all people were excluded from forest maps
at all times, however, and the inclusion of people
was also a mechanism for exerting control. The
location of settlements and their relationships to
the feudal manor or cities have been important

pieces of information to be included on maps.
[...] As the types of rights to land and resources
changed in importance, maps became more explicit means of controlling resource access. [...]

Contrary to the conclusion on hegemony that
Harley draws from his extensive research on the
politics of mapping (1989:301), maps can be used
to pose alternatives to the languages and images of
power and become a medium of empowerment or
protest. Alternative maps, or "counter-maps" as I
call them here, greatly increase the power of people
living in a mapped area to control representations
of themselves and their claims to resources (see,
e.g., Orlove, 1989). Local people may exert control directly by making their own maps or entrust a
representative of their choice, such as a local
NGO, to perform the task. Counter-maps thus
have the potential for challenging the omissions
of human settlements from forest maps, for contesting the homogenization of space on political,
zoning, or property maps, for altering the categories of land and forest management, and for ex-
pressing social relationships in space rather than
depicting abstract space in itself [...]. Counter-
mapping can be used for alternative boundary-
making and "to depict strategies of resistance:
where to block... unwise development, to identify
landscapes that have been damaged, to describe
alternatives to the incremental destruction of sustaining habitats" (Aberley, 1993:4).

An analogous challenge to elite power historically was the secularization of the language of
print. The replacement of Latin manuscripts with
books, pamphlets, and newspapers written in the
vernacular languages of Europe (and subsequently
replacing colonial newspapers with those in local
or lingua franca languages in Asia and other
places) revolutionized the lives of millions of
people (Anderson 1991:37–40). [...] Although it
is difficult to imagine the spread of mapping skills
as having anywhere near the impact of the spread
of print and the capacity to read, there are several
ways in which counter-mapping can have a major
impact.

I would argue that while counter-mapping has
some potential to transform the role of mapping
from "a science of princes" (Harley, 1988: 281),
it is unlikely to become a "a science of the masses"
simply because of the level of investment required
by the kind of mapping with the potential to challenge the authority of other maps. Investment in
specialized computers and software and knowledge will make the costs of mapping prohibitive
for most local people, particularly in poor areas.
This of course creates openings for new types of

power relations around the control and knowledge of mapping technologies, both in local class relations and in the relationships between NGOs and local villagers. [...]. What ultimately may be more important for the "masses" is not the technology itself, but the content of the maps produced and the way the knowledge and information on the maps is distributed.

[...]

Indonesian Forests and Forest Mapping

[...] In Kalimantan, forest land use planning effectively began with the passing of Basic Forestry Law No. 5/1967,[1] which empowered the national government to control, manage, and administer all state forest lands (Barber, 1989; Zerner, 1990). Until 1966, Indonesia's first president, Sukarno, had pursued economic policies oriented toward domestic self-sufficiency, shunning most foreign investment, particularly by the "Western" (Europe, North America, Australia) capitalist countries. When Suharto took over as president in 1967, he immediately set the stage for foreign investment and capitalist development. [...] Foreign logging industries from Japan, the Philippines, the USA, and Europe were granted timber concessions, called HPH (*Hak Pengusahaan Hutan* – Permit for Forest Industry) in the Outer Islands (Manning, 1972). [...]

The first of three mapping episodes directed at "forest management" in Kalimantan [...] consisted of notoriously inaccurate and secretive concession locations. Anecdotal evidence indicates that these maps revealed border conflicts, multiple permitting of territories, and illegal entry of one concession operator onto the concessions granted another. They ignored the physical conditions of the forest itself in designating these concession areas for timber production and whether competing claims and forms of management were already in place. [...]

These maps were replaced between 1981 and 1985 when provincial foresters collaborated with colleagues in agriculture, public works, and agrarian affairs, to develop plans and maps. [...] Once again, no account was taken of local people's previous claims to these lands, nor of existing vegetative cover (Potter, 1995:12). [...]

The third and most recent state attempt to map forests in Kalimantan and other "outer" islands of Indonesia is the Regional Physical Planning Programme for Transmigration (generally known as RePPProt), a collaborative effort between the GOI's Ministry of Transmigration and the Land Resources Department of the Overseas Development Administration (ODA) in London. The maps are part of a larger regional planning effort, which in the case of Kalimantan is to involve the resettlement of millions of people from Java, Bali, and Lombok and the creation of agricultural estates – principally for palm oil and rubber. The labor for these estates will be drawn from both immigrant and locally born populations.

Using Landsat data and aerial photographs, actual land use cover is being mapped and the areas included in different forest land use categories are being reconsidered. The discrepancies between the earlier TGHK maps and the RePPProt maps are striking. [...]

These latest planning maps also include settlement areas around urban areas and villages, cultivated fields outside of these settlements and planned forest areas. The maps underestimate, indeed, lack knowledge of, forest-based populations' claims to and management of forest territories, as well as their actual patterns of forest and agricultural land use.

[...]

The RePPProt planners have not completely ignored their lack of knowledge of customary systems, but they have neither emphasized their importance in the executive summary, nor made recommendations about what to do for the purposes of their map-making exercise. [...] The executive summary recommends further studies of customary rights, land use, and land ownership. [...]

Planning is apparently proceeding without further consideration of local institutions. Much of the forest considered "Convertible" encompasses large areas of community forests long protected by local peoples (Momberg, 1994; Sirait et al., 1994; *Kompas*, 1993). The allocation of these forests to plantation managers, transmigration planners, and other development planners proceeds according to the map.

Not only do planners *not* know the boundaries and types of customary rights and claims of local people, they are not even sure how many people there are. [...]

Both in Indonesian law and by verbal consensus, Indonesian planners recognize that extensive systems of customary law and practice (*hukum adat* and *hak ulayat*) exist throughout Indonesia, and often overlap with forest territories and resources claimed by the state, though they have no maps or other documents formally indicating their extent. Forest Law No. 5 states that the rights of indigenous peoples to land and resources covered by *adat* should be respected, except when these conflict with national or the (undefined) "public interest." [...] Earlier legal efforts were made to erase some of the ambiguities of the dual Indonesian law imposed under Dutch colonialism. Basic Agrarian Act No 5/1960, for example, was meant to replace the dual system of *adat* and statutory law by providing legal rights to all Indonesian citizens. All land was to be registered according to this law, so the status of ownership was clear and treated legally under a single system, common to all parts of the country. The enormity of such a registration system notwithstanding, the Act has had little impact on most of the land in Kalimantan, where many people have not even heard of it (Moniaga, 1993:139).

Territorial Claims and Counter-mapping

Mapping by government land-use planners focuses on the land itself. In other words, maps are part of a larger resource management strategy with a strong territorial component. [...] State land use planners [...] only recognize local people's *territorial* rights to areas they define as "permanent cultivation" (GOI, n.d., Executive Summary:30). Forest planners recognize people's *adat* claims to certain forest trees and plants producing products such as rattan, fruit, honey, illipe nut, resins (damar), and rubber, even when these occur in state-claimed forest territories. State recognition of individual trees in the forest, however, does not translate into recognition of villagers' claims to portions of the forest *as territorial entities*. In fact, exactly the opposite is true: certain species and individual claims to them are recognized in part to allow the state to claim the forest as territory and to allocate exploitation rights (to corporations, not to villages, as a general rule) as it sees fit. Such rights include rights to harvest timber (through concessions) and rights to convert the forest to plantation tree cropping, whether oil palm, rubber, or pulpwood species (in the case of lands categorized "Convertible Forest"). The drive to maintain territorial sovereignty also reflects efforts by state managers to distribute the jurisdictions among themselves – e.g., land parcels are transferred from forest production to forest protection or conservation agencies, to transmigration and resettlement authorities, or to the Department of Plantations.

Government officials refer to Dayak[2] agriculture as "shifting agriculture" (*perladangan berpindah-pindah*), a pejorative term dating back to the colonial period. In practice, the system is more rotational than shifting. As mentioned above, some groups have hardly shifted at all. It is noteworthy, however, that shifting cultivation areas were grouped by RePPProt mappers with areas of scrub, regrowth, and grassland, all of which are "considered available for development planning" (Executive Summary:31). That local people's territorial forest rights are not recognized is evident in the significant increase in lands included in the category of "Convertible Forest" [...].

Local counter-mapping initiatives and territoriality

Two different counter-mapping strategies have been developed in response to this situation. The first is through efforts of outsiders working for international organizations. They have suggested mapping as a way of clearly depicting and protecting local claims to territory and resources to a government that in the past ignored them. The second has been initiated by Indonesian NGOs who request or contract the services of key international groups to learn the uses of counter-mapping strategies to document forest uses, claims, and population distribution. Both strategies involve 1) the uses of low and high technology mapping techniques necessitating villagers' formation of political alliances with international NGOs and foreign experts, and 2) the assertion of specific and permanent territorial claims to resources. The key theoretical questions about the impacts of counter-mapping on resource control are to what degree new notions of territoriality reflect older ones; how the reinvention of these traditions benefits or works to the detriment of customary practice, law, and resource distribution; and how the intervention of NGOs (whether locally, nationally, or internationally based) affects the villagers' access to and control over forest resources.

[...] In both the past and present, Dayak forest and land management strategies have included territorial and non-territorial components. Swidden cultivation, practiced by most rural Dayaks, imparts territorial rights. Once old growth forest has been cleared, territorial rights are vested in either the clearer's direct descendants or in the clearer's longhouse/village (see Appell, n.d.). Swiddening, for many swiddening groups, is a form of rotational agroforestry, practiced on a relatively broad regional basis, and involving the management of not only swidden fields but also of swidden fallows in multiple stages of development, including standing forests. [...]

Dayak forest managers differentiate activities within different types of forest, although they do not always establish rigid land use categories. [...] These forest management categories are neither understood nor recognized by state forest managers and other government officials.

In swidden fallows of different ages and in other types of forest, Dayaks actively manage production of both timber and non-timber products, with "rules" guiding access rights varying widely across and within groups. [...] Although access to and management of these resources are not discussed in terms of territoriality, their management is partially territorial, in the sense that once planted or otherwise claimed, others may not clear these plants to use the land where they occur. This situation gives implicit territorial control to the individuals and groups who claim trees and other forest products.

These systems have changed in response to shifting market opportunities, and more recently, to the large influx of immigrant settlers from other parts of Indonesia. International markets have stimulated extraction and production of forest and agroforestry products in Kalimantan for at least two thousand years, with the demanded products ranging from camphor, to incense wood, birds nests, resins, latexes, rattan, and wildlife (Peluso, 1992). Both planned and spontaneous migration of other Indonesian peoples to the island has increased pressure on the land, and will soon make the Dayaks a minority group in their own homeland.

Counter-mapping as a joint forest management strategy

One of the two counter-mapping strategies described here has been applied in the Kayan Mentarang Reserve. [...] Culturally and biologically diverse, it contains potentially important archeological remains and is home to 12 distinct ethnolinguistic groups. [...] Since approximately 1990, the Worldwide Fund for Nature, The Indonesian Department of Forest and Nature Conservation (PHPA) and the Indonesian Institute of Sciences have been cooperating to develop a long-term conservation program in this 1.6 million hectare reserve, one of the largest in Asia. Their activities include an inventory of the reserve's extensive human and natural resources, documentation of local knowledge and resource management systems, and, most recently, efforts to record this information on maps. The maps are intended to

form the basis of talks for identifying customary forest tenure boundaries in order to assess how

indigenous ways of organizing and allocating space might support or conflict with the objectives of forest protection, for evaluating different means of coordinating indigenous resource management systems with government-instituted systems of management, and as a basis for formal legal recognition and protection of customary forest tenure arrangements

(Sirait et al., 1994).

With funding from the Ford Foundation, a subproject within the reserve area was established, called the "Culture and Conservation" project. The goal of the project was to record oral histories, indigenous knowledge, and village dynamics related to resource management. [...] Using a method developed by Fox (1990), sketch maps of local land use and resource territories were constructed. Sketch maps reflecting local people's ways of talking about resources and their claims to them were combined with points on the GPS. A geographic information system was used to match field data with data on official land use and topographic maps. In this way, the counter-mapping agencies hoped to identify territorial conflicts, establish resource use boundaries, and better understand the ways local people conceptualize their resources.

[...]

In sharp contrast to the locally produced maps, the land uses on the TGHK maps show no regard for current village uses or claims. On the basis of these maps, and with no ground checks, government forest planners allocated more than 50 percent of the village's land – mostly its standing forest – to two external users: the Kayan Mentarang Reserve and a timber concession. [...] Were the villagers to prevail in a decision over whose maps to use, the outcome would be more standing forest than the government has presently planned.

The question raised by these discrepancies is whether the counter map has a chance of recognition by the government. [...] Two major things need to happen to give the villagers' total jurisdiction over their forest. First, the status of the Kayan Mentarang Nature Reserve would need to be changed to a National Park or a Biosphere Reserve, in order to allow some "traditional" uses of the forest by local people. [...] However, since the counter-map was made, a request to change the reserve's status was put forth. A concurrent request by the logging company for permission to build a road through the proposed park to the timber concession led the Minister to turn down both (Fox, pers. comm., 1995).

The second change required would be to alter the forest concession agreement. This would entail changing the boundaries of the concession, a much more expensive and contestable task than changing from one conservation status to another. [. . .]

[. . .] The "Culture and Conservation" mapping project has several factors operating in its favor. First, as it is one of the biggest contiguous reserves/parks in Asia, developments within it are likely to have an important impact regionally, particularly if it successfully integrates people into the planning process and the majority of local people feel they have benefited after implementation. Second is the participation of international institutions with a history of involvement in and influence on resource management policy in Indonesia.[3] Some of these programs have emphasized taking the needs of local people into account. A key question, however, is whether the Worldwide Fund for Nature (WWF) in particular will be willing to make commitments to a conservation strategy that gives local people a strong or even dominant voice in determining how and what to conserve. [. . .] The organization has not historically opted for such "radical" people-oriented conservation strategies. A third element in the mapping project's favor is the appropriation of the government's own mapping methods and planning tools, including the topographic map series and the GPS. Indonesia has invested considerable funds in GIS technologies, satellite technology, and computerized resource management tools; acquisitions that now make the state somewhat vulnerable to counter-mapping strategies. Moreover, when peasant groups meet government mappers on their own ground, as it were, their efforts have greater legitimacy than if the maps were simple sketches.

Finally, counter-mappers have allies within the Indonesian state itself. The Ministry of Forestry has been involved in reserve planning and oversight since the beginning, including at least some discussions concerning the roles and status of indigenous peoples living in or adjacent to the park. [. . .] As forests and their protection will likely retain a place on the world political stage for some time, the choices made in this reserve could serve as precedent elsewhere, at the same time giving the beleaguered MOF some relief from the attacks made frequently on its production and protection policies.

Counter-mapping strategies initiated by local NGOs

Both structurally and in terms of goals, mapping projects initiated by local NGOs unfold somewhat differently. In Kalimantan, as in parts of eastern Indonesia, several local NGOs have requested the services of mapping experts to teach and aid them in mapping village land use. [. . .] These NGOs work autonomously: they do not share management of the project with government agencies, or with internationally-based NGOs like WWF. [. . .]

Some of these NGOs' goals in mapping include documenting current and historical land uses and claims as well as locating and counting forest-dependent populations by ethnicity. In doing so, they intend to legitimate claims to areas that have not already been "converted" into production forests or plantations. They also hope to counter the impact of the national census which inadequately represents the diversity of local populations and therefore works against local claims formerly protected by customary law (*adat*). [. . .] However, the notion of *adat* as aboriginal customary law is itself problematic, largely because its forms and rules have been interpreted, written, and rewritten by Dutch scholars and anthropologists, and most recently by government officials seeking to homogenize variations of practice and understanding of these rules within the various sub-ethnic groups. [. . .] These inherent problems with the concept have not been generally acknowledged by the villagers themselves or by the activists assisting them. *Adat* as an institution has generally been romanticized as the way resources were locally managed prior to the rise of foreign investment and forest industry in the 1960s. [. . .] [*Adat*] is a [. . .] dynamic institution which has repeatedly changed in response to forces impinging on particular localities from the "outside," such as markets and other political-economic influences.

[. . .] Ethnic diversity and identity, expressed among other ways, through resource management and control strategies, and codified by *adat*, is an important aspect of what these local NGOs wish to document. Relating population figures to forest maps is thus a first step in understanding where conflict might arise between claimants with aboriginal or historical claims and newcomers to the local scene, including both newly settled migrants and government-sponsored resource exploitation projects. In a less formal, but no less territorialized manner, the NGOS want to help local people document their claims to the resources within particular lands and the rights to convert forest to other land uses, as they did for centuries before the nationalization of forest land. Local NGOs are also trying to learn more effective ways to use available data such as census data. [. . .]

Both mapping strategies described above necessarily involve more educated, often urbanized members of these subethnic groups, representing "local" situations of which they may no longer be a permanent part. The technology being used necessitates this – at least in these early stages. Moreover, they are providing a voice from these localities which has been missing from previous representations of these forested spaces. The more detailed these maps become, however, the more important will become the question of which local voices are represented.

Discussion and Conclusion

Counter-mapping is a uniquely late-twentieth century phenomenon, made possible in part by both technological developments and the last decade's push toward participatory politics and management strategies. This paper presents two means by which local people are gaining access to the tools of the powerful – maps and mapping technologies developed by and for state international resource planners and managers – and shows how they are using them to legitimize their claims to land and resources. Regardless of their future success or failure in changing state policy and state maps, however, the cases raise several critical theoretical issues. Most critical, perhaps, is the potential maps have for "freezing" the dynamic social processes which are referred to as "customary law." Secondly, will an independent strategy to map and claim resources fare better than an inclusive one that works with government forest agencies and international environmental groups with a strong presence in Indonesia?

As Foucault, Anderson, Giddens and others have discussed, the use of a new medium of expression, in this case maps, to express social relations has transformative power. The fear of "freezing" custom is not a new argument for Indonesia (or the former Dutch East Indies). Many writers have argued that the codification of customary law, the writing down of oral traditions, the legalizing of flexible law codes, generally resulted in "freezing" these traditions, taking away their characteristic flexibility, and therefore changing their very nature (Lev, 1985; cf. van Vollenhoven in Holleman, 1981). Similar arguments were made in colonial debates about customary law in Africa as well (Moore, 1986). In some ways, we have seen how this is so: particularly in the reification of *adat* by some contemporary NGOs as a timeless, local system, unaffected by the turbulent political economic changes of the past.

Since mapping is the visual or representational aspect of the "writing" of custom, it too can be accused of affecting the flexibility of land use and claims to resources. Certain common land and forest uses may not be clearly defined or separable from local viewpoints. Long-term rotational agroforestry strategies, for example, are not easily accommodated on maps (although they could be by using some types of GIS). Moreover, future uses are difficult to predict, given local people's responsiveness to changes in the political-economic and environmental circumstances in which they find themselves. The question is whether maps will *preclude* future changes that ignore the information on the map. I think the answer to this question in terms of land use is no: maps may or may not be a covenant, despite the current fascination with them as a planning tool. Whether a user will harvest all or some of the rattan on his or her land all at once or gradually, whether they will plant rice, stringbeans, or rubber and fruit, are decisions unlikely to be made solely on the basis of the lines on the map. Once a group's map is empowered by both state recognition and local acceptance, the map can become a tool for negotiation of local land use controls – separating protection forest from agricultural land, for example. But empowerment should also bring the ability to change the map, to renegotiate its terms, and to alter the contents of what may remain somewhat abstract space at a larger scale. In addition, many of the boundaries on the ground are unlikely to remain as strict and clear as they will appear on maps. Maps may influence the direction and impact of change, but change, like flexibility, is an important part of customary practice or law. Like customary rules transmitted orally, or even like written customary or statutory laws, maps can be changed as practice, use, and values change, or as rights are transferred between generations or out of the hands of the original holders. [. . .]. In addition to formalizing some past claims, counter-maps will set in motion new dynamics for making claims to the forest.

Not all local people will be happy with these changes. One change which a majority may regard as beneficial may be the transformation of more nature reserves to biosphere reserve or national park status, either alternative allowing more human use. However, some people may use the establishment of boundary lines between and within villages as a permanent indicator of private property rights. Detailed local maps which serve as alternatives or precursors to cadastral maps would increase flexible options of one person at the expense of another. Local maps will also transform blurry boundaries between forest villages to fixed ones, another potentially contentious issue (see, e.g., Peluso, 1992a).

A second, related, issue has to do with the transformation of customary rights to forests [. . .]. Some land use categories might be structurally impossible to allocate as individual territory. For example, territorializing rights to mature fruit forests (*tembawang*) would undoubtedly lead to conflict. In these social forests, multiple descent groups claim ancestral rights to fruit, resin, and trees. Virtually every tree has a set of owners which differs from the set claiming the next tree (Peluso, 1993, 1994). Thus, the degree of detail in mapping claims within the village becomes important, particularly in seeking ways to represent resource claims which cannot be territorialized.

In general, however, the use of maps requires the re-definition of customary forest rights which emphasized standing forest resources and products to an emphasis on the territory itself. [. . .] By purposely making maps "empty" or "homogenous space," counter-mappers can reduce the potentially negative effects of such a territorialization. In other words, communities can retain the most internal flexibility in interpreting and changing land uses if individual rights within the village are not mapped. While broad land use categories such as protection forests, *tembawang*, or agricultural areas may be mapped, the detailing of individual claims to trees or other resources within them could lead to local conflict. Leaving out the details of resource use within each category allows local people much more freedom to determine individual or descent group rights of access and to change management practices (Fox, pers. comm.).

In sum, although mapping has until now been peripheral to the politics of customary rights and forest access, its role is likely to increase. Mapping is a tool that speaks a language both national and international resource planners and managers can understand. Given the drive in Indonesia and elsewhere in Southeast Asia to zone land uses, such as production forests, agricultural lands, and areas of urban settlement, and parallel efforts to register private lands in cadastral surveys, the use of maps to recognize the bounds of community-controlled resources is an appropriate and timely tool. Indeed, communal or group-held properties are among the only categories of land that the government has never really mapped, nor does the government have concrete plans to do so. Because RePPProt planners have stated the need to understand customary claims to the resources and lands

mapped under their auspices, counter-mappers could incorporate government planners into their own plans.

The main purpose of the maps described here is to document and establish boundaries between forest villagers and external claimants, from the local point of view, and to re-claim for local people some of the territory being appropriated by state and international forest mapping projects. Local notions of territoriality have had to change as extensive land-based projects have threatened them; they will change further with mapping. Yet, given the alternate futures – of not being on the map, as it were, being obscured from view and having local claims obscured, there almost seems to be no choice. Both in forest mapping and generally in Indonesia's natural resource politics, local people's views and claims have not been adequately recognized, and even more rarely accepted on their own terms. Some translation is needed into the terms of those who would claim them. Maps give local people the power to do so.

NOTES

1 Based on Article 33 of the 1945 Indonesian Constitution.
2 The indigenous or autochthonous peoples of Borneo (comprised of Indonesian Kalimantan, Malaysian Sarawak and Sabah, and Brunei) are collectively called Dayak and Punan/Penan. Though the Dayak peoples of Borneo have a wide variety of rituals, customs, social organization, and even resource management practices, they share some patterns of resource management. For the sake of consistency, my remarks here refer only to Dayak peoples, although they may be also relevant for some settled Punan and some rural Malays.
3 For example, the Ford Foundation, The Worldwide Fund for Nature, and the East-West Center.

REFERENCES

Aberley, D. (1993) *Boundaries of Home: Mapping for Local Empowerment*. Gabriola Island, B.C., New Society Publishers.

Anderson, B. R. O'G. (1991, first printing 1983). *Imagined Communities: Reflections on the Origins and Spread of Nationalism*. London: Verso.

Appell, G. N. (n.d.) Observational procedures for land tenure and kin groupings in the cognatic societies of Borneo. Unpublished manuscript.

Barber, C. V. (1989) "The State, the Environment, and Development: The Genesis and Transformation of

Social Forest Policy in New Order Indonesia." Unpublished PhD dissertation, University of California, Berkeley.

Fox, J. (1990) Sketch mapping as a diagnostic tool in forest management. In Mark Proffenberger (Ed.) *Keepers of the Forest: Land Management Alternatives for Southeast Asia.* Westport: Kumarian Press 119–133.

Giddens, A. (1984) *The Constitution of Society.* Berkeley: University of California Press.

Girot, P. and B. Nietschmann (1993) The geopolitics and ecopolitics of the Rio San Juan. *Research and Exploration* 8: 52–63.

Government of Indonesia (GOI) (n.d.) Regional Physical Planning Programme for Transmigration (RePPPProt). Jakarta: ODA and Department Transmigrasi.

Harley, J. B. (1988) Maps, Knowledge, and power. In D. Cosgrove and S. Daniels (Eds.) *The Iconography of Landscape.* New York: Cambridge University Press, pp. 277–312.

Harley, J. B. (1989) Deconstructing the map. *Cartographica* 26: 1–20.

Harley, J. B. (1992) *History of Cartography.* Vol. 1. Chicago: University of Chicago Press.

Hobsbawm, E. and T. Ranger (Eds.) (1983) *The Invention of Tradition.* Cambridge: Cambridge University Press.

Holleman, J. F. (Ed.). 1981. *Van Vollenhoven on Indonesian Adat Law: Selections from "Het Adatrecht van Nederlandsch-Indie Vol. 1, 1918."* The Hague: Martinus Nijhoff.

Kain, R. J. P., and E. Baigent (1992) *The Cadastral Map in the Service of the State: A History of Property Mapping.* Chicago: University of Chicago Press.

Kompas (1993) Hutan Adat Jelmu Sibak Dijadikan HTI Trans. 18 September: 8. Jakarta.

Lev, D. (1985) Colonial law and the genesis of the Indonesian State. *Indonesia* No., 40.

Manning, C. (1972) The timber boom in East Kalimantan. *Bulletin of Indonesian Economic Studies* 7: 30–61.

Menzies, N. K. (1992) Strategies of inclusion and exclusion in China's forest management. *Modern Asian Studies.* 26: 719–733.

Momberg, F. (1994) Participatory Tools for Community Forest Profiling and Zonation of Conservation Areas: Experiences from the Kayang-Mentarang Nature Reserve, East Kalimantan, Indonesia. Paper presented at the Borneo Research Council Third Biennial International Conference, Pentavank, July 1–14.

Moniaga, S. (1993) Toward community-based forestry and recognition of adat property rights in the Outer Islands of Indonesia. In J. Fox (Ed.) *Legal Frameworks for Forest Management in Asia: Case Studies of Community/State Relations.* Honolulu: East-West Center Occasional Papers of the Program on Environment, pp. 131–150.

Moore, S. F. (1986) *Social Facts and Fabrications: "Customary" Law on Kilimanjaro, 1880–1980.* Cambridge: Cambridge University Press.

Orlove, B. S. (1989) "Maps of Lake Titicaca: The Politics of Representation in Encounters between Peasants and the State in Peru." Unpublished manuscript.

Peluso, N. L. (1992a) *Rich Forests, Poor People: Resource Control and Resistance in Java.* Berkeley: University of California Press.

Peluso, N. L. (1992b) The ironwood problem: (Mis-)management and development of an extractive rainforest product. *Conservation Biology* 6: 210–219.

Peluso, N. L. (1993) Coercing conservation: The politics of state resource control. *Global Environmental Change* 4(2). 199–217.

Peluso, N. L. (1994) Fruit trees and family trees: property rights, ethics of access, and environmental change in West Kalimantan. Under revision for *Comparative Studies in Society and History.*

Potter, L. (1995) Forest degradation, deforestation, and reforestation in Kalimantan: Towards a sustainable land use? In C. Padoch and N. L. Peluso (Eds.) *Borneo in Transition: People, Forests, Conservation, and Development.* Kuala Lumpur: Oxford University Press.

Sirait, M., S. Prasodjo, N. Podger, A. Flavell, and J. Fox (1994) Mapping customary land in East Kalimantan, Indonesia. *Ambio* 23 (7): 411–17.

Vandergeest, P. and N. L. Peluso (1995) Territorialization and the Thai State. *Theory and Society* (in press).

Zerner, C. (1990) *Legal Options for the Indonesian Forestry Sector.* Jakarta, Indonesia: United Nations Food and Agriculture Organization.

21

Misreading Africa's Forest History

James Fairhead and Melissa Leach

Introduction

This chapter examines the contrast between the formulation of problems in development policy and the perspectives of villagers whose views have been subjugated, and everyday activities criminalized, within this formulation. We attempt to identify the conditions in which certain demonstrably false ideas about environmental change have come to acquire validity in policy circles, while others, more correct and espoused by inhabitants, have been excluded from consideration and investigation.

Several authors have recently spotlighted the presence of particular off-the-shelf 'narratives', current in development institutions, which come to define development problems and justify interventions, particularly in conditions where data are poor, time is short, national agendas are overruled and local consultation impossible (Hoben 1993; Roe 1991, 1995). Narrative construction is the stuff of synthesis overview writing within development agencies and policy research institutes, and of interagency analytical alignment in development approaches. Narratives help decision-makers confidently fill the gap between ignorance and expediency.

With the spotlight on the narrative, less attention has been given to the ways in which the discursive processes which condition narrative construction also condition knowledge produced about development problems, including the generation of credible 'data' – often in large amounts. Adherents to the environmental-degradation view explored in this chapter think that there is abundant evidence to support their conviction. Focusing on these nar-ratives also encourages analysis to treat the relationship between international and local agendas as one of dislocation, divided by a gulf which the increasing use of development-institutionally acceptable research methods, apparently responsive to local concerns, might help bridge. Less attention is given to ways in which different sections of local society become involved in the discursive processes in which development-policy knowledge is produced. Such involvement may have developed over long periods, given that present development concerns frequently build on old debates which have already been incorporated into local political processes.

Environmental issues [...] particularly invite critical analysis because of the clarity with which global issues and constituencies as well as local ones are involved in defining and responding to the development problem. The analysis summarised in this chapter (for a detailed treatment, see Fairhead and Leach 1996a) [...] question[s] the readings of environmental change which have been driving development policies, revealing major contrasts between external perspectives and locally experienced realities. Contrasting definitions of the environmental problem contain particular images of local practices and justify contrasting development paradigms, commonly amounting to repression of, as opposed to support for, local techniques and institutions (e.g. Behnke and Scoones 1991; Leach and Mearns 1996; Thompson, Hatley and Warburton 1986; Tiffen, Mortimore and Gichuki 1993). The case considered in this chapter concerns ongoing 'savanni-zation' of tropical forest which is not, in fact, taking place.

Forest Loss Perceived

The vegetation of Guinea's Kissidougou prefecture reflects its position in West Africa's forest-savannah transition zone, consisting of patches of dense, high, semi-deciduous rainforest dispersed in savannah. For at least a century, environmental policy-makers have considered the forest patches, which surround old and new village sites, as the last endangered relics of a once extensive natural-forest cover now destroyed by local farming and fire-setting, a destruction they have continually sought to redress. But the experiences of most of Kissidougou's Kissi and Kuranko inhabitants, as well as archival and air photographic comparisons, do not support this view. Instead, they show forest islands to be the result of human management, created around villages in savannah by their inhabitants. They also show the woody vegetation cover of savannahs to have been increasing during the period when policy-makers have believed the opposite (Fairhead and Leach 1996a, 1996b).

West African vegetation maps, which show vegetation zones in more or less horizontal bands, easily lend themselves to interpretation as temporal as well as spatial transitions. Whether from desertification, sahelianization or savannization of forest, observers have been tempted to see each zone as the anthropogenically degraded derivate of a prior vegetation type. On many maps, the forest-savannah transition zone is marked explicitly as a 'derived savannah', or ex-forest, zone. And in Guinea, policy-makers since the turn of the century have been convinced of this southwards shift, with the conflation of spatial and temporal transitions incorporated into the scientific canon informing national and regional environmental policy. The first forest reserves established in Kissidougou in 1932 were conceived of as a protective 'curtain' to halt the southwards spread of fire- and farming-induced savannization. In 1993, the same conflation of spatial with temporal zones provided the logic for a major donor-funded environmental rehabilitation project to take forty Kissidougou farmers on a journey to northern Mali, to see the future of their own landscape should protective measures not be undertaken.

Within each vegetation zone, the iconography of spatiotemporal shifts on the vegetation map is complemented by the iconography of 'divergence from a climax vegetation type', the notional maximum vegetation which could exist given climatic conditions. This contains the idea of the previous existence of a 'bigger' and 'better' vegetation type 'prior to human disturbance', and closer to the 'Eden' which Africa's environment so often represented in colonial imaginations. In this way, present conditions in each vegetation zone may be envisaged as the anthropogenically degraded derivate of their predecessor. And so in Kissidougou, climate (e.g. annual rainfall levels over 1600 mm) and the presence of humid forest species and patches are taken as indicative of high forest potential and hence of its past existence.

The assumption of anthropogenic degradation of a prior natural forest formation was integral to the first delineation of West African vegetation zones in the early colonial period by the botanist Chevalier. This analysis was transferred directly into contemporary policy, since Chevalier was, at the time, the most senior advisor to the French West African colonial administrations responsible for environmental concerns. Subsequently, deductions made from analysis of the botanical composition ('phytosociology') of vegetation forms in these zones by botanists such as Aubréville, Adam and Schnell reinforced the hypothesis that the forest-savannah mosaic was in temporal transition. Observing the tree species characteristic of forest patch boundaries, for instance, botanists deduced that they indicated savannized forest (e.g. Adam 1948, 1968). They did not consider other possibilities: that this 'transition woodland' could represent a stable intermediate form, the establishment of forest in savannah, or the complex outcome of inhabitants' management strategies.

As Aubréville and Adam in turn became senior figures in French West Africa's forestry administrations, so their phytosociology, interpreted within the degradation logic, became institutionalized as the principal methodology for assessing regional vegetation change, and their publications became key texts in comprehending West African environmental history more generally (e.g. Aubréville 1949). Characteristically, these botanists directly observed landscape features and deduced history and people's impact from them. Their disciplinary position and the social conditions of their fieldwork reinforced their pejorative visions of local farming and fire-management practices, rendering it both difficult and seemingly unnecessary to verify change with local people themselves.

It has remained 'scientifically' acceptable to interpret vegetation history and anthropogenic impact from snapshot landscape observations, with deductions from plant and other indicators, vegetation surveys and remotely sensed imagery now adding to the repertoire. For example, modern observers of Kissidougou often take the presence of oil palms to indicate that forest has retreated from the area, while the team preparing Guinea's forestry action plan (République de Guinée 1988) deduced from their air photographic 'snapshots' and vegetation surveys that southern Kissidougou was a 'post-forest' zone. Similar social distance and pre-conviction as characterized the colonial botanists enables today's analysts too to overlook both local people's environmental experiences and management, and historical methods (e.g. oral histories and archive consultation) in comprehending environmental influences and trends.

Historical data sets are nevertheless available today, and their examination produces a very different picture of vegetation change. We compiled a picture of Kissidougou's vegetation dynamics through elderly people's oral recollections concerning vegetation use and management, and conducted comparative analysis of 1952, 1982 and 1991 air photographs and 1989/92 SPOT satellite data, and landscape descriptions found in archives dating from 1893. Social-anthropological fieldwork in Kissi and Kuranko villages throughout 1992 and 1993 provided an understanding of inhabitants' agro-ecological concepts and techniques and the social conditions of their application in the present, enabling closer enquiry into land-use change.

Far from being relics, Kissidougou's forest islands prove to have been created by local populations. In the majority of villages, elders describe how their ancestors encouraged forest-patch formation around settlements which had been founded either in savannah or beside gallery forests. The formation and growth of forest islands around recently established village sites is often visible when 1952 and modern air photographs are compared. Villagers also suggest that woody cover on the upland slopes and plateaux between the forest islands has generally increased during this century, and not declined as has been thought. In the north and east of the prefecture, grass savannahs have become more densely wooded with relatively fire-resistant savannah trees and oil palms. Indeed, the fact that oil palms have spread north into savannahs, encouraged by villagers, suggests that they may be better seen as outposts of anthropogenic forest advance than as relic indicators of forest retreat. Even more strikingly, in the south and south-east, large expanses of grass and sparse shrub savannah have ceded entirely to forest fallow vegetation: the area

is actually a 'post-savannah', not a 'post-forest' zone. These southerly savannah-forest transitions are not only evident in air-photograph comparison but are strongly indicated by changes in everyday resource use: for example, the introduction of tree-felling in agricultural operations, greater availability of preferred fuelwood species, changes in roofing and thatching materials, and changes in termite species associated with particular edible fungi. These demonstrable changes, which reflect long-term interactions between the populations of Kissidougou and their forest-savannah vegetation (Fairhead and Leach 1996a, 1996b) strongly challenge the view of a continuing shift of vegetation zones to the south.

Equally, evaluating 'degradation' in terms of a vegetation climax is revealed as inadequate when one takes the impact of long-term climate history into account. Given that West Africa has experienced both long-period, deep climatic fluctuations and changes in climatic variability [. . .], the history of vegetation form begins to appear as a history of continual transition rather than of divergence from a single, once extant climax. Recent ecological analysis suggests that such ceaseless transitions depend on multi-factor complexes rather than trends in one particular variable [. . .] (Behnke and Scoones 1991; Dublin, Sinclair and McGlade 1990). The various forest and savannah forms in the transition zone can be seen as such multiply-determined states dependent on fire, soil, water, seed availability, animal-related and other conditions. [. . .]. By altering the balance of interacting factors, people can initiate shifts between states which might be unattainable, or much less likely, through 'natural' ecological processes alone. The shifts from savannah to forest in Kissidoguou could be seen in this way (Fairhead and Leach 1996b).

Yet within Guinea, environmental services have been so convinced of the degradation they are combating that they find it unnecessary to compare their commissioned aerial and satellite images with those from 1952, let alone question their interpretative framework. Even when comparative interpretations are carried out, they are frequently not independent of preconceived ideas of vegetation change. In Kissidougou, the incredulous reactions of forestry staff when presented with 1952 and 1990 air photographs showing increased woody vegetation led them to a sceptical search for ways to render the comparison invalid (the photographs were taken in a-typical years, or incomparable seasons). In other parts of West Africa, similarly surprising results have simply been disbelieved and dismissed [...] (Houghton, Unruh and Lefebre 1993). In contrast, justifiable scepticism was cast aside when a comparison of eastern Guinea satellite images taken ten years apart seemed to show significant vegetation degradation, on which basis major donor funds for a regional environmental rehabilitation programme were secured (Grégoire, Flasse and Malingreau 1988).

The images of environmental change derived from these 'scientific' analyses have been incorporated not only into Guinean environmental institutions, but also into formal sector education and the popular consciousness of state functionaries. They are regularly reproduced in school geography lessons and national university curricula and theses. For those educated within this vision, casual readings of the landscape come to serve as confirmatory evidence; dry season bush fire is taken as proof of a worsening problem, and the conversion to farmland of a few forest islands near the town for urban market-gardening is taken to suggest forest-island diminution everywhere. Such casual landscape readings are often made during the dry season, when external consultants, forestry agents and urban nationals' visits to villages are concentrated. This is the destructive part of villagers' normal seasonal cycle, when bush is cleared for farming, fires sweep the savannah and trees are cut for construction or sale. Regeneration during the rainy season, anyway more subtle to observe, escapes attention within this seasonal bias (Chambers 1983).

Interpretations of vegetation degradation are reinforced not only by local observation, but also by the global and regional level analyses with which they are in keeping, and which carry the weight of international authority. Given FAO figures concerning rapid forest loss in West Africa (FAO 1990), for example, it appears inconceivable that Kissidougou should be experiencing anything else. Such figures, so frequently publicized in the more glossy development literature and on the radio, are far more accessible to the environmental administrations and urban public concerned with Kissidougou than are analyses of the locality itself. Equally the rhetoric of shared environmental crisis, made so apparent in the 1992 UNCED conference in Rio, appeals far more powerfully to local officials than the statements of the villagers who are supposedly experiencing these problems. This was made evident in the 1993 'Journées de l'Environnement' conference designed to raise awareness of Kissidougou prefecture's environmental problems, where both the Prefect and Kis-

sidougou's urban-based environmental NGO framed their speeches in terms of global concern with biodiversity loss and the common West African struggle against desertification. The projection of global and regional concerns on to Kissidougou's environment has recently increased, but it is not new; it has informed administrative perceptions since the early colonial period. A concern that deforestation in Kissidougou would damage regional climate and hydrology was apparent in the earliest writings of Chevalier (e.g. 1909) and underlay a major watershed rehabilitation programme first outlined in the 1930s, funded in the 1950s following the 1948 Goma inter-African soil conference, and launched again in 1991.

This analysis of environmental change which informs local policy cannot be separated from the financial context in which environmental institutions operate. In Guinea, early colonial administrations first became concerned with the perceived destructiveness of African environmental management because the colonial economy was heavily dependent on 'threatened' natural resources: initially wild rubber, and then, in Kissidougou, oil-palm products and tree crops grown in forest patches (Fairhead and Leach 1995). In the later colonial and post-colonial periods, more regional and global economic imperatives joined these national ones. [...] Recently, administrative solvency and development activities have come to rely even more heavily on foreign aid and thus become subject to various forms of 'green conditionality' (Davies 1992; Davies and Leach 1991). This greening of aid, and the specific forms it takes, reflects donors' need to satisfy home political constituencies heavily influenced by media images and northern environmental NGOs, as well as their own institutional assessments of African environmental problems.

In Guinea [...] a new generation of heavily funded environmental projects has emerged. [...] In agricultural and other development activities too, overt environmental sustainability components are important in attracting future funds. Kissidougou's prefecture administration, agriculture and forestry services are well aware of the packages which satisfy the donors in this respect: agroforestry programmes, forest conservation and improvement, bush-fire control, and rationalization and reduction of shifting cultivation in favour of intensive wetland rice. During Kissidougou's 'Journées de l'Environnement', the prefecture's number-two administrator stated explicitly: 'Donors are interested principally in environmental projects, so we must solicit their aid to ensure the development of the prefecture.' He suggested that other localities learn from the example of the Niger protection project zones, where schools, water and other infrastructural developments were provided in exchange for local participation in environmental protection. The emergence of local, urban-based environmental NGOs such as Kissidougou's 'Friends of Nature' society has also been encouraged by recent donor interest, not only in environmental issues but also in the claimed capacity of NGOs to achieve 'participatory' development. In short, presenting a degrading or threatened environment has become an imperative to gain access to donors' funds. In this respect, our own findings were often considered subversive, threatening to the prefecture's future financial and development interests, and to the continued employment and material privileges of environmental project administrators and extension workers.

Considering the environment as degrading and threatened is equally crucial to the solvency of state environmental institutions when they do not receive donor support. Since their inception, francophone West African forestry services have derived revenues from the sale of permits and licences for timber and wildlife exploitation, and from fines for what became environmental crimes in breaking state environmental laws. In Guinea, setting bush fires actually carried the death penalty during the 1970s (Law 08/ AN/ 72 of 14 September 1972). Environmental services have been able to gain such revenues only by taking control of the management of natural resources (e.g. fire and trees), and this through deeming villagers to be incapable and destructive resource custodians. Revenues are thus ensured by a reading of the landscape as degraded and degrading, of forest islands as disappearing relics in an increasingly grassy savannah, not as created in an increasingly woody one. The importance to forestry staff of informal receipts gained while applying policies of repression only accentuates the imperative for this environmental reading, while the antagonistic relationship thus engendered between forestry agents and villagers bars communication about villagers' own environmental experiences. Thus at local and national as well as international levels, the economic structures within which environmental agencies operate frame the ways that information is derived.

The attitudes of forestry staff depend not only on their financial and educational status as forestry service members, but also on their socio-cultural positions. They share with many other formally educated, urban-based Guineans a particular vision of villagers' resource management capabilities. This image of the rural farmer as environmental destroyer and of rural farming and forestry techniques as backward, in need of modernization, conforms with and helps justify urban intellectuals' self-definition as modern and progressive. [...] Just as urban circles benefited from the agricultural modernization which wrested resource control from villagers, so they have become the main beneficiaries of environmental control, keeping the moral high ground, while gaining from policies such as those removing timber-cutting rights from 'irresponsible' villagers.

Images of forest loss in Kissidougou are also reinforced as part of processes of ethnic distinction, which depend on colonial portrayals and their subsequent incorporation into local political discourse. From the outset, colonial constructions of ethnic difference among Kissidougou's populations rested partly on stereotypes concerning their environmental behaviour. [...]

[...]

During the First Republic, Sekou Touré's state regime encouraged villages to move out of the 'mystified obscurity' of their forest islands into 'the open', into the 'clarity' and 'modernity' upheld by the regime's cultural demystification policy, and into the roadside world more accessible to its demands (Rivière 1969). This policy drew on and reinforced ethnic stereotypes, deepening their construction in terms of forest. Maninka self-representations often draw on the ideal of social clarity, of openness and simplicity in language and expression, and make an explicit contrast between their clear 'savannah language' (*kan gbe*) and the secrecy and obscurity of the forest culture and languages, which they find difficult to learn. Many Kissia perceived Sekou Touré's regime as Maninka-biased, and considered the attempts it made to evict them from their forests and suppress 'sacred forest' schools as attempts to disempower the institution which had hitherto defended the Kissia from Maninka domination, whether cultural or military. The political conditions from 1958 to 1984 therefore reinforced the significance of forest symbolism in Kissidougou's local and ethnically charged political discourse.

In this context, both the present privileging of the forest, and the view that it is threatened as portrayed by the forestry service, coincide with the broader politico-ethnic interests of urban Kissia, interests heightened in the run-up to multiparty electoral processes beginning in December

1993. Sharing one forest – where the forest islands of neighbouring villages have come to touch each other – is one of the strongest metaphors of Kissi political solidarity, linked as it used to be to alliance in warfare and forest initiation. [. . .]

Distinctions between urban-institutional and rural villagers' perceptions of environmental change also derive from different valuations of vegetation quality. For urban observers and the forestry service, high value is accorded to large forest trees, whether for recent global reasons or for the commercial gains to be made from timber exploitation, which has recently become big business in Kissidougou. Villagers do not share this valuation, not least because the forestry laws designed to regulate timber exploitation (i.e. to preserve the environment) deny them all but an insignificant royalty from trees cut by outsiders in their forest islands. Their values are conditioned, instead, by the importance of different vegetation types and species in agriculture, gathering, settlement and tree-crop protection and cultural practices, and in which lower bush fallow vegetation is frequently more useful than high forest (Leach and Fairhead 1994). The large trees of forest islands are, in fact, more the 'fortuitous' consequence of villagers' environmental management for other reasons than a deliberately encouraged feature. While the felling of these trees may be of little consequence to villagers (or to forest area in the long term), to urban and official observers it epitomizes, and thus reinforces their conviction of, environmental destruction.

Forest Loss Explained

The image of environmental degradation in Kissidougou is supported by apparently successful explanations for it in terms of local land-use practices and their changing socio-economic, demographic and institutional contexts. [. . .]

Policy-makers' thinking has long been dominated by the view that local land use encourages savannization and reduces savannah tree cover and soil quality. These apparent processes of degradation are readily observable in the short term, in, for example, the clearing and burning of wooded lands for farming and the setting of fire by hunters and herders. But less attention is paid to processes of regeneration and the impact of local practices on them. In villagers' experience, their land use has, in the long run, maintained or enhanced woody vegetation cover and soil quality. The logic of local cultivation practices which encourage the advance of forest in this region has

been documented in Guinea by ourselves (Fairhead and Leach 1996a) and in neighbouring Côte d'Ivoire by Blanc-Pamard and Spichiger (1973). Villagers tend to consider themselves as improving once less-productive lands, rather than reducing the productivity of once 'naturally' productive ones.

Nevertheless, the contrasting external image of local land-use as inevitably degrading is combined with particular theories about the impact of demographic and social change to account for the long-term degradation which policy-makers believe has taken place. Discussions in development circles of the links between population and environment, poverty and environment, and social organization and environmental management have set the terms of debate which guide causal interpretations by development personnel, consultants and national institutions. Given that it is explanations of supposed environmental degradation which are being sought – and given the prevailing intellectual, social and fiscal structures which condition causal analysis – all but the dominant strands of thinking within these debates tend to be suppressed at the project level. Thus it is Malthusian views of the relationship between population and environment, the deduction that impoverishment forces villagers to draw down their natural resources and the notion of a 'tragedy of the commons', which are used to explain increasing environmental degradation in Kissidougou.

Environmental degradation is attributed to assumed demographic trends by policy-makers who believe that, since local land use is degrading, more people must mean more degradation, principally through extra upland use. An image of low pre-colonial population densities is commonly linked to the supposed existence then of extensive forest cover, and rapid population growth during this century (and now refugee settlements) are held to account for forest decline. Short fallows and long cultivation periods on savannah uplands are often taken as evidence of modern population pressure. That local farmers use intensive cultivation practices for positive ecological and economic reasons, unrelated to population pressure, is not considered. Nor does the possibility that population growth could lead to environmental improvement receive attention. Yet in Kissidougou, where there are more villages, there are more forest islands, and more people can mean that there is more intensive, soil- and vegetation-enhancing savannah cultivation and more generalized fire control.

Socio-economic theories to explain supposed recent environmental degradation attribute it partly to modern poverty, forcing villagers to sacrifice sustainable long-term resource management in favour of short-term uses assumed to be degrading. Recent environmental degradation is also explained through the idea that modern resource use is disorganized and individualistic, a vision shared by many local administrators as much as external consultants and university academics. In many versions of this narrative, a picture of people in greater 'harmony' with their forested environment is projected on to the pre-colonial period, a harmony maintained either by efficacious traditional authority (Green 1991; Stiegelitz 1990) or, in more sophisticated terms, by the integration of fire control within intra and inter-village social, cultural and political relationships (Zerouki 1993). An armoury of factors is held to have ruptured this controlled harmony, including socio-economic change, the weakening of traditional authority, new economic and cultural aspirations and social divisions, and the alienation of local resource control to state structures. The logical policy implication is that resource use can be rendered sustainable by improving forms of 'regulation', 'authority' and 'organization', whether by greater state control (e.g. over timber-cutting and fire) or, in recent policy emphasis, by 're-building' community institutions. These dominant social and demographic explanations for degradation and the idea of degradation itself seem to be mutually sustaining. From within this complex, the actual history of people's environmental use and the complex influences on it fail to receive serious attention.

The institutional and financial structures in which social science is applied to environmental problems in Guinea strongly support such uncritical explanations of degradation. Studies are commissioned by donor agencies and projects who need (or at least, must be seen to have sought) socio-economic information to help them tackle the environmental problems integral to their institutional survival in more 'appropriate' and 'participatory' ways. The environmental problem is thus built into the very terms of reference of consultants who have neither the time nor the social position to investigate village natural-resource management and its changes on any other terms. This problem is not necessarily solved when consultants are Guinean, nor even when they are working in their own areas; indeed, it can be compounded by the urban intellectual images which such local consultants bring to bear. Furthermore,

as the dominant social and demographic explanations of environmental degradation are the stuff of academic debate, consultancy reports phrased in their terms gain easy acceptance and credibility.

The interface between environmental-development agencies and villagers, which has developed over more than half a century, often in antagonistic ways, renders the communication of local environmental experiences highly problematic. Villagers, faced by questions about deforestation and environmental change, have learned to confirm what they know the questioners expect to hear. This is not only because of fear, politeness and an awareness that the truth will be met with incredulity, but also because of the desire to maintain good relations with authoritative outsiders who may bring as yet unknown benefits – a school, road or advantageous recognition to the village, for example. In such discussions, the historical ecology that villagers portray is as politically inflected as in their oral histories concerning settlement foundation, where images of initial vacancy (high forest, empty savannah, or abundant wild animals) often justify the first-comer status of current residents (Dupré 1991; Hill 1984). Like the prefecture administration, many village authorities realize the benefits which can accompany community participation in environmental rehabilitation, and in this context they may publicly agree to the 'urgent need' to plant trees, establish village environmental management committees and so on. Nevertheless, acceptance is not without anxiety over losing land to 'project' trees, over losing control over management of local ecologies to outsiders ignorant of their specificities, and over the unknown future demands that apparently generous projects of unknown origin and intent, huge financial resources and foreign interests, may later exact. Everyday forms of resistance thus frequently underlie overt participation: letting project tree nurseries and plantations burn in the dry season, for example, and ensuring that necessary fires are set in ways contrary to agreed project procedures.

It has been surprising to us how little the personal lifetime experiences of development workers from the prefecture influence the way that Kissidougou's environment has come to be perceived. This may be because personal environmental histories have too limited a spatial coverage to challenge a generality, or because unbroken personal histories are themselves rare: state officials are frequently transferred and are posted in preference to areas with which they are unfamiliar, so they have frequently been away from their childhood village environments for long periods. Such people almost invariably justify their perceptions of historical deforestation with examples drawn from roadsides and urban peripheries, with which they have more continuous familiarity, but which in Kissidougou are the proverbial exceptions to the rule.

Scientific challenge to the dominant analysis in Guinea is also rare. This is partly because the scientific information and ecological theory which questions the derived savannah model, and which often proves to support the farmers' explanations we have investigated, is dispersed among different disciplines and their specialist academic journals. These are largely inaccessible to policy makers and national academic institutions. Information from each discipline alone (e.g. botany, hydrology, soil science, demography and climate history) is insufficient to shift thinking in a sufficiently fundamental way; lack of inter-disciplinary criticism seems, indeed, to promote consistency. In any case, little such discussion enters the information bulletins of multinational organisations (e.g. FAO), NGOs, development journals or the media, the sources on which most development personnel rely for environmental science information. Fundamentally, the precepts basic to local science which challenge conventional savannization wisdom are not easily apprehended by researchers ill-disposed either to listen or to understand.

Conclusions

This environmental case illustrates in a particularly striking way how development problems and policies are constituted within diverse, seemingly disparate relations. The vision of environmental degradation in Kissidougou, to which so many people are drawn for different reasons, has, for a hundred years now, been sustained within their scientific, social, political, institutional and financial relationships. These relationships have evolved in ways which mean that today the degradation vision is not associated only with donor agencies and their narratives. It is partly the product of a long history of interaction with, and incorporation into, local social and political processes, and is thus today partly sustained within these. This is not to say that villagers' everyday ecological practice is influenced by the deforestation reasoning, but merely that their ecological reasoning is subjugated in much political interaction, development activities included.

Degradation visions have justified external authorities in exerting various forms of control over people and their resources, often compromising villagers' resource management and attracting considerable animosity. As one man from the north of the prefecture explained bitterly:

During the period of taxes and hunger, which weighed heavily on us during the First Republic, forest guards prevented us from felling trees, from setting fire even in the field, from cutting chewing sticks, from fishing and from hunting even on our own territory. We were worried and disorientated in land management, feeling ourselves to be strangers on our own lands and robbers from the State.

Nevertheless, villagers have needed to continue many of their agro-ecological strategies despite their criminalization, and have therefore adopted assorted strategies of resistance, whether covert fire-setting or tree-felling, or offering largesse to forest guards. As it was once expressed to us: 'We came to judge it best to continue managing our land as before, giving the forest guards money every year, because it is clearly money that is their priority, rather than any concern with forest protection.' That Kissidougou's farmers have been able to maintain landscape productivity in the face of such repression is in part testimony to the effectiveness of such resistance (Fairhead and Leach 1995). Cognisant of rural ill-will towards the environmental services, politicians have found promises to curb their repressive activities to be an effective electoral campaign strategy, although following elections, the other imperatives which this chapter documents have generally taken hold. It is only very recently that, under both internal and international pressure, Guinea's forest service has begun to undergo significant reforms, and their outcomes remain to be seen.

To date, villagers' own ecological knowledge and experience have been unable successfully to challenge the landscape readings driving policy. This is partly because of the power relations at the farmers' interface with environmental agencies and urban intellectuals. But it is also because views of degradation in Kissidougou are sustained not on the basis of ignorance, but through the continual production of supportive knowledge. Those who are convinced of deforestation and savannization do not lack data to support their convictions, and it is within this methodologically supported certainty that alternative methods and data sets have been disqualified as inadequate, naive, unscientific or simply improbable.

The Kissidougou case highlights a misreading of the forest-savannah transition landscape which a growing body of evidence suggests may well be relevant elsewhere in West Africa and beyond. [. . .] The case of Kissidougou is pertinent in illustrating how powerfully certain visions of environmental change and their linked development problems can arise and be maintained in policy circles, producing knowledge which excludes considerable counter-evidence. It is becoming clear that similar processes are at work in many African environmental contexts, from drylands through savannah grasslands and highlands to humid rainforests (Leach and Mearns 1996), and that, all too frequently, it is local land users whose perspectives and priorities are thus marginalized.

REFERENCES

Adam, J.G. (1948), 'Les reliques boisées et les essences des savanes dans la zone préforestière en Guinée francaise', *Bull. Soc. Bot. Fr.*, 98: 22–6.

—— (1968), 'Flore et végétation de la lisière de la forêt dense en Guinée, *Bulletin IFAN*, 30/3: 920–52.

Aubréville, A. (1949), *Climats, forêts et désertification de l'Afrique tropicale*, Paris: Société d'Edition de Géographie Maritime et Coloniale.

Behnke, R. and I. Scoones (1991), 'Rethinking Rangeland Ecology: Implications for Rangeland Management in Africa', *ODI/IIED Issues Paper*, 33.

Blanc-Pamard, C. and R. Spichiger (1973), 'Contact forêt-savane et recru forestier en Côte d'Ivoire', *L'Espace Géographique*, 3: 199–206.

Chambers, R. (1983), *Rural Development: Putting the Last First*, London: Longman.

Chevalier, A. (1909), *Rapport sur les nouvelles recherches sur les plantes à caoutchouc de la Guinée francaise*, Senegalese National Archives, 1G276.

Davies, S. (1992), 'Green Conditionality and Food Security: Winners and Losers from the Greening of Aid', *Journal of International Development*, 4/2: 151–65.

—— and M. Leach (1991), 'Globalism versus Villagism: Food Security and the Environment at National and International Levels', *IDS Bulletin*, 22/3: 43–50.

Dublin, H., A. Sinclair and J. McGlade (1990), 'Elephants and Fire as Causes of Multiple Stable States in the Serengeti-Mara Woodlands', *Journal of Animal Ecology*, 59: 1147–64.

Dupré, G. (1991), 'Les arbres, le fourré et le jardin: les plantes dans la société de Aribinda, Bukina Faso', in G. Dupré (ed.), *Savoirs paysans et développeement*, Paris: Karthala-ORSTOM.

FAO (1990), *Interim Report on Forest Resources Assessment*, Committee on Forestry, tenth session, 24–28 September 1990, Rome: United Nations Food Organization.

Fairhead, J. and M. Leach (1995), 'Reading Forest History Backwards: The Interaction of Policy and Local Land Use in Guinea, 1893–1993', *Environment and History*, 1/1.

—— (1996a), *Misreading the African Landscape: Society and Ecology in a Forest-savanna Mosaic*, Cambridge: Cambridge University Press (African Studies Series).

—— (1996b), 'Enriching the Landscape: Social History and the Management of Transition Ecology in the Forest-savannah Mosaic (Republic of Guinea)', *Africa*, 66/1: 14–36.

—— (forthcoming), *Forests of Statistics: Reframing Environmental History in West Africa*, London: Global Environmental Change Series, Routledge.

Green, W. (1991), *Lutte contre les feux de brousse*, Report for project DERIK, Développement Rural Intégré de Kissidougou.

Grégoire, J.M., S. Flasse and J.P. Malingreau (1988), *Evaluation de l'action des feux de brousse, de novembre 1987 à février 1988, dans la région frontalière Guinée-Sierra Leone*, Projet Régional FED-CILSS-CCR, 'Surveillance des ressources naturelles renouvables au Sahel-Volet Guinée', ISPRA, EEC.

Hill, M. (1984), 'Where to Begin? The Place of Hunter Founders in Mende Histories', *Anthropos*, 79: 653–6.

Hoben, A. (1993), 'The Political Economy of Land Tenure and Environmental Policy in Ethiopia', Draft summary of paper presented at African Studies Association meeting, Boston, December 1993.

Houghton, C.S., J.D. Unruh and P.A. Lefebre (1993), 'Current Land Cover in the Tropics and its Potential for Sequestering Carbon', *Global Biogeographical Cycles*, 7/2: 305–20.

Leach, M. and J. Fairhead (1994), The Forest Islands of Kissidougou: Social Dynamics of Environmental Change in West Africa's Forest-savannah Mosaic, Report to ESCOR of the Overseas Development Administration, London.

—— and R. Mearns (eds) (1996), *The Lie of the Land: Challenging Received Wisdom on the African Environment*, London: James Currey Publishers and Heinemann.

République de Guinée (1988), *Politique forestiére et plan d'action*, TFAP 1988, Conakry.

Rivière, C. (1969), 'Fétichisme et démystification: l'exemple guinéen', *Afrique documents*, 102–103: 131–68.

Rivière, C. (1976), 'Bourgeoisies du tracteur', *Revue Francaise d'Etudes Africaines*, 123: 74–101.

Roe, E. (1995), 'Except Africa: Postscript to a Special Section on Development Narratives', *World Development*, 19/4: 287–300.

Stiegelitz, F.V. (1990), *Exploitation forestière rurale et réhabilitation des forêts: premiers résultats d'un projet de recherche interdisciplinaire en Haute-Guinée*, Berlin.

Thompson, M., T. Hatley and M. Warburton (1986), *Uncertainty on a Himalayan Scale*, London: Ethnographica.

Tiffen, M., M. Mortimore and F. Gichuki (1993), *More People, Less Erosion: Environmental Recovery in Kenya*, Chichester: Wiley.

Zerouki, B. (1993), *Etude relative au feu auprès des populations des bassins versants types du Haut Niger*, Conakry: Programme d'amenagement des bassins versants types du Haut Niger.

22

Colonial Encounters in Postcolonial Contexts: Patenting Indigenous DNA and the Human Genome Diversity Project

Hilary Cunningham

Introduction

[...]

In this article, I examine how the Human Genome Diversity Project (HGDP) – a project which aspires to document human genetic diversity by extracting and studying blood and tissue samples from indigenous populations – has raised some significant ethical, conceptual and methodological issues for anthropologists. In 1992, shortly after the commencement of the HGDP, the project became the target of vociferous opposition and was renamed by many indigenous organizations as the 'Vampire Project'. Because several anthropologists are involved with the HGDP, the controversy surrounding the project has had implications not only for the field of anthropology in general, but also specifically for archaeologists, social-cultural anthropologists and biological anthropologists working with indigenous populations. The 14 March 1995 patenting of a cell line from a Hagahai man from Papua New Guinea not only fuelled the flames of discord between the HGDP and its opponents, but also gave the controversy new impetus.

[...]

Ethnographic Knowledge and Issues of Location

The enmity surrounding the Diversity Project, and its disputed connection to the recent Papua New Guinea (PNG) patent (withdrawn in 1996),[1] calls into question, yet again, the relationship between anthropological research and systems of power. Critical reflection on power and the production of ethnographic knowledge, of course, is not new to anthropology. Since at least the early 1970s, when several anthropologists began to reflect on colonialism and anthropology (Nash, 1975; Stocking, 1983), the concept of the anthropologist as a 'located subject' has received sustained attention in the discipline's deconstruction of the ethnographic process. For many anthropologists, it has been the publication of classics in this genre such as Maquet's 'Objectivity in Anthropology' (1964), Asad's *Anthropology and the Colonial Encounter* (1973) and Hymes's *Reinventing Anthropology* (1972) that have challenged and in many respects recast the practice of anthropological research by not only countering notions of an objective social scientist, but also, perhaps more importantly, forcing anthropologists to deconstruct their 'locatedness' in terms of political economy.

As this article intimates, however, the task of delineating the 'locatedness' of the anthropologist perdures, and anthropologists from all the sub-disciplines have continued to confront issues of locatedness within shifting configurations of political-economic power. Nowhere has this struggle with locatedness been more apparent among anthropologists than those working with indigenous populations. Virtually all anthropologists working with indigenous communities over the last 20 or so years have had to confront significant issues of locatedness: archaeologists with the repatriation of native skeletal remains and cultural artifacts and social-cultural anthropologists with access to native communities. As the Diversity Project controversy and the PNG patent reveal, biological anthropologists too are increasingly being drawn into political contexts in which the collection of biological data has become a politically embedded practice constitutive of larger relationships of power.

It is not my intention here, however, as a social-cultural anthropologist, to suggest that the Diversity Project controversy is germane only to biological anthropologists, nor to imply that HGDP's public relations problems are representative of genetic anthropology, itself a rather diverse field (see Marks, 1995b). Rather, the perspective adopted here suggests that the HGDP is an important case study relevant to all types of anthropologists, not only because it represents an opportunity to continue in the tradition of a reflexive anthropology, but also because, perhaps more importantly, it demonstrates how international economic trends are creating and cementing new global economies, and how these in turn are problematizing anthropological research vis-a-vis indigenous populations.

The contemporary political-economic context which challenges both the work and locatedness of archaeologists, social-cultural and biological anthropologists is, I suggest, characterized by two distinct trends, both of which I explore in relation to the HGDP and the PNG patent.

The first trend, the globalization of the economy (under the hegemony of a neo-liberal agenda), points to the changing context of political-economic power in which anthropological research is conducted. Global political-economic trends have significantly restructured the global flow of cultural, intellectual and natural resources, thereby reconstituting relationships between anthropologists and field subjects. While this restructuring of the global economy reflects an ongoing historical process several centuries old, new developments within global capitalism, particularly in the areas of intellectual property rights and biotechnology patents, have profound implications for the movement and control of both cultural and material knowledge. Anthropologists who collect and analyze either ethnographic knowledge or material artifacts thus find themselves ensconced in a larger political economy directing the flow of these resources in specific ways. This article examines how global commercial trends as well as multi-lateral and bilateral trade accords cementing the new global economy (such as the [WTO]) have problematized not only the specific anthropological goals of the Diversity Project, but also anthropological research vis-a-vis indigenous populations in general.

A second trend is the recognition of a new political context for anthropological self-critique. While the first volumes on anthropology and the colonial encounter were produced largely through an 'internal audit,' i.e. by anthropologists themselves, and were read largely by other anthropologists, current criticism of the field has newly *politicizing* participants: namely, indigenous organizations themselves and a growing network of advocacy groups active on behalf of indigenous rights. Although some anthropologists have collaborated with indigenous groups through organizations such as Cultural Survival, the International Working Group on Indigenous Affairs, Survival International and the Anthropology Resource Center, critiques from indigenous constituencies have remained largely peripheral to the field. Indigenous groups, for example, have not traditionally participated in academic conferences, responses to anthropological research by field subjects generally have not been published, and indigenous representation in anthropology faculties remains modest to say the least. The indigenous critique of the anthropological encounter, however, has a new political context which includes novel forms of political activism. This politicization has developed largely owing to the growth of new communication technologies and the emergence of new political spaces within an international milieu. Indigenous groups now have access to both new forms of political organization and new technological resources for disseminating opinions and agendas. The ongoing critique of anthropology, then, as a 'colonial encounter' is no longer confined simply to an academic arena. Anthropologists now find themselves negotiating not only the goals and execution of their studies, but also their own political identities with increasingly sophisticated, politicized and internationalized 'research subjects'.

[. . .]

The Politicization of Genetic Research: The Human Genome Diversity Project

In 1992 the Human Genome Diversity Project was formed as a consortium of mainly molecular biologists and biological anthropologists who proposed to study human genetic diversity by collecting DNA samples from indigenous populations around the world. The HGDP had its provenance in a letter published in the journal *Genomics* [. . .] The project's principal figures – geneticists Luca Cavalli-Sforza, Mary-Claire King, Charles Cantor, R.M. Cook-Deegan, the late Allan Wilson and population geneticist Kenneth Kidd – were critical of a multi-billion dollar project launched in the United States in October 1990 called the Human Genome Project (HGP) (see Roberts, 1989, 1991b). Sponsored by the National Institute of Health (NIH) and the Department of Energy (DOE), the HGP proposed to chart the roughly 100,000 genes that make up the human genome. The authors of the letter argued that the HGP was flawed because it was confining its genetic sampling to largely white, northern populations, thereby betraying an ethnocentric bias by being too narrowly focused on Anglo-European populations. Seeking to correct this, the authors felt that a broader sampling of ethnic populations would not only better the project's goal to combat common human diseases, but also enable anthropological efforts to reconstruct the story of human evolution and explore issues of human adaptation (see Kidd et al., 1993). In the letter to *Genomics*, Cavalli-Sforza, Cook-Deegan and Wilson asked researchers worldwide to collect DNA samples from indigenous populations and establish a genetic database before these populations became extinct (Ross, 1993: 17). Their plan was to have researchers extract blood samples from 25 individuals in each population and have them preserved in permanent cell lines for further research and study (Lock, 1994: 603).

In the year following the *Genomics* letter, the HGDP established an International Executive Committee along with two standing committees (one on ethics and the other on informatics) and the HGDP International Executive began to encourage member countries to establish regional committees.[2] The North American Executive Committee of the HGDP was among the first regional boards to form and its original 13-member directorate consisted of anthropologists, geneticists, a law school professor and a sociologist.

One of the first tasks of the HGDP was to establish a list of ethnic populations which would make logical subjects of genetic research. Consequently, in October 1992, HGDP geneticists, anthropologists and linguists gathered at Pennsylvania State University and identified 722 indigenous populations from around the world that they believed constituted highly desirable candidates for genetic study.

Trouble, however, quickly followed the creation of this list when the HGDP released it to the Rural Advancement Foundation International (RAFI), a Canadian-based NGO which had for its 20-year history forcefully opposed the commercial exploitation of Third World plant and animal resources.

RAFI's adverse reaction to the list was immediate and marked. While HGDP proponents considered the indigenous populations mentioned in the list to be 'genetically distinct', critics observed that those listed were also peoples who had suffered any one of a number of social ills at the hands of Western colonialism. Many of the groups on the list had been colonized or enslaved, pushed off their lands and forced onto reservations. Others had been virtually wiped out by diseases introduced into their communities by Europeans. Others still had been exposed to nuclear weapons testing on their homelands by colonial powers and were, in some cases, the only surviving members of their traditional societies. In short, according to critics, the HGDP list was also an amazingly comprehensive record of victims of so-called Western 'progress'.

Information about the HGDP list, communicated largely via the Internet and through RAFI's electronic communiqués (see RAFI, 1993, 1994a, 1994b), created a stir among indigenous coalitions and NGOs dedicated to indigenous rights. Several coalitions, upon receiving the list, consequently decided that the HGDP was yet another manifestation of First World exploitation, in this case a collaboration of scientists who were intent upon 'mining' indigenous communities for raw materials which now included their DNA (see Harry, 1994). Between 1992 and 1995, RAFI and several other groups began to publicize information on patent applications developed from indigenous samples.[3] Then, in October 1995, RAFI discovered that a patent on a cell line from an indigenous man from Papua New Guinea had been granted to the US government several months earlier.

The PNG Patent

First, how did the PNG patent come about?

In the mid-1980s a census and research team ventured into north-central Papua New Guinea to establish contact with the Hagahai, a hunter-gatherer people who had recently been reduced by disease to a group of roughly 300. Carol Jenkins, a medical anthropologist affiliated with the PNG Institute of Medical Research (IMR), a statutory body of the PNG government, joined the team and visited the Hagahai five times between 1985 and 1986 in order to investigate the causes underlying the Hagahai's decline and document the consequences of outside contact for their biological and cultural survival (Jenkins, 1987: 413). Jenkins, funded by the US National Geographic Society, collected ethnographic, demographic, linguistic and nutritional information on the Hagahai, and had blood samples drawn from roughly 25 Hagahai individuals. Her research revealed some alarming health trends among the Hagahai who showed pronounced incidences of tinea imbricata, upper respiratory infections, malaria, splenomegally, ulcers, severe otitis media, scabies, dysentery, conjunctivitis and chronic colds (Jenkins, 1987: 418–19). Moreover, Jenkins discovered that a high number of Hagahai were infected carriers of hepatitis. [...]

During a 1987 laboratory analysis of the blood samples in Australia, however, it became evident that the Hagahai were not only a culturally isolated people suffering the devastating consequences of cultural contact, but also possessed some genetically distinct traits: researchers discovered that the Hagahai were among a small group of indigenous groups infected with a variant of a T-cell leukemia lymphoma virus (called HTLV-1). (Usually the virus produces a severe form of leukemia, but the variant virus in the Hagahai is benign.) Consequently, the thymus lymphocytes (T-cells) were separated from the blood, maintained in a culture and sent to NIH labs near Washington, DC where they offered scientists a chance to better understand how the human body generates an immune response to leukemia-associated diseases.

On 24 August 1990, however, the research on the Hagahai samples took a commercial direction when the US government field for a patent on a cell line derived from a healthy, 20-year-old Hagahai male. The incentive for the patent, it appears, was the commercial possibility (potentially millions of dollars) of developing HTLV-related diagnostic tests as well as vaccines. Then, on 14 March 1995, the US government obtained a patent on the cell line.

When the public became aware of the PNG patent several months later, indigenous groups, political activists, religious leaders and academics from different disciplines began to condemn it. While for some groups the condemnation included a denunciation of the patenting of human biological products in general, for others it reflected special concern over the possible exploitation of indigenous populations in genetic research – especially those groups designated as 'genetically unique' or 'genetically endangered' (i.e. susceptible to extinction or genetic assimilation). The Hagahai patent, compounding the concerns of those critical of the HGDP, seemed to be confirmation of the new form of colonialism so many human rights activists feared – a colonialism in which wealthy corporate interests (aligned with

powerful national governments) sought to control the very molecular basis of life by exploiting the most vulnerable and poorest members of the human family.

Molecular biologists, the US government (as the holder of the PNG patent) and northern pharmaceutical companies soon became targets of this protest (see RAFI, 1996a) – but they were not the only ones. The role of a medical anthropologist in the Hagahai research and patent – Jenkins was one of the inventors listed on the PNG patent – engendered a kind of controversy around the discipline of anthropology that, although not new to the field, evoked some serious concerns. Consequently, indigenous groups have not only raised questions about the humanitarian objectives of the Hagahai project, but also more serious queries about the discipline of anthropology itself and the connection of biological anthropologists to the commercialization of indigenous DNA.

While the blood samples involved in the PNG patent were not drawn under the auspices of the HGDP, at least one prominent biological anthropologist, also active in Papua New Guinea and the Solomons, had a connection to the HGDP. While director of the Physical Program at the National Science Foundation, Jonathan Friedlaender had strongly supported the formation of the HGDP. For groups opposed to the HGDP, Friedlaender became the 'missing link', as it were, between the HGDP and the patenting of indigenous DNA for commercial profit. HGDP scientists, particularly those who had spearheaded the project, thus found themselves in the midst of an ugly political controversy in which opponents had connected them to exploitative pharmaceutical and biotech interests.[4]

The Controversy within Anthropology

Indigenous groups and NGOs were not, however, the only ones disturbed by the creation of the HGDP and the increasing role indigenous populations were assuming in commercial genetic research (see Roberts, 1992a, 1992b). While the scientific objectives and methodology of the project received criticism from several anthropologists (see, for example, Marks, 1995a), other anthropologists were concerned about the 'colonial' flavor of the endeavor (Goodman, 1996; Lock, 1997: 231–4).

First, HGDP scientists seemed concerned that the listed populations were rapidly going extinct and that the time for obtaining blood samples was limited. They did not, however, express any explicit concern over why these populations were going extinct or what might be done to prevent this. Such an attitude suggested that the HGDP, despite its scientific merits, was nevertheless based in an acquisitive ideology that objectified the 'primitive' as an exotic and rare source of knowledge that had to be quickly tapped before it vanished.

Second, several anthropologists – many of them influenced by social-cultural critiques of colonialism – felt uncomfortable with the more subtle implication in HGDP discourse that indigenous populations somehow held the key to understanding human evolution. Again, the indigenous populations named by the Diversity Project were treated too much like the 19th-century anthropological 'primitive', who, envisioned as vestiges of an earlier moment in human history, represented a mirror on to the past. The HGDP seemed ideologically founded on attitudes that implied indigenous populations were a last chance for 'modern man' to see 'himself' in a former manifestation – an opportunity, as Adam Kuper has commented in his work on the creation of primitive society, to take a glimpse into the human past in order understand who the human was in the present (Kuper, 1988: 5). For several anthropologists, then, HGDP statements about using indigenous genetic samples to reconstruct human history smacked uncomfortably of the tradition of primitivism in anthropology (Lock, 1997: 233).

While several biological anthropologists assumed critical postures vis-a-vis the HGDP, questions about the HGDP also found a foothold in sub-disciplinary divides. When HGDP founder Cavalli-Sforza commented, for example, that critics of the project were largely cultural types, who were not 'real' scientists but more like 'philosophers or social critics' (Gutin, 1994: 74), he was not only incorrect in the light of the biological critique but also exacerbated the troublesome schism between biological and social anthropologists (see Holden, 1993). Needless to say, such dismissals of HGDP critics as simply 'anti-science' or 'soft' intellectuals did little to foster cross-disciplinary dialogue.

The Commercialization of Genetic Research

Between the dispersal of the Diversity list in 1992 and the discovery of the PNG patent by RAFI in 1995, relations between indigenous groups and the HGDP rapidly worsened. Native L set up an electronic discussion group to keep the lines of communication open, but opposition to the pro-

ject mounted steadily.[5] Internationally as well, the HGDP suffered considerable setbacks owing to its troubled image and lack of clear guidelines for conducting research. In September 1995, for example, Cavalli-Sforza attended UNESCO's International Bioethics Committee to raise support for the project, but UNESCO's working group on population genetics, after representatives from indigenous coalitions spoke against the project, distanced itself from the HGDP (see Butler, 1995: 37).

Yet, despite the deepening conflict engulfing the HGDP, there were some who continued to ask, so why all the fuss? The practice of taking blood samples from field subjects, after all, was not something new to anthropology (Gutin, 1994: 72). Moreover, the HGDP had, particularly in its North American Model Ethical Protocol, acknowledged that sensitivity to the sampled populations had to be shown. (No indigenous groups, however, were invited to or consulted about the project during its planning stages [Marks, 1995a].)

Perhaps one of the most significant factors to take into consideration when attempting to explain what engendered such a vociferous response to the HGDP is the project's relationship to the trajectory of biological imperialism. While distinctive in terms of its scope, the HGDP proposes to draw blood and tissue samples from indigenous populations from under the shadow of at least two (some would argue considerably more) centuries of what might be termed ecological colonization. Indeed, the linkage between natural history, botany and the expansion of empire is not new to the late 20th century, and indeed the terms 'biocolonialism' and 'biopiracy' are equally suited to the last century as they are to the current one. The controversy over the commercialization of human biology generated by the HGDP and PNG patent, then, clearly has historical precedents. And yet there are some significant differences about current biocolonial practices which are linked to the notion that humanity is entering into a new 'Age of Biology', a phrase used by both proponents and critics of biotechnology to distinguish the 21st century as an era in which products made from chemicals and metals are to be replaced by those made from biological materials (Khor, 1995: 1–2). In this new context, biological products, molecular research and geneticists have all assumed a novel economic identity and importance – indeed the term 'scientist-entrepreneur' has acquired a new currency in light of these developments. [. . .]

[. . .]

On 20 June 1991, for example, the HGP took an explicit commercial direction when it edged its way into the global marketplace. Craig Venter, then an NIH researcher, filed patents applications with the US Patent and Trademarks Office (PTO) for 337 gene sequences from the human brain (Roberts, 1991a).[6] At the time, Venter, a US-government employee, submitted the patents on behalf of the US government. While the PTO office eventually denied his claims in 1992, Venter's applications raised a storm of protest about the commercialization of genome research and the involvement of government agencies in commercializing genetic research (see Anderson, 1991: 485; Gorman, 1993: 57; Marshall, 1994: 25; Roberts, 1991a: 11).[7]

Venter's patent claims sparked a kind of 'gene fever' among organizations working on the human genome.[8] Government-affiliated institutes such as INSERM in France and the MRC in Britain, which had hoped to keep the project free of commercial interests, quickly condemned the patent applications but nevertheless felt pressure not to be 'edged out' by aggressive US interests. In August 1992, for example, England's Medical Research Council (MRC) staged a 'counter attack' by filing for 1100 patents on its gene sequences (Aldhous, 1991: 785). Indeed, the push to patent genes has led some critics of biotechnology to speculate that the entire human genome will have been patented by governments, and biotech and pharmaceutical companies by the year 2000 (Rifkin, 1993: viii).

[. . .]

The rapidly blurring lines between government and commercial research, between independent university and corporate pharmaceutical research, has raised some serious questions about how genetic research and its medical products will be distributed to 'mankind'. Who will benefit from gene therapies? How much are gene therapies going to cost? And finally, are gene therapies likely to benefit all populations equally or will only wealthier nations be able to afford them?

Perhaps even more controversial, however, is the prospect that genetic research itself is being increasingly controlled by commercial interests. The very character of genetic research – the way in which data is collected, accessed, stored, analyzed and released to the public – is now profoundly structured by commercial institutions. [. . .]

While the HGDP has declared itself a non-commercial enterprise, it does not oppose the patenting of human biological materials (such as DNA). [. . .] Can the HGDP guarantee [. . .] that the research institutions and researchers with whom it is affiliated will eschew the commercial exploitation of indigenous populations? Genetic research recently conducted in Colombia, for example, has already created difficulties for the HGDP. In this particular case, blood samples were collected from remote indigenous groups across Colombia under the auspices of the Genetics Institute of Javeriana University, Bogota. The project, called 'The Great Human Expedition', received funding from a number of public institutions as well as several large biotech firms (including Hoechst and Pfizer). The Institute, however, is also a leading player in the implementation of the HGDP in Colombia. To make matters worse for the HGDP, a British filmmaker produced a documentary on the project in 1995 which showed scientists from the Bogota-based Genetics Institute collaborating with scientists from the pharmaceutical giant Hoffman-La Roche as they draw blood from the Asario Indians of Colombia. The scientists take blood samples without informing the Asario of either the nature of their research or possible scientific and/or commercial uses of the samples. In fact, the subjects who give blood are told that they are being tested for diabetes as part of a medical effort.[9]

The North–South Dynamic

As the above example suggests, the commercialization of biological research, while significantly altering the nature of scientific research and the role of the scientist, is also embedded in a specific North–South economic dynamic. To be added to the litany of queries raised above, then, are important questions about where biological products originate, who 'discovers' them, and who acquires profits emerging from their development.[10]

The most coveted 'artifacts' – ranging from soil micro-organisms to animals and human DNA – desired by biotech and pharmaceutical companies have become the biological resources from the Third World, especially given that tropical rainforests (which contain over 50 percent of the world's plant species) are rapidly being destroyed through development. [. . .]

The trend to use indigenous blood samples in commercial genetic research has also become a significant variable in this north–south dynamic. Just after the Hagahai patent was issued, for example, RAFI reported that scientists from Sequana Therapeutics (a California-based 'genomic' company) in conjunction with scientists from the Samuel Lunenfeld Research Institute of

Canada (affiliated with the University of Toronto), collected blood samples from the people of Tristan da Cuñha, a tiny island of just under 300 inhabitants located halfway between Brazil and South Africa. The inhabitants, who are all descendants of the island's original seven families, exhibit one of the world's highest incidences of asthma (30 percent of the population suffer from asthma and 20 percent are carriers). In 1995, Sequana indicated that it had the information necessary to identify and eventually patent the gene or genes which predispose people to asthma. Sequana subsequently sold the licensing rights to a diagnostic test for asthma to a German firm (Boehringer Ingelheim) for $70 million. In another recent case, RAFI documented that scientists from the Rockefeller Institute in New York, who, in conjunction with their research on obesity genes in lab mice, extracted blood samples from the inhabitants of Kosrae, an island in the Federated States of Micronesia in the South Pacific where obesity has a high incidence. Aiming to identify the obesity gene in humans in order to understand how the amount of fat stored in the body is regulated, the project's sponsor, Rockefeller University, was offered $20 million by Amgen, a California-based pharmaceutical company, for licensing rights to the obesity gene and was promised additional payments of up to $90 million (see Leff, 1994; RAFI, 1993, 1994a, 1994b, 1995). The substantial profits to be gained from the use of these samples, then, has made indigenous DNA a potentially valuable commodity within the biotech industry (see Calestous, 1995; Shiva, 1991, 1993).

Significantly, while the profits derived from biological development are in and of themselves substantial, biotech and pharmaceutical companies are frustrated with the lack of universal patenting laws and enforcements. The Chemical Manufacturers Association, for example, has claimed annual losses of US $6 billion owing to lax patent laws; the Pharmaceutical Manufacturers Association losses of US $4 billion; and US drug companies have argued that they annually lose US $150 million owing to Brazil's failure to enforce copyrights (ECEJ, 1993: 6). The solution, for many of these companies, has been not only to push for the universalization of patent legislation that makes all life forms patentable, but also to create tough sanctioning measures to ensure that the patents are respected. Because 99 percent of all patents are currently held by northern companies, it is clear that large pharmaceutical and biotech firms stand the most to gain financially from a stringently enforced and uniform system of patent laws.

Patenting Biology on a Global Scale

Traditionally, intellectual property rights (IPRs) have been handled by national governments and monitored by a few international agencies such as The World Intellectual Property Organization (WIPO). While previous IPR treaties have tended to promote a balance between the owners of patents and the general public, the emphasis has recently shifted to protecting the rights and royalty entitlements of patent holders on a global scale (ECEJ, 1993: 5–6). As a result, IPRs buttressing private capital have become a critical item on the agenda of the [...] World Trade Organization (WTO). The Trade-Related Intellectual Property Rights (TRIPs) of the Uruguay Round of the GATT, for example, extended patent rights over pharmaceutical products (the majority of which have been developed by US, European and Japanese companies) and have made the patentability of micro-organisms mandatory. In addition, it increased the duration of patent protection to 20 years from the date of application and has strengthened the rights of patent-holders by instituting tough reprisal measures for countries who do not adhere to the TRIPs guidelines (Correa, 1995). [...] TRIPs does not strictly obligate signatories to allow for the patenting of animals, plants and human materials although the ambiguity of the TRIPs statement on the patenting of life forms does not preclude this development. It is clear, however, and based on the lobbying efforts of organizations such as the Pharmaceutical Manufacturing Association (PMA) and the Industrial Biotechnological Association (IBA, which represents over 80 percent of private US corporations investing in biotechnology), that international patent laws protecting private research and development have become, and will remain, an important issue in future trade agreements.

[...]

NOTES

1   On 24 October 1996, the National Institutes of Health (NIH), the holder of the PNG patent, filed paperwork to disclaim the patent. See RAFI (1996b).

2   In its literature, the HGDP specifies that it is not part of the Human Genome Project (HGP). As of January 1994 it officially came under the auspices of the Human Genome Organization (HUGO), a

non-profit, non-governmental group of scientists who play an advisory role in coordinating international human genetic research. HUGO has stated that it does not oppose the patenting of life forms but objects to the patenting of partial DNA sequencing technologies that are 'increasingly mechanical and straightforward'.

3   In addition to the Papua New Guinea patent application, these included patents that the United States filed on a cell line of a 26-year-old Guaymi Indian woman from Panama (withdrawn); a patent for the human T-cell line of a 40-year-old woman from Morovo Lagoon in Western Province and a 58-year-old man from Guadalcanal, both of the Solomon Islands.

4   Although they would be extremely useful to an analysis of this patent as a 'colonial encounter', the specific details of the negotiations among Jenkins, the IMR and the Hagahai remain unclear. Defenders of the patent have claimed that informed consent was obtained from the Hagahai and that an agreement (specifying that 50 percent of all profits arising from the patent would go to the Hagahai) was signed. To date, however, no documents showing a record of informed consent or this financial agreement have been released to the public. See also Ibeji and Korowai (1996), Taubes (1995).

5   This is not to suggest that all indigenous groups respond negatively to the possible uses of their blood samples. See Liloqula (1996) and Mead (1996).

6   Venter's applications eventually included requests for 6122 patents on human brain sequences.

7   Venter eventually left the NIH to start his own multi-million dollar company, Human Genome Sciences, Inc., which established profitable links with a major pharmaceutical firm, Smithkline Beecham.

8   What has made the commercial nature of genetic research ever more chaotic, however, has been the nature of Venter's first patent applications. Venter's applications were for DNA sequences whose function was unknown, a move that has led to a kind of 'gene prospecting' whereby companies apply for patents without really knowing what the scientific value of the DNA is. As some scientists critical of this practice have remarked, this 'speculative patenting' is equivalent to the kind of gold prospecting that went on in the last century whereby prospectors bought claims to mineral deposits beneath land they had never seen, let alone tested for gold.

9   The film was released by Films for the Humanities as *The Gene Hunters* (1995) and includes interviews with geneticist Alberto Gomez, George Annas, Professor of Medical Ethics at the Massachusetts Institute of Technology, and Leonora Zalabata, spokeswoman for the Arhuaco of northern Colombia. *The Gene Hunters* was originally broadcast in the UK on 26 February 1995.

10 For an alternative analysis of how biotechnology can assist Third World countries see Calestous (1995).

REFERENCES

Aldhous, Peter (1991) 'Tit for Tat on Patents?' *Nature* 371: 785.

Anderson, Christopher (1991) 'US Patent Application Stirs up Gene Hunters', *Nature* 353: 485–6.

Anderson, Christopher (1993) 'Genome Project Goes Commercial', *Science* 259: 300–2.

Asad, T. (1973) *Anthropology and the Colonial Encounter*. New York: Humanities.

Butler, D. (1995) 'Genetic Diversity Proposal Fails to Impress International Ethics Panel', *Nature* 377: 373.

Calestous, Juma (1995) *The Gene Hunters: Biotechnology and the Scramble for Seeds*. Princeton, NJ: Princeton University Press.

Correa, Carlos (1995) *The Social Costs of New Patent Rules*. Penang, Malaysia: Third World Network Features.

ECEJ [Ecumenical Council for Economic Justice] (1993) 'Free Trade and Patenting Life: Is Nothing Sacred?', *Economic Justice Report* (4) (2).

Goodman, A. (1996) *Glorification of the Genes: Genetic Determinism and Racism in Science*. London: Intermediate Technological Publishers.

Gorman, Christinen (1993) 'The Race to Map Our Genes', *Time* 144 (8 February): 57.

Gutin, Joann (1994) 'End of the Rainbow', *Discover* 15: 70–5.

Harry, Debra (1994) 'The HGDP: Implications for Indigenous', *Abya Yala News* 8 (winter).

Holden, C. (1993) 'Failing to Cross the Biology – Culture Gap', *Science* 262: 1641–2.

Hymes, D. (1972) *Reinventing Anthropology*. New York: Pantheon Books.

Ibeji, Y. and G. Korowai (1996) 'The Hagahai Patent Controversy: In Their Own Words', *Cultural Survival Quarterly* 33 (summer): 33.

Jenkins, Carol L. (1987) 'Medical Anthropology in the Western Schrader Range, Papua New Guinea', *National Geographic Research* 3: 412–30.

Khor, Martin (1996) 'Bucking Biopiracy: What Activists are Doing to Stem the Tide', *Utne Reader* (March/April): 91–3.

Kidd, Judith R., Kenneth K. Kidd and Kenneth M. Weiss (1993) 'Human Genome Diversity Initiative', *Human Biology* 65: 1–6.

Kuper, Adam (1988) *The Invention of Primitive Society*. London and New York: Routledge.

Leff, David (1994) 'Just Discovered Obesity Gene Points to (Distant) Future Slimming Therapy', *BioWorld Today* 5: 33.

Liloqula, K. (1996) 'Value of Life: Saving Genes Versus Saving Indigenous Peoples', *Cultural Survival Quarterly* 42 (summer): 42–5.

Lock, Margaret (1994) 'Interrogating the Human Genome Diversity Project', *Social Science and Medicine* 39: 603–6.

Lock, Margaret (1997) 'The Human Genome Diversity Project: A Perspective from Cultural Anthropology', in Bartha Maria Knoppers (ed.) *Human DNA. Law and Policy*. The Hague: Kluwer Law International.

Maquet, J. (1964) 'Objectivity in Anthropology', *Current Anthropology* 5: 47–55.

Marks, Jonathán (1995a) 'The Human Genome Diversity Project', *AAA Newsletter* 36 (4): 72.

Marks, Jonathan (1995b) *Human Biodiversity*. New York: Aldine de Gruyter.

Marshall, Eliot (1994) 'HGS Opens its Data Banks – For a Price', *Science* 266: 25.

Mead, A. (1996) 'Genealogy, Sacredness and the Commodities Market', *Cultural Survival Quarterly* 46 (summer): 46–51.

Nash, June (1975) 'Nationalism and Fieldwork', *Annual Review of Anthropology* 4. Palo Alto, CA: Annual Reviews Inc.

RAFI (1993) 'Communiqué: Patents, Indigenous Peoples, and Human Genetic Diversity' (May). Ottawa: Rural Advancement Foundation International.

RAFI (1994a) 'Communiqué: The Patenting of Human Genetic Material' (January/February). Ottawa: Rural Advancement Foundation International.

RAFI (1994b) 'Communiqué: "Gene Boutiques" Stake Claim to Human Genome' (May/June). Ottawa: Rural Advancement Foundation International.

RAFI (1995) 'Communiqué: Gene Hunters in Search of "Disease Genes" Collect Human DNA from Remote Island Populations' (May/June). Ottawa: Rural Advancement Foundation International.

RAFI (1996a) 'Communiqué: New Questions About Management and Exchange of Human Tissues at NIH' (April). Ottawa: Rural Advancement Foundation International.

RAFI (1996b) 'Press Release: US Government Dumps the Hagahai Patent' (3 December). Ottawa: Rural Advancement Foundation International.

Rifkin, J. (1993) 'Introduction', in Andrew Kimbrell, *The Human Body Shop*. New York: Harper San Francisco.

Roberts, Leslie (1989) 'Genome Project Under Way, At Last', *Science* 243: 167–8.

Roberts, Leslie (1991a) 'Genome Patent Fight Erupts', *Science* 254: 184–6.

Roberts, Leslie (1991b) 'Genetic Survey Gains Momentum: Proposal to Collect DNA Samples from Aboriginal Populations', *Science* 254: 517.

Roberts, Leslie (1992a) 'Anthropologists Climb (Gingerly) on Board', *Science* 258: 1300–1.

Roberts, Leslie (1992b) 'How to Sample the World's Genetic Diversity', *Science* 257: 1204.

Ross, Philip E. (1993) 'Endangered Genes', *Scientific American* 268: 17.

Schiebinger, Londa (1993) *Nature's Body*. Boston: Beacon Press.

Shiva, Vandana (1991) *The Violence of the Green Revolution*. Penang, Malaysia: Third World Network.

Shiva, Vandana (1993) *Monocultures of the Mind: Biodiversity, Biotechnology and the Third World*. Penang, Malaysia: Third World Network.

Stocking, George W., Jr (1983) 'The Ethnographers Magic: Fieldwork in British Anthropology from Tylor to Malinowski', in George W. Stocking Jr (ed.) *Observers Observed: Essays on Ethnographic Fieldwork, History of Anthropology*, Vol. 1. Madison: University of Wisconsin Press.

Taubes, Gary (1995) 'Scientists Attacked for "Patenting" Pacific Tribe', *Science* 270 (17 November).

PART VII

Inside Development Institutions

Introduction

How do anthropologists put their knowledge to work inside development agencies? What dilemmas arise when they attempt to assist people who are the targets of official development projects? The authors of articles included in Part VII take on those challenges.[1] They offer inside views of powerful development agencies such as the International Monetary Fund (Harper), ethical issues that confront anthropologists who work or consult for the World Bank (Fox), and ways to improve or supersede the standard narratives of "blueprint development" (Roe).

Richard Harper's chapter presents an inside view of how the International Monetary Fund gathers the data that later appear in its reports and that inform its discussions with national governments. As Harper points out, the IMF is often invoked as a malevolent force in ethnographic and other analyses of underdevelopment, yet few anthropologists have actually bothered to investigate the production of IMF agreements or, more generally, the macroeconomic context in which they are sought, negotiated and enacted. His account suggests that ethnographers are perfectly capable, given the right circumstances, of carrying out innovative, revealing work on powerful institutions. It is also significant for the insight it provides into how data sources become naturalized and "written in stone." While anthropologists increasingly question the production of certain kinds of data sets, such as maps (see Nancy Peluso's chapter in Part VI of this volume), they have often accepted other varieties of official, published data with little understanding of how they are created or of the epistemological problems they might raise (Edelman and Seligson 1994; Moore 2001). Harper describes how IMF and national government representatives jockey over the figures that come to represent economic "reality." He devotes relatively little attention, however, to the macroeconomic or human consequences of accepting a given set of numbers or to the critical voices from the Global South who have denounced the IMF's data production process as a kind of pernicious "statistical trickery" (Budhoo 1990:27).

Jonathan Fox is an unusual scholar who has studied movements opposed to the World Bank, the impact of Bank projects in diverse regions, internal Bank policy-making and debates, and the anthropologists who work for the Bank (Clark et al. 2003; Fox and Brown 1998). In the chapter below, he discusses how anti-Bank movements had origins in the students' and citizens' power structure research of the 1960s and in grassroots opposition to Bank mega-projects, especially giant dams that had harmful environmental consequences. As transnational civil society networks have become increasingly effective as "early warning systems" about potentially problematical World Bank loans, the institution responded to criticisms by becoming more transparent and by emphasizing environmental sustainability and the empowerment of the poor and women. Fox questions the extent to which this new discourse reflects real changes in Bank thinking and policies. He also outlines significant ethical issues for anthropologists who work or consult for the Bank. These include their accountability to their research subjects and their frequent failure to demystify Bank projects or to seek genuine input from local communities and organizations or provide these with copies of their reports. He notes that World Bank-funded projects frequently produce clientelism, turning intended beneficiaries into petitioners rather than active participants in development.

Emery Roe is not an anthropologist but a public policy expert on science, technology, and environmental controversies. Yet his work directly engages anthropology and has significantly influenced development studies in many disciplines. We include here Roe's article on how scholars and practitioners can better use – rather than simply cirticize and dismiss – the standard narratives that give rise to blueprint development. His focus is the story-like structure and content of persistent narratives such as the "tragedy of the commons," which offer compelling scenarios that reduce the empirical ambiguities and complexities development agencies find difficult to digest. Conveyed in such blueprint narratives are misleading notions about processes such as environmental change or de/reforestation that can be surprisingly difficult to dislodge even on the basis of careful research (see also Leach and Fairhead's chapter in Part VI of this volume).

The complexity and predictive uncertainty of anthropological analyses of development situations, as discussed in this volume's Introduction, often make them less appealing to development practitioners and bureaucrats than the simplifying, universalising, predictive models of economists and agronomists (see also Ferguson's chapter in Part II of this volume). Yet it may be, as Dove (1999:236) suggests, that if anthropologists are to effectively counter the simplified or monolithic representations of development situations offered by states or development agencies, they must "employ language that is no less simplistic or essentializing." They may need to avoid explicit reflexivity and questioning of their own roles or of local representations of reality. In similar fashion, Scheper-Hughes (1995: 417, quoted in Dove 1999: 236) observes that her South African informants did not want "the anthropology of deconstruction and the social imaginary but the anthropology of the really real, in which the stakes are high, values are certain, and ethnicity (if not essentialized) is certainly essential." Furthermore, apprehension about the use to which ethnographic writing may be put, and about its possibly unintended consequences often rests on questionable assumptions about supposed past control over the consequences of ethnographic writing or about a "normal," apolitical ethnographic audience (Dove 1999: 240–241). Pressing development concerns demand much more attention to these critical issues in anthropology.

NOTE

1   See also this volume's Introduction for discussion of the contributions and challenges of development anthropology.

REFERENCES CITED

Budhoo, Davison L., 1990 Dear Mr. Camdessus...Open Letter of Resignation to the Managing Director of the International Monetary Fund. New York: New Horizons Press.

Clark, Dana, Jonathan Fox, and Kay Treakle, eds., 2003 Demanding Accountability: Civil-Society Claims and the World Bank Inspection Panel. Lanham, MD: Rowman & Littlefield.

Dove, Michael, 1999 Writing for, Versus about, the Ethnographic Other: Issues of Engagement and Reflexivity in Working with a Tribal NGO in Indonesia. Identities 6(2–3): 225–253.

Edelman, Marc, and Mitchell A. Seligson, 1994 Land Inequality: A Comparison of Census Data and Property Records in Twentieth-Century Southern Costa Rica. Hispanic American Historical Review 74(3) (Aug.): 445–491.

Fox, Jonathan A., and L. David Brown, eds., 1998 The Struggle for Accountability: The World Bank, NGOs, and Grassroots Movements. Cambridge, MA: MIT Press.

Moore, Sally Falk, 2001 The International Production of Authoritative Knowledge: The Case of Drought-Stricken West Africa. Ethnography 2(2):161–190.

Scheper-Hughes, Nancy, 1995 The Primacy of the Ethical: Propositions for a Militant Anthropology. Current Anthropology 36(3): 409–440.

23

Advocacy Research and the World Bank: Propositions for Discussion[1]

Jonathan Fox

Making a Difference: How Do We Know?

Researchers committed to the public interest work hard to avoid being 'merely academic'. Commitment is necessary but not sufficient for making a difference, however. Any discussion of how researchers can make a difference requires a broader assessment of whether the campaigns they work on are having an impact. From a research point of view, it turns out that assessing whether and how public interest campaigns *are* indeed having an impact is one of the hardest challenges. After all, most of the time, progress in dealing with powerful élite institutions inherently takes place through partial and uneven changes. Even more problematic, advocacy impact often needs to be assessed in terms of the terrible things that actually *did not* happen or were avoided – damage control – and this leads one onto the slippery terrain of the 'counter-factual'. For example, is the World Bank doing more nasty things now than it did almost two decades ago, when what came to be known as the Multilateral Development Bank (MDB) campaign first took off? If so, what would that tell us about the efficacy of the many civil society efforts to challenge the Bank's actions? Is the World Bank doing more decent things nowadays, having adopted a very enlightened-sounding series of official policies, public discourses, and NGO partners? Could *both* propositions be true at the same time, because the Bank is a contradictory institution that does lots of different things at once, some much worse than others?

When considering different approaches to and criteria for assessing advocacy impact it helps to keep one key proposition in mind: where you stand depends on where you sit. Policy changes that may seem quite small in San Francisco or London – for better or for worse – often loom much larger when seen from below, at the receiving end.

Participant Observation: Help Folks to Follow the Money

This essay is organised in terms of several propositions for discussion that link advocacy and research dilemmas. An early strategy for using research to empower campaigns to influence the World Bank came out of one of the intellectual traditions of the US social movements of the 1960s, namely that of researching power structures. The focus was on revealing to the public how powerful institutions were governed, how they made their decisions, and whose interests they served. This tradition drew on the power of transparency to question the legitimacy of 'business as usual'. One of the key tools was the 'citizen's guide', an accessible manual disclosing the inner workings of dominant institutions, such as government agencies, universities, and private corporations. These handbooks serve to guide action by revealing where the pressure points in the system are, as well as by highlighting cross-sectoral alliance possibilities. The phrase '*follow the money*' sums it up.

The power structure analysis was complemented by the 'case study' approach, which evolved into the most politically effective action-research strategy. Especially vivid cases of development disasters were documented in media-savvy ways, to show the world that if the Bank is capable of funding...(fill in the blank) then it must be an institution with deeply systemic flaws.

What's New Since Seattle?

The Seattle events of 1999 opened a new cycle in the campaigns against top-down globalisation, but the international campaigns to challenge the World Bank began in the mid-1980s. In spite of being muted since the attacks of 11 September 2001 on US targets, what *is* new since 1999 is that the campaign generated a broader, more mobilised social base in the USA than ever before, reaching far beyond its usual core of full-time professional advocacy staff. Did the 16 April 2000 (A16) protest marches in Washington DC have an impact on the World Bank? After so many years of terrible press, Bank decision makers had grown a fairly thick skin. How would we be able to tell?

One clear-cut example of impact that does come to mind concerns a Bank project that spectacularly failed to comply with its own, enlightened-sounding policies – the China Western Poverty Reduction project. Critics showed that the project would contribute to the long-standing Chinese policy of encouraging migration in order to dilute the nomadic ethnic Tibetan and Mongol populations, as senior Bank managers later privately admitted. In spite of the Bank's vast and very sophisticated public relations operations, this project managed to trip over one of the world's most influential and well-known indigenous rights movements, leading this movement to unite with the campaign on the Bank. Controversy raged at the highest levels, and between the US and Chinese governments behind the scenes. Affected Tibetans also filed a claim with the Bank's six-year-old, relatively autonomous ombudsperson office, the Inspection Panel, charging violations of the Bank's own policies.

The case turned into a make-or-break test for the Inspection Panel – the Bank's in-house watchdog commission, responsible for investigating the Bank's possible violations of its own social and environmental policies. Borrowing governments – which the Bank needs, since it has an imperative to lend – reacted defensively, claiming that this violated national sovereignty. The more general A16 protests helped this specific campaign because the mass media were already receptive and the Tibetan solidarity movement was already energised and had targeted the Bank. By June and July they were able to put vocal protesters downstairs at exactly the same time as the World Bank's board of executive directors was upstairs, deciding whether or not to move ahead and fund the project. Campaigners calculated that the board could actually hear the chants from the streets below. As far as I know, this was the first ever *mass* protest that directly targeted a board's loan decision-making process, and the protestors won – China was obliged to withdraw the project proposal. Following this embarrassment, Bank policy makers redesigned their internal procedures to make it more difficult for staff to ignore ostensibly mandatory 'safeguard' social and environmental policies.

So what's new here? Ten or fifteen years ago, protesters generally criticised projects that were *already* underway, and so had already been causing environmental and social damage for years. The best that could be hoped for, then, was some kind of mitigation or damage control. Reparations were (and still are) in order, but campaigners lacked the clout to extract them. Nowadays, specific projects at least can be stopped or changed before they start. While that doesn't necessarily change the overall direction the Bank is moving in, or improve compliance with reform policies more systematically, these project-specific victories matter a lot to those who would have been directly affected on the ground. The movement's capacity to do this is the combined result of past battles won and lost, the Bank's own reforms in response to public pressure exercised via threats to its congressional funding, and the broadening and deepening of transnational civil society networks that act as early-warning systems.

Wars of Movement Versus Wars of Position

When looking back on almost two decades of campaigning to change the World Bank, it is useful to reflect on political theorist Antonio Gramsci's classic distinction between wars of movement and wars of position. His military analogy refers to battles over institutions and ideas, because if one is interested in systemic change, then storming the barricades only gets one just so far. Wars of position evoke slow, slogging, trench warfare. The concept refers to the difficult and gradual process of challenging hegemonic ideas and institutions, especially during the long periods when the balance of forces keeps more radical change off the agenda. Wars of movement, in contrast, refer to fluid, rapidly changing dynamics involving the element of surprise and the mobilisation of concentrated pressure – as in Seattle, Prague, Genoa, or Barcelona.

For an important example, recall the World Bank's 50th anniversary in 1994, when the media resonance of the 'Fifty Years is Enough' protest campaign made it difficult for the Bank to celebrate too much. The 1993/94 period was unusual primarily because two political opportunities converged. In India, the mass movement of tribal peoples and farmers against the Narmada dam was highly mobilised and had just been legitimated by an independent study, commissioned by the Bank itself, which concluded that the movement was right and the Bank was wrong. At the same time, in the USA, because the Democrats controlled both the Congress and the presidency, a few progressive congressional leaders were emboldened to respond to the international Narmada campaign and used their control over foreign aid to force the Bank to make critical policy concessions – opening up public access to information and creating the Inspection Panel. What this suggests is that transnational civil society coalitions are key, but so is the degree of domestic leverage over the US government's own policy processes. This case also underscores the challenge of assessing impact. The Narmada campaign obliged the Bank to pull out, and then won several years of relative stability thanks to a national court decision, but the political winds shifted within India and the water level was raised – threatening thousands. It turns out that international advocacy campaigns cannot escape the challenge of domestic power politics.

Thinking about Bank campaigns more generally over the last 15 years, we see brief waves of intense mass mobilisation and unusual vindication in the dominant media (thanks to accessible images like burning rainforests, dam-flooded villages, and leaky oil pipelines). These moments were punctuated by long interludes when lower profile, more specialised watchdog groups kept up the more technical, less splashy work of monitoring and exposing the Bank. These efforts won occasional battles in relation to specific projects and provided key information and other resources that empowered allies both on the ground and in national capitals around the world.

Situating Official Discourse: Look at What They Do, Not Just What They Say

There is no doubt that important elements of World Bank discourse now sound remarkably enlightened. They have learned to talk the talk. This poses a puzzle for those scholars who see 'developmentalist discourse' in and of itself as inherently and always all-powerful. What does it mean when the World Bank changes its discourse to call for substantial policy changes and financial investments in sustainable development, gender equality, and poor people's empowerment? The 2000/2001 *World Development Report*, the Bank's flagship annual synthesis of 'state-of-the-art' research on a given theme, focuses on poverty alleviation. One of its main themes is that economic growth is necessary but not sufficient, that public institutions themselves must become 'pro-poor', that poor people must become empowered, and that ethnic and gender discrimination are key obstacles that must be overcome. As far as official lines go, this is new. The draft of this document was made public on the Internet and subjected to a systematic international consultation effort coordinated by the British NGO coalition, the Bretton Woods Project. Before the author could incorporate the comments that were made, a backlash from conservative economists and the US Treasury Department provoked him to resign in protest, leading most critics to assume that the final report would be gutted before it saw the light of day. Curiously, though, the final report is not all that different from the public draft. Some observers contend that the author's resignation effectively 'inoculated' the report, protecting its main message because the first version was still available for comparison – perhaps a case of the power of transparency.

How do we assess this shift in the official discourse? Is it just for show? One hypothesis is that the new *World Development Report* lines reflect the combination of shifting internal debates and the failure of the Bank's conventional wisdom in practice, under the pressure of years of civil society criticism. The *Report* projects the views of the World Bank's usually subordinated minority of non-economist social scientists. At the same time, in almost all other arenas that matter, the Bank's macroeconomists clearly remain hegemonic. It is still too soon to tell whether the *World Development Report*'s legitimation of more heterodox views will make much difference, but it poses an analytical puzzle for analysts. Is more enlightened discourse going to be just as influential as the classic developmentalist ideology we have all critiqued so thoroughly? Certainly not – but why not? When, where, and how will it matter, if at all? Probably when its advocates within the Bank manage to partner with similar reform-minded counterparts in borrowing governments and civil society – but only then. A search for the answers requires us to embed our analysis of official discourses in an understanding of the contending ideas and interests *within* the institutions that generate and propagate them.

To understand the relative weight of Bank discourse, we need to situate it in terms of Bank *policies*. Bank policies are supposed to guide the design and implementation of projects, so they are, in effect, an important potential bridge between discourse and institutional practice. There are two main kinds – safeguard policies and 'good practices' policies. The safeguard policies are in the 'first do no harm' category, including environmental assessment, indigenous peoples, resettlement – and they are supposed to be mandatory. The 'good practices' policies are merely recommended, and advocate, for example, gender equality, collaboration with NGOs, and informed participation by poor people. In short, some of the enlightened discourse is translated into policies that are optional, while other elements are translated into ostensibly mandatory policies that turn out to be systematically violated. As a result of the Bank's problem with reform policy compliance, it is now in a long-term process of trying to water them down – to make compliance easier.

What Side Are the Bank's Anthropologists On?

The anthropologists who work for the Bank are not so different from those who work for any large, powerful bureaucracy that is not accountable to those it is supposed to serve. Here the observation of a Latin American activist anthropologist colleague is very relevant. As he put it, 'I think all anthropologists have problems when they reach power. The point is: they think they know more about the needs of the natives than the natives themselves.'

From my own experience of studying them, most anthropologists who pursue a Bank career follow one of three kinds of paths. First, as you might expect, some get fully co-opted – assimilating the institution's norms and applying their skills to blunting just a bit of sharp edge of what the Bank funds (for example, figuring out how to convince people to move out of the way before the bulldozers actually show up). Second, there are those who take principled stands some of the time, but are inconsistent. This means that they have difficulty sustaining coalitions with directly affected groups. In part because of their limited influence inside the institution, they end up doing a kind of everyday triage, picking their battles carefully to avoid finding themselves on the outside looking in.

A third group, very small to be sure, manages to stick to its principles most of the time while still functioning within the institution. Some focus on carving out small niches where they can promote participatory, innovative development projects that are so tiny, by Bank standards, that they don't threaten the rest of what the Bank does. Still, those cracks in the system matter a lot for the grassroots organisations that find new room for manoeuvre. Other insider reformists sometimes manage to block nasty projects before they gather unstoppable momentum. When that doesn't work, they play critical roles in empowering public interest groups in their campaigns. As Bank critics marshal their evidence to reveal why certain projects are 'development disasters', you often hear the phrase 'even Bank documents show … how horrible they are'. Well, somebody had to write those documents, and somebody had to put them into the right hands. Recall Professor Ted Downing's consultant study for the Bank on the disastrous social effects of the Bío Bío dam in Chile on the Mapuche people, which led to an official complaint by the American Anthropological Association.

Clearly this is just a schematic set of distinctions, very much in the eye of the beholder, and sometimes the same individual shifts from one category to another. More importantly, this proposition does not imply that *any* of these categories is very large or very influential, for three main reasons. First, there are very few anthropologists who are actual Bank staff. Second, they are involved in a very small fraction of the total number of projects, since most of the money goes to structural adjustment and other kinds of macro-institutional changes. And third, even where they are involved, they are more often ignored than heeded.

The Need for More Civil Society Monitoring from Below

Those who do grassroots field research in developing countries probably come up against the World Bank often without knowing it – you deal with the local clinic or school, or with the municipal government. Most of the Bank's money no longer goes on the classic highways through the rainforest or the hydroelectric dams that flood villages. First, such projects provoked such effective environmental/human rights coalitions that it is just much harder to get away with them now than it used to be – especially in countries that have active, mobilised civil societies. Elsewhere, the Bank's social and environmental policies risk being sidestepped, as occurred in Chad, whose president received a US$25 million 'signing bonus' from an oil consortium once the Bank loan for a pipeline was approved, of which US$4.5 million was spent on arms (Farah and Ottaway 2000). But, second, infrastructure projects account for only a minority of Bank funding – most of the loans go to macro-structural adjustment (oscillating between just less than a half and two thirds of the total over the last few years), and a significant fraction goes to social and environmental projects. These projects may or may not be good for society or the environment, but one can be sure that whatever *is* wrong with them is far less obvious, and will require much more field research and institutional analysis than the emblematic 'road through the rainforest'.

For example, the role of the World Bank in Mexico's social policy process was completely secret until recently, but, since the Bank's 1994 information disclosure reforms, it turns out that many of the government's anti-poverty pro-grammes were supported by World Bank loans targeted to the poorest and most rural states (see, for example, Fox 2000). What is the government's main strategy in each of these sectors? Decentrali-sation. Where did the World Bank fit in? The availability of World Bank loans gave added ideo-logical and economic leverage to those sectors within the national government that were promot-ing a rapid decentralisation of social policies to the governments of the poorest states. This was a process of blind decentralisation, however, be-cause even in the World Bank's technical logic, there was no empirical evidence that those state governments had the capacity to manage health and education services more efficiently than the federal government. After many years and literally billions of dollars in loans – which the Mexican people will have to pay back with interest – it still remains unclear just how effective those social investments have been. Why is it not clear? Be-cause, in spite of the World Bank's own policies, none of the large anti-poverty loans included any measures to encourage the independent monitor-ing and evaluation of governmental performance – particularly the state and municipal governments now responsible for many anti-poverty invest-ments. At least some of these projects may have contributed to the violent unrest in Chiapas – culminating in the 1997 Acteal massacre – since the Funds were administered by local government structures which were more part of the problem than of the solution (Fox 2000:623). *Proving* this hypothesis, of course, is easier said than done, but that's where anthropologists come in – researchers who understand how nation-states actually oper-ate within communities, up close and personal.

Most of the problems with anti-poverty loans are less spectacular than in Chiapas, involving everyday forms of resistance and collective action to win the right to participatory, accountable gov-ernance. To mention examples of some of the projects that we monitor in Mexico, the Bank lends money to the government for ostensibly par-ticipatory indigenous agricultural development, rural health clinics, and local village-run anti-pov-erty projects. When seen from the point of view of the independent peasants and indigenous organ-isations that want to monitor and influence the policy process, there is a lot to learn from the methodology developed to defend communities against the classic infrastructure mega-projects that were the main focus of the first wave of the MDB campaign in the 1980s.

For example, many have learned how to follow the money through the system, to figure out where possible pressure points are, and to begin to disen-tangle the respective roles of the World Bank and the national government – which in the Mex-ican case remains quite autonomous of the Bank. At the same time, they need to adjust this ap-proach because in the case of anti-poverty and environmental projects their main goal is not to *stop* such projects but to make sure that they actually meet their goals. Here the Bank's paper policies become potential weapons for grassroots organisations. These organisations are trying to use the Bank's commitment to public information access and informed participation by indigenous peoples in policies that affect them as levers to open up space in their 500 years of struggle with the state.

One of the most promising advocacy strategies now being adopted by civil society involves the *vertical integration* of monitoring, advocacy, and campaigning. Vertical integration refers to the sys-tematic coordination between diverse levels of civil society – from local to provincial, national, and international arenas – to monitor and offset the parallel partnerships between the World Bank and national, provincial, and local governments. This approach is being pursued systematically in both Brazil, which has the broadest and deepest civil society advocacy coalition, Rede Brasil, and in Mexico, where the Oaxaca-based NGO watch-dog Trasparencia works closely with diverse indi-genous organisations to monitor and influence social and environmental projects in rural areas. Like many other grassroots-oriented advocacy campaigns in the South, they are trying to democ-ratise the triangular relationship between their own government, the MDBs, and civil society.

A Proposal from Mexico: A Code of Ethics for Bank Anthropologists

This essay concludes by sharing some reflections by Manuel Fernández Villegas, director of Trasparencia:

The role of anthropologists in World Bank activities: A wake-up call

World Bank operations often incorporate the participation of anthropologists (as well as other social experts) in the analyses that form part of the evaluations and technical studies involved in preparing their development investment programmes.

In addition to the small number of anthropologists who work as permanent employees of the Bank, it often hires such specialists as consultants...Sometimes these temporary contracts are carried out with the intermediation of academic institutions or research centres. These researchers, during their fieldwork, present themselves as academics and do not always clearly explain – to the organisations and communities that are the focus of their diagnoses – the role they are playing, nor the final destiny of their reports.

It is easy to imagine that those who are interviewed might well choose to present their proposals and opinions differently if they knew that the reports went directly to the offices of the World Bank and the government officials with whom they share these technical studies. It is not the same to converse with a 'nice guy' academic researcher, as it is with a consultant in the service of the Bank who is collecting information as part of the investment logic it shares with the government institutions who actually carry out the projects...

From our point of view, this is quite delicate, and it would be worthwhile to propose something like a code of ethics for those social development professionals who work as consultants, involving their relationships with the communities and social organisations who are the target of their research.

For example, it is very rare for the communities and organisations mentioned in the reports and diagnoses to receive a copy of them, so that they are not even aware of what is said about them, much less have the opportunity to state their opinion or revise the way in which the results that are obtained during their (always brief) field visits [are presented].

Clearly, in practice, the counter-argument that the consultants offer is that the final reports are the property of those who commissioned them ... (the Bank) and they cannot be shared without its authorisation.

Yes, this is the logic of contractual relations for those who sell their consulting services, but (from our point of view) this means giving priority to their source of temporary employment, over and above the interests and rights of the communities and social organisations who are trying to defend their autonomy and their right to decide and to participate in the government programmes that are carried out in their area of influence – [already] a complicated and difficult challenge...

Anthropologists...could well be very useful to communities and grassroots organisations if they would help us to understand the World Bank and its development projects. From the grassroots perspective, it is not always easy to understand the logic of multilateral financing for specific public policies.

It seems that for many ordinary citizens, the World Bank and the projects it promotes are foreign and remote, almost magical, the target of prejudices – true modern myths. [The officials] seem distant and somehow superior – their direct physical presence is an act of 'coming down' to be in contact with us, [who are the ones] interested in whether or not they support us.

These institutions' power and technical expertise creates the appearance of being supposedly 'objective'. They project the image of being capable of resolving problems and changing the painful reality of poverty if they were to decide to do so – if we could only convince them. Their visiting missions of experts create a climate in which we are expected to try to win them over by courting them with polite proposals.

In practice, however, discussions with Bank missions often turn ostensible beneficiaries into petitioners rather than real participants or partners. Lack of information among grassroots actors about the World Bank and the policy process more generally often creates a fertile ground for manipulative and clientelistic practices, especially during election time. Anti-poverty funding is often seen as a discretionary donation by the powerful, who expect loyalty and gratitude in exchange, rather than as an exercise of economic, social, and political rights.

[In summary, then]...grassroots organisations also need the technical services of anthropologists and social analysts, to be able to provide us with the diagnoses and field research that would allow us to better understand the customary laws of the

multilateral institutions and [their government partners].... We need some of them on our side.

NOTE

1   This essay draws on long-term partnerships, including a process of independent civil society monitoring of World Bank projects in rural Mexico led by Manuel Fernández de Villegas, Fernando Melo, and the team at Trasparencia (www.trasparencia.org.mx); a research collection co-edited with L. David Brown of the Institute for Development Research and Harvard University's Hauser Center (*The Struggle for Accountability: The World Bank, NGOs and Grassroots Movements*, Cambridge, MA: MIT Press, 1998); conversations with the Brazilian Network on Multilateral Financial Institutions (www.rbrasil.org.br); ongoing collaboration with the Washington-based public interest group Bank Information Center (www.bicusa.org), as well as a recent book co-edited with Dana Clark and Kay Treakle (*Demanding Accountability: Civil Society Claims and the World Bank's Inspection Panel*, Lanham, MD: Rowman and Littlefield, 2003).

REFERENCES

Farah, Douglas and David Ottaway (2000) 'World Bank Reassesses Chad Pipeline Deal', *Washington Post 5* December: A38.

Fox, Jonathan (2000) 'Los Flujos y reFlujos de préstamos sociales y ambientales del Banco Mundial en México', in A. Alvarez Béjar et al. (eds.) *Las nuevas fronteras del siglo XXI: Dimensiones culturales, politicas y socioeconómicas de las relaciones, México-Estados Unidos*, Mexico City: UNAM/La Jornada Ediciones.

World Bank (2000) *World Development Report 2000/ 2001: Attacking Poverty*, New York: OUP and World Bank.

24

Development Narratives, Or Making the Best of Blueprint Development

Emery M. Roe

1. Introduction

No one has a good word for blueprint development. The notion that rural development can be stenciled whole-cloth from premade plans and blueprints has been taken to task by many well-known critics. [. . .] Invariably, the remedy recommended is to abandon blueprint development in favor of a learning process approach, one that conceives development as trial and error, where projects are hypotheses and what is called "failure" is part of, or should be part of, a broader learning curve (e.g., Chambers, 1983, pp. 211–212). The comparative advantage of the learning process approach is taken to be its flexibility and adaptability, given that the "probability of planned actions going wrong is high in an environment characterized by instability and uncertainty," as is the case for many regions of the developing world (Hyden, 1983, p. 157). Unfortunately, this last point undermines, rather than reinforces, the purported advantages of the learning process approach.

The reasons we do not learn more from past rural development efforts are precisely the same reasons we cannot plan better for future ones. If planning is difficult, so too must be learning, and the performance record of rural development points overwhelmingly in one direction: planning has left much to be desired (Caiden and Wildavsky, 1974; Johnston and Clark, 1982, Chapter 1; for an exception, see Cohen and Lewis, 1987). The preconditions for successful project and national planning – low environmental uncertainty, stability in goals and national objectives, institu-tional memory, and redundant resources – are precisely the same preconditions for "learning better from experience," and it is these preconditions that are woefully lacking across wide parts of the developing world. It is the impression of learning less and less over time while being more and more vulnerable to error which characterizes some 30 years of sub-Saharan African livestock projects, for example.[1] Those caught in its clutches find little consolation in being told that they should "embrace" error in order to learn better (e.g., Korten, 1980, p. 498).

The learning process approach, or some more potent remedy, could of course win the day. But what do we do, as development practitioners, if blueprint development is here to stay for the time being? How can we make the best of a bad situation? These are the questions addressed by this paper. Rather than focusing on how one might improve the learning process approach, attention is given below to ways practitioners can better utilize blueprint development.

2. Four Development Narratives

First it must be understood that blueprint development persists for precisely the same reason said to warrant the learning process approach. Rural development is a genuinely uncertain activity, and one of the principal ways practitioners, bureaucrats and policy makers articulate and make sense of this uncertainty is to tell stories or scenarios that simplify the ambiguity. Indeed, the pressure to generate narratives about development is directly proportional to the ambiguity decision makers experience over the development process. The more uncertain things seem at the microlevel, the greater the tendency to see the scale of uncertainty at the macrolevel to be so enormous as to require broad explanatory narratives that can be operationalized into standard approaches with widespread application. The unresolved failure of project blueprints derived from development narratives thus often serves only to reinforce, not lessen, the perceived need for some sort of narrative that accounts for the resulting increase in uncertainty.

These considerations raise the question of whether rural development could be more productively improved by identifying ways to make better use of those narratives that give rise to the blueprints. To see how this might be done, four development narratives are examined below. The examples are from Africa, but could be from anywhere in the world. Each of these narratives has persisted in the face of strong empirical evidence against its storyline and it is this persistence which, the paper argues, can be more effectively exploited. Rather than continuing to focus on trying to undermine the narrative evidentially, our efforts should shift to creating and engaging counternarratives to the more objectionable narrative or modifying that narrative to make it less objectionable. In order to strengthen this argument, the four examples have been chosen precisely because they appear at first glance to demonstrate the worst in blueprint development and to cry out for rectification through a learning process approach. By arguing that blueprint development can be improved through better manipulating the narratives upon which it is based, the examples seek to underscore that practitioners will have to deal much more enterprisingly with a form of development that persists regardless and, at times, in spite of what is learned in the field.

A preliminary definition of "development narratives" stresses both their status as stories or arguments and their differences from other notions more familiar to the development practitioner, namely, ideology, myth and conventional wisdom. The narratives discussed below follow the common definition of "story." Each has a beginning, middle, and end (or premises and conclusions, when cast in the form of an argument) and revolves around a sequence of events or positions in which something happens or from which something follows.[2] Typically less hortatory and normative than ideology, development narratives tell scenarios not so much about what should happen as about what will happen – according to their

tellers – if the events or positions are carried out as described. Even when their truth-value is in question, these narratives are explicitly more programmatic than myths and have the objective of getting their hearers to believe or do something. In addition, the narratives, at least the four to which we now turn, are treated by many of their tellers and hearers as continuing to retain some general explanatory or descriptive power even after a number of the specific conventional wisdoms upon which they are based are understood to be subject to serious qualification.[3] How these and other features of development narratives operate, and with what implications, will become clearer in the examples.

(a) The "tragedy of the commons"

The most obvious feature of the "tragedy of the commons" is oddly the least commented on, namely, its status as narrative. Its most famous expositor, Garrett Hardin, goes out of his way to tell the tragedy of the commons as a story having all the classic properties of a beginning, middle, and end. "The tragedy of the commons develops in this way. Picture a pasture open to all...," begins Hardin in what surely is the most quoted passage in all of the common property literature. We soon are in the middle of things – "the rational herdsman concludes that the only sensible course for him to pursue is to add another animal to his herd. And another... But this is the conclusion reached by each and every rational herdsman sharing a commons" – and the end comes rapidly and palpably into sight: "Ruin is the destination toward which all men rush, each pursuing his own best interest in a society that believes in the freedom of the commons" (Hardin, 1977, p. 20).

Reality and story, however, congrue imperfectly. When the tragedy of the commons argument is probed empirically – for example, just what is the evidence that desertification is caused by overgrazing? – the data turn out to be much more ambiguous or outright contradictory (Sandford, 1983, Chapter 1). Even where people agree with Hardin that range degradation is taking place and that many commons today are open access free-for-alls, they often part company with him over causes. For these critics, long-term climatological changes along with growing and competing land uses have led to degradation more than the existence of the commons – a commons which, the critics hasten to add *contra* Hardin, was often managed in a restricted access, not open access, fashion until these exogenous pressures undermined local management efforts (see Panel on Common Property Resource Management, 1986; McCay and Acheson, 1987).

Hardin merits a much closer reading than some of his critics have given him. "It must not be supposed that all commons are bad in all situations," Hardin tells us, "... when there were only a few million people in the world, it was all right to run the hunting grounds as a commons, though even then an area was no doubt often managed as tribal property" (Hardin, 1977, pp. 47–48). Hardin does not say that the commons cannot be managed. The "commons, if it is justifiable at all, is justifiable only under conditions of low-population density" (p. 28). His pivotal point is that herders find it to their individual advantage not to cooperate in limiting herd numbers or ensuring range quality even when each and every herder recognizes that the overall stocking rate on the commons exceeds its carrying capacity, and that range deterioration and liveweight loss are on the rise (Hardin, 1977, p. 72). In such a situation, corrective measures are largely outside the initiative of the individual herder. Either the commons has to be legislated as private property or other coercive devices, such as taxes and user regulations, have to be instituted from the outside (p. 22).

In short, if we subscribe to Hardin's argument, we should expect to find at least two states of affairs pertaining when a rangeland tragedy of the commons is said to exist. First, even when herders agree that the range is in poor or already heavily-stocked condition, they still act in a non-cooperative, competitive fashion. They evince few if any collective practices for managing that commons, which in turn encourages its further over-utilization. Second, a tragedy of the commons supposes that a privatized rangeland will be better managed (e.g., have a better range condition), than if it were a commons, other things being equal.

The best test to date of Hardin's comprehensive version of the tragedy of the commons can be found in a series of publications based on data collected during the 1979–80 Botswana Water Points Survey. [...] Rural eastern Botswana [...] has repeatedly been described by both those inside and outside the Botswana government as in the throes of a rangeland tragedy of the commons. First, do rural Batswana themselves perceive overgrazing to be taking place? The evidence here is mixed. While the range condition was found to be already at low levels in much of the eastern communal areas when assessed by standard range ecology measures, a number of survey households indicated that variation in rainfall rather than livestock numbers was taken to be the major explanation of overstocking and overgrazing (Fortmann and Roe, 1981; Bailey, 1982). Yet there is sufficient grounds – in the form of low cattle carcass weights and other interview findings – to suppose that a significant proportion of Batswana, albeit not a majority, did in fact believe that increasing numbers of livestock were leading to overutilization of the range in the late 1970s and early 1980s. Moreover, Botswana must be one of the few countries in sub-Saharan Africa that has enshrined the tragedy of the commons argument into its national rangeland policy (see in particular, Republic of Botswana, 1975, p. 1).

On the assumption that overgrazing is taking place, do rural Batswana cooperate in the management of their communal resources and have management practices to do so? An in-depth survey by Fortmann of communal dams constructed in eastern Botswana during 1974–80 found that this was indeed the case (Fortmann and Roe, 1981). Of the 24 dams surveyed, 21 had some sort of collective management, be it in the form of maintenance, regulation, or revenue collection. In particular, all 21 dam groups had users who jointly regulated the use of these dams. Restrictions on numbers of users, types of use, the manner of use, and the time of use were found in force.

Did communal management have a positive effect on the surrounding range condition and if so, how did it compare to privatized resource management? An analysis of grazing conditions around a sample of 46 water points found that those water points owned or managed by government or groups had better dry season range conditions than privately-owned water points (Roe, 1984). No one-to-one correlation was found between private ownership, private management, and the actual restriction of livestock watering access. Indeed, the finding that private rights and better range condition do not go hand-in-hand has been confirmed on a number of occasions in Botswana. Only three years after the first leasehold fenced ranches were occupied under the World Bank's First Livestock Development Project, two-thirds of them were already overstocked (Odell and Odell, 1986, p. 7). Conditions did not improve under the Bank's Second Livestock Development Project. Bekure and Dyson-Hudson (1982) found that range management and condition on these leasehold ranches was often no better than in the communal areas. In a related fashion, roughly 15 years of government grazing trials undertaken periodically from the 1950s through the 1970s could show no significant difference in range conditions between those found under various fenced rotational systems and that observed under a continuous "single paddock" grazing regime approximating the communal system (see Roe and Fortmann, 1981, p. 71; Animal Research Production Unit, 1980, pp. 85–86). Communal management of the dams studied in the Water Points Survey was found not only to be ecologically efficient relative to the next best private alternative, but cost figures indicated that this management was economically efficient as well (Fortmann and Roe, 1986). In short, the evidence is far from conclusive that privatization of the Botswana commons increases the likelihood of improving range conditions there.

These and other negative findings across the world have been around for some time and it is increasingly tempting to dismiss the tragedy of the commons as some kind of old-fashioned fable. But to do so would be misguided and would miss the point altogether. As a development narrative, the tragedy of the commons continues to have staying power in large part because these negative findings and critiques in no way dispel the chief virtue of the narrative: it has helped to stabilize and underwrite the assumptions needed for decision making. Policy makers resort to the tragedy of the commons model in order to understand what is going on and what must be done in lieu of more elaborate and demanding analysis, particularly when such analysis leads only to doubts and uncertainties about just what the story is behind rural resource utilization. Critiques of the tragedy of the commons are doubly troublesome for the decision maker, since they can generate rather than reduce uncertainty. They both undermine the assumptions of decision making and leave that decision maker without the means to make the transition from the discredited narrative to whatever is to replace it. In fact, the more the tragedy of the commons is criticized and found substantively wanting, the more uncertain policy makers can become – why indeed did Batswana manage their water points collectively? – and the more pressure they feel to hold onto the simple heuristics they have, no matter how worn around the edges they now appear. In short, a critique, like that based on the Botswana data, never tells its own story – its point-by-point rebuttal does not have its own beginning, middle, and end – and often serves only to raise doubts that the critique itself cannot answer.

What displaces a development narrative are not just the negative findings that seem to refute it. Displacement also requires an equally straightfor-

ward narrative that tells a better story. The appeal of the tragedy of the commons to livestock rangeland project designers has been its blueprinted design implications for privatizing the commons and legislating stock controls. If project designers are to reject the blueprint, they must have another story whose design implications are equally as obvious to them. The operating assumption here is that if decision makers are to move beyond the prevailing model of an entirely unmanaged and open-access commons, they will do so not merely by being told that reality is more complex than has been thought, but also by having a counternarrative which can predict when common property management will take place or not and what are the implications of either event.

Moreover, the counternarrative will have to be as parsimonious as the tragedy of the commons argument, but comprehensive enough to explain not only when management of the commons occurs, but when the tragedy takes places instead. Indeed, the ideal counternarrative for the project designer and policy maker would be like the tragedy of the commons in having to rely on nothing more sophisticated than introductory microeconomics (for an example of one such model, see Roe, 1987). While such a conclusion will offend many social scientists, its dismissal is surely premature, as we all wait for a counternarrative – *any* counternarrative – to the tragedy of the commons that is more substantial than the critiques offered up so far.

(b) Land registration and increased agricultural productivity

For at least the past 35 years, one of the most potent development narratives in Kenya has been that land registration leads to increased agricultural productivity. Once land is adjudicated, consolidated and registered, so this argument goes, the landowner will be in a position to use the title deed as collateral for securing credit with which to invest in improving and intensifying agricultural production on the land concerned. Dating from (if not before) the blueprint laid out in the government's 1954 Swynnerton Plan (Colony and Protectorate of Kenya, 1954, pp. 8–9), the argument remains extremely popular among Kenyan politicians, senior civil servants and social scientists [. . .].

Empirical studies have repeatedly failed to find a positive causal link connecting the government's land registration program to expanded credit opportunities and thereby to increased agricultural productivity. Over the years, the effects of land registration in one district (Embu) have been studied in detail by different researchers, while others have undertaken point-in-time research on the same topic – much of it in the form of household surveys at the farm level – for localities in at least 13 other districts [. . .] covering much of the country's most agriculturally productive cropland. All the studies have failed to confirm or have raised serious doubts about the scenario linking land registration to agricultural production (Sorrenson, 1967; Barber, 1970; Bernard, 1972; Gray, 1972; Wilson, 1971; Coldham, 1979; Hunt, 1984; Njeru, 1978; Brokensha and Njeru, 1977; Haugerud, 1981, 1983, and 1989; Shipton, 1985; Odingo, 1985; Green, 1985; Fleuret, 1988; see also Wangari, forthcoming, and Olouch-Kosura, forthcoming)[4]. [. . .] This general finding is made all the more significant by the equally demonstrated interregional ethnic and socioeconomic diversity of the country's rural households.

In contrast to the narrative, the cumulative picture left by the research suggests that once landowners are registered, many do not bother to obtain their title deeds (they would never risk losing them on anything as uncertain as loan defaults); of those landowners who do obtain titles, not all of them do so to obtain credit (they may have to sell their land or parts of it to meet school fees and other household expenses); of those who want to use their titles to obtain loans, not all actually receive credit (farmers may not know where to go for credit or meet other requirements of the lending institution, which in turn might not have the funds to lend); of those landowners who actually succeed in using their titles for securing credit, a number of them use the loans for nonagricultural investments (e.g., their off-farm businesses); once the registered landowner dies or sells off parcels, the new landowner frequently does not reregister; and those who do not reregister or who could not legally register in the first place – mostly women – are ineligible for title-secured loans.

Nor has the problem only been one of a low conditional probability that, once registered, credit will be obtained and agriculture intensified. In some cases, land registration and increasing agricultural production may actually be negatively related. When registered, some landowners feel (i) they can leave the land idle without fear of someone else claiming it because no one was planting there; (ii) they have the "freedom" to sell land without real consent from those dependent on it and whose labor makes it as productive as it is; and (iii) they can enter land transactions for speculation purposes only. As a result of these and other factors, several authorities have concluded that Kenya's land registration program has increased insecurity, rather than the security, of tenure in many parts of the country.

Yet, the recurrent finding that registration does not increase production via the credit mechanism has not changed one iota the belief of many respected Kenyans that registration has a positive and widespread effect on agriculture. What then is the policy maker to do if he or she feels compelled to pursue the topic of land registration's supposedly positive effect on agricultural productivity? One could, of course, continue to analyze the subject of agricultural credit on the assumption that land registration would intensify agriculture if only credit is made more timely, convenient, and adequate to more smallholders. Pushing credit, however, has continually proven to afford about as much leverage in Kenya's agricultural sector as pushing string does elsewhere (e.g., World Bank, 1985). Another option would be to explore the other links between registration and agriculture that appear to have potential in offering up a counternarrative relevant for policy and program development. [. . .] Nevertheless, if past research is any indication, this approach will yield mixed signals for the policy maker. Land concentration has boosted agricultural productivity in the view of one study, while another finds otherwise; fragmentation is an ecologically valid, risk-averse response of farmers to some researchers, while others focus on what they see as increasingly subeconomic holdings (e.g., see Shipton, 1985; Haugerud, 1983). The policy maker who chooses this option, as noted earlier, will have to balance the findings of increasing complexity at the microlevel with the widening scale of Kenya's land problems that seem to demand standard approaches to their management and amelioration.

A very different option suggests itself, however, if the operating assumption is that both the popular narrative linking registration to production and its blueprint, the government's land registration program, will persist for the foreseeable future in the absence of any viable alternative and regardless of empirical findings that erode their credibility. Assuming this is so, the question then becomes one of focusing the policy maker's attention on those few topics where land registration offers some promise of actually expanding agricultural production.

One prospect stands out in its priority and scale – estimating the extent to which the implementation of a progressive land tax in Kenya could intensify agricultural production by discouraging land speculation, absentee management, uneconomic fragmentation, and nonproductively large holdings. The records of the land registration program as to who is registered or holds title deed will greatly facilitate the operation of such a tax, if and when it is introduced. Moreover, it is difficult to conceive of a more efficient way to up-date these records for the unregistered subdivisions mentioned earlier, i.e., the levy could serve as the necessary incentive for the reregistration of land currently registered in the names of other owners, since the tax would presumably be assessed on those whose names show up in the records. Even though land taxation is controversial in Kenya (albeit the government is proposing to introduce a tax on agricultural production), a focus on the promising positive links between registration and agriculture has the considerable merit of being consistent with the development narrative that has hitherto resisted all manner of assaults on it. Indeed, the narrative's blueprint becomes one way of altering rather than displacing the narrative itself. The existence of a huge and growing ministry, staff and budget – all committed to ensuring that land registration is the blueprint across the country – will inevitably increase pressure to justify their purported programmatic effect on intensifying agriculture, even if the specific mechanism for linking registration and production is no longer principally that of title secured credit.

(c) Systems analysis and sectoral integration

Systems thinking suffuses the practitioner's approach to rural development. The field of livestock rangeland development provides an especially good illustration of the development narrative in question. For example, few specialists would quarrel with the following:

> Pastoral production is normally and correctly part of wider production systems; changes in any element have ramifications in all others (Galaty and Aronson, 1981, p. 21).

> Livestock production is a very complex system which has many interrelated components such as climate, soil, plants and obviously animals operating with a high degree of interaction within a certain economic and social environment (Sidahmed and Koong, 1984, p. 61).

> [. . .]

But why stop at "region"? The "system" entails, after a point, supraregional levels in a long chain of behavioral links which

starts with land managers and their direct relations with the land (. . . stocking densities . . . and so on). Then on the next link concerns their relations with each other, other land users, and groups in the wider society who affect them in any way, which in turn determines land management. The state and the world economy constitute the last links in the chain (Blaikie and Brookfield, 1987, p. 27).

Once something has evolved into such a long-linked "system," description frequently becomes prescription. [. . .]

[. . .] Making a systems critique can be easier than living with its implications. The development syllogism in the critique seems inescapable: integrated system, integrated intervention. As many readers already know, a number of integrated rural development programs (particularly in the agricultural sector) have been "disintegrating agricultural development" (Leonard, 1984). Ministerial portfolios, based often on apparent sectoral divisions in the political economy, seem as a rule not to accommodate the need for intersectoral coordination and integration. Moreover, once one accepts the validity of a narrative that posits a long chain of putative causality between the international economy and the local herder, the probability of finding something wrong along the way increases exponentially. Critics continually find projects that are local successes, but system failures, in a world where localized interventions, such as projects, provide little leverage in correcting what are perceived to be systemic dysfunctions. [. . .]

Yet the practitioner who objects to the systems approach to rural development runs the risk of always having to recant the objection. [. . .] After all, what rural development practitioner is foolish enough to operate as if cause and effect had been suspended?

One of the more recent and salutary developments in the systems approach has been to introduce the distinction between tightly and loosely coupled systems. [. . .] For example, Moris and Thom argue that irrigation scheme managers in many parts of Africa must contend with what is best characterized as a loosely coupled system where a myriad of agencies, levels of authority, and formal as well as informal networks of communication are relevant to the manager's activities, but not coordinated for the purposes of facilitating his or her management (1987, pp. 430–431).

In fact, many rural development processes are best understood as a *mix* of tightly coupled and loosely coupled systems. [...]

[...]

(d) Repetitive budgeting by national governments

Disarray in budgeting by governments at the national level is patently evident. Neither the developing world nor the developed countries can cope budgetarily. [...]

It is in the developing world, however, where repetitive budgeting has received the greatest attention. [...] For example, there have in the past been substantial differences between what is printed in the government of Kenya's five-year national development plan and what the government eventually budgets in its three-year forward budget, between that printed forward budget and what has been budgeted annually in the published estimates, between what the ministries formally requested to have budgeted in the annual estimates and what ended up being allocated to them by way of official Treasury warrants, and between that allocation and what audit reports subsequently show was actually spent (Roe, 1986; for similar gaps in the US federal budgetary process, see Caiden, 1984). Accordingly, a very large gap can exist between what was originally planned and what is eventually implemented, and it is this gap which motivates many of more critical accounts on the failure of large-scale government programs in both the developing and developed worlds.

The facts, however, do not always accord with this universalized narrative linking repetitive budgeting at the national level to poor project implementation at the local level. It simply is not the case, for example, that sub-Saharan governments all budget or implement alike, notwithstanding blanket terms like "the crisis in Africa." [...]

More empirical work on intercountry differences is needed and would certainly go some way in undermining the grim narrative's depiction of African national budgeting. In the absence of these case studies, are there other ways to weaken the narrative? Several options have been suggested in the previous sections. In theory, one could try to create a counternarrative; use the blueprints generated by the narrative to alter it; or fill in the "details" of the narrative in order to make it less misleading. There are probably many cases, however, where the practitioner has little leeway to be creative. The best he or she may be able to do is to engage another already existing narrative, which, once engaged, conflicts with the more objectionable one.

[...]

3. Conclusion

[...] Blueprint planning and a learning process need not be mutually exclusive, at least to the extent the latter operates within the context of the former. Counternarratives to the tragedy of the commons, for example, can and have been based on what has been learned in the field about common property resource management (Roe, 1987). Similarly, no one is arguing that since budget computerization seems to have worked in Kenya, it should be copied in Bolivia in the absence of learning to what extent, if at all, "computerization improves budgeting" is even a development narrative there. The argument here has not been that blueprint development that suits one country should suit them all, but rather a more modest claim. Blueprint development can be made more suitable to the needs of a given country by first learning how to better manipulate the development narratives that support these blueprints. Such a conclusion, however, should not be taken to mean that development narratives are to be evaluated solely on the grounds of how well learning introduces a measure of realism into them. In the four cases discussed above, it is not a question of which narratives are more accurate or have greater verisimilitude.[5]

It may be best to conceive of many development narratives as functionally equivalent to the early animated cartoon convention that animals have four instead of five fingers. The convention tells us at once that these cartoon figures are supposed to be more "like" us than not – after all they have fingers – without, however, being us just because they otherwise behave as we do. So too for development narratives: they tell us at once that things happen "like" the way they are described – after all narratives relate things causally – without, however, reflecting the fact that things happen in rural development so uncertainly. Narratives may be caricatures of reality, but there is no pretense otherwise for many of them. Believing a narrative and acting upon it is just like watching a story unfold on the screen and being moved by it in the same manner as one is moved by real events. Indeed, when one story more than any other becomes the way we best articulate our "real" feelings or make sense of the uncertainties and ambiguities around and in us, then the force of the narrative in question becomes compelling. Obviously, the day rural development becomes less uncertain and riddled with disagreement is the day we can begin to dispense with some of the development narratives that populate our profession. Until then, rural development practitioners must think more positively than has sometimes been the case about how to make the best of what we already have, meager and troubling as it often is.

The above remarks have been devoted to a class of development narratives that have, by and large, remained narratives only. What deserves much more attention is why and how a few of these narratives cease to be just that and become plausible assertions. Plausible assertions are those development narratives that can be justified as applicable to a site on the basis of long experience and observation. They are more than the latest imported development fad, but much less than an empirical generalization, let alone a testable hypothesis. Perhaps the best known plausible assertion in the rural development literature, and one that started out as a development narrative, is the scenario revolving around how road construction in an area can greatly facilitate the surrounding economic growth. The assertion clearly cannot be generalized to all developing countries or to all regions in some countries. Nor is it a hypothesis that can always be tested, since the scenario is very frequently cast in the past tense, i.e., had transportation infrastructure been constructed then, it would have led to more development later. Nor is the assertion really based on learning in the sense of trial and error. It is plausible solely because very different people would nonetheless be able to interrogate and defend the scenario on the basis of their detailed involvement, knowledge and familiarity with the area in question, notwith-standing the absence there of any major road construction program in the past. Case studies on the tangled and highly selective process whereby one of many development narratives is transformed into a plausible assertion are a matter of priority, if not urgency.

NOTES

1 For a discussion of this phenomenon as it is found in irrigation projects, see Roe (1988).
2 This definition of narrative and story is a standard one (e.g., see the respective entries in Prince, 1987).
3 How the truth of a narrative does not necessarily derive from or depend upon the truth of its constituent parts is discussed in Roth (1989), pp. 456 ff.

4 Studies listed as forthcoming when this chapter was originally published have been updated here.
5 This is not to argue against criticizing development narratives for their lack of realism. For examples of conventional wisdoms, puzzles, myths and folktales in rural development that deserve much greater scrutiny, see Roe (1987b, 1988c, 1989b, and 1989c).

REFERENCES

Animal Production Research Unit, *Beef Production and Range Management in Botswana* (Gaborone, Botswana: Ministry of Agriculture, 1980).

Bailey, Charles, *Cattle Husbandry in the Communal Areas of Eastern Botswana*, PhD dissertation (Ithaca, New York: Cornell University, 1982).

Barber, William, "Land reform and economic change among African farmers in Kenya," *Economic Development and Cultural Change*, Vol. 19, No. 1 (October 1970), pp. 6–24.

Bekure, Solomon, and Neville Dyson-Hudson, *The Operation and Viability of the Second Livestock Development Project (1497–BT): Selected Issues*, Report (Gaborone, Botswana: Ministry of Agriculture, 1982).

Bernard, Frank, *East of Mount Kenya: Meru Agriculture in Transition* (Munich: Weltforum Verlag, 1972).

Blaikie, Piers, and Harold Brookfield, *Land Degradation and Society* (London: Methuen, 1987).

Brokensha, David, and E. H. N. Njeru, "Some consequences of land adjudication in Mbere Division, Embu," Working Paper No. 320 (Nairobi: Institute of Development Studies, University of Nairobi, 1977).

Caiden, Naomi, "The new rules of the federal budget game," *Public Administration Review*, Vol. 44, No. 2 (March/April, 1984), pp. 109–118.

Caiden, Naomi, and Aaron Wildavsky, *Planning and Budgeting in Poor Countries* (New York: John Wiley & Sons, 1974).

Chambers, Robert, *Rural Development: Putting the Last First* (London: Longman, 1983).

Cohen, John, and David Lewis, "Role of government in combating food shortages: Lessons from Kenya 1984–85," in Michael Glantz (Ed.), *Drought and Hunger in Africa* (Cambridge: Cambridge University Press, 1987).

Coldham, Simon, "Land-tenure reform in Kenya: The limits of the law," *The Journal of Modern African Studies*, Vol. 17, No. 4 (December 1979), pp. 615–627.

Colony and Protectorate of Kenya, *A Plan to Intensify the Development of African Agriculture in Kenya* (compiled by R. J. M. Swynnerton, Nairobi: Government Printer, 1954).

Fleuret, Anne, "Some consequences of tenure and agrarian reform in Taita, Kenya," in R. E. Downs and S. P. Renya (Eds.), *Land and Society in Contem-*

porary Africa (Hanover, New Hampshire: University Press of New England, 1988).

Fortmann, Louise, and Emery Roe, "Common property management of water in Botswana," in *Proceedings of the Conference on Common Property Resource Management* (Washington, DC: National Academy Press, 1986).

Fortmann, Louise, and Emery Roe, *The Water Points Survey*, Report (Gaborone, Botswana: Ministry of Agriculture and Center for International Studies, Cornell University, 1981).

Galaty, John, and Dan Aronson, "Research priorities and pastoralist development: What is to be done?" in John Galaty, Dan Aronson, Philip Salzman, and Amy Chouinard (Eds.), *The Future of Pastoral Peoples: Proceedings of a Conference Held in Nairobi, Kenya, 4–8 August, 1980* (Ottawa: International Development Research Center, 1981).

Gray, Nancy, "Acceptance of land adjudication among the Digo," Discussion Paper No. 37 (Nairobi: Institute of African Studies, 1972).

Green, Joy, "Evaluating the impact of consolidation of holdings, individualization of tenure, and registration of title: Lessons from Kenya," LTC Paper No. 129 (Madison: Land Tenure Center, University of Wisconsin, 1985).

Hardin, Garrett, "The tragedy of the commons," in Garrett Hardin and John Baden (Eds.), *Managing the Commons* (San Francisco: W. H. Freeman and Company, 1977) [originally published in 1968].

Haugerud, Angelique, "Land tenure and agrarian change in Kenya," *Africa*, Vol. 59, No. 1 (1989), pp. 61–90.

Haugerud, Angelique, "The consequences of land tenure reform among smallholders in the Kenya Highlands," *Rural Africana*, Nos. 15–16 (Winter 1983), pp. 65–89.

Haugerud, Angelique, "Development and household economy in two eco-zones of Embu District," Working Paper No. 382 (Nairobi: Institute of Development Studies, University of Nairobi, 1981).

Hunt, Diana, *The Impending Crisis in Kenya: The Case for Land Reform* (Aldershot, England: Gower Publishing Company, 1984).

Hyden, Goren, *No Shortcuts to Progress: African Development Management in Perspective* (Berkeley: University of California Press, 1983).

Johnston, Bruce, and William Clark, *Redesigning Rural Development: A Strategic Perspective* (Baltimore: The Johns Hopkins University Press, 1982).

Korten, David, "Community organization and rural development: A learning process approach," *Public Administration Review*, Vol. 40, No. 5 (September/October 1980), pp. 480–511.

Leonard, David, "Disintegrating agricultural development," *Food Research Institute Studies*, Vol. XIX, No. 2 (1984), pp. 177–186.

McCay, Bonnie, and James Acheson (Eds.), *The Question of the Commons: The Culture and Ecology of Communal Resources* (Tucson: The University of Arizona Press, 1987).

Migot-Adholla, Shem. E., Frank Place, and W. Oluch-Kosura, "Security of Tenure and Land Productivity in Kenya," in John W. Bruce and Shem E. Migot-Adholla (Eds.), *Searching for Land Tenure Security in Africa* (Dubuque, Iowa: Kendall/Hunt Publishing Co, 1991).

Moris, Jon, and Derrick Thom, *African Irrigation Overview: Main Report*, Water Management Synthesis Report 37 (Logan: Utah State University, 1987).

Njeru, E. H. N., "Land adjudication and its implications for the social organization of the Mbere," Research Paper No. 73 (Madison: Land Tenure Center, University of Wisconsin, 1978).

Odell, Malcolm, and Marcia Odell, "Communal area livestock development in Botswana: Lessons for the World Bank's Third Livestock Development Project," Paper presented to the World Bank (Amesbury, MA: Synergy International, 1986).

Odingo, Richard, "The dynamics of land tenure reform and of agrarian systems in Africa: Land tenure study in the Nakuru, Kericho and Machakos Areas of the Kenya Highlands" (Rome: FAO, 1985).

Panel on Common Property Resource Management, *Proceedings of the Conference on Common Property Resource Management* (Washington, DC: National Academy Press on behalf of the Board on Science and Technology for International Development, Office of International Affairs, National Research Council, 1986).

Prince, Gerald, *A Dictionary of Narratology* (Lincoln: University of Nebraska Press, 1987).

Republic of Botswana, *White Paper of 1975: National Policy on Tribal Grazing Land* (Gaborone, Botswana: Government Printer, 1975).

Roe, Emery, "Perspectives from organization theory on irrigation bureaucracies in East and West Africa," in Norman Uphoff with Prithi Ramamurthy and Roy Steiner, *Improving Performance of Irrigation Bureaucracies: Suggestions for Systematic Analysis and Agency Recommendations* (Ithaca, New York: Cornell University, 1988).

Roe, Emery, "Last chance at the African kraal: Reviving livestock projects in Africa," in J. T. O'Rourke (Ed.), *Proceedings of the 1987 International Rangeland Development Symposium* (Morrilton, Arizona: Winrock International Institute for Agricultural Development, 1987).

Roe, Emery, "The ceiling as base: National budgeting in Kenya," *Public Budgeting and Finance*, Vol. 6, No. 2 (Summer 1986), pp. 87–103.

Roe, Emery, "Range conditions around water sources in Botswana and Kenya." *Rangelands*, Vol. 6, No. 6 (December 1984), pp. 247–249.

Roe, Emery, and Louise Fortmann, *Allocation of Water Points at the Lands* (Gaborone, Botswana Ministry of Local Government and Lands and the Center for International Studies, Cornell University, 1981).

Roth, Paul, "How narratives explain," *Social Research*, Vol. 56, No. 2 (Summer 1989), pp. 449–478.

Sandford, Stephen, *Management of Pastoral Development in the Third World* (Chichester, England: John Wiley & Sons, 1983).

Shipton, Parker, *Land, Credit and Crop Transitions in Kenya: The Luo Response to Directed Development in Nyanza Province*, PhD dissertation (Cambridge: University of Cambridge, 1985).

Sidahmed, Ahmed, and L. Koong, "Application of systems analysis to nomadic livestock production in the Sudan," in James Simpson and Phylo Evangelou (Eds.), *Livestock Development in Subsaharan Africa: Constraints, Prospects, Policy* (Boulder, Colorado: Westview Press, 1984).

Sorrenson, M. P. K., *Land Reform in the Kikuyu Country: A Study in Government Policy* (Nairobi and London: Oxford University Press, 1967).

Wangari, Esther, Effects of land registration on small-scale farming in Kenya: The case of Mbeere Ph.D. dissertation, 1993.

Wilson, Rodney, "The Economic implications of land registration in Kenya's smallholder areas," Staff Working Paper No. 91 (Nairobi: Institute of Development Studies, University of Nairobi, 1971).

World Bank, *Kenya: Agricultural Credit Policy Review*, Report No. 5619-KE (Washington, DC: August 1985).

25

The Social Organization of the IMF's Mission Work

Richard Harper

[. . .]

The International Monetary Fund ('the Fund') [. . .] is of great consequence, and though its work can be conceived of as a kind of auditing of national economies, it has remained beyond the scope of ethnographic enquiry. This is all the more surprising given how the IMF is often invoked in anthropological ethnographies of underdeveloped communities as the single organization that has caused more strife than any other. Such accusations (irrespective of whether they are right or wrong) are made with little knowledge of how the Fund does its business. As Gardner and Lewis (1996) remark, macro-economics – the stuff of the IMF's work – has remained uninvestigated territory for anthropology.

One may ask why this is. It may be that the view anthropological ethnographers have of the Fund has been so negative that any entreaty they may have made for access has been unacceptable to the Fund itself. I certainly heard numerous stories to that effect when undertaking my study. (It needs to be remembered that I do not present myself as an anthropologist.) Another reason may be that anthropologists have wanted to examine both the Fund and one of the governments it works with. Doing so would enable the anthropologist to examine what one might call, following Power, [1997] the 'audit loop'. Such requests are likely to be spurned for the simple fact that they would require agreement from too many people.

[. . .]

An Ethnography of the IMF

[. . .]

I focus on one of the main activities of the Fund, namely the point when it gathers its auditing data.

This primarily occurs during what are called Fund missions. A description of one of these forms the centrepiece of this chapter. I describe how this mission, and by example all missions (at least the common sort, known as an article IV), consist of a division of labour which supports an iterative process whereby a mixture of arithmetical, econometric and meeting skills are used to create data that are reconciled and measured against the data collected by others within the mission. This process results in an overall picture – an audit – of an economy. This is then used as a basis for discussion with the local (or member) authorities, and ultimately is used to create various documents, the most important of which is called a staff report. These documents, or textual devices to give them a fashionable sociological name, are the vehicles through which the Fund presents and justifies its auditing work.

This chapter does not so much focus on the way in which these devices are used by the Fund itself (i.e. after a mission) as on their production during missions, and in particular, on certain aspects of missions which, it is suggested, are fundamental to the social organization of international auditing, at least of the kind the Fund undertakes. What I have in mind are those phenomena which Fund staff themselves call the facts of life. It is these they have to contend with, orient toward and work around. These 'facts of life' are interesting ethnographically because they consist of the matters of practical relevance constitutive of the rationalities deployed by Fund staff. [. . .]

Amongst the facts of life I will consider is how data work on missions in a deeply social process and not just one that involves economic analysis. For, although data may be found in a variety of different places (namely, different offices within the various institutions of the member authority government agencies), only certain persons within those offices have the rank to sanction the relevant interpretations and associated numbers. These people provide the stamp of approval. A Fund mission must seek these out. On the mission described here, one individual had a particularly important role in this. For though this individual was not able to give official sanction to every single number, his data, his views on that data, his explanations and accounts of policy were treated as absolutely essential and vital to the mission's ability to comprehend the situation. [...]

A sketch of the International Monetary Fund

The Fund, based in Washington DC, is a financial 'club' whose members consist of most of the countries of the world. Member countries contribute to a pool of resources which can then be used to provide low interest, multi-currency loans should a member find itself facing balance of payments problems. The Fund has some 3,000 staff, of whom 900 are professional economists. These economists analyse economic policies and developments – especially in the macroeconomic arena. They have particular interest in the circumstances surrounding the emergence of financial imbalances (including those that lead to a balance of payments crisis), the policies to overcome such imbalances, and the corrective policy criteria for making loans. This involves going on missions to the country in question.

The Fund is divided into a number of departments. The most important are 'area' departments responsible for particular member countries divided up into contiguous geographic blocks (Western Hemisphere, Middle Eastern). The area departments are divided into divisions, each with responsibility for certain countries. The divisions are populated by desk officers and chiefs. Desk officers are economists who develop and maintain expertise on any particular country. A chief will manage several countries and desk officers, and hence will be responsible for the information the Fund has about any particular set of member countries.

A case study of a Fund mission

I confine my exposition to the main process of Fund missions and supplement this with three vi-

gnettes of particular events. The first, the team's first meeting, provides the opportunity to begin explaining how mission work is in large part a social process. It will also provide an opportunity to explain how members of a mission team assume that the materials they gather as part of this process have what one might call 'understandable' problems: numbers get added up incorrectly, miscategorization occurs, and spreadsheet tables get lost. These are part of the 'facts of life' in mission work and these are the things with which the team must deal, come what may. I will then characterize in general terms the data-gathering activities undertaken by this particular mission before providing a second vignette, this time of one of the meetings undertaken by two members of the mission with a key official in the authorities. Here I point towards how a mission needs to get a perspective that can enable it to distinguish between usable and unusable numbers. Some numbers are good for certain tasks, but not for others. I then discuss how the chosen numbers have to be 'socially validated'. In this case, the senior official could only sanction some and not all of the numbers of interest. Finally, in a third vignette, I will describe one of the policy meetings that occurred at the end of the mission. Here I draw attention to the ritualizing effects of these meetings (desired but not always achieved), important not only in giving those meetings the status they have but in transforming the numbers presented in those meetings into ones that count.

Before I start my exposition, two remarks need to be made. First, the mission team I describe consisted of a chief and his deputy, an administrative assistant, the desk officer responsible for the country in question, a fiscal economist, and a junior economist called an 'EP' (basically on trial through the Economists' Program). Second, for the sake of confidentiality, I call the country in question 'Arcadia'.

The First Day: Vignette One

The team left Washington together except for the chief and the administrative assistant who were to follow later. The departing team consisted of four economists, including the deputy chief, and myself. The first view we had of Arcadia came with a parting of clouds as we approached the airport: a blue sea, smooth coastline and ochre landscape pockmarked with little confusions of grey and white villages. In the distance, slowly emerging in the haze, was the great swathe of the capital city of Arcadia itself, a muddled warren of creamy white buildings at its heart, wide sweeping roads and modernist blocks in the suburbs, dusty olive green mountains behind.

On arrival, the team were the first to depart the plane. They were greeted with swoops and bows by a smiling official and a coterie of uniformed customs officers. The official directed customs officers to remove the team's luggage and lead them to passport control. There, he shooed the passport officials away, explaining to them that the team had diplomatic status and therefore didn't need visas. The desk officer pointed towards me. After some confusion, it was decided that I be given a tourist visa. Meanwhile, another smiling official arrived and presented the desk officer with a huge stack of documents. We were then introduced to two more individuals who would be our chauffeurs. Whilst negotiations were undertaken about how to load us and our luggage into the cars, the desk officer started to browse the papers he had been given. His head began to drop as he looked more closely, and he glanced at the rest of the team with an expression of glee and concern. 'Look', he said, 'Here are two copies of the budget, some other tables. I don't know what they are, but there are also four sets of the national accounts, all with the same bottom line. But look: they have different numbers. What is this?'

[. . .]

During check-in, the deputy announced that the team would be given half an hour to unpack before the first team meeting.

By the time I had arrived for the meeting, the deputy chief was already discussing with the desk officer the papers that he had been given at the airport. The desk officer pointed towards them and was saying: 'Well these are what we want. I have sorted them out. I assume that they must have included some early drafts. It is not a problem. It is the bottom line that matters at this point. Besides, I can see from the way they have been working which is the most recent so I will use that. I can clarify things with officials later on. Still, here are some materials that each of you can use to help build up your tables.' [. . .]

The deputy [. . .] then outlined what meetings had been arranged, and a list was handed out. She pointed out who amongst the team would be meeting with which official and when. She turned to ask each economist: 'Do you know what you can get out of this person? What information will you still need after this meeting? Do you know who you will need to meet afterwards? Can I have those meetings arranged for you now?' [. . .]

The deputy then made a little speech. She explained that, in her opinion, the 'shift in credit towards the government' would be the crux of the staff report (by this she meant the question of how the government was financing itself, the mechanisms for this and the resulting influence on investment in the economy at large, including exports of manufactures). She wanted to reiterate that it was therefore going to be the main focus of the mission. [. . .]

Comment

[. . .] There are two telling aspects of the day's events on which I want to reflect: first, the attitude of the desk officer to the materials he was given at the airport, and, second, the deputy's concern with whom the mission members would be meeting.

As regards the first: the oddness of documents given the desk officer. Essentially what he found was that four sets of national accounts did not consist of the same individual numbers. It is extremely important to grasp his perspective on this. For example, a conspiratorial desk officer might have contended that the oddity was a reflection of deliberate obfuscation on the part of Arcadian officials. But this desk officer did not think this. Rather, his assumption was that the problem in the documents had to do with the nature of the material used in the Fund's work. To paraphrase, his view was that this material had to be worked up, crafted, and polished. Further, in this process mistakes can be made, sometimes simple and sometimes more complex. In this case, the oddness was actually the result of a clerical error: in his words, 'some early drafts of the tables had been picked up'. He did not view the numbers used in the Fund's work as existing in some tidy, clean and perfect world, a world, say, akin to a scientific laboratory. Instead, he assumed that these materials are produced in the ordinary world of offices, over-filled with paperwork and filing cabinets. In a phrase, these materials were produced in the mundane world where simple mistakes get made for all too ordinary reasons.

[. . .]

The second issue to raise has to do with how and why the mission team displayed a concern with how its work involved a *social process*. The fact that the deputy wanted to talk about which meetings were arranged with whom, and therefore what would be the outcome of those meetings was not, I would argue, a reflection of the mere fact that data have to [be] produced by someone. It is rather a recognition of the fact that in policy work, *numbers and persons go hand in hand.* [...] The team were recognizing and depending upon the relationship between an individual's role in an organization and the understanding that individual will have as a result of that position. This may seem a banal point, but it is fundamental to mission activity. For mission work is all about creating analysis through the social process of agreeing and determining the facts in question. What is of concern to members of a mission is not that this is so. It is rather what in practice this means: which people and in what ways can these things (agreement of the facts) be achieved in any particular instance.

Ordinary work

[...] The first few days of the mission were spent marching around the various buildings of the Arcadian authorities, gathering more numbers, and discussing with those responsible for their production issues to do with how to interpret those numbers, and on that basis, how to use them. Each member of the mission would have their own 'circuit' of meetings and officials to work around.

This data collection process consisted of various stages, akin to the peeling of an onion. First was collecting the first set of data. This would supplement the data the desk officer had already collected over the year or via the questionnaire he had sent to the authorities prior to the mission. These data would be collected in meetings at such places as the Central Bank for balance of payments and foreign currency holdings data, and the Ministry of Finance for fiscal figures. At the end of each day, each economist would add the figures to their increasingly extensive spreadsheets. The figures for one 'sector' would then be reconciled with the figures in the other sectors. When there was a problem of reconciliation between two or more sectors, the team would decide what might be the cause. They would conjecture, say, that the numbers collected for the fiscal sector were not up to date in comparison with figures from other sectors. To investigate this, the fiscal economist would be asked to enquire into when the figures were calculated in their next round of meetings. This may be thought of as a further stage of the mission, a further peeling of the onion.

Sorting out the facts in the facts

Key to the data-gathering tasks is not simply gathering the raw numbers but also gathering insight into how to understand or interpret those numbers. On the Arcadia mission, one official in the Ministry of Planning had an almost unique insight into the economic position of Arcadia. This was based in part on years of work in various ministries and in part on his current role in the Ministry of Planning. His connections with missions in the past had also resulted in the growth of considerable trust between him and Fund staff. The deputy chief and the desk officer wanted to talk with this individual not only to gather certain figures, but also to get some guidance on how to read and interpret the figures that the team as a whole were gathering. From this view he was the mission's 'chief informant'.

The deputy chief and desk officer were after two things. First, they wanted some advice on how to separate what they called the flotsam from the main body of economic fact, for the figures that would be collected consisted both of long-term trends or 'underlying movements' and elements reflecting one-off events. For instance, the Arcadians had bought two Airbuses in the previous year which had impacted on the current account and ultimately the Arcadian balance of payments. But the mission needed to separate out this fact since this was unique, or an exceptional item as it is sometimes called. It did not reflect the underlying trend. The mission was after this trend in the current account and in the balance of payments. The official in the Ministry of Planning could provide this 'inside information'. The second purpose of these meetings related to the fact that the official could share with them the authorities' own perspective on the current economic trends. Here concern was for the mission to understand the weight given to some issues and the indifference felt towards others. Ultimately there would be a good chance that these views would be shared with the team during the policy discussions that concluded the mission, but the team wanted to get an understanding before those events so as to tailor their investigations in such a way as to enable them to 'talk to those views'.

Trust between the official and the team was also such that the official could offer frank remarks which might be more difficult to make in the formalized and partly ritual events of policy discussion. For example, the official was quite willing to say that the authorities 'really didn't know' why some trend was manifesting itself in the figures whereas in the policy meetings such admissions would be difficult. It is important to realize that such frankness was not pointing towards failings on the part of the authorities. By and large they had a view of and considerable understanding about the matters at hand. It was just that there was a handful of issues that they were unsure about. This was a fact of life.

[...]

Discussing the Facts Among the Facts: Vignette Two

[...] On the second day of the mission, the topic of [the] meeting was 'the macroeconomic framework and review of overall developments'. The official had already supplied some tables to the mission, and these formed the basis of the meeting. These tables consisted of consolidated balance of payments tables for the previous four years (including targets), as well as detailed tables of exports of goods, services and transfers, and the equivalent import tables. Much data on these tables would be very important at a later stage in the mission, but at the outset, these data could not be used. As the desk officer put it, they needed to learn 'how to read these tables'. Their concern was to know something about 'what lay behind the figures', to understand what they meant. [...]

There were two components to this concern. The first was understanding what the figures for 'actuals' represented, and the second was understanding the relationship between the actuals and the related projections. The tables which had been supplied consisted of two columns for each year, one with the actuals and the other for the projected or estimated figures. [...]

Once formalities had been completed, the desk officer said that the mission wanted to get some explanation as to why there had been a lowering of export volumes and an increase in imports over projections in the most recent quarterly figures. He pointed towards the relevant numbers in the tables. The official responded by saying the answer(s) lay not in the general but in the particular, and suggested that they go through each sub-category of exports and imports. [...]

The first of these happened to be textiles. It also happened to be the case that this particular category bucked the general trend, since here had been an increase in textile exports over and above projections. The desk officer asked if the official could explain this: 'I suppose shirts are in demand!' He then smiled and said: 'I cannot fully say why textiles have been doing so well. The manufacturers are reporting that business has never been so good. They claim that their designs and quality makes for a good product. I don't think there is anything else I can say on that number.'

[...] 'Mechanical and electrical goods: these are down on projections: why?'

'There is poor demand for these goods. It reflects the general weakening of demand in the world economy.'

'But if this is the case why has there been an increase in imports of raw materials given that there appears to be a slow down in the economy as a whole?'

'Well, because there has been an increase in investments in tourism. This has caused an increase in imports of raw materials – building goods. This is seasonal: it is the time when many buildings need rebuilding. It is not a trend.'

'Okay, whilst on the subject of tourism, let's move down the table to numbers for tourism: how is that there has been a decline? Or rather, how is it that there has been a reduction: receipts for tourism are down.'

'Tourism? There are more tourists this year but they spend less. I think it is that we went down-market a bit. The tourists who are coming this year spend less than those who came last year. [...]

On certain categories of numbers the discussions became [...] more detailed. Partly this was a reflection of what numbers were available. For example, the imports numbers had the following categories which led the deputy chief and desk officer to ask for quite specific accounts: 'Why has there been such a large increase in agriculture and food stuffs? Look, this figure here: milk and yoghurt.'

'Well, it has become fashionable. I think it is to do with healthy eating.'

'But this is a huge increase, this is millions of litres. No, seriously!'

'Yes, what can I say? People in Arcadia didn't used to drink milk. It's not traditional. This year everyone is drinking it. I think young people think it will make them look like athletes.' The official then patted his stomach and said: 'I've not been drinking it!'

The desk officer and deputy chief looked at each other and laughed. 'Okay, let's not worry about that one, it won't show itself in the final total anyway.'

At other times the questions started out being rather more general but ended up being specific: 'Can we consider the totals for consumer imports for this period compared with the previous quarter. According to the tables you gave us there has been a large increase in demand...'

'No. Look, one problem is that the figures for the last quarter can't really be compared with the previous quarter because this quarter was Ramadan. So imports for consumer goods and agricultural goods will go up in Ramadan. It is a period of celebration.'

'I thought Ramadan was a period of fast.'

'Yes it is in [*a neighbouring country*] but not in Arcadia. It is like your Christmas here. Except that it lasts a month!'

'That's why it is such good place to live!'

[...]

Sanctioning numbers

As the week passed so the focus of concern changed in these meetings. Gradually, the team began to build up a higher-level picture where things such as oddities in the current accounts disappeared from view. Discussions were also undertaken on fairly complex problems such as how to determine the Arcadians' international competitiveness, and hence the optimum exchange rate for the Arcadian currency. A focus here was on the selection of the so-called 'basket of currencies' used to calculate these matters. The Arcadians opted for a different set from the mission team.

I do not describe these discussions, however, since the main point to draw from these meetings with the official in the Ministry of Planning is how he was able to give inside information – information that derived from his location within the government and at the centre of information production. Meetings with him comprised an informal nexus whereby the team were able to sort out the 'facts amongst the facts' and to learn about the authorities' perspectives. The many years of contact between members of the mission team and this official also gave the meeting an informal character, where matters of little importance were treated as an opportunity for jocularity. But this should not distract from the serious intent of these meetings nor the extent of professional understanding and expertise deployed in them.

It is important to note that as the team moved towards completion of the data-gathering stage of the mission, so they embarked on another cycle of activity. Here the role of this official changed. For though he was able to give very useful comment on many of the numbers in question, he was only able to *sanction* a sub-set. The team needed to get all of its figures sanctioned before they could start on the analysis of policy and prepare their efforts to discuss policy with the authorities.

[...]

Building up a picture

[...] The team gradually aggregated the numbers, crosschecking and validating them, until they were confident enough to use the data to build integrated representations of those data. One of the most important of these representations was the *key economic indicators table*. Others were the *medium-term projection tables*. Ultimately the work undertaken with these tables enabled the team to embark on the last component of the mission – the policy discussions with the Arcadians. [...]

The team's construction, built out of the residues of the hours they spent in meetings with various officials, deriving from their spreadsheets and elaborated in such things as the medium-term projections, was not 'merely' a description of the economy. The output of their work could not be measured on, say, the basis of completeness, comprehensiveness or accuracy alone. Rather, the product of their activities was a perspective about the present from which to reason through policy alternatives into the future.

This is a key feature of the Fund's auditing work. Whereas the kinds of auditing done in commercial enterprises is strictly limited to assessing the adequacy of the processes of number production, the Fund adds to that a concern with probing into the future: what it calls policy analysis. In this sense the Fund's auditing work looks more like management accounting in that it attempts to wrest from the routinely audited numbers sufficient materials to support policy analysis. Indeed, it is difficult to underestimate the importance attached to this future prognosis work.

[...]

[...] The team worked hard to prepare themselves. The tables upon which the discussions would be based were examined again and again. They attempted to determine what the figures still being crafted 'would turn out to be'. They spent a great deal of time considering how to express and articulate their views. It was particularly important that the team got the tenor and emphasis of this 'just right'. For they did not want to misrepresent the authorities' intentions and past policy motivations. Questions included whether they should *recommend* the authorities to pursue such things as restraint on credit to the government or should be *forcefully urged* to do so. Such distinctions were important in conveying the extent of understanding the team had of the Arcadian authorities' past conduct and current intentions. For example, to *forcefully urge* would give the impression that the team believed the authorities were unwilling to pursue this policy; *to recommend* would give the impression that the authorities were more willing to do so. The latter was deemed more appropriate since it reflected what the mission believed were the Arcadians' genuine attempts to keep government credit within practical limits. It also reflected the particular form of relations between the authorities and the mission. The mission had a role rather like that of external auditors: they enquired into how things were done, then offered correctives, encouragements and advice for the future. [. . .]

[. . .]

Policy Discussions: Vignette Three

When the team gathered early in the morning of the first day of the policy meetings, there was an atmosphere of relief – the worst was over. For, by this time, the economists had become exhausted. As each day of the mission had passed and the amount of data they had collected had increased, so they spent more and more time on data entry tasks and spreadsheet analysis. This work had reached such a fever pitch that in the days immediately prior to the policy discussions they had had little sleep, instead working late into the night keying in data, and finding the task taking ever longer as their minds and fingers became increasingly tired. But the atmosphere of relief was tinged with a degree of apprehension. For policy discussions can also be difficult occasions, not only in themselves – the local authorities being surprised and worried, for example, by issues the mission presents – but also because the upshot of these discussions can be that a mission team has to go back to revisit its calculations.[1] This was an outcome the team were loath to consider. It would mean more late nights, more exhaustion, and further delays before they could get home. Hence they loaded themselves into the official cars with a strange mix of smiles and weariness. The economists knew that they wouldn't be doing much during the discussions and that the chief would be the centre of attention. This was his day. But they knew also that the outcome of these meetings could either be the completion of the mission on schedule or the need for more work and delay.

On this particular day, there were to be two meetings: the first with the Ministry of Finance, the second with the Central Bank. I focus on the latter.

Meeting with the Central Bank

Officials were waiting for the delegation at the entrance to the bank, and led the team into a meeting room. The chief entered first, followed by his staff. Whilst waiting for the bank officials to arrive, the chief asked for his economists to sit either side of him. He took some spreadsheet tables from his briefcase and placed them on the desk in front. He began to move them around like a painter preparing his palette. He then asked the desk officer for one of the medium-term projections tables, which he added to his collection on the table. Finally, he took some handwritten notes from his jacket pocket and placed them in the centre of his documents. An official then burst in and announced the imminent arrival of the bank Governor. The team stood up. The Governor arrived with a flurry of officials and secretaries behind him. The Governor sat down directly opposite the chief, similarly surrounded by his cohorts.

After formalities, the chief stood up and commenced what can best be described as an oration. It was an oration in the sense that it had a formal structure, but more importantly it demanded a response or a reply, as we shall see. He began by complimenting the Arcadians on the work that had been achieved in the past year and the impressive performance in certain areas of the economy. He commented also on the continuing frailties in certain areas. He noted that there had been some practical difficulties in preparing the data during the mission as regard such things as the collection of the foreign debt figures and totals for credit to the government. But with the hard work of his team and the energies of the Arcadians themselves, the mission had been able to ascertain the basic features of the Arcadian economy. These were to be the basis of the discussions in the meeting.

The chief then started to run through the team's figures, explaining that these indicated that there would be a growth in the money supply of 6.5 per cent in the forthcoming year. Further, if government bonds were included in the figures, this would increase to 10.6 per cent. As he explained this, he moved his hands over the tables in front of him, occasionally lifting one to read, as if looking at an oracle. He then remarked on the fact that the team calculated certain figures differently from the Arcadians. [. . .]

The chief then came to what the mission believed was the heart of the matter. For it was the team's view that the authorities were clearly exceeding their projected credit levels to the government. There were a number of reasons, including lower than expected growth in some sectors and, most noticeably, an unexpected growth in expenditure in agricultural stocks, particularly for olives. Related to this, there was a reduction in the revenues from the sale of olives in export markets – all of this in a year where the harvest had been unusually good. The chief explained that, as a result of this situation, the Arcadian authorities would find their foreign reserves getting reduced to a very low level, little more than one week's imports, or even lower. This was, according to the chief, too little, and necessitated immediate corrective polices. Failure to adopt the correct policies could lead the Arcadians to seek assistance from the Fund in the near future.

When the chief finished his oration there was a long silence. Then the Governor turned to his officials and beckoned them to gather round his chair. For some minutes the Arcadians discussed matters quietly amongst themselves. All the mission could see was a wall of individuals with their backs facing outward. Gradually, officials started to peel off and return to their seats. Eventually, the Governor turned round to face the table again. There was some momentary discussions as to who should speak: the Governor instructed the official on his right to ask the first question. This individual, having looked either side, proceeded to say: 'We are not sure of all the figures you have presented. Could you go over them again and this time in a little more detail? We want to make sure we agree with them all.'

The chief preceded to reiterate the key figures. Several Arcadian officials had by this time taken their pocket calculators out and had placed them on the table. As the chief went through the numbers so they keyed the figures in. At last the chief finished. Again a pause. The officials with the calculators read out their totals. They confirmed the mission's calculations. It was suggested that the chief do a run through for a third time during which process each number would be 'checked' by the Arcadians. By this I mean that one of the bank officials had to agree or disagree with the numbers. The process involved calling out each number in turn and waiting for someone to accept it (or not). As with earlier stages, the numbers were all agreed to.

After this point the Governor and his staff formed a little group again and began to talk intensively amongst themselves. After a while, the officials turned round and asked the chief to explain where his team had received its figures.

The chief responded by reporting on those individuals who had provided important numbers in institutions other than the bank. He asked his staff to help list these persons. The chief also explained how these figures had been consolidated with the figures his team had received from the Central Bank staff. The Arcadians then talked amongst themselves again. After a few more minutes had passed, the Governor explained that his staff did indeed agree with the figures that the chief had presented. They recognized the difficulties envisaged by the mission, and commented also on the fact that the team had been able 'to consolidate some figures that we were expecting to receive shortly.'

The chief then spoke up again and suggested that perhaps they should examine the olive and cereal stock figures in detail, and to begin to unpack the related issues. The desk officer quickly scribbled down the stock figures on a piece of paper and slid it in front of the chief who then read them out [...]. There was a 71 per cent increase for olive stocks[2] since the past year. The chief then explained that, the question for the meeting was how the costs of this, combined with a reduction in revenues from the sale of olives, would impact upon the credit available in the economy. The chief explained that, in the mission's view, the situation would have a significant impact in the allocation of credit in the economy. It would mean that there would be a substantial growth in credit to the government, and this in turn would have an impact on growth and on the GDP. An increase in credit to the government would also result in continuing growth in money supply but without allowing a growth in investment and productivity. These would be 'squeezed out'. Accordingly, the chief went on, the authorities would need to revise their estimates for growth and reserves and revise their policy stance to achieve new projections. Otherwise, the government would take a larger share of credit in the economy, further adding pressures on the balance of payments.

Once this stage of the meeting was complete, participants started investigations of the detailed implications of the credit issue and its potential impact on other figures. The problem they had to solve was where exactly those connections between credit and other issues, such as growth, inflation and the balance of payments, would show themselves. This was to be found out in the process of working up the monetary tables. [...] In the first 'run through', the Arcadians suggested that their projections for inflation be slightly increased. The chief turned to his team and discussed what they would view as an acceptable alternative projection for inflation. Their concern was not to make up any inflation figure, but to determine what would be a 'reasonable variance' in the inflation rate. After some discussion, both sides agreed to a variation that increased inflation by 1.3 per cent. Once this had been determined, the impact of that variation upon other variables, such as government borrowing and balance of payments, could be calculated.

These investigations took some time. The meeting then proceeded to alter other variables to see what impact those changes might have on the economic situation. By the time they had done all this, they had spent nearly five hours together.

Comment

[...]

There were a number of outcomes from these meetings. One was a finalized and jointly agreed set of key economic indicators. These would be presented in a Selected Economic Figures Table in the staff report. A second outcome was a specification of the salient factors in policy. For, once the basic figures had been agreed, investigations into the future were to be undertaken. [...] In the meeting described, both sides came to an agreement as to what was of central concern to policy – namely, the current levels of government borrowing and the levels of growth in the economy and what this would mean for the future.

More specifically, these investigations of the future resulted in the realization that the current credit problems could lead the Arcadians to the Fund in the future. Alternatively, these current problems might be reduced by larger than expected revenues from export growth. Both possibilities looked plausible from the basic facts at hand. The team took this evidence to subsequent meetings on the last days of the mission, and used them to make persuasive arguments to the effect that the Arcadians should reduce structural impediments (manifest, for instance, in such things as complex and restrictive investment codes) to help ensure that the potential growth in the economy turned into a reality. These arguments were also presented in the staff report.

[...]

Meetings that count

The meeting described here consisted of two main parts, with a watershed in the middle. The chief's oration flowed across both stages. His oration commenced with a presentation not just of what the team had been working on, but what the team's view had become at that point in time. Given that the team was invested by the Fund to act on its behalf, this view was effectively the Fund's view. Moreover, the relationship between the mission and the authorities was one wherein the team was instructing the Arcadians as to what were the salient issues. In this respect, they were in a subordinate role as regards the mission. This was symbolized in the oration: the chief reported on the conduct of the authorities; he offered correctives; he gave guidance. This was more of a paternalistic relationship than one of equals. Accordingly, it was presented with all the solemnity it deserved. This was not an opportunity for the discussion of opinions or for jokes and levity.

Nonetheless, the Arcadians still had the power to reject the view offered by the chief. They had to respond to his oration. To this extent, this was paternalism without power. For though Arcadians had been involved in the development of this view – some more than others as we have seen – the Arcadian authorities had not officially accepted it and were under no obligation to do so. The period during which the Governor and his officials turned away and discussed the chief's remarks was the opportunity for them to decide whether to accept or reject it. It was therefore a moment pregnant with tension for the mission team. As it happens, in this process some of the figures could have been revised or amended, but none were in the meeting I described. Irrespective of that, the bottom line was that it was only once the Arcadians had announced acceptance that the next stage of the meeting could occur.

[...] In accepting the numbers the Arcadians transformed the meeting into a ritual one, or rather one that had ritual effects. For their acceptance resulted in the numbers being ones that could be acted upon. They were transformed from being mere numbers into resources for policy. An important point to understand is that such ritual transformations cannot be guaranteed. If the Arcadians had rejected the numbers, this transformation would not have occurred. This is to reiterate the importance of the events and hence of the concern that participants had about them beforehand. After all, this was why the mission team were so apprehensive when they waited in the hotel lobby that morning: they knew the meetings could turn out to have the desired effect but they could also turn out quite otherwise.

This second stage also involved the chief standing up and making a speech – continuing his oration – but this time his remarks had a different character. If before they were descriptive, now they became an opportunity to outline issues to be investigated. It is in this respect that there was a watershed in the centre of the meeting. For after the Governor's acceptance, the chief's presentation became the common ground upon which both sides undertook subsequent analytical work.

[...]

construct, in this case, a construction based on audited numbers. If so, then it might lead one to believe that the concern of a mission and their counterparts in the authorities is not the real, hard, economic facts, but to ensure that the process of building a picture results in agreement, the difficulties in achieving this notwithstanding. This would give the impression that the exact nature of the picture does not matter, the main concern being simply that two sides, mission and authorities, agree to it.

[...]

The raw and the cooked

The process of converting 'raw numbers' into meaningful and 'useable' information constitutes, in part, a *moral transformation* and not just an arithmetical or econometric one. [...] Mission work as a whole consists of a process of gathering data, subjecting these data to various assessments and sanctionings and, if the data pass these tests, using them in analytical tasks. This is in part a moral process because the data in question will often remain the same (i.e. the actual numbers at issue) irrespective of whether they are signed off, as in earlier stages of a mission, or ritually accepted, as in the policy meetings at the end. [...] Once data have been transformed (signed off), they come to exist in a moral field. By this I mean that when a number is signed off, it can jostle other numbers, sometimes resulting in those other numbers being ejected or returned to a non signed-off status (that is, thrown out of the figures). In this regard, one might say that missions are to some extent in the business of creating a moral order, an order upon which the Fund's analytical apparatus can operate.

It is worth noting that this process did not appear to involve a preference to seek agreement in the sense that both sides always try to agree with each other, as is the case with ordinary conversation. In this mission, there were distinct occasions when difficulties reaching agreement were confronted. These difficulties were solved through small, 'intimate' meetings between the chief and his equals in the authorities, including the Governor of the Central Bank. The chief and the mission team believed that these meetings would be difficult, and so asked for them to be held *in camera*. The Arcadians too asked for certain meetings to held in the same private manner.

Be that as it may, all this discussion of the moral transformation of economic facts could lead one to think that economic reality is 'merely' a social

Conclusion

Each and every Fund mission is unique; furthermore, the pattern of relations between the Fund and particular members is also always unique, reflecting the kinds of problems a member has, its expertise, its institutional structures and so on. In this case, the member authorities were somewhat reliant on the Fund mission to guide and instruct them on policy work. As one of the Arcadians quipped toward the end of the mission: 'We've been waiting for you [*the mission*] to come back again to help us solve these policy dilemmas. You should come back more often!' The specifics of the Arcadian institutions also showed themselves in the mission process and in the character of the policy meetings. The desk officer explained to me (during the event) that one of the reasons why the Central Bank staff took so long deliberating on the figures the chief presented was that they were trying to determine which of those figures were their responsibility and which were other departments' within the government. They were concerned to make sure that the numbers they had produced did not indicate that they had done a bad job.

These particularities aside, I [...] highlight a number of general, key features of mission work whether it be to Arcadia or anywhere else. I have shown that getting to the right information involves both an analytic and social process. It is analytical in the sense that it requires the understanding of the representational apparatus that will be given to a mission (the numbers, the tables, the National Accounts). It is social in the sense that it means talking to those who devise this apparatus, which enables a mission to understand the motives and purposes behind these tools. It is also social in the sense that when a mission begins to develop an apparatus of its own (their own set of numbers, tables, and so forth), they have to have it signed off by the authorities.

I reiterate, however, that mission work itself is fraught with the possibility of not coming to understand what the policy situation is, not in the sense that the two sides (mission and authorities) might not agree, but because determination of the facts of the case may be difficult to achieve. The Arcadian team became more and more tired towards the end of the mission not simply because they were trying to get all the work done in time but because the work was turning out to be very difficult. Of course they wanted to get the work done in time, but first and foremost they had to get the numbers right. This holds true for all missions. Mission work is, in other words, a hands-on empirical science, albeit bound up with and immersed in social practice.

Finally, [...] missions come to an agreement as to the numbers representing the economic situation not in a fashion that is 'merely ritualistic' (that is, an agreement that is inevitable). The numbers a mission team generates achieve transformation in the very useability of numbers only because the analytical work for the construction of those numbers is done successfully. This may take more time, or it may take less. Such transformations are likely to be salient in all organizations and institutional contexts subject to audit. Here the numbers represent the enormously complex and indeed vast scale of national economies; in other situations they may represent much finer grained phenomena. As I mentioned at the outset, the ubiquity of auditing is affecting all aspects of our lives. It goes without saying that such auditing is being undertaken with a view to assess quality, productivity, and so on. Often doing so is treated as essential to a rational society. But if it is the case that the transformations I have described are common to all audit processes, then the society we are moving toward – Power's Audit Society – is perhaps much less rational in the Weberian sense than we may think. It may well be that though the raw material of those processes may be wholly mundane, agreeing to count them may make them seem sacred. The empirical materials I have presented from the IMF lead me to make this suggestion; it is for others to investigate whether this is so.

NOTES

1 Sometimes local authorities 'reject' the figures and analysis of Fund missions, and insist that a mission goes through its numbers again.
2 It should be added that costs for stocks were carried by the government since it had a policy of purchasing unsold stocks off the suppliers.

REFERENCES

Gardner, L. and Lewis, D. (1996) *Anthropology, Development and the Postmodern Challenge*, London: Pluto Press.

Power, M. (1997) *The Audit Society: Rituals of Verification*, Oxford: Oxford University Press.

Part VIII

Development Alternatives, Alternatives to Development

Introduction

The chapters in Part VIII explore imagined alternatives *to* development (a position that entails renunciation of the entire discourse); possible reforms *within* the development apparatus; and the successes, failures, and potentialities of capitalism and socialism. This section opens with a landmark article by Arturo Escobar, a leading proponent of the alternatives-to-development position (see this volume's Introduction) and one of the first to incorporate Foucauldian perspectives into the anthropological analysis of development.[1] Here he emphasizes the mid-1940s as a watershed in development discourses and institutions, a moment when development acquired a powerful hold on the imaginations of both rich and poor. Decades later, critiques of development had reached an impasse and now more radical alternative futures must be imagined, Escobar argues. Such alternatives require "a theoretical and practical transformation in existing notions of development, modernity and the economy" – a transformation to be achieved through social movements that can "create alternative visions of democracy, economy and society."

In contrast to Escobar's stance on the need for alternatives *to* development, Katy Gardner and David Lewis argue, in chapter 27, that anthropologists should not shun practical involvement in the work of development agencies, though they should be careful about the form it takes. Gardner and Lewis affirm both the value of deconstructing development and the need for anthropologists to "make the vital connection between knowledge and action" if they are to "make politically meaningful contributions to the worlds in which they work." In their view, both anthropologists of development and development anthropologists should be producing ideas about how to change it. As noted in this volume's Introduction, Gardner and Lewis's analysis is informed both by post-structural and other contemporary theoretical approaches and by their own experiences inside the aid industry. They comment on the ethics of such involvement, the challenges of offering constructive criticism, and the risks of having critical or participatory agendas coopted and watered down by developers.

Elizabeth Isichei's chapter explores symbolic or imaginative dimensions of development as revealed through African village intellectuals' myths, prophecies, and fables. These expressive forms represent conscious attempts to explain Africa's poverty and Europe's riches, colonial conquest, and political and socio-economic change. They include predictions about what Isichei terms the "victory of the cash nexus," forced labor, and visions of moral economy and an imagined past. Particularly perplexing to village intellectuals, Isichei writes, was the question of Africa's poverty and Europe's wealth. Their narratives on this theme "are the result of conscious reflection on the shape of history and its injustices. At their heart is a determination to make experience morally intelligible." Thus some of their stories construe poverty as punishment and "wealth and power as signs of divine favor." Other tales attribute European wealth to a Faustian pact, or they denounce Europeans for their avarice, or portray them as Tricksters (archetypal figures who are physically weak but cunning, or greedy and duplicitous). Some texts explain white prosperity, while others condemn it. In short, these narratives, and others like them outside of Africa, mirror development theory in their attempts to explain or judge global economic inequalities.

During the past three decades, the Indian state of Kerala has become known as an international success story. It is among the handful of cases that Nobel Prize-winning economist Amartya Sen has cited repeatedly in support of the idea that countries (or in this case, a subnational polity) with low or modest per-capita incomes can, by implementing the right policies, attain extraordinarily high levels of well-being (measured in terms of life expectancy, infant mortality, and literacy, among other indicators).[2] Kerala has managed to do this within a framework of political democracy, unlike Cuba or pre-reform China, which also achieved major improvements in health, education, and equity.

Richard Franke and Barbara Chasin's chapter employs the Kerala story as a test of several approaches to development, including modernization theory, targeted poverty-reduction programs, appropriate technology, and radical redistribution of income and wealth. They conclude that Kerala's successes are largely the result of redistributive policies. Many of these are similar to policies in the affluent European social democracies, though Kerala, were it an independent country, would be among the world's poorest nations. The Communist Party of India-Marxist (CPI-M), which engineered most of Kerala's reforms, has had to compete in elections (that it sometimes loses) and thus must be sensitive to public opinion, unlike the situation in the state of West Bengal, where a long string of less competitive elections resulted in CPI-M governments that were less successful in overcoming entrenched, caste-based forms of clientelism and exploitation. While some scholars insist that the Kerala model is economically unsustainable (Tharamangalam 1998), much recent research suggests that Kerala remains an important center of development innovations. The World Bank and the Indian state, for example, have – since the 1990s – pushed administrative decentralization as a means of streamlining bureaucracies and assuring government accountability, and Kerala remains among a handful of places within India or worldwide where massive mobilization of civil society has given decentralization a genuinely democratic character (Alyar 2002; Heller 2001; Isaac and Franke 2002).[3]

Katherine Verdery, whose chapter examines the systemic contradictions that contributed to the demise in the late 1980s and early 1990s of the Soviet Union and its allies, is one of the pioneers of the anthropological study of socialism and post-socialism.[4] Central planning, as Verdery describes in detail, had unresolvable, inherent contradictions, notably the system of production targets that perversely contributed to shortages and hoarding and to making information flows between planners, on the one hand, and factory administrators and suppliers, on the other, highly unreliable. The problem of targets (or "plan indicators," as they were also called) was that they had to be expressed in quantitative terms that were inevitably inadequate whenever there was any sort of product mix. Electricity, an undifferentiated product, could be reliably demanded in kilowatt-hours, but demand for, say, nails, measured in tons, could lead, as in a famous cartoon published in the Soviet satirical magazine *Krokodil*, to a single giant nail – and to shortages of the mixed-size, small nails that carpenters might actually need (Nove 1977:96–97). Verdery deftly analyzes how central planning connected to a system of socialist paternalism – and to conspicuous discrepancies between official discourse and lived realities – that weakened individual initiative, required an underground, quasi-market-based informal economy, and fostered cynicism and resentment of the authorities.

While Verdery devotes little attention to the cost of the arms race and geopolitical competition with the West as factors contributing to the collapse of socialism, she does note that the Eastern European countries in particular became highly indebted to Western banks in the 1970s and ultimately suffered a debt crisis similar to that which afflicted Latin America in the 1980s. Her rich discussion of what socialism was includes an original analysis of how consumption became a key locus of contention between the state and the citizenry and a major element in the formation of oppositional identities. For seven decades in the twentieth century, "actually existing socialism" was an alternative of sorts to the crises and irrationality of capitalism and, even shortly before its collapse, some leading scholars argued that market-based adjustments to the system could make it a "feasible" solution for humanity's future (Nove 1983). This conclusion is harder to maintain in the early 21st century, after twenty-five years of neoliberalism, but even today, as the free-market Washington Consensus crumbles, advocates of the decommodification of essential human needs again have an audience among those seeking alternative forms of development (Esping-Anderson 2002).

Poverty alleviation is, many would argue, the most fundamental task of development policy. John Gledhill's chapter tackles the ideological rise of the "Third Way" idea, associated with Tony Blair, Bill Clinton, and theorist Anthony Giddens (1998). Giddens considers the "Third Way" a "renewal of social democracy" or an alternative to both bureaucratic socialism and the unfettered free market (critics often contend that it is nothing more than pragmatic neoliberalism).[5] Gledhill paints a grim picture of the misery that the majority of Mexicans have experienced since 1994, when the North American Free Trade Agreement (NAFTA) came into effect. And while poverty in Mexico of course predates NAFTA and neoliberalism, as Gledhill remarks, "the data show that evil old statism reduced poverty quite substantially, whereas neoliberalism has brought the statistics back more or less to where they were 30 years ago."

Two main issues – inequality and labor rights – are fundamental to Gledhill's critique of the "Third Way." Giddens (1998:100) has described inequality as an "obsession" that matters little if minimal safety nets are in place to protect those unable to defend themselves against market-induced change. Gledhill suggests instead that inequality does indeed matter, both for ethical reasons and because highly inegalitarian societies tend to become politically polarized and to resort to coercion to control discontent. Similarly, ensuring that labor has the capacity to organize is, he indicates, one of the few ways to rein in corporate capital's efforts to restructure Mexico and the world.

The search for development alternatives and alternatives to development is among the richest areas of contemporary debate (Cavanagh et al. 2002; Sandbrook 2003). It also highlights connections between the historic field of development studies and the more recent rise of globalization studies. From social tariffs and currency transaction taxes to efforts to institute internationally recognized labor standards, from "delinking" and "localization" to new forms of global governance, few discussions are likely to be as wide ranging or to have such critical consequences for humanity.

NOTES

1   Somewhat earlier, James Ferguson wrote a path-breaking analysis of development in Lesotho (1990) that drew on Foucault and characterized development as an "anti-politics machine." Ferguson's and Escobar's analyses and findings differ in important ways, as noted in this volume's Introduction.

2   Other cases Sen cites include pre-reform China, pre-civil war Sri Lanka, and Costa Rica (Sen 1999).

3   Another much-debated case of democratic decentralization that attempts to go beyond the World Bank's technocratic approach is the Brazilian city of Porto Alegre, which implemented a widely admired though controversial participatory budgeting process (Baierle 2002; Heller 2001). This innovation was part of what led the World Social Forum, a coalition of global justice activists, to hold its first two annual gatherings in Porto Alegre.

4   It has, of course, been easier for anthropologists and other social scientists to carry out first-hand, on-the-ground studies of post-socialism than it was for them to study socialism and this has contributed to a boom in the relevant literature. Among the more interesting studies are Gal and Kligman (2000) and Hann (2002).

5   The large critical literature on the "Third Way" includes Callinicos (2001) and Kurtz (2002). See also Giddens (2000).

REFERENCES

Alyar, Mani Shankar, 2002 Panchayati Raj: The Way Forward. Economic and Political Weekly (3 Aug.) http://www.epw.org.in/ showArticles.php?root=2002&lear= 08&filename

Baierle, Sergio, 2002 The Porto Alegre Thermidor? Brazil's "Participatory Budget" at the Crossroads. *In* Fighting Identities: Race, Religion and Ethno-Nationalism, Leo Panitch and Colin Leys, eds., pp.305–328. New York: Monthly Review Press.

Callinicos, Alex, 2001 Against the Third Way. Cambridge: Polity.

Cavanagh, John et al., 2002 Alternatives to Economic Globalization: A Better World is Possible. San Francisco: Berrett-Koehler Publishers.

Esping-Anderson, Gøsta, 2002 Towards the Good Society, Once Again? *In* Why We Need a New Welfare State, Gøsta Esping-Anderson et al., pp.1–25. Oxford: Oxford University Press.

Gal, Susan and Gail Kligman, 2000 The Politics of Gender after Socialism. Princeton, NJ: Princeton University Press.

Giddens, Anthony, 1998 The Third Way: The Renewal of Social Democracy. Cambridge: Polity.

—— 2000 The Third Way and its Critics. Cambridge: Polity.

Hann, C.M., ed., 2002 Postsocialism: Ideals, Ideologies and Practices in Eurasia. London: Routledge.

Heller, Patrick, 2001 Moving the State: The Politics of Decentralization in Kerala, South Africa, and Porto Alegre. Politics and Society 29(1) (March): 131–163.

Isaac, T.M. and Richard W. Franke, 2002 Local Development and Democracy: The Kerala People's Campaign for Decentralized Planning. Lanham, MD: Rowman & Littlefield.

Kurtz, Geoffrey, 2002 Anthony Gidden's Third Way: A Critique. Logos 1(3) (Summer): 88–106.

Nove, Alec, 1977 The Soviet Economic System, 2nd edition. London: George Allen & Unwin.

—— 1983 The Economics of Feasible Socialism. London: George Allen & Unwin.

Sandbrook, Richard, ed., 2003 Civilizing Globalization: A Survival Guide. Albany: SUNY Press.

Sen, Amartya, 1999 Development as Freedom. New York: Anchor Books.

Tharamangalam, Joseph, 1998 The Perils of Social Development without Economic Growth: The Development Debacle of Kerala, India. Bulletin of Concerned Asian Scholars 30(1) (Jan.-Mar.) http://csf.Colorado.edu/bcas/ kerala/kerther1.htm

26

Imagining a Post-Development Era

Arturo Escobar

If I knew for a certainty that a man was
coming to my house with the conscious
design of doing me good, I should run for
my life ... for fear that I should get some of
his good done to me.

(Thoreau 1977: 328)

Introduction

For some time now, it has been difficult to talk
about development, protest or revolution with the
same confidence and encompassing scope with
which intellectuals and activists once spoke
about these vital matters. It is as if the elegant
discourses of the 1960s – the high decade of both
Development and Revolution – have been suspended, caught in mid-air as they strove toward
their zenith, and, like fragile bubbles, exploded,
leaving a scrambled trace of their glorious path
behind. [...] A new discourse has set in: that of
the 'crisis of development,' on the one hand, and
of 'new social actors' and 'new social movements,'
on the other. Many scholars even propose a radical
reinterpretation of social and political reality
based on a new set of categories such as 'alternative development,' new identities, radical pluralism, historicity and hegemony.

Until recently, [...] development was chiefly a
matter of capital, technology, and education and
the appropriate policy and planning mechanisms
to combine these elements successfully. Resistance, on the other hand, was primarily a class
issue and a question of imperialism. Nowadays
this distinction has been muddled, and even imperialism and class are thought to be the object of
innumerable mediations. But while innovative research into the nature of resistance and political

practice is growing, the same cannot be said for
development. The theory of social movements, in
particular, has become one of the key arenas for
social science and critical thought over the last
decade or so (Touraine 1981; Laclau and Mouffe
1985; Slater 1985; Kothari 1987; Shet 1987;
Melucci 1989; Shiva 1988; Calderón *et al.* 1992;
Escobar and Alvarez 1992).

The same vitality does not characterize the
second key arena with which this chapter is
concerned, that of 'development.' While many
consider development dead, or that it has failed
miserably, few viable alternative conceptualizations and designs for social change are offered
in its place. Thus the imaginary of development
continues to hold sway. In social movement
theory new social orders are clearly imaginable,
but in the arena of development the picture is
blurred, adumbrating a future 'developed' society
where only 'basic needs' are met. But to arrive
at this society (assuming that it were possible)
would entail that all the fuss about plurality,
difference and autonomy – notions central to
social movement discourse – would have been
in vain.

The seeming inability to imagine a new domain
which finally leaves behind the imaginary of development, and transcends development's dependence on Western modernity and historicity raises a
number of questions: why has development been
so resistant to radical critique? What kinds of
critical thought and social practice might lead
to thinking about Third World reality differently?
Can the hegemonic discourses of development –
inscribed in multiple forms of knowledge, political
technologies and social relations – be significantly modified? The emergence of a powerful

alternative social movement discourse raises further questions: how do popular actions become objects of knowledge in social movement discourse? If new discourses and practices are appearing that contribute to shaping the reality to which they refer (Foucault 1985), what is the domain that this discourse makes visible? Who can 'know,' according to what rules, and what are the pertinent objects? What criteria of politics does it put into effect, with what consequences for popular actors? Finally, what is the relationship between the demise of development and the emergence of social movements?

This chapter aims to bridge these two areas of enquiry. The argument can be summarized in three propositions. First, most critiques of development have reached an impasse. The present impasse does not call for a 'better' way of doing development, nor even for 'another development.' A critique of the discourse and practice of development can help to clear the ground for a more radical imaginging of alternative futures. Second, development is not simply an instrument of economic control over the physical and social reality of Asia, Latin America and Africa. It is also an invention and strategy produced by the 'First World' about the 'underdevelopment' of the 'Third World.' Development has been the primary mechanism through which the Third World has been imagined and imagined itself, thus marginalizing or precluding other ways of seeing and doing. Third, to think about 'alternatives to development' requires a theoretical and practical transformation in existing notions of development, modernity and the economy. This can best be achieved by building upon the practices of the social movements, especially those in the Third World. These movements are essential to the creation of alternative visions of democracy, economy and society.

The Hegemony of Development

The making of the Third World through development discourses and practices has to be seen in relation to the larger history of Western modernity, of which development seems to be one of the last and most insidious chapters (Escobar 1995). From this perspective, development can best be described as an apparatus that links forms of knowledge about the Third World with the deployment of forms of power and intervention, resulting in the mapping and production of Third World societies. Development constructs the contemporary Third World, silently, without our noticing it. By means of this discourse, individuals,

governments and communities are seen as 'underdeveloped' and treated as such.

Needless to say, the peoples of Asia, Africa and Latin America did not always see themselves in terms of 'development.' This unifying vision goes back only as far as the post-war period, when the apparatuses of Western knowledge production and intervention (such as the World Bank, the United Nations, and bilateral development agencies) were globalized and established their new political economy of truth (see Sachs 1992; Escobar 1984, 1988). To examine development as discourse requires an analysis of why they came to see themselves as underdeveloped, how the achievement of 'development' came to be seen as a fundamental problem, and how it was made real through the deployment of a myriad of strategies and programmes.

Development as discourse shares structural features with other colonizing discourses, such as Orientalism, which, as Said argues:

Can be discussed and analyzed as the corporate institution for dealing with the Orient – dealing with it by making statements about it, by teaching it, settling it, ruling over it; in short, Orientalism as a Western style for dominating, restructuring and having authority over the Orient. [...] (Said 1978: 3)

Likewise, development has functioned as an all-powerful mechanism for the production and management of the Third World in the post-1945 period. The previous knowledge production system was replaced by a new one patterned after North American institutions and styles (Fuenzalida 1983, 1987; Escobar 1989). This transformation took place to suit the demands of the post-war development order, which relied heavily on research and knowledge to provide a reliable picture of a country's social and economic problems. Development disciplines and sub-disciplines – including development economics, the agricultural sciences, the health, nutrition and educational sciences, demography, and urban planning – proliferated.

The Third World countries thus became the target of new mechanisms of power embodied in endless programmes and 'strategies.' Their economies, societies and cultures were offered up as new objects of knowledge that, in turn, created new possibilities of power. The creation of a vast institutional network (from international organizations and universities to local development agencies) ensured the efficient functioning of this apparatus. Once consolidated, it determined what could be said, thought, imagined; in short, it defined a perceptual domain, the space of development. Industrialization, family planning, the 'Green Revolution,' macroeconomic policy, 'integrated rural development' and so on, all exist within the same space. All repeat the same basic truth, namely, that development is about paving the way for the achievement of those conditions that characterize rich societies: industrialization, agricultural modernization, and urbanization. Until recently, it seemed impossible to get away from this imaginary of development. [...] Development colonized reality, it became reality.

A critique of development as discourse has begun to coalesce in recent years (Mueller 1987a, 1987b; Ferguson 1990; Apffel Marglin and Marglin 1990; Sachs 1992). The critics aim to examine the foundations of an order of knowledge about the Third World, the ways in which the Third World is constituted in and through representation. Third World reality is inscribed with precision and persistence by the discourses and practices of economists, planners, nutritionists, demographers, and the like, making it difficult for people to define their own interests in their own terms – in many cases actually disabling them from doing so (Illich 1977). Development proceeded by creating abnormalities ('the poor,' 'the malnourished,' 'the illiterate,' 'pregnant women,' 'the landless') which it would then treat or reform. Seeking to eradicate all problems, it actually ended up multiplying them indefinitely. Embodied in a multiplicity of practices, institutions and structures, it has had a profound effect on the Third World: social relations, ways of thinking, visions of the future are all indelibly marked and shaped by this ubiquitous operator.

The view of development as a discourse differs significantly from analyses carried out from the perspective of political economy, modernization, or even 'alternative development.' Such analyses have generated proposals to modify the current regime of development: ways to improve upon this or that aspect, revised theories or conceptualizations, even its redeployment within a new rationality (for instance, socialist, anti-imperialist, or ecological). These modifications, however, do not constitute a radical positioning in relation to the discourse; they are instead a reflection of how difficult it is to imagine a truly different domain. Critical thought should help recognize the pervasive character and functioning of development as a paradigm of self-definition. But can it go further and contribute to the transformation or dismantling of the discourse?

First one must ask whether such a domain can be imagined. Philosophers have made us aware that we cannot describe exhaustively the period in which we happen to live, since it is from within its rules that we speak and think, and since it provides the basis for our descriptions and our own history (Benjamin 1969: 253–64; Foucault 1972; 130–1; Guha 1989: 215–23). [...] The critiques of development by dependency theorists, for instance, still functioned within the same discursive space of development, even if seeking to attach it to a different international and class rationality. We may now be approaching the point at which we can delimit more clearly the past era. Perhaps we are beginning to inhabit a gap between the old order and a new one, slowly and painfully coming into existence. Perhaps we will not be obliged to speak the same truths, the same language, and prescribe the same strategies.

Inordinate care must be taken to safeguard this new discourse from attempts to salvage development through fashionable notions such as 'sustainable development,' 'grassroots development,' 'women and development,' 'market-friendly development,' and the like, or to restructure the Third World in line with the symbolic and material requirements of a new international division of labour based on high technology (Castells 1986; Harvey 1989; Amin 1990; López Maya 1991). Critical thought can rouse social awareness about the power that development still has in the present. It will also help in visualizing some possible paths along which communities can move away from development into a different domain, yet unknown, in which the 'natural' need to develop is finally suspended, and in which they can experiment with different ways of organizing societies and economies and of dealing with the ravages of four decades of development.

The number of Third World scholars who agree with this prescription is growing. Rather than searching for development alternatives, they speak about 'alternatives to development,' that is, a rejection of the entire paradigm. They see this reformulation as a historical possibility already underway in innovative grassroots movements and experiments. In their assessment, these authors share a number of features: a critical stance with respect to established scientific knowledge; an interest in local autonomy, culture and knowledge; and the defence of localized, pluralistic grassroots movements, with which some of them have worked intimately (Esteva 1987; Kothari 1987; Nandy 1987, 1989; Shet 1987; Fals Borda 1988; Rahnema 1988a, 1988b; Shiva

1988; Parajuli 1991; Sachs 1992). For these authors, as the links between development and the marginalization of people's life and knowledge become more evident, the search for alternatives also deepens. The imaginary of development and 'catching up' with the West is drained of its appeal. In sum, new spaces are opening up in the vacuum left by the colonizing mechanisms of development, either through innovation or the survival and resistance of popular practices.

What is at stake is the transformation of the political, economic and institutional regime of truth production that has defined the era of development. This in turn requires changes in institutions and social relations, openness to various forms of knowledge and cultural manifestations, new styles of participation, greater local autonomy over the production of norms and discourses. Whether or not this leads to significant transformations in the prevailing regime remains to be seen. [. . .] Social movements constitute an analytical and political terrain in which the weakening of development and the displacement of certain categories of modernity (for example, progress and the economy), can be defined and explored. It is in terms of social movement discourse that 'development,' and its foundational role in the constitution of the 'Third World' and the post-war international economic order, can be put to the test.

Social Movements and the Transformation of the Development Order

There is little point in speculating in the abstract about the character of a post-development era. If we accept that critical thought must be 'situated' (Haraway 1989; Fraser 1989), then a discussion of these issues should be practice-oriented, engaging with the politicized claims and actions of oppositional movements. In the long run, it is these movements which would largely determine the scope and character of any possible transformation. Hence it is important to link proposals for the transformation of development with the ongoing work of social movements.

[. . .] Questions about daily life, democracy, the state, political practice, and the redefinition of development can be most fruitfully pursued in the context of social movements. But how are the practices of social movements to be studied? How can social science make visible the domain of popular practices and the inter-subjective meanings that underlie them? How can the self-interpretation of agents be accounted for? What is the

field of meanings in which popular actions are inscribed and how has this field been generated by processes of domination and resistance, strategies and tactics, scientific knowledges and popular knowledges and traditions? What are the relations between cultural definitions of social life and political culture? How do collective actors build collective identities, and how do they create new cultural models?

The importance of daily life and its practices for the study of social movements is increasingly appreciated in Latin America. Reflection on daily life has to be located at the intersection of the microprocesses of meaning production, and the macroprocesses of domination. Inquiry into social movements from this perspective seeks to restore the centrality of popular practices *without reducing the movements to something else*: the logic of domination or capital accumulation, the struggle of the working class or the labour of parties. This procedure privileges the value of everyday practices in producing the world in which we live. [. . .]

Much of the recent literature takes for granted that a significant social transformation has already taken place, perhaps the coming of a new period altogether. The 'old' is often yoked to analyses of modernization or dependency; to politics centred around traditional actors like parties, vanguards, and the working class who struggle for the control of the State; and to a view of society as composed of more or less immutable structures and class relations that only great changes (i.e. massive development schemes or revolutionary upheavals) can alter in a significant way. The 'new,' by contrast, is invoked in analyses based not on structures but on social actors; the promotion of democratic, egalitarian and participatory styles of politics; and the search not for grand structural transformations but rather for the construction of identities and greater autonomy through modifications in everyday practices and beliefs.

Social movement discourse thus identifies two orders – the old and the new – characterized by specific historical features. In the process, the many continuities between the two regimes – as well as the ways in which, for instance, old styles of politics are still pervasive among the new movements – are overlooked. Equally important, the past is endowed with features that are not completely accurate (for instance, the claim that all styles of politics in the past were clientilistic and non-participatory). To acknowledge the continuities existing between the two periods – both at the level of theories of politics, development, the economy, and that of popular practices – is important (Cardoso 1987; Mires 1987; Alvarez 1989). A more rigorous characterization of the nature of the change that is taking place is needed.

The demise of old models is arguably brought about by the failure of the developmentalist state to bring about lasting improvements, and of political mechanisms, on either Left or Right, to deal with that failure. Moreover, the untenability of the old models is reflected in the present crisis. This dual crisis of paradigms and economies is forcing a new situation, a 'social reconfiguration,' as Mires (1987) has aptly put it. [. . .] Crisis is conceptualized mostly in economic and political terms, but many questions remain: what, for instance, are the inherent contradictions of today's models? What specific problems of system control seem to be critical? What structures are being strained? How are legitimation, fiscal and economic crises interrelated in specific Latin American countries?

Still other questions are raised by the premise that culture and ideology are embedded in production and politics: what cultural features seem to pose limits to accumulation and the persistence of old political forms? Is the loosening of economic and political structures leading to new traditions and identities? What specific institutions are disintegrating? What groups of people feel their identity particularly threatened, and in what ways? If old systems of group identity are losing their integrating power, what are the new systems for identity formation? What new goals and values are being formulated? What new discourses are being put in circulation as the usual mechanisms for social and cultural discourse production are upset? These questions do not arise simply in relation to the very real and dramatic dislocations that Latin America suffers today. It is also necessary to probe deeper into the shifts and fluctuations in institutional arrangements, meanings and practices that result, in part, from the crisis.

The number and quality of studies of social movements in Latin America has grown steadily over the last decade. Amongst those studied are urban popular movements, Christian communities, peasant mobilizations, new types of workers' organizations and novel forms of popular protest (for basic needs and local autonomy, for example). Increasing attention is being paid to women's and ethnic movements and grassroots movements of various kinds; on the other hand, few studies exist of the gay (McRae 1990) and ecology movements (Viola 1987; García 1992). Human rights and defence of life issues, as well as youth forms of protest, have also attracted some attention. [. . .]

Social movements are defined precisely in terms of what they supposedly bring about: new forms of politics and sociality whose definition in turn is left unproblematized. The 'new forms of doing politics' comprise not a new conception of politics but an expansion of the political domain to encompass everyday practices. Even the future of the movements is seen in relatively conventional terms: small organizations will branch out vertically and horizontally, non-party formations will give way to parties, short-term protest to long-term efforts. Similarly, social scientists see social movements as pursuing goals that look very much like conventional development objectives (chiefly, the satisfaction of basic needs). More radical questions about the redefinition of the political and the dismantling of development are thus overlooked. This is compounded by the fact that there is no agreement as to what counts as a 'movement' and what makes it 'new.'

Despite these difficulties, studies of social movements have clarified a number of macro issues. The relationships among crisis, social movements and democracy have been broadly defined. The reasons for the emergence of new actors have also been identified. These include the exclusionary character of development, increased fragmentation and precarious urbanization, general social decomposition and violence, the growth of the informal sector, loss of confidence in the government and political parties, the breakdown of cultural mechanisms, and so forth. Others have argued that the displacement of spaces and identities (from the working class to new actors, from the factory to the city, from the public sphere to the household, from the plaza to the neighbourhood) accounts for the new movements. Some of the movements have arguably achieved a transition 'from the micro to the macro, and from protest to proposal,' as they connect with each other in the building of coalitions and political movements, such as the Workers' Party in Brazil, the M-19 Democractic Alliance in Colombia, and the Cardenista movement in Mexico (Fals Borda 1992).

[. . .]

Issues in Social Movement Research: Knowledge, Politics and Needs

The intellectual and political challenges of social movements have provoked a significant academic reappraisal of civil society, the importance of the microsociology and politics of everyday life, the possibility for new types of pluralist democracies and alternative ways of satisfying basic needs (Calderón *et al.* 1992). There is, then, a sort of 'thematic renewal' which, despite conflicting demands and the existence of conservative tendencies (such as neo-liberalism), is having a great impact on the social sciences in Latin America (López Maya 1991).

This does not mean that European and North American theories are not important. Post-structuralism, post-modernism and post-marxism have significantly influenced Latin American social movements theory. The most influential notions are Touraine's concept of historicity, Laclau and Mouffe's elaboration of articulation of identities and radical democracy, and Melucci's proposal of the social as a submerged network of practices and meanings. Touraine's and Melucci's work foreground the cultural aspects of collective mobilization. For the French sociologist, social movements struggle for the control of 'historicity,' defined as the 'set of cultural models that rule social practice' (Touraine 1988: 8). In other words, social movement actors recognize that there is a cultural project at stake, not merely a struggle for organizational control, services, or economic production. Melucci emphasizes the cultural character of contemporary collective action at an even deeper level. For this author, social movements have a very important symbolic function; collective actions 'assume the form of networks submerged in everyday life.... What nourishes [collective action] is the daily production of alternative frameworks of meaning, on which the networks themselves are founded and live from day to day' (Melucci 1988: 248). This also means that what we usually empirically observe as 'movements' is usually the manifestation of a larger, latent reality that involves continuous symbolic and cultural production.

For Laclau and Mouffe (1985), the collective identities that define a given movement (whether peasant, working-class, feminist, gay, ecologist, indigenous, or what have you) are never given from the start, but are the result of processes of 'articulation.' This process of articulation is always discursive, to the extent that it always entails a plurality of orientations and subject positions. The processes of negotiation, interaction, building of common interests, and relations to the social and political environment – like all social life – is endowed with and apprehended through meaning. From the dominant side, the process of discursive articulation results in a hegemonic formation; on the side of social movements, the logic

of articulation can lead to radical democracy – groups and movements organizing in autonomous spheres, but also creating the possibility of articulations with other groups and movements, and, in the long run, the possibility of 'counter-hegemonic' formations.

While these works have been influential in Latin America, it should not be concluded that their application to that context, or that theory production, is a one-way street. Indeed as Calderón *et al.* (1992: 21) argue, one must question 'whether in spite of the richness of these foreign analyses there may not be something present in the social movements of the region impervious to the analytical categories provided by European theorists.' They conclude that Latin American researchers might actually be leading the way in the reformulation of social movements theory and methodology through continuous reflection on the practice of the movements. In sum, the belief that theory is produced in one place and applied in another is no longer acceptable practice. There are multiple sites of production and multiple mediations in the generation and production of theory. [. . .]

Jean Cohen (1985) has introduced a useful distinction between those social movements primarily concerned with resource mobilization and those which emphasize struggles to constitute new identities as a means to open democratic spaces for more autonomous action. The focus of the identity-centered paradigm is primarily on social actors and collective action. This is true of the three most influential European conceptualizations of social movements already mentioned – those of Alain Touraine, Ernesto Laclau and Chantal Mouffe, and Alberto Melucci (see Escobar (1992: 35–41) for a critique).

However, as Alvarez (1989) has remarked, disregard for the North American resource mobilization paradigm has had a high cost in Latin America. Many types of popular action have been crudely characterized in terms of groups 'reclaiming their identity' or searching for 'new ways of doing politics.' This leaves unexplained complex issues that impinge on the movements, such as organizational and institutional development, the role of external factors, constraints and opportunities *vis-à-vis* local or national politics, and so on. Some authors (Alvarez 1989; Tarrow 1988) argue that both paradigms should be combined for a more realistic portrayal of social movements in Latin America and elsewhere.

The recent work of the *Subaltern Studies* group of Indian historians provides rich insights for thinking 'the political' in a new manner.

According to this group, conventional views of Indian politics, of the Right or the Left, are indelibly shaped by the institutions of colonialism, thus overlooking the existence of a whole different political domain:

Parallel to the domain of elite politics there existed throughout the colonial period another domain of Indian politics in which the principal actors were not the dominant groups of the indigenous societies or the colonial authorities but the subaltern classes and groups.[. . .] (Guha 1988: 401)

Recognition of the existence of the subaltern domain of politics is the basis, according to Guha, for developing alternative conceptions of popular consciousness and mobilization, independent of conventional politics. In the case of peasant resistance in colonial India, for example, mobilization was achieved through horizontal rather than vertical integration; it relied on traditional forms such as kinship and territoriality; it sometimes grew out of outrage, even crime, to insurgency and uprisings; it was collective and often destructive and total; and it practised various styles of class, ethnic and religious solidarity. Nationalist leaders, on the other hand, tried to make the masses conform to a conventional politics with recognizable organizations and strategies (Guha 1983).

Much of the discussion of social movements in Latin America assumes a single political domain. Popular struggles sometimes resemble Guha's notion of subalternity but one of the effects of bourgeois hegemony has been the belief in a single political domain. [. . .] With few exceptions, the possibility of a subaltern domain has been overlooked in Latin America even though scholars have tried to recuperate popular resistance as part of a theoretical and practical discussion of political practice and process. The conventional view of politics shapes any 'normal' understanding of the political, entrenched as it is in structures and everyday practices (including the state, interests groups, parties, forms of rationality and behaviour such as strikes, visible mobilizations, and so on). A redefinition of politics cannot occur without changing this political discourse. [. . .]

Critical reflection on the politics of knowledge and the state is also crucial for transforming our understanding of social movements and development. Although social movements are usually thought of in terms of their connection to the state, they are also well beyond it. In the first place, relations of power exist outside the state,

in a whole network of other relations (at the level of knowledge, the family, and so on) (Foucault 1980a, 1980b). Social movements may also hinder the consolidation of extra-social bodies such as the state. If the state is arborescent (characterized by unity, hierarchy, order), the new social movements are rhizomic (assuming diverse forms, establishing unexpected connections, adopting flexible structures, moving in various dimensions – the family, the neighbourhood, the region) (see Deleuze and Guattari 1987). Social movements are fluid and emergent, not fixed states, structures, and programmes. They might even be considered 'nomadic.' In perpetual interaction with the state and other megaforms like multinational corporations, they are irreducible to them.

A similar situation is found in the field of knowledge. State science and 'nomad' science coexist but the former is always trying to appropriate the latter. State science proceeds by territorializing, creating boundaries and hierarchies, producing certainties, theorems, and identities. Nomad (or popular) knowledge has a very different form of operation, opposed to that of the State and the economy, with its division of social space into rulers and governed, intellectual and manual labour. Nomad science stays closer to the everyday, seeking not to extract constants but to follow life and matter according to changing variables. [. . .]

These features of new social movements – a certain independence of the state and the existence of a domain of popular knowledge – are hinted at in some of the literature. Fals Borda (1992), for instance, sees Latin American social movements as fostering 'parallel networks of power' and a kind of 'neo-anarchism' resulting from the movements' search for greater autonomy from the state and conventional political parties. Some see today's social movements as 'nomad forms' which, although expanding the cultural and political terrain, may or may not coalesce into larger networks of action (Arditi 1988). Similarly, other systems of knowledge are invoked in the literature on alternatives to development (Apffel Marglin and Marglin 1990). Such alternative forms of knowledge are practised in the popular domain, particularly among women (Shiva 1989) and indigenous people. Participatory action research is based on this belief, focusing on the encounter between modern and popular forms of knowledge (Fals Borda 1988; Fals Borda and Rahman 1991).

[. . .] Movements would not merely be a reflection of the current crisis or any other principle, but would have to be understood in terms of their own rationality and the organization they themselves produce. Our knowledge of this history, of course, can only be fragmentary and dependent on our own systems of interpretation. Like hypotheses of the existence of subaltern domains of politics and knowledge, we need to be aware of the mediations that inevitably condition our perceptions of people's histories.

The Politics of Needs

The question of 'needs' is central to social movements analysis. The definition of needs presumes the knowledge of experts who certify 'needs,' and the institutionalization of 'social services' by the state. Needs discourses, as elaborated by development experts, universities, social welfare agents, and all kinds of professionals can be seen as 'bridge discourses, which mediate the relations between social movements and the state . . . expert discourses play this mediating role by translating the politicized needs claimed by oppositional movements into potential objects of state administration' (Fraser 1989: 11). Most often, the interpretation of people's needs is taken as unproblematic, although it can easily be shown to be otherwise. There is an officially recognized idiom in which needs can be expressed: the means of satisfying 'needs' position people as 'clients' in relation to the state. Models of needs satisfaction are stratified along class, gender and ethnic lines. In other words, needs discourses constitute veritable 'acts of intervention' (Fraser 1989: 166) to the extent that the political status of a given need is an arena of struggle over how it is interpreted.

Social movements necessarily operate within dominant systems of need interpretation and satisfaction. But they do tend to politicize those interpretations by refusing to see needs purely as 'economic' or 'domestic.' This process contributes to the consolidation of alternative social identities by subaltern groups, especially if they manage to invent new forms of discourse for interpreting needs. [. . .] Whereas expert discourses (such as those of the agents of development) reposition groups as 'cases' for the state and the development apparatus, thus depoliticizing needs, popular actors challenge expert interpretations with varying degrees of success; for instance, rural development programmes may spawn movements for the recuperation of land.

In the Third World the process of needs interpretation and satisfaction is clearly and inextricably linked to the development apparatus. The 'basic human needs' strategy, pushed by the World Bank and adopted by most international agencies, has played a crucial role in this regard (World Bank 1975a; Leipziger and Streeten 1981). This strategy, however, is based on a liberal human rights discourse and on the rational, scientific assessment and measurement of 'needs.' Lacking a significant link to people's everyday experience, 'basic human needs' discourse does not foster greater political participation. This is why the struggle over needs interpretation is a key political arena of struggle for new social actors involved in redirecting the apparatuses of development and the state. The challenge for social movements – and the 'experts' who work with them – is to come up with new ways of talking about needs and of demanding their satisfaction in ways that bypass the rationality of development with its 'basic needs' discourse. The 'struggle over needs' must be practised in a way conducive to redefining development and the nature of the political. Finally, the language of 'needs' itself must be reinterpreted as one of the most devastating legacies of modernity and development, as Ivan Illich (1992) argues. These are open challenges that remain to be explored.

Conclusion

The possibility for redefining development rests largely with the action of social movements. Development is understood here as a particular set of discursive power relations that construct a representation of the Third World. Critical analysis of these relations lays bare the processes by which Latin America and the rest of the Third World have been produced as 'underdeveloped.' Such a critique also contributes to devising means of liberating Third World societies from the imaginary of development and for lessening the Third World's dependence on the episteme of modernity. While this critical understanding of development is crucial for those working within social movements, awareness of the actions of the movements is equally essential for those seeking to transform development.

As regards social movement research, significant ambiguities and confusions still exist. A critical view of modernity, for instance, emphasizes the need to resist post-Enlightenment universals (such as those of economy, development, politics and liberation); a reflection on historicity allows us to foreground the cultural aspects of the new movements; the discussion of meaning and background cultural practices provides a way to study the connection between cultural norms, definitions of social life and movement organization; this discussion also provides a conceptual tool for exploring the more profound effects of social movements, namely, those that operate at the level of life's basic norms.

Similarly, the notion of autopoiesis suggests that social movements are not merely a reflection of the crisis, but have to be understood in terms of the organization they themselves produce. They are, in important ways, self-producing, self-referential systems, even if their effects disseminate across large areas of economic, social and cultural life. In conceptualizing social movements as autopoietic entities, conventional definitions of the political, of knowledge, and of the relation between social movements and the state need to be scrutinized. Even if popular knowledge and politics are in continuous relation to the state, they nevertheless may have their own rationality and rules of operation.

To conclude, we may postulate the existence of three major discourses in Latin America with the ability to articulate forms of struggle. First, there is the discourse of the democratic imaginary (including the fulfilment of 'needs,' economic and social justice, human rights, class, gender and ethnic equality). Although it originates in the egalitarian discourses of the West, it does not necessarily have to follow the West's experience. This discourse offers the possibility of material and institutional gains and the emergence of more pluralistic societies. Second, there is the discourse of difference, which includes cultural difference, alterity, autonomy and the right of each society to self-determination. This possibility originates in a variety of sources: anti-imperialist struggles, struggles of ethnic groups and women, the challenge to European ethnocentrism and conventional epistemologies, revisions of history, and so on. The potential here is for the strategic release and furthering of some of these struggles. Third, there are anti-development discourses proper, which originate in the current crisis of development and the work of grassroots groups. The potential here is for more radical transformations of the modern capitalist order and the search for alternative ways of organizing societies and economies, of satisfying needs, of healing and living.

It should be clear by now that struggles in the Third World cannot be seen as mere extensions of the 'democratic revolution' or the consolidation of modernity. Although they may be necessary to help weather the precariousness of life conditions and to democratize social and economic life, the recent struggles in the Third World go well beyond

the principles of equality, relations of production and democracy. [...] Social movements are not ruled by the logic of all or nothing; they must consider the contradictory and multiple voices present in such experiences without reducing them to a unitary logic.

In the long run, new ways of seeing, new social and cultural self-descriptions, are necessary to displace the categories with which Third World groups have been constructed by dominant forces. [...]

Perhaps social movements, as symbols of resistance to the dominant politics of knowledge and organization of the world, provide some paths in the direction of this calling, that is, for the re-imagining of the 'Third World' and a post-development era.

REFERENCES

Alvarez, S. (1989) 'Conceptual problems and methodological impasses in the study of contemporary social movements in Brazil and the Southern Cone', paper presented at the XV International Conference of the Latin American Studies Association, Miami, Florida.

Amin, S. (1990) *Maldevelopment: Anatomy of a Global Failure*, London: Zed Books.

Apffel Marglin, F. and Marglin, S. (eds.) (1990) *Dominating Knowledge: Development, Culture and Resistance*, Oxford: Clarendon Press.

Arditi, B. (1988) 'La sociedad a Pesar del Estado', in F. Calderón (ed.) *La Modernidad en La Encrucijada Postmoderna*, Buenos Aires: CLACSO.

Benjamin, W. (1969) 'Theses on the philosophy of history', in W. Benjamin (ed.) *Illuminations*, New York: Schocken Books.

Calderón, F., Píscitelli, A., and Reyna, J.L. (1992) 'Social movements: actors, theories, expectations', in A. Escobar and S. Alvarez (eds.) *The Making of Social Movements in Latin America: Identity, Strategy and Democracy*, Boulder, Colorado: Westview Press.

Cardoso, R.C.L. (1987) 'Movimientos sociais na América Latina', *Revista Brasileira de Ciências Sociais* 3, 1: 27–37.

Castells, M. (1986) 'High technology, world development, and structural transformation: the trends and the debate', *Alternatives* 11, 3: 297–344.

Cohen, J. (1985) 'Strategy or identity: new theoretical paradigms and contemporary social movements', *Social Research* 52, 4.

——(1987) *A Thousand Plateaus: Capitalism and Schizophrenia*, Minneapolis: University of Minnesota Press.

Escobar, A. (1984) 'Discourse and power in development: Michel Foucault and the relevance of his work to the Third World', *Alternatives* 10: 377–400.

—— (1988) 'Power and visibility: the invention and management of development in the Third World', *Cultural Anthropology* 4, 4: 428–443.

—— (1989) 'The professionalization and institutionalization of "development" in Colombia in the early post-World War II period', *International Journal of Educational Development* 9, 2: 139–154.

—— (1992) 'Imagining a post-development era? critical thought, development and social movements', *Social Text*, 31/32: 20–54.

—— (1995) *Encountering Development. The Making and Unmaking of the Third World*, Princeton: Princeton University Press.

Escobar, A. and Alvarez, S. (eds.) (1992) *The Making of Social Movements in Latin America: Identity, Strategy and Democracy*, Boulder, Colorado: Westview Press.

Esteva, G. (1987) 'Regenerating people's space', *Alternatives* 10, 3: 125–152.

Fals Borda, O. (1988) *Knowledge and People's Power*, Delhi: Indian Social Institute.

—— (1992) 'Social movements and political power in Latin America', in A. Escobar and S. Alvarez (eds.) *The Making of Social Movements in Latin America: Identity, Strategy and Democracy*, Boulder, Colorado: Westview Press.

Fals Borda, O. and Rahman, A. (eds.) (1991) *Action and Knowledge: Breaking the Monopoly with Participatory Action-Research*, New York: Apex Press.

Ferguson, J. (1990) *The Anti-Politics Machine: 'Development', Depoliticisation and Bureaucratic Power in Lesotho*, Cambridge: Cambridge University Press.

Foucault, M. (1972) *The Archaelogy of Knowledge and the Discourse on Language*, New York: Tavistock Publications.

—— (1980a) *The History of Sexuality*, New York: Random House.

—— (1980b) *Power/Knowledge: Selected Interviews and Other Writings, 1972–1977,*

—— (1985) *The Use of Pleasure*, New York: Vintage Books.

Fraser, N. (1989) *Unraly Practices: Power, Discourse and Gender in Contemporary Social Theory*, Minneapolis: University of Minnesota Press.

Fuenzalida, E. (1983) 'The reception of 'scientific sociology' in Chile', *Latin American Research Review* 18, 1: 95–112.

—— (1987) 'La reorganización de las Instituciones de Enseñanza Superior e de Investigación en América Latina entre 1950 y 1980 sus Interpretaciones', *Estudios Sociales* 52: 115–137.

García, M., del Pilar (1992) 'The Venezuelan ecology movement: symbolic effectiveness, social practice, and political strategies', in A. Escobar and S. Alvarez (eds.) *The Making of Social Movements in Latin America: Identity, Strategy and Democracy*, Boulder, Colorado: Westview Press.

Guha, R. (1983) *Elementary Aspects of Peasant Insurgency in Colonial India*, Delhi: Oxford University Press.

—— (1988) 'On some aspects of the historiography of colonial India', in R. Guha and G. Spivak (eds.) *Selected Subaltern Studies*, Delhi: Oxford University Press.

—— (1989) 'Dominance without hegemony and its historiography', in R. Guha (ed.) *Subaltern Studies*, Delhi: Oxford University Press.

Haraway, D. (1989) *Primate Visions: Gender, Race and Nature in the World of Modern Science*, London: Routledge.

Harvey, D. (1989) *The Condition of Postmodernity: An Enquiry into the Origins of Cultural Change*, Oxford: Basil Blackwell.

Ilich, I. (1977) *Toward a History of Needs*, Berkeley: Heyday Books.

—— (1992) 'Needs', in W. Sachs (ed.) *The Development Dictionary: A Guide to Knowledge as Power*, London: Zed Books.

Kothari, R. (1987) 'On humane governance', *Alternatives* 12, 3: 277–290.

Laclau, E. and Mouffe, C. (1985) *Hegemony and Socialist Strategy*, London: Verso.

Leipziger, D.M. and Streeten, P. (eds.) (1981) *Basic Needs to Development*, Cambridge, Mass.: Oelgeschlager, Gunn and Hain Publishers.

López Maya, M. (ed.) (1991) *Pensamiento Crítico. Un Diálogo Interregional, 3. Desarollo y Democracia*, Caracas: Universidad Central/Nueva Sociedad.

McRae, E. (1990) *A Construçáo da Igualdade. Identidade Sexual e Política no Brasil da 'Abertura'*, São Paulo: Universidade Estadual de Campinas.

Melucci, A. (1988) 'Social movements and the democratization of everyday life', in J. Keane (ed.) *Civil Society and the State: New European Perspectives*, London: Verso.

—— (1989) *Nomads of the Present*, Philadelphia: Temple University Press.

Mires, F. (1987) 'Continuidad y ruptura en el discurso politico', *Nueva Sociedad* 91: 129–140.

Mueller, A. (1987a) 'Peasants and professionals: the social organization of women in development knowledge', unpublished Ph.D. thesis, Ontario Institute for Studies in Education, Toronto.

—— (1987b) 'Peasants and professionals: the production of knowledge about women in the Third World', paper presented at the Association for Women in Development, Washington, D.C.

Nandy, A. (1987) *Traditions, Tyranny and Utopias: Essays in the Politics of Awareness*, Delhi: Oxford University Press.

—— (1989) 'Shamans, savages and the wilderness: on the audibility of dissent and the future of civilisations', *Alternatives* 14, 3: 263–278.

Parajuli, P. (1991) 'Power and knowledge in development discourse: new social movements and the state in India', *International Social Science Journal* 127: 173–190.

Rahnema, M. (1988a) 'A new variety of AIDS and its pathogens: homo economicus, development and aid', *Alternatives* 13, 1: 117–136.

——(1988b) 'Power and regenerative processes in micro-spaces', *International Social Sciences Journal* 117: 361–375.

Sachs, W. (ed.) (1992) *The Development Dictionary: A Guide to Knowledge as Power*, London: Zed Books.

Said, E. (1978) *Orientalism*, New York: Pantheon.

Shet, D.L. (1987) 'Alternative development as political practice', *Alternatives* 12, 2: 155–171.

Shiva, V. (1988) *Staying Alive: Women, Ecology and Development*, London: Zed Books.

Slater, D. (ed.) (1985) *New Social Movements and the State in Latin America*, Amsterdam: CEDLA.

Tarrow, S. (1988) 'National politics and collective action: recent theory and research in Western Europe and the United States', *Annual Review of Sociology* 14:421–440.

Thoreau, H.D. (1977) *The Portable Thoreau*, New York: Penguin Books.

Touraine, A. (1981) *The Voice and the Eye: An Analysis of Social Movements*, Cambridge: Cambridge University Press.

——(1988) *The Return of the Actor*, Minneapolis: University of Minnesota Press.

Viola, E. (1987) 'O movimento ecológico no Brasil (1974–1986)', *Revista Brasileria de Ciencias Sociais* 1, 3: 5–25.

World Bank (1975a) *Assault on World Poverty*, Baltimore: Johns Hopkins University Press.

27

Beyond Development?

Katy Gardner and David Lewis

[...] Anthropology's relationship to development is riven with contradiction. While on the one hand anthropologists have for many generations worked within governmental and non-governmental organisations, demonstrating how much the discipline has to offer in terms of improving the work of developers, other anthropologists are engaged in a radical critique of the very notion of development, arguing that as a concept it is morally, politically and philosophically corrupt. [...]

In the post-modern/post-structuralist context of the 1990s [...] the two approaches appear to be further apart than ever. In this [...] chapter we shall suggest that this need not necessarily be the case. Indeed, while it is absolutely necessary to unravel and deconstruct 'development', if anthropologists are to make politically meaningful contributions to the worlds in which they work they must continue to make the vital connection between knowledge and action. [...]

This 'involved anthropology' is undoubtedly fraught with danger. In this sense it is perhaps the most testing and problematic domain for individual anthropologists to work in, whether as detached critics or as consultants hired by aid agencies. But this should not mean that they shun practical involvement, although they may need to be careful about what form it takes. Anthropologists should also not expect involvement to be easy. If they have any collective responsibility it is endlessly to question and problematise their positions, to be uncomfortable, and with their questions to make others uncomfortable. This is a source of creativity, as well as a form of political engagement. It is also, however, a perilous path to take.

Unpicking Development

As Ferguson (1990: xiii) has pointed out:

Like 'civilisation' in the nineteenth century, 'development' is the name not only for a value, but also for a dominant problematic or interpretive grid through which the impoverished regions of the world are known to us. Within this intepretive grid, a host of everyday observations are rendered intelligible and meaningful.

Laying bare the assumptions behind such 'interpretive grids', and thus indicating the relationship between knowledge, discourse and the reproduction of power, is one of the most important tasks of the contemporary anthropology of development, a project which has burgeoned in recent years.

[...]

The new anthropology of development can be used to deconstruct the knowledge of developers as well as those 'to be developed'. Although often caricatured as simply involving 'scientific rationality', this is also more complex, in much the same way that 'indigenous knowledge' is. [...] Development plans are often far from rational, and relationships within development institutions are as hierarchical, unequal and culturally embedded as any of the societies usually studied by anthropologists. The interface between developers and those to be developed is not simply a case of binary oppositions: modern ('scientific') versus traditional ('indigenous') thought. Instead, the paradigms within which developers work are as contextually contingent, culturally specific and contested as those of the social groups whom they target. What must not be lost sight of, however, is that discourses of development are produced by those in power and often result (even if unintentionally) in reproducing power relations between areas of the world and between people.

These perspectives help anthropologists turn a highly critical eye on the assumptions which lie behind those who speak of 'development' in both the resource-rich Northern countries and the economically poor countries of the South. They help reveal how the language used in the North to describe the Third World is not neutral, but reflects the continuing inequalities arising from the histories of colonisation, the need for Northern states to maintain their position of economic dominance and the limited vision that those in richer countries may have of the global future. It also becomes clear how development has been institutionalised, and the people who work within its projects professionalised. Important issues are raised concerning the production and uses of knowledge, about the legitimacy or otherwise of the 'experts' who provide advice, about the level of participation of local people in projects and about the intended and unintended economic and political consequences of the whole development enterprise as it is carried out across the world.

Anthropology and Development: Moving On

Discomforting, but nonetheless crucial, questions are also asked about the involvement in development work of anthropologists, who are frequently accused of 'buying in' to the dominant discourse and thus perpetuating global inequality even while attempting to 'do good'. As one of its fiercest critics, Arturo Escobar (1991, 674–7), puts it:

Development institutions are part and parcel of how the world is put together so as to ensure certain processes of ruling. Under these conditions, development anthropology almost inevitably upholds the main tenets of development...for all its claim to relevance to social problems, to cultural sensitivity...[development anthropology]...has done no more than recycle and dress in more localised fabrics, the discourses of modernisation and development.

Such perspectives are vital in the ongoing task of rethinking and thus remaking the world. [...] Anthropologists must continue to ask difficult questions of themselves and of others. But as well as showing that the very concept of development and all of its discursive paraphernalia (including the role of development anthropology) is deeply problematic, anthropologists in and of development should also be producing ideas on how to change it. For them to criticise the inability of 'development' to deliver is relatively easy; understanding and supporting the alternatives are more difficult.

Why should anthropologists remain involved? Reading through some of the texts produced by post-structuralists it might appear that the problems of Southern countries are simply a construct, a figment of the post-colonial imagination, and a justification for the continuing domination of the South by the North. It is certainly true that every effort must be made to move beyond perceiving the 'Third World' in crude and debilitating stereotypes which negate the agency, dynamism and self-reliance of those who are labelled 'the poor'. It should also be recognised that the 'Third World' – if this is to be understood in terms of marginalisation – also exists within the North; witness the scandal of homelessness and social deprivation within the cities of Britain and the US. Lastly, those from materially richer societies need to recognise the degree to which their views are embedded within their own cultural assumptions.

Yet while it is important to acknowledge that not everyone perceives the world in the same terms, global inequalities and poverty cannot simply be explained away as culturally relative. The first problem with this stance is that it relies upon the notion of bounded and separate cultures, all of which have their own internal logic; in this view there are clearly no universals. [...] [Yet] it is increasingly recognised that the world and its cultures are highly interconnected. People are not simply separated by the invisible and impermeable walls of culture. Although there is of course great diversity among societies, there are also great similarities.

Second, while as an ideological position cultural relativism may be 'politically correct', it can lead to complacency, at both an individual and a state level. It may also negate the struggles and perceptions of those fighting to change conditions within their societies, who may request and welcome the solidarity of outsiders. In these cases, the relativism of post-modernist approaches is in danger of collapsing into depoliticised irresponsibility. As Micaela di Leonardo (1991: 24) comments:

In other words, there is no place for any morally evaluative or politically committed stance within the disintegrating logic of post-structuralism. It is fundamentally nihilist...Ironically, given its sometime association with radical political stances, post-structuralism does not challenge the status quo in an increasingly retrograde era.

Similar issues have been hotly debated within feminism. While the 'politics of difference' (the recognition of the diversity of feminist voices and experience and, by extension, the critique of white, Western feminists' representations) has been central to debates within feminist theory in recent years, some feminists worry that an ideal of endless difference might cause feminism to self-destruct. For the feminist movement to have any meaning, there must therefore be post-modern 'stopping points' (Nicholson, 1990: 8), a recognition that there *are* globalised structures of dominance and subordination. These are not simply a construct (Bordo, 1990: 149).

Another major problem with the deconstructionalist stance is that it makes active involvement in processes of change difficult, for the terms in which such change is thought of are themselves suspicious, as is any Northern involvement in Southern societies. Those from the North[1] therefore become silenced, unable to act beyond producing hostile critiques of the work of those who are involved. But if this is all they do, their contribution becomes reductive: they detract while adding nothing. Although unpicking 'development' is clearly a political as well as an academic act, the irony of post-structuralism is that it can thus also be inherently depoliticising.

If anthropologists are to retain a commitment to improving the world they therefore need to move beyond deconstruction, taking with them its critical insights, but leaving behind the political apathy that it sometimes evokes. There are moral absolutes in the world; people are not merely atomised individuals, endlessly fragmented by diversity, with wholly different perceptions and experiences. People have a right to basic material needs; they also have a right to fulfil their individual potential, whether this involves becoming literate, retaining their cultural identity or their freedom, having the means to generate an income, or whatever. Yet many millions of people throughout the world are denied these rights. We therefore make no apologies for arguing that professionally as well as personally anthropologists should be actively engaged in attempting to change the conditions which produce poverty, inequality and oppression.

One way in which anthropologists can move forward is to shift their focus away from development and on to relations of poverty and inequality. This means that there is still an important role for anthropologists working within development, for from their positions as participants they can continually insist that inequality and poverty – as social relationships – remain at the top of the agenda. [...] They can also work on the institutions concerned, whether these are donor agencies, governments or NGOs, insisting that the development discourse itself changes. [...]

Working from Within

As insiders in the aid industry, anthropologists can play a part in ensuring that the issues of equity and participation within the 'development process' (as opposed to the simpler, more measurable notions of economic growth and technological change) are uppermost in the approaches and practices of those working in development. These are in many ways 'anthropological' issues, for the traditional subject matter of anthropology – small-scale, low-income rural communities – has generated a wealth of information about how the different elements of a society fit together, and how, by extension, things could be improved. [...] Anthropologists ask crucial questions regarding people's access to resources and the differential effects of change. It is vital that these questions stay on the developers' agenda, for [...] many planners have limited insight into the effects of their work; they need to be constantly reminded that change is inherently social.

One role that anthropologists can play is therefore to keep the developers under control. Mair wrote in her study of anthropology and development that one of the main roles of the social anthropologist is to 'beg the agents of development to keep their eyes open' (1984: 13) and to represent the interests and the discontent of those people passed over by the new order(s) created by economic progress. But Mair's view remains to some extent one of the anthropologist mediating between the developer and the developed along the inevitable path of progress. When she points out that the anthropologist can usefully warn developers of 'resistance likely to be met' (ibid.: 4), this is a far cry from the anthropologist as, ideally, a full participant in questioning development itself or facilitating the participation of people in those processes.

Anthropology has other types of contributions to make beyond being a mediator between the developers and those to be 'developed'. Anthropologists are trained sceptics: they tend to argue that situations and ideas are usually more complicated than is immediately apparent; they believe that no fact or detail is too trivial to be considered; they may prefer quality to quantity; they are rarely ready to offer conclusions or advice in terms of a straightforward course of action. All these qualities are of course of immense value in informing planned change, but they sit uneasily within the time-frames and priorities of the world of development practice. To some development practitioners, anthropologists are therefore an administrative nightmare, because the knowledge and ideas in which they deal seem to have very little practical applicability and, worse still, can raise endless problems. Yet the uneasiness and frustration sometimes created by the presence of an anthropologist can be harnessed in development work and is arguably anthropologists' greatest strength, if it can be deployed constructively.

As we have seen, anthropology can be used in the project setting for a number of purposes. Anthropologists are well equipped to monitor the process of project implementation, which in effect is the task of monitoring social change. [. . .] Anthropologists in the course of monitoring need to assess whether three-way communication is taking place between planners, implementors and population. This is needed to make projects needs-based and to reduce ethnocentric assumptions.

Anthropologists are trained to see beyond the immediate formal relationships which might exist. While their questions might appear irrelevant to technocrats, they often probe beyond what is immediately apparent. Are the project boundaries drawn too narrowly? For example, are there new or adapting sets of patron–client relationships which are being fed by the project and its resources? What are the distributional effects of the project? Finally, survey data can be supplemented with case studies, which capture dynamism and complexity and therefore add dimension to more static data collection.

On a directly practical level, anthropology has helped to provide a model, through its traditional participatory fieldwork methodology, of information gathering which is more sensitive to people. This not only improves the quality of the information needed by policy-makers and practitioners, but can increase the opportunities for local people to contribute more directly to the evolution of policies and programmes. The use of anthropological methodology in participatory techniques such as PRA is an example. In turn, anthropologists can question and thus help redesign such techniques, ensuring that they do not ossify into rigid exercises which have lost their meaning.

If anthropologists are to become involved in development work in the South, a number of practical issues need to be considered. Before turning to the question of ethics, let us consider these.

How Should Anthropologists Become Involved?

[. . .] One important indicator or warning sign which the anthropologist should look out for when considering a practical involvement is the history of a project. Has it been drawn up with the participation of an anthropologist, or is the anthropologist part of an attempt to 'fix up' a project which has run into trouble?

When working in a team, or with other organisations or government agencies, the anthropologist may need to keep in mind the lack of wider knowledge or misconceptions which can exist about anthropology during the work. An important part of such work will be a preparedness to discuss anthropological ideas and outlooks with members of an interdisciplinary team or with project staff or administrators. [. . .]

The anthropologist needs to be aware of the difference between the way academic anthropology is written up and presented and the more immediate requirements of project or agency reports and documents. Reports will have to be well structured, so that relevant sections can be read separately by those who wish to access information quickly. They should be clearly written, with unfamiliar anthropological terms avoided unless necessary. [. . .]

It is also important to be constructively critical: it makes little sense if the anthropologist fails to take responsibility for the practical implications of critical points. If certain assumptions or ideas have been shown to be false, alternatives can often be suggested which will create more appropriate courses of action. Many project staff will be pleased to experiment with new ideas, but will be frustrated by relentless negativity. A knowledge of the administrative culture in which many development initiatives take place is an essential prerequisite for this type of applied work.

The Ethics of Involvement

There can be little doubt that anthropologists can do much to change and improve the work of developers. Their involvement, however, remains deeply problematic. While setting out to reformulate and change from within, the danger is that anthropologists become profoundly compromised. No discussion of anthropology and development can therefore ignore the difficult issue of ethics [...]

One of the most complex questions for anthropologists concerns on what terms to get involved in development work. Little can be done if the project has been poorly designed or based on unfounded assumptions, and the 'legitimising role' of the anthropologist may indeed make matters worse rather than better. The involvement of the anthropologist will always be a matter of individual conscience, but informed choices can be made by asking some preliminary questions. At what stage is the anthropologist being asked to participate in a project? How much time will the anthropologist have to undertake the research? How much credibility will be given to the findings? By participating in development, does the anthropologist simply become part of the prevailing discourse and help to oil the 'anti-politics machine'?

Another set of ethical issues surrounds the roles of expatriates and nationals. This can lead to the loss of scarce local employment opportunities, and in the longer term may have implications for the development and strengthening of local educational and research institutions. [...] Expatriate researchers can easily undermine the work of local practitioners by taking jobs or by using local workers in subordinate positions. Foreign anthropologists need to take responsibility for developing, through their work, the abilities of local researchers to carry out applied and other research. The 'fly in, fly out' expert role is one most anthropologists would wish to avoid, except to provide general support, as such activities can weaken the practice of local research.

[...]

Cooption by Developmental Discourse

The increasing use of anthropological research by developers is to be applauded, but we must beware of our work being forced into narrow, institutionally defined boundaries, thus becoming part of the discourse which we should be objectively criticising. Since they may be funding it, the danger is that developers can dictate what type of research is carried out, and on what terms. [...]

In their insistence that research should be practically 'useful', developers usually presuppose that they know already what the most important issues are. But as we have seen, some of the most interesting anthropology of development does not simply ask questions about policy; it examines

change within its wider context. By insisting that the research agenda concentrates on certain issues and that findings are presented in a certain way, development may therefore absorb anthropology – potentially its most radical critic – into the dominant development discourse, which, give or take a few adjustments, remains unchanged.

This has already happened to various important concepts, which have been appropriated for development and watered down to the point of a grotesque parody. The use of the term 'participation' is a good example of the dangers, since it can easily be 'coopted' by those with power and influence. [...]

Participation all too easily slips into empty rhetoric, can serve the interests of the status quo and can readily lend itself to the fate of being 'veneered'.

Likewise, the insights of anthropologists working on gender relations have, in some cases, been reformulated to fit into the dominant discourse, thus becoming depoliticised and institutionally 'safe'. By creating posts for WID officers, or adding WID to the list of policy commitments, institutions may feel that they have dealt with the problem, when in reality the changes are little more than cosmetic. [...]

[...] Since most development work is carefully planned, fitted around bureaucratic tools such as the 'project framework', social change is often forced into the constraints of institutional agendas and phrases. Social development becomes an 'output' to be measured (usually through quantifiable criteria such as numbers of people trained, loans taken out or meetings attended). Likewise, research which points to potential problems in project implementation must be presented in report form, with practical recommendations or 'action points' listed. Reports which are too critical are condemned as being irrelevant or useless and are not acted upon, for they do not fit into the discourse (Ferguson, 1990:69). It would seem that anthropology is welcomed by some developers, but only on their terms.

Breaking Out of the Discourse

These tendencies must be continually guarded against by involved anthropologists, and it is here that those working within development and those studying development as discourse may have most to say to each other. We need to reassess endlessly how particular concepts are used, especially perhaps those which seem on the surface to be anthropologically friendly – whether social or community development, WID / GAD, participation, or whatever. This involves research not only into their meanings at the managerial or institutional level, but also into how they are transformed at different stages in the project chain. How do local government workers who have received gender training carry those concepts into their work? What does community development mean to the community development workers employed in projects? How do those participating in projects view things?

It is important to recognise that the agenda is not wholly predetermined. Anthropology can be used to re-radicalise those concepts which have been absorbed by it and stripped of their more progressive connotations: as Rahnema (1992: 122) argues, 'no-one learns who claims to know in advance'. The discourse is already changing to a degree, despite the dangers of cooption. Indeed, by highlighting the problems we do not wish to undermine the contribution of many dedicated professionals working within development agencies and NGOs who are actively engaged in changing it. Perhaps too, we need to be rather more confident. We urge our colleagues working within development agencies to think beyond the immediate constraints of their institutional culture. Are project frameworks really necessary? Must social issues always be treated as a poor relative, allowed to eat at the same table as the economists and technocrats, but only on their terms? Rew (1985) is right to point out the various skills which applied anthropologists must learn (working in a team and writing reports), but let us not be too subservient: the developers too must change.

Beyond 'Anthropologists as Experts'

Another way of moving forward is to ensure that anthropological insights and methods are not confined to a small elite group of experts. [...] As a way of seeing, and of working, anthropology does not have to be confined to experts from the North. Anthropology has the potential to be taken up, utilised and 'owned' by people in countries where talk about 'development' is high on the agenda. Anthropological insights need not be solely the property or the domain of academic or professional anthropologists, but can be opened up to those working in different contexts – such as within NGOs.

In Bangladesh, for example, the discipline is a new one, but is already providing a framework through which people can re-examine the development process and indigenise a local anthropology. There is a danger that academic neutrality may be discouraged and that the new field will be controlled by foreign donors, who, by paying for the work, will set its agendas and define the limits of its activities. Anthropologists in the South must not become mere social researchers, funded by foreigners, on the development projects underway in their own countries. They are generating ideas within their own societies and understand and express its needs, but they also need to be supported with opportunities to work elsewhere, in order to bring back ideas and insights. What can these anthropologists and other outsider anthropologists tell us about development issues in both the North and the South?

[...] Anthropological knowledge, and in particular anthropological methodologies, are readily accessible to the non-anthropologist and can be used by development practitioners and indeed everyone. While anthropology shows up the limitations of the popularly used survey methodology for reflecting social and economic realities, what can it offer instead?

The provision of PRA training provides an opportunity for public servants and NGO staff to examine their assumptions and their modes of working in order to make them more people-centred. Even if development projects were to disappear overnight, every society has ongoing relationships and situations in which people interact with outsiders and experts. For example, the agricultural extension worker from the local government office can either 'lord it' over the farmers, relying more on status than on an interest in understanding their possible needs, or she or he can work towards developing a more equal relationship in which a two-way exchange of information takes place, putting her or himself at the service of the clients. A nurse in a local health centre can either patronise his or her patients, or can take time to listen to their needs and develop lasting, two-way relationships. Such methodologies may be adapted or distorted or abused in the process, as when PRA becomes a means of legitimising existing practices with only cursory consultation or forced participation. But ultimately there is no 'proper' way of doing things. More broadly, this type of knowledge and methodology is also useful in its deployment in critical, oppositional, questioning roles, in questioning ethnocentric assumptions and economism.

Meanwhile, many grassroots organisations have been working anthropologically for several decades, without the involvement of experts. [...]

NGOs have developed approaches which may be changing the ways in which development is conceived and practised. Their fieldworkers may be drawn from the local community and may provide a sympathetic and accountable link with events and resources locally and more widely. They may be engaged in work which makes outside anthropologists less relevant, but both can have something to learn from each other. Social movements are also potential vehicles for change which may express local aspirations and initiatives. So far, few anthropologists have been involved in such initiatives as either researchers or activists, but this does not mean that potential roles do not exist, although the anthropologist may have to take sides and abandon some customary (and often illusory) detachment.

For the moment at least, the rhetoric of development and to some extent its practice is moving in directions which bring it closer to what might be termed 'anthropological' territory. [. . .] While the development arena provides anthropologists with a site that is rich in potential for analysing the ways power is exercised and change achieved in the post-modern world, it may also simultaneously contribute, as Johanssen has hinted (1992), to the reimagining of anthropology itself, as local political realites are moved centre-stage.

Conclusion

It would be ridiculous to suggest that anthropology holds all the solutions. Although it may be able to contribute to problematising and changing aspects of development discourse, there are far wider issues involved over which individual anthropologists and their methods have little influence. Ultimately, for the quality of people's lives in poorer countries to improve, global conditions must change. Poverty and inequality are products of a range of global conditions, of which development discourse is only one part. International trade, war, political oppression and so on are all of central importance. Anthropologists traditionally have had little to say about these: while they may comment upon their social and cultural consequences, with a few exceptions they are less practised in analysing them as interconnected phenomena. Instead, they tend to concentrate on the 'micro level' and on face-to-face relations.

Anthropology's contribution to positive post-developmental change is therefore part of a larger effort. But this does not mean that it is not worthwhile. [. . .] Development discourse is central to how the world is represented and controlled by those with the most power, and anthropology has much to say about it. [. . .] It tells us that any causal, engineering model of social change is bound to exclude and indeed repress the richness and diversity of people's lives. We have argued that anthropology offers no simple formula for bringing about positive change. Anthropology cannot bring to bear a set of practical tools to be applied as 'means to ends'.

Instead, anthropology promotes an attitude and an outlook: a stance which encourages those working in development to listen to other people's stories, to pay attention to alternative points of view and to new ways of seeing and doing. This outlook continually questions generalised assumptions that we might draw from our own culture and seek to apply elsewhere, and calls attention to the various alternatives that exist in other cultures. Such a perspective helps to highlight the richness and the diversity of human existence as expressed through different languages, beliefs and other aspects of culture. Anthropology tries to show the interconnectedness of social and economic life and the complex relationships which exist between people under conditions of change. Finally, anthropology encourages us to dig as deeply as possible, to go beyond what is immediately apparent, and to uncover as much of the complexity of social and economic life that we can.

The relationship between anthropology and development will never be a straightforward one. Anthropology cannot simply be put at the service of development or of 'the people', whoever they might be. What anthropology has to offer is a continuous questioning of the processes, assumptions and agencies involved in development. But while they do this, and while they stimulate others to do the same, anthropologists have a role to play in unpicking, analysing and changing development practice over time. There is therefore scope for anthropology to take part in this 'gradualist' challenge, because the problems which development has thrown up, as well as the problems which development seeks to solve, will not be changed or disappear overnight. We do not see the point of simply wishing them away or rejecting them as invalid.

Clearly anthropologists have a choice. [. . .] Anthropology exposes the limitations of so much which is done in the name of development – its ethnocentric assumptions, its expression of the imbalance of power, its self-delusion, its economic biases – while at the same time offering ideas for challenging constructively the world of development and suggesting how this can be changed. Are these changes possible, or is an involved anthropology only ever going to reproduce neocolonial discourses? Should we reject the project of development altogether? We are less pessimistic than this rejectionist position allows, and can see important roles for the anthropologist in reconstructing ideas and practice in order to overcome poverty and improve the quality of life across the world.

NOTE

1 Whatever the criteria for this are. It should be recognised that people's positioning as 'Northern' or 'Southern' is often far from fixed.

REFERENCES

Bordo, S. (1990) 'Feminism, post-modernism and gender-scepticism' in Nicholson, L., ed. *Feminism/Post-Modernism*. London: Routledge, pp. 133–53.

Di Leonardo, M. (1991) *Gender at the Crossroads of Knowledge: Feminist Anthropology in the Postmodern Era*. London: Macmillan.

Escobar, A. (1991) 'Anthropology and the development encounter: the making and marketing of development anthropology', *American Ethnologist* vol. 18, no. 4, pp. 658–81.

Ferguson, J. (1990) *The Anti-Politics Machine: 'Development', Depoliticisation, and Bureaucratic Power in Lesotho*. Cambridge: Cambridge University Press.

Johannsen, A.M. (1992) 'Applied anthropology and post-modernist ethnography', *Human Organisation* vol. 51, no. 1, pp. 71–81.

Mair, L. (1984) *Anthropology and Development*. London: Macmillan.

Malinoswki, B. (1922) *Argonauts of the Western Pacific*. London: Routledge and Kegan Paul.

Nicholson, L., ed. (1990) *Feminism/Post-Modernism*. London: Routledge.

Rahnema, M. (1992) 'Participation' in Sachs, W., ed. *The Development Dictionary: A Guide to Knowledge as Power*. London: Zed, pp. 116–32.

Rew, A. (1985) 'The organizational connection: multi-disciplinary practice and anthropological theory' in Grillo, R. and Rew, A., eds. *Social Anthropology and Development Policy* (ASA Monographs 23). London: Tavistock, pp. 185–98.

28

Village Intellectuals and the Challenge of Poverty

Elizabeth Isichei

"Why are blacks poor and whites rich? is one of the hardest questions to answer, and one which is put again and again by the younger generation."
(Aylward Shorter on East Africa, in 1985)[1]

[...] A study of the Shambaa of northern Tanzania refers to "Peasant Intellectuals,"[2] and the terminology is echoed in this chapter's title. While still expressed chiefly in metaphor, symbol, and myth, the sources to which we now turn embody conscious attempts to interpret experience and make it morally intelligible. Above all, what seemed to need explaining was Africa's poverty vis-à-vis the wealth and power of the West and its representatives. But there are many other dimensions in this search for understanding. One of the most striking is a widespread pattern in which past prophets were remembered, re-interpreted, or, even, invented. They are said to have foretold, in remarkable detail, the nature of the colonial experience. Perhaps, in some instances, these extraordinary intellectuals were historic figures, who understood, with striking insight, the ongoing historical processes affecting their diverse worlds. Alternatively, later traditions may have attributed new prophecies to historic figures. And some prophets may be later inventions – attempts to locate uncontrollable and overwhelming experiences within the sphere of African foreknowledge. The tide of colonial conquest could not be halted, but it had been anticipated.

Prophets

Prophets were the intellectuals of their societies, who described, often with extraordinary insight,

patterns of political and socio-economic change.[3] Ewenihi is remembered as a nineteenth-century Igbo seer, a member of the Aguinyi clan, who is thought to have anticipated, with striking accuracy, the shape of things to come. "He was said to have foretold the coming of the whiteman, telling the people that he 'saw them white and reflecting in the wilderness,' and that they would usurp the children of the clan." "Those quarrelling over political powers are merely fighting over another's property." He predicted the way in which the sale of land would replace traditional rights of usufruct, and the escalation of land values, saying that those who wanted land would need twenty thousand cowries. He anticipated the decline of traditional religion, when the gods would be left to starve to death, and those that survived would have hot oil put in their eyes.[4]

Of the many East African prophets said to have predicted the colonial experience, perhaps the most notable was the Fipa seer, Kaswa, from southern Tanzania, [who predicted] an age of cannibals and the victory of the cash nexus. [...]

He said: "There are monstrous strangers coming,
Bringing war, striking you unawares, relentlessly,
O you people, you're going to be robbed of your
  country."[5]

He is said to have foretold the way in which the aged would be left alone, as their children departed for the towns.

And he said: "The grasshoppers are your children,
And they are flying away, all of them!
You remain behind, old and dying, and to the very
  end they are not there! ... "

Kaswa said: "A person will clothe his whole body,
Even his eyes.
Everything will have its price...."[6]

In Shambaa, in northern Tanzania, a prophet foretold an expanded population, and a pattern of resettlement produced by road construction. [...]
There were similar prophets in Kenya. A Turkana diviner said in c. 1875, "I have seen a great vulture, coming down from the sky, and scooping up the land of Turkana in its talons."[7] A Kamba woman prophet, Syokimau, said people would come with skins like meat, who spoke like birds [that is, unintelligibly] and that there would be a long snake [the railway].[8] A number of Meru prophets, from the 1860s on, also foretold the long snake, in whose service warriors would dig like women.[9]
In the 1930s, when white ascendancy in Kenya seemed immovable, Jomo Kenyatta wrote of a Kikuyu prophet who foretold

that strangers would come to Gikuyuland from out of the big water, the colour of their body would resemble that of a small light-coloured frog... which lives in water, their dress would resemble the wings of butterflies; that these strangers would carry magical sticks which would produce fire.... The strangers... would later bring an iron snake [which] would spit fires and would stretch from the big water in the east to another big water in the west of the Gikuyu country.[11]

Railways were an important instrument of colonial control, a fact which these metaphors reflect; the snake is deadly, and many workers died in railway (or road) construction. These True Fictions contrast with the rhetoric of empire. In the early twentieth century, Winston Churchill visited East Africa. He called the Uganda railway "one slender thread of scientific civilisation, of order, authority and arrangement, drawn across the primeval chaos of the world."[12]
Prophets had real power to shape events, as colonial officials discovered. A woman prophet, Chanjiri, appeared in Malawi in 1907 and said

that she had a magic to spread darkness over the land where the white men lived and they would all disappear; therefore, there was no need to pay taxes. The people left their jobs and flocked to the woman. The Government at first did not take the matter seriously until it discovered that the tax returns had shown a shortage....[13]

Legends about Kupe, the magic mountain in Cameroon, published in 1930, froze popular perceptions at a particular moment in time.[14] Local sorcerers were given credit for the advent of the Europeans (in the interests of progress) and vied with them for the symbols of political supremacy. [...] The literate were said to possess "the ekong [sorcery] of the European," and a mission station was a halting place for sorcerers on their journey to Kupe. In their astral struggles for supremacy, black and white meet on equal terms. Black sorcerers emulate the feats of white technology and travel on astral trains. Europeans appear all-powerful, but are acting out a scenario determined by Africans. It was a different way of restoring African autonomy to recent history.
[...]

Prophetic Madness

In Africa, as elsewhere, prophecy is often close to madness – the familiar paradox of Shakespeare's King Lear. The insane are alienated from "reality" as others perceive it; standing outside society, they may understands its deficiencies more clearly. Having nothing to lose, they are sometimes empowered to utter a penetrating critique, which no one else has the insight or courage to provide. When Kaswa had completed his prophetic utterances, he disappeared into the earth in a place called Loss of Mind.[14] Ewenihi is remembered as insane, a consequence of the loss of his only son in a local war. [...] Aylward Shorter writes of a "madman," in a Tanzanian village, in late 1982, who, at a time of economic hardship, criticized government policies when others were afraid to do so.[15]
All this is mirrored in fiction. In Ouloguem's Le devoir de violence, the sorcerer Bouremi becomes mad and is able, for the first time, to denounce oppression. "[M]adness is a fine thing, a marvelous alibi, sweet and terrible."[16] [...]
In Tansi's L'anté-peuple, set in West Central Africa, insanity becomes a way of escaping from the intolerable oppression of the state.[17] The hero, once a Training College Principal, now disguised as a naked lunatic, assassinates a politician, but his action leads only to a wholesale massacre of the insane.[18]

A Remembrance of Things Past

While real or invented prophets perceived the shape of things to come, particular visions of moral economy were often formulated in terms of an imagined past. In Africa and elsewhere, the invention of a vanished Golden Age has often been used to critique the present. In the mid eighteenth century it was used to condemn the Atlantic slave trade.[19] Another nineteenth-century Igbo prophet called himself Restorer of the Primitive Style.[20]

The colonial era offered new opportunities and new freedoms. Some individuals became more prosperous, but growing socio-economic disparities led to the sense of tension and division that underlay the extraordinary proliferation of anti-witchcraft movements. Popular inventions of history described the erosion of a sense of community. [. . .]

The golden age has not always been located in the past. In the context of independence struggles, or even of a return to civilian rule in a military state, the future has often become the focus of reasonable and unreasonable hopes.

> Independence will mean that our women and children will be healthy, sickness and death will no longer be as they are now, and our villages will be crowded.[21]

They were soon disappointed. In 1974, the author of a letter to a Nigerian newspaper borrowed the eloquent words of T. E. Lawrence.

> We lived many lives in those swirling campaigns . . . yet when we had achieved, and the new world dawned, the old men came out again and took from us our victory, and remade it in the likeness of the former world they knew. . . . We stammered that we had worked for a new heaven and a new earth, and they thanked us very kindly and made their peace.[22]

In 1979, Nigerians hoped for great things from a return to civilian rule, and queued patiently to vote, on five successive Saturdays. Twenty years later, there was another return to civilian rule, and another election. An Igbo electrician said, "the whole process is irrelevant to me. . . . Politics is a pastime for rich businessmen and corrupt military men." Neo-traditional religion had come to fill the nurturing role once hoped for from the state. The custodian of an Igbo shrine said, "This is where people feel they get real help."[23]

Nothing speaks more eloquently of the disappointments of contemporary Africa than its silences. A Zambian mine worker said in the mid 1980s, "We black people are unable to speak of the future. We can only talk about the past."[24] In the late 1990s, a member of the Nigerian elite told a journalist, "Nigeria is the land of no tomorrow."[25]

The Problem of Poverty

The question perplexing village intellectuals above all others was that of Africa's poverty, vis-à-vis the West. [According to] one symbolic answer, Western goods were made by enslaved African souls for white sorcerers under the sea. Rodney's *How Europe Underdeveloped Africa* (1972) was extremely popular among students in Africa because it attempted to provide an explanation.

Many scattered village intellectuals have struggled with this question. Their narratives are the result of conscious reflection on the shape of history and its injustices. At their heart is a determination to make experience morally intelligible. [. . .] Scores of similar myths have been recorded, over hundreds of years, in West and West Central Africa.[26] The constant recreation of similar stories is as significant as the details of their content.

These commentaries on Europe's wealth and Africa's poverty are a form of bricolage, assembled from traditions at once indigenous and changing and from various kinds of encounters with strangers. Here I analyze only a small selection from the many instances known to me. They fall into four overlapping categories. The first explains, through stories of a primal choice, why Europeans are rich and Africans poor. The second category ascribes the wealth and power of Europeans to their Trickster qualities. The third consists of retold biblical narratives of apparently arbitrary preference. In the fourth category, the whites are denounced for avarice; in one compelling narrative, a cosmic rebel against God is also the king of the Europeans.

A Cosmic Choice

A black and a white brother – women rarely appear in these texts – take it in turns to select a symbolic object. The consequences of their decisions are momentous, but are concealed from them. The black brother has the first choice, reflecting either his seniority or God's special love for him. The white brother's share is a symbol of literacy.

In the earliest version of the myth, recorded in c.1700, the question which demanded explanation was why Europeans were slave-owners and Africans slaves. By the late nineteenth century, it seemed important to understand how a small minority of Europeans were able to establish and sustain the conquest states we call colonies. In the post-colony, the basic question endures – "Why are blacks poor and whites rich?"

These accounts are abundant, not only because they were so often reinvented, but also because Europeans had a particular interest in recording them. A hidden subtext is that Europeans perceived them as flattering, because of their explicit acknowledgment of white material and technical superiority. The German who recorded a Bakossi (Cameroon) myth in 1893 observed:

> We whites are not only more handsome and intelligent than the blacks. We also possess immense powers of witchcraft. And, most important of all, we need not work with our hands. All these advantages are thought to be an indication that God loves the whites more than the blacks.[27]

But if we look at the details of the myth he narrates, we find that white delusions of supremacy are rejected and Europeans are portrayed as mere middlemen between Africa and superior beings who

> live on the shore of the other world and are half human, half spirit. Their mental power allows them to make themselves invisible and to obtain whatever they want from God.... Now comes the commerce between the three! Actually, it is us, the whites, who have the role of middlemen. We whites rule over the islands and the sea, between this world of the blacks and the other world where the superior beings live. We carry on the trade between them both and make enormous profit from it.[28]

Eurocentric notions of white supremacy are explicitly rejected.

Myths about a momentous choice between symbolic commodities are adaptations of a much wider and probably ancient genre. In the tiny western Igbo polity of Agbor, a little-known story is told to explain its relative weakness vis-à-vis its great neighbor, Benin. Both kings were asked to make a momentous choice between two boxes. The king of Agbor chose one containing axes and cutlasses; the ruler of Benin was left with a box of snail shells filled with sand. He spread the sand to create dry land, and this explains his seniority.[29]

In the earliest account of symbolic choices made by Africans and Europeans, recorded in the Gold Coast in about 1700, Africans chose gold, leaving literacy for Europeans. "God granted their Request, but being incensed at their Avarice, resolved that the Whites should for ever be their Masters, and they obliged to wait on them as their slaves."[30]

A similar myth was recorded at the Asante court, in 1817. The European obtains paper and knowledge and learns how to build ships and embark on international commerce, accurately perceived as the key to white prosperity. African deprivation is due to "the blind avarice of their forefathers."[31] The poor are poor through their own fault. In a missionary version, the Europeans' reward is true religion.[32] In a text collected in Dahomey in the 1880s, Africans again choose gold, leaving literacy to Europeans; God then gives the whites the power to govern the blacks.[33] Now the consequence of black cupidity is colonial encroachment.

In a legend from Ivory Coast published early this century, the African chose a canoe, and the European, a steamer. The former went to a distant country, where his white brother brought him gifts – cloth, tobacco, and manufactured goods. He gave him livestock and chickens in return.

> The white replied, "But I have not sold anything to you, I have made you a gift." But the black did not understand, so his brother, in annoyance, said to him, "I wanted to give you a present, you have not accepted it, from now on, although you are my brother, when I bring you something, it will be as trade."[34]

The cash nexus governing the relations of black and white becomes the black's fault, the result of his refusal to accept a gift gracefully.

[...]

These West African narratives have many Central African counterparts. A merchant who traded on the Cabinda coast from 1869 to 1873 recorded a version where Mane [king] Pouta [Portugal, Europe] had two sons – Mane Kongo and Zonga.

> Zonga took paper, pens, a telescope, a gun, and powder. Mani Congo preferred copper bracelets, iron swords and bows and arrows.[35]

The brothers parted and Zonga crossed the ocean and became the ancestor of the Europeans.[36]

[...]

Stories of symbolic choices are still told in the post-colony. One was collected among the Balanta of Guinea-Bissau, in 1995. Here the choice was between a large bowl of food and a small plate – but a hoe went with the bowl, and a pen with the plate. The African chose the former, and the European the latter.[37] Again, there is the (implicit) condemnation of a fictitious black ancestor's greed, and the assertion of the crucial role of literacy.

A disquieting aspect of many of these stories is the way in which the African is marginalized. He is not merely mistaken, but also greedy and avaricious. Perhaps this is an example of the phenomenon described long ago by Fanon, where the colonized internalize the values of the colonizer. Another disconcerting aspect is the way in which agricultural tools become identified with subordination and suffering. Agriculture was at the heart of these communities' livelihoods and their traditional values. The symbolic importance of iron tools (and weapons) was mirrored in a multitude of rituals found across West and Central Africa. These narratives of symbolic choices reflect the relative deprivation of the peasant farmer, the marginalization and poverty of rural life, and the overpowering attraction of white-collar employment.

The Power of Literacy

The object(s) acquired by the African vary, but the European's share almost always includes a symbol of literacy, which is seen as the key to the progressive accumulation of knowledge and thus to power. Literacy often seemed to have a magical power of its own. Members of a dance society on the East African coast sang:

To be able to read and speak the language of Europe,
The gates of Heaven are opened for us.[38]

Alternatively the power and prosperity of the Europeans was ascribed to secret knowledge of a ritual, rather than technical, nature. Missionaries were associated with the superior technology of the whites, and with the military victories of colonial powers. It was at first hoped that they would share the secret ritual knowledge that made this possible. As time went on, and many Christians remained as poor as before, it was often believed that the missionaries were keeping this crucial information secret. The discovery that the Protestant Bible excluded the Apocrypha – and that all Bibles omit Gnostic tests such as the Gospel of Thomas – seemed to confirm this.

In the late 1950s, in Ghana, a society appeared "whose aim was to find out the wonder-working secret magics by means of which Jesus wrought miracles."[39] In the western Niger Delta, there is a tradition of "a lost Bible, far fuller and richer in content than the usual version in use, which was originally given.... to Isoko Christians, but was then taken away and either lost or destroyed by the missionaries."[40] A tract written in Gabon was called, *La Bible Secrète des noirs selon le Bouity* (The Secret Bible of the Blacks according to Bwiti).[41]

The Colonial Trickster

The archetypal Trickster of African story tellers is physically weak – Anansi the spider, among the Akan, the tortoise among the Igbo – but overcomes more powerful adversaries by his cunning. Often, the Trickster is greedy as well as duplicitous.

The power and wealth of Europeans were often explained by the fact that they had the qualities of Tricksters. The Fang of Gabon initially explained the material resources of the whites by identifying them with the ancestors or ascribing supernatural powers to them, as in the white sorcerers under the sea. Later, "there... appeared a tendency to assimilate them to the power of evil, and, in various myths, to ascribe their superiority to trickery and duplicity."[42] [...] In Swahili, the word for European is *Mzungu*. Its dictionary meanings include, "something wonderful, startling, surprising, ingenuity, cleverness, a feat, a trick, a wonderful device."[43] In Malagasy, Europeans are *vazaha*, a word which also means "crafty," and is, Bloch tells us, "a quality which is typical of Europeans and which is more feared than admired."[44]

[...]

Texts that identify colonial Europeans with Tricksters are a form of subversive discourse. Like stories of white sorcerers who enslave African souls under the sea, they embody a powerful critique of what they represent.

Biblical Echoes

The Hebrew Bible is full of instances of apparently arbitrary parental or divine preference, and many of the stories that explain the different fortunes of black and white appear to be influenced by biblical narratives or explicitly retell them. These narratives are reshaped, in an intricate process of bricolage, to such an extent that they are sometimes almost unrecognizable.

Often, the story retold is Genesis 9:20–28, where, after the Flood, Noah lay drunken and naked in his tent. Ham saw him and told his brothers, who, with their eyes averted, covered their father. When Noah found out, he cursed Ham's descendants, saying that they would be slaves.

In the 1880s, Bentley referred to the circulation of the story in the Kongo kingdom from the time of the earlier Catholic missionaries.[45] An (unbiblical) gloss to the effect that Africans are the descendants of Ham, condemned by Noah's curse to servitude, was used to justify slavery in the New World, and apartheid in South Africa. It may well have figured in missionary exegesis.

A bitter and eloquent version collected in Senegal in the late nineteenth century reflects the persistent tendency to marginalize the story's African protagonist. Noah's eldest son, Toubab, was white; his health was delicate but he was intelligent, with a particular talent for commerce (Europeans are called Toubab in modern francophone West Africa). The second son, Hassan, was brown and an expert pastoralist. The third, Samba, was "the colour of the Wolofs," that is, black. He was stronger than his brothers and an outstanding farmer, whose produce was often sold to Toubab in exchange for luxuries.

Noah died and left his wealth to be equally shared among his sons. While Samba slept in a drunken stupor, Toubab took Noah's valuables, including his cloth, firearms, and gunpowder, to sea in an ark, and settled elsewhere. Hassan took Noah's herds to the desert. When Samba awoke, he experienced a moment of despair, but soon consoled himself with brandy and tobacco.

> This is why, for a very long time, the whites have sailed on the sea, with the ark and valuables, and with qualities inherited from Toubab, making a lot of money from trade.
> This is why the Moors have fine herds and willingly disappear into the depths of the desert.
> This is why the blacks, who are the descendants of Samba, are always deceived by the whites and by the Moors, finding consolation for their sad condition only in tobacco and brandy.[46]

European prosperity is due to their ocean-going steamers and their resultant hegemony in international trade. Once more, the African is poor through his own fault.

An elaborate Kitawala (Watchtower) version of the Genesis stories of the Creation and the sons of Noah, collected in Zaire/Congo, was published in 1962. It is too long to paraphrase in its entirety, but an episode is significant. [. . .] In an extended and complex narrative, the black son is punished for unfilial behavior. But it is a black man who invents all the technological wonders of the western world. The white man enslaves him, and steals his secrets, part of a popular Kongo history of colonialism, in which Europeans used mission teaching and the violence of the colonial state to destroy both metal-working skills and indigenous medicine – so that the sick needed to consult foreign doctors, who sometimes enslaved their souls (echoes of the zombie motif). "Stories are told of

local geniuses who were prevented by the Belgians from making trucks or airplanes."[47] In the second issue of the Kongo newspaper, *Kongo Dieto*, in 1959, it was said,

> Our elders knew how to make iron tools, guns and many other things, but when [the Europeans] came to steal our freedom, the old [skills] disappeared.[48]

[. . .]

[. . .] Changes effected in biblical narratives reflect both the incorporation of motifs from local cultures and the oral and haphazard way in which they were encountered by those unable to read – in sermons, often at second or third hand.

The West Condemned

In many of these narratives, poverty, understandably enough, is seen as a punishment, and wealth and power as signs of divine favor. In some sources, however, the wealth of the whites is attributed to a Faustian pact, or a primal rebellion from God.

An officer who took part in a West African military expedition in 1891–2 recorded a conversation with his Wolof servant, Moussa N'Diaye, who asked, why, if France was so beautiful, were the French invading Africa?

> The devil knows that the whites have beautiful women; every year he comes to the edge of the hole, say the ignorant,[49] to the shore, say the well informed, like Moussa, and there he demands the most beautiful of our companions in return for wonderful inventions. And this is why we are in the Sudan. Having given our women to the devil, we are obliged to look for them elsewhere. The new whites who disembark each year are those who have just traded their wives for some new application of steam or electricity.... We are a colony of voluntary widowers, a colony of the victims of the love of progress.[50]

Here, a Faustian pact is made, not by a witch, but by Europeans. The technical achievements of the whites are paid for by the sacrifice of their wives, a choice of wealth in things rather than wealth in people.

[. . .] In Tanganyika, a Nyakusa song, recorded in the 1930s, contrasted Western avarice with the core values of the traditionalist and of the Christian.

> The chiefs, the chiefs to whom do they pray!
> To the shades! To the shades! . . .
> The Europeans, the Europeans to whom do they
>   pray?

To money! To money!...
The baptized, the baptized to whom do they pray?
To Jesus! to Jesus![51]

A popular Kongo song, published in 1963, ran:

> The White left Europe
> To get money.
> The White came to Africa
> In search of money.[52]

This is echoed in contemporary central African fiction. "Whites worshipped no other God but money."[53] A Yoruba invocation to Aje, god of wealth, is very similar:

> The white man who sailed across the sea to set up a tent
> Is driven by the desire to make money
> Like a deadly insect that bites people in the forest.[54]

In some texts, white prosperity is explained, and in others, it is condemned.

Conclusion

Legends which ascribe African poverty or colonial rule to the folly or greed of an African ancestor make uncomfortable reading, not least because they were welcomed by Europeans in the heyday of colonialism. The felt need to explain the unequal global distribution of resources was not peculiar to Africa. The story of the sons of Noah was also retold in the Pacific, where the descendants of Ham were banished to New Guinea or, alternatively, goods meant for Melanesians were stolen by white Tricksters. "Why are blacks poor and whites rich?" is as much a burning question in the Pacific as it is in East Africa. And if these various explanations seem unsatisfactory, this perhaps reflects both the inadequacy of other explanatory models, and the fact that the experts who analyze global injustice have not, as yet, provided solutions for it.

NOTES

1 Aylward Shorter, *Jesus and the Witch Doctor* (London, 1985), 72.

2 S. Feierman, *Peasant Intellectuals: Anthropology and History in Tanzania* (London, 1990).

3 For a discussion of African prophets, see "Introduction" in D. M. Anderson and D. H. Johnson (eds.), *Revealing Prophets* (London and Nairobi, 1995), 1–27.

4 Oral histories collected in Aguinyi by J. I. Ejiofor in 1972; extract in E. Isichei, *Igbo Worlds* (Basingstoke and Philadelphia, 1978), 198.

5 R. Willis, "Kaswa: Oral Traditions of a Fipa Prophet," *Africa* (1970): 253. The word translated as "monstrous strangers" has overtones of cannibalism.

6 Ibid., 253.

7 J. Lamphear, *The Scattering Time: Turkana Responses to Colonial Rule* (Oxford, 1992), 48.

8 J. Forbes Munro, *Colonial Rule and the Kamba* (London, 1975), 27 n. 3.

9 J. Fadiman, *When We Began, There Were Witchmen* (Berkeley, 1993), 101–102.

10 J. Kenyatta, *Facing Mount Kenya: The Tribal Life of the Gikuyu* (1938, London, 1953), 42; he names the seer as Mogo wa Kebiro, Muriuki as Cege wa Kibiru. G. Muriuki, *A History of the Kikuyu 1500–1900* (Nairobi and London, 1974), 137.

11 Winston Churchill, *My African Journey*, quoted in J. C. Gruesser, *White on Black* (Urbana and Chicago, 1992), 5.

12 Quoted in G. Shepperson, *Myth and Reality in Malawi* (Evanston 1966), 22.

13 J. Ittmann, "Der Kupe in Aberglauben der Kameruner," *Der Evangelische Heidenbote* (Basel, 1930), 77–80, 94–95, 111–13.

14 Willis, "Kaswa: Oral Traditions of a Fipa Prophet," 253–54.

15 A. Shorter, *Jesus and the Witchdoctor: An Approach to Healing and Wholeness* (London, 1985), 73. See also J. L. and J. Comaroff, "The Madman and the Migrant: Work and Labor in the Historical Consciousness of a South African People," *American Ethnologist* (1987): 191–209.

16 Y. Ouologuem, *Bound to Violence*, trans. R. Manheim (Oxford, 1971), 82.

17 Sony Labou Tansi, *The Antipeople*, trans. J. A. Underwood (London and New York, 1988), 155.

18 Ibid., 163–70.

19 W. Smith, *A New Voyage to Guinea* (London, 1744), 266, citing Charles Wheeler on the Gold Coast.

20 Church Misionary Society Archives (Consulted in London, now in Birmingham, Eng.) CA/3/037/86A, J. C. Taylor, journal entry, 23 Nov. 1864.

21 *Kongo Dieto* (Kinshasa) 25 Oct. 1959, quoted in W. MacGaffey, "The West in Congolese Experience," in P. D. Curtin (ed.), *Africa and the West* (Wisconsin, WI, 1972), 59.

22 Quoted in a letter to the editor, *The [Enugu, Nigeria] Renaissance*, 22 Jan. 1974.

23 A. Duval Smith, "Nigeria Votes out the Tricky and the Greedy," *The Independent on Sunday* (London), 28 Feb. 1999.

24 J. Ferguson, "The Country and the City on the Copperbelt," *Cultural Anthropology* (1992): 86.

25 K. Maier, *The House Has Fallen: Midnight in Nigeria* (New York, 2000), xviii.

26 There are numerous examples in V. Görög-Karady, *Noirs et blancs: leur image dans la litérature orale africaine; étude, anthologie* (Paris, 1976) and V. Görög, "*L'origine de l'inégalité des races: Étude de trente-sept contes africains,*" in *Cahiers d'Études africaines* (1968): 290–309.

27 F. Autenrieth, *Inner-Hochland von Kamerun* (Stuttgart-Basel, 1900), 44–6, quoted in H. Balz, *Where the Faith Has to Live: Studies in Bakossi Society and Religion* (Basel, 1984), 112. Balz's translation.

28 Ibid.

29 Chief Nwokoro Obuseh of Agbor, 30 Sept. 1979 (recorded by Peter Obue); similar versions were collected from a number of other informants.

30 W. Bosman, *A New and Accurate Description of the Coast of Guinea* (1705), 2nd ed. (London, 1967), 147.

31 T. E. Bowdich, *Mission from Cape Coast Castle to Ashante*, 3rd ed. (London, 1966), 261–62. See also A. B. Ellis, *The Tshi Speaking Peoples of the Gold Coast of West Africa* (London, 1887), 339.

32 A. J. N. Tremeane (compiler), J. Martin, diary extracts, *Man* (1912): 141.

33 E. Foà, *Le Dahomey* (Paris, 1885), 214.

34 G. Thomann, *Essai de manuel de la langue néoulé* (Paris, 1905), 129–32. I omit the first part of the story, which concerns European and African dining customs, to the detriment of the latter.

35 C. Jeannest, *Quatre Années au Congo* (Paris, 1883), 97–8.

36 Ibid., 98–9.

37 I owe this source to email from Walter Hawthorne on 13 Nov. 1996.

38 H. Lambert, "The Beni Dance Songs," *Swahili, Journal of the East African Swahili Committee* 33 (Dar es Salaam, 1962–3): 21, quoted in G. Shepperson, *Myth and Reality in Malawi* (Evanston, IL, 1966), 20.

39 M. Field, *Search for Security: An Ethno-Psychiatric Study of Rural Ghana* (London, 1960), 267–68.

40 S. Barrington-Ward, "The Centre Cannot Hold": Spirit Possession as Redefinition," in E. Fasholé-Luke et al. (eds.), *Christianity in Independent Africa* (London, 1978), 463–64.

41 J. Fernandez, "Fang Representations Under Acculturation," in P. Curtin (ed.), *Africa and the West* (Madison, WI, 1972), 27 n.52.

42 Ibid., 26.

43 *Standard Swahili-English Dictionary* (London, 1955) cited in T. Beidelman, "A Kaguru Version of the Sons of Noah: A Study in the Inculcation of the Idea of Racial Superiority," *Cahiers d'Études africaines* (1963): 477 n.14.

44 M. Bloch, *Placing the Dead* (London and New York, 1971), 31.

45 W. H. Bentley, *Pioneering on the Congo* (London, 1900), I: 251.

46 J. B. Berenger-Feraud, *Recueil de contes populaires de la Senegambie* (Paris, 1885; reprint, Nendeln, 1970), 77.

47 MacGaffey, "The West in Congolese Experience," 59.

48 *Kongo Dieto* (Kinshasa) 25 Oct. 1959, quoted in MacGaffey, "The West in Congolese Experience," 59.

49 Some believed that France was located in a huge hole in the sea.

50 A. Baratier, *A travers l'Afrique* (Paris, 1912), 138–39.

51 M. Wilson, *Communal Rituals of the Nyakusa* (London, 1959), epigraph.

52 G. Balandier, "Les mythes politiques de colonisation et de décolonisation en Afrique," *Cahiers internationaux de Sociologie* (1963): 90.

53 Tansi, *The Antipeople*, 26

54 Belasco, *The Entrepreneur as Cultural Hero*, 143; the last noun is "jungle," in Belasco's text.

29

Kerala: Radical Reform as Development in an Indian State

Richard W. Franke and Barbara H. Chasin

Kerala is more than a tiny exotic subtropical [state] of the world's second-most-populous country. It is a region in which radical reforms over the past several decades have brought about some of the world's highest levels of health, education, and social justice. Kerala is *an experiment in radical reform as a modern development strategy.*

Kerala is overwhelmingly poor. If it were a separate country, it would be the ninth poorest in the world, with a per capita income of only $182 in 1986. Despite its poverty, Kerala displays a set of unusually high development indicators [. . .], and stands out among low-income countries and in comparison with the rest of India. [For example, per capita GNP (in 1986 dollars) was $182 in Kerala, $290 in India, $200 in countries other than China and India that the World Bank designates as "low income," and $17,480 in the United States. Adult literacy in 1986 was 78 percent in Kerala and 43 percent in India. Life expectancy was 68 years in Kerala and 57 in India. Infant mortality was 27 per 1,000 births in Kerala and 86 per 1,000 in India. The birth rate in Kerala was 22 per 1,000 population and 32 per 1,000 in India.] These particular indicators are so important because – except for GNP – they all measure things that must be available to wide sections of the population to show up statistically. The GNP per capita is an average of *all* income divided by the number of persons. If wealth is highly concentrated in the hands of a few, the average could be high while most people have little. But the literacy rate can only improve as more and more people learn to read and write. Average life expectancy will also not go up much if only the elite live longer, because even *they* can only live about 75 to 80 years no matter how rich they may be.

Similarly, infant mortality and birth rates change little unless large numbers have received the benefits of modern medicine. Thus, these four indicators reliably measure the impact of social and economic development as it spreads to large sections of the population.

Kerala's achievements are not limited only to a *general* expansion of education and health care. One of the striking features of the state is that quality of life benefits are fairly equally distributed among men and women, urban and rural areas, and low and high castes [. . .].

Literacy, for example, exhibits a 9 point spread between males and females in Kerala, while for India as a whole the difference is 22 points in favor of males. Urban India is nearly twice as literate as the rural areas, while in Kerala the disparity is only 76 percent vs. 69 percent. Kerala's low caste population is now as literate as India's urban people, while low castes in the nation as a whole are still nearly 80 percent illiterate. Even for tribal groups living mostly in the mountains, literacy is nearly twice the all-India average, although it remains far below the level of Kerala's other groups. In Kerala tribal groups account for 1 percent of the state's population, while for India as a whole they make up nearly 8 percent. Thus, Kerala's shortcoming in this category has less absolute impact than in the country as a whole.

Looking at infant mortality and birth rates, we see that rural areas in Kerala are only slightly behind the urban centers, where medical care is easier to provide. For India as a whole, urban–rural differences are especially severe in mortality, with the incredibly high figure of 124 (more than one in ten) infants dying before they reach the age of one year. In fact, Kerala's *rural* infant mortality rate is about one third less than India's overall *urban* rate, a remarkable achievement.

A different way of looking at Kerala's development achievements, comes from a series of studies done by various Indian agencies on productivity and basic services. In agriculture, Kerala ranks first among all Indian states in the rupees value of output per unit of land area. In addition, the state is first in India on fifteen of twenty measures of basic services within two or five kilometers of villages and very high on five others. [These include the percentage of (1) villages with all-weather roads within two kilometers (98 percent as compared with 48 percent in India as a whole); (2) secondary schools (99 percent as opposed to 44 percent in India); and health dispensaries (91 percent compared with 25 percent in India as a whole). Ninety-seven percent of Kerala villages had electricity in the late 1970s, as compared with 33 percent in India as a whole.] In short, Kerala stands above other Indian states in providing basic services to its people, despite the fact that in 1980–81, it ranked seventh among 22 Indian states with a per capita income of 1,421 rupees versus the all-India average of 1,559 rupees.

Kerala in the Development Debate

Why are all these figures so important? Of course, their foremost meaning is to the people of Kerala, who benefit from them. But the data have implications also at the level of international development studies, where Kerala's achievements assume a great importance. Let us briefly summarize the leading points of view on how third world countries can develop, so that we can look both more closely and more broadly at the complex reality that underlies Kerala's statistical profile.

In the forty-year history of development theory, numerous ideas have been suggested. The various writings seem to boil down to four major approaches: growth and modernization theory, basic needs theory, appropriate technology theories, and radical and revolutionary theories. Each of these approaches has several variants. We shall therefore summarize only the main features along with the most important subtheories.

Growth and modernization theory

The earliest and still most widely accepted theory of development in the United States is based on the success of Western industrial capitalism. If only the poor countries can get their economies to grow and modernize, they will become like us,

wealthy and developed. One group of modernizers has looked for cultural or psychological reasons for the continuing poverty in the third world. Are peasants economically irrational? Do non-Western peoples lack the individualistic, achievement orientation that helped produce modern capitalism? Are third world cultures sufficiently rationalist and scientific to create modern economies?

A second and more influential group of modernizers rejects the idea of cultural limitations. According to this subgroup, third world people are as rational and can become as individualistic and achievement oriented as anyone else. What is needed is sufficient capital, infrastructure, and management education to stimulate their economies. Growth and modernization theories have been popular among establishment economists and other social scientists in the United States and Western Europe.

But what about the poor? According to the mainstream of modernization theory, the underdeveloped nations can follow the approximate path of the already wealthy. This means that in the earliest stages of economic growth, inequality and poverty might actually *increase* (as happened in nineteenth-century Europe), but as growth continues, distribution will become more just. This is the subtheory of equitable growth. Advocates of this approach view Taiwan and South Korea as examples of the success of their theories. [. . .] From Kerala's low per capita GNP figure we can see that it does not conform to any of these approaches.

Basic needs and special targeting

Many experts have demanded a response to the glaring fact that despite a lot of economic growth in the poor countries in the past forty years, enormous segments of their populations have remained in abysmal poverty. Basic needs theory is the response. According to this theory, we need to focus on "first things first"[1] by targeting certain assistance to the very poorest to "relieve as quickly as is possible absolute poverty . . . [and] . . . to meet the needs of all in terms . . . such as food, clothing, shelter and fuel."[2] Basic needs theory has become popular among international lending agencies such as the World Bank and AID, the Agency for International Development, as a supplement, but not an alternative, to growth and modernization theory.

A recent further modification of basic needs is the theory of the "ultrapoor." Here it is argued that development is proceeding rather well in the poor countries in general, but certain groups are being bypassed and could be left out entirely. Because of urban bias in development strategies, nearly all of the very poorest are found in the vast rural areas of the third world. They are so poor and so deprived of basic productive assets that special targeting efforts are required to reach them. Thus, normal growth and modernization should continue, but extra programs should be initiated to reach those who are not benefiting from the growth.[3] Basic needs experts see themselves as the agents of the redistribution that growth and modernization theory await in the future.

[. . .] We might conclude that Kerala supports the basic needs theory. However, Kerala's achievements result not primarily from a few enlightened policy makers with humane ideas and a lot of foreign aid. Instead, its achievements have been produced by a redistribution of wealth brought about by the organized strength and militant activity of poor people allied with committed and often self-sacrificing radicals from higher-income groups.

Appropriate technology

"Small is beautiful" theories focus on the need to give development aid that can be used directly by the people most in need. China's barefoot doctors and inexpensive biogas plants using animal waste to produce methane gas and fertilizer are seen as more effective in the short run *and* more environmentally sound in the long run than high-tech medical centers or huge hydroelectric plants to generate industrial power. Appropriate technology appeals to wealthy country ecology advocates, but many in the poor countries argue that large-scale industrial development is the only real means to the higher standards of living they desire.[4] Although Kerala's reformers are experimenting with some appropriate technologies such as low-cost smokeless ovens to reduce health risks from rural kitchens, the state is not a major center of this development approach.

Radical and revolutionary theories

These have developed largely in response to the apparent failures of growth and modernization theory. According to these approaches, capitalism itself, though once a source of development for today's rich countries, now stands in the way of that very development for third world nations. One variation is called dependency theory or world systems theory. Its advocates argue that the heavy dependency of the poor countries on the rich for technology and investment distorts their economies so that they are always kept behind the wealthy. A more directly Marxist version is the theory of imperialism in which it is argued that the wealthy countries actually *extract* income and resources from underdeveloped countries through repatriating profits to the wealthy countries and maintaining repressive military regimes in the poor countries to keep workers and peasants from exercising political power. This relationship is the original cause of rich country wealth built on the exploitation of small farmers and workers in the third world. According to this view, socialist revolution and a fundamental break with the international capitalist world is the main prerequisite to effective development. Such theorists point to nations such as Cuba and China where substantial quality-of-life improvements have taken place without the large-scale growth in per capita GNP advocated by the modernization school. A modified version in the Soviet Union [was] called noncapitalist development. It emphasizes the need to develop the public sector in the poor countries without necessarily having a socialist revolution. Like the more revolutionary versions, this perspective also supports radical reforms in the distribution of wealth and power where possible. Kerala has not had a socialist revolution, but its large and well-organized peasant and worker movements make it an example of the radical-revolutionary approach.

The Redistribution Debate

Within the broad development debate a single issue has come to dominate most writings: which is more effective, growth or redistribution? Although in a perfect world one might wish to have both, it seems to many that the two goals are usually incompatible. Governments must choose whether to proceed with generating more economic output through stimulating capitalist enterprise or to dampen growth by redistributing wealth and then undertaking some form of government-sponsored investment.

Advocates of both positions can find strong support in the data. Research shows overwhelmingly that higher levels of income generally produce longer life, more education, fewer infant deaths, and the like. This seems to close the debate in favor of growth. But studies also show that for any given level of average per capita income countries choosing redistribution (mostly socialist) provide substantially better education, longer life, lower infant mortality, etc., than do those choosing growth alone. The advantages of redistribution are relatively greater in countries with the lowest per capita incomes.[5]

In the redistribution debate, Kerala's experience takes on special significance. Little growth has occurred and per capita income is very low. The state has not had a socialist revolution, but Kerala's people have organized and struggled for basic reform policies that resemble many of the socialist countries. [...]

[...] Only three underdeveloped countries [Taiwan and both Koreas] have succeeded in achieving both growth and redistribution [...]. Many, including the countries of Latin America, the Middle East, and Southeast Asia, have achieved considerable growth, but have had little or no redistribution [...]. Several, including some of the world's least developed countries, have failed on both counts [most of Africa and South Asia]. Of the small number of cases representing substantial redistribution with little growth in per capita GNP, two – China and Cuba – have experienced large-scale revolutions and require separate consideration. This leaves only Tanzania, Sri Lanka, and Kerala to represent the effects of choosing redistribution as a primary means to development, while remaining broadly within the capitalist world system.

Kerala's Special Political Circumstances

While development theory usually focuses on the nation-state as its unit of analysis, Kerala is one of twenty-two states within the Indian federal system. States in India have substantial administrative powers, but they are ultimately under the control of the powerholders in New Delhi. India has so far not had a Communist or Left Front government and many of Kerala's reforms have been blunted by policies from the center. The most important of these was the 1959 dismissal by the president of India of Kerala's first Communist government, elected in 1957.[6] This delayed and undermined [...] radical land reform [...]. On at least three occasions the central government manipulated food supplies to undercut left-wing governments.[7] During Indira Gandhi's "Emergency" of the mid-1970s, hundreds of leftist activists were arrested despite their decades-long commitment to democratic and parliamentary politics.[8]

[More] recently, Kerala may have been subjected to manipulations of its finances and development budget by the antileft government of Rajiv Gandhi.[9] Kerala's achievements have thus been accomplished without the state power usually associated with revolutionary governments. This makes Kerala especially relevant to local organizers and reformers in third world countries where they cannot hope for an immediate opportunity to hold state power.

What Is Redistribution?

Redistribution can include many types of programs and policies. The most radical and far-reaching involve government seizure of private assets such as land and factories and the redistribution of surplus through wage controls and strict limits on private accumulation of wealth. Less profound reorganization involves massive public health and welfare schemes to benefit the poorest groups. The typical package of redistribution policies includes land reform, price controls on food and other necessities, public housing, free or inexpensive medical care, expanded educational services, and any number of special programs to increase social and economic mobility among the poorest groups. Kerala has undertaken virtually all of these policies as keystones of its approach to development.

How successful has Kerala been? The state's people live longer, are better educated, and have better access to health care than almost any population [in the Middle East, South and Southeast Asia, the Pacific Islands, and most of Latin America and Africa which include the majority of the world's people. ...]

NOTES

1 Streeten et al. 1981.
2 Webster 1990:34.
3 Lipton 1977, 1988.
4 Schumacher 1973; Webster 1990:169–187.
5 Cereseto and Waitzkin 1988. The authors of this article contrasted one hundred capitalist countries with thirteen socialist countries and ten recent revolutionary countries grouped into five income categories on ten major development indicators.
6 Nossiter 1988:74–76.
7 Sathyamurthy 1985:183, 197, 238.
8 Sathyamurthy 1985:315; Nossiter 1982:258; Nossiter 1988:99.
9 Menon 1988:5.

REFERENCES

Cereseto, Shirley, and Howard Waitzkin. 1988. Economic development, political-economic system, and the physical quality of life. *Journal of Public Health Policy*, Spring 1988:104–120.

Lipton, Michael. 1977. Why *Poor People Stay Poor: Urban Bias in World Development*. Cambridge: Harvard University Press.

——1988. *The Poor and the Poorest: Some Interim Findings*. The World Bank. Discussion Paper No. 25. Washington, D. C.

Menon, V. Viswanatha. 1988. *Budget Speech 1988–89*. Trivandrum: Government of Kerala.

Nossiter, T. J. 1982. *Communism in Kerala: A Study in Political Adaptation*. Delhi: Oxford University Press.

——1988. *Marxist State Governments in India*. London: Pinter Publishers.

Sathyamurthy, T. V. 1985. *India Since Independence: Studies in the Development of the Power of the State. Volume 1: Centre-State Relations, the Case of Kerala*. Delhi: Ajanta.

Schumacher, E. F. 1973. *Small is Beautiful: Economics as if People Mattered*. New York: Harper and Row.

Streeten, Paul, Shahid Javed Burki, Mahbub Ul Haq, Norman Hicks, and Frances Stewart. 1981. *First Things First: Meeting Basic Human Needs in Developing Countries*. New York: Oxford University Press. Published for the World Bank.

Webster, Andrew. 1990. *Introduction to the Sociology of Development*. London: The Macmillan Press Ltd. Second Edition.

30

What Was Socialism, and Why Did It Fall?

Katherine Verdery

The startling disintegration of Communist Party rule in Eastern Europe in 1989, and its somewhat lengthier unraveling in the Soviet Union between 1985 and 1991, rank among the century's most momentous occurrences. [...]

What Was Socialism?

The socialist societies of Eastern Europe and the Soviet Union differed from one another in significant respects – for instance, in the intensity, span, and effectiveness of central control, in the extent of popular support or resistance, and in the degree and timing of efforts at reform. Notwithstanding these differences within "formerly existing socialism," I follow theorists such as Kornai in opting for a single analytical model of it.[1] The family resemblances among socialist countries were more important than their variety, for analytic purposes, much as we can best comprehend French, Japanese, West German, and North American societies as variants of a single capitalist system. Acknowledging, then, that my description applies more fully to certain countries and time periods than to others. I treat them all under one umbrella.

For several decades, the analysis of socialism has been an international industry, employing both Western political scientists and Eastern dissidents. Since 1989 this industry has received a massive infusion of new raw materials, as once-secret files are opened and translations appear of research by local scholars (especially Polish and Hungarian) into their own declining socialist systems.[2] My taste in such theories is "indigenist": I have found most useful the analyses of East Europeans concerning the world in which they

lived. The following summary owes much to that work, and it is subject to refinement and revision as new research appears.[3] [...]

Production

[...]

[Despite the image of totalitarian power, socialist states were relatively weak. Their] fragility begins with the system of "centralized planning," which the center neither adequately planned nor controlled. Central planners would draw up a plan with quantities of everything they wanted to see produced, known as targets. They would disaggregate the plan into pieces appropriate for execution and estimate how much investment and how many raw materials were needed if managers of firms were to fill their targets. Managers learned early on, however, that not only did the targets increase annually but the materials required often did not arrive on time or in the right amounts. So they would respond by bargaining their plan: demanding more investments and raw materials than the amounts actually necessary for their targets. Every manager, and every level of the bureaucracy, padded budgets and requests in hopes of having enough, in the actual moment of production. (A result of the bargaining process, of course, was that central planners always had faulty information about what was really required for production, and this impeded their ability to plan.) Then, if managers somehow ended up with more of some material than they needed, they hoarded it. Hoarded material had two uses: it could be kept for the next production cycle, or it could be exchanged with some other firm for something one's own firm lacked. These exchanges or barters of material were a crucial component of behavior within centralized planning.

A result of all the padding of budgets and hoarding of materials was widespread shortages, for which reason socialist economies are called economies of shortage.[4] Shortages were sometimes relative, as when sufficient quantities of materials and labor for a given level of output actually existed, but not where and when they were needed. Sometimes shortages were absolute, since relative shortage often resulted in lowered production, or – as in Romania – since items required for production or consumption were being exported. The causes of shortage were primarily that people lower down in the planning process were asking for more materials than they required and then hoarding whatever they got. Underlying their behavior was what economists call soft budget constraints – that is, if a firm was losing money, the center would bail it out. In our own economy, with certain exceptions (such as Chrysler and the savings and loan industry), budget constraints are hard: if you cannot make ends meet, you go under. But in socialist economies, it did not matter if firms asked for extra investment or hoarded raw materials; they paid no penalty for it.

A fictitious example will help to illustrate – say, a shoe factory that makes women's shoes and boots. Central planners set the factory's targets for the year at one hundred thousand pairs of shoes and twenty thousand pairs of boots, for which they think management will need ten tons of leather, a half ton of nails, and one thousand pounds of glue. The manager calculates what he would need under ideal conditions, if his workers worked consistently during three eight-hour shifts. He adds some for wastage, knowing the workers are lazy and the machines cut badly; some for theft, since workers are always stealing nails and glue; some to trade with other firms in case he comes up short on a crucial material at a crucial moment; and some more for the fact that the tannery always delivers less than requested. The manager thus refuses the plan assigned him, saying he cannot produce that number of shoes and boots unless he gets thirteen rather than ten tons of leather, a ton rather than a half-ton of nails, and two thousand rather than one thousand pounds of glue. Moreover, he says he needs two new power stitchers from Germany, without which he can produce nothing. In short, he has bargained his plan. Then when he gets some part of these goods, he stockpiles them or trades excess glue to the manager of a coat factory in exchange for some extra pigskin. If leather supplies still prove insufficient, he will make fewer boots and more shoes, or more footwear of small size, so as to use less leather; never mind if women's feet get cold in winter, or women with big feet can find nothing to wear.

With all this padding and hoarding, it is clear why shortage was endemic to socialist systems, and why the main problem for firms was not whether they could meet (or generate) demand but whether they could procure adequate supplies. So whereas the chief problem of economic actors in Western economies is to get profits by selling things, the chief problem for socialism's economic actors was to procure things. Capitalist firms compete with each other for markets in which they will make a profit; socialist firms competed to maximize their bargaining power with suppliers higher up. In our society, the problem is other sellers, and to outcompete them you have to befriend the buyer. Thus our clerks and shop owners smile and give the customer friendly service because they want business; customers can be grouchy, but it will only make the clerk try harder. In socialism, the locus of competition was elsewhere: your competitor was other buyers, other procurers; and to outcompete them you needed to befriend those higher up who supplied you. Thus in socialism it was not the clerk – the provider, or "seller" – who was friendly (they were usually grouchy) but the procurers, the customers, who sought to ingratiate themselves with smiles, bribes, or favors. The work of procuring generated whole networks of cozy relations among economic managers and their bureaucrats, clerks and their customers. We would call this corruption, but that is because getting supplies is not a problem for capitalists: the problem is getting sales. In a word, for capitalists salesmanship is at a premium; for socialist managers, the premium was on acquisitionsmanship, or procurement.

[...] Among the many things in short supply in socialist systems was labor. Managers hoarded labor, just like any other raw material, because they never knew how many workers they would need. Fifty workers working three eight-hour shifts six days a week might be enough to meet a firm's targets – *if* all the materials were on hand all month long. But this never happened. Many of those workers would stand idle for part of the month, and in the last ten days when most of the materials were finally on hand the firm would need 75 workers working overtime to complete the plan. The manager therefore kept 75 workers on the books, even though most of the time he needed fewer; and since all other managers were doing the same, labor was scarce. This provided a convenient if unplanned support for the regimes' guaranteed employment.

An important result of labor's scarcity was that managers of firms had relatively little leverage over their workers. Furthermore, because supply shortages caused so much uncertainty in the production process, managers had to turn over to workers much control over this process, lest work come to a standstill. That is, structurally speaking, workers under socialism had a somewhat more powerful position relative to management than do workers in capitalism. Just as managers' bargaining with bureaucrats undercut central power, so labor's position in production undercut that of management.

More than this, the very organization of the workplace bred opposition to Party rule. Through the Party-controlled trade union and the frequent merger of Party and management functions, Party directives were continually felt in the production process – and, from workers' viewpoint, they were felt as unnecessary and disruptive. Union officials either meddled unhelpfully or contributed nothing, only to claim credit for production results that workers knew were their own. Workers participated disdainfully – as sociologist Michael Burawoy found in his studies of Hungarian factories – in Party-organized production rituals, such as work-unit competitions, voluntary workdays, and production campaigns; they resented these coerced expressions of their supposed commitment to a wonderful socialism.[5] Thus instead of securing workers' consent, workplace rituals sharpened their consciousness and resistance. Against an official "cult of work" used to motivate cadres and workers toward fulfilling the plan, many workers developed an oppositional cult of nonwork, imitating the Party bosses and trying to do as little as possible for their paycheck. Cadres often found no way around this internal sabotage, which by reducing productivity deepened the problems of socialist economies to the point of crisis.

[...]

Surveillance and paternalistic redistribution

In each country, some equivalent of the KGB was instrumental in maintaining surveillance, with varying degrees of intensity and success. Particularly effective were the Secret Police in the Soviet Union, East Germany, and Romania, but networks of informers and collaborators operated to some extent in all. These formed a highly elaborate "production" system parallel to the system for producing goods – a system producing paper, which contained real and falsified histories of the people over whom the Party ruled. Let us call the immediate product "dossiers," or "files," though the ultimate product was political subjects and subject dispositions useful to the regime. This parallel production system was at least as important as the system for producing goods, for producers of files were much better paid than producers of goods. [...]

The work of producing files (and thereby political subjects) created an atmosphere of distrust and suspicion dividing people from one another. One never knew whom one could trust, who might be informing on one to the police about one's attitudes toward the regime or one's having an American to dinner. Declarations might also be false. Informers with a denunciation against someone else were never asked what might be their motive for informing; their perhaps-envious words entered directly into constituting another person's file – thus another person's sociopolitical being. Moreover, like all other parts of the bureaucracy, the police too padded their "production" figures, for the fact of an entry into the file was often more important than its veracity.[6] [...]

If surveillance was the negative face of these regimes' problematic legitimation, its positive face was their promises of social redistribution and welfare. At the center of both the Party's official ideology and its efforts to secure popular support was "socialist paternalism," which justified Party rule with the claim that the Party would take care of everyone's needs by collecting the total social product and then making available whatever people needed – cheap food, jobs, medical care, affordable housing, education, and so on. Party authorities claimed, as well, that they were better able to assess and fill these needs than were individuals or families, who would always tend to want more than their share. Herein lay the Party's paternalism: it acted like a father who gives handouts to the children as he sees fit. The Benevolent Father Party educated people to express needs it would then fill, and discouraged them from taking the initiative that would enable them to fill these needs on their own. The promises – socialism's basic social contract – did not go unnoticed, and as long as economic conditions permitted their partial fulfillment, certain socialist regimes gained legitimacy as a result. But this proved impossible to sustain.

[...]

The promise of redistribution was an additional reason, besides my earlier argument about shortages, why socialism worked differently from capitalism. Socialism's inner drive was to accumulate not profits, like capitalist ones, but distributable resources. This is more than simply a drive for autarchy, reducing dependency on the outside: it aims to increase dependency of those within. Striving to accumulate resources for redistribution involves things for which profit is totally irrelevant. In capitalism, those who run lemonade stands endeavor to serve thirsty customers in ways that make a profit and outcompete other lemonade stand owners. In socialism, the point was not profit but the relationship between thirsty persons and the one with the lemonade – the Party center, which appropriated from producers the various ingredients (lemons, sugar, water) and then mixed the lemonade to reward them with, as it saw fit. Whether someone made a profit was irrelevant: the transaction underscored the center's paternalistic superiority over its citizens – that is, its capacity to decide who got more lemonade and who got less.

Controlling the ingredients fortified the center's capacity to redistribute things. But this capacity would be even greater if the center controlled not only the lemons, sugar, and water but the things they come from: the lemon trees, the ground for growing sugar beets and the factories that process them, the wells and the well-digging machinery. That is, most valuable of all to the socialist bureaucracy was to get its hands not just on resources but on resources that generated *other* usable resources, resources that were themselves further productive. Socialist regimes wanted not just eggs but the goose that lays them. Thus if capitalism's inner logic rests on accumulating surplus value, the inner logic of socialism was to accumulate means of production.

The emphasis on keeping resources at the center for redistribution is one reason why items produced in socialist countries so often proved uncompetitive on the world market. Basically, most of these goods were not being made to be sold competitively: they were being either centrally accumulated or redistributed at low prices – effectively given away. Thus whether a dress was pretty and well made or ugly and missewn was irrelevant, since profit was not at issue: the dress would be "given away" at a subsidized price, not sold. In fact, the whole point was *not* to sell things: the center wanted to keep as much as possible under its control, because that was how it had redistributive power; and it wanted to give away the rest, because that was how it confirmed its legitimacy with the public. Selling things competitively was therefore beside the point. So too were ideas of

"efficient" production, which for a capitalist would enhance profits by wasting less material or reducing wages. But whatever goes into calculating a profit – costs of material or labor inputs, or sales of goods – was unimportant in socialism until very late in the game. Instead, "efficiency" was understood to mean "the full use of existing resources," "the maximization of given capacities" rather than of results, all so as to redirect resources to a goal greater than satisfying the population's needs. In other words, what was rational in socialism differed from capitalist rationality. Both are stupid in their own way, but differently so.

Consumption

Socialism's redistributive emphasis leads to one of the great paradoxes of a paternalist regime claiming to satisfy needs. Having constantly to amass means of production so as to enhance redistributive power caused Party leaders to prefer heavy industry (steel mills, machine construction) at the expense of consumer industry (processed foods, or shoes). After all, once a consumer got hold of something, the center no longer controlled it; central power was less served by giving things away than by producing things it could continue to control. The central fund derived more from setting up a factory to make construction equipment than from a shoe factory or a chocolate works. In short, these systems had a basic tension between what was necessary to legitimate them – redistributing things to the masses – and what was necessary to their power – accumulating things at the center. The tension was mitigated where people took pride in their economy's development (that is, building heavy industry might also bring legitimacy), but my experience is that the legitimating effects of redistribution were more important by far.

Each country addressed this tension in its own way. For example, Hungary after 1968 and Poland in the 1970s gave things away more, while Romania and Czechoslovakia accumulated things more; but the basic tension existed everywhere. The socialist social contract guaranteed people food and clothing but did not promise (as capitalist systems do) quality, ready availability, and choice. Thus the system's mode of operation tended to sacrifice consumption, in favor of production and controlling the products. This paradoxical neglect of consumption contributed to the long lines about which we heard so much (and we heard about them, of course, because we live in a system to which consumption is crucial).

In emphasizing this neglect of consumption as against building up the central resource base, I have so far been speaking of the *formally* organized economy of socialism – some call it the "first" or "official" economy. But this is not the whole story. Since the center would not supply what people needed, they struggled to do so themselves, developing in the process a huge repertoire of strategies for obtaining consumer goods and services. These strategies, called the "second" or "informal" economy, spanned a wide range from the quasi-legal to the definitely illegal.[7] In most socialist countries it was not illegal to moonlight for extra pay – by doing carpentry, say – but people doing so often stole materials or illegally used tools from their workplace; or they might manipulate state goods to sell on the side. Clerks in stores might earn favors or extra money, for example, by saving scarce goods to sell to special customers, who tipped them or did some important favor in return. Also part of the second economy was the so-called "private plot" of collective farm peasants, who held it legally and in theory could do what they wanted with it – grow food for their own table or to sell in the market at state-controlled prices. But although the plot itself was legal, people obtained high outputs from it not just by virtue of hard work but also by stealing from the collective farm: fertilizer and herbicides, fodder for their pigs or cows, work time for their own weeding or harvesting, tractor time and fuel for plowing their plot, and so on. The second economy, then, which provisioned a large part of consumer needs, was parasitic upon the state economy and inseparable from it. It developed precisely because the state economy tended to ignore consumption. To grasp the interconnection of the two economies is crucial, lest one think that simply dismantling the state sector will automatically enable entrepreneurship – already present in embryo – to flourish. On the contrary: parts of the second economy will wither and die if deprived of the support of the official, state economy.

It is clear from what I have said that whereas consumption in our own society is considered primarily a socioeconomic question, the relative neglect of consumer interests in socialism made consumption deeply political. In Romania in the 1980s (an extreme case), to kill and eat your own calf was a political act, because the government prohibited killing calves: you were supposed to sell them cheap to the state farm, for export. Romanian villagers who fed me veal (having assured themselves of my complicity) did so with special satisfaction. It was also illegal for urbanites to go and buy forty kilograms of potatoes directly from the villagers who grew potatoes on their private plot, because the authorities suspected that villagers would charge more than the state-set price, thus enriching themselves. So Romanian policemen routinely stopped cars riding low on the chassis and confiscated produce they found inside.

Consumption became politicized in yet another way: the very definition of "needs" became a matter for resistance and dispute. "Needs," as we should know from our own experience, are not given: they are created, developed, expanded – the work especially of the advertising business. It is advertising's job to convince us that we need things we didn't know we needed, or that if we feel unhappy, it's because we need something (a shrink, or a beer, or a Marlboro, or a man). Our need requires only a name, and it can be satisfied with a product or service. Naming troubled states, labeling them as needs, and finding commodities to fill them is at the heart of our economy. Socialism, by contrast, which rested not on devising infinite kinds of things to sell people but on claiming to satisfy people's *basic* needs, had a very unadorned definition of them – in keeping with socialist egalitarianism. Indeed, some Hungarian dissidents wrote of socialism's relationship to needs as a "dictatorship." As long as the food offered was edible or the clothes available covered you and kept you warm, that should be sufficient. If you had trouble finding even these, that just meant you were not looking hard enough. No planner presumed to investigate what kinds of goods people wanted, or worked to name new needs for newly created products and newly developed markets.

[. . .]

As people became increasingly alienated from socialism and critical of its achievements, then, the politicization of consumption also made them challenge official definitions of their needs. They did so not just by creating a second economy to grow food or make clothes or work after hours but also, sometimes, by public protest. Poland's Communist leaders fell to such protest at least twice, in 1970 and in 1980, when Polish workers insisted on having more food than government price increases would permit them. Less immediately disruptive were forms of protest in which people used consumption styles to forge resistant social identities. The black markets in Western goods that sprang up everywhere enabled alienated consumers to express their contempt for their governments through the kinds of things they chose to buy. You could spend an entire month's salary on a pair of blue jeans, for instance, but it was worth

it: wearing them signified that you could get something the system said you didn't need and shouldn't
have. Thus consumption goods and objects con-
ferred an identity that set you off from socialism,
enabling you to differentiate yourself as an individual in the face of relentless pressures to homogenize
everyone's capacities and tastes into an undifferentiated collectivity. Acquiring objects became a way
of constituting your selfhood against a deeply unpopular regime.

Bureaucratic factionalism and markets

Before turning to why these system fell, I wish to
address one more issue: politicking in the Party
bureaucracy. [. . .] One way of thinking about
these various divisions is that they distinguish
ownership from management; or the people who
oversaw the paperwork of administration from
those "out in the field," intervening in actual social
life.[8] We might then look for conflicting
tendencies intra-Party between the central
"owners" or paperworkers, on one hand, who
might persist in policies that accumulated means
of production without concern for things like
productivity and output, and the bureaucratic
managers of the allocative process or its fieldworkers, on the other, who *had* to be concerned
with such things. Although the power of the
system itself rested on continued accumulation,
such tendencies if unchecked could obstruct the
work of those who had actually to deliver resources or redistribute them. Without actual investments and hard material resources, lower-level
units could not produce the means of production
upon which both bureaucracy and center relied. If
productive activity were so stifled by "overadmi-
nistration" that nothing got produced, this would
jeopardize the redistributive bureaucracy's power
and prestige.

Thus when central accumulation of means of
production began to threaten the capacity of
lower-level units to produce [. . .] then pressure
arose for a shift of emphasis. The pressure was
partly from those in the wider society to whom
not enough was being allocated and partly from
bureaucrats themselves whose prestige and, increasingly, prospects of retaining power depended
on having more goods to allocate. One then heard
of decentralization, of the rate of growth, of productivity – in a word, of matters of output, rather
than the inputs that lay at the core of bureaueratic
performance. This is generally referred to as the
language of "reform."
[. . .]

Why Did It Fall?

[. . .]
   In event-history terms, the proximate cause of
the fall of East European and Soviet socialism was
an act of the Hungarian government: its dismantling of the barbed wire between Hungary and
Austria, on the eve of a visit by President George
Bush, and its later renouncing the treaty with the
GDR that would have prevented East German
emigration through Hungary. This culmination
of Hungary's long-term strategy of opening up to
the West gave an unexpected opportunity for some
East German tourists to extend their Hungarian
vacations into West Germany; the end result, given
that Gorbachev refused to bolster the East
German government with Soviet troops in this
crisis, was to bring down the Berlin Wall. To
understand the conjuncture in which Hungary
could open its borders and Gorbachev could
refuse Honecker his troops requires setting in
motion the static model I have given above and
placing it in its international context. This includes
asking how socialism's encounter with a changing
world capitalism produced or aggravated factional divisions within Communist Parties.

International solutions
to internal problems

My discussion of socialism indicated several
points of tension in its workings that affected the
system's capacity for extended reproduction.
Throughout their existence, these regimes sought
to manage such tensions in different ways, ranging
from Hungary's major market reforms in the
1960s to Romania's rejection of reform and its
heightened coercive extraction. In all cases, managing these tensions involved decisions that to a
greater or lesser degree opened socialist political
economies to Western capital. The impetus for this
opening – critical to socialism's demise – came
chiefly from within, as Party leaders attempted to
solve their structural problems without major
structural reform. Their attitude in doing so was
reminiscent of a "plunder mentality" that sees the
external environment as a source of booty to be
used as needed in maintaining one's own system,
without thought for the cost. This attitude was
visible in the tendency of socialist governments to
treat foreign trade as a residual sector, used to
supplement budgets without being made an integral part of them.[9] Because of how this opportun-
istic recourse to the external environment brought

socialism into tighter relationship with capitalism, it had fateful consequences.

The critical intersection occurred not in 1989 or 1987 but in the late 1960s and early 1970s, when global capitalism entered the cyclical crisis from which it is still struggling to extricate itself. Among capitalists' possible responses to the crisis (devaluation, structural reorganization, etc.), an early one was to lend abroad; facilitating this option were the massive quantities of petrodollars that were invested in Western banks, following changes in OPEC policy in 1973. By lending, Western countries enabled the recipients to purchase capital equipment or to build long-term infrastructure, thereby expanding the overseas markets for Western products.[10]

The loans became available just at the moment when all across the socialist bloc, the first significant round of structural reforms had been proposed, halfheartedly implemented, and, because profitability and market criteria fit so poorly with the rationale of socialism, largely abandoned. Reluctance to proceed with reforms owed much, as well, to Czechoslovakia's Prague Spring, from which the Party apparatus all across the region had been able to see the dangers that reform posed for its monopoly on power. Instead of reforming the system from within, then, most Party leaderships opted to meet their problems by a greater articulation with the surrounding economy: importing Western capital and using it to buy advanced technology (or, as in Poland, to subsidize consumption), in hopes of improving economic performance. Borrowing thus became a substitute for extensive internal changes that would have jeopardized the Party's monopoly over society and subverted the inner mechanisms of socialism. In this way, the internal cycles of two contrasting systems suddenly meshed.

The intent, as with all the international borrowing of the period, was to pay off the loans by exporting manufactured goods into the world market. By the mid-1970s it was clear, however, that the world market could not absorb sufficient amounts of socialism's products to enable repayment, and at the same time, rising interest rates added staggeringly to the debt service. With the 1979–80 decision of the Western banking establishment not to lend more money to socialist countries, the latter were thrown into complete disarray. I have already mentioned several features that made socialist economies inapt competitors in the international export market. [. . .] To [these] was added the fact that socialist economies were "outdated": as Jowitt put it, "After 70 years of murderous effort, the Soviet Union had created a German industry of the 1880s in the 1980s."[11]

In these circumstances, the balance of power tilted toward the faction within the Communist Party of the Soviet Union that had long argued for structural reforms, the introduction of market mechanisms, and profit incentives, even at the cost of the Party's "leading role." The choice, as Gorbachev and his faction saw it, was to try to preserve either the Soviet Union and its empire (by reforms that would increase its economic performance and political legitimacy) or collective property and the Party monopoly. Gorbachev was ready to sacrifice the latter to save the former but ended by losing both.

While Western attention was riveted on the speeches of policy-makers in the Kremlin, the more significant aspects of reform, however, were in the often-unauthorized behavior of bureaucrats who were busily creating new property forms on their own. Staniszkis describes the growth of what she calls "political capitalism," as bureaucrats spontaneously created their own profit-based companies from within the state economic bureaucracy. Significantly for my argument that socialism's articulation with world capitalism was crucial to its fall, the examples she singles out to illustrate these trends are all at the interface of socialist economies with the outside world – in particular, new companies mediating the export trade and state procurement of Western computers.[12] In fact, she sees as critical the factional split between the groups who managed socialism's interface with the outside world (such as those in foreign policy, counterintelligence, and foreign trade) and those who managed it internally (such as the Party's middle-level executive apparatus and the KGB). Forms of privatization already taking place as early as 1987 in Poland and similar processes as early as 1984 in Hungary[13] show the emerging contours of what Staniszkis sees as the reformists goal: a dual economy. One part of this economy was to be centrally administered, as before, and the other part was to be reformed through market/profit mechanisms and selective privatization of state property. The two were to coexist symbiotically.

[. . .]

It is possible (though unlikely) that socialist regimes would not have collapsed if their hard-currency crisis and the consequent intersection with capitalism had occurred at a different point in capitalism's cyclicity. The specifics of capitalism's own crisis management, however, proved unmanageable for socialist systems. Without wanting to present recent capitalism's "flexible specialization" as either unitary or fully dominant (its forms differ from place to place, and it coexists with other socioeconomic forms), I find in the literature about it a number of characteristics even more inimical to socialism than was the earlier "Fordist" variant, which Soviet production partly imitated. These characteristics include: small-batch production; just-in-time inventory; an accelerated pace of innovation; tremendous reductions in the turnover time of capital via automation and electronics; a much-increased turnover time in consumption, as well, with a concomitant rise in techniques of need-creation and an increased emphasis on the production of events rather than goods; coordination of the economy by finance capital; instantaneous access to accurate information and analysis; and an overall decentralization that increases managerial control (at the expense of higher-level bodies) over labor.

How is socialism to mesh with this? – socialism with its emphasis on large-scale heroic production of means of production, its resources frozen by hoarding – no just-in-time here! – its lack of a systemic impetus toward innovation, the irrelevance to it of notions like "turnover time," its neglect of consumption and its flat-footed definition of "needs," its constipated and secretive flows of information (except for rumors!) in which the center could have no confidence, and the perpetual struggle to retain central control over all phases of the production process? Thus, I submit, it is not simply socialism's embrace with capitalism that brought about its fall but the fact that it happened to embrace a capitalism of a newly "flexible" sort. David Harvey's schematic comparison of "Fordist modernity" with "flexible post-modernity" clarifies things further: socialist systems have much more in common with his "Fordist" column than with his "flexible" one.[14]

[...] Increasing numbers of scholars note that accompanying the change in capitalism is a change in the nature of state power: specifically, a number of the state's functions are being undermined. The international weapons trade has made a mockery of the state's monopoly on the means of violence. The extraordinary mobility of capital means that as it moves from areas of higher to areas of lower taxation, many states lose some of their revenue and industrial base, and this constrains their ability to attract capital or shape its flows. Capital flight can now discipline all nation-state governments. The coordination of global capitalism by finance capital places a premium on capital mobility, to which rigid state boundaries are an obstacle. And the new computerized possibilities for speculative trading have generated strong pressures to release the capital immobilized in state structures and institutions by diminishing their extent.

This has two consequences for the collapse of socialism. First, groups inside socialist countries whose structural situation facilitated their fuller participation in the global economy now had reasons to expand their state's receptivity to capital – that is, to promote reform. Second, the control that socialist states exerted over capital flows into their countries may have made them special targets for international financial interests, eager to increase their opportunities by undermining socialist states. These internal and international groups each found their chance in the interest of the other. It is in any case clear from the politics of international lending agencies that they aim to reduce the power of socialist states, for they insist upon privatization of state property – the basis of these states' power and revenue. Privatization is pushed even in the face of some economists' objections that "too much effort is being invested in privatization, and too little in creating and fostering the development of new private firms" – whose entry privatization may actually impede.[15]

[...]

What Comes Next?

The outcome of the confluence between socialist and capitalist systemic crises is far more complicated than "capitalism triumphant," however. Ken Jowitt captures this with an unexpected metaphor, that of biological extinction and its attendant erasure of formerly existing boundaries among forms of life. In his brilliant essay "The Leninist Extinction," he pursues the metaphor's implications as follows:

[One feature] of mass extinctions ... is that they typically affect more than one species. In this respect, the collapse of European Leninism may be seen more as a political volcano than as an asteroid. A volcano's eruption initially affects a circumscribed area (in this case limited to Leninist regimes), but, depending on its force, the effects gradually but dramatically become global. The Leninist volcano of 1989 will have a comparable effect on liberal and "Third World" biota around the globe.[16]

After describing the new regime "species" that have emerged with changed forms of government in Poland, Hungary, Romania, and elsewhere, as well as other new forms of political life arising out of Yugoslavia and the Soviet Union, he ponders the larger question of the end of the Cold War:

> For half a century we have thought in terms of East and West, and now there is no East as such. The primary axis of international politics has "disappeared." Thermonuclear Russia hasn't, but the Soviet Union/Empire most certainly has. Its "extinction" radically revises the framework within which the West, the United States itself, the Third World, and the countries of Eastern Europe, the former Russian Empire, and many nations in Asia have bounded and defined themselves.
>
> The Leninist Extinction will force the United States [not to mention all those others] to reexamine the meaning of its national identity.[17]

What the Leninist Extinction confronts us with, then, is a conceptual vacuum. Jowitt concludes by invoking the biblical story of Genesis ("the world was without form, and void"), whose theme is bounding and naming new entities, as the "narrative" most appropriate to the immediate future.

In my view, not only is Jowitt absolutely right but one could go even further. It is not just new political identities, including our own, that we will have the task of bounding and naming – a task which, if the example of Bosnia is any indication, is of awesome magnitude. It is also the entire conceptual arsenal through which Western institutions and social science disciplines have been defined in this century. As one reads scholarship on the postsocialist processes of "privatization," the creation of "property rights," the development of "democracy" or "civil society" or "constitutions" – in short, the proposed building of a "liberal state" – profound confusion sets in. One begins to see that these terms do not label useful concepts: they are elements in a massive political and ideological upheaval that is by no means restricted to the "East."

If this is true, then everything we know is up for grabs, and "what comes next" is anyone's guess.

NOTES

1 János Kornai, *The Socialist System: The Political Economy of Communism* (Princeton: Princeton University Press, 1992).

2 See especially Elemér Hankiss, *East European Alternatives* (New York: Oxford University Press, 1990); Ágnes Horváth and Árpád Szakolczai, *The Dissolution of Communist Power: The Case of Hungary*

(New York: Routledge, 1992); and Jadwiga Staniszkis, *The Dynamics of the Breakthrough in Eastern Europe: The Polish Experience* (Berkeley and Los Angeles: University of California Press, 1991) and *The Ontology of Socialism* (New York: Oxford University Press, 1992).

3 In particular: Pavel Campeanu, *The Origins of Stalinism: From Leninist Revolution to Stalinist Society* (Armonk, NY: M. E. Sharpe, 1986) and *The Genesis of the Stalinist Social Order* (Armonk, NY: M. E. Sharpe, 1988); Ferenc Fehér, Agnes Heller, and György Márkus, *Dictatorship over Needs: An Analysis of Soviet Societies* (New York: Blackwell, 1983); George Konrád and Ivan Szelényi, *The Intellectuals on the Road to Class Power: A Sociological Study of the Role of the Intelligentsia in Socialism* (New York: Harcourt, Brace, Jovanovich, 1979); and János Kornai, *The Socialist System*, and *Economics of Shortage* (Amsterdam: North-Holland Publishing, 1980).

4 See Kornai, *Economics of Shortage* and *The Socialist System*.

5 Michael Burawoy and János Lukács, *The Radiant Past: Ideology and Reality in Hungary's Road to Capitalism* (Chicago: University of Chicago Press, 1992), chapter 5.

6 These observations show how fraught is the use of files in assessing fitness for political office (as in the Czech practice of "lustration").

7 See, e.g., István Gábor, "The Second (Secondary) Economy," *Acta Oeconomica* 3–4 (1979): 291–311; and Steven Sampson, "The Second Economy in Eastern Europe and the Soviet Union." *Annals of the American Association of Political and Social Science* 493 (1986): 120–36.

8 Campeanu, *The Genesis of the Stalinist Social Order*, pp. 143–57; and Horváth and Szakolczai, *The Dissolution of Communist Power*, pp. 204–5.

9 Paul Hare, "Industrial Development of Hungary since World War II," *Eastern European Politics and Societies* 2 (1988): 115–51.

10 David Harvey, *The Condition of Postmodernity* (Oxford: Blackwell, 1989), p. 184.

11 Ken Jowitt, "The Leninist Extinction," in Daniel Chirot, ed., *The Crisis of Leninism and the Decline of the Left* (Seattle: University of Washington Press, 1991), p. 78.

12 Jadwiga Staniszkis, "'Political Capitalism' in Poland," *East European Politics and Societies* 5 (1991): 129–30.

13 David Stark, "Privatization in Hungary: From Plan to Market or from Plan to Clan?" *East European Politics and Societies* 4 (1990): 364–65.

14 Harvey, *The Condition of Postmodernity*, pp. 340–41.

15 Peter Murrell, "Privatization Complicates the Fresh Start," *Orbis* 36 (1992): 325.

16 Jowitt, "The Leninist Extinction," pp. 80–81.

17 Ibid., pp. 81–82.

31

"Disappearing the Poor?": A Critique of the New Wisdoms of Social Democracy in an Age of Globalization

John Gledhill

Introduction

The architects of neoliberalism, in both the North Atlantic countries and Latin America, conventionally respond to critics with the phrase: "There is no alternative." Yet as the inevitable consequences of structural adjustment, reduction of the state's responsibilities for social welfare and economic globalization became all too apparent, this refrain became qualified, both in political circles and within the transnational agencies of global transformation, including the World Bank. In this paper I consider the claims of the so-called "politics of the Third Way" to provide an alternative to neoliberalism. What is interesting about Third Way discourse is that it has internationalized quite successfully, despite differences of emphasis in different national contexts. Its advocates are to be found among a cosmopolitan elite in Latin America as well as Europe and North America. Its master concepts, notably that of social exclusion, have become part of a global discourse that government research councils and private foundations have made central to the agendas of fundable social science research.

Focusing in particular on the approach of Anthony Giddens, I will argue that there is a sense in which Third Way theorists replicate the arguments of elites at the dawn of the industrial capitalist era. This resonance is particularly striking in the way they deploy the ideas of "social stability," controlling "dangerous classes," and enforcing "participation" in the normal life process of market society. Yet this rhetoric can also be seen as a response to new circumstances provoked by glob-

alization, including the rise of identity politics and the formation of transnational ties between NGOs and concerned citizens' groups and local social movements.

Third Way theorists generally advocate a strengthening of "civil society" to tame the power of global corporations, and welcome the potential role of global networks of NGOs and "third sector" voluntary organizations in promoting "responsible capitalism" (Giddens 2000: 144). They tend, however, to disapprove of all forms of "community-based" identity politics as potentially divisive and exclusionary, "difficult to reconcile with the principles of tolerance and diversity on which an effective civil society depends" (Giddens 2000: 64). The cornerstone of contemporary Third Way positions is that rights must be matched by responsibilities, a concept of social citizenship that applies equally to rich and poor, business corporations and private individuals (Giddens 2000:52). I argue that this construction of social citizenship provides intellectuals who have grown comfortable with the corporate wealth-creating world with a series of profoundly disingenuous ways of ignoring the social realities of contemporary capitalism and the bases of growing global income polarization. But far worse, it provides a framework for dismissing some of the most significant manifestations of the existence of popular alternatives to the world as it is and for legitimating the suppression of many forms of dissidence.

[...]

One of the reasons [Giddens's] arguments might be seen as pernicious rather than simply misguided is that they provide a reformist discourse that resonates rather better with Latin American sensibilities than the more technocratic kind of neoliberal rhetoric. Third Way politics focus on the individual citizen, and are inimical to collective claims based on black or indigenous identities. This is a message that can resonate with many poorer citizens who feel marginalized by the growth of identity-based politics as well as alienated from the statism and clientelism that characterized the regimes that preceded the neoliberal turn of the region. The danger here is that Third Way political rhetoric will be used to disempower social movements that use identity-based claims as part of a broader program to contest the shape of capitalist development, and as a cover for the reinforcement of increasingly predatory forms of capitalist development in Latin America.

A further danger lies in the way Giddens attempts to sever connections between North and South in the production of global social inequalities. As far as the problems of the South are concerned, he adopts a strong "blame the victim" posture:

> Most of the problems that inhibit the economic development of the impoverished countries don't come from the global economy itself, or from self-seeking behaviour on the part of the richer nations. They lie mainly in the societies themselves: in authoritarian government, corruption, conflict, over-regulation and the low level of emancipation of women. Mobile investment capital will give such countries a wide berth, since the level of risk is unacceptable (Giddens 2000: 129).

Leaving aside the somewhat counter-experiential final remark in this quotation, its general thrust of blaming global inequalities on local pathologies that are completely disconnected from the past or contemporary effects of Northern hegemony clearly fits a wider pattern of post-Cold War discourse (Gledhill 1999). Giddens is not concerned with making connections or exploring uncomfortable causal relationships (such as those between Southern political mafias and respectable Northern financial institutions). His argument rests on the assumption that an acceptable social order for the majority of citizens can be achieved within a national frame by a judicious blend of policing and investment in "human capital."

Contextualizing the New Social Democracy

From the point of view of a majority of Mexican citizens, there has been little to celebrate in the fifteen years of economic transformations that have followed the country's entry into the GATT and subsequent "partnership" with the United States and Canada under the NAFTA. During the administration of President Ernesto Zedillo (1994–2000), the numbers of urban Mexicans living in extreme poverty doubled, to two out of every five inhabitants, while the number living above the poverty line fell to less than a third of the urban population (Boltvinik and Hernández 2000). As peasant agriculture at best stagnated, and in most regions declined, under the pressure of withdrawal of subsidies and exposure to competition from cheaper (and often subsidized) imports (Wiggins et al. 1999), the longstanding association of rural areas with an even higher incidence of extreme poverty intensified. The consequences of rural collapse were partially disguised by an increase in outmigration from rural communities to both the United States and the cities, and, in a different way, by the growth of the drug economy, though the latter's violence also contributed to rural abandonment in some regions.

The apparent political breakthrough represented by the ending of the 70 year rule of the Institutional Revolutionary Party (PRI) with the victory of Vicente Fox, candidate of the National Action Party (PAN) in 2000, needs to be set in the context of this sustained process of immiseration. [...]

[...] Latin American politicians have not ignored the starkness of the social impacts of orthodox neoliberal policies in Latin America, which include the resurgence of 19th century diseases of poverty as well as diminished public services and protection from everyday crime and violence. In this respect, the reemergence of contested electoral politics is nontrivial, even where many citizens remain skeptical of the value of democracy and abstain from voting. The fall of the PRI was to some extent at least a consequence of the old regime's increasing failure to deliver material benefits to any of its mass constituencies. The 1990s saw a variety of governments elected throughout Latin America on the basis of neopopulist rhetoric that promised an alternative to neoliberalism, even if many of these promises rapidly proved deceptive, as exemplified by the case of Bucaram in Ecuador. Yet although neoliberal governments have survived in Ecuador with U.S.-sponsored local military backing, the mass support enjoyed by the campaign of the Confederación de Nacionalidades Indígenas (CONAIE) against the dollarization of the economy, privatization and military cooperation with the United States, continues to focus minds in that region. The interest of a significant group of Latin American intellectuals and politicians in Third Way politics might thus been seen as a response to the threat of further escalation of popular (or populist) resistance to globalization.

For many critics, the Third Way is simply neoliberalism in another guise, though this is [...] something that Giddens himself disputes. What is undisputed, however, is that there are a variety of Third Way positions. As Giddens himself concedes, the term Third Way is hardly new. It appeared during the Cold War as a label for a social democratic alternative to North American market liberalism and Soviet communism respectively, fading from view until its revival, after the collapse of the Soviet empire, by the U.S. Democrats under Clinton and British "New Labour" under Blair (Giddens 2000: 1). [...] A previous Latin American incarnation was the Catholic Church's efforts to chart an alternative to free-market capitalism and socialism in the late 19th and early 20th century, which, as ultimately embodied in Mexico's *sinarquista* movement in the 1930s and 1940s, constituted the Latin American version of fascism (Meyer 1977). Nevertheless, as in the case of continental Europe, whose Third Way theorists also tend to favor a rather greater role for the state and public expenditure than their Anglo-Saxon counterparts, contemporary Latin American Third Wayers tend to describe themselves as a "democratic left" or "modernizing social democrats." All argue that their approach is a response to irreversible social changes brought about by globalization, that state-led development failed and that traditional left projects are obsolete.

[...]

[...] The position adopted by Giddens (and other Europeans) resonates with that of many Left intellectuals in Latin America. Surely, they argue, the neoliberals were right to critique the evils of statism? This is not simply about buying into the "welfare cultures of dependency model," whose Mexican equivalent, articulated by writers such as Gustavo Gordillo[1] (1988), is "the paternalistic state versus the infantilized poor." It is also a critique of pervasive corruption, the featherbedding of domestic capital and the futility of achieving greater social justice under conditions in which public investment simply encourages rent-seeking. Whatever this model looked like to Europeans and North Americans, it certainly managed to resonate not merely with intellectuals but with a great many citizens in Latin American countries (even if they retained conscientious doubts about the rest of the neoliberal package or saw it, quite explicitly, as a vehicle for advancing domestic and foreign capitalist interests, potentially at their own expense). The only fly in the ointment for "evidence-based social research," as we will see, is that in the Mexican case the data show that evil old statism reduced poverty quite substantially, whereas neoliberalism has brought the statistics back more or less to where they were 30 years ago. And even the most superficial glance at the nature of the neoliberal model implemented in Mexico suggests that we are dealing with a very special case. Mexico's version of neoliberal economic strategy is peculiarly disadvantageous to working people and has sharply differentiating impacts at the regional level.

Anthony Giddens: Life Politics and the Normalization of Inequality

[...]

Giddens's claim to represent a "modernizing Left" rests in part on a claim that an old model had become exhausted and demonstrated its bankruptcy, opening the way for neoconservative and neoliberal positions to gain a political initiative that must now be recaptured. There are alternative ways of reading this history: in terms, for example, of the fiscal crisis of the state, accumulation crisis and global economic shifts associated both with the management of impending crisis by states and the evolution of both transnational corporations and global financial markets (as means of hedging increasing risks and as circuits of accumulation in their own right). Nor is it hard to discern that the lightening of the bureaucratic hand of the state on some actors under neoliberalism is accompanied by increasing regulatory intervention in others. [...]

It has, however, proved easier to critique the new dispensation than to defend the old, especially in the form of the defunct actually existing socialisms. On that one, Giddens rests his case on the proposition that the world has experienced irreversible social change to which the "Old Left" simply failed to react theoretically. Much of what he actually has to say here covers very familiar and rather dubious ground. Part of it simply revamps the de-industrialization argument for the irrelevance of class, with a particular focus on the way the emergence of an IT-based middle class of "wired workers" breaks down past divisions between "Left" and "Right." These people care about GM foods and human rights, but don't want to pay more taxes. A great deal of this is arguably rather silly. For example, if we look at what "wired workers" actually earn, we find that wage trends for white-collar and college-educated workers were not particularly favorable through the 1990s. Even newly hired engineers and scientists in the IT industry were earning less in 1997 than their counterparts did in 1989 (Mishel et al. 2001). The generalized experience of white collar workers in the 1990s mirrored that of blue-collar workers in the 1980s: wage losses, displacement from downsizing and job instability (Mishel 1999). The kinds of statistics Giddens bandies about do not appear to distinguish the staff of call centers from software engineers, his version of California appears to lack sweatshops and low-pay service occupations, and terms such as "race" scarcely appear in his text at any point. The Giddens perspective on globalization ("not really a negative development overall and essentially new") has already attracted its fair share of critical discussion. But what it seems most important to recognize is that the way he approaches globalization seeks to displace the issue of real income inequalities from a central place in the discussion.

Although Giddens argues that income inequalities are diminishing in some places (including the United States),[2] he is quite happy to accept that global trends towards rising income inequality may exist, urging us to take a broader view of what social inequality is. On this front, we are offered the countervailing trend of women becoming more equal to men in social and cultural terms, or rather aspiring to such greater equality. One could, of course, readily turn this line of argument on its head and say that even where income inequality is declining, qualitative changes in lifestyles and working patterns might diminish the returns to people and social life of such changes. One of the most obvious downsides of the United States's improvements of living standards under Clinton was growth in the hours worked (and work pressures and insecurities) experienced by even the better-off sectors of the workforce (Mishel et al. 2001). Another is the staggering rise in consumer personal debt behind the apparent rise in living standards. But the main problem with Giddens is that he is not really interested in the exploration of life-worlds in an ethnographic sense or seeking to capture the subjective experience of change from any vantage point other than his own. This is readily apparent in his approach to poverty and the new master concept of social exclusion.

Giddens argues that "recent research" has shown three things: first, that a surprising number of people escape from poverty; second, that an equally surprising number of people experience poverty at some point in their lives; and third, that people often slip back into poverty after escaping it. There is a particular irony in Giddens's invocation of the principle that people escape from poverty in significant numbers. This just happens to be a front on which the United Kingdom and United States share a low success rate (26%) in comparison with the more regulated economies of continental Europe (and Canada) which manage between 36% and 44% (OECD data, Economic Policy Institute Website, http://epinet.org/webfeatures/snapshots/archive/2000/071900/snapshots071900.html).

Leaving that issue aside, Giddens is on firmer ground in arguing that there are different causes of poverty and different processes that keep people in poverty. "The poor" are not passive victims, but active agents. We need to ask "why" people are poor. There are different answers for different people, so "the poor" must be divided up into different categories.

Yet although this sounds perfectly reasonable (if scarcely as revolutionary as Giddens would have us believe) his conclusions about how the policy debate should shift are not. Giddens argues that well-intentioned policies have produced intractable problems, such as the creation of housing estates on the edges of cities that become sinks of criminality and youth delinquency. There are new policies that we should favor to help poor people's own efforts to get out of poverty, such as investment in human capital through micro-credit and welfare-to-work schemes. Giddens also touches on the problem of disabled people here, arguing that it makes sense to "help mobilize their action potential and reduce dependency." This perspective is evidently not well adapted to countries in which dependency is not focused on the state, but on family structures that are under pressure from global economic change, and in which women often bear the lion's share of the costs of "adjustment."

The master-concept underlying all this is the distinction between "poverty" and "social exclusion." Giddens argues that social exclusion is essentially about mechanisms of social separation. If upper-income families decide to live in gated communities and elites are unwilling to pay taxes to fund social services or play their role in public life, they are also promoting it. But if we are talking about social exclusion at the bottom, we are talking about social mechanisms that produce or sustain deprivation. These include being spatially separated in run-down housing estates and lacking "access to normal labor market opportunities."

[...]

Though evidently anxious not to be seen as espousing the discourse of the Right, Giddens is somewhat stuck when it comes to finding remedies for the problems he has identified. He lives in hopes that everyone will be able to find decently paid and socially fulfilling jobs, and get access to education and training. He is hard on "corporate greed" and although he does not seem to think there's a great deal "we" can do about it, he holds out hope for the "merely affluent" signing up for an ethic of "civic responsibility." We need good state (public) schools so that people will not educate their kids privately, and we need to stop crime in the inner cities so that the merely affluent won't retreat to the suburbs. As usual in Giddens's text there is some confusion of cause and effect here, or at any rate a refusal to engage with that issue. But it is the bottom-line of the argument that is most striking. What we are being offered in Giddens's calls for "civic responsibility" is a moralizing slogan. We are back to the 19th century, with calls on the rich to be philanthropic and appeals to us all to give to charity. The poor are called upon to accept the logic of capitalist restructuring and help themselves into the opportunities provided. Giddens is quite right to say that many people do that spontaneously. But the logic of his argument is that those who choose some other way of making it in the world should be stopped from doing so by all means available.

One obvious problem with this perspective is that it abstracts from two possible features of "pathological" adaptations to late capitalist realities. One is that the people who participate in these "perverse" livelihood strategies may obtain better material living standards and/or subjectively superior "senses of self" by doing so. That Giddens doesn't have a clue what it might be like to be a Pakistani in Manchester, a cholo in a Lima shantytown, a Cambodian in Stockton, California, or "poor white trash" in Louisiana is not surprising. That he doesn't regard such issues as interesting or important is more worrying. Struggles to infuse personal and collective lives with meaning seem more rather than less central to urbanized mass societies in the 21st century. The other problem is that the growth of "informal" and "illegal" economies are an integral part of those late capitalist realities, cannot be separated from other dimensions of globalization, and

involve the participation of different social classes. "Corporate greed" versus "civic responsibility" may not really cut it in that context.

[...]

In arguing that the old "emancipatory projects of the left" are rendered obsolete by social change, Giddens opts for a focus on the individual in "society" rather than subgroups of actors and forms of sociality that might defy normalization. He argues that today's routes to emancipation should be based on a personal "life politics" that enables individuals to feel "fulfilled" by, for example, being allowed to continue to work past the normal age of retirement (Giddens 2000: 40). Modernizing social democracy (like liberalism) is focused on equality of opportunity, and its advocates should be prepared to accept higher rather than lower levels of income inequality as a correlate of the incentives and freedoms integral to the model (Giddens 2000: 86). Giddens suggests that high levels of social and cultural diversity are to be counted among the gains of reconciling equality with pluralism and "lifestyle diversity," "since individuals and groups have the opportunities to develop their lives as they see fit" (Giddens 2000: 86). Policies to promote equality should focus on enhancing "social capabilities" in Amartya Sen's sense (1992). Inter alia, this will still require some mechanisms for redistribution of income to guarantee that the children of today's (relative) "failures" have an equal chance of self-realization.

As far as Giddens is concerned, freedoms defined as the capability to pursue well being by making use of social and material goods are distinct from neoliberal freedoms in that they are exercised through membership of groups, communities and "cultures"[3] (Giddens 2000: 88). He insists that Third Way politics are not a variant of neoliberalism. They not only advocate the continuing provision of public goods, but also the subjection of market-based decisions to social and ethical criteria defined by a "healthy" civil society capable of consummating a "democratization of democracy" through devolution of power (Giddens 2000: 33,61). Civil society is "fundamental to constraining the power of both markets and government" and itself "supplies the grounding of citizenship" (Giddens 2000: 65).

A stable civil society "incorporates norms of trust and social decency" (Giddens 2000: 165). Poverty cannot simply be measured in terms of material deprivation, since even if an unemployed person receives an income similar to someone in work, he may still feel a lack of social esteem that limits his sense of well being (Giddens 2000: 88).

Yet Giddens is not interested in the kinds of arguments anthropologists such as Ferguson (1992) have made about the difficulties of measuring wealth and poverty on a linear scale. Those arguments are fundamentally concerned with the power relations that shape social change and the way differentiated social actors contest and negotiate such change. What is ultimately underscored in Giddens's recent work, in contrast, is the idea that the ability to "function" in capitalist society should become the key to all forms of self-fulfillment. Let us, then, turn to see how that proposition looks from south of the Río Grande.

The View from the South

Giddens may be right to insist that we should look more carefully at the social diversity and temporality of situations of poverty in the contemporary world. Although the perspective from south of the Rio Grande seems to privilege persistent situations of marginality and mass impoverishment, such a perspective is simplistic in a sense. It is not difficult to find examples of pockets of small-scale enterprise dynamism, especially in regions where the earnings of US migrants were substantial enough to be reinvested and conditions, including government schemes to match investments peso for peso, were favorable to such investments.

Yet a persistent official discourse on the need to encourage "micro-enterprises" during the 1990s did not prevent vast numbers of small and medium-sized businesses failing thanks to other aspects of economic policy. The work of Boltvinik and Hernández (2000) on the movement of national income distribution and poverty indicators in Mexico during the period of neoliberal transition makes depressing reading. Noting that all studies demonstrate that poverty levels diminished rapidly in the period 1968 to 1981, to half of their 1968 level by the end of the period of import-substituting industrialization and state intervention, Boltvinik and Hernández argue that the macro-picture from 1981 to 1996 was one of virtually continuous pauperization and "social retrocession." Worse, the period since 1996 brought further deterioration before a leveling off which leaves the administration of Fox with a severe problem.

Looking at urban poverty in the 38 principal cities of the country, Boltvinik and Hernández show a relative increase between 1994 and 1999 of 70% in the number of people who would be classified as "indigent" (per capita income of half the value set for the poverty line), and 20% absolute increases in the numbers living in poverty and extreme poverty. It might be argued that the more dynamic centers linked to the growth of the export economy would present a more favorable picture. Yet this study demonstrates that, Tijuana aside, where the increase in poverty is the lowest, at 7.9%, this hope fails to be realized. Guadalajara, Mexico's Silicon Valley, has one of the largest increases, along with other border economic dynamos such as Matamoros and Cuidad Juárez.

Much of this rise in poverty figures represents the progressive impoverishment of working families. With minimum wages set below the levels needed to meet real family needs, the neoliberal anti-poverty programs of the Salinas and Zedillo administrations simply look like palliatives that fail to address the true social costs of Mexico's new economic model. Neoliberalism pulled the plug on a state sector that had guaranteed minimum standards of livelihood and some opportunities for building on them through household economic strategies during the 1970s. Vast numbers of Mexicans never directly enjoyed the benefits of statism, but the impact of the declining fortunes of the beneficiaries on the rest of the population are apparent enough, both in the cities and in regions devastated by an agricultural collapse worsened by the NAFTA. Although renewed growth generated more jobs, and even produced labor shortages in some regions, Vicente Fox himself conceded quite openly that translating this into rising real incomes for a still growing economically active population under the current NAFTA arrangements is a forlorn hope. So, it appears, are his suggestions that the United States help him to solve this problem through new arrangements for the legal entry of Mexican guest workers and longer-term progress towards a European-style customs union. The context is therefore one in which neoliberal policies seem incapable of alleviating social polarization and impoverishment. Indeed, some would see them as leading Mexico along a path leading to something not dissimilar to the "savage capitalism" provoked by "market reform" in Eastern Europe. A strong neoliberal approach is thus becoming increasingly difficult to defend politically, opening the space for an "alternative" that seeks to preserve the coherence of the state and allow a greater role for public expenditure (without a return to the past evils of "statist" economic management). The aim is to fund anti-poverty programs by increasing the tax take of the national state without deviating in other respects from the model of private enterprise, economic openness and market-driven development.

What has actually happened under neoliberal governments in Mexico makes it quite clear that wages are an issue. The Mexican model has catastrophically depressed real wages. In 1975, Mexican industrial wages in leading sectors were 23% of their U.S. equivalents. Twenty years later they were 9% (Paul Kay, personal communication). Mexico's industrial base has been pulverized, with assembly production orientated to the U.S. market spreading from the border zone deep into the country. Old industrial cores such as Mexico City or Puebla have declined as this new system of production has developed, but to no great advantage to the inhabitants of the most "dynamic" regions located nearer to the United States, as the poverty data indicate. Much of the new export-orientated industry has not even been directly financed by the US transnationals that are driving these developments, and it has become increasingly vulnerable to recession in the North as the domestic market has become increasingly insignificant. Mexico has become a vast sweatshop, in which even marginalized areas such as Chiapas can become prey to the predation of transnational enterprises interested in the varied forms of exploitation of tropical resources. A model this catastrophic in social terms only makes sense to a national economic elite that is already transnational in orientation and profoundly distanced socially from the rest of the population. It is an elite that contributes surprisingly little in taxes (and nothing in the case of the capital gains made so plentiful by Mexico's manner of regulating financial markets and backstage deals on privatization). It is an elite which has a long history of moving its own capital across the border, exacting a heavy toll in bribes from the Mexican state at the expense of those who do actually pay their taxes.

[...]

Alternatives

There are, of course, alternatives. Even neoliberalism does not have to mirror the Mexican model, as Chile demonstrates particularly clearly, but the Chilean model rests on different historical conditions (and would require a different critique). What we see in Mexico is not neoliberalism in general, but a peculiarly disadvantageous form of integration into the global economy managed by a technocratic elite, backed by force when hegemony crumbled, on behalf of a transnational capitalist alliance that covers both the legal and illegal economy.

There are now some emergent alternatives to all forms of neoliberalism. One is the Hugo Chávez approach in Venezuela. Chávez is essentially a caudillo, and in this respect, Fox in Mexico may follow his political style. By resolutely attacking the oligarchy and its institutions, however, Chávez has maintained his popular base while embarking on policies which, somewhat unconventionally, seek to restore economic life to the countryside. We might see this as a rare governmental response to popular reassertions of the social rights and economic possibilities offered by possession of land embodied in the Zapatista autonomous communities in Chiapas and the Sem Terra movement in Brazil. However factionalized these movements may now have become on the ground, their combination of agrarian demands with an alternative cultural politics of social dignification is significant. In rejecting the legitimacy of the social niches laid out for the poor by global capitalism and the non-identities that go with them, they maintain a real challenge to the ability of neoliberal elites of all kinds to define the social good in terms of the individual consumer-worker-citizen. Even in the case of the movements where indigenous identity and autonomy are foregrounded, it is important to acknowledge that this vision is being sustained (to the extent that it is being sustained) by appropriation of land and practices of collective production.

[...]

The Third Way critique of neoliberalism ultimately shares its concern to efface the social personalities of the poor in their diversity and make them manageable subjects of bourgeois governmentality as worker-consumer-citizens. Like liberals such as Rawls or Dworkin who seek to produce models of "justice and fairness" that can reduce social inequalities, Giddens does not seek to question the basic structures of contemporary Northern societies. This leads to complacency about the power relations shaping social relations, and the inevitability of the suppression of certain dissident forms of life incompatible with the dominant consensus. It also fosters a lack of interest in the capacity of such dissidence to offer alternative models for structures.

As a more "liberal" doctrine than that of the conservative Right, "Third Wayism" does not advocate the combination of extreme deregulation of the market economy with a state that is utterly coercive in the personal moral sphere. Rights to diversity can be recognized in such areas as sexual preference and in those cultural or lifestyle practices that find expression in a commodified

"personhood." But people cannot be allowed the freedom to practice non-capitalist economic strategies that respond to their own needs and aspirations in rainforests whose biodiversity is commercially exploitable. And they certainly cannot be allowed to turn urbanized spaces into places that run by rules that offend and perhaps threaten "the rest of us." Such positions only seem reasonable if we assume that the rights of corporate capital to restructure the world (and its boundaries) in whatever manner may suit it are now unassailable, or at any rate only marginally negotiable. This seems a rather odd position to take in a world in which much of the blurring of the traditional boundaries between social movements of the Right and the Left seems to turn precisely on unhappiness with that particular proposition. And this does highlight a weak link in the imperialist chain, or perhaps better, what might now be seen as a new form of global hegemony of which "The Third Way" is itself another expression. It invokes the possibility of global revulsion against countries turned into sweatshops and a renewal of the idea that there must be a better way that has something to do with how much people get paid and the conditions under which they work.

NOTES

1 Gordillo was a former adviser to a major militant peasant movement and leading example of a generation of intellectuals who embraced a Maoist model of putting grassroots work first. His entry into the cabinet of Carlos Salinas de Gortari reflected that administration's ability to attract militants with this kind of perspective at all levels. Much of the new bureaucracy formed to manage the reform (and hoped for eventual privatization) of the land reform sector consisted of young activists from independent Left organizations (Moguel 1994; Nuijten 1998). Gordillo did not find life in government agreeable and is now director of the FAO in Latin America.

2 This is virtually the only point at which he touches base with the issue of "race," arguing that the income share of Blacks and Latinos in the United States is now rising. Although he does not offer any explanations, positive income trends seem to be basically a result of declining rates of unemployment within minority groups, rather than reductions in wage disparities. Recent improvements represent a very modest and potentially rapidly reversible advance on an historically dismal picture. Despite the widespread improvements in living standards of the last few years, very little of the 20.5% increase in productivity achieved in the USA between 1989 and 1999 went to working people. Wage inequality increased, and the share of

income distribution accruing to the owners of business increased steadily, magnifying the gap between top and middle income earners (Mishel et al. 2001). This leaves inequality in the United States high in historic terms, and more significantly, high in comparison with other industrialized countries, since low-wage workers and the growing number of men and women in "non-standard occupations" earn less in real terms. The percentage of children living in poverty is double that of other advanced countries. Of these one in five poor children, Black and Latino families registered the highest proportion (Mishel et al. 2001). Health service coverage of the workforce was lower in 1998 than in 1979 (62.9%) and only half the workforce had pension coverage.

3 Like many sociologists and social policy theorists, Giddens insists on using a concept of "culture" that most anthropologists would hopefully find archaic.

REFERENCES CITED

Boltvinik, Julio, and Enrique Hernández Laos (2000). Pobreza y distribución del ingreso en México. Mexico City: Siglo XXI Editores.

Ferguson, James (1992). The Cultural Topography of Wealth: Commodity Paths and the Structure of Property in Rural Lesotho, American Anthropologist 94(1): 55–73.

Giddens, Anthony (2000). The Third Way and Its Critics. Cambridge: Polity Press.

Gledhill, John (1999). Official Masks and Shadow Powers: Towards an Anthropology of the Dark Side of the State. Urban Anthropology and Studies of Cultural Systems and World Economy 28(3–4): 199–251.

Gordillo, Gustavo (1988). El leviatán rural y la nueva sociabilidad política. IN Las Sociedades Rurales Hoy, Jorge Zepeda Patterson (ed.). Zamora: El Colegio de Michoacán, pp. 223–254.

Meyer, Jean A. (1977) Le sinarquisme: un fascisme mexicain? 1937–1947. Paris: Hachette.

Mishel, Lawrence (1999). The "New Economy." Article in Viewpoints section of Economic Policy Institute website, http://epinet.org. Originally published in the Las Vegas Review, 14th February, 1999.

Mishel, Lawrence, Jared Bernstein and John Schmitt (2001). The State of Working America. Cornell: Cornell University Press. Extracts available from http://epinet.org.

Moguel, Julio (1994). The Mexican Left and the Social Program of Salinismo. IN Transforming State-Society Relations in Mexico: The National Solidarity Strategy, Wayne A. Cornelius, Ann L. Craig and Jonathan Fox (eds.). La Jolla: Center for U.S.-Mexican Studies, UCSD, pp. 167–176.

Nuijten, Monique (1998). In the Name of the Land: Organization, Transnationalism and the Culture of the State. Ph.D. thesis, Wageningen: Landbouwuniversiteit Wageningen.

Sen, Amartya (1992). Inequality Reexamined. Oxford: The Clarendon Press.

Wiggins, Steve, Nicola Keilbach, Kerry Preibisch, Sharon Proctor, Gladys Rivera Herrejón and Gregoria Rodrí-guez Muñoz (1999). Changing Livelihoods in Rural Mexico. Research Report, DFID-ESCOR Grant R6528. London: Department for International Development.

Index